Bilingual Dictionary

English-German
German-English
Dictionary

Compiled by
Bicskei Hedwig

STAR Foreign Language BOOKS

© Publishers

ISBN : 978 1 908357 39 7

This Edition : 2023

Published by

STAR Foreign Language BOOKS

a unit of

Star Books

56, Langland Crescent
Stanmore HA7 1NG, U.K.
info@starbooksuk.com
www.bilingualbooks.co.uk

Printed in India at
Star Print-O-Bind, New Delhi-110 020

About this Dictionary

Developments in science and technology today have narrowed down distances between countries, and have made the world a small place. A person living thousands of miles away can learn and understand the culture and lifestyle of another country with ease and without travelling to that country. Languages play an important role as facilitators of communication in this respect.

To promote such an understanding, **STAR Foreign Language BOOKS** has planned to bring out a series of bilingual dictionaries in which important English words have been translated into other languages, with Roman transliteration in case of languages that have different scripts. This is a humble attempt to bring people of the word closer through the medium of language, thus making communication easy and convenient.

Under this series of *one-to-one dictionaries*, we have published almost 57 languages, the list of which has been given in the opening pages. These have all been compiled and edited by teachers and scholars of the relative languages.

Publishers

Bilingual Dictionaries in this Series

English-Afrikaans / Afrikaans-English	Abraham Venter
English-Albanian / Albanian-English	Theodhora Blushi
English-Amharic / Amharic-English	Girun Asanke
English-Arabic / Arabic-English	Rania-al-Qass
English-Bengali / Bengali-English	Amit Majumdar
English-Bosnian / Bosnian-English	Boris Kazanegra
English-Bulgarian / Bulgarian-English	Vladka Kocheshkova
English-Burmese (Myanmar) / Burmese (Myanmar)-English	Kyaw Swar Aung
English-Cambodian / Cambodian-English	Engly Sok
English-Cantonese / Cantonese-English	Nisa Yang
English-Chinese (Mandarin) / Chinese (Mandarin)-Eng	Y. Shang & R. Yao
English-Croatian / Croatain-English	Vesna Kazanegra
English-Czech / Czech-English	Jindriska Poulova
English-Danish / Danish-English	Rikke Wend Hartung
English-Dari / Dari-English	Amir Khan
English-Dutch / Dutch-English	Lisanne Vogel
English-Estonian / Estonian-English	Lana Haleta
English-Farsi / Farsi-English	Maryam Zaman Khani
English-French / French-English	Aurélie Colin
English-Georgian / Georgina-English	Eka Goderdzishvili
English-Gujarati / Gujarati-English	Sujata Basaria
English-German / German-English	Bicskei Hedwig
English-Greek / Greek-English	Lina Stergiou
English-Hindi / Hindi-English	Sudhakar Chaturvedi
English-Hungarian / Hungarian-English	Lucy Mallows
English-Italian / Italian-English	Eni Lamllari
English-Japanese / Japanese-English	Miruka Arai & Hiroko Nishimura
English-Korean / Korean-English	Mihee Song
English-Latvian / Latvian-English	Julija Baranovska
English-Levantine Arabic / Levantine Arabic-English	Ayman Khalaf
English-Lithuanian / Lithuanian-English	Regina Kazakeviciute
English-Malay / Malay-English	Azimah Husna
English-Nepali / Nepali-English	Anil Mandal
English-Norwegian / Norwegian-English	Samuele Narcisi
English-Pashto / Pashto-English	Amir Khan
English-Polish / Polish-English	Magdalena Herok
English-Portuguese / Portuguese-English	Dina Teresa
English-Punjabi / Punjabi-English	Teja Singh Chatwal
English-Romanian / Romanian-English	Georgeta Laura Dutulescu
English-Russian / Russian-English	Katerina Volobuyeva
English-Serbian / Serbian-English	Vesna Kazanegra
English-Sinhalese / Sinhalese-English	Naseer Salahudeen
English-Slovak / Slovak-English	Zuzana Horvathova
English-Slovenian / Slovenian-English	Tanja Turk
English-Somali / Somali-English	Ali Mohamud Omer
English-Spanish / Spanish-English	Cristina Rodriguez
English-Swahili / Swahili-English	Abdul Rauf Hassan Kinga
English-Swedish / Swedish-English	Madelene Axelsson
English-Tagalog / Tagalog-English	Jefferson Bantayan
English-Tamil / Tamil-English	Sandhya Mahadevan
English-Thai / Thai-English	Suwan Kaewkongpan
English-Tigrigna / Tigrigna-English	Tsegazeab Hailegebriel
English-Turkish / Turkish-English	Nagme Yazgin
English-Ukrainian / Ukrainian-English	Katerina Volobuyeva
English-Urdu / Urdu-English	S. A. Rahman
English-Vietnamese / Vietnamese-English	Hoa Hoang
English-Yoruba / Yoruba-English	O. A. Temitope

STAR Foreign Language BOOKS

ENGLISH-GERMAN

A

a *a.* ein
aback *adv.* rückwärts
abandon *v.t.* verlassen
abase *v.* gedemütigen
abashed *adj.* Beschämt
abate *v.t.* vermindern
abbey *n.* Abtei {f}
abbot *n.* Abt {m}
abbreviate *v.t.* kürzen
abbreviation *n.* Abkürzung {f}
abdicate *v.t.* entsagen
abdication *n.* Abdankung {f}
abdomen *n.* Bauch {m}
abdominal *a.* abdominal
abduct *v.t.* entführen
abduction *n.* Entführung {f}
aberrant *adj.* anomal
aberration *n.* Verirrung {f}
abet *v.* begünstigen
abeyance *n.* Unentschiedenheit {f}
abhor *v.* verabscheuen
abhorrence *n.* Abscheu {f}
abhorrent *adj.* zuwider
abide *v.i* verweilen
abiding *adj.* verweilend
ability *n.* Begabung {f}
abject *adj.* elend
abjure *v.* abschwören
ablaze *adv.* lodernd
able *adj.* fähig
ablutions *n.* Waschung {f}
abnormal *adj.* unnormal

aboard *adv.* anwesend
abode *n.* bleiben
abolish *v.t* abschaffen
abolition *n.* Abschaffung {f}
abominable *adj.* abscheulich
abominate *v.* verabscheuen
aboriginal *adj.* eingeboren
abort *v.i* abbrechen
abortion *n.* Abtreibung {f}
abortive *adj.* nutzlos
abound *v.i.* strotzen
about *adv.* über
about *prep.* etwa
above *adv.* oben
above *prep.* oberhalb
abrasion *n.* Abrieb {m}
abrasive *adj.* abrasiv
abreast *adv.* nebeneinander
abridge *v.t* verkürzen
abroad *adv.* überallhin
abrogate *v.* aufheben
abrupt *adj.* hastig
abscess *n.* Abszess {m}
abscond *v.* flüchten
absence *n.* Abwesenheit {f}
absent *adj.* abwesend
absentee *n.* Abwesende {m,f}
absolute *adj.* absolut
absolution *n.* Absolution {f}
absolve *v.* freisprechen
absorb *v.* einsaugen
abstain *v.* enthalten
abstinence *n.* Enthaltung {f}
abstract *adj.* abstrakt

abstruse	adj.schwerverständlich	accomplish v.	vollbringen
absurd adj.	absurd	accomplished	adj. ausgeführt
absurdity n.	Albernheit {f}	accomplishment n.	Ausführung {f}
abundance n.	Überfluss {m}	accord v.	übereinstimmen
abundant adj.	reichlich	accordance n.	Übereinstimmung {f}
abuse v.	missbrauchen	according adv.	gemäß
abusive adj.	beleidigend	accordingly adv.	Entsprechend
abut v.	angrenzen	accost v.	ansprechen
abysmal adj.	miserabel	account n.	Konto {m}
abyss n.	Abgrund {m}	accountable adj.	verantwortlich
academic adj.	akademisch	accountancy n.	Buchhaltung {f}
academy n.	Akademie {f}	accountant n.	Buchhalter {m}
accede v.	beitreten	accoutrement n.	Ausstattung {f}
accelerate v.	beschleunigen	accredit v.	beglaubigen
accelerator n.	Beschleuniger {m}	accredited adj.	beglaubigt
accent n.	Akzent {m}	accretion n.	Wachstum {n}
accentuate v.	akzentuieren	accrue v.t.	entstehen
accept v.	annehmen	accumulate v.	anhäufen
acceptable adj.	annehmbar	accumulation n.	Häufung {f}
acceptance n.	Annahme {f}	accurate adj.	richtig
access n.	Zugriff {m}	accusation n.	Anklage {f}
accessible adj.	zugänglich	accuse v.	beschuldigen
accession n.	Akzession {f}	accustom v.	gewöhnen
accessory n.	Zusatz {m}	accustomed adj.	gewöhnt
accident n.	Unglücksfall {m}	ace n.	As {n}
accidental adj.	versehentlich	acerbic adj.	scharfzüngig
acclaim v.	zujubeln	acetate n.	Azetat {n}
acclimatise v.t	gewöhnen	acetone n.	Azeton {n}
accolade n.	Auszeichnung {f}	ache n.	Schmerzen {pl}
accommodate v.	anpassen	achieve v.	erreichen
accommodation n.	Versorgung {f}	achievement n.	Vollendung {f}
accompaniment n.	Begleitung {f}	acid n.	Säure {f}
accompany v.	begleiten	acidity n.	Azidität {f}
accomplice n.	Komplize {m}	acknowledge	v.anerkennen

acknowledgement *n.* Danksagung {f}

acme *n.* Höhepunkt {m}

acne *n.* Akne {f}

acolyte *n.* Messgehilfe {f}

acorn *n.* Eichel {f}

acoustic *adj.* Akustik {f}

acquaint *v.* bekanntmachen

acquaintance *n.* Bekanntschaft {f}

acquiesce *v.* dulden

acquiescence *n.* Ergebung {f}

acquire *v.* erwerben

acquisition *n.* Anschaffung {f}

acquit *v.* freisprechen

acquittal *n.* Freispruch {m}

acre *n.* Acker {m}

acrid *adj.* gallig

acrimony *n.* Bitterkeit {f}

acrobat *n.* Akrobat {m}

acrobatic *adj.* akrobatisch

across *adv.* durch

acrylic *adj.* acrylsauer

act *v.* agieren

acting *n.* Schauspielerei {f}

acting *adj.* stellvertretend

actinium *n.* Actinium {n}

action *n.* Arbeitsgang {m}

actionable *adj.* verklagbar

activate *v.* aktivieren

active *adj.* aktiv

activist *n.* Aktivist {m}

activity *n.* Tätigkeit {f}

actor *n.* Schauspieler {m}

actress *a.* Schauspielerin {f}

actual *adj.* tatsächlich

actually *adv.* eigentlich

actuary *n.* Versicherungsstatistiker {m}

actuate *v.* antreiben

acumen *n.* Scharfsinn {m}

acupuncture *n.* Akupunktur {f}

acute *adj.* intensiv

adamant *adj.* unerbittlich

adapt *v.* angleichen

adaptation *n.* Adaptierung {f}

add *v.* summieren

addendum *n.* Beifügung {f}

addict *n.* Süchtige {m,f}

addicted *adj.* süchtig

addiction *n.* Sucht {f}

addition *n.* Ergänzung {f}

additional *adj.* zusätzlich

additive *n.* Zusatzstoff {m}

addled *adj.* verdarb

address *n.* Anschrift {m}

addressee *n.* Empfänger {m}

adduce *v.* erbringen

adept *adj.* erfahren

adequacy *n.* Angemessenheit {f}

adequate *adj.* angemessen

adhere *v.* anhaften

adherence *n.* Anhänglichkeit {f}

adhesive *n.* Klebstoff {m}

adieu *n.* Lebewohl

adjacent *adj.* danebenliegend

adjective *n.* Adjektiv {n}

adjoin *v.* angrenzen

adjourn *v.* aufschieben

adjournment *n.* Vertagung {f}

adjudge *v.t.* zusprechen

9

adjudicate	v.	urteilen	
adjunct	n.	Zubehör {n}	
adjust	v.	anpassen	
adjustment	n.	Abgleich {m}	
administer	v.	verwalten	
administration	n.	Verwaltung {f}	
administrative	adj.	verwaltungsmäßig	
administrator	n.	Verwalter {m}	
admirable	adj.	bewundernswert	
admiral	n.	Admiral {m}	
admiration	n.	Bewunderung {f}	
admire	v.	bewundern	
admissible	adj.	zulässig	
admission	n.	Zulassung {f}	
admit	v.	zulassen	
admittance	n.	Zutritt {m}	
admonish	v.	ermahnen	
ado	n.	Getue {n}	
adobe	n.	Lehmstein {m}	
adolescence	n.	Jugend {f}	
adolescent	adj.	pubertär	
adopt	v.	adoptieren	
adoption	n.	Adoption {f}	
adoptive	adj.	angenommen	
adorable	adj.	anbetungswürdig	
adoration	n.	Verehrung {f}	
adore	v.t.	verehren	
adorn	v.	zieren	
adrift	adj.	haltlos	
adroit	adj.	geschickt	
adsorb	v.	adsorbieren	
adulation	n.	Schmeichelei {f}	
adult	n.	Erwachsener {m}	
adulterate	v.	verfälschen	

adulteration	n.	Verfälschung {f}	
adultery	n.	Ehebruch {m}	
advance	v.	fortschreiten	
advance	n.	Fortschritt {m}	
advancement	n.	Beförderung {f}	
advantage	v.t.	begünstigen	
advantage	n.	Vorteil {m}	
advantageous	adj.	vorteilhaft	
advent	n.	Advent {m}	
adventure	n.	Abenteuer {n}	
adventurous	adj.	abenteuerlich	
adverb	n.	Adverb {n}	
adversary	n.	Gegner {m}	
adverse	adj.	feindlich	
adversity	n.	Missgeschick {n}	
advertise	v.	werben	
advertisement	n.	Propaganda {f}	
advice	n.	Ratschlag {m}	
advisable	adj.	ratsam	
advise	v.	anraten	
advocate	n.	Anwalt {m}	
advocate	v.	verfechten	
aegis	n.	Ägide {f}	
aerial	n.	Antenne {f}	
aeon	n.	Äon {m}	
aerobatics	n.	Kunstflug {m}	
aerobics	n.	Ärobic {f}	
aerodrome	n.	Flugplatz {m}	
aeronautics	n.	Luftfahrttechnik {f}	
aeroplane	n.	Flugzeug {n}	
aerosol	n.	Ärosol {n}	
aerospace	n.	Raumfahrt {f}	
aesthetic	adj.	ästhetisch	
aesthetics	n.	Ästhetik {f}	

afar	*adv.*	fern
affable	*adj.*	freundlich
affair	*n.*	Geschäft {n}
affect	*v.*	bewegen
affectation	*n.*	Ziererei {f}
affected	*adj.*	beeinträchtigt
affection	*n.*	Zuneigung {f}
affectionate	*adj.*	liebevoll
affidavit	*n.*	Zustellungsurkunde {f}
affiliate	*v.*	verknüpfen
affiliation	*n.*	Verwandtschaft {f}
affinity	*n.*	Affinität {f}
affirm	*v.*	bekräftigen
affirmation	*n.*	Bekräftigung {f}
affirmative	*adj.*	zustimmend
affix	*v.t.*	befestigen
afflict	*v.*	quälen
affliction	*n.*	Leid {n}
affluence	*n.*	Wohlstand {m}
affluent	*adj.*	wohlhabend
afford	*v.t.*	leisten
afforestation	*n.*	Aufforstung {f}
affray	*n.*	Schlägerei {f}
affront	*n.*	Beleidigung {f}
afield	*adv.*	draußen
aflame	*adj.*	in Flammen
afloat	*adj.*	schuldenfrei
afoot	*adv.*	im Gange
afraid	*adj.*	befürchtend
afresh	*adv.*	wieder
African	*adj.*	afrikanisch
aft	*adv.*	hinten
after	*adv.*	hinterher
after	*conj.*	gemäß

after	*prep.*	nachdem
again	*adv.*	nochmals
against	*prep.*	entgegen
agate	*n.*	Achat {m}
age	*n.*	Alter {n}
aged	*adj.*	gealtert
ageism	*n.*	Altersdiskriminierung {f}
ageless	*adj.*	zeitlos
agency	*n.*	Vermittlung {f}
agenda	*n.*	Tagesordnung {f}
agent	*n.*	Wirkungsmittel {n}
agglomerate	*v.*	aufhäufen
aggravate	*v.*	gravieren
aggravation	*n.*	Verschlimmerung {f}
aggregate	*n.*	Aggregat {n}
aggression	*n.*	Angriff {m}
aggressive	*adj.*	aggressiv
aggressor	*n.*	Angreifer {m}
aggrieve	*v.*	betrüben
aghast	*adj.*	bestürzt
agile	*adj.*	beweglich
agility	*n.*	Lebendigkeit {f}
agitate	*v.*	erregen
agitation	*n.*	Angst {f}
agnostic	*n.*	Agnostiker {m}
ago	*adv.*	vorher
agog	*adj.*	gespannt
agonize	*v.*	quälen
agony	*n.*	Qual {f}
agrarian	*adj.*	landwirtschaftlich
agree	*v.*	beipflichten
agreeable	*adj.*	angenehm
agreement	*n.*	Abkommen {n}
agricultural	*adj.*	Ackerbautreibend

11

agriculture	*n.*	Ackerbau {m}
aground	*adj.*	gestrandet
ahead	*adv.*	vorn
aid *n.*		Mithilfe {f}
aide	*n.*	Helfer {m}
aids	*n.*	Beihilfen {pl}
ail *v.*		kränkeln
ailing	*adj.*	kränkelnd
ailment *n.*		Unpässlichkeit {f}
aim	*v.i.*	zielen
aim	*n.*	Ziel {n}
aimless *adj.*		ziellos
air *n.*		Luft {f}
aircraft *n.*		Luftfahrzeug {n}
airy	*adj.*	luftig
aisle	*n.*	Seitenschiff {n}
ajar	*adv.*	angelehnt
akin	*adj.*	verwandt
alacritous	*adj.*	heiter
alacrity *n.*		Bereitwilligkeit {f}
alarm	*n*	Alarm {m}
alarm	*v*	alarmieren
alas	*conj.*	leider
albeit	*conj.*	obgleich
album	*n*	Album {n}
albumen	*n.*	Eiweiß {n}
alchemy	*n.*	Alchemie {f}
alcohol *n.*		Alkohol {m}
alcoholic	*adj.*	alkoholisch
alcove	*n.*	Nische {f}
ale *n.*		Tal {n}
alert	*adj.*	wachsam
algebra *n.*		Algebra {f}
alias	*adv.*	alias

alias	*n.*	Pseudonym {n}
alibi	*n.*	Alibi {n}
alien	*adj.*	Außerirdischer {m}
alienate	*v.i.*	entfremden
alight	*v.t.*	landen
align	*v.*	ausrichten
alignment	*n.*	Gruppierung {f}
alike	*adj.*	gleich
alimony	*n.*	Unterhalt {m}
alive	*adj.*	lebendig
alkali	*n.*	alkali
all *adj.*		alle
allay	*v.*	beschwichtigen
allegation	*n.*	Behauptung {f}
allege	*v.*	behaupten
allegiance *n.*		Untertanentreue {f}
allegory	*n.*	Allegorie {f}
allergen	*n.*	Allergiestoffe {pl}
allergic *adj.*		allergisch
allergy *n.*		Allergie {f}
alleviate	*v.*	lindern
alleviation	*n.*	Linderung {f}
alley	*n.*	Allee {f}
alliance *n.*		Allianz {f}
allied	*adj.*	verbündet
alligator	*n.*	Alligator {m}
alliterate	*n.*	Analphabet {m}
alliteration	*n.*	Alliteration {f}
allocate	*v.*	belegen
allocation	*n.*	Besetzung {f}
allot	*v.*	zuwiesen
allotment	*n.*	Anteil {m}
allow	*v.*	bewilligen
allowance	*n.*	Erlaubnis {f}

12

alloy *n.*	Legierung {f}	
allude *v.t.*	hinweisen	
allure *n.*	Lockung {f}	
alluring *adj.*	verlockt	
allusion *n.*	Anspielung {f}	
ally *n.*	Verbündete {m,f}	
almanac *n.*	Almanach {n}	
almighty *adj.*	allmächtige	
almond *n.*	Mandel {f}	
almost *adv.*	fast	
alms *n.*	Almosen {pl}	
aloft *adv.*	oben	
alone *adv.*	allein	
along *prep.*	längs	
alongside *prep.*	entlang	
aloof *adj.*	fern	
aloud *adv.*	laut	
alpha *n.*	Alpha {m}	
alphabet *n.*	Alphabet {n}	
alphabetical *adj.*	alphabetisch	
alpine *adj.*	Alpin	
already *adv.*	bereits	
also *adv.*	auch	
altar *n.*	Altar {m}	
alter *v.*	verändern	
alteration *n.*	Veränderung {f}	
altercation *n.*	Zank {m}	
alternate *v.t.*	abwechseln	
alternative *adj.*	alternativ	
although *conj.*	obwohl	
altitude *n.*	Höhe {f}	
altogether *adv.*	vollkommen	
altruism *n.*	Altruismus {m}	
aluminium *n.*	Aluminium {n}	

alumnus *n.*	Absolvent {m}	
always *adv.*	immer	
amalgam *n.*	Amalgam {n}	
amalgamate *v.*	vereinigen	
amalgamation *n.*	Vermischung {f}	
amass *v.*	ansammeln	
amateur *n.*	Anfänger {m}	
amateurish *adj.*	dilettantisch	
amatory *adj.*	verliebt	
amaze *v.*	erstaunen	
amazement *n.*	Schrecken {m}	
amazon *n.*	Amazone {f}	
ambassador *n.*	Botschafter {m}	
amber *n.*	Bernstein {m}	
ambient *adj.*	umgebend	
ambiguity *n.*	Doppelsinnigkeit {f}	
ambiguous *adj.*	unklar	
ambit *n.*	Geltungsbereich {m}	
ambition *n.*	Ehrgeiz {m}	
ambitious *adj.*	ambitioniert	
ambivalent *adj.*	ambivalent	
amble *v.*	schlendern	
ambrosia *n.*	Götterspeise {f}	
ambulance *n.*	Ambulanz {f}	
ambush *n.*	Hinterhalt {m}	
ameliorate *v.*	verbessern	
amelioration *n.*	Aufbesserung {f}	
amend *v.*	gefügigen	
amendment *n.pl.*	Verbesserung {f}	
amenable *adj.*	gefügig	
amiable *adj.*	liebenswürdig	
amicable *adj.*	freundschaftlich	
amid *prep.*	mittenunter	
amiss *adj.*	fehlend	

13

amity *n.*	Freundschaftlichkeit {f}	**analyst** *n.*	Analytiker {m}
ammunition *n.*	Munition {f}	**analytical** *adj.*	analytisch
amnesia *n.*	Amnesie {f}	**anarchism** *n.*	Anarchismus{f}
amnesty *n.*	Amnestie {f}	**anarchist** *n.*	Anarchist {m}
amok *adv.*	Amok {m}	**anarchy** *n.*	Anarchie {f}
among *prop.*	zwischen	**anatomy** *n.*	Anatomie {f}
amoral *adj.*	amoralisch	**ancestor** *n.*	Vorfahr {m}
amorous *adj.*	verliebt	**ancestral** *adj.*	angestammt
amorphous *adj.*	formlos	**ancestry** *n.*	Abstammung {f}
amount *n.*	Summe {f}	**anchor** *n.*	Anker {m}
ampere *n.*	Amperezahl {f}	**anchorage** *n.*	Ankergrund {m}
ampersand *n.*	Kaufmanns-Und {n}	**ancient** *adj.*	ehemalig
amphibian *n.*	Amphibie {f}	**ancillary** *adj.*	untergeordnet
amphitheatre *n.*	Amphitheater {n}	**and** *conj.*	und
ample *adj.*	groß	**android** *n.*	Androide {m}
amplification *n.*	Verstärkung {f}	**anecdote** *n.*	Androide {m}
amplifier *n.*	Verstärker {m}	**anew** *adv.*	neue
amplify *v.*	erweitern	**angel** *n.*	Engel {m}
amplitude *n.*	Weiten {pl}	**anger** *n.*	Zorn {m}
amulet *n.*	Amulett {n}	**angina** *n.*	Angina {f}
amuse *v.*	unterhalten	**angle** *n.*	Winkel {m}
amusement *n.*	Vergnügung {f}	**angry** *adj.*	aufgebracht
an *adj.*	ein	**anguish** *n.*	Pein {f}
anachronism *n.*	Anachronismus {m}	**angular** *adj.*	winklig
anaemia *n.*	Anämie {f}	**animal** *n.*	Tier {n}
anaesthesia *n.*	Anästhesie {f}	**animate** *v.*	animieren
anaesthetic *n.*	Anästhetikum {n}	**animated** *adj.*	animiert
anal *adj.*	anal	**animation** *n.*	Animation {f}
analgesic *n.*	Schmerztablette {f}	**animosity** *n.*	Feindlichkeit {f}
analogous *adj.*	analog	**aniseed** *n.*	Anissamen {m}
analogue *adj.*	analog	**ankle** *n.*	Fußknöchel {m}
analogy *n.*	Analogie {f}	**anklet** *n.*	Fußring {m}
analyse *v.*	analysieren	**annals** *n.*	Annalen {pl}
analysis *n.*	Analyse {f}	**annex** *v.*	anfügen

14

annexation *n.*	Hinzufügung {f}	**anthology** *n.*	Zusammenstellung {f}
annihilate *v.*	vernichten	**anthropology** *n.*	Menschenkunde {f}
annihilation *n.*	Vernichtung {f}	**anthrax** *n.*	Milzbrand {m}
anniversary *n.*	Jahrestag {m}	**anti** *n.*	anti
annotate *v.*	anmerken	**antibiotic** *n.*	Antibiotikum {n}
announce *v.*	ankündigen	**antibody** *n.*	Gegenkörper {m}
announcement *n.*	Bekanntmachung {f}	**antic** *n.*	Possen {pl}
annoy *v.*	nerven	**anticipate** *v.*	vorahnen
annoyance *n.*	Verdruss {m}	**anticipation** *n.*	Vorausnahme {f}
annual *adj.*	jährlich	**anticlimax** *n.*	Antiklimax {f}
annuity *n.*	Jahresrente {f}	**antidote** *n.*	Gegenmittel {n}
annul *v.*	annullieren	**antioxidant** *n.*	Antioxidant {n}
anode *n.*	Anode {f}	**antipathy** *n.*	Antipathie {f}
anoint *v.*	salben	**antiperspirant** *n.*	Deo {n}
anomalous *adj.*	anormal	**antiquarian** *adj.*	antiquarisch
anomaly *n.*	Anomalie {f}	**antiquated** *adj.*	veraltet
anonymity *n.*	Anonymität {f}	**antique** *adj.*	antik
anonymous *adj.*	namenlos	**antiquity** *n.*	Antiquität {f}
anorexia *n.*	Appetitlosigkeit {f}	**antiseptic** *adj.*	antiseptisch
another *adj.*	ander	**antisocial** *adj.*	unsozial
answer *n.*	Antwort {f}	**antithesis** *n.*	Antithese {f}
answerable *adj.*	beantwortbar	**antler** *n.*	Geweih {n}
ant *n.*	Ameise {f}	**antonym** *n.*	Antonym {n}
antacid *adj.*	Magensäuremittel {n}	**anus** *n.*	After {m}
antagonism *n.*	Gegensatz {m}	**anvil** *n.*	Amboss {m}
antagonist *n.*	Gegenmittel {n}	**anxiety** *n.*	Beklemmung {f}
antagonize *v.*	entgegenwirken	**anxious** *adj.*	ängstlich
Antarctic *adj.*	Antarktis {f}	**any** *adj.*	irgendeiner
antecedent *n.*	Vorrang {m}	**anyhow** *adv.*	irgendwie
antedate *v.*	vordatieren	**anyone** *pron.*	irgendjemand
antelope *n.*	Antilope {f}	**anything** *pron.*	etwas
antenna *n.*	Antenne {f}	**anywhere** *adv.*	irgendwo
anthem *n.*	Hymne {f}	**apace** *adv.*	schnell
		apart *adv.*	abgesondert

15

apartheid	n.	Rassentrennung {f}
apartment	n.	Wohnung {f}
apathy	n.	Apathie {f}
ape	n.	Affe {m}
aperture	n.	Blende {f}
apex	n	Scheitelpunkt {m}
aphorism	n.	Gedankensplitter {m}
apiary	n.	Bienenhaus {n}
aplomb	n.	Selbstbewusstsein {n}
apocalypse	n.	Apokalypse {f}
apologize	v.	entschuldigen
apology	n.	Entschuldigung {f}
apoplectic	adj.	apoplektisch
apostate	n.	Abtrünnige {m,f}
apostle	n.	Apostel {m}
apostrophe	n.	Hochkomma {n}
appal	v.	erschrecken
apparatus	n.	Ausrüstung {f}
apparel	n.	Kleidung {f}
apparent	adj.	offenbar
appeal	v.t.	ansprechen
appear	v.	erscheinen
appearance	n.	Anschein {m}
appease	v.	beruhigen
append	v.	anhangen
appendage	n.	Anhang {m}
appendicitis	n	Blinddarmentzündung {f}
appendix	n.	Anhang {m}
appetite	n.	Appetit {m}
appetizer	n.	Aperitif {m}
applaud	v.	applaudieren
applause	n.	Applaus {m}
apple	n.	Apfel {m}
appliance	n.	Gerät {n}

applicable	adj.	einsetzbar
applicant	n.	Bewerber {m}
application	n.	Verwendung {f}
apply	v.t.	anwendet
appoint	v.	bestimmen
appointment	n.	Bestimmung {f}
apportion	v.t.	zuteilen
apposite	adj.	treffend
appraise	v.	bewerten
appreciable	adj.	merkbar
appreciate	v.	schätzen
appreciation	n.	Dankbarkeit {f}
apprehend	v.	erfassen
apprehension	n.	Besorgnis {f}
apprehensive	adj.	bedenklich
apprentice	n.	Lehrling {m}
apprise	v.	benachrichtigen
approach	v.	anmarschieren
appropriate	adj.	annähern
appropriation	n.	Besitznahme {f}
approval	n.	Genehmigung {f}
approve	v.	zustimmen
approximate	adj.	angleichend
apricot	n.	Aprikose {f}
apron	n.	Schurz {m}
apt	adj.	geeignet
aptitude	n.	Begabung {f}
aquarium	n.	Aquarium {n}
aquatic	adj.	aquatisch
aqueous	adj.	wässrig
Arab	n.	Araber {m}
Arabian	n.	arabisch
Arabic	n.	arabisch
arable	adj.	kulturfähig

16

arbiter *n.* Schiedsmann {m}	**armada** *n.* Armada {m}
arbitrary *adj.* willkürlich	**Armageddon** *n.* Weltuntergang {m}
arbitrate *v.* schlichten	**armament** *n.* Aufrüstung {f}
arbitration *n.* Schiedsgerichtsbarkeit {f}	**armistice** *n.* Waffenstillstand {m}
arbitrator *n.* Schiedsrichter {m}	**armour** *n.* Panzer {m}
arbour *n.* Laube {f}	**armoury** *n.* Vorrat {m}
arc *n.* Bogen {m}	**army** *n.* Landstreitkräfte {f}
arcade *n.* Bogengang {m}	**aroma** *n.* Aroma {f}
arch *n.* Fußrücken {m}	**aromatherapy** *n.* Aromatherapie {f}
archaeology *n.* Archäologie {f}	**around** *adv.* herum
archaic *adj.* veraltet	**arouse** *v.* aufwecken
archangel *n.* Erzengel {m}	**arrange** *v.* anfechten
archbishop *n.* Erzbischof {m}	**arrangement** *n.* Vereinbarung {f}
archer *n.* Bogenschütze {m}	**arrant** *adj.* völlig
architect *n.* Architekt {m}	**array** *n.* Reihe {f}
architecture *n.* Architektur {f}	**arrears** *n.* Schulden {pl}
archives *n.* Archiv {n}	**arrest** *v.* verhaften
Arctic *n.* Arktis {f}	**arrival** *n.* Anreise {f}
ardent *adj.* sehnlich	**arrive** *v.* ankommen
ardour *n.* Überschwang {m}	**arrogance** *n.* Hochmut {m}
arduous *adj.* anstrengend	**arrogant** *adj.* überheblich
area *n.* Zone {f}	**arrogate** *v.* anmaßen
arena *n.* Arena {f}	**arrow** *n.* Richtungspfeil {m}
argue *v.* argumentieren	**arsenal** *n.* Arsenal {n}
argument *n.* Argument {n}	**arsenic** *n.* Arsen {n}
argumentative *adj.* Beweiskräftig	**arson** *n.* Brandstiftung {f}
arid *adj.* dürr	**art** *n.* Kunst {f}
arise *v.* entspringen	**artefact** *n.* Artefakt {n}
aristocracy *n.* Aristokratie {f}	**artery** *n.* Arterie {f}
aristocrat *n.* Aristokrat {m}	**artful** *adj.* kunstvoll
arithmetic *n.* Arithmetik {f}	**arthritis** *n.* Arthritis {f}
arithmetical *adj.* arithmetisch	**artichoke** *n.* Artischocke {f}
ark *n.* Arche {f}	**article** *n.* Abschnitt {m}
arm *n.* Armlehne {f}	**articulate** *adj.* wortgewandt

17

artifice	*n.*	Kunstgriff {m}	
artificial	*adj.*	künstlich	
artillery	*n.*	Artillerie {f}	
artisan	*n.*	Handwerker {m}	
artist	*n.*	Künstler {m}	
artistic	*adj.*	künstlerisch	
artless	*adj.*	schlicht	
as	*adv.*	so	
asbestos	*n.*	Asbest {m}	
ascend	*v.*	steigen	
ascendant	*adj.*	steigend	
ascent	*n.*	Aufstieg {m}	
ascertain	*v.*	ermitteln	
ascetic	*adj.*	enthaltsam	
ascribe	*v.*	zuschreiben	
aseptic	*adj.*	aseptisch	
asexual	*adj.*	ungeschlechtlich	
ash	*n.*	Asche {f}	
ashamed	*adj.*	beschämt	
ashore	*adv.*	an Land	
Asian	*adj.*	asiatisch	
aside	*adv.*	daneben	
asinine	*adj.*	dumm	
ask	*v.*	fragen	
askance	*adv.*	schief	
askew	*adv.*	schräg	
asleep	*adj.*	schlafend	
asparagus	*n.*	Spargel {m}	
aspect	*n.*	Aspekt {m}	
asperity	*n.*	Schroffheit {f}	
aspersions	*n.*	Verleumdungen {pl}	
asphyxiate	*v.*	ersticken	
aspirant	*n.*	Kandidat {m}	
aspiration	*n.*	Aufsaugung {f}	

aspire	*v.*	aufstreben	
ass	*n.*	Dummkopf {m}	
assail	*v.*	anstürmen	
assassin	*n.*	Mörder {m}	
assassinate	*v.*	ermorden	
assassination	*n.*	Ermordung {f}	
assault	*n.*	Körperverletzung {f}	
assemblage	*n.*	Versammlung {f}	
assemble	*v.*	assemblieren	
assembly	*n.*	Baugruppe {f}	
assent	*n.*	Zustimmung {f}	
assert	*v.*	behaupten	
assess	*v.*	veranlagen	
assessment	*n.*	Feststellung {f}	
asset	*n.*	Vermögen {n}	
assiduous	*adj.*	emsig	
assign	*v.*	zuweisen	
assignation	*n.*	Zuweisung {f}	
assignment	*n.*	Auslosung {f}	
assimilate	*v.*	anpassen	
assimilation	*n.*	Angleichung {f}	
assist	*v.*	assistieren	
assistance	*n.*	Hilfestellung {f}	
assistant	*n.*	Assistant	
associate	*v.*	vereinigen	
association	*n.*	Gesellschaft	
assonance	*n.*	Assonanz {f}	
assorted	*adj.*	sortiert	
assortment	*n.*	Sortiment {n}	
assuage	*v.*	erleichtern	
assume	*v.*	annehmen	
assumption	*n.*	Vermutung {f}	
assurance	*n.*	Zusicherung {f}	
assure	*v.*	beteuern	

18

assured	*adj.*	bestärkt	
asterisk	*n.*	Stern {m}	
asteroid	*n.*	Asteroid {m}	
asthma *n.*		Asthma {n}	
astigmatism *n.*		Astigmatismus {m}	
astonish	*v.*	verwunderlichen	
astonishment	*n.*	Erstaunen {n}	
astound	*v.*	verblüffen	
astral *adj.*		sternförmig	
astray *adv.*		verloren	
astride *prep.*		rittlings	
astrologer	*n.*	Astrologe {m}	
astrology	*n.*	Astrologie {f}	
astronaut	*n.*	Astronaut {m}	
astronomer *n.*		Astronom {m}	
astronomy	*n.*	Sternkunde {f}	
astute *adj.*		scharfsinnig	
asunder	*adv.*	auseinander	
asylum *n.*		Heim {n}	
at *prep.*		an	
atavistic	*adj.*	rückschlagig	
atheism	*n.*	Atheismus {m}	
atheist *n.*		Atheist {m}	
athlete *n.*		Athlet {m}	
athletic *adj.*		sportlich	
atlas	*n.*	Atlas {m}	
atmosphere *n.*		Atmosphäre {f}	
atoll	*n.*	Atoll {n}	
atom	*n.*	Atom {n}	
atomic *adj.*		atomar	
atone	*v.*	sühnen	
atonement	*n.*	Sühne {f}	
atrium	*n.*	Vorhalle {f}	
atrocious	*adj.*	scheußlich	

atrocity *n.*		Schreckenstat {f}	
attach	*v.*	anfügen	
attaché *n.*		Attache {m}	
attachment	*n.*	Anlage {f}	
attack	*v.*	überfallen	
attain	*v.*	erreichen	
attainment	*n.*	Erreichung {f}	
attempt *v.*		versuchen	
attend	*v.*	begleiten	
attendance	*n.*	Besuch {m}	
attendant	*n.*	Bedienstete {m,f}	
attention	*n.*	Achtung {f}	
attentive	*adj.*	achtsam	
attest	*v.*	beglaubigen	
attic	*n.*	Dachstube {f}	
attire	*v.*	kleiden	
attitude *n.*		Attitüde {f}	
attorney	*n.*	Rechtsanwalt	
attract	*v.*	anziehen	
attraction	*n.*	Attraktion {f}	
attractive	*adj.*	reizvoll	
attribute	*v.*	zuschreiben	
aubergine	*n.*	Aubergine {f}	
auction *n.*		Auktion {f}	
audible *adj.*		akustisch	
audience	*n.*	Zuhörerschaft {f}	
audio	*n.*	Audio {n}	
audit	*n.*	Rechnungsprüfung {f}	
audition	*n.*	Vorsprechung {f}	
auditorium	*n.*	Aula {f}	
augment	*v.*	Vergrößerung {f}	
August *n*		August {m}	
aunt	*n.*	Tante {f}	
aura	*n.*	Heiligenschein {m}	

19

auspicious *adj.* glücksverheißend	**avid** *adj.* begierig
austere *adj.* streng	**avidly** *adv.* gierig
Australian *n.* australisch	**avocado** *n.* Avokado {f}
authentic *adj.* authentisch	**avoid** *v.* vermeiden
authenticity *n.* Rechtsgültigkeit {f}	**avoidance** *n.* Vermeidung {f}
author *n.* Verfasser	**avow** *v.* bekennen
authoritative *adj.* herrisch	**avuncular** *adj.* onkelhaft
authority *n.* Machtvollkommenheit {f}	**await** *v.* erwarten
authorize *v.* ermächtigen	**awake** *v.* wecken
autism *n.* Autismus {m}	**award** *v.* gewinnen
autobiography *n.* Autobiografie {f}	**aware** *adj.* bewusst
autocracy *n.* Autokratie {f}	**away** *adv.* abwesend
autocrat *n.* Autokrat {m}	**awe** *n.* Ehrfurcht {f}
autocratic *adj.* autokratisch	**awesome** *adj.* furchteinflößend
autograph *n.* Autograph {m}	**awful** *adj.* schrecklich
automatic *adj.* automatisch	**awhile** *adv.* eine Weile
automobile *n.* Kraftfahrzeug {n}	**awkward** *adj.* peinlich
autonomous *adj.* autonom	**awry** *adv.* krumm
autopsy *n.* Autopsie {f}	**axe** *n.* Axt {f}
autumn *n.* Herbst {m}	**axis** *n.* Achse {f}
auxiliary *adj.* hilfend	**axle** *n.* Achse {f}
avail *v.* nützen	
available *adj.* verfügbar	**B**
avalanche *n.* Lawine {f}	**babble** *v.* Störgeräusch {n}
avarice *n.* Geldgier {f}	**babe** *n.* Kindlein {n}
avenge *v.* rächen	**Babel** *n.* Stimmengewirr {n}
avenue *n.* Straße {f}	**baboon** *n.* Pavian {m}
average *n.* Durchschnittsbetrag {m}	**baby** *n.* Baby {n}
averse *adj.* abgeneigt	**bachelor** *n.* Junggeselle {m}
aversion *n.* Aversion {f}	**back** *n.* zurück
avert *v.* abwenden	**backbone** *n.* Rückgrat {n}
aviary *n.* Vogelhaus {n}	**backdate** *v.* (zu)rückdatieren {v}
aviation *n.* Fliegen {n}	**backdrop** *n.* Kulisse {f}
aviator *n.* Flieger {m}	**backfire** *v.* Gegenfeuer {n}

background	n.	Hintergrund {m}
backhand	n.	Rückhand {f}
backing	n.	Begleitung {f}
backlash	n.	Rückwirkung {f},
backlog	n.	Rückstand {m}
backpack	n.	Rucksack {m}
backside	n.	Rückseite {f}
backstage	adv.	Garderobenräume {pl}
backtrack	v.	zurückverfolgen {v}
backward	adj.	rückwärts
backwater	n.	Stauwasser {n}
bacon	n.	Schinkenspeck {m}
bacteria	n.	Bakterien {pl}
bad	adj.	schlimm
badge	n.	Abzeichen {n}
badly	adv.	schlecht
badminton	n.	Federball {n}
baffle	v.	Schallwand {f}
bag	n.	Koffer {m}
baggage	n.	Reisegepäck {n}
baggy	adj.	ausgebeult
baguette	n.	Baguette {n}
bail	n.	Bürgschaft {f}
bailiff	n.	Gerichtsvollzieher {m}
bait	n.	Köder {m}
bake	v.	backen {v}
baker	n.	Bäcker {m}
bakery	n.	Bäckerei {f}
balance	n.	Abgleich {m}
balcony	n.	Balkon {m}
bald	adj.	schmucklos
bale	n.	Ballen {m}
ball	n.	Ball {m}
ballad	n.	Ballade {f}

ballet	n.	Ballett {n}
balloon	n.	Luftballon {m}
ballot	n.	Wahlgang {m}
balm	n.	Balsam {n}
balsam	n.	Balsam {n}
bamboo	n.	Bambus {n}
ban	v.	verboten
banal	adj.	banal
banana	n.	Banane {f}
band	n.	Trupp {m}
bandage	n.	Wundverband {m}
bandit	n.	Räuber {m}
bane	n.	Verderben {n}
bang	n.	Schlag {m}
banger	n.	Knallkörper {m}
bangle	n.	Armreif {m}
banish	v.	verbannen
banishment	n.	Verbannung {f}
banisters	n.	Geländer {n}
banjo	n.	Banjo {n}
bank	n.	Bank {f}
banker	n.	Bankier {m}
bankrupt	adj.	bankrott
bankruptcy	n.	Bankrott {m}
banner	n.	Fahne {f}
banquet	n.	Bankett {n}
banter	n.	Geplänkel {n}
baptism	n.	Taufe {f}
Baptist	n.	Täufer {m}
baptize	v.	taufen
bar	n.	Riegel {m}
barb	n.	Widerhaken {m}
barbarian	n.	Barbar {m}
barbaric	adj.	barbarisch

21

barbecue	*n.*	Grill {m}
barbed	*adj.*	mit Widerhaken
barber	*n.*	Friseur {m}
bard	*n.*	Barde {f}
bare	*adj.*	knapp
barely	*adv.*	kaum
bargain	*n.*	Angebot {n}
barge	*n.*	Lastkahn {m}
bark	*n.*	Bellen {n}
barley	*n.*	Gerste {f}
barn	*n.*	Scheune {f}
barometer	*n.*	Barometer {n}
baron	*n.*	Baron {m}
barrack	*n.*	Baracke {f}
barracuda	*n.*	Barrakuda {f}
barrage	*n.*	Barriere {f}
barrel	*n.*	Fass {n}
barren	*adj.*	unfruchtbar
barricade	*n.*	Schutzwall {m}
barrier	*n.*	Absperrung {f}
barring	*prep.*	ausgenommen
barrister	*n.*	Rechtsanwalt {m}
barter	*v.*	Tauschgeschäft {n}
base	*n.*	Basis {f}
baseless	*adj.*	grundlos
basement	*n.*	Kellergeschoss {n}
bashful	*adj.*	verschämt
basic	*n.*	grundlegend
basil	*n.*	Basilikum {n}
basilica	*n.*	Basilika {f}
basin	*n.*	Becken {n}
basis	*n.*	Basis {f}
bask	*v.*	sich sonnen
basket	*n.*	Korb {m}

bass	*n.*	Bass {m}
bastard	*n.*	Bastard {m}
baste	*v.*	verprügeln
bastion	*n.*	Bastion {f}
bat	*n.*	Fledermaus {f}
batch	*n.*	Schub {m}
bath	*n.*	Bad {n}
bathe	*v.*	baden
bathos	*n.*	Gemeinplatz {m}
batik	*n.*	Batist {m}
baton	*n.*	Stab {m}
battalion	*n.*	Bataillon {n}
batten	*n.*	gedeihen
batter	*n.*	zerschmettert
battery	*n.*	Batterie {f}
battle	*n.*	Kampf {m}
bauble	*n.*	Spielerei {f}
baulk	*v.*	Hindernis {n}
bawl	*v.*	grölen
bay	*n.*	Erker {m}
bayonet	*n.*	Seitengewehr {n}
bazaar	*n.*	Basar {m}
bazooka	*n.*	Panzerfaust {f}
be	*v.*	sein
beach	*n.*	Badestrand {m}
beacon	*n.*	Leuchtfeuer {n}
bead	*n.*	Wulst {f}
beady	*adj.*	perlend
beagle	*n.*	Spürhund {m}
beak	*n.*	Schnabel {m}
beaker	*n.*	Messbecher {m}
beam	*n.*	Leitstrahl {m}
bean	*n.*	Bohne {f}
bear	*v.t*	tragen

bear	n.	Bär {m}	
beard	n.	Bart {m}	
bearing	n.	Dulden {n}	
beast	n.	Biest {n}	
beastly	adj.	tierisch	
beat	v.	Schlag {m}	
beautician	n.	Kosmetikerin {f}	
beautiful	adj.	schön	
beautify	v.	verschönern	
beatitude	n.	Seligkeit {f}	
beauty	n.	Schönheit	
beaver	n.	Biber {m}	
becalmed	adj.	beruhigt	
because	conj.	weil	
beck	n.	Wink {m}	
beckon	v.	winken	
become	v.	werden	
bed	n.	Bett {n}	
bedding	n.	Bettung {f}	
bedlam	n.	Tollhaus {n}	
bedraggled	adj.	beschmutzt	
bee	n.	Biene {f}	
beech	n.	Buche {f}	
beef	n.	Rindfleisch {n}	
beefy	adj.	fleischig	
beep	n.	akustisches Zeichen	
beer	n.	Bier {n}	
beet	n.	Rübe {f}	
beetle	n.	Käfer {m}	
beetroot	n.	Rote Beete {f}	
befall	v.	zustoßen	
befit	v.	ziemen	
before	adv.	vorher	
beforehand	adv.	zuvor	

befriend	v.	befreunden
befuddled	adj.	berauscht
beg	v.	abbitten
beget	v.	zeugen
beggar	n.	Bettler {m}
begin	v.	beginnen
beginning	n.	Anfang {m}
beguile	v.	täuschen
behalf	n.	namens
behave	v.	benehmen
behaviour	n.	Verhalten {n}
behead	v.	enthaupten
behemoth	n.	Riesentier {n}
behest	n.	Geheiß {n}
behind	prep.	dahinter
behold	v.	erblicken
beholden	adj.	verpflichtet
beige	n.	beige
being	n.	Wesen {n}
belabour	v.	durchprügeln
belated	adj.	verspätet
belay	v.	festmachen
belch	v.	aufstoßen
beleaguered	adj.	belagert
belie	v.	lügen
belief	n.	Glauben {m}
believe	v.	glauben
belittle	v.	verkleinern
bell	n.	Klingel {f}
belle	n.	Schönheit {f}
bellicose	adj.	kriegerisch
belligerent	adj.	streitlustig
bellow	v.	brüllen
bellows	n.	Federbalg {m}

belly	*n.*	Bauch {m}	**beside** *prep.*	neben
belong	*v.*	zusammengehören	**besiege** *v.*	überhäufen
belongings	*n.*	Eigentum {n}	**besmirch** *v.*	besudeln
beloved	*adj.*	geliebt	**besom** *n.*	Besen {m}
below	*prep.*	unten	**besotted** *adj.*	liebestrunken
belt	*n.*	Gürtel {m}	**bespoke** *adj.*	bestellt
bemoan	*v.*	beklagen	**best** *adj.*	am besten
bemused	*adj.*	verwirrt	**bestial** *adj.*	tierisch
bench	*n.*	Sitzbank {f}	**bestow** *v.*	schenken
bend	*v.*	Krümmung {f}	**bestride** *v.*	reiten
beneath	*adv.*	unterhalb	**bet** *v.*	wetten
benediction	*n.*	Segnung {f}	**betake** *v.*	begeben
benefactor	*n.*	Wohltäter {m}	**betray** *v.*	verraten
benefice	*n.*	Benefizium {n}	**betrayal** *n.*	Verrat {m}
beneficent	*adj.*	wohltätig	**better** *adj.*	besser
beneficial	*adj.*	nützlich	**between** *adv.*	zwischen
benefit *n.*		Vorteil {m}	**bevel** *n.*	Fase {f}
benevolence	*n.*	Wohlwollen {n}	**beverage** *n.*	Getränk {n}
benevolent *adj*		wohlwollend	**bevy** *n.*	Schwarm {m}
benign *adj.*		harmlos	**bewail** *v.*	klagen
bent	*adj.*	gebogen	**beware** *v.*	vermeiden
bequeath	*v.*	vermachen	**bewilder** *v.t*	verwirren
bequest	*n.*	Erbe {n}	**bewitch** *v.*	verhexen
berate *v.*		auszanken	**beyond** *adv.*	jenseits
bereaved *v.*		berauben	**bi** *comb.*	bi
bereavement	*n.*	Verlust {m}	**biannual** *adj.*	zweimal jährlich
bereft *adj.*		beraubend	**bias** *n.*	Vorspannung {f}
bergamot	*n.*	Bergamotte {f}	**biased** *adj.*	voreingenommen
berk	*n.*	Dussel {m}	**bib** *n.*	Latz {m}
berry	*n.*	Beere {f}	**Bible** *n.*	Bibel {f}
berserk *adj.*		wütend	**bibliography** *n.*	Literaturangabe {f}
berth	*n.*	Liegeplatz {m}	**bibliophile** *n.*	Bücherfreund {m}
beseech	*v.*	ersuchen	**bicentenary** *n.*	Jubiläum {n}
beset	*v.*	verfolgen	**biceps** *n.*	Bizeps {pl}

24

bicker	v.	zanken	
bicycle	n.	Fahrrad {n}	
bid	v.	bieten	
biddable	adj.	anbietend	
bidder	n.	Anbieter {m}	
bide	v.	erwarten	
bidet	n.	Sitzwaschbecken {n}	
biennial	adj.	zweijährig	
bier	n.	Bahre {f}	
bifocal	adj.	bifokal	
big	adj.	groß	
bigamy	n.	Bigamie {f}	
bigot	n.	Fan {m}	
bigotry	n.	Engstirnigkeit {f}	
bike	n.	Drahtesel {m}	
bikini	n.	Bikini {m}	
bilateral	adj.	zweiseitig	
bile	n.	Galle {f}	
bilingual	adj.	zweisprachig	
bill	n.	Anklageschrift {f}	
billet	n.	Knüppel {m}	
billiards	n.	Billard {n}	
billion	n.	Milliarde {f}	
billionaire	n.	Milliardär {m}	
billow	v.	wogen	
bin	n.	Eimer {m}	
binary	adj.	binär	
bind	v.	binden	
binding	n.	Anbindung {f}	
binge	n.	Gelage {n}	
binocular	adj.	binokular	
biochemistry	n.	Biochemie {f}	
biodegradable	adj.	abbaubar	
biodiversity	n.	Biodiversität {f}	

biography	n.	Biographie {f}	
biologist	n.	Biologe {m}	
biology	n.	Biologie {f}	
biopsy	n.	Biopsie {f}	
bipartisan	adj.	Parteienvertretend	
birch	n.	Birke {f}	
bird	n.	Vogel {m}	
bird flu	n.	Vogelgrippe {f}	
birth	n.	Geburt {f}	
biscuit	n.	Keks {m}	
bisect	v.	halbieren	
bisexual	adj.	bisexuell	
bishop	n.	Bischof {m}	
bison	n.	Wisent {m}	
bit	n.	Bit {n}	
bitch	n.	Hündin {f}	
bite	v.	beißen	
biting	adj.	beißend	
bitter	adj.	bitter	
bizarre	adj.	bizarr	
blab	v.	ausplaudern	
black	adj.	schwarz	
blackberry	n.	Brombeere {f}	
blackboard	n.	Kreidetafel {f}	
blacken	v.	schwärzen	
blacklist	n.	Liste(schwarze) {f}	
blackmail	n.	Erpressung {f}	
blackout	n.	Ausfall {m}	
blacksmith	n.	Schmied {m}	
bladder	n.	Blase {f}	
blade	n.	Klinge {f}	
blain	n.	Pustel {f}	
blame	v.	schuldigen	
blanch	v.	bleichen	

bland *adj.*	sanft	
blank *adj.*	unausgefüllt	
blanket	*n.*	Tuch {n}
blare *v.*	schmettern	
blarney *n.*	Flunkerei {f}	
blast *n.*	Explosion {f}	
blatant *adj.*	lärmend	
blaze *n.*	Brand {m}	
blazer *n.*	Klubjacke {f}	
bleach *adj.*	ausbleichend	
bleak *adj.*	öde	
bleat *v. i*	meckern	
bleed *v.*	bluten	
bleep *n.*	Piepsen {n}	
blemish	*n.*	Schönheitsfehler {m}
blench *v.*	zurückschrecken	
blend *v. t*	verblenden	
blender *n.*	Mixer {m}	
bless *v.*	segnen	
blessed	*adj.*	gesegnet
blessing	*n.*	Segen {m}
blight *n.*	Pesthauch {m}	
blind *adj.*	blind	
blindfold	*v.*	verbinden (Augen)
blindness *n.*	Blindheit {f}	
blink *v.*	anblinzeln	
blinkers	*n.*	Scheuklappen {pl}
blip *n.*	Markierung {f}	
bliss *n.*	Glück {n}	
blister *n.*	Brandblase {f}	
blithe *adj.*	heiter	
blitz *n.*	Blitzkrieg {m}	
blizzard	*n.*	Schneesturm {m}
bloat *v.*	aufblasen	

bloater *n.*	Bückling {m}	
blob *n.*	Farbfleck {m}	
bloc *n.*	Ostblock {m}	
block *n.*	Block {m}	
blockade	*n.*	Blockade {f}
blockage	*n.*	Blockierung {f}
blog *n.*	Blog {n}	
bloke *n.*	Bursche {m}	
blonde *adj.*	blond	
blood *n.*	Blut {n}	
bloodshed	*n.*	Blutvergießen {n}
bloody *adj.*	blutig	
bloom *v.*	blühen	
bloomers	*n.*	Pluderhosen {pl}
blossom	*n.*	Blüte {f}
blot *n.*	Schandfleck {m}	
blotch *n.*	Fleckigkeit {f}	
blouse *n.*	Bluse {f}	
blow *v.*	blasen	
blowsy *adj.*	schlampig	
blub *v.*	heulen	
bludgeon	*n.*	Knüppel {m}
blue *adj.*	blau	
bluff *v.*	täuschen	
blunder	*n.*	Fehler {n}
blunt *adj.*	stumpf	
blur *v.*	verwischen	
blurb *n.*	Klappentext {m}	
blurt *v.*	herausplatzen	
blush *v.*	erröten	
blusher *n.*	Schamröte {f}	
bluster *v.*	toben	
boar *n.*	Eber {m}	
board *n.*	Vorstand {m}	

boast *v.*	prahlen
boat *n.*	Boot {n}
bob *v.*	auftauchen
bobble *n.*	Bommel {f,m}
bode *v.*	erwarten
bodice *n.*	Taille {f}
bodily *adv.*	körperlich
body *n.*	Körper {m}
bodyguard *n*	Leibwache {f}
bog *n.*	Moor {n}
bogey *n.*	Kobold {m}
boggle *v.*	zurückschrecken
bogus *adj.*	gefälscht
boil *v.i.*	kochen
boiler *n.*	Kocher {m}
boisterous *adj.*	ungestüm
bold *adj.*	heftig
boldness *n.*	Mut {m}
bole *n.*	Baumstamm {m}
bollard *n.*	Poller {m}
bolt *n.*	Bolzen {m}
bomb *n.*	Bombe {f}
bombard *v.*	bestürmen
bombardment *n.*	Bombenangriff {m}
bomber *n.*	Bomber {m}
bonafide *adj.*	gutgläubig
bonanza *n.*	Glücksfall {m}
bond *n.*	Anleihe {f}
bondage *n.*	Unfreiheit {f}
bone *n.*	Knochen {m}
bonfire *n.*	Freudenfeuer {n}
bonnet *n.*	Mütze {f}
bonus *n.*	Prämie {f}
bony *adj.*	knöcherne

book *n.*	Buch {n}
booklet *n.*	Bändchen {n}
bookmark *n.*	Lesemarke {f}
bookseller *n.*	Buchhändler {m}
bookish *adj.*	buchgelehrt
boom *n.*	Donner {m}
boon *n.*	Wohltat {f}
boor *n.*	Lümmel {m}
boost *v.*	verstärken
booster *n.*	Spannungsverstärker {m}
boot *n.*	Stiefel {m}
booth *n.*	Stand {m}
bootleg *adj.*	Raubpressung {f}
booty *n.*	Beute {f}
border *n.*	Begrenzung {f}
bore *v.*	langweilen
born *adj.*	geboren
borough *n.*	Stadtgemeinde {f}
borrow *v.*	ausleihen
bosom *n.*	Busen {m}
boss *n.*	Oberhaupt {n}
bossy *adj.*	diktatorisch
botany *n.*	Pflanzenkunde {f}
both *adj. & pron.*	beide
bother *v.*	belästigen
bottle *n.*	Flasche {f}
bottom *n.*	Fußgrund {m}
bough *n.*	Ast {m}
boulder *n.*	Feldstein {m}
boulevard *n.*	Boulevard {n}
bounce *v.*	springen
bouncer *n.*	Türsteher {m}
bound *v.*	verbunden
boundary *n.*	Rand {m}

27

boundless	*adj.*	grenzenlos
bountiful	*adj.*	freigebig
bounty *n.*		Freigebigkeit {f}
bouquet	*n.*	Blumenstrauß {m}
bout *n.*		Runde {f}
boutique	*n.*	Laden {m}
bow *n.*		Bogen {m}
bow *v.*		verbeugen
bowel *n.*		Darm {m}
bower *n.*		Laube {f}
bowl *n.*		Becken {n}
box *n.*		Schachtel {f}
boxer *n.*		Boxer {m}
boxing *n*		Boxen {n}
boy *n.*		Junge {m}
boycott	*v.*	boykottieren
boyhood	*n*	Jugend {f}
bra *n.*		BH {m}
brace *n.*		Tragband {n}
bracelet	*n.*	Armband {n}
bracket *n.*		Klammer {f}
brag *v.*		prahlen
Braille *n.*		Blindenschrift {f}
brain *n.*		Hirn {n}
brake *n.*		Bremse {f}
branch *n.*		Ast {m}
brand *n.*		Brandmal {n}
brandish	*v.*	schwingen
brandy *n.*		Weinbrand {m}
brash *adj.*		aufdringlich
brass *n.*		Messing {n}
brave *adj.*		tapfer
bravery	*n.*	Tapferkeit {f}
brawl *n.*		Schlägerei {f}

bray *v.*		zerreiben
breach *v.*		brechen
bread *n.*		Brot {n}
breadth	*n.*	Breite {f}
break *v.*		unterbrechen
breakage	*n.*	Bruchstelle {f}
breakfast	*n.*	Frühstück {n}
breast *n.*		Brust {f}
breath *n.*		Atem {m}
breathe	*v.*	atmen
breech *n.*		Verschluss {m}
breeches	*n.*	Kniehosen {pl}
breed *v.*		züchten
breeze *n.*		Lärm {m}
brevity *n.*		Kürze {f}
brew *v.*		brauen
brewery	*n.*	Brauerei {f}
bribe *v. t.*		bestechen
brick *n.*		Backstein {m}
bridal *adj.*		brautlich
bride *n.*		Braut {f}
bridegroom *n.*		Bräutigam {m}
bridge *n.*		Brücke {f}
bridle *n.*		Zaum {m}
brief *adj.*		kurz
briefing *n.*		Beratung {f}
brigade	*n.*	Brigade {f}
brigadier	*n.*	Brigadier {m}
bright *adj.*		hell
brighten	*v.*	aufhellen
brilliance	*n.*	Glanz {m}
brilliant	*adj.*	strahlend
brim *n.*		Rand {m}
brindle *adj.*		scheckig

28

brine	n.	Salzlauge {f}	brusque	adj.	schroff
bring	v.	bringen	brutal	adj.	brutal
brink	n.	Rand {m}	brute	n.	Tier {n}
brisk	adj.	lebhaft	bubble	n.	Luftblase {f}
bristle	n.	Borste {f}	buck	n.	Bock {m}
British	adj.	britisch	bucket	n.	Schaufel {f}
brittle	adj.	spröde	buckle	n.	Schnalle {f}
broach	adj.	anstechend	bud	n.	Knospe {f}
broad	adj.	breit	budge	v.	bewegen
broadcast	v. t	übertragen	budget	n.	Kostenrahmen {m}
brocade	n.	Brokat {n}	buffalo	n.	Büffel {m}
broccoli	n.	Brokkoli {m}	buffer	n.	Stoßdämpfer {m}
brochure	n.	Broschüre {f}	buffet	n.	Buffet {n}
broke	adj.	zerbrochen	buffoon	n.	Witzbold {m}
broken	adj.	kaputt	bug	n.	Insekt {n}
broker	n.	Makler {m}	buggy	n.	Kinderwagen {m}
bronchial	adj.	bronchial	bugle	n.	Waldhorn {n}
bronze	n.	Bronze {f}	build	v.	bauen
brood	n.	Brut {f}	building	n.	Gebäude {n}
brook	n.	Bach {m}	bulb	n.	Blumenzwiebel {f}
broom	n.	Besen {m}	bulge	n.	Zunahme {f}
broth	n.	Fleischbrühe {f}	bulimia	n.	Fresssucht {f}
brothel	n.	Puff {m}	bulk	n.	Masse {f}
brother	n.	Bruder {m}	bulky	adj.	klotzig
brotherhood	n.	Brüderschaft {f}	bull	n.	Stier {m}
brow	n.	Braue {f}	bulldog	n.	Bulldogge {f}
brown	n.	braun	bullet	n.	Kugel {f}
browse	v.	grasen	bulletin	n.	Bericht {m}
browser	n.	Betrachter {m}	bullion	n.	Goldbarren {m}
bruise	n.	Prellung {f}	bullish	adj.	dickköpfig
brunch	n.	Gabelfrühstück {n}	bullock	n.	Ochse {m}
brunette		Brünette {f}	bully	n.	Raufbold {m}
brunt	n.	Hauptstoß {m}	bulwark	n.	Bollwerk {n}
brush	n.	Bürste {f}	bum	n.	Gammler {m}

29

bumble v.	herumwursteln	
bump n.	Plumps {m}	
bumper n.	Stoßstange {f}	
bumpkin n.	Bauernlümmel {m}	
bumpy adj.	holperig	
bun n.	Teilchen {n}	
bunch n.	Strauß {m}	
bundle n.	Bündel {n}	
bung n.	Spund {m}	
bungalow n.	Bungalow {n}	
bungle v.	vermasseln	
bunk n.	Quatsch {m}	
bunker n.	Bunker {m}	
buoy n.	Boje {f}	
buoyant adj.	schwimmend	
buoyancy n.	Lebenskraft {f}	
burble v.	plappern	
burden n.	Last {f}	
bureau n.	Büro {n}	
bureaucracy n.	Bürokratie {f}	
bureaucrat n.	Bürokrat {m}	
burgeon v.	knospen	
burger n.	Hamburger {m}	
burglar n.	Einbrecher {m}	
burglary n.	Einbruch {m}	
burial n.	Leichenbegräbnis {n}	
burlesque n.	Posse {f}	
burn v.	anbrennen	
burner n.	Brenner {m}	
burning adj.	anbrennend	
burrow n.	Kaninchenbau {m}	
bursar n.	Schatzmeister {m}	
bursary n.	Schatzamt {n}	
burst v.	explodieren	

bury v.	vergraben	
bus n.	Autobus {m}	
bush n.	Busch {m}	
bushy adj.	buschig	
business n.	Betrieb {m}	
businessman n.	Geschäftsmann {m}	
bust n.	Busen {m}	
bustle v.	hasten	
busy adj.	geschäftig	
but conj.	aber	
butcher n.	Metzger {m}	
butler n.	Diener {m}	
butter n.	Butter {f}	
butterfly n.	Schmetterling {m}	
buttock n.	Hinterbacke {f}	
button n.	Knopf {m}	
buy v.	kaufen	
buyer n.	Einkäufer {m}	
buzz n.	Anruf {m}	
buzzard n.	Bussard {m}	
buzzer n.	Summer {m}	
by prep.	durch	
by-election n.	Zwischenwahl {f}	
bygone adj.	vergangen	
byline n.	Nebenlinie {f}	
bypass n.	Umgehung {f}	
byre n.	Kuhstall {m}	
bystander n.	Zuschauer {m}	
byte n.	Byte {n}	

C

cab n.	Taxi {n}	
cabaret n.	Kabarett {n}	
cabbage n.	Kraut {n}	

30

cabin	n.	Kabine {f}	
cabinet	n.	Kabinett {n}	
cable	n.	Kabel {n}	
cacao	n.	Kakao {m}	
cache	n.	Pufferspeicher {m}	
cachet	n.	Merkmal {m}	
cackle	v.	gackeln	
cactus	n.	Kaktus {m}	
cad	n.	Prolet {m}	
cadaver	n.	Kadaver {m}	
caddy	n.	Teedose {f}	
cadaver	n.	Kadaver	
cadet	n.	Kadett {m}	
cadmium	n.	Cadmium {n}	
cadre	n.	Kader {m}	
caesarean	n.	Kaiserschnitt {m}	
cafe	n.	Café {n}	
cafeteria	n.	Cafeteria {f}	
cage	n.	Schaltkäfig {m}	
cahoots	n.	Teilhaberschaften {pl}	
cajole	v.	schmeicheln	
cake	n.	Kuchen {m}	
calamity	n.	Katastrophe {f}	
calcium	n.	Calcium {n}	
calculate	v.	rechnen	
calculator	n.	Rechner {m}	
calculation	n.	Berechnung {f}	
calendar	n.	Kalender {m}	
calf	n.	Kalb {n}	
calibrate	v.	kalibrieren	
calibre	n.	Kaliber {n}	
call	v.	rufen	
calligraphy	n.	Kalligraphie {f}	
calling	n.	Aufruf {m}	

callous adj. schwielig,
callow adj. nackt
calm adj. still
calorie n. Kalorie {f}
calumny n. Verleumdung {f}
camaraderie n. Kameradschaftsgeist {m}
camber n. Bombage {f}
cambric n. Batist {m}
camcorder n. Camcorder {m}
camel n. Kamel {n}
cameo n. geschnittener Stein
camera n. Kamera {f}
camp n. Lager {n}
campaign n. Kampagne {f}
camphor n. Kampfer {m}
campus n. Campus {m}
can n. Kanister {m}
can v. konnen
canal n. Kanal {m}
canard n. Zeitungsente {f}
cancel v. kündigen
cancellation n. Absage {f}
cancer n. Krebs {m}
candela n. Candela
candid adj. aufrichtig
candidate n. Bewerber {m}
candle n. Kerze {f}
candour n. Aufrichtigkeit {f}
candy n. Bonbon {n}
cane n. Stock {m}
canine adj. hundeartig
canister n. Kanister {m}
cannabis n. Cannabis {m}
cannibal n. Kannibale {m}

31

cannon *n.*	Kanone {f}
canny *adj.*	umsichtig
canoe *n.*	Paddelboot {n}
canon *n.*	Stiftsherr {m}
canopy *n.*	Thronhimmel {m}
cant *n.*	Schräge {f}
cantankerous *adj.*	zänkisch
canteen *n.*	Gemeinschaftsküche {f}
canter *n.*	Kanter {m}
canton *n.*	Bezirk {m}
cantonment *n.*	Quartier {f}
canvas *n.*	Leinwand {f}
canvass *v.*	prüfen
canyon *n.*	Schlucht {f}
cap *n.*	Mütze {f}
capability *n.*	Leistungsfähigkeit {f}
capable *adj.*	fähig
capacious *adj.*	geräumig
capacitor *n.*	Kondensator {m}
capacity *n.*	Kapazität {f}
caparison *n.*	Schabracke {f}
cape *n.*	Umhang {m}
capital *n.*	Kapital {n}
capitalism *n.*	Kapitalismus {m}
capitalist *n.&adj.*	Kapitalist {m}
capitalize *v.*	kapitalisieren
capitation *n.*	Zahlung {f}
capitulate *v.*	aufgeben
caprice *n.*	Kaprize {f}
capricious *adj.*	launisch
capsicum *n.*	Paprika {m}
capsize *v.*	kentern
capstan *n.*	Rollenantrieb {m}
capsule *n.*	Kapsel {f}

captain *n.*	Mannschaftskapitän {m}
captaincy *n.*	Kapitänsamt {n}
caption *n.*	Bildlegende {f}
captivate *v.*	fesseln
captive *n.*	Gefangener
captivity *n.*	Gefangenschaft {f}
captor *n.*	Fänger {m}
capture *v.*	gefangennehmen
car *n.*	Auto {n}
caramel *n.*	Karamell {n}
carat *n.*	Karat {n}
caravan *n.*	Wohnwagen {m}
carbohydrate *n.*	Kohlehydrat {n}
carbon *n.*	Kohlenstoff {m}
carbonate *adj.*	karbonisiert
carcass *n.*	Körper {m}
card *n.*	Karte {f}
cardamom *n.*	Kardamom {n}
cardboard *n.*	Karton {m}
cardiac *adj.*	herzkrank
cardigan *n.*	Strickjacke {f}
cardinal *n.*	Kardinal {m}
cardiograph *n.*	Kardiographie {f}
cardiology *n.*	Kardiologie {f}
care *n.*	Sorge {f}
career *n.*	Karriere {f}
carefree *adj.*	sorgenlos
careful *adj.*	sorgfältig
careless *adj.*	leichtsinnig
carer *n.*	Pflegekraft {f}
caress *v.*	liebkosen
caretaker *n.*	Verwalter {m}
cargo *n.*	Ladung {f}
caricature *n*	Karikatur {f}

32

carmine	n.	karminrot
carnage	n.	Blutbad {n}
carnal	adj.	fleischlich
carnival	n.	Karneval {m}
carnivore	n.	Raubtier {n}
carol	n.	Weihnachtslied {n}
carpal	adj.	karpal
carpenter	n.	Bautischler {m}
carpentry	n.	Zimmerhandwerk {n}
carpet	n.	Teppich {m}
carriage	n.	Schreibwagen {m}
carrier	n.	Spediteur {m}
carrot	n.	Karotte {f}
carry	v.	tragen
cart	n.	Einkaufswagen {m}
cartel	n.	Kartell {n}
cartilage	n.	Knorpel {m}
carton	n.	Schachtel {f}
cartoon	n.	Zeichentrickfilm {m}
cartridge	n.	Steckmodul {n}
carve	v.	schnitzen
carvery	n.	Schnitzlerei {f}
Casanova	n.	Casanova {m}
cascade	n.	Wasserfall {m}
case	n.	Kiste {f}
casement	n.	Fensterflügel {m}
cash	n.	Bargeld {m}
cashew	n.	Acajoubaum {m}
cashier	n.	Kassenbeamte {m}
cashmere	n.	Kaschmir {m}
casing	n.	Schalung {f}
casino	n.	Kasino {n}
cask	n.	Fass {n}
casket	n.	Transportbehälter {m}

casserole	n.	Kasserolle {f}
cassock	n.	Soutane {f}
cast	v.	Besetzung {f}
castaway	n.	Verworfene {m,f}
caste	n.	Kaste {f}
castigate	v.	züchtigen
casting	n.	Rollenbesetzung {f}
castle	n.	Schloss {n}
castor	n.	Fahrrolle {f}
castrate	v.	kastrieren
castor oil	a.	Rizinusöl {n}
casual	adj.	gelegentlich
casualty	n.	Verlust {m}
cat	n.	Katze {f}
cataclysm	n.	Katastrophe {f}
catalogue	n.	Katalog {m}
catalyse	v.	katalysieren
catalyst	n.	Katalysator {m}
cataract	n.	Katarakt {m}
catastrophe	n.	Katastrophe {f}
catch	v.	fangen
catching	adj.	auffangend
catchy	adj.	schwierig
catechism	n.	Katechismus {m}
categorical	adj.	kategorisch
categorize	v.	kategorisieren
category	n.	Kategorie {f}
cater	v.	heranschaffen
caterpillar	n.	Raupe {f}
catharsis	n.	Entspannung {f}
cathedral	n.	Kathedrale {f}
catholic	adj.	katholisch
cattle	n.	Rindvieh {n}
catty	n.	katzig

Caucasian	*adj.*	kaukasisch
cauldron	*n.*	Kessel {m}
cauliflower	*n.*	Blumenkohl {m}
causal *adj.*	ursächlich
causality	*n.*	Kausalität {f}
cause	*n.*	Ursache {f}
causeway	*n.*	Damm {m}
caustic *adj.*	ätzend
caution	*n.*	Vorsicht {f}
cautionary	*adj.*	warnend
cautious	*adj.*	zurückhaltend
cavalcade	*n.*	Kavalkade {f}
cavalier	*adj.*	hochmütig
cavalry *n.*	Reiterei {f}
cave	*n.*	Höhle {f}
caveat *n.*	Einspruch {f}
cavern *n.*	Höhle {f}
cavernous	*adj.*	porös
cavity *n.*	Aushöhlung {f}
cavort *v.*	umherspringen
cease *v.*	enden
ceasefire	*n.*	Feuerpause {f}
ceaseless	*adj.*	unaufhörlich
cedar *n.*	Zeder {f}
cede *v.*	überlassen
ceiling *n.*	Zimmerdecke {f}
celandine	*n.*	Scharbockskraut {n}
celebrant	*n.*	Zelebrant {m}
celebrate	*v.*	feiern
celebration *n.*	Fest {n}
celebrity	*n.*	Berühmtheit {f}
celestial	*adj.*	himmlisch
celibacy	*n.*	Zölibat {n}
celibate	*adj.*	unverheiratet

cell	*n.*	Zelle {f}
cellar	*n.*	Keller {m}
cellphone	*n.*	Mobiltelefon {n}
cellular *adj.*	zellig
cellulite	*n.*	Cellulite {f}
celluloid	*n.*	Zelluloid {n}
cellulose	*n.*	Zellstoff {m}
Celsius *n.*	Celsius
Celtic	*adj.*	keltisch
cement	*n.*	Zement {m}
cemetery	*n.*	Friedhof {m}
censer *n.*	Rauchfass {n}
censor *n.*	Kritiker {m}
censorship *n.*	Zensur {f}
censorious	*adj.*	mäkelig
censure	*v.*	tadeln
census *n.*	Volkszählung {f}
cent	*n.*	Cent
centenary	*n.*	Jahrhundert {n}
centennial	*n.*	Hundertjahrfeier {f}
center	*n.*	Zentrum
centigrade	*adj.*	hundertgradig
centimetre	*n.*	Zentimeter
centipede	*n.*	Tausendfuß {m}
central *adj.*	zentral
centralize	*v.*	zentralisieren
centre	*n.*	Mitte {f}
century *n.*	Jahrhundert {n}
ceramic	*n.*	Keramik {f}
cereal	*n.*	Getreide {n}
cerebral	*adj.*	zerebral
ceremonial *adj.*	feierlich
ceremonious	*adj.*	zeremoniös
ceremony	*n.*	Zeremonie {f}

34

certain	*adj.*	bestimmt	
certainly	*adv.*	gewiss	
certifiable	*adj.*	feststellbar	
certificate	*n.*	Bescheinigung {f}	
certify	*v.*	bescheinigen	
certitude	*n.*	Sicherheit {f}	
cervical	*adj.*	Hals {m}	
cessation	*n.*	Einstellung {f}	
cession	*n.*	Abtretung {f}	
chain	*n.*	Kette {f}	
chair	*n.*	Vorsitz {m}	
chairman	*n.*	Vorsitzende {m}	
chaise	*n.*	Liege {f}	
chalet	*n.*	Sennhütte {f}	
chalice	*n.*	Kelch {m}	
chalk	*n.*	Kreide {f}	
challenge	*n.*	Kampfansage {f}	
chamber	*n.*	Kammer {f}	
chamberlain	*n.*	Kammerherr {m}	
champagne	*n.*	Champagner {m}	
champion	*n.*	Meister {m}	
chance	*n.*	Möglichkeit {f}	
chancellor	*n.*	Kanzler {m}	
Chancery	*n.*	Kanzleigericht {n}	
chandelier	*n.*	Lüster {m}	
change	*v.*	Veränderung {f}	
channel	*n.*	Kanal {m}	
chant	*n.*	Kirchenlied {n}	
chaos	*n.*	Chaos {n}	
chaotic	*adj.*	chaotisch	
chapel	*n.*	Kapelle {f}	
chaplain	*n.*	Geistliche {m,f}	
chapter	*n.*	Abschnitt {m}	
char	*v.*	Zeichen {n}	

character	*n.*	Beschaffenheit {f}	
characteristic	*n.*	Ausprägung {f}	
charcoal	*n.*	Aktivkohle {f}	
charge	*v.*	Ladung {f}	
charge	*n.*	laden	
charger	*n.*	Ladegerät {n}	
chariot	*n.*	Kulissenwagen {m}	
charisma	*n.*	Ausstrahlung {f}	
charismatic	*adj.*	charismatisch	
charitable	*adj.*	wohltätig	
charity	*n.*	Mitleid {n}	
charlatan	*n.*	Quacksalber {m}	
charm	*n.*	Lieblichkeit {f}	
charming	*adj.*	bezaubernd	
chart	*n.*	Schaubild {n}	
charter	*n.*	Befrachtung {f}	
chartered	*adj.*	verfrachtet	
chary	*adj.*	vorsichtig	
chase	*v.*	verfolgen	
chassis	*n.*	Fahrgestell {n}	
chaste	*adj.*	rein	
chasten	*v.*	kasteien	
chastise	*v.*	bestrafen	
chastity	*n.*	Keuschheit {f}	
chat	*v. i.*	Plauderei {f}	
chateau	*n.*	Landhaus {n}	
chattel	*n.*	Habe {n}	
chatter	*v.*	schnattern	
chauffeur	*n.*	Fahrer {m}	
chauvinism	*n.*	Chauvinismus {m}	
chauvinist	*n. &adj.*	chauvinist	
cheap	*adj.*	billig	
cheapen	*v. t.*	verbilligen	
cheat	*v.*	betrügen	

35

cheat	*n.*	Falschspieler {m}	
check	*v.*	prüfen	
checkmate	*n*	Schachmatt {n}	
cheek	*n.*	Backe {f}	
cheeky	*adj.*	frech	
cheep	*v.*	piepsen	
cheer	*v. t.*	jubeln	
cheerful	*adj.*	heiter	
cheerless	*adj.*	trostlos	
cheery	*adj.*	froh	
cheese	*n.*	Käse {m}	
cheetah	*n.*	Gepard {m}	
chef	*n.*	Chefkoch {m}	
chemical	*adj.*	chemisch	
chemist	*n.*	Chemiker {m}	
chemistry	*n.*	Chemie {f}	
chemotherapy	*n.*	Chemotherapie {f}	
cheque	*n.*	Scheck {m}	
cherish	*v.*	schätzen	
chess	*n.*	Schach {n}	
chest	*n.*	Koffer {m}	
chestnut	*n.*	Kastanie {f}	
chevron	*n.*	Sparren {m}	
chew	*v.*	kauen	
chic	*adj.*	schick	
chicanery	*n.*	Schikane {f}	
chicken	*n.*	Huhn {n}	
chickpea	*n.*	Kichererbse {f}	
chide	*v.*	schelten	
chief	*n.*	Anführer {m}	
chiefly	*adv.*	hauptsächlich	
chieftain	*n.*	Häuptling {m}	
child	*n.*	Kind {n}	
childhood	*n.*	Kindheit {f}	

childish	*adj.*	kindisch
chill	*n.*	Kältegefühl {n}
chilli	*n.*	Chili {m}
chilly	*adj.*	frostig
chime	*n.*	Ton {m}
chimney	*n.*	Schornstein {m}
chimpanzee	*n.*	Schimpanse {m}
chin	*n.*	Kinn {n}
china	*n.*	Porzellan {n}
chip	*n.*	Chip {m}
chirp	*v.*	zirpen
chisel	*n.*	Meißel {m}
chit	*n.*	Kindchen {n}
chivalrous	*adj.*	galant
chivalry	*n.*	Rittertum {n}
chlorine	*n.*	Chlor {n}
chloroform	*n.*	Chloroform {n}
chocolate	*n.*	Schokolade {f}
choice	*n.*	Wahlmöglichkeit {f}
choir	*n.*	Chor {m}
choke	*v.*	würgen
cholera	*n.*	Cholera {f}
choose	*v. t*	wählen
chop	*v.*	zerhacken
chopper	*n.*	Zerhacker {m}
chopstick	*n.*	Essstäbchen {n}
choral	*adj.*	choral
chord	*n.*	Profilsehne {f}
chorus	*n.*	Chor {m}
Christ	*n.*	Christus {m}
Christian	*adj.*	christlich {adj}
Christianity	*n.*	Christentum {n}
Christmas	*n.*	Weihnachten {n}
chrome	*n.*	Chrom {n}

chronic	*adj.*	chronisch	citric	*adj.* zitrus

chronic *adj.* chronisch

chronicle *n.* Aufzeichnung {f}

chronology *n.* Chronologie {f}

chronograph *n.* Chronograph {m}

chuckle *v.* glucken

chum *n.* Kumpel {m}

chunk *n.* Klotz {m}

church *n.* Kirche {f}

churchyard *n.* Kirchhof {m}

churn *v.* Butterfass {n}

chutney *n.* Chutney {n}

cider *n.* Apfelsaft {m}

cigar *n.* Zigarre {f}

cigarette *n.* Zigarette {f}

cinema *n* Kino {n}

cinnamon *n.* Zimt {m}

circle *n.* Kreis {m}

circuit *n.* Schaltung {f}

circular *adj.* kreisförmig

circulate *v.* zirkulieren

circulation *n.* Blutkreislauf {m}

circumcise *v.* beschneiden

circumference *n.* Kreisumfang {m}

circumscribe *v.* umschreiben

circumspect *adj.* vorsichtig

circumstance *n.* Umstand {m}

circus *n.* Zirkus {m}

cist *n.* Steinkiste {f}

cistern *n.* Zisterne {f}

citadel *n.* Zitadelle {f}

cite *v.* zitieren

citizen *n.* Staatsbürger {m}

citizenship *n.* Staatsangehörigkeit {f}

citrus *n.* Zitrus

citric *adj.* zitrus

city *n.* Stadt {f}

civic *adj.* staatsbürgerlich

civics *n.* Bürgerpflicht {f}

civil *adj.* zivil

civilian *n.* Zivilist {m}

civilization *n.* Zivilisation {f}

civilize *v.* zivilisieren

clad *adj.* kaschiert

cladding *n.* Ausmauerung {f}

claim *v.* klagen

claimant *n.* Antragsteller {m}

clammy *adj.* feuchtkalt

clamour *n.* Geschrei {n}

clamp *n.* Steigbügel {m}

clan *n.* Sippe {f}

clandestine *adj.* heimlich

clap *v.* klatschen

clarify *v.* abklären

clarification *n.* Aufklärung {f}

clarion *adj.* Kriegsfanfare {f}

clarity *n.* Übersichtlichkeit {f}

clash *v.* zusammenstoßen

clasp *v.* umklammern

class *n.* Klasse {f}

classic *adj.* klassisch

classical *adj.* klassischer

classification *n.* Aufgliederung {f}

classify *v.* einstufen

clause *n.* Klausel {f}

claustrophobia *n.* Klaustrophobie {f}

claw *n.* Fang {m}

clay *n.* Ton {m}

clean *adj.* sauber

cleanliness	*n.*	Reinlichkeit {f}	
cleanse	*v.*	reinigen	
clear	*adj.*	deutlich	
clearance	*n.*	Klärung {f}	
clearly	*adv.*	klar	
cleave	*v.*	kleben	
cleft	*n.*	Riss {m}	
clemency	*n.*	Nachsicht {f}	
clement	*adj.*	nachsichtig	
Clementine	*n.*	Klementine	
clench	*v.*	zusammen beißen	
clergy	*n.*	Geistliche {m,f}	
cleric	*n.*	Kleriker {m}	
clerical	*adj.*	kirchlich	
clerk	*n.*	Schreiber {m}	
clever	*adj.*	klug	
click	*n.*	Klick {m}	
client	*n.*	Kunde {m}	
cliff	*n.*	Felsvorsprung {m}	
climate	*n.*	Klima {n}	
climax	*n.*	Höhepunkt {m}	
climb	*v.i*	klettern	
clinch	*v.*	anheften	
cling	*v.*	anschmiegen	
clinic	*n.*	Klinik {f}	
clink	*n.*	Ziegelstein {m}	
clip	*n.*	Klemme {f}	
cloak	*n.*	Mantel {m}	
clock	*n.*	Uhr {f}	
cloister	*n.*	Kreuzgang {m}	
clone	*n.*	Clone {n}	
close	*adj.*	nah	
closet	*n.*	begehbarer Schrank	
closure	*n.*	Verschluss {m}	

clot	*n.*	Klumpen {m}	
cloth	*n.*	Tuch {n}	
clothe	*v.*	kleiden	
clothes	*n.*	Kleidung {f}	
clothing	*n.*	Kleidung {f}	
cloud	*n.*	Wolke {f}	
cloudy	*adj.*	wolkig	
clove	*n.*	Nelke {f}	
clown	*n.*	Clown {m}	
cloying	*adj.*	anwidernd	
club	*n.*	Club {m}	
clue	*n.*	Hinweis {m}	
clumsy	*adj.*	plump	
cluster	*n.*	Haufen {m}	
clutch	*v. t.*	packen	
coach	*n.*	Trainer {m}	
coal	*n.*	Steinkohle {f}	
coalition	*n.*	Koalition {f}	
coarse	*adj.*	ungeschliffen	
coast	*n.*	Küste {f}	
coaster	*n.*	Küstenfahrer {m}	
coat	*n.*	Jackett {n}	
coating	*n.*	Beschichtung {f}	
coax	*v.*	Koaxialkabel {n}	
cobalt	*n.*	Kobalt {n}	
cobble	*n.*	Stümper {m}	
cobbler	*n.*	Schuster {m}	
cobra	*n.*	Brillenschlange {f}	
cobweb	*n.*	Spinnennetz {n}	
cocaine	*n.*	Kokain {n}	
cock	*n.*	Hahn {m}	
cockade	*n.*	Kokarde {f}	
cockpit	*n.*	Kanzel {f}	
cockroach	*n.*	Kakerlake {f}	

cocktail	n. Cocktail {n}	collaborate	v.zusammen arbeiten
cocky	adj. eingebildet	collaboration	n. Mitarbeit {f}
cocoa	n. Kakao {m}	collage n.	Collage {f}
coconut	n. Kokosnuss {f}	collapse	v. zusammenbrechen
cocoon n.	Kokon {m}	collar n.	Halsband {n}
code	n. Kode {m}	collate v.	kollationieren
co-education	n. Koedukation {f}	collateral	n. Kollateral
coefficient	n. Koeffizient {m}	colleague	n. Kollege {m}
coerce v.	zwingen	collect v.	sammeln
coeval adj.	gleichzeitig	collection	n. Sammlung {f}
coexist	v. koexistieren	collective	adj. eingesammelt
coexistence	n. Koexistenz {f}	collector	n. Kollektor {m}
coffee n.	Kaffee {m}	college	n. Fachhochschule
coffer n.	Kasten {m}	collide v.	kollidieren
coffin n.	Totenschrein {m}	colliery n.	Kohlenbergwerk {n}
cog n.	Radzahn {m}	collision	n. Karambolage {f}
cogent adj.	zwingend	colloquial	adj. umganglich
cogitate v.	überlegen	collusion	n. Kollusion {f}
cognate adj.	verwandt	cologne	n. Kölnisch Wasser {n}
cognizance n.	Erkenntnis {f}	colon n.	Dickdarm {m}
cohabit v.	kohabitieren	colonel	n. Oberst {m}
cohere v.	zusammenhängen	colonial	adj. kolonial
coherent adj.	zusammenhängend	colony n.	Siedlung {f}
cohesion n.	Kohäsion {f}	colossal	adj. riesig
cohesive adj.	zusammenhaltend	colossus n.	Riese {m}
coil n.	Wicklung {f}	column n.	Stütze {f}
coin n.	Münze {f}	colour n.	Farbe {f}
coinage n.	Münzwesen {n}	colouring n.	Färbung {f}
coincide v.	übereinstimmen	colourless	n. farblos
coincidence n.	Zufall {m}	coma n.	Koma {n}
coir n.	Kokoswandplatte {f}	comb n.	Kamm {m}
coke n.	Koks {m}	combat n.	Bekämpfung {f}
cold adj.	kalt	combatant n.	Kämpfer {m}
colic n.	Kolik {f}	combination	n. Kombination {f}

39

combine	v.	vereinigen	commitment	n.	Verbindlichkeit {f}
combustible	adj.	entflammbar	committee	n.	Ausschuss {m}

combine *v.* vereinigen
combustible *adj.* entflammbar
combustion *n.* Verbrennung {f}
come *v.* kommen
comedian *n.* Schauspieler {m}
comedy *n* Komödie {f}
comet *n.* Komet {m}
comfort *n.* Trost {m}
comfort *v.* trösten
comfortable *adj.* trostreich
comic *adj.* komisch
comma *n.* Komma {n}
command *v.* befehlen
commandant *n.* Kommandant {m}
commander *n.* Kapitän {m}
commando *n.* Kommandotruppe {f}
commemorate *v.* gedenken
commemoration *n.*Gedenkfeier {f}
commence *v.* anfangen
commencement *n.* Anfang {m}
commend *v.* empfehlen
commendable *adj.* lobenswert
commendation *n.* Belobigung {f}
comment *n.* Anmerkung {f}
commentary *n.* Kommentar {m}
commentator *n.* Kommentator {m}
commerce *n.* Handel {m}
commercial *adj.* kaufmännisch
commiserate *v.* bemitleiden
commission *n.* Weisung {f}
commissioner *n.* Bevollmächtigte
commissure *n.*Nervenfaserbündel {pl}
commit *v.* verüben

commitment *n.* Verbindlichkeit {f}
committee *n.* Ausschuss {m}
commode *n.* Kommode {f}
commodity *n.* Bedarfsartikel {m}
common *adj.* allgemein
commoner *n.* Bürger {m}
commonplace *adj.* banal
commonwealth *n.*Staatenbund {m}
commotion *n.* Unruhe {f}
communal *adj.* kommunal
commune *n.* Gemeinde {n}
communicable *adj.* mitteilbar
communicant *n.* Kommunikant {m}
communicate *v.* mitteilen
communication *n.* Mitteilung {f}
communion *n.* Kommunion {f}
communism *n.* Kommunismus {m}
community *n.* Gemeinschaft {f}
commute *v.* pendeln
compact *adj.* kompakt
companion *n.* Gefährte {m}
company *n.* Unternehmen {n}
comparative *adj.* vergleichend
compare *v.* vergleichen
comparison *n.* Vergleich {m}
compartment *n.* Abteilung {f}
compass *n.* Kompass {m}
compassion *n.* Mitleid {n}
compatible *adj.* verträglich
compatriot *n.* Landsmann {m}
compel *v.* zwingen
compendious *adj.* zusammen gefasst
compendium *n.* Handbuch {n}
compensate *v.* kompensieren

40

compensation	n.	Entschädigung {f}	
compere	v.	moderieren	
compete	v.	konkurrieren	
competence	n.	Zuständigkeit {f}	
competent	adj.	sachkundig	
competition	n.	Wettbewerb {m}	
competitive	adj.	konkurrenzfähig	
competitor	n.	Konkurrent {m}	
compile	v.	übersetzen	
complacent	adj.	selbstgefällig	
complain	v.	klagen	
complaint	n.	Beschwerde {f}	
complaisant	adj.	gefällig	
complement	n.	Gegensatz {m}	
complementary	adj.	ergänzend	
complete	adj.	vollständig	
completion	n.	Vervollständigung {f}	
complex	adj.	aufwändig	
complexity	n.	Umfang {m}	
complexion	n.	Gesichtsfarbe {f}	
compliance	n.	Zustimmung {f}	
compliant	adj.	gefällig	
complicate	v.	komplizieren	
complication	n.	Komplikation {f}	
complicit	adj.	mitschuldig	
complicity	n.	Mitschuld {f}	
compliment	n.	Kompliment {n}	
compliment	v. i	loben	
comply	v.	erfüllen	
component	n.	Bestandteil {m}	
comport	v.	sich betragen	
compose	v.	zusammenstellen	
composer	n.	Komponist {m}	
composite	adj.	gemischt	

composition	n.	Aufsatz {m}
compositor	n.	Setzer {m}
compost	n.	Kompost {m}
composure	n.	Gelassenheit {f}
compound	n.	Verbindung {f}
comprehend	v.	begreifen
comprehensible	adj.	Nachvollziehbar
comprehension	n.	Verständnis {n}
comprehensive	adj.	reichhaltig
compress	v.	komprimieren
compression	n.	Stauchung {f}
comprise	v.	umfassen
compromise	n.	Kompromiss {m}
compulsion	n.	Zwang {m}
compulsive	adj.	zwingend
compulsory	adj.	obligatorisch
compunction	n.	Gewissensbisse {pl}
computation	n.	Errechnung {f}
compute	v.	rechnen
computer	n.	Computer {m}
computerize	v.	computerisieren
comrade	n.	Kamerad {m}
concatenation	n.	Dateienverknüpfung {f}
concave	adj.	gewölbt
conceal	v.	kaschieren
concede	v.	einräumen
conceit	n.	Eingebildetheit {f}
conceivable	adj.	absehbar
conceive	v. t	ersinnen
concentrate	v.	konzentrieren
concentration	n.	Konzentration {f}
concept	n.	Entwurf {m}
conception	n.	Auffassung {f}
concern	v.	betreffen

concerning	*prep.*	betreffend	
concert	*n.*	Konzert {n}	
concerted	*adj.*	vereinbart	
concession	*n.*	Zugeständnis {n}	
conch	*n.*	Meeresschnecke {f}	
conciliate	*v.*	vermitteln	
concise	*adj.*	knapp	
conclude	*v.*	beenden	
conclusion	*n.*	Schlussfolgerung {f}	
conclusive	*adj.*	endgültig	
concoct	*v.*	zusammenbrauen	
concoction	*n.*	Gebräu {n}	
concomitant	*adj.*	gleichzeitig	
concord	*n.*	Übereinstimmung {f}	
concordance	*n.*	Übereinstimmung {f}	
concourse	*n.*	Zusammentreffen {n}	
concrete	*n.*	Beton {m}	
concubine	*n.*	Konkubine {f}	
concur	*v.*	mitwirken	
concurrent	*adj.*	simultan	
concussion	*n.*	Gehirnerschütterung {f}	
condemn	*v.*	verurteilen	
condemnation	*n.*	Verurteilung {f}	
condense	*v.*	kondensieren	
condescend	*v.*	geruhen	
condiment	*n.*	Würze {f}	
condition	*n.*	Bedingung {f}	
conditional	*adj.*	bedingt	
conditioner	*n.*	Balsam	
condole	*v.*	kondolieren	
condolence	*n.*	Beileid {n}	
condom	*n.*	Kondom {n}	
condominium	*n.*	Eigentumswohnung {f}	
condone	*v.*	verziehen	

conduct	*n.*	Aufführung {f}
conduct	*v.*	geleiten
conductor	*n.*	Dirigent {m}
cone	*n.*	Konus {m}
confection	*n.*	Konfekt {n}
confectioner	*n.*	Zuckerbäcker {m}
confectionery	*n.*	Konditorwaren {pl}
confederate	*adj.*	vereinigt
confederation	*n.*	Staatenbund {m}
confer	*v.*	vergleichen
conference	*n.*	Konferenz {f}
confess	*v.*	beichten
confession	*n.*	Beichte {f}
confidant	*n.*	Vertraute {m}
confide	*v.*	Vertrauen
confidence	*n.*	Vertrauen {n}
confident	*adj.*	vertrauensvoll
confidential	*adj.*	vertraulich
configuration	*n.*	Konfiguration {f}
confine	*v.*	begrenzen
confinement	*n.*	Gefangenschaft {f}
confirm	*v.*	bestätigen
confirmation	*n.*	Bestätigung {f}
confiscate	*v.*	Beschlagnehmen
confiscation	*n.*	Konfiszierung {f}
conflate	*v.*	verbinden
conflict	*n.*	Konflikt {m}
confluence	*n.*	Zusammenfluss {m}
confluent	*adj.*	zusammen fließend
conform	*v.*	anpassen
conformity	*n.*	Übereinstimmung {f}
confront	*v.*	gegenüberstellen
confrontation	*n.*	Gegenüberstellung {f}
confuse	*v.*	verlegen

42

confusion	n.	Verwechslung {f}
confute v.		widerlegen
congenial	adj.	sympathisch
congenital	adj.	angeboren
congested	adj.	verkehrsreich
congestion	n.	Überlastung {f}
conglomerate	n.	Konglomerat
conglomeration	n.	Anhäufung {f}
congratulate		v. Beglückwünschen
congratulation	n.	Beglückwünschung {f}
congregate	v.	versammeln
congress	n.	Kongress {m}
congruent	adj.	deckungsgleich
conical	adj.	kegelförmig
conjecture	n. &v.	Vermutung {f}
conjugal	adj.	ehelich
conjugate	v.	konjugieren
conjunct	adj.	vereint
conjunction	n.	Verbindung {f}
conjunctivitis	n.	Bindehautentzündung
conjuncture	n.	Umstand {m}
conjure v.		gezaubern
conker	n.	Kastanie {f}
connect	v.	verbinden
connection	n.	Verbindung {f}
connive	v.	dulden
conquer	v.	erobern
conquest	n.	Eroberung {f}
conscience	n.	Gewissen {n}
conscious	adj.	bewusst
consecrate	v.	segnen
consecutive	adj.	fortlaufend
consecutively	adv.	nachfolgen
consensus	n.	Konsens {m}

consent	n.	Genehmigung {f}
consent	v.t.	genehmigen
consequence	n.	Folge {f}
consequent	adj.	folgend
conservation	n.	Bewahrung {f}
conservative	adj.	konservativ
conservatory	n.	Konservatorium {n}
conserve	v. t	konservieren
consider	v.	bedenken
considerable	adj.	beträchtlich
considerate	adj.	bedachtsam
consideration	n.	Rücksichtnahme {f}
considering	prep.	erachtend
consign	v.	übergeben
consignment	n.	Warensendung {f}
consist	v.	bestehen aus
consistency	n.	Beschaffenheit {f}
consistent	adj.	konsistent
consolation	n.	Zuspruch {m}
console	v. t.	trösten
consolidate	v.	konsolidierung
consolidation	n.	Festigung {f}
consonant	n.	Konsonant {m}
consort	n.	Prinzgemahl {m}
consortium	n.	Vereinigung {f}
conspicuous	adj.	auffallend
conspiracy	n.	Verschwörung {f}
conspirator	n.	Verschwörer {m}
conspire	v.	verschwören
constable	n.	Polizist {m}
constabulary	n.	Polizeitruppe {f}
constant	adj.	konstant
constellation	n.	Konstellation {f}
consternation	n.	Bestürzung {f}

43

constipation	n. Darmverstopfung {f}	contemptuous	adj. Geringschätzig
constituency	n. Wahlkreis {m}	contend	v. disputieren
constituent	adj. zugehörig	content adj. zufrieden	
constitute	v. errichten	content	n. Inhalt {m}
constitution	n. Konstitution {f}	contention	n. Wettstreit {m}
constitutional	adj. gesetzmäßig	contentment	n. Zufriedenheit {f}
constrain	v. zwingen	contentious	adj. streitsüchtig
constraint	n. Einschränkung {f}	contest	n. Wettkampf {m}
constrict	v. zusammen ziehen	contestant	n. Wettkämpfer {m}
construct	v. bauen	context	n. Zusammenhang {m}
construction	n. Konstruktion {f}	contiguous	adj. zusammen hängend
constructive	adj. konstruktiv	continent	n. Kontinent {m}
construe	v. konstruieren	continental	adj. kontinental
consul	n. Konsul {m}	contingency	n. Möglichkeit {f}
consular	n. konsularisch	continual	adj. dauernd
consulate	n. Konsulat {n}	continuation	n. Fortführung {f}
consult	v. Befragen {n}	continue	v. fortsetzen
consultant	n. Fachberater {m}	continuity	n. Fortbestand {m}
consultation	n. Beratung {f}	continuous	adj. kontinuierlich
consume	v. verbrauchen	contort	v. Umriss {m}
consumer	n. Verbraucher {m}	contour	n. umrissen
consummate	v. vollenden	contra	prep. gegen
consumption	n. Verbrauch {m}	contraband	n. Konterbande {f}
contact	n. Kontakt {m}	contraception	n.
contagion	n. Ansteckung {f}	Schwangerschaftsverhütung {f}	
contagious	adj. ansteckend	contraceptive	n. Verhütungsmittel
contain	v.t. enthalten	{n} contract	n. Vertrag {m}
container	n. Container {m}	contractual	adj. vertraglich
containment	n. Eindämmung {f}	contractor	n. Bauunternehmer {m}
contaminate	v. verseuchen	contraction	n. Zusammenziehung {f}
contemplate	v. betrachten	contradict	v. widersprechen
contemplation	n. Betrachtung {f}	contradiction	n. Widerspruch {m}
contemporary	adj. zeitgenössisch	contrary	adj. entgegengesetzt
contempt	n. Verachtung {f}	contrast	n. Gegensatz {m}

44

contravene	v.	verstoßen	
contribute	v.	beitragen	
contribution	n.	Beitrag {m}	
contrivance	n.	Vorrichtung {f}	
contrive	v.	erfinden	
control	n.	Kontrolle {f}	
controller	n.	Steuereinheit {f}	
controversial	adj.	brisant	
controversy	n.	Kontroverse {f}	
contusion	n.	Kontusion {f}	
conundrum	v. t	Scherzfrage {f}	
conurbation	n.	Ballungsgebiet {n}	
convene	v.	berufen	
convenience	n.	Komfort {m}	
convenient	adj.	bequem	
convent	n.	Kloster {n}	
convention	n.	Konvention {f}	
converge	v.	konvergieren	
conversant	adj.	vertraut	
conversation	n.	Gespräch {n}	
converse	v.	Umkehrung {f}	
conversion	n.	Umsetzung {f}	
convert	v.	übertragen	
convert	v.	verwandeln	
convey	v.	versenden	
conveyance	n.	Spedition {f}	
convict	n.	Zuchthäusler {m}	
convict	v.	verurteilen	
conviction	n.	Verurteilung {f}	
convince	v.	überzeugen	
convivial	adj.	festlich	
convocation	n.	Einberufung {f}	
convoy	n.	Geleit {n}	
convulse	n.	erschüttern	

convulsion	n.	Zuckung {f}	
cook	n.	Koch {m}	
cook	v.	kochen	
cooker	n.	Kocher {m}	
cookie	n.	Keks {m}	
cool	adj.	kühl	
coolant	n.	Kühlmittel {n}	
cooler	n.	Kühler {m}	
cooper	n.	Küfer {m}	
cooperate	v.	zusammenwirken	
cooperation	n.	Kooperation {f}	
cooperative	adj.	Zusammenwirkend	
coordinate	v. t	koordinieren	
coordination	n.	Koordinierung {f}	
cope	v.	meistern	
copier	n.	Kopierer {m}	
copious	adj.	reichlich	
copper	n.	Kupfer {n}	
copulate	v.	begatten	
copy	n.	Abschrift {f}	
copy	v.	kopieren	
coral	n.	Koralle {f}	
cord	n.	Strick {m}	
cordial	adj.	herzlich	
cordon	n.	Kordon {m}	
core	n.	Kernstück {n}	
coriander	n.	Koriander {m}	
cork	n.	Korken {m}	
corn	n.	Getreide {n}	
cornea	n.	Hornhaut {f}	
corner	n.	Winkel {m}	
cornet	n.	Horn {n}	
coronation	n.	Krönung {f}	

45

coroner *n.* Untersuchungsrichter {m} **coronet** *n.* Diadem {n}
corporal *n.* Korporal {m}
corporate *adj.* vereinigt
corporation *n.* Gesellschaft {f}
corps *n.* Korps
corpse *n.* Leiche {f}
corpulent *adj.* beleibt
correct *adj.* richtig
correct *v.* korregieren
correction *n.* Korrektur {f}
corrective *adj.* fehlerbehebend
correlate *v.* beziehen
correlation *n.* Korrelation {f}
correspond *v.* korrespondieren
correspondence *n.* Briefwechsel {m}
correspondent *n.* Korrespondent {f}
corridor *n.* Korridor {m}
corroborate *v.* bekräftigen
corrode *v.* beizen
corrosion *n.* Korrosion {f}
corrosive *adj.* korrosiv
corrugated *adj.* gerillt
corrupt *adj.* korrupt
corruption *n.* Korruption {f}
cortisone *n.* Kortison {n}
cosmetic *adj.* kosmetisch
cosmetic *n.* Schönheitspflege {f}
cosmic *adj.* kosmisch
cosmology *n.* Kosmologie {f}
cosmopolitan *adj.* kosmopolit
cosmos *n.* Kosmos {m}
cost *v.* kosten
costly *adj.* aufwändig

costume *n.* Anzug {m}
cosy *adj.* gemütlich
cot *n.* Hütte {f}
cottage *n.* Häuschen {n}
cotton *n.* Baumwolle {f}
couch *n.* Liege {f}
couchette *n.* Liegewagen {m}
cough *v.* husten
council *n.* Rat {m}
councillor *n.* Ratsmitglied {n}
counsel *n.* Ratschlag {m}
counsel *v.* raten
counsellor *n.* Ratgeber {m}
count *v.* zählen
countenance *n.* Ermutigung {f}
counter *n.* Zähler {m}
counter *v.t.* durchkreuzen
counteract *v.* entgegenwirken
counterfeit *adj.* nachgemacht
counterfoil *n.* Kontrollabschnitt {m}
countermand *v.* abbestellen
counterpart *n.* Entsprechung {f}
countless *adj.* zahllos
country *n.* Land {n}
county *n.* Grafschaft {f}
coup *n.* Putsch {m}
coupe *n.* Coupé {n}
couple *n.* Paar {n}
couplet *n.* Verspaar {n}
coupon *n.* Coupon {m}
courage *n.* Mut {m}
courageous *adj.* mutig
courier *n.* Eilbote {m}
course *n.* Rennbahn {f}

court	n.	Hof {m}	
courteous	adj.	höflich	
courtesan	n.	Kurtisane {f}	
courtesy	n.	Verbindlichkeit {f}	
courtier	n.	Höfling {m}	
courtly	adj.	vornehm	
courtship	n.	Liebeswerben {n}	
courtyard	n.	Hofraum {m}	
cousin	n.	Vetter {m}	
cove	n.	Gewölbe {n}	
covenant	n.	Pakt {m}	
cover	n.	Deckel {m}	
cover	v.	decken	
covert	adj.	versteckt	
covet	v.	begehren	
cow	n.	Kuh {f}	
coward	n.	Feigling {m}	
cowardice	n.	Feigheit {f}	
cower	v.	hocken	
coy	adj.	schüchtern	
cozy	adj.	lieblich	
crab	n.	Krabbe {f}	
crack	n.	Bresche {f}	
crack	v.	knacken	
cracker	n.	Keks {m}	
crackle	v.	knistern	
cradle	n.	Wiege {f}	
craft	n.	Fahrzeug {n}	
craftsman	n.	Handwerker {m}	
crafty	adj.	listig	
cram	v.	mästen	
cramp	n.	Krampf {m}	
crane	n.	Kran {m}	
crinkle	v.	knittern	

crash	v.	zerbrechen	
crass	adj.	prüde	
crate	n.	Kiste {f}	
cravat	n.	Krawatte {f}	
crave	v. t	flehen	
craven	adj.	feige	
crawl	v.	kriechen	
crayon	n.	Buntstift {m}	
craze	n.	Haarriss {m}	
crazy	adj.	verrückt	
creak	n.	knarr	
creak	v.	knarren	
cream	n.	Creme {f}	
crease	n.	Falte {f}	
create	v.	erzeugen	
creation	n.	Erzeugung {f}	
creative	adj.	schöpferisch	
creator	n.	Erschaffer {m}	
creature	n.	Lebewesen {n}	
crèche	n.	Kinderhort {m}	
credentials	n.	Berechtigungsnachweis {m}	
credible	adj.	zuverlässig	
credit	n.	Darlehen {n}	
creditable	adj.	anerkennenswert	
creditor	n.	Gläubigerin {f}	
credulity	adv.	Leichtgläubigkeit {f}	
creed	n.	Glaubensbekenntnis {n}	
creek	n.	Flüsschen {n}	
creep	v.	Kriechen	
creeper	n.	Kriecher {m}	
cremate	v.	einäschern	
cremation	n.	Feuerbestattung {f}	
crematorium	n.	Krematorium {n}	
crescent	n.	Mondsichel {f}	

47

crest	n.	Mähne {f}	crucial	adj. entscheidend
crew	n.	Mannschaft {f}	crude	adj. grob,
crib	n.	Behälter {m}	cruel	adj. schrecklich
cricket	n.	Grille {f}	cruelty	adv. Grausamkeit {f}

crest   n.   Mähne {f}
crew   n.   Mannschaft {f}
crib   n.   Behälter {m}
cricket   n.   Grille {f}
crime   n.   Verbrechen {n}
criminal   n.   Verbrecher {m}
criminology n.   Kriminologie {f}
crimson   n.   karmesinrot
cringe   v.   kriechen
cripple   n.   Krüppel {m}
crisis   n.   Notstand {m}
crisp   adj. knusprig
criterion   n.   Kriterium {n}
critic   n.   Kritiker {m}
critical   adj. kritisch
criticism   n.   Kritik {f}
criticize   v.   beurteilend
critique n.   kritische Abhandlung
croak   n.   quaken
crochet n.   häkeln
crockery   n.   Geschirr {n}
crocodile n.   Krokodil {n}
croissant   n.   Hörnchen {n}
crook   n.   Ganove {m}
crooked   adj. krumm
crop   n.   Ernte {f}
cross   n.   Kreuz {n}
crossing   n.   Straßenkreuzung {f}
crotchet   n.   Viertelnote {f}
crouch   v.   Hockstellung {f}
crow   n.   Krähe {f}
crowd   n.   Menge {f}
crown   n.   Zahnkrone {f}
crown   v.   krönen

crucial adj. entscheidend
crude adj. grob,
cruel adj. schrecklich
cruelty adv. Grausamkeit {f}
cruise v.   Kreuzfahrt {f}
cruiser n.   Kreuzfahrtschiff {n}
crumb n.   Brotkrume {f},
crumble v.   abbröckeln
crumple v.   zerknitternd
crunch v.   zermalmen
crusade n.   Kreuzzug {f}
crush v.   zerdrücken
crust n.   Kruste {f}
crutch n.   Krücke {f}
crux n.   Haken {m}
cry n.   Schrei {m}
cry v.   weinen
crypt n.   Krypta {f}
crystal n.   Kristall {m}
cub n.   Flegel {m}
cube n.   Würfel {m}
cubical adj. kubisch
cubicle n.   Zelle {f}
cuckold n.   Hahnerei {f}
cuckoo n.   Kuckuck {m}
cucumber n.   Salatgurke {f}
cuddle v.   verhätscheln
cuddly adj. kuschelig
cudgel n.   Knüppel {m}
cue n.   Auslösereiz {m}
cuff n.   Manschette {f}
cuisine n.   Küche {f}
culinary adj. kulinarisch
culminate v.   kulminierend

culpable	adj.	strafbar
culprit	n.	Schuldige {m,f}
cult	n.	Kult {m}
cultivate	v.	kultivieren
cultural	adj.	kulturell
culture	n.	Kultur {f}
cumbersome	adj.	schwerfällig
cumin	n.	Kreuzkümmel {m}
cumulative	adj.	gesamt
cunning	adj.	schlau
cup	n.	Pokal {f}
cupboard	n.	Schrank {m}
cupidity	n.	Habgier {f}
curable	adj.	heilbar
curative	adj.	heilend
curator	n.	Museumsdirektor {m}
curb	v. t	zügeln
curd	n.	Weißkäse {m}
cure	v. t.	heilen
curfew	n.	Ausgangssperre {f}
curiosity	n.	Merkwürdigkeit {f}
curious	adj.	neugierig
curl	n.	Locke {f}
currant	n.	Korinthe {f}
currency	n.	Währung {f}
current	adj.	jetzig
current	n.	Stromstärke {f}
curriculum	n.	Studienplan {m}
curry	n.	striegel {m}
curse	n.	fluch [m]
cursive	adj.	kursiv
cursor	n.	Cursor {m}
cursory	adj.	oberflächliche
curt	adj.	knapp

curtail	v.	kürzen
curtain	n.	Gardine {f}
curve	n.	Krümmung {f}
cushion	n.	Kissen {n}
custard	n.	Eierkrem {f}
custodian	n.	Aufseher {m}
custody	n.	Haft {f}
custom	n.	Zoll {m}
customary	adj.	gewöhnlich
customer	n.	Kunde {m}
customize	v.	anpassen
cut	v.	reduzieren
cute	adj.	süß
cutlet	n.	Schnitzel {m}
cutter	n.	Zuschneider {m}
cutting	n.	Schneiden {n}
cyan	n.	Zyan
cyanide	n.	Zyanid {n}
cyber	comb.	künstlich…
cyberspace	n.	Cyberspace {m}
cycle	n.	Zyklus {m}
cyclic	adj.	periodisch
cyclist	n.	Radfahrer {m}
cyclone	n.	Zyklon {m}
cylinder	n.	Zylinder {m}
cynic	n.	Zyniker {m}
cynosure	n.	Anziehungspunkt {m}
cypress	n.	Zypresse {f}
cyst	n.	Zyste {f}
cystic	adj.	Blasen {pl}

D

dab	v.	abtupfen

49

dabble v.	bespritzen
dad n	Papa {m}
daffodil n.	Narzisse {f}
daft adj.	doof
dagger n.	Dolch {m}
daily adj.	täglich
dainty adj.	mäkelig
dairy n.	Milchgeschäft {n}
dais n.	Podium {n}
daisy n.	Gänseblümchen {n}
dale n.	Tal {n}
dally v.	trödeln
dalliance n.	Liebelei {f}
dam n.	Staudamm {m}
damage n.	Beschädigung {f}
dame n.	Dame {f}
damn v.	verurteilen
damnable adj.	verdammenswert
damnation n.	Verurteilung {f}
damp adj.	feucht
dampen v.	entmutigen
dampern.	Dampfer {m}
dampness n.	Feuchtigkeit {f}
damsel n.	Maid {f}
dance v.	Tanz {m}
dancer n.	Tänzer {m}
dandelion v.	Löwenzahn {m}
dandle v.	wiegen
dandruff n.	Schuppen {pl}
dandy n.	Stutzer {m}
danger n.	Gefahr {f}
dangerous adj.	gefährlich
dangle v. i.	baumeln
dank adj.	feucht

dapper adj.	adrett
dapple v.	sprenkeln
dare v.	wagen
daring adj.	wagemutig
dark adj.	dunkel
darkness n.	Dunkelheit {f}
darken v.	verdunkeln
darling n.	Liebling {m}
darn v.	verfluchen
dart n.	Pfeil {m}
dash v.	zerschmettern
dashboard n.	Armaturenbretter {pl}
dashing adj.	zerschmetternd
dastardly adj.	heimtückisch
data n.	Daten {pl}
database n.	Datenbank {f}
date n.	Termin {m}
date n.	Bezugspunkt {m}
datum n.	Bezugspunkt {m}
daub v.	schmieren
daughter n.	Tochter {f}
daughter-in-lawn.	Schwiegertochter {f}
daunt v.	entmutigen
dauntless adj.	unerschrocken
dawdle v.	vertrödeln
dawn n.	Morgenrot {n}
day n.	Tag {m}
daze v.	betäuben
dazzle v. t.	blenden
dead adj.	tot
deadline n.	Stichtage {pl}
deadlock n.	Verklemmung {f}
deadly adj.	tödlich
deaf adj.	taub

deafening	adj.	betäubend
deal	n.	Handel {m}
deal	v. i	handeln
dealer	n.	Händler {m}
dean	n.	Dekan {m}
dear	adj.	lieber
dearly	adv.	teuer
dearth	n.	Mangel {m}
death	n.	Tod {m}
debacle	n.	Katastrophe {f}
debar	v. t.	ausschließen
debase v.		verschlechtern
debatable	adj.	streitig
debate	n.	Debatte {f}
debate	v. t.	debattieren
debauch	v.	verführen
debauchery	n.	Ausschweifung {f}
debenture	n.	Anleihe {f}
debilitate	v.	schwächen
debility	n.	Schwächezustand {m}
debit	n.	Lastposten {m}
debonair	adj.	höflich
debrief v.		Nachbesprechung {f}
debris	n.	Schutt {m}
debt	n.	Schuld {f}
debtor	n.	Schuldner {m}
debunk v.		entlarven
debut	n.	Debüt {n}
debutante	n.	Debütant {m}
decade n.		Dekade {f}
decadent	adj.	dekadent
decaffeinated		adj. entkoffeiniert
decamp	v.	aufbrechen
decant v.		abgießen

decanter	n.	Karaffe {f}
decapitate	v.	köpfen
decay v. i		verfallen
decease	n.	Sterbefall {m}
deceased	adj.	gestorben
deceit	n.	Betrug {m}
deceitful	adj.	betrügerisch
deceive v.		betrügen
decelerate	v.	verlangsamen
December	n.	Dezember {m}
decency	n.	Anstand {m}
decent adj.		anständig
decentralize v.		dezentralisieren
deception	n.	Täuschung {f}
deceptive	adj.	täuschend
decibel n.		Dezibel {n}
decide v.		entscheiden
decided	adj.	beschlossen
decimal	adj.	dezimal
decimate	v.	dezimieren
decipher	v.	entziffern
decision	n.	Entscheidung {f}
decisive	adj.	entscheidungsfreudig
deck	n.	Verdeck {n}
declaim	v.	vortragen
declaration	n.	Erklärung {f}
declare v.		erklären
declassify	v.	deklassieren
decline v. t.		ablehnen
declivity	n.	Abhang {m}
decompose v.		zerlegen
decomposition	n.	Zersetzung {f}
decompress	v.	dekomprimieren

51

decongestant	*n.* abschwellendes Mittel	**defence**	*n.*	Verteidigung {f}
deconstruct *v.*	dekonstruieren	**defend** *v.*	verteidigen	
decontaminate	*v.* entgiften	**defendant**	*n.*	Angeklagte {f}
decor *n.*	Bühnenausstattung {f}	**defensible**	*adj.* vertretbar	
decorate	*v.* schmücken	**defensive**	*adj.* defensiv	
decoration	*n.* Verzierung {f}	**defer** *v.*	verschieben	
decorative	*adj.* dekorativ	**deference**	*n.*	Ehrerbietung {f}
decorous	*adj.* anständig	**defiance**	*n.*	Herausforderung {f}
decorum	*n.* Anstand {m}	**deficiency**	*n.*	Mangel {m}
decoy *n.*	ködern	**deficient**	*adj.* mangelhaft	
decrease	*v.* Verkleinerung {f}	**deficit** *n.*	Fehlbetrag {m}	
decree *n.*	Dekret {n}	**defile**	*v. t* defilieren	
decrement	*v. t.* vermindern	**define** *v.*	definieren	
decrepit	*adj.* altersschwach	**definite** *adj.*	bestimmt	
decriminalize	*v.* entkriminalisieren	**definition**	*n.*	Definition {f}
decry *v.*	anprangen	**deflate** *v.*	entleeren	
dedicate	*v.* widmen	**deflation**	*n.*	Entleerung {f}
dedication	*n.* Widmung {f}	**deflect** *v.*	ablenken	
deduce *v.*	ableiten	**deforest**	*v.* abforsten	
deduct *v.*	abrechnen	**deform** *v.*	entstellen	
deduction	*n.* Abstrich {m}	**deformity**	*n.*	Missbildung {f}
deed *n.*	Urkunde {f}	**defraud** *v.*	betrügen	
deem *v.*	erachten	**defray** *v.*	zahlen	
deep *adj.*	tief	**defrost** *v.*	entfrosten	
deer *n.*	Hirsch {m}	**deft** *adj.*	gewandt	
deface *v.*	verunstalten	**defunct** *adj.*	verstorben	
defamation *n.*	Verleumdung {f}	**defuse** *v.*	entschärfen	
defame *v.*	verleumden	**defy** *v.*	herausfordern	
default *n.*	Grundzustand {m}	**degenerate** *v.*	entarten	
defeat *v. t.*	besiegen	**degrade**	*v.* degradieren	
defeatist	*n.* Miesmacher {m}	**degree** *n.*	Grad {m}	
defecate	*v.* reinigen	**dehumanize** *v.*	entmenschlichen	
defect *n.*	Fehler {m}	**dehydrate**	*v.* dörren	
defective	*adj.* fehlerhaft	**deify**	*v.* vergöttern	

52

deign	v.	geruhen	**delve** v.	erforschen
deity	n.	Gottheit {f}	**demand** n.	Forderung {f}
déjà vu n.		Déjà-Vu {n}	**demanding** adj.	verlangend
deject	v.	entmutigen	**demarcation** n.	Abgrenzung {f}
dejection	n.	Kotentleerung {f}	**demean** v.	erniedrigen
delay	v. t	verzögern	**demented** adj.	wahnsinnig
delectable	adj.	köstlich	**dementia** n.	Schwachsinn {m}
delectation	n.	Ergötzen {n}	**demerit** n	Minuspunkt {m}
delegate	n.	Abgesandte {m}	**demise** n.	Besitzübertragung {f}
delegation	n.	Delegation {f}	**demobilize** v.	demobilisieren
delete	v. i	zerstören	**democracy** n.	Demokratie {f}
deletion	n.	Tilgung {f}	**democratic** adj.	demokratisch
deleterious	adj.	schädlich	**demography** n.	Demografie {f}
deliberate	adj.	beabsichtigt	**demolish** v.	demolieren
deliberation	n.	Überlegung {f}	**demon** n.	Teufel {m}
delicacy	n.	Delikatesse {f}	**demonize** v.	verteufeln
delicate	adj.	feinfühlig	**demonstrate** v.	demonstrieren
delicatessen	n.	Zartheit {f}	**demonstration** n.	Vorführung {f}
delicious	adj.	appetitlich	**demoralize** v.	demoralisieren
delight	v. t.	erfreuen	**demote** v.	degradieren
delightful	adj.	entzückend	**demur** v.	einwenden
delineate	v.	begrenzen	**demure** adj.	nüchtern
delinquent	adj.	straffällig	**demystify** v.	entmystifizieren
delirious	adj.	irreredend	**den** n.	Höhle {f}
delirium	n.	Säuferwahnsinn {m}	**denationalize** v.	entstaatlichen
deliver	v.	liefern	**denial** n.	Aberkennung {f}
deliverance n.		Überlieferung {f}	**denigrate** v.	verunglimpfen
delivery	n.	Auslieferung {f}	**denomination** n.	Benennung {f}
dell	n.	Tal {n}	**denominator** n.	Nenner {m}
delta	n.	Delta {n}	**denote** v. t	bezeichnen
delude	v.	täuschen	**denounce** v.	anklagen
deluge	n.	Wolkenbruch {m}	**dense** adj.	dicht
delusion	n.	Wahn {m}	**density** n.	Gedrängtheit {f}
deluxe	adj.	luxus	**dent** n.	Kerbe {f}

53

dental *adj.*	zahnärztlich	**deputy** *n.*	Vertreter {m}
dentist *n.*	Zahnarzt {m}	**derail** *v. t.*	entgleisend
denture*n.*	Gebiss {n}	**deranged** *adj.*	verwirrte, gestört
denude*v.*	entblößen	**deregulate** *v.*	abordnen
denunciation *n.*	Denunziation {f}	**deride** *v.*	verspotten
deny *v. i.*	leugnen	**derivative** *adj.*	Ableitung {f}
deodorant *n.*	Deodorant {n}	**derive** *v.*	ableiten
depart *v.*	abfahren	**derogatory** *adj.*	nachteilig
department *n.*	Ressort {n}	**descend** *v.*	herunterkommen
departure *n.*	Abreise {f}	**descendant** *n.*	Abkomme {m}
depend*v.*	abhängen	**descent** *n.*	Landung {f}
dependant *n.*	Abhängige {m,f}	**describe** *v.*	beschreiben
dependency*n.*	Schutzgebiet {n}	**description** *n.*	Beschreibung {f}
dependent *adj.*	abhängig	**desert** *v.*	Wüsten
depict *v.*	schildern	**deserve** *v. t.*	verdienen
depilatory *adj.*	Enthaarungsmittel {n}	**design** *n.*	Planung {f}
deplete*v.*	dezimieren	**designate** *v.*	bezeichnen
deplorable *adj.*	bedauerlich	**desirable** *adj.*	wünschenswert
deploy *v.*	eingesetzt	**desire** *n.*	Trieb {m}
deport *v. t*	abschieben	**desirous** *adj.*	begierig
depose*v.*	entheben	**desist** *v.*	ablassen
deposit*n.*	Depot {n}	**desk** *n.*	Tisch {m}
depository *n.*	Kontoinhaber {m}	**desolate** *adj.*	wüst
depot *n.*	Betriebswerk {n}	**despair***n.*	Verzweiflung {f}
deprave *v.*	verderben	**desperate** *adj.*	verzweifelt
deprecate *v.*	missbilligen	**despicable** *adj.*	verächtlich
depreciate *v.*	herabsetzen	**despise** *v.*	verachten
depreciation *n.*	Minderung {f}	**despite***prep.*	trotz
depress *v.*	bedrücken	**despondent***adj.*	mutlos
depression *n.*	Unterdruck {m}	**despot** *n.*	Despot {m}
deprive *v.*	berauben	**dessert***n.*	Dessert {n}
depth *n.*	Tiefe {f}	**destabilize** *v.*	destabilisieren
deputation *n.*	Abordnung {f}	**destination** *n.*	Reiseziel {n}
depute *v.*	deputierend	**destiny***n.*	Schicksal {n}

destitute	*adj.* mittellos		devil	*n.* Teufel {m}
destroy*v.*	zerstören		devious	*adj.* abwegig
destroyer	*n.* Zerstörer {m}		devise	*v.* ausdenken
destruction	*n.* Zerstörung {f}		devoid *adj.* leer	
detach	*v.* ablösen		devolution	*n.* Befugnisübergabe {f}
detachment	*n.* Trennung {f}		devolve	*v.* übertragen
detail	*n.* Detail {n}		devote	*v.* hingeben
detain	*v. t* abhalten		devotee	*n.* Anhänger {m}
detainee	*n.* Häftling {m}		devotion	*n.* Hingebung {f}
detect	*v.* entdecken		devour	*v.* verschlingen
detective	*n.* Detektiv {m}		devout *adj.* andächtig	
detention	*n.* Vorenthaltung {f}		dew	*n.* Tau {m}
deter	*v.* abschrecken		dexterity	*n.* Fertigkeit {f}
detergent	*n.* Waschmittel {n}		diabetes	*n.* Zuckerkrankheit {f}
deteriorate	*v.* verschlechtern		diagnose	*v.* diagnostizieren
determinant *adj.* bestimmend			diagnosis	*n.* Diagnose {f}
determination	*n.* Entschluss {m}		diagram	*n.* Diagramm {n}
determine	*v. t* ausschlaggeben		dial	*n.* Wählscheibe {f}
deterrent	*n.* Abschreckungsmittel {n}		dialect	*n.* Mundart {f}
detest	*v.* verabscheuen		dialogue	*n.* Gespräch {n}
dethrone	*v.* entthronen		dialysis*n.* Dialyse {f}	
detonate	*v.* explodieren		diameter	*n.* Diameter {m}
detour	*n.* Umweg {m}		diamond	*n.* Diamant {m}
detoxify	*v.* entgiften		diaper	*n.* Windel {f}
detract	*v.* Herabsetzung {f}		diarrhoea	*n.* Durchfall {m}
detriment	*n.* Schaden {m}		diary	*n.* Notizbuch {n}
detritus*n.* Geröll {n}			Diaspora	*n.* Diaspora {f}
devalue	*v.* abwerten		dice	*n.* Würfel {pl}
devastate	*v.* verheeren		dictate	*n.* Diktat {n}
develop	*v.* entwickeln		dictation	*n.* Diktat {n}
development	*n.* Bildung {f}		dictator*n.* Diktator {m}	
deviant *adj.* Abweichung {f}			diction	*n.* Wortwahl {f}
deviate	*v.* abschwenken		dictionary	*n.* Wörterbuch {n}
device	*n.* Laufwerk {n}		dictum	*n.* Machtspruch {m}

didactic	*adj.* didaktisch	**dinner**	*n.*	Mahl {n}

didactic *adj.* didaktisch
die *v.* sterben
diesel *n.* Diesel {m}
diet *n.* Diät {f}
dietitian *n.* Diätspezialist {m}
differ *v.* unterscheiden
difference *n.* Verschiedenheit {f}
different *adj.* unterschiedlich
difficult *adj.* diffizil
difficulty *n.* Schwierigkeit {f}
diffuse *v.* verbreiten
dig *v.* graben
digest *v.* verdauen
digestion *n.* Verdauung {f}
digit *n.* Zahl {f}
digital *adj.* digital
dignified *adj.* würdevoll
dignify *v.* ehren
dignitary *n.* Würdenträger {m}
dignity *n.* Erhabenheit {f}
digress *v.* abschweifen
dilapidated *adj.* baufällig
dilate *v.* erweitern
dilemma *n.* Dilemma {n}
diligent *adj.* fleißig
dilute *v.* verdünnen
dim *adj.* dunkel
dimension *n.* Abmessung {f}
diminish *v.* reduzieren
diminution *n.* Verminderung {f}
din *n.* Getöse {n}
dine *v.* dinieren
diner *n.* Restaurantgast {m}
dingy *adj.* schäbig

dinner *n.* Mahl {n}
dinosaur *n.* Dinosaurier {m}
dip *v. t* tauchen
diploma *n.* Diplom {n}
diplomacy *n.* Diplomatie {f}
diplomat *n.* Diplomat {m}
diplomatic *adj.* diplomatisch
dipsomania *n.* Alkoholsucht {f}
dire *adj.* grässlich
direct *adj.* gerade
direction *n.* Richtung {f}
directive *n.* Richtlinie {f}
directly *adv.* geradezu
director *n.* Direktor {m}
directory *n.* Adressbuch {n}
dirt *n.* Verschmutzung {f}
dirty *adj.* dreckig
disability *n.* Unfähigkeit {f}
disable *v.* unfähig machend
disabled *adj.* geschäftsunfähig
disadvantage *n.* Benachteiligung {f}
disaffected *adj.* unzufrieden
disagree *v.* nicht zustimmend
disagreeable *adj.* widerwärtig,
disagreement *n.* Uneinigkeit {f}
disallow *v.* verweigernd
disappear *v.* verschwindend
disappoint *v.* enttäuschend
disapproval *n.* Missfallen {n}
disapprove *v.* missbilligend
disarm *v.* abrüstend
disarmament *n.* Abrüstung {f}
disarrange *v.* verwirrend
disarray *n.* Unordnung {f}

disaster	n.	Unglück {n}
disastrous	adj.	unheilvoll
disband	v.	entlassen
disbelief	n.	Unglaube {m}
disburse	v.	bezahlen
disc	n.	Radschüssel {f}
discard	v.	ausrangieren
discern	v.	erkennen
discharge	v.	absetzen
disciple	n.	Disziplin {f}
discipline	n.	disziplinieren
disclaim	v.	dementieren
disclose	v.	verlautbaren
disco	n.	Disko {f}
discolour	v.	verfärben
discomfit	v.	besiegen
discomfort	n.	Unbehagen {n}
disconcert	v.	verdutzend
disconnect	v.	trennen
disconsolate	adj.	trostlos
discontent	n.	Unzufriedenheit {f}
discontinue	v.	unterbrechen
discord	n.	Zwietracht {f}
discordant	adj.	uneinig
discount	n.	Rabatt {m}
discourage	v.	entmutigen
discourse	n.	Diskurs {m}
discourteous	adj.	unhöflich
discover	v.	entdecken
discovery	n.	Entdeckung {f}
discredit	v.	anzweifeln
discreet	adj.	diskret
discrepancy	n.	Abweichung {f}
discrete	adj.	diskret

discriminate	v.	benachteiligen
discursive	adj.	abschweifend
discuss	v.	diskutieren
discussion	n.	Besprechung {f}
disdain	v.	verachten
disease	n.	Erkrankung {f}
disembark	v.	landen
disembodied	adj.	entkörperlicht
disempower	v.	entmachten
disenchant	v.	desillusionieren
disengage	v.	freimachen
disentangle	v.	entwirren
disfavour	n.	Missfallen {n}
disgrace	n.	Schande {f}
disgruntled	adj.	verärgert
disguise	v.	Verstellung {f}
disgust	n.	Abstoß {m}
dish	n.	Gericht {n}
dishearten	v.	entmutigen
dishonest	adj.	unehrlich
dishonour	n.	Ehrlosigkeit {f}
disillusion	v.	desillusionieren
disincentive	n.	Abhaltung {f}
disinfect	v.	desinfizieren
disingenuous	adj.	unaufrichtig
disinherit	v.	enterben
disintegrate	v.	zersetzen
disjointed	adj.	zerfahren
dislike	v.	ablehnen
dislocate	v.	ausrenken
dislodge	v.	vertreiben
disloyal	adj.	treubrüchig
dismal	adj.	düster
dismantle	v.	demontieren

dismay	n.	Bestürzung {f}	disreputable	adj.	verrufen
dismiss	v.	entlassen	disrepute	n.	Schande {f}
dismissive	adj.	respektlos	disrespect	n.	Respektlosigkeit {f}
disobedient	adj.	ungehorsam	disrobe	v.	entkleiden
disobey	v.	missachten	disrupt	v.	zerreißen
disorder	n.	Unordnung {f}	dissatisfaction	n.	Unzufriedenheit {f}
disorganized	adj.	ungeordnet	dissect	v.	zerlegen
disorientate	v.	desorganisieren	dissent	v.	Unstimmigkeit {f}
disown	v.	verableugnend	dissertation	n.	Dissertation {f}
disparity	n.	Disparität {f}	dissident	n.	Dissident {m}
dispassionate	adj.	leidenschaftslos	dissimulate	v.	verheimlichen
dispatch	v.	abfertigen	dissipate	v.	zerteilend
dispel	v.	zerstreuen	dissolve	v. t	scheiden
dispensable	adj.	entbehrlich	dissuade	v.	abraten
dispensary	n.	Arzneiausgabe {f}	distance	n.	Entfernung {f}
dispense	v.	dispensieren	distant	adj.	entfernt
disperse	v.	auseinandertreiben	distaste	n.	Widerwille {m}
dispirited	adj.	mutlos	distil	v.	abdestillieren
displace	v. t	verschieben	distillery	n.	Schnapsbrennerei {f}
display	v.	zeigen	distinct	adj.	ausgeprägt
displease	v.	missfallen	distinction	n.	Auszeichnung {f}
displeasure	n.	Missfallen {n}	distinguish	v. t	hervorheben
disposable	adj.	verfügbar	distort	v.	sinnentstellen
disposal	n.	Verfügung {f}	distract	v.	verwirren
dispose	v. t	anordnen	distraction	n.	Verstörtheit {f}
dispossess	v.	enteignen	distress	n.	Elend {n}
disproportionate	adj.	Unverhältnismäßig	distribute	v.	verteilen
disprove	v.	widerlegen	distributor	n.	Streugerät {n}
dispute	v. i	streiten	district	n.	Revier {n}
disqualification	n.	Disqualifikation {f}	distrust	n.	Misstrauen {n}
disqualify	v.	disqualifizieren	disturb	v.	verwirren
disquiet	n.	Unruhe {f}	ditch	n.	Wassergraben {m}
disregard	v. t	missachten	dither	v.	Schwanken {n}
disrepair	n.	Verfall {m}	ditto	n.	dito

dive	*v.*	tauchen	domestic	*adj.*	häuslich
diverge	*v.*	divergierender	domicile	*n.*	Wohnsitz {m}
diverse	*adj.*	verschieden	dominant	*adj.*	beherrschend
diversion	*n.*	Abzweigung {f}	dominate	*v.*	dominieren
diversity	*n.*	Diversität {f}	dominion	*n.*	Herrschaft {f}
divert	*v. t*	ablenken	donate	*v.*	schenken
divest	*v.*	entblößen	donkey	*n.*	Esel {m}
divide	*v.*	teilen	donor	*n.*	Spender {m}
dividend	*n.*	Kapitalertragsteuer {f}	doom	*n.*	Verdammung {f}
divine	*adj.*	göttlich	door	*n.*	Tür {f}
divinity	*n.*	Gottheit {f}	dormitory	*n.*	Schlafsaal {m}
division	*n.*	Trennung {f}	dose	*n.*	Dosis {f}
divorce	*n.*	Ehescheidung {f}	dossier	*n.*	Dossier {n}
divorcee	*n.*	Geschiedene {m,f}	dot	*n.*	Punkt {m}
divulge	*v.*	enthüllen	dote	*v.*	sabbeln
do	*v.*	tun	double	*adj.*	doppelt
docile	*adj.*	gelehrig	doubt	*n.*	Zweifel {m}
dock	*n.*	Anklagebank {f}	dough	*n.*	Teig {m}
docket	*n.*	Prozessliste {f}	down	*adv.*	runter
doctor	*n.*	Doktor {m}	downfall	*n.*	Untergang {m}
doctorate	*n.*	Doktorat {n}	download	*v.*	laden
doctrine	*n.*	Doktrin {f}	downpour	*n.*	Regenguss {m}
document	*n.*	Dokument {n}	dowry	*n.*	Mitgift {f}
documentary	*n.*	dokumentarische	doze	*v. i*	dösen
dodge	*v. t*	abwedeln	dozen	*n.*	Dutzend {n}
doe	*n.*	Ricke {f}	drab	*adj.*	eintönig
dog	*n.*	Hund {m}	draft	*n.*	Entwurf {m}
dogma	*n.*	Dogma {n}	drag	*v. t*	ziehen
dogmatic	*adj.*	dogmatische	dragon	*n.*	Drache {m},
doldrums	*n.*	Flaute {f}	drain	*v. t*	entwässern
doll	*n.*	Puppe {f}	drama	*n.*	Drama {n}
dollar	*n.*	Dollar {m}	dramatic	*adj.*	dramatisch
domain	*n.*	Besitz {m}	dramatist	*n.*	Dramatiker {m}
dome	*n.*	Dom {m}	drastic	*adj.*	drastisch

draught	n.	Luftzug {m}	duct	n.	Röhre {f}
draw	v.	nachziehen	dudgeon	n.	Groll {m}
drawback	n.	Nachteil {m}	due	adj.	schuldig
drawer	n.	Trassant {m}	duel	n.	Zweikampf {m}
drawing	n.	Zeichnung {f}	duet	n.	Duett {n}
dread	v.t	fürchten	dull	adj.	stumpf
dreadful	adj.	grässlich	dullard	n.	Dummkopf {m}
dream	n.	Traum {m}	duly	adv.	ordnungsmäßig
dreary	adj.	trostlos	dumb	adj.	blöd
drench	v.	durchnässen	dummy	n.	Dummi {m}
dress	v.	Kleid {n}	dump	n.	Auslistung {f}
dressing	n.	Dressing {n}	dung	n.	Dung {m}
drift	v.	treiben	dungeon	n.	Kerker {m}
drill	n.	Drill {m}	duo	n.	Duo {n}
drink	v.t	trinken	dupe	v.	übertölpeln
drip	v.i	Tropfen {m}	duplex	n.	Verdopplung {f}
drive	v.	fahren	duplicate	adj.	vervielfältig
driver	n.	Fahrer {m}	duplicity	n.	Doppelzüngigkeit {f}
drizzle	n.	Sprühregen {m}	durable	adj.	langlebig
droll	adj.	drollig	duration	n.	Dauer {f}
droop	v.	schlaff	during	prep.	während
drop	v.	abwerfen	dusk	n.	Abenddämmerung {f}
dross	n.	Schlacke {f}	dust	n.	Staub {m}
drought	n.	Trockenheit {f}	duster	n.	Staubtuch {n}
drown	v.	ertrinken	dutiful	adj.	pflichtgemäß
drowse	v.	schlummern	duty	n.	Abgabe {f}
drug	n.	Droge {f}	duvet	n.	Bettdecke {f}
drum	n.	Trommel {f}	dwarf	n.	Zwerg {m}
drunkard	adj.	Trunkenbold {m}	dwell	v.	wohnte
dry	adj.	herb	dwelling	n.	Behausung {f}
dryer	n.	Trockener {m}	dwindle	v.t	schwinden
dual	adj.	zweifach	dye	n.	färbte
dubious	adj.	zweifelhaft	dynamic	adj.	dynamisch
duck	n.	Ente {f}	dynamics	n.	Dynamik {f}

dynamite	*n.*	Dynamit {n}
dynamo	*n.*	Gleichstromerzeuger {m}
dynasty	*n.*	Dynastie {f}
dysentery	*n.*	Ruhr {f}
dysfunctional	*adj.*	störend {f}
dyslexia	*n.*	Legasthenie {f}
dyspepsia	*n.*	Verdauungsstörung {f}

E

each	*adj.*	jede
eager	*adj.*	eifrig
eagle	*n.*	Adler {m}
ear	*n.*	Ohr {n}
earl	*n.*	Graf {m}
early	*adj.*	früh
earn	*v.*	verdienen
earnest	*adj.*	ernst
earth	*n.*	Welt {f}
earthen	*adj.*	erdig
earthly	*adj.*	weltlich
earthquake	*n.*	Erdbeben {n}
ease	*n.*	Leichtigkeit {f}
east	*n.*	Orient {m}
Easter	*n.*	Ostern {n}
eastern	*adj.*	österlich
easy	*adj.*	unschwer
eat	*v.*	essen
eatery	*n.*	Esslokal {n}
eatable	*adj.*	essbar
ebb	*n.*	Ebbe {f}
ebony	*n.*	Ebenholz {n}
ebullient	*adj.*	überschäumend
eccentric	*adj.*	exaltiert
echo	*n.*	Widerhall {m}

eclipse	*n.*	Finsternis
ecology	*n.*	Ökologie {f}
economic	*adj.*	wirtschaftlich
economical	*adj.*	haushälterisch
economics	*n.*	Volkswirtschaftslehre {f}
economy	*n.*	Wirtschaftlichkeit {f}
ecstasy	*n.*	Ekstase {f}
edge	*n.*	Kante {f}
edgy	*adj.*	nervös
edible	*adj.*	essbar
edict	*n.*	Erlass {m}
edifice	*n.*	Gebäude {n}
edit	*v.*	bearbeiten
edition	*n.*	Auflage
editor	*n.*	Editor {m}
editorial	*adj.*	redaktionell
educate	*v.*	bilden
education	*n.*	Ausbildung {f}
efface	*v.*	auslöschen
effect	*n.*	Auswirkung {f}
effective	*adj.*	wirksam
effeminate	*adj.*	verweichlicht
effete	*adj.*	entkräftet
efficacy	*n.*	Wirkungskraft {f}
efficiency	*n.*	Leistungsfähigkeit {f}
efficient	*adj.*	wirkungsvoll
effigy	*n.*	Nachbildung {f}
effort	*n.*	Mühe {f}
egg	*n.*	Ei {n}
ego	*n.*	Ego {n}
egotism	*n.*	Egoismus {m}
eight	*adj. & n.*	acht
eighteen	*adj. & n.*	achtzehn
eighty	*adj. & n.*	achtzig

either	adv.	entweder
ejaculate	v.	ausstoßen
eject	v. t	vertreiben
elaborate	adj.	ausgearbeitet
elapse	v.	vergehen
elastic	adj.	elastisch
elbow	n.	Ellenbogen {m}
elder	adj.	älter
elderly	adj.	ältlich
elect	v.	auserwählen
election	n.	Erwählung {f}
elective	adj.	wahlberechtigt
electorate	n.	Wählerschaft {f}
electric	adj.	elektrisch
electrician	n.	Elektriker {m}
electricity	n.	Elektrizität {f}
electrify	v.	elektrisieren
electrocute	v.	hinrichten
electronic	adj.	elektronisch
elegance	n.	Eleganz {f}
elegant	adj.	elegant
element	n.	Element {n}
elementary	adj.	elementar
elephant	n.	Elefant {m}
elevate	v.	erheben
elevator	n.	Fahrstuhl {m}
eleven	adj.& n.	elf
elf	n.	Kobold {m}
elicit	v.	hervorlocken
eligible	adj.	wahlfähige
eliminate	v.	auslöschen
elite	n.	Elite {f}
ellipse	n.	Ellipse {f}
elocution	n.	Rhetorik {f}

elongate	v.	verlängern
elope	v.	entlaufen
eloquence	n.	Eloquenz {f}
else	adv.	sonst
elucidate	v. t	erläutern
elude	v.	umgehen
elusion	n.	Ausflucht {f}
elusive	adj.	trügerisch
emaciated	adj.	abgemagert
email	n.	Email {m}
emancipate	v. t	emanzipieren
emasculate	v.	entmannen
embalm	v.	einbalsamieren
embankment	n.	Eindämmung {f}
embargo	n.	Handelssperre {f}
embark	v. t	einschiffen
embarrass	v.	beschämt
embassy	n.	Botschaft {f}
embattled	adj.	aufstellend
embed	v.	eingeschlossen
embellish	v.	verschönern
embitter	v.	verbittern
emblem	n.	Abzeichen {n}
embodiment	n.	Darstellung {f}
embolden	v.	ermutigen
emboss	v.	stanzen
embrace	v.	umarmen
embroidery	n.	Stickerei {f}
embryo	n.	Embryen {pl}
emend	v.	verbessern
emerald	n.	Smaragd {m}
emerge	v.	auftauchen
emergency	n.	Notsituation {f}
emigrate	v.	auswandern

eminence	n.	Eminenz {f}	encompass v.	umgeben
eminent	adj.	hervorragend	encore n.	Zugabe {f}
emissary	n.	Sendbote {m}	encounter v.	begegnen
emit v.		ausgeben	encourage v.	ermuntern
emollient	adj.	gelindert	encroach v.	eingreifen
emolument	n.	Vergütung {f}	encrypt v.	verschlüsseln
emotion	n.	Gefühl {n}	encumber v.	belasten
emotional	adj.	gefühlsmäßig	encyclopaedia n.	Enzyklopädie {f}

eminence   n.   Eminenz {f}
eminent   adj.   hervorragend
emissary   n.   Sendbote {m}
emit   v.   ausgeben
emollient   adj.   gelindert
emolument   n.   Vergütung {f}
emotion   n.   Gefühl {n}
emotional   adj.   gefühlsmäßig
emotive   adj.   gefühlserregend
empathy   n.Einfühlungsvermögen {n}
emperor   n.   Kaiser {m}
emphasis   n.   Betonung {f}
emphasize   v.   betonen
emphatic   adj.   nachdrücklich
empire n.   Kaiserreich {n}
employ v.   beschäftigen
employee   n.   Beschäftigte {m,f}
employer   n.   Firma {m}
empower   v.   befähigen
empress   n.   Kaiserin {f}
empty adj. leer
emulate   v. t   nacheifern
enable v.   ermöglichen
enact   v.   verordnen
enamel n.   Lack {m}
enamour   v. t   verlieben
encapsulate v.   verkapseln
encase v.   eingeschlossen
enchant   v.   bezaubern
encircle   v. t   einkreisen
enclave n.   Enklave {f}
enclose   v.   einschließen
enclosure   n.   Beilage {f}
encode v.   verschlüsseln

encompass v.   umgeben
encore n.   Zugabe {f}
encounter   v.   begegnen
encourage   v.   ermuntern
encroach   v.   eingreifen
encrypt v.   verschlüsseln
encumber   v.   belasten
encyclopaedia   n.   Enzyklopädie {f}
end   n.   Schluss {m}
endanger   v.   gefährden
endear v.   einschmeicheln
endearment n.   Zärtlichkeit {f}
endeavour   v.   bemühen
endemic   adj.   endemisch
endorse   v.   indossieren
endow v.   ausstatten
endure v.   aushalten
enemy n.   Feind {m}
energetic   adj.   energetisch
energy n.   Energie {f}
enfeeble   v.   entkräften
enfold v.   umfasst
enforce   v.   erzwingen
enfranchise   v.   befreien
engage   v.   beschäftigen
engagement   n.   Einstellung {f}
engine n.   Motor {m}
engineer   n.   Ingenieur {m}
English n.   Englisch {n}
engrave   v.   gravieren
engross   v.   beanspruchen
engulf v.   versinken
enigma n.   Rätsel {n}
enjoy   v.   genießen

63

enlarge v.	erweitern	entrance	n.	Eintritt {m}
enlighten v.	erleuchten	entrap v. t.		einfangen
enlist v.	beteiligen	entreat v.		ersuchen
enliven v.	beleben	entreaty	n.	Flehen {n}
enmity n.	Feindschaft {f}	entrench	v.	verschanzen
enormous adj.	gewaltig	entrepreneur	n.	Unternehmer {m}
enough adj.	ausreichend	entrust v.		anvertrauen
enquire v.	erkundigen	entry	n.	Eintragung {f}
enquiry n.	Erkundigung {f}	enumerate	v. t	aufzählen
enrage v.	erzürnen	enunciate	v.	ausdrücken
enrapture v.	hinreißen	envelop	v.	entwickeln
enrich v.	anreichern	envelope	n.	Umschläge {m}
enrol v.	einstellen	enviable	adj.	beneidenswert
enshrine v.	verehren	envious	adj.	neidisch
enslave v.	unterjochen	environment	n.	Ausstattung {f}
ensue v.	folgen	envisage	v.	vorstellen
ensure v.	sichern	envoy	n.	Gesandte {m,f}
entangle v.t.	verwickeln	envy	n.	Neid {m}
enter v.	Eintrag {m}	epic	n.	Epos {n}
enterprise n.	Unternehmung {f}	epicure	n.	Genießer {m}
entertain v.	unterhalten	epidemic	n.	Epidemie {f}
entertainment	n. Unterhaltung {f}	epidermis	n.	Epidermis {f}
enthral v.	begeistern	epigram	n.	Sinngedicht {n}
enthrone v.	inthronisieren	epilepsy	n.	Epilepsie {f}
enthusiasm n.	Begeisterung {f}	epilogue	n.	Epilog {m}
enthusiastic n.	Schwärmer {m}	episode	n.	Abschnitt {m}
entice v.	locken	epistle n.		Epistel {f}
entire adj.	vollständig	epitaph n.		Grabschrift {f}
entirety n.	Ganze {n}	epitome	n.	Epitome {f}
entitle v.	berechtigen	epoch n.		Epoche {f}
entity n.	Eigenheit {f}	equal	adj.	gleich
entomology n.	Insektenkunde {f}	equalize	v. t	ausgleichen
entourage n.	Umgebung {f}	equate v.		gleichstellen
entrails n.	Innereien {pl}	equation	n.	Gleichung {f}

64

equator	n.	Äquator {m}	
equestrian	adj.	Reiter {m}	
equidistant	adj.	abstandsgleich	
equilateral	adj.	gleichseitig	
equilibrium	n.	Gleichgewicht {n}	
equip	v.	ausrüsten	
equipment	n.	Ausstattung {f}	
equitable	adj.	gerecht	
equity	n.	Gerechtigkeit {f}	
equivalent	adj.	gleichwertig	
equivocal	adj.	mehrdeutig	
era	n.	Ära {f}	
eradicate	v.	ausrotten	
erase	v.	löschen	
erect	adj.	errichtet	
erode	v.	erodieren	
erogenous	adj.	erogen	
erosion	n.	Erosion {f}	
erotic	adj.	erotisch	
err	v.	irren	
errand	n.	Botengang {m}	
errant	adj.	irrend	
erratic	adj.	fahrig	
erroneous	adj.	irrtümlich	
error	n.	Fehler {m}	
erstwhile	adj.	ehemals	
erudite	adj.	gelehrt	
erupt	v.	ausbrechen	
escalate	v.	eskalieren	
escalator	n.	Rolltreppe {f}	
escapade	n.	Streich {m}	
escape	v.i	entkommen	
escort	n.	Begleitung {f}	
esoteric	adj.	esoterisch	

especial	adj.	vornehmlich	
especially	adv.	insbesonders	
espionage	n.	Spionage {f}	
espouse	v.	unterstützen	
espresso	n.	Espresso {m}	
essay	n.	Versuch {m}	
essence	n.	Essenz {f}	
essential	adj.	unerlässlich	
establish	v.	errichten	
establishment	n.	Anstalt {f}	
estate	n.	Besitztum {n}	
esteem	n.	Schätzung {f}	
estimate	v. t	bewerten	
estranged	adj.	entfremdet	
et cetera	adv.	usw. -und so weiter	
eternal	adj.	ewig	
eternity	n.	Ewigkeit {f}	
ethic	n	Ethik {f}	
ethical	adj.	ethisch	
ethnic	adj.	ethnisch	
ethos	n.	Ethos {n}	
etiquette	n.	Etikett {n}	
etymology	n.	Etymologie {f}	
eunuch	n.	Eunuch {m}	
euphoria	n.	Euphorie {f}	
euro	n.	Euro {m}	
European	n.	Europäer {m}	
euthanasia	n.	Euthanasie {f}	
evacuate	v.	entleeren	
evade	v. t	ausweichen	
evaluate	v. i	auswerten	
evaporate	v.	verdampfen	
evasion	n.	Umgehung {f}	
evasive	adj.	ausweichende	

eve	*n.*	Vorabend {m}	**excerpt** *n.*		Auszug {m}
even	*adj.*	gerade	**excess** *n.*		Exzess {m}
evening	*n.*	Abend {m}	**excessive**	*adj.*	überschüssig
event	*n.*	Fall {m}	**exchange**	*v. t*	austauschen
eventually	*adv.*	schließlich	**exchequer**	*n.*	Fiskus {m}
ever	*adv.*	jemals	**excise** *n.*		Verbrauchssteuer {f}
every	*adj.*	jeder	**excite**	*v.i*	reizen
evict	*v.*	exmittieren	**excitement**	*n.*	Angst {f}
eviction	*n.*	Exmission {f}	**exclaim** *v.*		ausrufen
evidence	*n.*	Zeugenaussage {f}	**exclamation** *n.*		Ausruf {m}
evident	*adj.*	einleuchtend	**exclude**	*v.*	ausschließen
evil	*adj.*	übel	**exclusive**	*adj.*	ausschließlich
evince	*v.*	bekunden	**excoriate**	*v.*	abschürfend
evoke	*v.*	hervorrufen	**excrete** *v.*		absondern
evolution	*n.*	Entwicklung {f}	**excursion**	*n.*	Ausflug {m}
evolve	*v.*	entwickeln	**excuse** *v.*		Entschuldigung {f}
exact	*adj.*	richtig	**execute**	*v.*	ausführen
exaggerate	*v.*	übertrieben	**execution**	*n.*	Abarbeitung {f}
exaggeration	*n.*	Übertreibung {f}	**executive**	*n.*	Führungskraft {f}
exalt	*v.*	verherrlichen	**executor** *n.*		Testamentsvollstrecker {m}
exam	*n.*	Prüfung {f}	**exempt**	*adj.*	frei
examination	*n.*	Examen {n}	**exercise**	*n.*	Aufgabe {f}
examine	*v.*	prüfen	**exert**	*v.*	bemühen
examinee	*n.*	Prüfling {m}	**exhale** *v.*		ausatmen
example	*n.*	Vorbild {n}	**exhaust**	*v.*	erschöpfen
exasperate	*v.*	ärgern	**exhaustive**	*adj.*	erschöpfend
excavate	*v.*	ausgraben	**exhibit** *v.*		ausstellen
exceed *v.*		überschritten	**exhibition**	*n.*	Ausstellung {f}
excel	*v.*	übertreffen	**exhilarate**	*v.*	erheitern
excellence	*n.*	Vortrefflichkeit {f}	**exhort** *v.*		ermahnen
excellency	*n.*	Exzellenz {f}	**exigency**	*n.*	Zwangslage {f}
excellent	*adj.*	ausgezeichnet	**exile**	*n.*	Exil {n}
except *prep.*		außer	**exist**	*v.*	existieren
exception	*n.*	Besonderheit {f}	**existence**	*n.*	Existenz {f}

exit	*n.*	Austritt {m}
exonerate	*v.*	entlasten
exorbitant	*adj.*	unerschwinglich
exotic	*adj.*	exotisch
expand	*v.*	erweitern
expanse	*n.*	Ausdehnung {f}
expatriate	*n.*	ausbürgern
expect	*v.*	erwarten
expectant	*adj.*	erwartungsvoll
expedient	*adj.*	zweckmäßig
expedite	*v.*	vorantreiben
expedition	*n.*	Entdeckungsreise {f}
expel	*v. t*	ausweisen
expend	*v.*	verausgaben
expenditure	*n.*	Aufwendung {f}
expense	*n.*	Aufwand {m}
expensive	*adj.*	teuer
experience	*n.*	Erfahrung {f}
experiment	*n.*	Experiment {n}
expert	*n.*	Experte {m}
expertise	*n.*	Know-how {n}
expiate	*v.*	sühnen
expire	*v.*	abeaufen
expiry	*n.*	Ablauf {m}
explain	*v.*	erklären
explicit	*adj.*	ausdrücklich
explode	*v.*	explodieren
exploit	*v. t*	ausbeuten
exploration	*n.*	Untersuchung {f}
explore	*v.*	erforschen
explosion	*n.*	Explosion {f}
explosive	*adj.*	explosiv
exponent	*n.*	Exponent {m}
export	*v. t.*	exportieren

expose	*v.*	belichten
exposure	*n.*	Ausgesetztsein {n}
express	*v.*	ausdrücken
expression	*n.*	Ausdruck {m}
expressive	*adj.*	aussagekräftig
expropriate	*v.*	enteignen
expulsion	*n.*	Vertreibung {f}
extant	*adj.*	übriggeblieben
extend	*v.*	erweitern
extension	*n.*	Ausdehnung {f}
extent	*n.*	Ausmaß {n}
exterior	*adj.*	äußerlich
external	*adj.*	extern
extinct	*adj.*	erloschen
extinguish	*v.*	auslöschen
extirpate	*v.*	ausrotten
extort	*v.*	erpressen
extra	*adj.*	extra
extract	*v. t*	herausziehen
extraction	*n.*	Entziehung {f}
extraordinary	*adj.*	Außergewöhnlich
extravagance	*n.*	Überspanntheit {f}
extravagant	*adj.*	Verschwenderisch
extravaganza	*n.*	Extravaganza {f}
extreme	*adj.*	extrem
extremist	*n.*	Extremist {m}
extricate	*v.*	befreien
extrovert	*n.*	Extravertiert {m}
extrude	*v.*	extrudieren
exuberant	*adj.*	überschäumend
exude	*v.*	ausschwitzen
eye	*n.*	Auge {n},
eyeball	*n.*	Augapfel {m}
eyesight	*n.*	Augenlicht {n}

eyewash	n.	Augenwasser {n}
eyewitness	n.	Augenzeuge {m}

F

fable	n.	Fabel {f}
fabric	n.	Bau {m}
fabricate	v.	fabrizieren
fabulous	adj.	märchenhaft
facade	n.	Fassade {f}
face	n.	Fläche {f}
facet	n.	Fassette {f}
facetious	adj.	witzig
facial	adj.	Gesicht-
facile	adj.	einfach
facilitate	v.	erleichtern
facility	n.	Einrichtung {f}
facing	n.	Verkleidung {f}
facsimile	n.	Reproduktion {f}
fact	n.	Tatsache {f}
faction	n.	Splitterpartei {f}
factitious	adj.	künstlich
factor	n.	Faktor {m}
factory	n.	Fertigungsanlage {f}
faculty	n.	Fähigkeit {f}
fad	n.	Hobby {n}
fade	v.i	verblassen
Fahrenheit	n.	Fahrenheit
fail	v.	misslingen
failing	n.	Durchfallen {n}
failure	n.	Versager {m}
faint	adj.	schwach
fair	adj.	schön
fairing	n.	Verkleidung {f}
fairly	adv.	ordentlich

fairy	n.	Zauberin {f}
faith	n.	Vertrauen {n}
faithful	adj.	treu
faithless		adj. treulos
fake	adj.	falsch
falcon	n.	Falke {f}
fall	v.	fallen
fallacy	n.	Täuschung {f}
fallible	adj.	fehlbar
fallow	adj.	falb
false	adj.	unrichtig
falsehood	n.	Falschheit {f}
falter	v.	schwanken
fame	n.	Ruhm {m}
familiar		adj. familiär
family	n.	Familie {f}
famine	n.	Hungersnot {f}
famished		adj. verhungert
famous		adj. berühmt
fan	n.	Fan {m}
fanatic	n.	Fanatiker {m}
fanciful	adj.	phantasiereich
fancy	n.	Kaprize {f}
fanfare	n.	Fanfare {f}
fang	n.	Fangzahn {m}
fantasize	v.	phantasieren
fantastic		adj. fantastisch
fantasy	n.	Phantasie {f}
far	adv.	fern
farce	n.	Posse {f}
fare	n.	Kost {f}
farewell	interj.	Lebewohl {n}
farm	n.	Bauernhof {m}
farmer	n.	Landwirt {m}

fascia	*n.*	Binde {f}	
fascinate	*v.*	bezaubern	
fascism	*n.*	Faschismus {m}	
fashion	*n.*	Mode {f}	
fashionable	*adj.*	modisch	
fast	*adj.*	schnell	
fasten	*v.*	befestigen	
fastness	*n.*	Schnelligkeit {f}	
fat	*n.*	Fett {n}	
fatal	*adj.*	tödlich	
fatality	*n.*	Verhängnis {n}	
fate	*n.*	Schicksal {n}	
fateful	*adj.*	schicksalhaft	
father	*n.*	Vater {m}	
fathom	*n.*	Ergründer {m}	
fatigue	*n.*	Ermüdung {f}	
fatuous	*adj.*	illusorisch	
fault	*n.*	Mangel {m}	
faulty	*adj.*	fehlerhaft	
fauna	*n.*	Fauna	
favour	*n.*	Gunst {f}	
favourable	*adj.*	gefällig	
favourite	*adj.*	favorit	
fax	*n.*	Fax {n}	
fear	*n.*	Befürchtung {f}	
fearful	*adj.*	furchtsam	
fearless	*adj.*	furchtlos	
feasible	*adj.*	praktikabel	
feast	*n.*	Fest {m}	
feat	*n.*	Kunststück {m}	
feather	*n.*	Feder {f}	
feature	*n.*	Fähigkeit {f}	
febrile	*adj.*	fiebernd	
February	*n.*	Februar {m}	

feckless	*adj.*	schwach	
federal	*adj.*	Föderal	
federate	*v.*	verbünden	
federation	*n.*	Föderation {f}	
fee	*n.*	Lohn {m}	
feeble	*adj.*	kraftlos	
feed	*v.*	bewirten	
feeder	*n.*	Einspeisung {f}	
feel	*v.*	fühlen	
feeling	*n.*	Gefühl {n}	
feign	*v.*	heucheln	
feisty	*adj.*	übellaunig	
felicitate	*v.*	beglückwünschen	
felicitation	*n.*	Glückwunsch {m}	
felicity	*n.*	Glück {n}	
fell	*v.*	fallen	
fellow	*n.*	Kumpel {m}	
fellowship	*n.*	Kameradschaft {f}	
felon	*n.*	Schwerverbrecher {m}	
female	*adj.*	weiblich	
feminine	*adj.*	feminin	
feminism	*n.*	Feminismus {m}	
fence	*n.*	Zaun {m}	
fencing	*n.*	Fechten {n}	
fend	*v.*	abwehren	
feng shui	*n.*	feng shui {n}	
fennel	*n.*	Fenchel {m}	
feral	*adj.*	wild	
ferment	*v.*	vergären	
fermentation	*n.*	Vergärung {f}	
fern	*n.*	Farn {n}	
ferocious	*adj.*	grausam	
ferry	*n.*	Fähre {f}	
fertile	*adj.*	fruchtbar	

69

fertility *n.*	Fruchtbarkeit {f}	fig *n.*	Feige {f}
fertilize *v.*	befruchten	fight *v.t*	kämpfen
fertilizer *n.*	Düngemittel {n}	fighter *n.*	Streiter {m}
fervent *adj.*	glühend	figment *n.*	Erfindung {f}
fervid *adj.*	inbrünstig	figurative *adj*	bildlich
fervour *n.*	Eifer {m}	figure *n.*	Gestalt {f}
fester *v.*	verfaulen	figurine *n.*	Figurine {f}
festival *n.*	Fest {n}	filament *n.*	Heizfaden {m}
festive *adj.*	festlich	file *n.*	Aktenordner {m}
festivity *n.*	Festlichkeit {f}	filings *n.*	Archivierung {f}
fetch *v.*	holen	fill *v.*	füllen
fete *n.*	Party {f}	filler *n.*	Spachtel {f}
fetish *n.*	Fetisch {m}	filling *n.*	Füllung {f}
fettle *n.*	Verfassung {f}	fillip *n.*	Nasenstüber {m}
fetus *n.*	Fötus {m}	film *n.*	Film {m}
feud *n.*	Fehde {f}	filter *n.*	Filter {m}
feudalism *n.*	Feudalismus {m}	filth *n.*	Schmutz {m}
fever *n.*	Fieber {n}	filtrate *v.*	filtern
few *adj.*	wenig	fin *n.*	Naht {f}
fey *adj.*	todgeweiht	final *adj.*	endgültig
fiancé *n.*	Verlobte {m}	finalist *n.*	Finalist {m}
fiasco *n.*	Fiasko {n}	finance *n.*	Finanz
fibre *n.*	Ballaststoff {m}	financial *adj.*	finanziell
fickle *adj.*	schwankend	financier *n.*	Finanzbeamte {m}
fiction *n.*	Fiktion {f}	find *v.*	finden
fictitious *adj.*	fiktiv	fine *adj.*	schön
fiddle *n.*	Fiedel {f}	finesse *n.*	Feinheit {f}
fidelity *n.*	Wiedergabetreue {f}	finger *n.*	Finger {m}
field *n.*	Feld {n}	finial *n.*	Kreuzblume {f}
fiend *n.*	Feind {m}	finicky *adj.*	affektiert
fierce *adj.*	grimmig	finish *v.*	beenden
fiery *adj.*	feurig	finite *adj.*	endlich
fifteen *adj. & n.*	fünfzehn	fir *n.*	Fichte {f}
fifty *adj. & n.*	fünfzig	fire *n.*	Feuer {n}

firewall *n.*	Schutzwall {m}		**flame** *n.*	Flamme {f}
firm *adj.*	fest		**flammable** *adj.*	entflammbar
firmament *n.*	Himmelszelt {n}		**flank** *n.*	Flanke {f}
first *adj.& n.*	frühest		**flannel** *n.*	Flannel {n}
first aid *n.*	Hilfe {f} -erste		**flap** *v.*	schlagen
fiscal *adj.*	steuerrechtlich		**flapjack** *n.*	Haferflockenplätzchen
fish *n.*	Fisch {m}		{n} **flare** *n.*	Leuchtgeschoss {n}
fisherman *n.*	Fischer {m}		**flash** *v.*	blitzen
fishery *n.*	Fischerei {f}		**flash light** *n.*	Taschenlampe {f}
fishy *adj.*	trüb		**flask** *n.*	Fläschchen {n}
fissure *n.*	Sprung {m}		**flat** *adj.*	Wohnung{f}
fist *n.*	Faust {f}		**flatten** *v.t.*	planieren
fit *adj.*	passt,		**flatter** *v.*	schmeicheln
fitful *adj.*	ruckartig		**flatulent** *adj.*	blähend
fitter *n.*	Einrichter {m}		**flaunt** *v.*	paradierend
fitting *n.*	Einbau {m}		**flavour** *n.*	Geschmack {m}
five *adj.& n.*	fünf		**flaw** *n.*	Fehlerstelle {f}
fix *v.*	befestigen		**flea** *n.*	Floh {m}
fixation *n.*	Fixierung {f}		**flee** *v.*	flüchten
fixture *n.*	Befestigungsorgan {n}		**fleece** *n.*	Vlies {n}
fizz *v.*	perlen		**fleet** *n.*	Flotte {f}
fizzle *v.*	zischend		**flesh** *n.*	Fleisch {n}
fizzy *adj.*	kohlensäurehaltig		**flex** *v.*	biegen
fjord *n.*	Fjord {m}		**flexible** *adj.*	flexibel
flab *n.*	Kreuzblume {f}		**flexitime** *n.*	Gleitzeit {f}
flabbergasted *adj.*	entgeistert		**flick** *v.*	schlagen
flabby *adj.*	schlapp		**flicker** *v.t*	flackern
flaccid *adj.*	schlaff		**flight** *n.*	Flug {m}
flag *n.*	Fahne {f}		**flimsy** *adj.*	schwache
flagellate *v.*	geißeln		**flinch** *v.*	zurückweichen
flagrant *adj.*	eklatant		**fling** *v.*	werfen
flair *n.*	Talent {n}		**flint** *n.*	Feuerstein {m}
flake *n.*	Kokosraspel {f}		**flip** *v.*	klapsen
flamboyant *adj.*	überladen		**flippant** *adj.*	leichtsinnig

71

flipper	n.	Flosse {f}
flirt	v.i	kokettieren
flit v.		wandern
float	v.	schwimmen
flock	n.	Schar {f}
floe	n.	Eisscholle {f}
flog	v.	peitschen
flood	n.	Überschwemmung {f}
floodlight	n.	Scheinwerfer {m}
floor	n.	Stockwerk {n}
flop	v.	plumpsen
floppy	adj.	schlappig
flora	n.	Flora {f}
floral	adj.	blumen
florist	n.	Florist {m}
floss	n.	Seide {f}
flotation	n.	Gründung {f}
flounce v.		zappeln
flounder	v.	zappeln
flour	n.	Mehl {n}
flourish v.		blühen
flow	v.i	Fließen
flower	n.	Blüte {f}
flowery adj.		blüten
flu n.		Grippe {f}
fluctuate	v.	schwanken
fluent	adj.	fließend
fluff	n.	Fluse {f}
fluid	n.	Flüssigkeit {f}
fluke	n.	Glücksbringer
fluorescent	adj.	fluoreszierend
fluoride n.		Fluorid {n}
flurry	n.	Windstoß {m}
flush	v.	scheuchen

fluster	v.	verwirren
flute	n.	Flöte {f}
flutter	v.	flattern
fluvial	adj.	flussartig
flux	n.	Strömung {f}
fly v.i		fliegen
foam	n.	Schaumstoff {m}
focal	adj.	fokal
focus	n.	Fokus {m}
fodder	n.	Tierfutter {n}
foe	n.	Feind {m}
fog	n.	Nebel {m}
foil	v.	vereiteln
fold	v.t	falten
foliage	n.	Laubwerk {n}
folio	n.	Seitenzahl {f}
folk	n.	Volk
follow	v.	folgen
follower	n.	Nachfolger {m}
folly	n.	Verrücktheit {f}
fond	adj.	verliebt
fondle	v.	liebkosen
font	n.	Schriftart {f}
food	n.	Lebensmittel {n}
fool	n.	Narr {m}
foolish	adj.	dümmlich
foolproof	adj.	kinderleicht
foot	n.	Fuß {m}
footage n.		Bildmaterial {n}
football n.		Fußball {m}
footing	n.	Fundament {n}
footling adj.		alberne
for	prep.	bei
foray	n.	Streifzug {m}

forbear v.	unterlassen	forgery n.	Fälschung {f}
forbid v.	abstoßen	forget v.	vergessen
force n.	Macht {f}	forgetful adj.	vergesslich
forceful adj.	kräftig	forgive v.	verzeihen
forceps n.	Zange {f}	forgo v.	verzichten auf
forcible adj.	gewaltsam	fork n.	Gabel {f}
fore adj.	vorn	forlorn adj.	trist
forearm n.	Vorderarm {m}	form n.	Formblatt {n}
forebear n.	Vorfahr {m}	formal adj.	formal
forecast v.t	voraussagen	formality n.	Förmlichkeit {f}
forefather n.	Vorfahr {m}	format n.	Format {m}
forefinger n.	Zeigefinger {m}	formation n.	Gliederung {f}
forehead n.	Stirn {f}	former adj.	ehemalig
foregoing adj.	vorhergehend	formerly adv.	ehemals
foreign adj.	fremd,	formidable adj.	furchtbar
foreigner n.	Ausländer {m}	formula n.	Formel {f}
foreknowledge n.	Voraussicht {f}	formulate v.	formulieren
foreleg n.	Vorderbein {n}	forsake v.	verlassen
foreman n.	Vorarbeiter {m}	forswear v.	abschwören
foremost adj.	erst, vorderst	fort n.	Kastell {n}
forename n.	Vorname {m}	forte n.	Stärke {f}
forensic adj.	gerichtlich	forth adv.	heraus
foreplay n.	Vorspiel {n}	forthcoming adj.	bevorstehend
forerunner n.	Vorbote {m}	forthwith adv.	unverzüglich
foresee v.	voraussehen	fortify v.	bekräftigen
foresight n.	Vorblick {m}	fortitude n.	Tapferkeit {f}
forest n.	Wald {m}	fortnight n.	vierzehn Tage
forestall v.	verhindern	fortress n.	Festung {f}
forestry n.	Forstwissenschaft {f}	fortunate adj.	glücklich
foretell v.	vorhersagen	fortune n.	Glück {n}
forever adv.	immer	forty adj.&n.	vierzig
foreword n.	Vorwort {n}	forum n.	Forum {n}
forfeit v.	Verwirkung {f}	forward adj.	weiter
forge v.t	schmieden	fossil n.	Versteinerung {f}

73

foster	v.	aufziehen
foul	adj.	schmutzig
found	v.	auffinden
foundation	n.	Fundament {n}
founder	n.	Gründer {m}
foundry	n.	Gießerei {m}
fountain	n.	Brunnen {m}
four	adj.&n.	vier
fourteen	adj.&n.	vierzehn
fourth	adj.&n.	viertes
fowl	n.	Geflügel {n}
fox	n.	Fuchs {m}
foyer	n.	Empfangshalle {f}
fraction	n.	Bruch {m}
fractious	adj.	mürrisch
fracture	v.t	brechen
fragile	adj.	brüchig
fragment	n.	Fragment {n}
fragrance	n.	Duftstoff {m}
fragrant	adj.	duftend
frail	adj.	zerbrechlich
frame	n.	Rahmen {m}
framework	n.	Fachwerk {n}
franchise	n.	Franchise
frank	adj.	offen
frankfurter	n.	Frankfurter
frantic	adj.	außer sich
fraternal	adj.	brüderlich
fraternity	n.	Brüderschaft {f}
fraud	n.	Betrug {m}
fraudulent	adj.	betrügerisch
fraught	adj.	voll
fray	v.	ausfransen
freak	n.	Freak {m}

freckle	n.	Sommersprosse {f}
free	adj.	frei
freebie	n.	Werbegeschenk {n}
freedom	n.	Freiheit {f}
freeze	v.	einfrieren
freezer	n.	Tiefkühltruhe {f}
freight	n.	Fracht {f}
freighter	n.	Frachter {m}
French	adj.	französisch
frenetic	adj.	frenetisch
frenzy	n.	Wahnsinn {m}
frequency	n.	Schwingungszahl {f}
frequent	adj.	häufig
fresh	adj.	frisch
fret	v.t.	Ärger {m}
fretful	adj.	ärgerlich
friable	adj.	bröcklig
friction	n.	Reibung {f}
Friday	n.	Freitag {m}
fridge	n.	Kühlschrank {m}
friend	n.	Freund {m}
fright	n.	Angst {f}
frighten	v.	beängstigen
frigid	adj.	kalt
frill	n.	Rüschen
fringe	n.	Rand {m}
frisk	v.	hüpfen
fritter	v.	verzetteln
frivolous	adj.	frivol
frock	n.	Kleid {n}
frog	n.	Frosch {m}
frolic	v.i.	scherzen
from	prep.	von
front	n.	Front {f}

74

frontbencher	*n.*	Vorderbänkler {m}
frontier *n.*		Landesgrenze {f}
frost	*n.*	Frost {m}
frosty	*adj.*	frostig
froth	*n.*	Schaum {m}
frown	*v.i*	missbilligen
frowsty	*adj.*	moderig
frugal	*adj.*	bedürfnislos
fruit	*n.*	Obst {n}
fruitful	*adj.*	fruchtbar
frump	*n.*	Schlampe {f}
frustrate	*v.*	frustrieren
fry	*v.*	braten
fudge	*n.*	Fälschung {f}
fuel	*n.*	Brennmaterial {n}
fugitive	*n.*	Flüchtling {m}
fulcrum *n.*		Stützpunkt {m}
fulfil	*v.*	vollziehen
fulfilment	*n.*	Erfüllung {f}
full	*adj.*	voll
fulsome	*adj.*	ekelhaft
fumble *v.*		umhertasten
fume	*n.*	Rauch {m}
fumigate	*v.*	desinfizieren
fun	*n.*	Spaß {m}
function	*n.*	Amt {n}
functional	*adj.*	amtlich
functionary *n.*		Funktionär {m}
fund	*n.*	Kapital {n}
fundamental	*adj.*	grundsätzlich
funeral *n.*		Beerdigung {f}
fungus *n.*		Pilz {m}
funky	*adj.*	bange
funnel	*n.*	Trichter {m}

funny	*adj.*	komisch
fur *n.*		Pelz {m}
furious	*adj.*	wütend
furl	*v.*	zusammenklappen
furlong *n.*		Achtelmeile {f}
furnace *n.*		Hochofen {m}
furnish *v.*		möblieren
furnishing	*n.*	Möblierung {f}
furniture	*n.*	Möbel {n}
furore	*n.*	Aufsehen {n}
furrow	*n.*	Furche {f}
further	*adv.*	ferner
furthermore *adv.*		außerdem
furthest	*adj*	weitest
fury	*n.*	Zorn {m}
fuse	*v.*	absichern
fusion	*n.*	Verschmelzung {f}
fuss	*n.*	Lärm {m}
fussy	*adj.*	heikel
fusty	*adj.*	muffig
futile	*adj.*	zwecklos
futility	*n.*	Vergeblichkeit {f}
future	*n.*	Zukunft {f}
futuristic	*adj.*	futuristisch

G

gab	*v.*	plappern
gabble	*v.t.*	schwätzen
gadget *n.*		Spielerei {f}
gaffe	*n.*	Ausrutscher {m}
gag	*n.*	Gag {m}
gaga	*adj.*	verblödet
gaiety	*n.*	Lustigkeit {f}

gaily	*adv.*	unbekümmert	**garden**	*n.*	Garten {m}
gain	*v.*	Zunehmen	**gardener**	*n.*	Gärtner {m}
gainful	*adj.*	einträglich	**gargle**	*v.*	gurgeln
gait	*n.*	Gang {m}	**garish**	*adj.*	auffallend
gala	*n.*	Gala {f}	**garland**	*n.*	Girlande {f}
galaxy	*n.*	Galaxie {f}	**garlic**	*n.*	Knoblauch {m}
gale	*n.*	Sturm {m}	**garment**	*n.*	Anzug {m}
gall	*n.*	Galle {f}	**garner**	*v.*	Getreidespeicher {m}
gallant	*adj.*	Kavalier {m}	**garnet**	*n.*	Granat {m}
gallantry	*n.*	Edelmut {m}	**garnish**	*v.*	garnieren
gallery	*n.*	Galerie {f}	**garret**	*n.*	Dachkammer {f}
gallon	*n.*	Gallone {f}	**garrulous**	*adj.*	geschwätzig
gallop	*n.*	Galopp {n}	**garter**	*n.*	Strumpfband {n}
gallows	*n.*	Galgen {m}	**gas**	*n.*	Benzin {n}
galore	*adj.*	in Menge	**gasket**	*n.*	Dichtung {f}
galvanize	*v.i.*	verzinken	**gasp**	*v.i*	keuchen
gambit	*n.*	Gambit {n}	**gastric**	*adj.*	magen-
gamble	*v.*	um Geld spielen	**gastronomy**	*n.*	Gastronomie {f}
gambler	*n.*	Spieler {m}	**gate**	*n.*	Sperre {f}
gambol	*v.*	herumtanzen	**gateau**	*n.*	Sahnetorte {f}
game	*n.*	Spiel {n}	**gather**	*v.*	versammeln
gamely	*adj.*	mutig	**gaudy**	*adj.*	farbenprächtig
gammy	*adj.*	lahm	**gauge**	*n.*	Maß {n}
gamut	*n.*	Farbskala {f}	**gaunt**	*adj.*	hager
gang	*n.*	Bande {f}	**gauntlet**	*n.*	Fehdehandschuh
gangling	*adj.*	schlaksig	**gauze**	*n.*	Gaze {f}
gangster	*n.*	Gangster {m}	**gawky**	*adj.*	einfältig
gangway	*n.*	Laufsteg {m}	**gay**	*adj.*	heiter
gap	*n.*	Lücke {f}	**gaze**	*v.*	anstarren
gape	*v.*	angaffen	**gazebo**	*n.*	Aussichtspunkt {m}
garage	*n.*	Garage {f}	**gazette**	*n.*	Zeitung {f}
garb	*n.*	Tracht {f}	**gear**	*n.*	Getriebe {f}
garbage	*n.*	Müll {m}	**geek**	*n.*	Versessener
garble	*v.*	verstümmeln	**gel**	*n.*	Gel

geld	v.	kastrieren	gesture	n.	Geste {f}
gem	n.	Edelstein {m}	get	v.	bekommen
gender	n.	Geschlecht {n}	geyser	n.	Geiser {m}
general	adj.	generell	ghastly	adj.	grausam
generalize	v.	verallgemeinern	ghost	n.	Gespenst {n}
generate	v.	erzeugen	giant	n.	Gigant {m}
generation	n.	Generation {f}	gibber	v.	Kauderwelsch reden
generator	n.	Generator {m}	gibe	v.	verspotten
generosity	n.	Großzügigkeit {f}	giddy	adj.	schwindlig
generous	adj.	freigiebig	gift	n.	Geschenk {n}
genesis	n.	Ursprung {m}	gifted	adj.	begabt
genetic	adj.	genetisch	gigabyte	n.	Gigabyte {m}
genial	adj.	großartig	gigantic	adj.	gigantisch
genius	n.	Genie {n}	giggle	v.t.	kichern
genteel	adj.	vornehm	gild	v.	vergolden
gentility	n.	vornehme Herkunft	gilt	adj.	vergoldet
gentle	adj.	mild	gimmick	n.	Ding {n}
gentleman	n.	Ehrenmann {m}	ginger	n.	Ingwer {m}
gentry	n.	Leute {pl}	gingerly	adv.	behutsam
genuine	adj.	echt	giraffe	n.	Giraffe {f}
geographer	n.	Geograph {m}	girder	n.	Tragbalken {m}
geographical	adj.	geographisch	girdle	n.	Gürtel {m}
geography	n.	Erdkunde {f}	girl	n.	Mädchen {n}
geologist	n.	Geologe {m}	girlish	adj.	mädchenhaft
geology	n.	Geologie {f}	giro	n.	Giro {n}
geometric	adj.	geometrisch	girth	n.	Gurt {m}
geometry	n.	Geometrie {f}	gist	n.	Hauptinhalt {m}
germ	n.	Keim {m}	give	v.	geben
German	n.	Deutsche {f}	given	adj.	angegeben
germane	adj.	zugehörig	glacial	adj.	eisig
germinate	v.	entkeimen	glacier	n.	Gletscher {m}
germination	n.	Sprossen {n}	glad	adj.	freudig
gerund	n.	Gerundium {n}	gladden	v.	erfreuen
gestation	n.	Schwangerschaft {f}	glade	n.	Waldwiese {f}

glamour	*n.*	Glanz {m}
glance	*v.i.*	Streifblick {m}
gland	*n.*	Drüse {f}
glare	*v.i*	anblitzen
glass	*v.t.*	verglasen
glaze	*v.*	glasieren
glazier	*n.*	Glaser {m}
gleam	*v.*	Schimmer {m}
glean	*v.*	sammeln
glee	*n.*	Fröhlichkeit {f}
glide	*v.*	gleiten
glider	*n.*	Segelflieger {m}
glimmer	*v.*	Schimmer {m}
glimpse	*n.*	Eindruck
glisten	*v.*	glitzern
glitch	*n.*	Spannungsspitze {f}
glitter	*v.*	funkeln
gloat	*v.*	sich freuen
global	*adj.*	umfassend
globalization	*n.*	Globalisierung {f}
globe	*n.*	Erdball {m}
globetrotter	*n.*	Weltenbummler {m}
gloom	*n.*	Trübsinn {m}
gloomy	*adj.*	düster
glorification	*n.*	Verschönerung {f}
glorify	*v.*	verherrlichen
glorious	*adj.*	prächtig
glory	*n.*	Glorie {f}
gloss	*n.*	Glosse {f}
glossary	*n.*	Wörterverzeichnis {n}
glossy	*adj.*	glatt
glove	*n.*	Handschuh {m}
glow	*v.*	glühen
glucose	*n.*	Glukose {f}

glue	*n.*	Leim {m}
glum	*adj.*	deprimiert
glut	*n.*	überhäufe
glutton	*n.*	Vielfraß {m}
gluttony	*n.*	Völlerei {f}
glycerine	*n.*	Glyzerin {n}
gnarled	*adj.*	rau
gnat	*n.*	Stechmücke {f}
gnaw	*v.*	zernagen
go	*v.t*	gehen
goad	*v.*	antreiben
goal	*n.*	Tor {n}
goalkeeper	*n.*	Torwart {m}
goat	*n.*	Ziege {f}
gob	*n.*	Klumpen {m}
gobble	*v.*	verschlingen
goblet	*n.*	Kelch {m}
god	*n.*	Gott {m}
godchild	*n.*	Patenkind {n}
goddess	*n.*	Göttin {f}
godfather	*n.*	Taufpate {f}
godly	*adj.*	fromm
godmother	*n.*	Patin {f}
goggle	*n.*	glotzen
going	*n.*	Gehen {n}
gold	*n.*	Gold
golden	*adj.*	golden
goldsmith	*n.*	Goldschmied {m}
golf	*n.*	Golf {n}
gondola	*n.*	Gondel {f}
gong	*n.*	Gong
good	*adj.*	gut
goodbye	*excl.*	lebewohl
goodness	*n.*	Tugend {f}

78

goodwill	n.	Wohlwollen {n}	
goose	n.	Gans {f}	
gooseberry	n.	Stachelbeere {f}	
gore	n.	Blut {n}	
gorgeous	adj.	prachtvoll	
gorilla	n.	Gorilla {m}	
gory	adj.	mörderisch	
gospel	n.	Evangelium {n}	
gossip	n.	Geschwätz {n}	
gouge	v.	ausmeißeln	
gourd	n.	Flaschenkürbis {m}	
gourmand	n.	Vielfraß {m}	
gourmet	n.	Feinschmecker {m}	
gout	n.	Gicht {f}	
govern	v.	regieren	
governance	n.	Regierungsgewalt {f}	
governess	n.	Erzieherin {f}	
government	n.	Landesregierung {f}	
governor	n.	Gouverneur {m}	
gown	n.	Abendkleid {n}	
grab	v.	angreifen	
grace	n.	Anmut {f}	
graceful	adj.	zierlich	
gracious	adj.	gnädig	
gradation	n.	Abstufung {f}	
grade	n.	Schulnote {f}	
gradient	n.	Steigung {f}	
gradual	adj.	stufenweise	
graduate	n.	promovieren	
graffiti	n.	Wandschmiererei {f}	
graft	n.	Schiebung {f}	
grain	n.	Samenkorn {n}	
gram	n.	Gramm {n}	
grammar	n.	Grammatik {f}	

gramophone	n.	Grammophon {n}	
granary	n.	Kornspeicher {m}	
grand	adj.	großartig	
grandeur	n.	Herrlichkeit {f}	
grandiose	adj.	bombastisch	
grandmother	n.	Großmutter {f}	
grange	n.	Farm {f}	
granite	n.	Granit {m}	
grant	v.	gewähren	
granule	n.	Körnchen {n}	
grape	n.	Weintraube {f}	
graph	n.	Graph {m}	
graphic	adj.	grafisch	
graphite	n.	Graphit {m}	
grapple	v.t.	anpacken	
grasp	v.	zupacken	
grass	n.	Gras {n}	
grasshopper	n.	Grashüpfer {m}	
grate	v.t	reiben	
grateful	n.	dankbar	
grater	n.	Reibeisen {n}	
gratification	n.	Genugtuung {f}	
gratify	v.	erfreuen	
grating	n.	Rasterung {f}	
gratis	adv. &adj.	gratis	
gratitude	n.	Erkenntlichkeit {f}	
gratuitous	adj.	unentgeltlich	
gratuity	n.	Gratifikation {f}	
grave	n.	Grab {n}	
gravel	n.	Kiesel {m}	
graveyard	n.	Friedhof {m}	
gravitas	n.	Gravität {f}	
gravitate	v.	gravitieren	
gravitation	n.	Gravitation {f}	

gravity	n.	Anziehungskraft {f}	
gravy	n.	Bratensoße {f}	
graze	v.	abgrasen	
grease	n.	Schmierfett {n}	
great	adj.	toll	
greatly	adv.	großartig	
greed	n.	Gier {f}	
greedy	adj.	gierig	
green	adj.&n.	grün	
greengrocer	n.	Gemüsehändler {m}	
greenery	v.t.	zubetonieren	
greet	n.	grüßen	
greeting	n.	Begrüßung {f}	
grenade	a.	Handgranate {f}	
grey	n.	grau	
greyhound	n.	Windhund {m}	
grid	n.	Gitter {n}	
griddle	n.	Kuchenblech {n}	
grief	n.	Kummer {m}	
grievance	n.	Kümmernis {n}	
grieve	v.	bekümmern	
grievous	adj.	schmerzlich	
grill	v.	Grill {m}	
grim	adj.	makaber	
grime	n.	Schmutz {m}	
grin	v.	grinsen	
grind	v.	Plackerei {f}	
grinder	n.	Schleifmaschine {f}	
grip	v.	ergreifen	
gripe	v.	fesseln	
grit	n.	Split {m}	
groan	v.	stöhnen	
grocer	n.	Lebensmittelhändler {m}	
grocery	n.	Lebensmittelgeschäft {n}	

groggy	adj.	betrunken	
groin	n.	Leiste {f}	
groom	v.	pflegen	
groove	n.	Riefe {f}	
grope	v.	tasten	
gross	adj.	dick	
grotesque	adj.	fratzenhaft	
grotto	n.	Grotte {f}	
ground	n.	Erdboden {m}	
groundless	adj.	grundlos	
group	n.	Gruppe {f}	
grouping	n.	Gruppierung {f}	
grout	n.	Grütze {f}	
grovel	v.	kriechen	
grow	v.i.	wachsen	
growl	v.	knurren	
growth	n.	Gewachs {n}	
grudge	n	Groll {m}	
grudging	adj.	neidisch	
gruel	n.	Haferschleim {m}	
gruesome	adj.	grausig	
grumble	v.	grummeln	
grumpy	adj.	kauzig	
grunt	v.i.	grunzen	
guarantee	v.t	garantieren	
guarantor	n.	Garant {m}	
guard	v.	Wächter {m}	
guarded	adj.	bewacht	
guardian	n.	Hüter {m}	
guava	n.	Guave	
gudgeon	n.	Zapfen {m}	
guerrilla	n.	Guerilla {m}	
guess	v.i	vermuten	
guest	n.	Gast {m}	

guffaw *n.*	Gelächter {n}	
guidance *n.*	Lenkung {f}	
guide *n.*	Anleitung {f}	
guidebook *n.*	Reiseführer {m}	
guild *n.*	Gilde {f}	
guile *n.*	List {f}	
guillotine *n.*	Schneidemaschine {f}	
guilt *n.*	Schuld {f}	
guilty *adj.*	schuldbewusst	
guise *n.*	Erscheinung {f}	
guitar *n.*	Gitarre {f}	
gulf *n.*	Golf {m}	
gull *n.*	Möwe {f}	
gullet *n.*	Wasserrinne {f}	
gullible *adj.*	leichtgläubig	
gully *n.*	Schlammfang {m}	
gulp *v.*	hinunterschlingen	
gum *n.*	Gummi {m}	
gun *n.*	Gewehr {n}	
gurdwara *n.*	Gurdwara {f}	
gurgle *v.*	gurgeln	
gust *n.*	Windstoß {m}	
gut *n.*	Darm {m}	
gutsy *adj.*	gefräßig	
gutter *n.*	Gosse {f}	
guy *n.*	Kerl {m}	
guzzle *v.*	verprassen	
gymnasium *n.*	Turnhalle {f}	
gymnast *n.*	Turner {m}	
gymnastic *n.*	Gymnastik {f}	
gynaecology *n.*	Gynäkologie {f}	
gypsy *n.*	Zigeuner {m}	
gyrate *v.*	kreisen	

H

habit *n.*	Gewohnheit {f}	
habitable *adj.*	bewohnbar	
habitat *n.*	Lebensraum {m}	
habitation *n.*	Wohnung {f}	
habituate *v.t.*	gewöhnen	
habitué *n.*	Stammgast {m}	
hack *v.*	hacken	
hackneyed *adj.*	abgedroschen	
haemoglobin *n.*	Hämoglobin {n}	
haemorrhage *n.*	Blutung {f}	
haft *n.*	Griff {m}	
hag *n.*	Hexe {f}	
haggard *adj.*	wild	
haggle *v.*	feilschen	
hail *n.*	Hagel {m}	
hair *n.*	Haar {n}	
haircut *n.*	Haarschnitt {m}	
hairstyle *n.*	Haartracht {f}	
hairy *adj.*	haarig	
hajj *n.*	Haddsch {m}	
halal *adj.*	halal	
hale *adj.*	gesund	
halitosis *n.*	Mundgeruch {m}	
hall *n.*	Saal {m}	
hallmark *n.*	Stempel {m}	
hallow *v.*	anbeten	
hallucinate *v.*	halluzinieren	
halogen *n.*	Halogen {n}	
halt *v.*	Halt {m}	
halter *n.*	Strick {m}	
halting *adj.*	zögerlich	
halve *v.*	halbieren	
halyard *n.*	Fall {m}	

ham	n.	Schinken {m}	happiness	n.	Fröhlichkeit {f}
hamburger	n.	Hamburger {m}	happy	adj.	glücklich
hamlet	n.	Teich {m}	harass	v.	belästigen
hammer	n.	Schlägel {m}	harassment	n.	Schikane {f}
hammock	n.	Hängematte {f}	harbour	n.	Hafen {m}
hamper	n.	Geschenkkorb {m}	hard	adj.	hart
hamster	n.	Hamster {m}	hard drive	n.	Festplattenlaufwerk {n}
hamstring	n.	Kniesehne {f}	hardback	n.	gebunden (Buch)
hand	n.	Hand {f}	harden	v.	gehärten
handbag	n.	Handtasche {f}	hardly	adv.	schwerlich
handcuff	n.	Handfesseln {pl}	hardship	n.	Not {f}
handbill	n.	Handzettel {m}	hardy	adj.	kühn
handbook	n.	Handbuch {n}	hare	n.	Hase {m}
handful	n.	handvoll	harelip	n.	Hasenscharte {f}
handicap	n.	Behinderung {f}	harem	n.	Harem {n}
handicapped	n.	behindert	hark	v.	horchen
handicraft	n.	Handwerk {n}	harlequin	n.	Harlekin {m}
handiwork	n.	Handarbeit {f}	harm	n.	Schaden {m}
handkerchief	n.	Taschentuch {n}	harmful	adj.	schändlich
handle	v.t	behandeln	harmless	adj.	harmlos
handout	n.	Zuteilung {f}	harmonious	adj.	harmonisch
handshake	n.	Händeschütteln {n}	harmonium	n.	Harmonium {n}
handsome	adj.	hübsch	harmonize	v.	harmonisieren
handy	adj.	nützlich	harmony	n.	Harmonie {f}
hang	v.i.	aufhängen	harness	n.	Gurtsatz {m}
hangar	n.	Flugzeughalle {f}	harp	n.	Harfe {f}
hanger	n.	Aufhänger {m}	harpy	n.	Harpyie {f
hanging	n.	Behang {m}	harrow	n.	Egge {f}
hangover	n.	Katzenjammer {m}	harrowing	adj.	eggend
hank	n.	Strähne {f}	harsh	adj.	brutal
haphazard	adj.	zufällig	harvester	n.	Erntearbeiter {m}
hapless	adj.	glücklos	hassock	n.	Grasbüschel {n}
happen	v.	geschehen	hasten	v.	beeilen
happening	n.	Ereignis {n}	hat	n.	Hut {m}

hatchet n.	Kriegsbeil {n}		hearse n.	Leichenwagen {m}
hateful adj.	verhasst		heart n.	Herz {n}
haulage n.	Schleppen {n}		heartache n.	Herzschmerz {m}
haunch n.	Hüfte {f}		heartbreak n.	Herzeleid {n}
haunt v.	verfolgen		heartburn n.	Sodbrennen {n}
haunted adj.	verfolgt		hearten v.	ermutigen
have v.	haben		heartening adj.	ermutigend
haven n.	Hafen {m}		heartfelt adj.	tiefgefühlt
havoc n.	Verwüstung {f}		hearth n.	Feuerstelle {f}
hawk n.	Falke {f}		heartless adj.	herzlos
hawker n.	Hausierer {m}		hearty adj.	herzhaft
hawthorn n.	Weißdorn {m}		heat n.	Wärme {f}
hay n.	Heu {n}		heater n.	Heizung {f}
hazard n.	Gefahr {f}		heath n.	Heideland {n}
hazardous adj.	riskant		heathen n.	Heide {m}
haze n.	Schleier {m}		heather n.	Heidekraut {n}
hazy adj.	nebelhaft		heating n.	Erwärmung {f}
he pron.	er		heave v.	heben
head n.	Kopf {n}		heaven n.	Himmel {m}
headache n.	Kopfschmerz {m}		heavenly adj.	himmlisch
heading n.	Ansetzungsform {f}		heavy adj.	schwer
headlight n.	Scheinwerfer {m}		heckle v.	zwischenrufen
headline n.	Überschrift {f}		hectare n.	Hektar {m}
headmaster n.	Direktor {m}		hectic adj.	hektisch
headphone n.	Kopfhörer {m}		hector v.	einschüchtern
headquarters n.	Hauptquartier {n}		hedge n.	Hecke {f}
headstrong adj.	eigensinnig		hedonism n.	Genussucht {f}
heady adj.	voreilig		heed v.	Beachtung {f}
heal v.	heilen		heel n.	Ferse {f}
health n.	Gesundheit {f}		hefty adj.	kräftig
healthy adj.	gesund		hegemony n.	Hegemonie {f}
heap n.	Haufen {m}		height n.	Höhe {f}
hear v.	hören		heighten v.	erhöhen
hearing n.	Gehör {n}		heinous adj.	abscheulich

heir	n.	Erbe {m}
helicopter	n.	Hubschrauber {m}
heliportn.		Hubschrauberlandeplatz {m}
hell	n.	Hölle {f}
helm	n.	Pinne {f}
helmet	n.	Helm {m}
help	v.	helfen
helpful	adj.	behilflich
helpingn.		helfend
helpless	adj.	hilflos
hem	n.	Saum {m}
hemisphere n.		Halbkugel {f}
hen	n.	Henne {f}
hence	adv.	infolgedessen
henceforth	adv.	fortan
henchman	n.	Handlanger {m}
henna	n.	Henna {f,n}
henpecked	adj.	dominiert
hepatitis	n.	Hepatitis {f}
heptagon	n.	Siebeneck {n}
her	pron.	ihr
herald	n.	Vorbote {m}
herb	n.	Kraut {n}
herculean	adj.	übermenschlich
herd	n.	Herde {f}
here	adv.	hier
hereabouts	adv.	hier herum
hereafter	adv.	nachher
hereby	adv.	hierdurch
hereditary	adj.	erblich
heredity	n.	Vererbung {f}
heritage	n.	Erbschaft {f}
hermetic	adj.	hermetisch
hermit	n.	Einsiedler {m}

hermitage	n.	Klause {f}
hernia	n.	Leistenbruch {m}
hero	n.	Held {m}
heroic	adj.	heldenhaft
heroinen.		Heldin {f}
herpes	n.	Herpes {f}
herring n.		Hering {m}
hers	pron.	ihre
herself	pron.	ihrer
hesitant	adj.	zögerlich
hesitate	v.	zögern
heterogeneous	adj.	Verschiedenartig
heterosexual	adj.	heterosexuell
hew	v.	hauen
hexogen	n.	Hexogen {n}
heyday n.		Höhepunkt {m}
hibernate	v.	überwintern
hiccup n.		Schluckauf {m}
hide	v.t	verstecken
hideous	adj.	abscheulich
hierarchy	n.	Rangordnung {f}
high	adj.	hoch
highlight	v.	hervorheben
highly	adv.	hoch
Highness	n.	Höhe {f}
highway	n.	Schnellstraße {f}
hijack	v.	entführen
hike	n.	Wanderung {f}
hilarious	adj.	vergnügt
hilarity n.		Heiterkeit {f}
hilln.		Hügel {m}
hillock	n.	Hügelchen {n}
hilt	n.	Griff {m}
him	pron.	ihm

himself *pron.*	Ihn	
hinder *v.*	verhindern	
hindrance *n.*	Verhinderung {f}	
hindsight *n.*	Nachhinein	
hinge *n.*	Scharnier {n}	
hint *n.*	Tipp {m}	
hip *n.*	Hüfte {f}	
hire *v.t*	anstellen	
hirsute *adj.*	haarig	
his *adj.*	seine	
hiss *v.i*	zischen	
histogram *n.*	Histogram {f}	
historian *n.*	Historiker {m}	
historic *adj.*	historisch	
historical *adj.*	geschichtlich	
history *n.*	Geschichte {f}	
hit *v.*	Treffer {m}	
hitch *v.*	rücken	
hither *adv.*	hierher	
hitherto	*adv.* bisher	
hive *n.*	Bienenstock {m}	
hoard *n.*	Schatz {m}	
hoarding *n.*	Vorrat {m}	
hoarse *adj.*	heiser	
hoax *n.*	Scherz {m}	
hob *n.*	Wälzfräser {m}	
hobble *v.*	humpeln	
hobby *n.*	Hobby {n}	
hobgoblin *n.*	Kobold {m}	
hockey *n.*	Hockey {n}	
hoist *v.*	hochziehen	
hold *v.t*	halten	
holdall *n.*	Reisetasche {f};	
hole *n.*	Loch {n}	

holiday *n.*	Feiertag {m}	
holistic *adj.*	holistisch	
hollow *adj.*	aushöhlend	
holly *n.*	Stechpalme {f}	
holmium *n.*	Holmium {n}	
holocaust *n.*	Holocaust {n}	
hologram *n.*	Hologram {n}	
holster *n.*	Pistolentasche {f}	
holy *adj.*	heilig	
homage *n.*	Huldigung {f}	
home *n.*	Heimat {f}	
homely *adj.*	häuslich	
homicide *n.*	Mord {m}	
homoeopath *n.*	Homöopath {m}	
homeopathy *n.*	Homöopathie {f}	
homogeneous *a.*	einheitlich	
homophobia *n.*	Homophobie {f}	
homosexual *n.*	homosexuell	
honest *adj.*	ehrlich	
honesty *n.*	Ehrlichkeit {f}	
honey *n.*	Honig {m}	
honeycomb *n.*	Honigwabe {f}	
honeymoon *n.*	Flitterwochen {pl}	
honk *n.*	Hupensignal {n}	
honorary *adj.*	ehrenamtlich	
honour *n.*	Ehre {f}	
honourable *adj.*	ehrenwert	
hood *n.*	Kapuze {f}	
hoodwink *v.*	täuschen	
hoof *n.*	Klaue {f}	
hook *n.*	Haken {m}	
hooked *adj.*	eingehakt	
hooligan *n.*	Rowdy {m}	
hoop *n.*	Reifen {m}	

hoopla	n.	Ringwerfen {n}	
hoot	n.	Gejohle {n}	
hoover	n.	Staubsauger {m}	
hop	v.	hüpfen	
hope	n.	Hoffnung {f}	
hopefully	adv.	hoffnungsvoll	
hopeless	adj.	hoffnungslos	
horde	n.	Horde {f}	
horizon	n.	Horizont {m}	
horizontal	adj.	horizontal	
hormone	n.	Hormon {n}	
horn	n.	Horn {n}	
hornet	n.	Hornisse {f}	
horoscope	n.	Horoskop {n}	
horrendous	adj.	horrend	
horrible	adj.	grausam	
horrid	adj.	grauenvoll	
horrific	adj.	entsetzlich	
horrify	v.	erschrecken	
horror	n.	Gräuel {m}	
horse	n.	Pferd {n}	
horsepower	n.	Pferdestärke	
horticulture	n.	Gartenbau {m}	
hose	n.	Schlauch {m}	
hosiery	n.	Strumpfware {f}	
hospice	n.	Hospiz {n}	
hospitable	adj.	gastfreundlich	
hospital	n.	Krankenhaus {n}	
hospitality	n.	Bewirtung {f}	
host	n.	Wirt {m}	
hostage	n.	Geisel {f}	
hostel	n.	Herberge {f}	
hostess	n.	Hostess {f}	
hostile	adj.	feindselig	

hostility n. Feindseligkeit {f}
hot adj. heiß
hotchpotch n. Mischmasch {m}
hotel n. Hotel {n}
hound n. Jagdhund {m}
hour n. Stunde {f}
house n. Haus {n}
housewife n. Hausfrau {f}
housing n. Unterkunft {f}
hovel n. Hütte {f}
hover v. schweben
how adv. wie
however adv. dennoch
howl n. heulen
howler n. Stilblüte {f}
hub n. Hub {m}
hubbub n. Lärm {m}
huddle v. Wirrwarr {n}
hue n. Geschrei {n}
huff n. Verärgerung {f}
hug v. Umarmung {f}
huge adj. riesig
hulk n. Koloss {m}
hull n. Hülle {f}
hum v. brummen
human adj. menschlich
humanism n. Humanismus {m}
humanitarian adj. humanitär
humanity n. Menschlichkeit {f}
humanize v. vermenschlichen
humble adj. demütig
humid adj. feucht
humidity n. Feuchtigkeit {f}
humiliate v. erniedrigen

86

humility	n.	Demut {f}
hummock	n.	Eishügel {m}
humorist	n.	Humorist {m}
humorous	adj.	humoristisch
humour	n.	Humor {m}
hump	n.	Buckel {m}
hunch	v.	vermuten
hundred	adj.& n.	hundert
hunger	n.	Hunger {m}
hungry	adj.	hungrig
hunk	n.	Brocken {m}
hunt	v.	jagen
hunter	n.	Jäger {m}
hurdle	n.	Hürde {f}
hurl	v.	schleudern
hurricane	n.	Wirbelsturm {m}
hurry	v.	eilen
hurt	v.	verletzen
hurtle	v.	zusammenprallen
husband	n.	Ehemann {m}
husbandry	n	Landwirtschaft {f}
hush	v.i	beruhigen
husk	n.	Hülse {f}
husky	adj.	kräftig
hustle	v.	stoßen
hut	n.	Hütte {f}
hutch	n.	Kasten {m}
hybrid	n.	Mischling {m}
hydrant	n.	Hydrant {n}
hydrate	v.	hydratisieren
hydraulic	adj.	hydraulisch
hydrofoil	n.	Tragflügelboot {n}
hydrogen	n.	Wasserstoff {m}
hyena	n.	Hyäne {f}

hygiene	n.	Gesundheitspflege {f}
hymn	n.	Hymne {f}
hype	n.	Rummel {m}
hyper	pref.	über
hyperactive	adj.	hyperaktiv
hyperbole	n.	Hyperbel {f}
hypertension	n.	Hypertonie {f}
hyphen	n.	Bindestrich {m}
hypnosis	n.	Hypnose {f}
hypnotism	n.	Hypnose {f}
hypnotize	v.	hypnotisieren
hypocrisy	n.	Heuchelei {f}
hypocrite	n.	Heuchler {m}
hypotension	n.	Hypotenuse {f}
hypothesis	n.	Hypothese {f}
hypothetical	adj.	hypothetisch
hysteria	n.	Hysterie {f}
hysterical	adj.	hysterisch

| I | | |

I	pron.	ich
ice	n.	Eis {n}
iceberg	n.	Eisberg {m}
ice-cream	n.	Speiseeis {n}
icicle	n.	Eiszapfen {m}
icing	n.	Glasur {f}
icon	n.	Ikone {f}
icy	adj.	eisig
idea	n.	Idee {f}
ideal	n.	ideal
ideally	adv.	idealerweise
idealism	n.	Idealismus {m}
idealist	n.	Idealist {m}
idealistic	adj.	idealistisch

87

idealize v.	idealisieren	**illegibility** n.	Unleserlichkeit {f}
identical adj.	identisch	**illegitimate** adj.	unehelich
identification n.	Erkennung {f}	**illicit** adj.	verboten
identity n.	Identität {f}	**illiteracy** n.	Analphabetentum {n}
identify v.	identifizieren	**illiterate** n.	Analphabet {m}
ideology n.	Ideologie {f}	**illness** n.	Krankheit {f}
idiocy n.	Schwachsinn {m}	**illogical** adj.	unlogisch
idiom n.	Mundart {f}	**illuminate** v.	erleuchten
idiomatic adj.	idiomatisch	**illumination** n.	Beleuchtung {f}
idiosyncrasy n.	Veranlagung {f}	**illusion** v.t.	Illusion {f}
idiot n.	Blödmann {m}	**illusory** adj.	illusorisch
idiotic adj.	idiotisch	**illustrate** n.	illustrieren
idle adj.	faul	**illustration** n.	Illustration {f}
idleness n.	Trägheit {f}	**illustrious** adj.	illuster
idler n.	Faulenzer {m}	**image** n.	Bild {n}
idol n.	Idol {n}	**imagery** n.	Bilder {pl}
idolatry n.	Vergötterung {f}	**imaginary** adj.	imaginär
idolize v.	vergöttern	**imagination** n.	Einbildung {f}
idyll n.	Idylle {f}	**imaginative** adj.	fantasievoll
if conj.	wenn	**imagine** v.t.	einbilden
igloo n.	Iglu {n}	**imbalance** n.	Ungleichgewicht {n}
igneous adj.	eruptiv	**imbibe** v.	aufsaugen
ignite v.	entzünden	**imbroglio** n.	Verwicklung {f}
ignition n.	Entzündung {f}	**imbue** v.	erfüllen
ignoble adj.	gemein	**imitate** v.	imitieren
ignominy n.	Unehre {f}	**imitation** n.	Nachahmung {f}
ignominious adj.	schändlich	**imitator** n.	Imitator {m}
ignoramus n.	Ignorant {m}	**immaculate** adj.	makellos
ignorance n.	Unwissenheit {f}	**immanent** adj.	immanent
ignorant adj.	unwissend	**immaterial** adj.	unkörperlich
ignore v.	ignorieren	**immature** adj.	unreif
ill adj.	krank	**immaturity** n.	Unreife {f}
illegal adj.	gesetzeswidrig	**immeasurable** adj.	unmessbar
illegible adj.	unleserlich	**immediate** adj.	unmittelbar

88

immemorial *adj.* uralt
immense *adj.* immens
immensity *n.* Grenzenlosigkeit {f}
immerse *v.* eintauchen
immersion *n.* Vertiefung {f}
immigrant *n.* Einwanderer {m}
immigrate *v.* einwandern
immigration *n.* Immigration {f}
imminent *adj.* drohend
immoderate *adj.* maßlos
immodest *n.* unbescheiden
immodesty *a.* Unbescheidenheit {f}
immolate *v.* opfern
immoral *adj.* unmoralisch
immorality *n.* Sittenlosigkeit {f}
immortal *adj.* unsterblich
immortality *n.* Unsterblichkeit {f}
immortalize *v.* verewigen
immovable *adv.* unbeweglich
immune *adj.* gefeit
immunity *n.* Sicherheit {f}
immunize *v.* immunisieren
immunology *n.* Immunologie {f}
immure *v.* einschließen
immutable *adj.* unveränderbar
impact *n.* Auswirkung {f}
impair *v.* beeinträchtigen
impalpable *adj.* unfühlbar
impart *v.* weitergeben
impartial *adj.* unparteiisch
impartiality *n.* Unvoreingenommenheit {f}
impassable *adj.* unbefahrbar
impasse *n.* Sackgasse {f}
impassioned *adj.* leidenschaftlich

impassive *adj.* teilnahmslos
impatient *adj.* ungeduldig
impeach *v.* anklagen
impeachment *n.* Amtsenthebungsverfahren {n}
impeccable *adj.* makellos
impede *v.* verhindern
impediment *n.* Hindernis {n}
impel *v.* antreiben
impending *adj.* drohend
impenetrable *adj.* unzugänglich
imperative *adj.* unbedingt
imperfect *adj.* unvollständig
imperfection *n.* Mangelhaftigkeit {f}
imperial *adj.* kaiserlich
imperialism *n.* Imperialismus {m}
imperil *v.* gefährden
impersonal *adj.* unpersönlich
impersonate *v.* verkörpern
impersonation *n.* Personifikation {f}
impertinence *n* Dreistigkeit {f}
impertinent *adj.* dummdreist
impervious *adj.* undurchdringlich
impetuous *adj.* heftig
impetus *n.* Anstoß {m}
impious *adj.* pietätlos
implacable *adj.* unerbittlich
implant *v.* einpflanzen
implausible *adj.* unwahrscheinlich
implement *n.* Ausführung {f}
implicate *v.* verwickeln
implication *n.* Folgerung {f}
implicit *adj.* implizit
implode *v.* implodieren
implore *v.t.* anflehen

89

imply	v.	implizieren
impolite	adj.	unhöflich
import	v.	einführen
importer	n.	Importeur {m}
importance	n.	Wichtigkeit {f}
important	adj.	wichtig
impose	v.	imponieren
imposing	adj.	auferlegend
imposition	n.	Auferlegung {f}
impossibility	n.	Unmöglichkeit {f}
impossible	adj.	unmöglich
imposter	n.	Gaukler {m}
impotence	n.	Impotenz {f}
impotent	adj.	impotent
impound	v.	beschlagnahmen
impoverish	v.	verarmen
impracticable	adj.	undurchführbar
impractical	adj.	unpraktisch
impress	v.	beeindrucken
impression	n.	Eindruck {m}
impressive	adj.	eindrucksvoll
imprint	v.	aufdrucken
imprison	v.	einschließen
improbable	adj.	unwahrscheinlich
improper	adj.	ungeeignet
impropriety	n.	Ungehörigkeit {f}
improve	v.	verbessern
improvement	n.	Verbesserung {f}
improvident	adj.	unvorsichtig
improvise	v.	improvisieren
imprudent	adj.	unbesonnen
impudent	adj.	frech
impulse	n.	Impuls {m}
impulsive	adj.	impulsiv

impunity	n.	Straflosigkeit {f}
impure	adj.	unrein
impurity	n.	Verunreinigung {f}
impute	v.	unterstellen
in	prep.	hinein
inability	n.	Unfähigkeit {f}
inaccurate	adj.	ungenau
inaction	n.	Tatenlosigkeit {f}
inactive	adj.	inaktiv
inadequate	adj.	mangelhaft
inadmissible	adj.	unzulässig
inadvertent	adj.	versehentlich
inane	adj.	gehaltlos
inanimate	adj.	leblos
inapplicable	adj.	ungeeignet
inappropriate	adj.	unangebracht
inarticulate	adj.	unartikuliert
inattentive	adj.	nachlässig
inaudible	adj.	unhörbar
inaugural	adj.	eingeführt
inaugurate	v.	einführen
inauspicious	adj.	ungünstig
inborn	adj.	angeboren
inbred	adj.	angeborene
incalculable	adj.	unabsehbar
incapable	adj.	unfähig
incapacity	n.	Unfähigkeit {f}
incarcerate	v.	einkerkern
incarnate	adj.	verkörpert
incarnation	n.	Verkörperung {f}
incense	n.	Weihrauch {m}
incentive	adj.	anreizend
inception	n.	Beginn {m}
incest	n.	Blutschande {f}

inch	n.	Zoll {n}		incumbent	adj.	obliegend

inch   n.   Zoll {n}
incidence   n.   Einfall {m}
incident   n.   Vorfall {m}
incidental adj. zufällig
incisive adj. schneidend
incite   v.   aufhetzen
inclination n.   Neigung {f}
incline   v.   neigen
include v.   erfassen
inclusion   n.   Einbeziehung {f}
inclusive   adj. inklusive
incoherent adj. Unzusammenhängend
income n.   Verdienst {m}
incomparable adj. unvergleichbar
incompatible adj. unverträglich
incompetent   adj. inkompetent
incomplete adj. unvollständig
inconclusive adj. ergebnislos
inconsiderate adj. rücksichtslos
inconsistent adj. folgewidrig
inconsolable adj. trostlos
inconspicuous adj. unscheinbar
inconvenience n.Unbequemlichkeit {f}
incorporate v. verbunden
incorporation n. Angliederung {f}
incorrect   adj. inkorrekt
incorrigible adj. unverbesserlich
incorruptible adj. unbestechlich
increase   v.   anwachsen
incredible adj. unglaublich
increment   n.   Zunahme {f}
incriminate v.i. beschuldigen
incubate   v.   ausbrüten
inculcate   v.   einschärfen

incumbent   adj. obliegend
incur   v.   zuziehen
incurable   adj. unheilbar
incursion   n.   Einfall {m}
indebted   adj. verschuldet
indecency   n.   Unanständigkeit {f}
indecent   adj. unanständig
indecision n.   Zögern {n}
indeed adv. allerdings
indefensible adj. unhaltbar
indefinite adj. unklar
indemnity   n.   Abfindung {f}
indent   v.   einkerben
indenture   n.   Vertrag {m}
independence n.   Eigenständigkeit {f}
independent   adj. selbstständig
indescribable adj. unbeschreiblich
index   n.   Index {m}
Indian   n.   indisch
indicate   v.   anzeigen
indication n.   Anzeichen {n}
indicative adj. hinweisend
indicator   n.   Indikator {m}
indict   v.   anklagen
indictment n.   Anklage {f}
indifference n.   Gleichgültigkeit {f}
indifferent adj. gleichgültig
indigenous adj. eingeboren
indigestible adj. unverdaulich
indigestion n.   Verdauungsstörung {f}
indignant   adj. ungehalten
indignation n.   Empörung {f}
indignity   n.   Beleidigung {f}
indigo n.   Indigo {n}

91

indirect *adj.* indirekt
indiscipline *n.* Indisziplin {f}
indiscreet *adj.* indiskret
indiscretion *n.* Indiskretion {f}
indiscriminate *adj.* unüberlegt
indispensable *adj.* unumgänglich
indisposed *adj.* abgeneigt
indisputable *adj.* unbestreitbar
indistinct *adj.* undeutlich
individual *adj.* individuell
individualism *n.* Individualismus {m}
individuality *n.* Individualität {f}
indivisible *adj.* unteilbar
indolent *adj.* träge
indomitable *adj.* unzähmbar
indoor *adj.* innen
induce *v.* veranlassen
inducement *n.* Veranlassung {f}
induct *v.* einweihen
induction *n.* Einarbeitung {f}
indulge *v.* nachgeben
indulgence *n.* Nachsicht {f}
indulgent *adj.* duldsam
industrial *adj.* industriell
industrious *adj.* arbeitsam
industry *n.* Industrie {f}
ineffective *adj.* unwirksam
inefficient *adj.* unwirksam
ineligible *adj.* ungeeignet
inequality *n.* Ungleichheit {f}
inert *adj.* inaktiv
inertia *n.* Trägheit {f}
inescapable *adj.* unentrinnbar
inevitable *adj.* unabwendbar

inexact *adj.* ungenau
inexcusable *adj.* unentschuldbar
inexhaustible *adj.* unerschöpflich
inexorable *adj.* unerbittlich
inexpensive *adj.* billig
inexperience *n.* Unerfahrenheit {f}
inexplicable *adj.* unerklärlich
inextricable *adj.* unentwirrbar
infallible *adj.* unfehlbar
infamous *adj.* schändlich
infamy *n.* Unverschämtheit {f}
infancy *n.* Kindheit {f}
infant *n.* Kleinkind {n}
infanticide *n.* Kindesmord {m}
infantile *adj.* kindisch
infantry *n.* Infanterie {f}
infatuate *v.* betören
infatuation *n.* Betörung {f}
infect *v.* anstecken
infection *n.* Ansteckung {f}
infectious *adj.* ansteckend
infer *v.* folgern
inference *n.* Folgerung {f}
inferior *adj.* untergeordnet
inferiority *n.* Minderwertigkeit {f}
infernal *adj.* höllisch
infertile *adj.* unfruchbar
infest *v.* heimsuchen
infidelity *n.* Veruntreuung {f}
infighting *n.* Nahkampf {m}
infiltrate *v.* eindringen
infinite *adj.* endlos
infinity *n.* Grenzenlosigkeit {f}
infirm *adj.* kraftlos

92

infirmity	n.	Gebrechlichkeit {f}
inflame v.		entflammen
inflammable adj.		entflammbar
inflammation	n.	Entzündung {f}
inflammatory	adj.	aufrührerisch
inflate v.		aufblasen
inflation	n.	Inflation {f}
inflect v.		biegen
inflexible	adj.	unbeweglich
inflict v.		zufügen
influence	n.	Einwirkung {f}
influential	adj.	einflussreich
influenza	n.	Grippe {f}
influx	n.	Einfuhr {f}
inform v.		benachrichtigen
informal	adj.	formlos
information n.		Angabe {f}
informative	adj.	informativ
informer	n.	Denunziant {m}
infrastructure	n.	Infrastruktur {f}
infrequent	adj.	selten
infringe v.		verletzen
infringement	n.	Rechtsverletzung {f}
infuriate	v.	ärgern
infuse v.		aufgießen
infusion	n.	Infusion {f}
ingrained	adj.	einbetten
ingratitude	n.	Undankbarkeit {f}
ingredient	n.	Bestandteil {m}
inhabit v.		bewohnen
inhabitable	adj.	bewohnbar
inhabitant	n.	Bewohner {m}
inhale v.		inhalieren
inhaler	n.	Inhalation {f}

inherent	adj.	eingewurzelt
inherit v.		erben
inheritance	n.	Erbschaft {f}
inhibit v.		verhindern
inhibition	n.	Hemmung {f}
inhospitable	adj.	ungastlich
inhuman	adj.	unmenschlich
inimical	adj.	feindlich
inimitable	adj.	einzigartig
initial	adj.	anfänglich
initiate v.		auslösen
initiative	n.	Initiative {f}
inject v.		einspritzen
injection	n.	Injektion {f}
injudicious	adj.	unüberlegt
injunction	n.	gerichtliche Verfügung
injure v.		schädigen
injurious	adj.	schädlich
injury	n.	Beschädigung {f}
injustice	n.	Ungerechtigkeit {f}
ink	n.	Tinte {f}
inkling	n.	Andeutung {f}
inland	adj.	Binnenland {n}
inmate	n.	Insasse {m}
inmost	adj.	innerst
inn	n.	Gasthaus {n}
innate	adj.	angeboren
inner	adj.	innerlich
innermost	adj.	innerst
innocence	n.	Unschuld {f}
innocent	adj.	unschuldig
innovate	v.	innovieren
innovation	n.	Neuerung {f}
innovator	n.	Wegbereiter {m}

93

innumerable	adj.	unzählig
inoculate	v.	impfen
inoculation	n.	Impfung {f}
inoperative	adj.	funktionsunfähig
inopportune	adj.	unangebracht
inpatient	n.	Bettenstation {f}
input	n.	Eingabe {f}
inquest	n.	Untersuchung {f}
inquire	v.	erkundigen
inquiry	n.	Erkundigung {f}
inquisition	n.	Untersuchung {f}
inquisitive	adj.	neugierig
insane	adj.	wahnsinnig
insanity	n.	Irrsinn {m}
insatiable	adj.	unersättlich
inscribe	v.	beschriften
inscription	n.	Aufschrift {f}
insect	n.	Insekt {n}
insecticide	n.	Insektengift {n}
insecure	adj.	unsicher
insecurity	n.	Unsicherheit {f}
insensible	adj.	unempfänglich
inseparable	adj.	untrennbar
insert	v.	Einsatz {m}
insertion	n.	Einschub {m}
inside	n.	Innern
insight	n.	Einblick {m}
insignificance	n.	Geringfügigkeit {f}
insignificant	adj.	bedeutungslos
insincere	adj.	unaufrichtig
insincerity	adv.	Unaufrichtigkeit {f}
insinuate	v.	andeuten
insinuation	n.	Andeutung {f}
insipid	adj.	fade

insist	v.	insistieren
insistence	n.	Insistenz {f}
insistent	adj.	hartnäckig
insolence	n.	Frechheit {f}
insolent	adj.	unverschämt
insoluble	adj.	unauflöslich
insolvency	n.	Zahlungsunfähigkeit {f}
insolvent	adj.	zahlungsunfähig
inspect	v.	beschauen
inspection	n.	Inspektion {f}
inspector	n.	Aufseher {m}
inspiration	n.	Eingebung {f}
inspire	v.	anregen
instability	n.	Unbeständigkeit {f}
install	v.	installieren
installation	n.	Installierung {f}
instalment	n.	Abzahlung {f}
instance	n.	Fall {m}
instant	adj.	augenblicklich
instantaneous	adj.	augenblicklich
instead	adv.	stattdessen
instigate	v.	anstiften
instil	v.	einträufeln
instinct	n.	Instinkt {n}
instinctive	adj.	instinktiv
institute	n.	Institut {n}
institution	n.	Anstalt {f}
instruct	v.	anleiten
instruction	n.	Befehl {m}
instructor	n.	Lehrer {m}
instrument	n.	Instrument {n}
instrumental	adj.	instrumentell
instrumentalist	n.	Instrumentalist {m}
insubordinate	adj.	aufsässig

insubordination	n.	Gehorsamsverweigerung
{f} insufficient	adj.	ungenügend
insular	adj.	insular
insulate	v.	isolieren
insulation	n.	Wärmedämmung {f}
insulator	n.	Isolator {m}
insulin	n.	Insulin {n}
insult	v.t.	beschimpfen
insupportable	adj.	unerträglich
insurance	n.	Versicherung {f}
insure	v.	versichern
insurgent	n.	Rebell {m}
insurmountable	adj.	Unüberbrückbar
insurrection	n.	Aufruhr {m}
intact	adj.	unbeschädigt
intake	n.	Ansaugung {f}
intangible	adj.	unfassbar
integral	adj.	eingebaut
integrity	n.	Unbescholtenheit {f}
intellect	n.	Intellekt {m}
intellectual	adj.	intellektuell
intelligence	n.	Intelligenz {f}
intelligent	adj.	intelligent
intelligible	adj.	verständlich
intend	v.	beabsichtigen
intense	adj.	intensiv
intensify	v.	verstärken
intensity	n.	Intensität {f}
intensive	adj.	intensiv
intent	n.	Absicht {f}
intention	n.	Absicht {f}
intentional	adj.	absichtlich
interact	v.	aufeinander wirken
intercede	v.	vermitteln

intercept	v.	abfangen
interception	n.	Unterbrechung {f}
interchange	v.	Austausch {m}
intercom	n.	Gegensprechanlage {f}
interconnect	v.	zusammen bindend
intercourse	n.	Verkehr {m}
interdependent	adj.	voneinander abhängig
interest	n.	Vorteil {m}
interesting	adj.	interessant
interface	n.	Grenzfläche {f}
interfere	v.	eingriffen
interference	n.	Eingriff {m}
interim	n.	vorläufig
interior	adj.	inner
interject	v.	einwerfen
interlink	v.	einfügen
interlock	v.	verzahnen
interlocutor	n.	Gesprächspartner {m}
interloper	n.	Eindringling {m}
interlude	n.	Zwischenprogramm {n}
intermediary	n.	Zwischenhändler {m}
intermediate	adj.	zwischenliegen
interminable	adj.	endlos
intermission	n.	Pause {f}
intermittent	adj.	unterbrochen
intern	v.	internieren
internal	adj.	innerbetrieblich
international	adj.	international
internet	n.	Internet {n}
interplay	n.	Wechselwirkung {f}
interpret	v.	dolmetschen
interpreter	n.	Interpret {m}
interracial	adj.	interrassisch
interrelate	v.	wechseln

interrogate v.	verhören	intrude v.	eindringen
interrogative	adj. fragend	intrusion n.	Eindringen {n}
interrupt v.	unterbrechen	intrusive	adj. zudringlich
interruption n.	Unterbrechung {f}	intuition n.	Ahnung {f}
intersect v.	durchschneiden	intuitive n.	wissend
interstate n.	zwischenstaatlich	inundate v.	überschwemmen
interval n.	Intervall {n}	invade v.	eindringen
intervene v.	dazwischenkommen	invalid n.	Kranke
intervention n.	Eingriff {m}	invalidate v.	entkräften
interview n.	Vorstellungsgespräch {n}	invaluable	adj. unschätzbar
intestine n.	Darm {m}	invariable	adj. unveränderlich
intimacy n.	Intimität {f}	invasion n.	Invasion {f}
intimate adj.	intim	invective n.	Schimpfwort {n}
intimidate v.	verschüchtern	invent v.	erfinden
intimidation n.	Einschüchterung {f}	invention n.	Erfindung {f}
into prep.	in	inventor n.	Erfinder {m}
intolerable adj.	unerträglich	inventory n.	Inventar {n}
intolerant adj.	intolerant	inverse adj.	invertiert
intone v.	anstimmen	invert v.	umkehren
intoxicate v.	berauschen	invest v.t.	investieren
intoxication n.	Rausch {m}	investigate v.	untersuchen
intractable adj.	unfügsam	investigation n.	Nachforschung {f}
intranet n.	Intranet {n}	investment n.	Investition {f}
intransitive adj.	intransitiv	invigilate adj.	Überwacht
intrepid adj.	unerschrocken	invigilator n.	Überwachungseinrichtung {f}
intricate adj.	kompliziert	invincible adj.	unbesiegbar
intrigue v.	intrigieren	inviolable adj.	unantastbar
intrinsic adj.	immanent	invisible adj.	unsichtbar
introduce v.	einweisen	invitation n.	Einladung {f}
introduction n.	Einleitung {f}	invite v.	einladen
introductory adj.	einleitend	inviting adj.	einladend
introspect v.	prüfen sich	invocation n.	Aufruf {m}
introspection n.	Selbstprüfung {f}	invoice n.	Rechnung {f}
introvert n.	introvertiert	invoke v.	aufrufen

involuntary	*adj.*	unfreiwillig	**isle**	*n.*	Eiland {n}
involve *v.*		verwickeln	**islet**	*n.*	Inselchen {n}
invulnerable	*adj.*	unverwundbar	**isobar** *n.*		Isobar {n}
inward *adj.*		einwärts	**isolate** *v.*		isolieren
irate	*adj.*	zornig	**isolation**	*n.*	Isolierung {f}
ire	*n.*	Zorn {m}	**issue**	*n.*	Streitfall {m}
iris	*n.*	Schwertlilie {f}	**it** *pron.*		es
irksome	*v.*	ermüdend,	**italic**	*adj.*	Kursiv
iron	*n.*	Eisen {n}	**itch**	*v.i.*	jucken
ironical *adj.*		ironisch	**itchy**	*adj.*	juckend
irony	*n.*	Ironie {f}	**item**	*n.*	Artikel {m}
irradiate	*v.*	bestrahlen	**iterate** *v.*		wiederholen
irrational	*adj.*	unvernünftig	**itinerary**	*n*	Reisetagebuch {n}
irreconcilable	*adj.*	unvereinbar	**itself**	*pron.*	selbst
irredeemable	*adj.*	unkündbar	**ivory**	*n.*	Elfenbein {n}
irrefutable	*adj.*	unwiderlegbar	**ivy** *n.*		Efeu {m}
irregular	*adj.*	unregelmäßig			
irregularity	*n.*	Unregelmäßigkeit {f}	**J**		
irrelevant	*adj.*	irrelevant	**jab**	*v.*	stechen
irreplaceable	*adj.*	unersätzlich	**jabber**	*v.*	plappern
irresistible	*adj.*	unaufhaltsam	**jack**	*n.*	Springer {m}
irresolute	*adj.*	unentschlossen	**jackal**	*n.*	Schakal {m}
irrespective *adj.*		rücksichtslos	**jackass** *n.*		Esel {m}
irresponsible	*adj.*	Verantwortungslos	**jacket**	*n.*	Jackett {n}
irreversible *adj.*		unumkehrbar	**jackpot** *n.*		Jackpot {m}
irrevocable	*adj.*	unwiderruflich	**Jacuzzi** *n.*		Whirlwanne {f}
irrigate *v.*		bewässern	**jade**	*n.*	Jade {m,f}
irrigation	*n.*	Bewässerung {f}	**jaded**	*adj.*	erschöpft
irritable *adj.*		reizbar	**jagged** *adj.*		zackig
irritant *n.*		irritativ	**jail** *n.*		Gefängnis {n}
irritate *v.*		irritieren	**jailer**	*n.*	Gefängniswärter {m}
irruption	*n.*	Einbruch {m}	**jam**	*v.t.*	einklemmen
Islam	*n.*	Islam {m}	**jam**	*n.*	Marmelade {f}
island *n.*		Insel {f}	**jamboree**	*n.*	Gaudi {m}

janitor	n.	Portier {m}	
January	n.	Januar {m}	
jar n.		Glas {n}	
jargon	n.	Jargon {m}	
jasmine	n.	Jasmin {m}	
jaundice	n.	Gelbsucht {f}	
jaunt	n.	Ausflug {m}	
jaunty	adj.	munter	
javelin	n.	Wurfspieß {m}	
jaw	n.	Klemmbacke {f}	
jay n.		Tölpel {m}	
jazz	n.	Jazz {m}	
jazzy	adj.	toll	
jealous adj.		eifersüchtig	
jealousy	n.	Eifersucht {f}	
jeans	n.	Jeans {f}	
jeep	n.	Jeep {m}	
jeer	v.	spotten	
jelly	n.	Gelee {n}	
jellyfish	n.	Meduse {f}	
jeopardize	v.	gefährden	
jeopardy	n.	Gefahr {f}	
jerk	n.	Trottel {m}	
jerkin	n.	Jacke {f}	
jerry can	n.	Benzinkanister {m}	
jersey n.		Trikot {n}	
jest	n.	scherzen	
jester	n.	Spaßmacher {m}	
jet n.		Strahl {m}	
jet lag	n.	Zeitzonenkater {m}	
jewel	n.	Juwel {n}	
jeweller n.		Juwelier {m}	
jewellery	n.	Juwelierwaren {pl}	
jibe	v.	zustimmen	

jig n.		Hilfsmittel {n}	
jiggle	v.	rütteln	
jigsaw	n.	Laubsägemaschine {f}	
jingle	v.	klingeln	
jinx	n.	Pechvogel {m}	
jitters	n.	Schwankungsbreite {f}	
job	n.	Stellung {f}	
jockey	n.	Jockey {m}	
jocose	adj.	drollig	
jocular	adj.	scherzhaft	
jog	v.	Joggen	
joggle	v.	schütteln	
join	v.	vereinigen	
joiner	n.	Schreiner {m}	
joint	n.	Verbindungsstelle {f}	
joist	n.	Balken {m}	
joke	n.	Scherz {m}	
joker	n.	Witzbold {m}	
jolly	adj.	vergnügt	
jolt	v.t.	rütteln	
jostle	v.t.	anrempeln	
jot	v.t.	hinwerfen	
journal n.		Tageblatt {n}	
journalism	n.	Journalismus {m}	
journalist	n.	Journalist {m}	
journey	n.	Reise {f}	
jovial	adj.	gemütlich	
joviality	n.	Heiterkeit {f}	
joy n.		Wonne {f}	
joyful	adj.	freudig	
joyous	adj.	erfreulich	
jubilant adj.		jubelnd	
jubilation	n.	Gejohle {n}	
jubilee n.		Jubiläum {n}	

judge	n.	Richter {m}		

judge *n.* Richter {m}
judgement *n.* Beurteilung {f}
judicial *adj.* gerichtlich
judiciary *n.* Justizgewalt {f}
judicious *adj.* urteilsfähig
judo *n.* Judo {n}
jug *n.* Krug {m}
juggle *v.* jonglieren
juggler *n.* Gaukler {m}
juice *n.* Saft {m}
juicy *adj.* saftig
July *n.* Juli {m}
jumble *n.* Mischmasch {m}
jumbo *adj.* Jumbo {m}
jump *v.i* springen
jumper *n.* Springer {m}
junction *n.* Verbindung {f}
juncture *n.* Verbindungspunkt {m}
June *n.* Juni {m}
jungle *n.* Dschungel {m}
junior *adj.* junior
junior *n.* Nachwuchs {m}
junk *n.* Ausschuss {m}
Jupiter *n.* Jupiter
jurisdiction *n.* Gerichtsbarkeit {f}
jurisprudence *n.* Rechtswissenschaft {f}
jurist *n.* Jurist {m}
juror *n.* Vereidigter {m}
jury *n.* Jury {m}
just *adj.* gerade
justice *n.* Gerechtigkeit {f}
justifiable *adj.* entschuldbar
justification *n.* Justierung {f}
justify *v.* rechtfertigen

jute *n.* Jute {f}
juvenile *adj.* jugendlich

K

kaftans *n.* Kaftan {m}
kaleidoscope *n.* Kaleidoskop {n}
kangaroo *n.* Känguru {n}
karaoke *n.* Karaoke {n}
karate *n.* Karate {n}
karma *n.* Schicksal {n}
kebab *n.* Kebab {m}
keel *n.* Kiel {m}
keen *adj.* eifrig
keenness *n.* Schärfe {f}
keep *v.* behalten
keeper *n.* Tierpfleger {m}
keeping *n.* Wahrung {f}
keepsake *n.* Andenken {n}
keg *n.* Lagerfass {n}
kennel *n.* Gosse {f}
kerb *n.* Bordstein {m}
kerchief *n.* Halstuch {n}
kernel *n.* Samenkern {m}
kerosene *n.* Kerosin {n}
ketchup *n.* Tomatensauce {f}
kettle *n.* Kessel {m}
key *n.* Schlüssel {m}
keyboard *n.* Keyboard {n}
keyhole *n.* Schlüsselloch {n}
kick *v.* treten
kid*n.* Kind {n}
kidnap *v.* entführen
kidney *n.* Niere {f}
kill *v.* töten

killing	*n.*	Tötung {f}
kiln	*n.*	Brennofen {m}
kilo	*n.*	Kilogramm {n}
kilobyte	*n.*	Kilobyte {n}
kilometre	*n.*	Kilometer {m}
kilt	*n.*	Schottenrock {m}
kimono	*n.*	Kimono {m}
kin	*n.*	Sippe {f}
kind	*n.*	Sorte {f}
kindergarten	*n.*	Kindergarten {m}
kindle	*v.*	anzünden
kindly	*adv.*	gütig
kinetic	*adj.*	kinetisch
king	*n.*	König {m}
kingdom	*n.*	Königreich {n}
kink	*n.*	Knick {m}
kinship	*n.*	Blutsverwandtschaft {f}
kiss	*v.t.*	küssen
kit	*n.*	Bausatz {m}
kitchen	*n.*	Küche {f}
kite	*n.*	Drachen {m}
kith	*n.*	Sack {m}
kitten	*n.*	Kätzchen {n}
kitty	*n.*	Kätzchen {n}
knack	*n.*	Kniff {m}
knacker	*v.*	kaputtmachen
knave	*n.*	Schurke {m}
knead	*v.*	kneten
knee	*n.*	Knie {n}
kneel	*v.*	knien
knickers	*n.*	Schlüpfer {pl}
knife	*n.*	Messer {n}
knight	*n.*	Ritter {m}
knighthood	*n.*	Ritterschaft {f}

knit	*v.*	stricken
knob	*n.*	Höcker {m}
knock	*v.*	klopfen
knot	*n.*	Knoten {m}
knotty	*adj.*	knotig
know	*v.*	wissen
knowing	*adj.*	wissend
knowledge	*n.*	Kenntnis {f}
knuckle	*n.*	Knöchel {m}
kosher	*adj.*	koscher
kudos	*n.*	Ansehen {n}
kung fu	*n.*	Kung fu {m}

L

label	*n.*	Kennsatz {m}
labial	*adj.*	labial
laboratory	*n.*	Labor {n}
laborious	*adj.*	arbeitsam
labour	*n.*	Arbeit {f}
labourer	*n.*	Arbeiter {m}
labyrinth	*n.*	Labyrinth {n}
lace	*n.*	Spitze {f}
lacerate	*v.*	zerfleischen
lachrymose	*adj.*	tränenreich
lack	*n.*	Mangel {m}
lackey	*n.*	Lakai {m}
lacklustre	*adj.*	glanzlos
laconic	*adj.*	lakonisch
lacquer	*n.*	Lack {m}
lacrosse	*n.*	Lacrosse {n}
lactate	*v.*	säugen
lactose	*n.*	Milchzucker {m}
lacuna	*n.*	Lücke {f}
lacy	*adj.*	spitzenartig

lad	n.	Jüngling {m}	lanky	adj.	schlaksig
ladder	n.	Leiter {f}	lantern	n.	Laterne {f}
laden	n.	Gesamtgewicht {n}	lap	n.	Schoß {m}
ladle	n.	Schöpflöffel {m}	lapse	n.	Verfehlung {f}
lady	n.	Dame {f}	lard	n.	Schweinefett {n}
ladybird	n.	Marienkäfer {m}	larder	n.	Speisekammer {f}
lag	v.	verzögern	large	adj.	groß
lager	n.	Lagerbier {n}	largesse	n.	Freigebigkeit {f}
laggard	n.	Zauderer {m}	lark	n.	Lerche {f}
lagging	n.	Nachhängen {n}	larva	n.	Larve {f}
lagoon	n.	Lagune {f}	larynx	n.	Kehlkopf {m}
lair	n.	Versteck {n}	lasagne	n.	Lasagne {f}
lake	n.	See {m}	lascivious	adj.	lüstern
lamb	n.	Lamm {n}	laser	n.	Laser {m}
lambast	v.	verprügeln	lash	v.	peitschen
lame	adj.	lahm	lashings	n.	Laschung {f}
lament	n.	Klage {f}	lass	n.	Freundin {f}
lamentable	adj.	beklagenswert	last	adj.	letzte
laminate	v.	schichten	lasting	adj.	dauerhaft
lamp	n.	Lampe {f}	latch	n.	Sperre {f}
lampoon	v.	verspotten	late	adj.	spät
lance	n.	Lanze {f}	lately	adv.	neulich
lancer	n.	Lanzenreiter {m}	latent	adj.	verborgen
lancet	n.	Lanzette {f}	lath	n.	Latte {f}
land	n.	Festland {n}	lathe	n.	Drehbank {f}
landing	n.	Landung {f}	lather	n.	Schaum {m}
landlady	n.	Hausbesitzerin {f}	latitude	n.	Breite {f}
landlord	n.	Hausbesitzer {m}	latrine	n.	Latrine {f}
landscape	n.	Landschaft {f}	latte	n.	Messlatte {f}
lane	n.	Gasse {f}	latter	adj.	modern
language	n.	Sprache {f}	lattice	n.	Gitter {n}
languid	adj.	schwach	laud	v.	loben
languish	v.	schmachten	laudable	adj.	löblich
lank	adj.	strähnig	laugh	v.	lachen

laughable	adj.	lächerlich	
laughter	n.	Lachen {n}	
launch	v.	lancieren	
launder	v.	waschen	
launderette	n.	Waschsalon {m}	
laundry	n.	Wäscherei {f}	
laurel	n.	Lorbeerbaum {m}	
laureate	n.	Preisträger {m}	
lava	n.	Lava {f}	
lavatory	n.	Klosett {n}	
lavender	n.	Lavendel {m}	
lavish	adj.	freigebig	
law	n.	Rechtswissenschaft {f}	
lawful	adj.	rechtmäßig	
lawless	adj.	gesetzlos	
lawn	n.	Liegewiese {f}	
lawyer	n.	Rechtsanwalt	
lax	adj.	locker	
laxative	n.	Abführmittel {n}	
laxity	n.	Laxheit {f}	
lay	v.	legen	
layer	n.	Auflage {f}	
layman	n.	Laie {f}	
laze	v.	faulenzen	
lazy	adj.	faul	
leach	v.	laugen	
lead	n.	Führung {f}	
lead	v.	führen	
leaden	adj.	schwer	
leader	n.	Führer {m}	
leadership	n.	Führung {f}	
leaf	n.	Blatt {n}	
leaflet	n.	Merkblatt {n}	
league	n.	Liga {f}	

leak	v.	Undichtigkeit {f}	
leakage	n.	Verlust {m}	
lean	v.	lehnen	
leap	v.	überspringen	
learn	v.	lernen	
learned	adj.	gelernt	
learner	n.	Lernende {m,f}	
learning	n.	Lernprozeß {m}	
lease	n.	Miete {f}	
leash	n.	Leine {f}	
least	adj	wenigsten	
leather	n.	Leder {n}	
leave	v.t.	verlassen	
lecture	n.	Lektüre {f}	
lecturer	n.	Dozent {m}	
ledge	n.	Platte {f}	
ledger	n.	Hauptbuch {n}	
leech	n.	Blutegel {m}	
leek	n.	Lauch {m}	
left	n.	links	
leftist	n.	Linkshänder {m}	
leg	n.	Bein {n}	
legacy	n.	Hinterlassenschaft {f}	
legal	adj.	rechtlich	
legality	n.	Gesetzmäßigkeit {f}	
legalize	v.	legalisieren	
legend	n.	Legende {f}	
legendary	adj.	sagenhaft	
leggings	n.	Gamasche {f}	
legible	adj.	lesbar	
legion	n.	Legion {f}	
legislate	v.	gesetzgeben	
legislation	n.	Gesetzgebung {f}	
legislative	adj.	gesetzgebend	

102

legislator	n.	Gesetzgeber {m}
legislature	n.	Legislative {f}
legitimacy	n.	Legitimierung {f}
legitimate	adj.	rechtmäßig
leisure	n.	Freizeit {f}
leisurely	adj.	gemächlich
lemon	n.	Zitrone {f}
lemonade	n.	Limonade {f}
lend	v.	ausleihen
length	n.	Länge {f}
lengthy	adj.	langwierig
leniency	n.	Nachsicht {f}
lenient	adj.	nachsichtig
lens	n.	Linse {f}
lentil	n.	Linse {f}
Leo	n.	Löwe {m}
leopard	n.	Leopard {m}
leper	n.	Aussätzige {m,f}
leprosy	n.	Lepra {f}
lesbian	n.	Lesbierin {f}
less	adj.	wenig
lessee	n.	Leasingnehmer {m}
lessen	v.	verringern
lesser	adj.	kleiner
lesson	n.	Lektion {f}
lessor	n.	Vermieter {m}
lest	conj.	geringere
let	v.	lassen
lethal	adj.	tödlich
lethargic	adj.	lethargisch
lethargy	n.	Lethargie {f}
letter	n.	Brief {m}
level	n.	Niveau {n}
lever	n.	Hebel {m}

leverage	n.	Hebelkraft {f}
levity	n.	Leichtsinn {m}
levy	v.	erheben
lewd	adj.	liederlich
lexical	adj.	lexikalisch
lexicon	n.	Lexikon {n}
liability	n.	Verpflichtung {f}
liable	adj.	verpflichtet
liaise	v.	vermitteln
liaison	n.	Liebesverhältnis {n}
liar	n.	Lügner {m}
libel	n.	Ehrenkränkung {f}
liberal	adj.	freiheitlich
liberate	v.	befreien
liberation	n.	Befreiung {f}
liberator	n.	Befreier {m}
liberty	n.	Freiheit {f}
libido	n.	Libido {f}
Libra	n.	Waage {f}
librarian	n.	Bibliothekar {m}
library	n.	Bibliothek {f}
licence	n.	Lizenz {f}
licensee	n.	Lizenznehmer {m}
licentious	adj.	unzüchtig
lick	v.	lecken
lid	n.	Topfdeckel {m}
lie	v.	lügen
liege	n.	Liege {f}
lien	n.	Pfandrecht {n}
lieu	n.	Abgeltung {f}
lieutenant	n.	Leutnant {m}
life	n.	Leben {n}
lifeless	adj.	leblos
lifelong	adj.	lebenslänglich

103

lift	*v.t.*	abheben	
ligament	*n.*	Ligament {n}	
light	*n.*	Licht {n}	
lighten	*v.*	erhellen	
lighter	*n.*	Feuerzeug {n}	
lighting *n.*	Beleuchtung {f}		
lightly	*adv.*	leicht	
lightening	*n.*	Blitz {m}	
lignite	*n.*	Braunkohle {f}	
like	*prep.*	ähnlich	
likeable *adj.*	sympathisch		
likelihood	*n.*	Wahrscheinlichkeit {f}	
likely	*adj.*	gleicht	
liken	*v.*	vergleichen	
likeness	*n.*	Ähnlichkeit {f}	
likewise	*adv.*	desgleichen	
liking	*n.*	Neigung {f}	
lilac	*n.*	Flieder {m}	
lily *n.*	Lilie {f}		
limb	*n.*	Glied {n}	
limber	*v.*	lockern	
limbo	*n.*	Rumpelkammer {f}	
lime	*n.*	Limette {f}	
limelight	*n.*	Rampenlicht {n}	
limerick	*n.*	Limerick {m}	
limit	*n.*	Grenzwert {m}	
limitation	*n.*	Begrenzung {f}	
limited *adj.*	eingeschränkt		
limousine	*n.*	Limousine {f}	
limp	*v.*	lahmen	
line	*n.*	Richtung {f}	
lineage *n.*	Abstammung {f}		
linen	*n.*	Leinen {n}	
linger	*v.*	verweilen	

lingerie *n.*	Damenunterwäsche {f}		
lingo	*n.*	Kauderwelsch {n}	
lingua	*n.*	Zunge {f}	
lingual	*n.*	Zungenlaut {m}	
linguist *n.*	Sprachwissenschaftler {m}		
linguistic	*adj.*	sprachlich	
lining	*n.*	Belag {m}	
link	*n.*	Verlinkung {f}	
linkage *n.*	Gestänge {n}		
linseed *n.*	Saat-Lein {m}		
lintel	*n.*	Oberschwelle {f}	
lion	*n.*	Löwe {m}	
lip *n.*	Lippe {f}		
liposuction	*n.*	Fettabsaugung {f}	
liquefy	*v.*	schmelzen	
liquid	*n.*	Flüssigkeit {f}	
liquidate	*v.*	tilgen	
liquidation	*n.*	Liquidation {f}	
liquor	*n.*	Saft {m}	
lisp	*v.*	lispeln	
lissom	*adj.*	geschmeidig	
list *n.*	Verzeichnis {n}		
listen	*v.*	anhören	
listener *n.*	Empfänger {m}		
listless *adj.*	lustlos		
literal	*adj.*	wörtlich	
literary *adj.*	literarisch		
literate *adj.*	gebildet		
literature	*n.*	Literatur {f}	
lithe	*adj.*	geschmeidig	
litigant *n.*	Prozessführer {m}		
litigate *v.*	prozessieren		
litigation	*n.*	Streitsache {f}	
litre	*n.*	Liter {m}	

litter	n.	Abfall {m}
little	adj.	klein
live	v.	leben
livelihood	n.	Lebensunterhalt {m}
lively	adj.	lebendig
liven	v.	beleben
liver	n.	Leber {f}
livery	n.	Tracht {f}
living	n.	Lebensweise {f}
lizard	n.	Eidechse {f}
load	n.	Beschickung {f}
loaf	n.	Laib {n}
loan	n.	Leihe {f}
loath	adj.	abgeneigt
loathe	v.	verabscheuen
loathsome	adj.	widerlich
lobby	n.	Interessengruppe {f}
lobe	n.	Lappen {m}
lobster	n.	Hummer {m}
local	adj.	örtlich
locale	n.	Schauplatz {m}
locality	n.	Örtlichkeit {f}
localize	v.	lokalisieren
locate	v.	festlegen
location	n.	Standort {m}
lock	n.	Verschluss {m}
locker	n.	Schrank {m}
locket	n.	Medaillon {n}
locomotion	n.	Fortbewegung {f}
locomotive	n.	Lokomotive {f}
locum	n.	Vertreter {m}
locus	n.	Ortskurve {f}
locust	n.	Heuschrecke {f}
locution	n.	Redewendung {f}

lodge	n.	Häuschen {n}
lodger	n.	Untermieter {m}
lodging	n.	Unterkunft {f}
loft	n.	Dachboden {m}
lofty	adj.	hochtrabend
log	n.	Kloben {m}
logarithm	n.	Logarithmus {m}
logic	n.	Logik {f}
logical	adj.	logisch
logistics	n.	Logistik {f}
logo	n.	Abzeichen {n}
loin	n.	Lende {f}
loiter	v.	trödeln
loll	v.	rekeln
lollipop	n.	Lutscher {m}
lolly	n.	Mäuse {pl}
lone	adj.	einsam
loneliness	n.	Alleinsein {n}
lonely	adj.	allein
loner	n.	Einzelgänger {m}
lonesome	adj.	einsam
long	adj.	langwierig
longevity	n.	Langlebigkeit {f}
longing	n.	Sehnsucht {f}
longitude	n.	Länge {f}
loo	n.	Klo {n}
look	v.	sehen
look	n	Blick {m}
lookalike	n.	Doppelgänger {m}
loom	n.	Auftauchen {n}
loop	n.	Schlaufe {f}
loose	adj.	locker
loosen	v.	lockern
loot	n.	Beute {f}

lop	v.	stutzen
lope	v.	traben
lopsided	adj.	einseitig
lord	n.	Gebieter {m}
lordly	adj.	großzügig
lore	n.	Überlieferung {f}
lorry	n.	Lastkraftwagen {m}
lose	v.	verlieren
loss	n.	Verlust {m}
lot n.		Haufen {m}
lotion	n.	Lotion {f}
lottery	n.	Lotterie {f}
lotus	n.	Lotus {m}
loud	adj.	laut
lounge	v.	faulenzen
lounge	n.	Aufenthaltsraum {m}
louse	n.	Laus {f}
lousy	adj.	mies
lout	n.	Lümmel {m}
Louvre	n.	Louvre {n}
lovable	adj.	liebenswert
love	n.	Liebe {f}
lovely	adj.	liebhaft
lover	n.	Geliebte {m,f}
low	adj.	niedrig
lower	adj.	niedriger
lowly	adj.	unten
loyal	adj.	loyal
loyalist	n.	Loyalist {m}
lozenge	n.	Rhombus {m}
lubricant	n.	Schmierstoff {m}
lubricate	v.	schmieren
lubrication	n.	Schmierung {f}
lucent	adj.	schillernd

lucid	adj.	deutlich
lucidity	n.	Klarheit {f}
luck	n.	Glück {n}
luckless	adj.	glücklos
lucky	adj.	froh
lucrative	adj.	lukrativ
lucre	n.	Gewinnsucht {f}
ludicrous	adj.	albern
luggage	n.	Reisegepäck {n}
lukewarm	adj.	lauwarm
lull	v.	einlullen
lullaby	n.	Schlaflied {n}
luminary	n.	Leuchtkörper {m}
luminous	adj.	leuchtend
lump	n.	Schwellung {f}
lunacy	n.	Irrsinn {m}
lunar	adj.	mond
lunatic	n.	Wahnsinnige {m,f}
lunch	n.	Mittagessen {n}
luncheon	n.	Mittagessen {n}
lung	n.	Lunge {f}
lunge	n.	Lunge {f}
lurch	v.	torkeln
lure	v.	ködern
lurid	adj.	grell
lurk	v.	lauern
luscious	adj.	üppig
lush	adj.	saftig
lust	n.	Begierde {f}
lustful	adj.	wollüstig
lustre	n.	Lüster {m}
lustrous	adj.	glänzend
lusty	adj.	kräftig
lute	n.	Laute {f}

luxuriant   *adj.* üppig
luxurious   *adj.* luxuriös
luxury   *n.* Luxus {m}
lychee   *n.* Litschi {f}
lymph   *n.* Lymphe {f}
lynch   *v.* lynchen
lyre   *n.* Leier {f}
lyric   *n.* Lyrik {f}
lyrical   *adj.* lyrisch
lyricist   *n.* Lyriker {m}

M

macabre   *adj.* grausig
machine   *n.* Maschine {f}
machinery   *n.* Maschinerie {f}
macho *adj.* Macho {m}
mackintosh *n.* Regenmantel {m}
mad *adj.* irre
madam *n.* Dame {f}
madcap   *adj.* toll
Mafia   *n.* Mafia {f}
magazine   *n.* Zeitschrift {f}
magenta   *n.* magenta
magic   *n.* Magie {f}
magician   *n.* Zauberer {m}
magisterial *adj.* behördlich
magistrate   *n.* Friedensrichter {m}
magnanimous   *adj.* großzügig
magnate   *n.* Magnat {n}
magnet *n.* Magnet {m}
magnetic   *adj.* magnetisch
magnetism   *n.* Magnetismus {m}
magnificent *adj.* herrlich
magnify   *v.* vergrößern

magnitude   *n.* Größenordnung {f}
magpie *n.* Elster {f}
mahogany   *n.* Mahagonibaum {m}
maid   *n.* Dienstmädchen {n}
maiden *n.* Magd {f}
mail   *n.* Post {f}
mail order   *n.* Bestellung {f}
maim   *v.* verstümmeln
main   *adj.* primär
mainstay   *n.* Hauptstütze {f}
maintain   *v.* aufrechterhalten
maintenance   *n.* Wartung {f}
maisonette *n.* Doppeletagenwohnung {f}
majestic   *adj.* majestätisch
majesty   *n.* Majestät {f}
major *adj.* hauptsächlich
majority   *n.* Mehrheit {f}
make   *v.* anfertigen
make-up   *n.* Schminke {f}
making *n.* Herstellung {f}
maladjusted *adj.* Verhaltensgestört
maladministration *n.* Misswirtschaft {f}
malady *n.* Krankheit {f}
malaise *n.* Unpässlichkeit {f}
malaria *n.* Malaria {f}
malcontent *adj.* unzufrieden
male   *n.* Männchen {n}
malediction *n.* Fluch {m}
malefactor   *n.* Missetäter {m}
malformation   *n.* Missbildung {f}
malfunction *v.* versagen
malice *n.* Bosheit {f}
malicious   *adj.* böswillig
malign *adj.* schädlich

malignant	*adj.*	maligne
mall	*n.*	Einkaufszentrum {n}
malleable	*adj.*	dehnbar
mallet	*n.*	Klüpfel {m}
malnutrition	*n.*	Unterernährung {f}
malpractice	*n.*	Untat {f}
malt	*n.*	Malz {n}
maltreat	*v.*	misshandeln
mammal	*n.*	Säugetier {n}
mammary	*adj.*	Brust-
mammon	*n.*	Mammon {m}
mammoth	*n.*	Mammut {m}
man	*n.*	Mensch {m}
manage	*v.*	handeln
manageable	*adj.*	handlich
management	*n.*	Geschäftsführung {f}
manager	*n.*	Direktor {m}
managerial	*adj.*	geschäftsführend
mandate	*n.*	Mandat {n}
mandatory	*adj.*	obligatorisch
mane	*n.*	Mähne {f}
manful	*adj.*	mannhaft
manganese	*n.*	Mangan {n}
manger	*n.*	Krippe {f}
mangle	*v.*	zerfleischen
mango	*n.*	Mango
manhandle	*v.*	meistern
manhole	*n.*	Kanalisationsschacht {m}
manhood	*n.*	Männlichkeit {f}
mania	*n.*	Wahnsinn {m}
maniac	*n.*	Wahnsinnige {m,f}
manicure	*n.*	Maniküre {f}
manifest	*adj.*	offenbar
manifestation	*n.*	Kundgebung {f}
manifesto	*n.*	Manifest {n}
manifold	*adj.*	mehrfach
manipulate	*v.*	manipulieren
manipulation	*n.*	Verarbeitung {f}
mankind	*n.*	Menschheit {f}
manly	*adj.*	männlich
mannequin	*n.*	Schaufensterpuppe {f}
manner	*n.*	Verhalten {pl}
mannerism	*n.*	Manieriertheit {f}
manoeuvre	*n.*	Manöver {n}
manor	*n.*	Gut {n}
manpower	*n.*	Arbeitskräfte {pl}
mansion	*n.*	Villa {f}
mantel	*n.*	Mantel {m}
mantle	*n.*	Decke {f}
mantra	*n.*	Mantra {n}
manual	*adj.*	manuell
manufacture	*v.*	gefertigen
manufacturer	*n.*	Handwerker {m}
manumission	*n.*	Freilassung {f}
manure	*n.*	Dünger {m}
manuscript	*n.*	Manuskript {n}
many	*adj.*	viele
map	*n.*	Karte {f}
maple	*n.*	Ahorn {m}
mar	*v.*	verheiraten
marathon	*n.*	Marathonlauf {m}
maraud	*v.*	plündern
marauder	*n.*	Plünderer {m}
marble	*n.*	Murmel {f}
march	*n.*	März {m}
march	*v.*	marschieren
mare	*n.*	Stute {f}
margarine	*n.*	Margarine {f}

margin *n.* Seitenrand {m}
marginal *adj.* marginal
marigold *n.* Ringelblume {f}
marina *n.* Jachthafen {m}
marinade *n.* Beize {f}
marinate *v.* marinieren
marine *adj.* marin
mariner*n.* Schiffer {m}
marionette *n.* Marionette {f}
marital *adj.* ehelich
maritime *adj.* maritim
mark *n.* Markierung {f}
marker *n.* Marke {f}
market *n.* Markt {m}
marketing *n.* Vertrieb {m}
marking *n.* Kennzeichnung {f}
marksman *n.* Präzisionsschütze {m}
marl *n.* Mergel {m}
marmalade *n.* Marmelade {f}
maroon*n.* Kastanienbraun
marquee *n.* Markise {f}
marriage *n.* Trauung {f}
marriageable *adj.* ehemündig
marry *v.* heiraten
Mars *n.* Mars {m}
marsh *n* Marsch {f}
marshal *n.* Polizeidirektor {m}
marshmallow *n.* Marshmellow
marsupial *n.* Beuteltier {m}
mart *n.* Handelszentrum {n}
martial *adj.* kriegerisch
martinet *n.* Leuteschinder {m}
martyr *n.* Märtyrer {m}
martyrdom *n.* Martyrium {n}

marvel *v.i* wundern
marvellous *adj.* wundervoll
Marxism *n.* Marxismus {m}
marzipan *n.* Marzipan {n}
mascara *n.* Mascara {f}
mascot*n.* Maskottchen {n}
masculine *adj.* männlich
mash *v.t* mischen
mask *n.* Maske {f}
masochism *n.* Masochismus {m}
mason *n.* Maurer {m}
masonry *n.* Mauerwerk {n}
masquerade *n.* Maskerade {f}
mass *n.* Messe {f}
massacre *n.* Massaker {n}
massage *n.* Massage {f}
masseur *n.* Masseur {m}
massive *adj.* massiv
mast *n.* Mast {m}
master *n.* Meister {m}
mastermind *n.* Vordenker {m}
masterpiece*n.* Meisterwerk {n}
mastery *n.* Herrschaft {f}
masticate *v.* mastizieren
masturbate *v.* masturbieren
mat *n.* Matte {f}
matador *n.* Matador {m}
match *n.* Ebenbild {n}
matchmaker *n.* Ehestifter {m}
mate *n.* Partner {m}
material *n.* Werkstoff {m}
materialism *n.* Materialismus {m}
materialize *v.* verkörperlichen
maternal *adj.* mütterlich

maternity	*n.*	Mutterschaft {f}
mathematical	*adj.*	mathematisch
mathematician	*n.*	Mathematiker {m}
mathematics	*n.*	Mathematik {f}
matinee	*n.*	Matinee {pl}
matriarch	*n.*	Matriarchat {n}
matricide	*n.*	Muttermord {m}
matriculate	*v.*	immatrikulieren
matriculation	*n.*	Immatrikulation {f}
matrimonial	*adj.*	ehelich
matrimony	*n.*	Ehestand {m}
matrix	*n.*	Matrix {f}
matron	*n.*	Matrone {m}
matter	*n.*	Stoff {m}
mattress	*n.*	Matratze {f}
mature	*adj.*	erwachsen
maturity	*n.*	Reife {f}
maudlin	*adj.*	rührselig
maul	*v.*	beschädigen
maunder	*v.*	faseln
mausoleum	*n.*	Mausoleum {n}
maverick	*n.*	Einzelgänger {m}
maxim	*n.*	Sprichwort {m}
maximize	*v.*	maximieren
maximum	*n.*	maximal
May	*n.*	Mai {m}
may	*v.*	durfen
maybe	*adv.*	vielleicht
mayhem	*n.*	Verstümmelung {f}
mayonnaise	*n.*	Mayonnaise {f}
mayor	*n.*	Bürgermeister {m}
maze	*n.*	Labyrinth {n}
me	*pron.*	ich
mead	*n.*	Aue {f}

meadow	*n.*	Au {f}
meagre	*adj.*	mager
meal	*n.*	Mahl {n}
mealy	*adj.*	mehlig
mean	*v.*	meinen
meander	*v.*	schlängeln
meaning	*n.*	Bedeutung {f}
means	*n.*	Mittel {n}
meantime	*adv.*	inzwischen
meanwhile	*adv.*	indes
measles	*n.*	Masern {pl}
measly	*adj.*	schäbig
measure	*v.*	messen
measure	*n.*	Maß {n}
measured	*adj.*	gemessen
measurement	*n.*	Messung {f}
meat	*n.*	Fleisch {n}
mechanic	*n.*	Mechaniker {m}
mechanical	*adj.*	mechanisch
mechanics	*n.*	Mechanik {f}
mechanism	*n.*	Mechanismus {m}
medal	*n.*	Medaille {f}
medallion	*n.*	Schaumünze {f}
medallist	*n.*	Olympiasieger {m}
meddle	*v.*	einmischen
media	*n.*	Media {f}
median	*adj.*	mittel
mediate	*v.*	vermitteln
mediation	*n.*	Vermittlung {f}
medic	*n.*	Arzt {m}
medical	*adj.*	medizinisch
medication	*n.*	Medikament {n}
medicinal	*adj.*	medizinisch
medicine	*n.*	Medizin {f}

medieval	adj.	mittelalterlich
mediocre	adj.	mittelmäßig
mediocrity	n.	Mittelmäßigkeit {f}
meditate	v.	meditieren
meditative	adj.	nachdenklich
Mediterranean	adj.	mediterran
medium	n.	Medium {n}
medley n.		Gemisch {n}
meek	adj.	hold
meet	v.	treffen
meeting	n.	Tagung {f}
mega	adj.	mega
megabyte	n.	Megabyte {n}
megahertz	n.	Megahertz {n}
megalith	n.	Megalith {n}
megalithic	adj.	groß
megaphone n.		Megafon {n}
megapixel	n.	Megapixel {n}
melamine	n.	Melamin {n}
melancholia n.		Schwermut {m}
melancholy n.		Wehmut {f}
melange	n.	Mischung {f}
meld	v.	erklären
melee	n.	Gewühl {n}
meliorate	v.	verbessern
mellow adj.		ausgereift
melodic	adj.	melodisch
melodious	adj.	klangvoll
melodrama n.		Melodrama {n}
melodramatic	adj.	melodramatisch
melody n.		Melodie {f}
melon	n.	Melone {f}
melt	v.	schmeltzen
member	n.	Mitglied {n}

membership	n.	Mitgliedschaft {f}
membrane	n.	Membrane {f}
memento	n.	Andenken {n}
memo	n.	Notiz {f}
memoir n.		Denkschrift {f}
memorable	adj.	denkwürdig
memorandum	n.	Memorandum {n}
memorial	n.	Denkmal {n}
memory	n.	Erinnerungsvermögen
{n} menace	n.	Drohung {f}
mend	v.	instandsetzen
mendacious adj.		verlogen
mendicant	adj.	betteln
menial	adj.	knechtisch
meningitis	n.	Hirnhautentzündung {f}
menopause n.		Menopause {f}
menstrual	adj.	menstruell
menstruation	n.	Menstruation {f}
mental	adj.	geistig
mentality	n.	Mentalität {f}
mention	v.	erwähnen
mentor n.		Mentor {m}
menu	n.	Menü {n}
mercantile	adj.	kaufmännisch
mercenary	adj.	käuflich
merchandise	n.	Ware {f}
merchant	n.	Kaufmann {m}
merciful	adj.	mitleidig
mercurial	adj.	lebhaft
mercury	n.	Quecksilber {n}
mercy n.		Mitleid {m}
mere	adj.	nur
meretricious	adj.	dirnenhaft
merge	v.	verschmelzen

111

merger *n.*	Verbinder {m}
meridian *n.*	Meridian {m}
merit *n.*	Verdienst {n}
meritorious *adj.*	verdienstlich
mermaid *n.*	Nixe {f}
merry *adj.*	heiter
mesh *n.*	Maschenweite {f}
mesmeric *adj.*	hypnotisch
mesmerize *v.*	hypnotisieren
mess *n.*	Schlamassel {m}
message *n.*	Nachricht {f}
messenger *n.*	Kurier {m}
messiah *n.*	Messias {m}
messy *adj.*	unordentlich
metabolism *n.*	Stoffwechsel {m}
metal *n.*	Metall {n}
metallic *adj.*	metallisch
metallurgy *n.*	Metallurgie {f}
metamorphosis *n.*	Wandlung {f}
metaphor *n.*	Metapher {n}
metaphysical *adj.*	metaphysisch
metaphysics *n.*	Metaphysik {f}
mete *v.*	messen
meteor *n.*	Meteor {m}
meteoric *adj.*	meteorisch
meteorology *n.*	Wetterkunde {f}
meter *n.*	Messgerät {n}
method *n.*	Methode {f}
methodical *adj.*	systematisch
methodology *n.*	Methodologie {f}
meticulous *adj.*	minuziös
metre *n.*	Meter {m,n}
metric *adj.*	metrisch
metrical *adj.*	metrisch

metropolis *n.*	Metropole {f}
metropolitan *adj.*	hauptstädtisch
mettle *n.*	Eifer {m}
mettlesome *adj.*	feurig
mew *v.*	miauend
mews *n.*	Stallung {f}
mezzanine *n.*	Halbgeschoss {n}
miasma *n.*	Miasma {n}
mica *n.*	Glimmer {m}
microbiology *n.*	Mikrobiologie {f}
microchip *n.*	Mikrochip {m}
microfilm *n.*	Mikrofilm {m}
micrometer *n.*	Mikrometer {n}
microphone *n.*	Mikrophon {n}
microprocessor *n.*	Mikroprozessor {m}
microscope *n.*	Mikroskop {n}
microscopic *adj.*	mikroskopisch
microsurgery *n.*	Mikrochirurgie {f}
microwave *n.*	Mikrowelle {f}
mid *adj.*	mittler
midday *n.*	Mittag {m}
middle *adj.*	Mittel
middleman *n.*	Mittelsmann {m}
middling *adj.*	mittelmäßig
midget *n.*	Zwerg {m}
midnight *n.*	Mitternacht {f}
midriff *n.*	Zwerchfell {n}
midst *adj.*	inmitten
midsummer *adj.*	Sommerwende {f}
midway *adv.*	Mittel
midwife *n.*	Geburtshelferin {f}
might *v.*	könnte
mighty *adj.*	mächtig
migraine *n.*	Migräne {f}

migrant	n.	Zugvogel {m}	mine	n.	Steinbruch {m}
migrate	v.	wandern	miner	n.	Bergmann {m}
migration	n.	Wanderung {f}	mineral	n.	Mineral {n}
mild	adj.	sanft	mineralogy	n.	Mineralogie {f}
mile	n.	Meile {f}	minestrone	n.	Eintopf {m}
mileage	n.	Kilometerleistung {f}	mingle	v.	mischen
milestone	n.	Meilenstein {m}	mini	adj.	mini
milieu	n.	Milieu {n}	miniature	n.	Miniatur {f}
militant	adj.	kämpferisch	minibus	n.	Minibus {m}
militant	n.	Militant {m}	minicab	n.	Minicab {n}
military	adj.	militärisch	minim	n.	Mindestbetrag {m}
militate	v.	widerstreiten	minimal	adj.	minimal
militia	n.	Miliz {f}	minimize	v.	verringern
milk	n.	Milch {f}	minimum	n.	Minimum {n}
milkshake	n.	Milchshake {m}	minion	n.	Günstling {m}
milky	adj.	milchig	miniskirt	n.	Minirock {m}
mill	n.	Mühle {f}	minister	n.	Pfarrer {m}
millennium	n.	Jahrtausend {n}	ministerial	adj.	amtlich
millet	n.	Hirse {f}	ministry	n.	Ministerium {n}
milligram	n.	Milligramm {n}	mink	n.	Nerz {m}
millimetre	n.	Millimeter {m,n}	minor	adj.	geringer
milliner	n.	Modistin {f}	minority	n.	Minderheit {f}
million	n.	Million {f}	minster	n.	Münster {m}
millionaire	n.	Millionär {m}	mint	n.	Minze {f}
millipede	n.	Doppelfüßer {m}	minus	prep.	abzüglich
mime	n.	Pantomime {f}	minuscule	adj.	klein
mimic	n.	Mimik {f}	minute	n.	Minute {f}
mimicry	n.	Gebärdensprache {f}	minute	adj.	winzig
minaret	n.	Minarett {n}	minutely	adv.	exakt
mince	v.	zerhacken	minx	n.	Range {f}
mind	n.	Verstand {m}	miracle	n.	Wunder {n}
mindful	adj.	eingedenk	miraculous	adj.	wundertätig
mindless	adj.	unbekümmert	mirage	n.	Luftspiegelung {f}
mine	pron.	mein	mire	n.	Sumpf {m}

113

mirror *n.*	Spiegel {m}	**misfit** *n.*	Außenseiter {m};
mirth *n.*	Fröhlichkeit {f}	**misfortune** *n.*	Missgeschick {n}
mirthful *adj.*	fröhlich	**misgive** *v.*	befürchten
misadventure *n.*	Missgeschick {n}	**misgiving** *n.*	Befürchtung {f}
misalliance *n.*	Missallianz {f}	**misguide** *v.*	verleiten
misapply *v.*	falschanwenden	**mishandle** *v.*	misshandeln
misapprehend *v.*	missverstehen	**mishap** *n.*	Malheur {n}
misapprehension *n.*	Missverständnis {n}	**misinform** *v.*	falschunterrichten
misappropriate *v.*	unterschlagen	**misinterpret** *v.*	missdeuten
misappropriation *n.*	Unterschlagung {f}	**misjudge** *v.*	verkennen
misbehave *v.*	schlechtbenehmen	**mislay** *v.*	verlegen
misbehaviour *n.*	Ungezogenheit {f}	**mislead** *v.*	beirren
misbelief *n.*	Irrglaube {m}	**mismanagement** *n.*	Misswirtschaft {f}
miscalculate *v.*	verkalkulieren	**mismatch** *n.*	Nichtübereinstimmung {f}
miscalculation *n.*	Kalkulationsfehler {m}	**misnomer** *n.*	Namensirrtum {m}
miscarriage *n.*	Fehlgeburt {f}	**misplace** *v.*	verlegen
miscarry *v.*	misslingen	**misprint** *n.*	Fehlbogen {m}
miscellaneous *adj.*	verschiedenartig	**misquote** *v.*	falschzitieren
mischance *n.*	Unfall {m}	**misread** *v.*	falschlesen
mischief *n.*	Schaden {m}	**misrepresent** *v.*	verdrehen
mischievous *adj.*	schadenfroh	**misrule** *v.*	schlechtregieren
misconceive *v.*	missverstehen	**miss** *n.*	Fräulein
misconception *n.*	Missverständnis {n}	**miss** *n.*	Fehlschuss {m}
misconduct *n.*	Verfehlung {f}	**missile** *n.*	Raketengeschoss {n}
misconstrue *v.*	missdeuten	**missing** *adj.*	verschollen
miscreant *n.*	Schurke {m}	**mission** *n.*	Sendung {f}
misdeed *n.*	Missetat {f}	**missionary** *n.*	Missionar {m}
misdemeanour *n.*	Vergehen {n}	**missive** *n.*	Sendschreiben {n}
misdirect *v.*	fehlleiten	**misspell** *v.*	falschbuchstabieren
miser *n.*	Geizhals {m}	**mist** *n.*	Nebel {m}
miserable *adj.*	erbärmlich	**mistake** *n.*	Fehler {m}
miserly *adj.*	geizig	**mistaken** *adj.*	vertan
misery *n.*	Not {f}	**mistletoe** *n.*	Mistelzweig {m}
misfire *v.*	fehlzünden	**mistreat** *v.*	schlechtbehandeln

114

mistress	n.	Gebieterin {f}
mistrust	v.	misstrauen
misty	adj.	nebelhaft
misunderstand	v.	missverstehen
misunderstanding	n.	Missverständnis {n}
misuse	v.	missbrauchen
mite	n.	Milbe {f}
mitigate	v.	strafmildern
mitigation	n.	Schadensminderung {f}
mitre	n.	Gehrungssäge {f}
mitten	n.	Fausthandschuh {m}
mix	v.	mixen
mixer	n.	Mischpult {n}
mixture	n.	Vermischung {f}
moan	v.	stöhnen
moat	n.	Burggraben {m}
mob	n.	Meute {f}
mobile	adj.	mobil
mobility	n.	Mobilität {f}
mobilize	v.	mobilisieren
mocha	n.	Mokka {m}
mock	v.	verspotten
mockery	n.	Spötterei {f}
modality	n.	Modalität {f}
mode	n.	Modus {m}
model	n.	Model {n}
modem	n.	Anschlussbox {f}
moderate	adj.	mittelmäßig
moderation	n.	Mäßigung {f}
moderator	n.	Diskussionsleiter {m}
modern	adj.	modern
modernity	n.	Moderne {f}
modernize	v.	modernisieren
modernism	n.	Modernismus {m}

modest	adj.	bequem
modesty	n.	Genügsamkeit {f}
modicum	n.	Teilchen {n}
modification	n.	Änderung {f}
modify	v.t.	ändern
modish	adj.	modisch
modulate	v.	modulieren
module	n.	Modul {n}
moil	v.	rackern
moist	adj.	feucht
moisten	v.	feuchten
moisture	n.	Feuchtigkeit {f}
moisturize	v.	befeuchten
molar	n.	Backenzahn {m}
molasses	n.	Melassesirup {m}
mole	n.	Maulwurf {m}
molecular	adj.	molekular
molecule	n.	Molekül {n}
molest	v.	belästigen
molestation	n.	Belästigung {f}
mollify	v.	besänftigen
molten	adj.	geschmolzen
moment	n.	Augenblick {m}
momentary	adj.	momentan
momentous	adj.	wichtig
momentum	n.	Moment {m}
monarch	n.	Monarch {m}
monarchy	n.	Monarchie {f}
monastery	n.	Kloster {n}
monastic	adj.	klösterlich
monasticism	n.	Mönchtum {n}
Monday	n.	Montag {m}
monetarism	n.	Geldwirtschaft {f}
monetary	adj.	monetär

115

money	n.	Geld {n}
monger	n.	Krämer {m}
mongoose	n.	Mungo {m}
mongrel	n.	Mischling {m}
monitor	n.	Bildschirm {m}
monitory	adj.	ermahnend
monk	n.	Mönch {m}
monkey	n.	Affe {m}
mono	n.	eins
monochrome	n.	monochrom
monocle	n.	Monokel {n}
monocular	adj.	einäugig
monody	n.	Stimmungsmensch {m}
monogamy	n.	Monogamie {f}
monogram	n.	Monogramm {n}
monograph	n.	Einzelwerk {n}
monolith	n.	Monolith {m}
monologue	n.	Monolog {m}
monophonic	adj.	monophon
monopolist	n.	Monopolist {m}
monopolize	v.	monopolisieren
monopoly	n.	Monopol {n}
monorail	n.	Einschienenbahn {f}
monosyllable	n.	einsilbige
monotheism	n.	Monotheismus {m}
monotheist	n.	Monotheist {m}
monotonous	adj.	monoton
monotony	n.	Eintönigkeit {f}
monsoon	n.	Monsun {m}
monster	n.	Monster {m}
monstrous	adj.	ungeheuer
montage	n.	Montage {f}
month	n.	Monat {m}
monthly	adj.	monatlich

monument	n.	Denkmal {n}
monumental	adj.	monumental
moo	v.	muhen
mood	n.	Stimmung {f}
moody	adj.	launisch
moon	n.	Mond {m}
moonlight	n.	Mondlicht {n}
moor	n.	Moor {n}
moorings	n.	Verankerung {f}
moot	adj.	streitig
mop	n.	Mopp {m}
mope	v.	waschen
moped	n.	Moped {n}
moraine	n.	Moräne {f}
moral	adj.	moralisch
morale	n.	Moral {f}
moralist	n.	Moralist {m}
morality	n.	Sittlichkeit {f}
moralize	v.	moralisieren
morass	n.	Morast {m}
morbid	adj.	morbid
morbidity	n.	Krankhaftigkeit {f}
more	adj.	mehr
moreover	adv.	außerdem
morganatic	adj.	luftsiegelig
morgue	n.	Leichenschauhaus {n}
moribund	adj.	sterbend
morning	n.	Morgen {m}
moron	n.	Schwachkopf {m}
morose	adj.	grämlich
morphine	n.	Morphium {n}
morphology	n.	Formenlehre {f}
morrow	n.	Zukunft {f}
morsel	n.	Bissen {m}

mortal *adj.*	tödlich	mould *n.*	Heizform {f}
mortality *n.*	Sterblichkeit {f}	moulder *n.*	Gießer {m}
mortar *n.*	Mörser {m}	moulding *n.*	Profil {n}
mortgage *n.*	Hypothek {f}	moult *v.*	mausern
mortgagee *n.*	Hypothekar {m}	mound *n.*	Erdwall {m}
mortgagor *n.*Hypothekenschuldner {m}		mount *v.*	erfassen
mortify *v.*	kränken	mountain *n.*	Gebirge {n}
mortuary *n.*	Leichenhalle {f}	mountaineer *n.*	Bergsteiger {m}
mosaic *n.*	Mosaik {n}	mountaineering *n.*	Bergsteigerei {f}
mosque *n.*	Moschee {f}	mountainous *adj.*	gebirgig
mosquito *n.*	Stechmücke {f}	mourn *v.*	trauern
moss *n.*	Moos {n}	mourner *n.*	Trauende {m,f}
most *n.*	höchst	mournful *adj.*	traurig
mote *n.*	Stäubchen {pl}	mourning *n.*	Trauerarbeit {f}
motel *n.*	Motel {n}	mouse *n.*	Maus {f}
moth *n.*	Falter {m}	mousse *n.*	Mousse {f}
mother *n.*	Mutter {f}	moustache *n.*	Schnurrbart {m}
motherboard *n.*	Hauptplatine {f}	mouth *n.*	Mund {m}
motherhood*n.*	Mutterschaft {f}	mouthful *n.*	mundvoll
mother-in-law *n.*	Schwiegermutter {f}	movable *adj.*	beweglich
motherly *adj.*	mütterlich	move *v.*	bewegen
motif *n.*	Motiv {n}	movement *n.*	Bewegung {f}
motion *n.*	Bewegung {f}	mover *n.*	Möbelspediteur {m}
motionless *adj.*	bewegungslos	movies *n.*	Kino {n}
motivate *v.*	motivieren	moving *adj.*	beweglich
motivation *n.*	Beweggrund {m}	mow *v.*	mähen
motive *n.*	Motiv {n}	mozzarella *n.*	Mozzarella {f}
motley *adj.*	scheckig	much *pron.*	viel
motor *n.*	Motor {m}	mucilage *n.*	Schleim {m}
motorcycle *n.*	Motorrad {n}	muck *n.*	Jauche {f}
motorist *n.*	Autofahrer {m}	mucous *adj.*	schleimig
motorway *n.*	Autobahn {f}	mucus *n.*	Schleim {m}
mottle *v.*	marmorieren	mud *n.*	Schmutz {m}
motto *n.*	Motto {n}	muddle *v.*	vermasseln

117

muesli *n.*	Müsli {n}	**municipality** *n.*	Stadtbezirk {m}
muffin *n.*	Teesemmel {f}	**munificent** *adj.*	freigebig
muffle *v.*	umhüllen	**munitions** *n.*	Munition {f}
muffler *n.*	Dämpfer {m}	**mural** *n.*	Mauer {f}
mug *n.*	Becher {m}	**murder** *n.*	Mord {m}
muggy *adj.*	schwül	**murderer** *n.*	Mörder {m}
mulatto *n.*	Mulatte {m}	**murk** *n.*	Dunkelheit {f}
mulberry *n.*	Maulbeerbaum {m}	**murky** *adj.*	finster
mule *n.*	Maultier {n}	**murmur** *v.*	raunen
mulish *adj.*	störrisch	**muscle** *n.*	Muskel {m}
mull *v.*	verpatzen	**muscovite** *n.*	Moskowiter {pl}
mullah *n.*	Mullah {m}	**muscular** *adj.*	muskulös
mullion *n.*	Mittelpfosten {m}	**muse** *n.*	Muse {f}
multicultural *adj.*	multikulturell	**museum** *n.*	Museum {n}
multifarious *adj.*	facettenreich	**mush** *n.*	Mus {n}
multiform *adj.*	vielförmig	**mushroom** *n.*	Pilz {m}
multilateral *adj.*	vielseitig	**music** *n.*	Musik {f}
multimedia *n.*	Multimedia	**musical** *adj.*	musikalisch
multiparous *adj.*	mehrgebärend	**musician** *n.*	Musiker {m}
multiple *adj.*	vielfach	**musk** *n.*	Moschus {m}
multiplex *n.*	Mehrfachbetrieb {m}	**musket** *n.*	Flinte {f}
multiplication *n.*	Multiplikation {f}	**musketeer** *n.*	Musketier {m}
multiplicity *n.*	Vielfachheit {f}	**Muslim** *n.*	Moslem {m}
multiply *v.*	multiplizieren	**muslin** *n.*	Musselin {m}
multitude *n.*	Menge {f}	**mussel** *n.*	Muschel {f}
mum *n.*	Mama {f}	**must** *v.*	müssen
mumble *v.*	murmeln	**mustang** *n.*	Mustang {m}
mummer *n.*	Vermummung {f}	**mustard** *n.*	Senf {m}
mummify *v.*	mumifizieren	**muster** *v.*	mustern
mummy *n.*	Mumie {f}	**musty** *adj.*	miefig
mumps *n.*	Mumps {m}	**mutable** *adj.*	veränderlich
munch *v.*	mampfen	**mutate** *v.*	verändern
mundane *adj.*	irdisch	**mutation** *n.*	Änderung {f}
municipal *adj.*	städtisch	**mutative** *adj.*	veränderlicher

mute	*adj.*	sprachlos	**nadir**	*n.*	Fußpunkt {m}

mute *adj.* sprachlos
mutilate *v.* verstümmeln
mutilation *n.* Verstümmelung {f}
mutinous *adj.* rebellisch
mutiny *n.* Meuterei {f}
mutter *v.* murmeln
mutton *n.* Hammel {m}
mutual *adj.* gegenseitig
muzzle *n.* Hundeschnauze {f}
muzzy *adj.* verschwommen
my *adj.* mein
myalgia *n.* Muskelschmerzen {pl}
myopia *n.* Kurzsichtigkeit {f}
myopic *adj.* kurzsichtig
myosis *n.* Muskelentzündung {f}
myriad *n.* Myriade {f}
myrrh *n.* Myrre {f}
myrtle *n.* Myrte {f}
myself *pron.* selbst
mysterious *adj.* mysteriös
mystery *n.* Geheimnis {n}
mystical *adj.* mystisch
mysticism *n.* Mystik {f}
mystify *v.* täuschen
mystique *n.* Geheimnis {n}
myth *n.* Mythos {n}
mythical *adj.* mythisch
mythological *adj.* mythologische
mythology *n.* Mythologie {f}

N

nab *v.* schnappen
nabob *n.* Nabob {m}
nacho *n.* Nacho {m}

nadir *n.* Fußpunkt {m}
nag *v.t.* keifen
nail *n.* Nagel {m}
naivety *n.* Naivität {f}
naked *adj.* nackt
name *n.* Name {m}
namely *n.* nämlich
namesake *n.* Namensvetter {m}
nanny *n.* Kindermädchen {n}
nap *n.* Noppe {f}
nape *n.* Nacken {m}
naphthalene *n.* Naphthalin {n}
napkin *n.* Mundtuch {n}
nappy *n.* Windel {f}
narcissism *n.* Narzissmus {m}
narcissus *n.* Narzisse {f}
narcotic *n.* Betäubungsmittel {n}
narrate *v.* erzählen
narration *n.* Erzählung {f}
narrative *n.* Geschichte {f}
narrator *n.* Erzähler {m}
narrow *adj.* eng
nasal *adj.* nasal
nascent *adj.* werdend
nasty *adj.* scheußlich
natal *adj.* geburts-
natant *adj.* geboren
nation *n.* Nation {f}
national *adj.* national
nationalism *n.* Nationalismus {m}
nationalist *n.* Nationalist {m}
nationality *n.* Staatsbürgerschaft {f}
nationalization *n.* Verstaatlichung {f}
nationalize *v.* verstaatlichen

119

native *n.* Einheimischer {m}
nativity *n.* Geburt {f}
natty *adj.* nett
natural *adj.* natürlich
naturalist *n.* Naturalist {m}
naturalize *v.* naturalisieren
naturalization *n.* Naturalisierung {f}
naturally *adv.* normalerweise
nature *n.* Natur {f}
naturism *n.* Naturismus {m}
naughty *adj.* böse
nausea *n.* Übelkeit {f}
nauseate *v.* verabscheun
nauseous *adj.* ekelhaft
nautical *adj.* nautisch
naval *adj.* naval
nave *n.* Kirchenschiff {n}
navigable *adj.* schiffbar
navigate *v.* schiffen
navigation *n.* Navigation {f}
navigator *n.* Seemann {m}
navy *n.* Schifffahrt {f}
nay *adv.* nein
near *adv.* nahe
nearby *adv.* dabei
near *v.i.* nähern
nearest *adj.* nächste
nearly *adv.* beinahe
neat *adj.* niedlich
nebula *n.* Nebelfleck {m}
nebulous *adj.* nebelig
necessarily *adv.* notwendigerweise
necessary *adj.* wichtig
necessitate *v.* erfordern

necessity *n.* Bedürfnis {n}
neck *n.* Nacken {m}
necklace *n.* Halskette {f}
necklet *n.* Halskette {f}
necromancy *n.* Zauberei {f}
necropolis *n.* Totenstadt {f}
nectar *n.* Nektar {m}
nectarine *n.* Nektarine {f}
need *v.* benötigen
needful *adj.* nötig
needle *n.* Nadel {f}
needless *adj.* nutzlos
needy *adj.* hilfsbedürftig
nefarious *adj.* ruchlos
negate *v.* vernein
negation *n.* Negation {f}
negative *adj.* negativ
negativity *n.* Negativität {f}
neglect *v.* vernachlässigen
negligence *n.* Nachlässigkeit {f}
negligent *adj.* nachlässig
negligible *adj.* vernachlässigbar
negotiable *adj.* verkäuflich
negotiate *v.* verhandeln
negotiation *n.* Verhandlung {f}
negotiator *n.* Unterhändler {m}
negress *n.* Negerin {f}
negro *n.* Neger {m}
neigh *n.* wiehern
neighbour *n.* Nachbar {m}
neighbourhood *n.* Stadtteil {m}
neighbourly *adj.* nachbarlich
neither *adj.* weder
nemesis *n.* Nemesis {f}

neoclassical	adj. neoklassisch	news n.	Neuigkeiten {pl}
Neolithic	adj. nölitisch	next adj.	nächstes
neon n.	Neon {n}	nexus n.	Verknüpfung {f}
neophyte n.	Neuling {m}	nib n.	Schreibfeder {f}
nephew n.	Neffe {m}	nibble v.	knabbern
nepotism n.	Vetternwirtschaft {f}	nice adj.	hübsch
Neptune n.	Neptunium {n}	nicety n.	Feinheit {f}
nerd n.	Streber {m}	niche n.	Nische {f}
Nerve n.	Nerv {m}	nick n.	Kerbe {f}
nerveless	adj. kraftlos	nickel n.	Nickel {n}
nervous	adj. nervös	nickname n.	Spitzname {m}
nervy adj.	nervösen	nicotine n.	Nikotin {n}
nescience n.	Agnostizismus {m}	niece n.	Nichte {f}
nest n.	Nest {n}	niggard n.	Geizhals {m}
nestle v.	kuscheln	niggardly	adj. geizig
nestling n.	Nesthäkchen {n}	nigger n.	Nigger {m}
net n.	Netz {n}	niggle v.	trödeln
nether adj.	unter	nigh	adv. nahe
netting n.	Ausgleichsprozess {m}	night n.	Nacht {f}
nettle n.	Nessel {f}	nightingale n.	Nachtigall {f}
network n.	Netzwerk {n}	nightmare n.	Alptraum {m}
neural adj.	neural	nightie n.	Nachthemd {n}
neurologist n.	Neurologe {m}	nihilism n.	Nihilismus {n}
neurology n.	Neurologie {f}	nil n.	Null {f}
neurosis n.	Neurose {f}	nimble adj.	flink
neurotic	adj. neurotisch	nimbus n.	Heiligenschein {m}
neuter adj.	sächlich	nine adj. & n.	neun
neutral adj.	neutral	nineteen	adj. & n. neunzehn
neutralize v.	neutralisieren	nineteenth adj. & n.	neunzehnte
neutron n.	Neutron {n}	ninetieth adj. & n.	neunzigste
never adv.	niemals	ninth adj. & n.	neunte
nevertheless	adv. dennoch	ninety adj. & n.	neunzig
new adj.	neu	nip v.	kniffen
newly adv.	neulich	nipple n.	Rohrstutzen {m}

121

nippy	*adj.*	spritzig		

nippy *adj.* spritzig
nirvana *n.* Nirvana {n}
nitrogen *n.* Stickstoff {m}
no *adj.* nicht
nobility *n.* Adelsgeschlecht {n}
noble *adj.* adelig
nobleman *n.* Adlige {m}
nobody *pron.* niemand
nocturnal *adj.* nächtlich
nod *v.* Nicken {n}
node *n.* Knoten {m}
noise *n.* Geräusch {n}
noisy *adj.* geräuschvoll
nomad *n.* Nomade {n}
nomadic *adj.* nomadisch
nomenclature *n.* Nomenklatur {f}
nominal *adj.* namentlich
nominate *v.* nominieren
nomination *n.* Ernennung {f}
nominee *n.* Kandidat {m}
non-alignment *n.* Fluchtlinie {f}
nonchalance *n.* Lässigkeit {f}
nonchalant *adj.* lässig
nonconformist *n.* Nichtübereinstimmung {f}
none *pron.* kein
nonentity *n.* Nichtsein {n}
nonplussed *adj.* verblüft
nonetheless *a.* trotz alledem
nonpareil *adj.* unvergleichlich
nonsense *n.* Unsinn {m}
nonstop *adj.* nonstop
noodles *n.* Nudeln {pl}
nook *n.* Schlupfwinkel {m}
noon *n.* Mittag {m}

noose *n.* Schlinge {f}
nor *conj.&adv.* weder noch
Nordic *adj.* nördlich
norm *n.* Norm {f}
normal *adj.* normal
normalcy *n.* Normalität {f}
normalize *v.* normalisieren
normative *adj.* normativ
north *n.* Norden {m}
northerly *adj.* nördlich
northern *adj.* nördlich
nose *n.* Nase {f}
nostalgia *n.* Nostalgie {f}
nostril *n.* Nasenloch {n}
nostrum *n.* Geheimmittel {n}
nosy *adj.* neugierig
not *adv.* nicht
notable *adj.* bemerkenswert
notary *n.* Notar {m}
notation *n.* Bezeichnung {f}
notch *n.* Ausschnitt {m}
note *n.* Note {f}
notebook *n.* Notizbuch {n}
noted *adj.* notiert
noteworthy *adj.* bemerkenswert
nothing *pron.* nichts
notice *n.* Kündigung {f}
noticeable *adj.* bemerkbar
noticeboard *n.* Anschlagbrett {n}
notifiable *adj.* anmeldepflichtig
notification *n.* Notiz {f}
notify *v.* bekannt geben
notion *n.* Begriff {m}
notional *adj.* begrifflich

notoriety	n.	Allbekanntheit {f}	
notorious	prep.	berüchtigt	
notwithstanding	prep.		ungeachtet
nougat n.		Nougat {m,n}	
nought n.		Null {f}	
noun n.		Substantiv {n}	
nourishv.		nähren	
nourishment	n.	Ernährung {f}	
novel n.		Roman {m}	
novelette	n.	Novelle {f}	
novelist	n.	Romanschriftsteller {m}	
novelty n.		Neuigkeit {f}	
november n.		November {m}	
novice n.		Anfänger {m}	
now	adv.	jetzt	
nowhere	adv.	nirgendwohin	
noxious	adj.	verderblich	
nozzle n.		Düse {f}	
nuance n.		Abstufung {f}	
nubile a.		mannbar	
nuclear adj.		nuklear	
nucleus	n.	Zellkern {m}	
nude	adj.	nackt	
nudge v.		anstößen	
nudist n.		Nudist {m}	
nudity n.		Nacktheit {f}	
nugatory	adj.	wertlos	
nugget n.		Klumpen {m},	
nuisance	n.	Belästigung {f}	
null	adj.	Null {f}	
nullification n.		Annullierung {f}	
nullify v.		beseitigen	
numb adj.		empfindungslos	
numbern.		Nummer {f}	

numberless	adj.	zahllos
numeral	n.	Zahl {f}
numerator	n.	Zähler {m}
numerical	adj.	numerisch
numerous	adj.	zahlreich
nun	n.	Nonne {f}
nunnery	n.	Nonnenkloster {n}
nuptial	adj.	hochzeitlich
nurse	n.	Krankenschwester {f}
nurseryn.		Kinderzimmer {n}
nurture	v.	pflegen
nut	n.	Schraubenmutter {f}
nutrient	n.	Nährstoff {m}
nutrition	n.	Ernährung {f}
nutritious	adj.	nahrhaft
nutritive	adj.	nahrhaft,
nutty	adj.	schmackhaft
nuzzle	v.	hätscheln
nylon	n.	Nylon {n}
nymph		Nymphe

O		
oaf	n.	Dumme {m}
oak	n.	Eiche {f}
oar	n.	Ruder {n}
oasis	n.	Oase {f}
oat	n.	Hafer {m}
oath	n.	Eid {m}
oatmeal	n.	Haferflocken {pl}
obduracy	n.	Verstocktheit {f}
obdurate	adj.	verstockt
obedience	n.	Folgsamkeit {f}
obedient	adj.	folgsam
obeisance	n.	Ehrerbietung {f}

123

obesity n.	Fettsucht {f}	obsession	n.	Besessenheit {f}

obesity n. Fettsucht {f}
obese adj. korpulent
obey v. gehorchen
obfuscate v. verfinstern
obituary n. Sterbeanzeige {f}
object n. Objekt {n}
objection n. Einwurf {m}
objectionable adj. widerwärti
objective adj. objektiv
objectively adv. sachlich
oblation n. Opfergabe {f}
obligated adj. verpflichtet
obligation n. Pflicht {f}
obligatory adj. verbindlich
oblige v. verpflichten
obliging adj. verbindlich
oblique adj. quer
obliterate v. tilgen
obliteration n. Vertilgung {f}
oblivion n. Nichtbeachtung {f}
oblivious adj. vergesslich
oblong adj. rechteckig
obloquy n. Verleumdung {f}
obnoxious adj. anstößig
obscene adj. obszön
obscenity n. Unzüchtigkeit {f}
obscure adj. dunkel
obscurity n. Dunkelheit {f}
observance n. Beachtung {f}
observant adj. achtsam
observation n. Beobachtung {f}
observatory n. Sternwarte {f}
observe v. beobachten
obsess v. quälen

obsession n. Besessenheit {f}
obsolescent adj. veraltend
obsolete adj. altmodisch
obstacle n. Hindernis {n}
obstinacy n Sturheit {f}
obstinate adj. starrköpfig
obstruct v. hemmen
obstruction n. Verstopfung {f}
obstructive adj. widersetzlich
obtain v. erhälten
obtainable adj. erhältlich
obtrude v. aufdrängen
obtuse adj. begriffsstutzig
obverse n. entsprechend
obviate v. vorbeugen
obvious adj. deutlich
occasion n. Gelegenheit {f}
occasional adj. gelegentlich
occasionally adv. verschiedentlich
occident n. Abendland {n}
occidental adj. westlich
occlude v. verstopfen
occult n. verborgen
occupancy n. Besitzergreifung {f}
occupant n. Besetzer {m}
occupation n. Beruf {m}
occupational adj. beruflich
occupy v. besetzen
occur v. auftreten
occurrence n. Fall {m}
ocean n. Ozean {m}
oceanic adj. ozeanisch
octagon n. Achteck {n}
octave n. Oktave {f}

octavo	n.	Oktavband {m}
October	n.	Oktober {m}
octogenarian	n.	Achtzigjähriger {m}
octopus	n.	Seepolyp {m}
octree	n.	Octree {m}
ocular	adj.	unmittelbar
odd	adj.	ungerade
oddity	n.	Seltsamkeit {f}
odds	n.	Ungleichheit {f}
ode	n.	Gedicht {n}
odious	adj.	verhasst
odium	n.	Abscheu {m,f}
odorous	adj.	riechend
odour	n.	Geruch {m}
odyssey	n.	Irrfahrt {f}
of	prep.	über
off	adv.	aus
offence	n.	Verstoß {m}
offend	v.	beleidigen
offender	n.	Angreifer {m}
offensive	adj.	angreifend
offer	v.	erbieten
offering	n.	Angebot {n}
office	n.	Büro {n}
officer	n.	Beamter {m}
official	adj.	offiziell
officially	adv.	offiziell
officiate	v.	amtieren
officious	adj.	übereifrig
offset	v.	ausgleichen
offshoot	n.	Sprössling {m}
offshore	adj.	offshore
offside	adj.	abseits
offspring	n.	Nachwuchs {m}

oft	adv.	oftmal
often	adv.	häufig
ogle	v.	liebäugeln
oil	n.	Öl {n}
oily	adj.	ölig
ointment	n.	Salbe {f}
okay	adj.	einverstanden
old	adj.	alt
oligarchy	n.	Oligarchie {f}
olive	n.	Olive {f}
Olympic	adj.	olympisch
omelette	n.	Omelette {n}
omen	n.	Vorbedeutung {f}
ominous	adj.	ahnungsvoll
omission	n.	Auslassung {f}
omit	v.	unterlassen
omnibus	n.	Omnibus {n}
omnipotence	n.	Allmacht {f}
omnipotent	adj.	allgewaltig
omnipresence	n.	Allgegenwart {f}
omnipresent	adj.	allgegenwärtig
omniscience	n.	Allwissenheit {f}
omniscient	adj.	allwissend
on	prep.	an
once	adv.	einmal
one	n. & adj.	eins
oneness	n.	Einheit {f}
onerous	adj.	lästig
oneself	pron.	eines
onion	n.	Zwiebel {f}
onlooker	n.	Zuschauer {m}
only	adv.	nur
onomatopoeia	n.	Onomatopöie {f}
onset	n.	Angriff {m}

onslaught	n.	Angriff {m}	optician	n.	Optiker {m}

onslaught   n.   Angriff {m}
ontology   n.   Ontologie {f}
onus   n.   Verpflichtung {f}
onward   adv. fortschreitend
onyx   n.   Onyx {m}
ooze   v.i. sickern
opacity n.   Undurchsichtigkeit {f}
opal   n.   Opal {m}
opaque adj. undurchsichtig
open   adj. offen
opening   n.   Marktlücke {f}
openly adv. offen
opera   n.   Oper {f}
operate v.   betätigen
operation   n.   Arbeitsgang {m}
operational adj. operativ
operative   adj. funktionsfähig
operator   n.   Operator {m}
opine   v.   meinen
opinion n.   Meinung {f}
opium   n.   Opium {n}
opponent   n.   Gegner {m}
opportune   adj. rechtzeitig
opportunism   n.   Opportunismus {m}
opportunity n. Gelegenheit {f}
oppose v.   gegenüberstellen
opposite   adj. gegenüberliegend
opposition   n.   Widerspruch {m}
oppress v.   unterdrücken
oppression   n.   Unterdrückung {f}
oppressive adj. gewaltsam
oppressor   n.   Schinder {m}
opt   v.   wählen
optic   adj. optisch

optician   n.   Optiker {m}
optimism   n.   Optimismus {m}
optimist   n.   Optimist {m}
optimistic   adj. optimistisch
optimize   v.   optimieren
optimum   adj. optimal
option   n.   Wahl {f}
optional   adj. freigestellt
opulence   n.   Reichtum {m}
opulent adj. reichlich
or   conj. oder
oracle   n.   Orakel {n}
oracular   adj. orakelhaft
oral   adj. mündlich
orally   adv. mündliche
orange n.   Orange {n}
oration n.   Rede {f}
orator   n.   Redner {m}
oratory n.   Redekunst {f}
orb   n.   Kugel {f}
orbit   n.   Augenhöhle {f}
orbital adj. kreisförmig
orchard   n.   Obstgarten {m}
orchestra   n.   Orchester {n}
orchestral   adj. orchestral
orchid   n.   Orchidee {f}
ordeal   n.   Geduldsprobe {f}
order   n.   Anordnung {f}
orderly adj. systematisch
ordinance   n.   Verordnung {f}
ordinarily   adv. gewöhnlich
ordinary   adj. alltäglich
ordnance   n.   Artillerie {f}
ore   n.   Erz {n}

organ *n.*	Orgel {f}	
organic *adj.*	organisch	
organism *n.*	organisch	
organization	*n.*	Organisation {f}
organize *v.*	organisieren	
orgasm *n.*	Orgasmus {m}	
orgy *n.*	Orgie {f}	
orient *n.*	Orient {m}	
oriental *adj.*	östlich	
orientate *v.*	orientieren	
origami *n.*	Origami {f}	
origin *n.*	Ursprung {m}	
original *adj.*	original	
originality *n.*	Echtheit {f}	
originate *v.*	entstehen	
originator *n.*	Erzeuger {m}	
ornament *n.*	Ornament {n}	
ornamental *adj.*	schmückend	
ornamentation	*n.*	Ausschmückung {f}
ornate *v.*	überladen	
orphan *n.*	Waise {m}	
orphanage *n.*	Waisenhaus {n}	
orthodox *adj.*	orthodoxe	
orthodoxy *n.*	Orthodoxie {f}	
orthopaedics	*n.*	Orthopädie {f}
oscillate *v.*	schwingen	
oscillation *n.*	Schwingung {f}	
ossify *v.*	verknöchern	
ostensible *adj.*	vordergründig	
ostentation *n.*	Zurschaustellung {f}	
osteopathy *n.*	Osteopathie	
ostracize *v.*	verbannen	
ostrich *n.*	Strauß {m}	
other *adj. & pron.*	anderes	

otherwise	*adv.* sonstig	
otiose *adj.*	müßig	
otter *n.*	Otter {m}	
ottoman *n.*	Osman {m}	
ounce *n.*	Unze {f}	
our *adj.*	unser	
ourselves *pron.*	uns selbst	
oust *v.*	enteignen	
out *adv.*	heraus	
outbid *v.*	überboten	
outboard *adj.*	außerhalb	
outbreak *n.*	Ausbruch {m}	
outburst *n.*	Ausbruch {m}	
outcast *n.*	Ausgestoßen {m}	
outclass *v.*	übertreffen	
outcome *n.*	Auswirkung {f}	
outcry *n.*	Aufschrei {m}	
outdated *adj.*	überaltert	
outdo *v.*	übertreffen	
outdoor *adj.*	draußen	
outer *adj.*	äußere	
outfit *n.*	Ausrüstung {f}	
outgoing *adj.*	abfahrend	
outgrow *v.*	auswachsen	
outhouse *n.*	Nebengebäude {n}	
outing *n.*	Ausflug {m}	
outlandish *adj.*	fremdartig	
outlast *v.*	überdauern	
outlaw *n.*	Geächtet {m}	
outlay *n.*	Aufwand {m}	
outlet *n.*	Abzug {m}	
outline *n.*	Entwurf {m}	
outlive *v.*	überleben	
outlook *n.*	Ausblick {m}	

outlying	adj.	entlegen
outmoded	adj.	veraltet
outnumber	v.	überlegen
outpatient	n.	Patient
outpost	n.	Außenposten {m}
output	n.	Arbeitsergebnis {n}
outrage	n.	Gewalttätigkeit {f}
outrageous	adj.	abscheulich
outrider	n.	Vorreiter {m}
outright	adv.	vollständig
outrun	v.	überschreiten
outset	n.	Anfang {m}
outshine	v.	überstrahlen
outside	n.	außen
outsider	n.	Außenseiter {m}
outsize	adj.	übergroß
outskirts	n.	Randgebiet {n}
outsource	v.	ausgliedern
outspoken	adj.	freimütig
outstanding	adj.	hervorragend
outstrip	v.	überholen
outward	adj.	äußerlich
outwardly	adv.	auswärts
outweigh	v.	überwiegen
outwit	v.	überlisten
oval	adj.	oval
ovary	n.	Fruchtknoten {m}
ovate	adj.	eiförmig
ovation	n.	Ovation {f}
oven	n.	Ofen {m}
over	prep.	vorüber
overact	v.	überspielen
overall	adj.	allumfassend
overawe	v.	einschüchtem

overbalance	v.	überwiegen
overbearing	adj.	anmaßen
overblown	adj.	bombastisch
overboard	adv.	über Bord
overburden	v.	überlasten
overcast	adj.	bewölkt
overcharge	v.	überfordern
overcoat	n.	Übermantel {m}
overcome	v.	überwinden
overdo	v.	übertreiben
overdose	n.	Überdosis {f}
overdraft	n.	Überziehung {f}
overdraw	v.	überziehen
overdrive	n.	Schnellgang {m}
overdue	adj.	überfällig
overestimate	v.	überschätzen
overflow	v.	Überlauf {m}
overgrown	adj.	überwuchernd
overhaul	v.	überholend
overhead	adv.	Mehraufwand {m}
overhear	v.	belauschen
overjoyed	adj.	überglücklich
overlap	v.	überlappen
overleaf	adv.	umseitig
overload	v.	überlasten
overlook	v.	übersehen
overly	adv.	übermäßig
overnight	adv.	am Vorabend
overpass	n.	Überführung {f}
overpower	v.	überwältigen
overrate	v.	überschätzen
overreach	v.	übervorteilen
overreact	v.	zureagieren
override	v.	überschrieben

overrule	v.	verwerfen
overrun	v.	überrollen
overseas	adv.	überseeisch
oversee	v.	beaufsichtigen
overseer	n.	Aufpasser {m}
overshadow	v.	überschatten
overshoot	v.	hinausschießen
oversight	n.	Übersicht {f}
overspill	n.	Bevölkerungsüberschuss {m}
overstep	v.	überschreiten
overt	adj.	offenkundig
overtake	v.	überholen
overthrow	v.	umstürzen
overtime	n	Überstunde {f}
overtone	n.	Oberschwingung {f}
overture	n.	Ouvertüre {f}
overturn	v.	umstoßen
overview	n.	Überblick {m}
overweening	adj.	anmaßend
overwhelm	v.	überwältigen
overwrought	adj.	überarbeitet
ovulate	v.	ausstoßen
owe	v.	schulden
owing	adj.	schuldend
owl	n.	Eule {f}
own	adj. & pron.	eigen
owner	n.	Besitzer
ownership	n.	Eigentumsrecht {n}
ox	n.	Ochse {m}
oxide	n.	Oxid {n}
oxygen	n.	Sauerstoff {m}
oyster	n.	Auster {f}
ozone	n	Ozon {n}

P

pace	n.	Stufe {f}
pacemaker	n.	Herzschrittmacher {m}
pacific	n.	Pazifik {m}
pacifist	n.	Pazifist {m}
pacify	v.	beruhigen
pack	n.	Pack {n}
package	n.	Paket {n}
packet	n.	Paket {n}
packing	n.	Verpackung {f}
pact	n.	Vertrag {m}
pad	n.	Stütze {f}
padding	n.	Füllung {f}
paddle	n.	Rührstange {f}
paddock	n.	Sattelplatz {m}
padlock	n.	Vorhängeschloss {n}
paddy	n.	Wutanfall {m}
paediatrician	n.	Kinderarzt {m}
paediatrics	n.	Pädiatrie {f}
paedophile	n.	Pädophile {m,f}
pagan	n.	Heide {m}
page	n.	Seite {f}
pageant	n.	Pomp {m}
pageantry	n.	Prunk {m}
pagoda	n.	Pagode {f}
pail	n.	Eimer {m}
pain	n.	Qual {f}
painful	adj.	schmerzhaft
painkiller	n.	Schmerzstiller {m}
painstaking	adj.	sorgfältig
paint	n.	Farbe {f}
painter	n.	Maler {m}
painting	n.	Gemälde {n}
pair	n.	Paar {n}

paisley *n.*	Paisleymuster {n}	**panic** *n.*	Panik {f}
pal*n.*	Kumpel {m}	**panorama** *n.*	Panorama {n}
palace *n.*	Palast {m}	**pant** *v.*	keuchen
palatable *adj.*	schmackhaft	**pantaloon** *n.*	Hose {f}
palatal *adj.*	gaumen...	**pantheism** *n.*	Pantheismus {m}
palate *n.*	Gaumen {m}	**pantheist** *adj.*	pantheist
palatial *adj.*	palastartig	**panther** *n.*	Panther {m}
pale *adj.*	blass	**panties** *n.*	Höschen {pl}
palette *n.*	Palette {f}	**pantomime** *n.*	Pantomime {f}
paling *n.*	Staket {n}	**pantry** *n.*	Speisekammer {f}
pall *n.*	Sargtuch {n}	**pants** *n.*	Unterhose {f}
pallet *n.*	Palette {f}	**papacy***n.*	Papsttum {n}
palm *n.*	Palme {f}	**papal** *adj.*	päpstlich
palmist*n.*	Wahrsager {m}	**paper** *n.*	Zeitung {f}
palmistry *n.*	Handlesekunst {f}	**paperback** *n.*	Taschenbuch {n}
palpable *adj.*	fühlbar	**par** *n.*	Pari
palpitate *v.*	klopfen	**parable***n.*	Parabel {m}
palpitation *n.*	Herzklopfen {n}	**parachute** *n.*	Fallschirm {m}
palsy *n.*	Lähmung {f}	**parachutist** *n.*	Fallschirmspringer {pl}
paltry *adj.*	dürftig	**parade** *n.*	Parade {f}
pamper*v.*	verzärteln	**paradise** *n.*	Paradies {n}
pamphlet *n.*	Merkblatt {n}	**paradox** *n.*	Paradox {m}
pamphleteer *n.*	Merkblatter {m}	**paradoxical** *adj.*	paradox
pan *n.*	Pfanne {f}	**paraffin***n.*	Paraffin {n}
panacea *n.*	Allheilmittel {n}	**paragon** *n.*	Musterknabe {m}
panache *n.*	Schwung {m}	**paragraph** *n.*	Absatz {m}
pancake *n.*	Eierkuchen {m}	**parallel***n.*	Parallele {f}
pancreas *n.*	Pankreas {n}	**parallelogram** *n.*	Parallelogramm {n}
panda *n.*	Panda {m}	**paralyse** *v.*	lähmen
pandemonium *n.*	Hölle {f}	**paralysis** *n.*	Paralyse {f}
pane *n.*	Fensterscheibe {f}	**paralytic** *adj.*	paralytisch
panegyric *n.*	Lobschrift {f}	**paramedic** *n.*	Rettungssanitäter {m}
panel *n.*	Paneel {n}	**parameter** *n.*	Parameter {m}
pang *n.*	Stechen {n}	**paramount** *adj.*	höchste

paramour	*n.*	Geliebte {m,f}	
paraphernalia	*n.*	Zubehör {n}	
paraphrase	*v.*	umschreiben	
parasite	*n.*	Parasit {m}	
parasol	*n.*	Sonnenschirm {m}	
parcel	*n.*	Päckchen {n}	
parched	*adj.*	geröstet	
pardon	*n.*	Verzeihung {f}	
pardonable	*adj.*	verzeihlich	
pare	*v.*	schälen	
parent	*n.*	Elternteil {n}	
parentage	*n.*	Abstammung {f}	
parental	*adj.*	elterlich	
parenthesis	*n.*	Klammer {f}	
pariah	*n.*	Ausgestoßene {m,f}	
parish	*n.*	Kirchgemeinde {f}	
parity	*n.*	Parität {f}	
park	*n.*	Park {m}	
parky	*adj.*	eisig	
parlance	*n.*	Ausdrucksweise {f}	
parley	*n.*	Unterredung {f}	
parliament	*n.*	Parlament {n}	
parliamentarian	*n.*	Parlamentarier {m}	
parliamentary	*adj.*	parlamentarisch	
parlour	*n.*	Wohnzimmer {n}	
parochial	*adj.*	beschränkt	
parody	*n.*	Parodie {f}	
parole	*n.*	Entlassener	
parricide	*n.*	Vatermord {m}	
parrot	*n.*	Papagei {m}	
parry	*v.*	parieren	
parse	*v.*	bestimmen	
parsimony	*n.*	Sparsamkeit {f}	
parson	*n.*	Pastor {m}	

part	*n.*	Einzelteil {n}	
partake	*v.*	teilnehmen	
partial	*adj.*	partiell	
partiality	*n.*	Parteilichkeit {f}	
participate	*v.*	beteiligen	
participant	*n.*	Teilnehmer {m}	
participation	*n.*	Beteiligung {f}	
particle	*n.*	Partikel {n}	
particular	*adj.*	besonders	
parting	*n.*	Trennung {f}	
partisan	*n.*	Vetternwirtschaft {f}	
partition	*n.*	Trennwand {f}	
partly	*adv.*	teilweise	
partner	*n.*	Teilnehmer {m}	
partnership	*n.*	Partnerschaft {f}	
party	*n.*	Party {f}	
pass	*v.*	vergehen	
passable	*adj.*	annehmbar	
passage	*n.*	Durchgang {m}	
passenger	*n.*	Passagier {m}	
passing	*adj.*	durchgehend	
passion	*n.*	Leidenschaft {f}	
passionate	*adj.*	leidenschaftlich	
passive	*adj.*	passiv	
passport	*n.*	Reisepass {m}	
past	*adj.*	Vergangenheit {f}	
pasta	*n.*	Nudeln {pl}	
paste	*n.*	Kleister {m}	
pastel	*n.*	Pastell {n}	
pasteurized	*adj.*	pasteurisiert	
pastime	*n.*	Zeitvertreib {m}	
pastor	*n.*	Pfarrer {m}	
pastoral	*adj.*	pastoral	
pastry	*n.*	Gebäck {n}	

pasture	n.	Viehweide {f}	pavement	n.	Straßenpflaster {n}

pasture   n.   Viehweide {f}
pasty n.   Pastete {f}
pat   v.   tätscheln
patch n.   Korrektur {f}
patchy adj. fleckig
patent n.   Patent {n}
paternal   adj. väterlich
paternity n.   Vaterschaft {f}
path   n.   Weg {m}
pathetic   adj. erbärmlich
pathology n.   Pathologie {f}
pathos n.   Pathos {m}
patience   n.   Geduld {f}
patient adj. geduldig
patient n.   Patient {m}
patio n.   Innenhof {m}
patisserie n.   Bäkerei {f}
patriarch n.   Patriarch {m}
patricide n.   Vatermord {m}
patrimony n.   Erbgut
patriot n.   Patriot {m}
patriotic adj. patriotisch
patriotism n.   Patriotismus {m}
patrol v.   Streifen
patron n.   Förderer {m}
patronage n.   Gönnerschaft {f}
patronize v.   beschützen
pattern n.   schwatzen
patty n.   Pastetchen {n}
paucity n.   Knappheit {f}
paunch n.   Speckbauch {m}
pauper n.   Sozialhilfeempfänger {m}
pause n.   Pause {f}
pave   v.   pflastern

pavement   n.   Straßenpflaster {n}
pavilion   n.   Pavillon {m}
paw   n.   Pfote {f}
pawn   n.   Bauer {m}
pawnbroker n.   Pfandleiher {m}
pay   v.   zahlen
payable   n.   zahlbar
payee n.   Zahlungsempfänger {m}
payment n.   Bezahlung {f}
pea   n.   Erbse {f}
peace n.   Friede {m}
peaceable adj. einlenkend
peaceful   adj. friedlich
peach n.   Pfirsich {m}
peacock n.   Pfau {m}
peahen n.   Pfauenhenne {f}
peak   n.   Spitze {f}
peaky adj. kränklich
peal   n.   Geläut {n}
peanut n.   Erdnuss {f}
pear   n.   Birne {f}
pearl n.   Perle {f}
peasant n.   Bauer {m}
peasantry n.   Landvolk {n}
pebble n.   Kieselstein {m}
pecan n.   Pecan {m}
peck   v.i. picken
peculiar   adj. eigenartig
pedagogue n.   Pädagoge {m}
pedagogy   n.   Pädagogik {pl}
pedal n.   Fußhebel {m}
pedant n.   Pedant {m}
pedantic   adj. pedantisch
peddle v.   hausieren

132

pedestal	n.	Sockel {m}	
pedestrian	n.	Fußgänger {m}	
pedicure	n.	Pediküre {f}	
pedigree	n.	Ahnentafel {f}	
pedlar	n.	Hausierer {m}	
pedometer	n.	Schrittmesser {m}	
peek	v.	gucken	
peel	n.	Schale {f}	
peep	v.	piepsen	
peer	n.	Beaufsichtigende {m,f}	
peer	v.	verbinden	
peerage	n.	Verbindung {f}	
peerless	adj.	unvergleichlich	
peg	n.	Stöpsel {m}	
pejorative	adj.	verschlimmernd	
pelican	n.	Pelikan {m}	
pellet	n.	Kraftfutter {n}	
pelmet	n.	Querbehang {m}	
pelt	v.	werfen	
pelvis	n.	Becken {n}	
pen	n.	Stift {m}	
penal	adj.	strafrechtlich	
penalize	v.	bestrafen	
penalty	n.	Strafe {f}	
penance	n.	Reue {f}	
penchant	n.	Hang {m}	
pencil	n.	Bleistift {m}	
pendant	n.	Schmuckanhänger {m}	
pendent	adj.	überhängend	
pending	adj.	schwebend	
pendulum	n.	Pendel {n}	
penetrate	v.	durchdringen	
penetration	n.	Eindringen {n}	
penguin	n.	Pinguin {m}	

peninsula	n.	Halbinsel {f}	
penis	n.	Penis {m}	
penitent	adj.	reuig	
penniless	adj.	mittellos	
penny	n.	Penny {m}	
pension	n.	Pension {f}	
pensioner	n.	Rentner {m}	
pensive	adj.	gedankenvoll	
pentagon	n.	Pentagon {n}	
penthouse	n.	Penthouse {n}	
penultimate	adj.	vorletzt	
people	n.	Leute {pl}	
pepper	n.	Pfeffer {m}	
peppermint	n.	Pfefferminz {n}	
peptic	adj.	peptisch	
per	prep.	für	
perambulate	v.t.	durchreisen	
perceive	v.	bemerken	
perceptible	adj.	wahrnehmbar	
percentage	n.	Prozentsatz {m}	
perceptible	adj.	erkennbar	
perception	n.	Auffassungskraft {f}	
perceptive	adj.	wahrnehmend	
perch	n.	Barsch {m}	
percipient	adj.	wahrnehmend	
percolate	v.	filtern	
percolator	n.	Kaffeemaschine {f}	
perdition	n.	Verderben {n}	
perennial	adj.	beständig	
perfect	adj.	perfekt	
perfection	n.	Vollkommenheit {f}	
perfidious	adj.	heimtückisch	
perforate	v.	perforieren	
perforce	adv.	zwangsläufig	

perform	v.	ausführen	perquisite	n.	Vergütung {f}
performance	n.	Leistung {f}	perry	n.	Birnenmost {m}
performer	n.	Darsteller {m}	persecute	v.	verfolgen
perfume	n.	Parfüm {n}	persecution	n.	Verfolgung {f}
perfume	adv.	parfümiert	perseverance	n.	Beharrlichkeit {f}
perfunctory	adj.	oberflächliche	persevere	v.i.	ausdauern
perhaps	adv.	eventuell	persist	v.	beharren
peril	n.	Gefahr {f}	persistence	n.	Fortdauer {f}
perilous	adj.	gefahrvoll	persistent	adj.	beharrlich
period	n.	Frist {f}	person	n.	Person {f}
periodic	adj.	periodisch	persona	n.	Rolle {f}
periodical	adj.	periodische	personage	n.	Persönlichkeit {f}
periphery	n.	Peripherie {f}	personal	adj.	persönlich
perish	v.	umkommen	personality	n.	Persönlichkeit {f}
perishable	adj.	vergänglich	personification	n.	Verkörperung {f}
perjure	v.	falsch schwören	personify	v.	personifizieren
perjury	n.	Eidbruch {m}	personnel	n.	Personal {n}
perk	v.	munter werden	perspective	n.	Durchblick {m}
perky	adj.	lebhaft	perspicuous	adj.	deutlich
permanence	n.	Konstanz {f}	perspiration	n.	Transpiration {f}
permanent	adj.	ständig	perspire	v.t.	schwitzen
permeable	adj.	durchlässig	persuade	v.	überreden
permissible	adj.	zulässig	persuasion	n.	Überzeugung {f}
permission	n.	Erlaubnis {f}	pertain	v.	gehören
permissive	adj.	tolerant	pertinent	adj.	einschlägig
permit	v.	Erlaubnisschein {m}	perturb	v.	beunruhigen
permutation	n.	Permutation {f}	perusal	n.	Durchsicht {f}
pernicious	adj.	verderblich	peruse	v.	durchgehen
perpendicular	adj.	senkrecht	pervade	v.	durchdringen
perpetrate	v.	verüben	perverse	adj.	pervers
perpetual	adj.	fortwährend	perversion	n.	Perversion {f}
perpetuate	v.t.	verewigen	perversity	n.	Pervertiertheit {f}
perplex	v.	ratlos	pervert	v.	pervertieren
perplexity	n.	Ratlosigkeit {f}	pessimism	n.	Pessimismus {m}

pessimist	*n.*	Pessimist {m}
pessimistic	*adj.*	pessimistisch
pest	*n.*	Landplage {f}
pester	*v.*	belästigen
pesticide	*n.*	Pestizid {n}
pestilence	*n.*	Seuche {f}
pet	*n.*	Haustier {n}
petal	*n.*	Blumenblatt {n}
petite	*adj.*	zierlich
petition	*n.*	Bitte {f}
petitioner	*n.*	Kläger {m}
petrify	*v.*	versteinern
petrol	*n.*	Benzin {n}
petroleum	*n.*	Erdöl {n}
petticoat	*n.*	Unterkleid {n}
pettish	*adj.*	empfindlich
petty	*adj.*	unbedeutend
petulance	*n.*	Gereiztheit {f}
petulant	*adj.*	gereizt
phantom	*n.*	Phantom {n}
pharmaceutical	*adj.*	Pharmazeutisch
pharmacist	*n.*	Pharmazeut {m}
pharmacy	*n.*	Apotheke {f}
phase	*n.*	Phase {f}
phenomenal	*adj.*	phänomenal
phenomenon	*n.*	Phänomen {n}
phial	*n.*	Fläschchen {n}
philanthropic	*adj.*	menschenfreundlich
philanthropist	*n.*	Philanthrop {m}
philanthropy	*n.*	Philanthropie {f}
philately	*n.*	Philatelie {f}
philological	*adj.*	philologisch
philologist	*n.*	Philologe {m}
philology	*n.*	Philologie {f}

philosopher	*n.*	Philosoph {m}
philosophical	*adj.*	philosophischen
philosophy	*n.*	Philosophie {f}
phlegmatic	*adj.*	phlegmatisch
phobia	*n.*	Phobie {f}
phoenix	*n.*	Phönix {m}
phone	*n.*	Telefon {n}
phonetic	*adj.*	phonetisch
phosphate	*n.*	Phosphat {n}
phosphorus	*n.*	Phosphor {n}
photo	*n.*	Foto {n}
photocopy	*n.*	Fotokopie {f}
photograph	*n.*	Fotografie {f}
photographer	*n.*	Fotograf {m}
photographic	*adj.*	fotografisch
photography	*n.*	Fotografie {f}
photostat	*n.*	fotokopieren
phrase	*n.*	Redewendung {f}
phraseology	*n.*	Ausdrucksweise {f}
physical	*adj.*	körperlich
physician	*n.*	Arzt {m}
physics	*n.*	Physik {f}
physiognomy	*n.*	Physiognomie {f}
physiotherapy	*n.*	Physiotherapie {f}
physique	*n.*	Körperbau {m}
pianist	*n.*	Pianist {m}
piano	*n.*	Klavier {n}
piazza	*n.*	Marktplatz {m}
pick	*v.*	pflücken
picket	*n.*	Pfahl {m}
pickings	*n.*	Reste {pl}
pickle	*n.*	Essiggurke {f}
picnic	*n.*	Picknick {n}
pictograph	*n.*	Piktogramm {n}

pictorial	*adj.*	bildhaften	**pioneer**	*n.*	Pionier {m}
picture *n.*		Gemälde {n}	**pious**	*adj.*	fromm
picturesque *adj.*		pittoresk	**pipe**	*n.*	Pfeife {f}
pie *n.*	Torte {f}		**pipette** *n.*		Pipette {f}
piece	*n.*	Stück {n}	**piquant** *adj.*		pikant
piecemeal	*adv.*	stückweise	**pique**	*n.*	reizen
pier	*n.*	Pfeiler {m}	**piracy**	*n.*	Seeräuberei {f}
pierce	*v.*	durchdrang	**pirate**	*n.*	Pirat {m}
piety	*n.*	Pietät {f}	**pistol**	*n.*	Pistole {f}
pig	*n.*	Schwein {n}	**piston**	*n.*	Kolben {m}
pigeon *n.*	Taube {f}		**pit**	*n.*	Box {f}
pigeonhole *n.*		Ablagefach {n}	**pitch**	*n.*	Tonhöhe {f}
piggery *n.*	Völlerei {f}		**pitcher** *n.*		Werfer {m}
pigment	*n.*	Pigment {n}	**piteous** *adj.*		erbärmlich
pigmy *n.*	Zwerg {m}		**pitfall**	*n.*	Fallgrube {f}
pike	*n.*	Hecht {m}	**pitiful**	*adj.*	mitleidig
pile	*n.*	Stoß {m}	**pitiless** *adj.*		erbarmungslos
pilfer	*v.*	mausen	**pity**	*n.*	Mitleid {m}
pilgrim *n.*	Pilger {m}		**pivot**	*n.*	Pivot {n}
pilgrimage *n.*		Pilgerschaft {f}	**pivotal** *adj.*		zentral
pill *n.*	Pille {f}		**pixel**	*n.*	Pixel {n}
pillar	*n.*	Pfeiler {m}	**pizza**	*n.*	Pizza {f}
pillow *n.*	Kissen {n}		**placard** *n.*		Plakat {n}
pilot	*n.*	Pilot {m}	**placate** *v.*		beschwichtigen
pimple *n.*	Pickel {m}		**place**	*n.*	Ort {m}
pin	*n.*	Nadel {f}	**placement**	*n.*	Hinstellen {n}
pincer *n.*	Kneifzange {f}		**placid**	*adj.*	sanft
pinch	*v.*	gekniffen	**plague** *n.*		Landplage {f}
pine	*v.*	Kiefer {f}	**plain**	*adj.*	einfach
pineapple	*n.*	Ananas {f}	**plaintiff** *n.*		Kläger {m}
pink	*adj.*	rosa	**plaintive**	*adj.*	traurig
pinnacle	*n.*	Zinne {f}	**plait**	*n.*	Zopf {m}
pinpoint	*v.*	festlegen	**plan**	*n.*	Plan {m}
pint	*n.*	Seidel {m}	**plane**	*n.*	Flugzeug {n}

planet	n.	Planet {m}
planetary	adj.	planetar
plank	n.	Planke {f}
plant	n.	Gewächs {n}
plantain	n.	Wegerich {m}
plantation	n.	Pflanzung {f}
plaque	n.	Zahnbelag {m}
plaster	n.	Gips {m}
plastic	n.	Plastik {f}
plate	n.	Teller {m}
plateau	n.	Plateau {n}
platelet	n.	Täfelchen {n}
platform	n.	Podium {n}
platinum	n.	Platin {n}
platonic	adj.	platonisch
platoon	n.	Polizeiaufgebot {n}
platter	n.	Servierplatte {f}
plaudits	n.	Beifall {m}
plausible	adj.	glaubhaft
play	v.i.	Spiel {n}
playground	n.	Spielplatz {m}
playwright	n.	Dramatiker {m}
player	n.	Spieler {m}
plaza	n.	Plaza {f}
plea	n.	Appell {m}
plead	v.	plädieren
pleasant	adj.	angenehm
pleasantry	n.	Hänselei {f}
please	v.	bitten
pleasure	n.	Vergnügung {f}
pleat	n.	Falte {f}
plebeian	adj.	plebejisch
plebiscite	n.	Plebiszit {n}
pledge	n.	Verpfändung {f}

plenty	pron.	Menge {f}
plethora	n.	Blutandrang {m}
pliable	adj.	gefügig
pliant	adj.	schmiegsam,
pliers	n.	Zange {f}
plight	n.	Gelöbnis {n}
plinth	n.	Plinthe {f}
plod	v.	schuften
plot	n.	Handlung {f}
plough	n.	Pflug {m}
ploughman	n.	Pflüger {m}
ploy	n.	List {f}
pluck	v.	gerupfen
plug	n.	Stecker {m}
plum	n.	Pflaume {f}
plumage	n.	Gefieder {n}
plumb	v.	erforschen
plumber	n.	Klempner {m}
plume	n.	Schadstofffahne {f}
plummet	v.	stürzen
plump	adj.	mollig
plunder	v.	plündern
plunge	v.	tauchen
plural	adj.	mehrfach
plurality	n.	Mehrheit {f}
plus	prep.	zuzüglich
plush	n.	Plüsch {m}
ply	n.	Schicht {f}
pneumatic	adj.	druckluftbetätigt
pneumonia	n.	Lungenentzündung {f}
poach	v.	pochieren
pocket	n.	Tasche {f}
pod	n.	Schale {f}
podcast	n.	Podcast {n}

podium *n.*	Podium {n}	**polo** *n.*	Polohemd {n}
poem *n.*	Gedicht {n}	**polyandry** *n.*	Polyandrie {f}
poet *n.*	Poet {m}	**polygamous** *adj.*	polygam
poetry *n.*	Dichtung {f}	**polygamy** *n.*	Polygamie {f}
poignancy *n.*	Schärfe {f}	**polyglot** *adj.*	vielsprachig
poignant *adj.*	scharf	**polygraph** *n.*	Polygraph {m}
point *n.*	Punkt {m}	**polytechnic** *n.*	Polytechnik
pointing *n.*	Hinweis {m}	**polytheism** *n.*	Polytheismus {m}
pointless *adj.*	sinnlos	**polytheistic** *adj.*	polytheistisch
poise *n.*	Haltung {f}	**pomegranate** *n.*	Granatapfel {m}
poison *n.*	Gift {n}	**pomp** *n.*	Gepränge {n}
poisonous *adj.*	giftig	**pomposity** *n.*	Wichtigtuerei {f}
poke *v.*	schürren	**pompous** *adj.*	prunkvoll
poker *n.*	Poker {m}	**pond** *n.*	Teich {m}
poky *adj.*	schäbig	**ponder** *v.*	grübeln
polar *adj.*	polar	**pontiff** *n.*	Hohepriester {m}
pole *n.*	Pfahl {m}	**pony** *n.*	Pony {n}
polemic *n.*	Polemik {f}	**pool** *n.*	Datenbasis {f}
police *n.*	Polizei {f}	**poor** *adj.*	arm
policeman *n.*	Polizist {m}	**poorly** *adv.*	dürftig
policy *n.*	Strategie {f}	**pop** *v.*	Pop {m}
polish *n.*	Politur {f}	**pope** *n.*	Papst {m}
polite *adj.*	höflich	**poplar** *n.*	Pappel {f}
politeness *n.*	Höflichkeit {f}	**poplin** *n.*	Popelin {m}
politic *adj.*	diplomatisch	**populace** *n.*	Pöbel {m}
political *adj.*	politisch	**popular** *adj.*	populär
politician *n.*	Politiker	**popularity** *n.*	Beliebtheit {f}
politics *n.*	Politik {f}	**popularize** *v.*	popularisieren
polity *n.*	Gemeinwesen {n}	**populate** *v.*	bevölkern
poll *n.*	Umfrage {f}	**population** *n.*	Bevölkerung {f}
pollen *n.*	Blütenstaub {m}	**populous** *adj.*	volkreich
pollster *n.*	Demoskop {m}	**porcelain** *n.*	Porzellan {n}
pollute *v.*	beschmutzen	**porch** *n.*	Veranda {f}
pollution *n.*	Verschmutzung {f}	**porcupine** *n.*	Stachelschwein {n}

pore	*n.*	Pore {f}	posterior	*adj.*	Hinterteil {n}
pork	*n.*	Schweinefleisch {n}	posterity	*n.*	Nachwelt {f}
pornography	*n.*	Pornographie {f}	postgraduate	*n.*	Graduierte {m,f}
porridge	*n.*	Brei {m}	posthumous	*adj.*	posthum
port	*n.*	Hafen {m}	postman	*n.*	Briefträger {m}
portable	*adj.*	tragbar	postmaster	*n.*	Postmeister {m}
portage	*n.*	Transport {m}	postmortem	*n.*	postmortal
portal	*n.*	Pforte {f}	postoffice	*n.*	Postamt {f}
portend	*v.*	deuten	postpone	*v.*	verschieben
portent	*n.*	Anzeichen {n}	postponement	*n.*	Aufschub {m}
porter	*n.*	Pförtner {m}	postscript	*n.*	Nachschrift {f}
portfolio	*n.*	Aktentasche {f}	posture	*n.*	Stellung {f}
portico	*n.*	Säulengang {m}	pot	*n*.	Topf {m}
portion	*n.*	Anteil {m}	potato	*n.*	Kartoffel {f}
portrait	*n.*	Portrait {n}	potency	*n.*	Potenz {f}
portraiture	*n.*	Porträtphotographie {f}	potent	*adj.*	potent
portray	*v.*	porträtieren	potential	*adj.*	potentiell
portrayal	*n.*	Darstellung {f}	potentiality	*n.*	Möglichkeit {f}
pose	*v.*	posieren	potter	*v.*	einlegen
posh	*adj.*	piekfein	pottery	*n.*	Töpfer {m}
posit	*v.*	postulieren	pouch	*n.*	Beutel {m}
position	*n.*	Lage {f}	poultry	*n.*	Geflügel {n}
positive	*adj.*	positiv	pounce	*v.*	bimsen
possess	*v.*	besitzen	pound	*n.*	Pfund
possession	*n.*	Besessenheit {f}	pour	*v.*	gießen
possessive	*adj.*	besitzanzeigend	poverty	*n.*	Armut {f}
possibility	*n.*	Möglichkeit {f}	powder	*n.*	Puder {n}
possible	*adj.*	möglich	power	*n.*	Kraft {f}
post	*n.*	Standpunkt {m}	powerful	*adj.*	kraftvoll
postage	*n.*	Porto {n}	practicability	*n.*	Durchführbarkeit {f}
postal	*adj.*	postalisch	practicable	*adj.*	durchführbar
postcard	*n.*	Postkarte {f}	practical	*adj.*	praktisch
postcode	*n.*	Postleitzahl {f}	practice	*n.*	Übung {f}
poster	*n.*	Poster {n}	practise	*v.*	praktizieren

practitioner *n.*	Praktiker {m}		**predicate** *n.*	Prädikat {n}
pragmatic *adj.*	pragmatisch		**predict** *v.*	vorhersagen
pragmatism *n.*	Pragmatismus {m}		**prediction** *n.*	Prophezeiung {f}
praise *v.t.*	loben		**predominance** *n.*	Vorherrschaft {f}
praline *n.*	Praline {f}		**predominant** *adj.*	vorherrschend
pram *n.*	Kinderwagen {m}		**predominate** *v.*	vorherrschen
prank *n.*	Possen {pl}		**pre-eminence** *n.*	Überlegenheit {f}
prattle *v.*	plaudern		**pre-eminent** *adj.*	hervorragend
pray *v.*	beten		**pre-empt** *v.*	erwerben
prayer *n.*	Gebet {n}		**prefabricated** *adj.*	vorfabriziert
preach *v.*	predigen		**preface** *n.*	Vorwort {n}
preacher *n.*	Prediger {m}		**prefect** *n.*	Prafekt
preamble *n.*	Präambel {f}		**prefer** *v.*	vorziehen
precarious *adj.*	unsicher		**preference** *n.*	Vorliebe {f}
precaution *n.*	Vorsorgemaßnahme {f}		**preferential** *adj.*	bevorzugt
precautionary *adj.*	vorbeugend		**preferment** *n.*	Beförderung {f}
precede *v.*	vorangehen		**prefix** *n.*	Präfix {n}
precedence *n.*	Priorität {f}		**pregnancy** *n.*	Schwangerschaft {f}
precedent *n.*	Präzedenzfall {m}		**pregnant** *adj.*	schwanger
precept *n.*	Vorschrift {f}		**prehistoric** *adj.*	prähistorisch
precinct *n.*	Bezirk {m}		**prejudge** *v.*	vorurteilen
precious *adj.*	geschätzt		**prejudice** *n.*	Schaden {m}
precipitate *v.*	ausfällen		**prejudicial** *adj.*	nachteilig
précis *n.*	Inhaltsangabe {f}		**prelate** *n.*	Prälat {n}
precise *adj.*	genau		**preliminary** *adj.*	vorläufig
precision *n.*	Präzision {f}		**prelude** *n.*	Vorspiel {n}
precognition *n.*	Vorkenntnis {f}		**premarital** *adj.*	vorehelich
precondition *n.*	Vorbedingung {f}		**premature** *adj.*	frühreif
precursor *n.*	Wegbereiter {m}		**premeditate** *v.*	vorsätzen
predator *n.*	Räuber {m}		**premeditation** *n.*	Vorsatz {m}
predecessor *n.*	Vorgänger {m}		**premier** *adj.*	erstaufgeführt
predestination *n.*	Prädestination {f}		**premiere** *n.*	Premiere {f}
predetermine *v.*	vorherbestimmen		**premise** *n.*	Prämisse {f}
predicament *n.*	Kategorie {f}		**premises** *n.*	Lokal {n}

premium	n.	Bonus {m}	
premonition	n.	Warnung {f}	
preoccupation	n.	Vertieftsein {n}	
preoccupy	v.	erfüllen	
preparation	n.	Vorbereitung {f}	
preparatory	adj.	vorbereitend	
prepare	v.	bereiten	
preponderance	n.	Übergewicht {n}	
preponderate	v.	überwiegen	
preposition	n.	Präposition {f}	
prepossessing	adj.	erfüllend	
preposterous	adj.	lächerlich	
prerequisite	n.	Voraussetzung {f}	
prerogative	n.	Vorrecht {n}	
presage	v.	Prophezeiung {f}	
prescience	n.	Vorherwissen {n}	
prescribe	v.	vorschreiben	
prescription	n.	Verordnung {f}	
presence	n.	Anwesenheit {f}	
present	adj.	präsent	
present	n.	Geschenk {n}	
present	v.	präsentieren	
presentation	n.	Präsentation {f}	
presently	adv.	zurzeit	
preservation	n.	Bewahrung {f}	
preservative	n.	Konservierungsmittel {f}	
preserve	v.	aufbewahren	
preside	v.	präsidieren	
president	n.	Präsident {m}	
presidential	adj.	präsidential	
press	v.	pressen	
pressure	n.	Druck {m}	
pressurize	v.	druckfest machen	
prestige	n.	Prestige {n}	

prestigious	adj.	prestigevoll	
presume	v.	vermuten	
presumption	n.	Vermutung {f}	
presuppose	v.	voraussetzen	
presupposition	n.	Voraussetzung {f}	
pretence	n.	Vortäuschung {f}	
pretend	v.	täuschen	
pretension	n.	Anmaßung {f}	
pretentious	adj.	anspruchsvoll	
pretext	n.	Scheingrund {m}	
prettiness	n.	Hübschheit {f}	
pretty	adj.	hübsch	
pretzel	n.	Bretzel {m}	
prevail	v.	überwiegen	
prevalence	n.	Vorherrschen {n}	
prevalent	adj.	herrschend	
prevent	v.	verhindern	
prevention	n.	Verhütung {f}	
preventive	adj.	vorsorglich,	
preview	n.	Vorschau {f}	
previous	adj.	vorherig	
prey	n.	Beute {f}	
price	n.	Preis {m}	
priceless	adj.	unbezahlbar	
prick	v.	stechen	
prickle	n.	Stachel {m}	
pride	n.	Stolz {m}	
priest	n.	Priester {m}	
priesthood	n.	Priesterschaft {f}	
prim	adj.	erst	
primacy	n.	Vorrang {m}	
primal	adj.	hauptsächlich	
primarily	adv.	erstrangig	
primary	adj.	zuerst	

primate	n.	Primat {m}	probation	n.	Bewährung {f}

primate n. Primat {m}
prime adj. wichtigste
primer n. Zündsatz {m}
primeval adj. urzeitlich
primitive adj. primitiv
prince n. Prinz {m}
princely adj. prinzlich
princess n. Prinzessin {f}
principal adj. wesentlich
principal n. Prinzipal {m}
principle n. Prinzip {n}
print v. drucken
printout n. Druckausgabe {f}
printer n. Druckerei {f}
prior adj. früher
priority n. Priorität {f}
priory n. Vorrang {m}
prism n. Prisma {n}
prison n. Gefängnis {n}
prisoner n. Gefangene {m,f}
pristine adj. ursprünglich
privacy n. Privatsphäre {f}
private adj. privat
privation n. Mangel {m}
privatize v. privatisieren
privilege n. Vorrecht {n}
privy adj. eingeweiht
prize n. Prämie {f}
pro n. Profi {m}
proactive adj. proaktiv
probability n. Wahrscheinlichkeit {f}
probable adj. wahrscheinlich
probably adv. voraussichtlich
probate v. bestätigen

probation n. Bewährung {f}
probationer n. Probekandidat {m}
probe n. Probe {f}
probity n. Rechtschaffenheit {f}
problem n. Problem {n}
problematic adj. problematisch
procedure n. Prozedur {f}
proceed v. ablaufen
proceedings n. Fortschritte {pl}
proceeds v. fortsetzen
process n. Vorgang {m}
procession n. Prozession {f}
proclaim v. proklamieren
proclamation n. Proklamation {f}
proclivity n. Neigung {f}
procrastinate v. zögern
procrastination n. Verschleppung {f}
procreate v. erzeugen
procure v. vermitteln
procurement n. Beschaffung {f}
prod v. stupsen
prodigal adj. verschwenderisch
prodigious adj. erstaunlich
prodigy n. Wunderkind {n}
produce v. Warenmarkt {m}
producer n. Hersteller {m}
product n. Produkt {n}
production n. Erzeugung {f}
productive adj. produktiv
productivity n. Produktivität {f}
profane adj. gotteslästerlich
profess v. erklären
profession n. Beruf {m}
professional adj. professionell

142

professor	n.	Professor {m}
proficiency	n.	Beschlagenheit {f}
proficient	adj.	tüchtig
profile	n.	Profil {n}
profit	n.	Profit {m}
profitable	adj.	vorteilhaft
profiteering	n.	Schiebergeschäfte {pl}
profligacy	n.	Lasterhaftigkeit {f}
profligate	adj.	liederlich
profound	adj.	tiefsinnig
profundity	n.	Tiefgründigkeit {f}
profuse	adj.	übermäßig
profusion	n.	Überfluss {m}
progeny	n.	Frucht {f}
prognosis	n.	Prognose {f}
prognosticate	v.	voraussagen
programme	n.	Programm {n}
progress	n.	Fortgang {m}
progressive	adj.	fortschrittlich
prohibit	v.	verboten
prohibition	n.	Verbot {n}
prohibitive	adj.	ausschließend
project	n.	Projekt {n}
projectile	n.	Projektil {n}
projection	n.	Projektion {f}
projector	n.	Projektor {m}
prolapse	v.	prolabieren
proliferate	v.	wuchern
proliferation	n.	Wucherung {f}
prolific	adj.	zahlreich
prologue	n.	Prolog {m}
prolong	v.	verlängern
prolongation	n.	Verlängerung {f}
promenade	n.	Gehweg {m}

prominence	n.	Bedeutung {f}
prominent	adj.	Prominente {m}
promiscuous	adj.	verworren
promise	n.	Versprechen {n}
promising	adj.	aussichtsvoll
promote	v.	befördern
promotion	n.	Beförderung {f}
prompt	v.	Anforderungszeichen {n}
prompter	n.	Souffleur {m}
promulgate	v.	verkündigen
prone	adj.	anfällig
pronoun	n.	Pronomen {n}
pronounce	v.	aussprechend
pronunciation	n.	Aussprache {f}
proof	n.	Probe {f}
prop	n.	Stütze {f}
propaganda	n.	Propaganda {f}
propagate	v.	verbreiten
propagation	n.	Verbreitung {f}
propel	v.	vorantreiben
propeller	n.	Propeller {m}
proper	adj.	korrekt
property	n.	Grundstück {n}
prophecy	n.	Prophezeiung {f}
prophesy	v.	prophezeien
prophet	n.	Prophezeier {m}
prophetic	adj.	prophetisch
propitiate	v.	versöhnen
proportion	n.	Anteil {m}
proportional	adj.	proportional
proportionate	adj.	anteilmäßig
proposal	n.	Vorschlag {m}
propose	v.	vorschlagen
proposition	n.	Satz {m}

propound *v.*	vorlegen
proprietary *adj.*	geschützt
proprietor *n.*	Besitzer {m}
propriety *n.*	Schicklichkeit {f}
prorogue *v.*	vertagen
prosaic *adj.*	prosaisch
prose *n.*	Prosa {f}
prosecute *v.*	betreiben
prosecution *n.*	Staatsanwaltschaft {f}
prosecutor *n.*	Staatsanwalt {m}
prospect *n.*	Sicht {f}
prospective *adj.*	voraussichtlich
prospectus *n.*	Werbeprospekt {n}
prosper *v.*	florieren
prosperity *n.*	Prosperität {f}
prosperous *adj.*	erfolgreich
prostate *n.*	Vorsteherdrüse {f}
prostitute *n.*	Prostituierte {m,f}
prostitution *n.*	Prostitution {f}
prostrate *adj.*	niederwerfend
prostration *n.*	Niederwerfung {f}
protagonist *n.*	Vorkämpfer {m}
protect *v.*	schützen
protection *n.*	Schutz {m}
protective *adj.*	geschützte
protectorate *n.*	Schirmherrschaft {f}
protein *n.*	Eiweiß {n}
protest *n.*	Protest {m}
protestation *n.*	Beteuerung {f}
protocol *n.*	Protokoll {n}
prototype *n.*	Prototyp {m}
protracted *adj.*	hingezogen
protractor *n.*	Winkelmesser {m}
protrude *v.*	vorstehen

proud *adj.*	stolz
prove *v.*	beweisen
provenance *n.*	Herkunft {f}
proverb *n.*	Sprichwort {m}
proverbial *adj.*	sprichwörtlich
provide *v.*	besorgen
providence *n.*	Vorsehung {f}
provident *adj.*	vorfürsorglich
providential *adj.*	glücklich
province *n.*	Provinz {f}
provincial *adj.*	kleinstädtisch
provision *n.*	Vorkehrung {f}
provisional *adj.*	provisorisch
proviso *n.*	Vorbehalt {m}
provocation *n.*	Herausforderung {f}
provocative *adj.*	aufreizend
provoke *v.*	provozieren
prowess *n.*	Tapferkeit {f}
proximate *adj.*	nächster
proximity *n.*	Näherung {f}
proxy *n.*	Vertretung {f}
prude *n.*	Prüde {f}
prudence *n.*	Klugheit {f}
prudent *adj.*	verständig
prudential *adj.*	klüglich
prune *n.*	Backpflaume {f}
pry *v.*	neugierig sein
psalm *n.*	Psalm {m}
pseudo *adj.*	schein...
pseudonym *n.*	Pseudonym {n}
psyche *n.*	Psyche {f}
psychiatrist *n.*	Psychiater {m}
psychiatry *n.*	Psychiatrie {f}
psychic *adj.*	psychisch

144

psychological	*adj.* psychologisch
psychologist	*n.* Psychologe {m}
psychology *n.*	Psychologie {f}
psychopath *n.*	Psychopathe {m}
psychosis *n.*	Psychose {f}
psychotherapy *n.*	Psychotherapie {f}
pub *n.*	Kneipe {f}
puberty *n.*	Pubertät {f}
pubic *adj.*	schamm
public *adj.*	öffentlich
publication *n.*	Veröffentlichung {f}
publicity *n.*	Werbung {f}
publicize *v.*	propagieren
publish *v.*	veröffentlichen
publisher *n.*	Verlagsbuchhändler {m}
pudding *n.*	Pudding {m}
puddle *n.*	Pfütze {f}
puerile *adj.*	kindlich
puff *n.*	Hauch {m}
puffy *adj.*	geschwollen
pull *v.*	ziehen
pulley *n.*	Scheibe {f}
pullover *n.*	Schlupfanorak {m}
pulp *n.*	Brei {m}
pulpit *n.*	Kanzel {f}
pulsar *n.*	Pulsschlag {m}
pulsate *v.*	pulsieren
pulsation *n.*	Pulsschlag {m}
pulse *n.*	Puls {m}
pummel *v.*	schlagen
pump *n.*	Pumpe {f}
pumpkin *n.*	Kürbis {m}
pun *n.*	Wortspiel {n}
punch *v.*	schlagen

punctual *adj.*	pünktlich
punctuality *n.*	Pünktlichkeit {f}
punctuate *v.*	unterstreichen
punctuation *n.*	Zeichensetzung {f}
puncture *n.*	Reifenpanne {f}
pungency *n.*	Beißende {f}
pungent *adj.*	stechend
punish *v.*	bestrafen
punishment *n.*	Strafe {f}
punitive *adj.*	strafend
punter *n.*	Stechkahnfahrer {m}
puny *adj.*	kümmerlich
pup *n.*	junger Hund
pupil *n.*	Schüler {m}
puppet *n.*	Marionette {f}
puppy *n.*	Welpe {m}
purblind *adj.*	kurzsichtig
purchase *v.*	kaufen
pure *adj.*	rein
purgation *n.*	Reinigung {f}
purgative *adj.*	abführend
purgatory *n.*	Fegefeuer {n}
purge *v.*	abführen
purification *n.*	Klärung {f}
purify *v.*	reinigen
purist *n.*	Purist {m}
puritan *n.*	Puritaner {m}
puritanical *adj.*	puritanisch
purity *n.*	Reinheit {f}
purple *n.*	Purpurr
purport *v.*	behaupten
purpose *n.*	Absicht {f}
purposely *adv.*	vorsätzlich
purr *v.*	Schnurren

purse *n.*	Geldbeutel {m}		**quaff** *v.*	zechen
purser *n.*	Chefsteward {m}		**quail** *n.*	Wachtel {f}
pursuance *n.*	Verfolgung {f}		**quaint** *adj.*	wunderlich
pursue *v.*	verfolgen		**quaintly** *adv.*	anheimelnd
pursuit *n.*	Verfolgung {f}		**quake** *v.*	beben
purvey *v.*	liefern		**quaker** *n.*	Quäker {m}
purview *n.*	Bereich {m}		**qualification** *n.*	Befähigung {f}
pus *n.*	Eiter {m}		**qualify** *v.*	qualifizieren
push *v.*	schieben		**qualitative** *adj.*	qualitativ
pushy *adj.*	aufdringlich		**quality** *n.*	Qualität {f}
puss *n.*	Miezchen {n}		**qualm** *n.*	Bedenken {n}
put *v.*	legen		**quandary** *n.*	Verlegenheit {f}
putative *adj.*	vermeintlich		**quango** *n.*	Verwaltungseinrichtung {f}
putrid *adj.*	verdorben		**quantify** *v.*	befähigen
puzzle *v.t.*	verwirren		**quantitative** *adj.*	quantitativ
pygmy *n.*	Pygmäe {m}		**quantity** *n.*	Größe {f}
pyjamas *n.*	Pyjama {f}		**quantum** *n.*	Betrag {m}
pyorrhoea *n.*	Parodontose {f}		**quarantine** *n.*	Quarantäne {f}
pyramid *n.*	Pyramide {f}		**quark** *n.*	Quark {n}
pyre *n.*	Scheiterhaufen {m}		**quarrel** *n.*	Auseinandersetzung {f}
pyromania *n.*	Pyromanie {f}		**quarrelsome** *adj.*	streitsüchtig
python	Pythonschlange {f}		**quarry** *n.*	Jagdbeute {f}
			quart *n.*	Quart {f}
Q			**quarter** *n.*	Viertel {n}
quack *v.i.*	quaken		**quarterly** *adj.*	vierteljährlich
quackery *n.*	Quacksalberei {f}		**quartet** *n.*	Quartett {n}
quad *n.*	vierfach		**quartz** *n.*	Quarz {m}
quadrangle *a.*	Viereck {n}		**quash** *v.*	verwerfen
quadrangular *n.*	viereckig		**quaver** *v.*	Achtelnote {f}
quadrant *n.*	Quadrant {m}		**quay** *n.*	Kai {m}
quadrilateral *n.*	vierseitig		**queasy** *adj.*	heikel
quadruped *n.*	Vierbeiner {m}		**queen** *n.*	Königin {f}
quadruple *adj.*	vierfach		**queer** *adj.*	wunderlich
quadruplet *n.*	Vierling {m}		**quell** *v.*	bezwingen

146

quench	v.	löschen	quorum	n.	Quorum {n}

quench v.   löschen
querulous   adj. verdrossen
query   n.   Frage {f}
quest   n.   Suche {f}
question   n.   Fragestellung {f}
questionable   adj. bedenklich
questionnaire   n.   Fragebogen {m}
queue   n.   Reihen {pl}
quibble   n.   ausgewichen
quick   adj. schnell
quicken   v.   beschleunigen
quickly adv. schnell
quid   n.   Pfund {n}
quiescent   adj. untätig
quiet   adj. leise
quieten v.   beruhigen
quietetude   n.   Ruhe {f}
quiff   n.   Tolle {f}
quilt   n.   Steppdecke {f}
quilted adj. wattierte
quin   n.   Quinärzahl {f}
quince n.   Quitte {f}
quinine n.   Chinin {n}
quintessence   n.   Quintessenz {f}
quip   n.   Stichelei {m}
quirk   n.   Eigenart {f}
quit   v.   verlassen
quite   adv. ziemlich
quits   adj. quitt
quiver v.   zittern
quixotic   adj. schwärmerisch
quiz   n.   Quiz {n}
quizzical   adj. komisch
quondam   adj. ehemalig

quorum   n.   Quorum {n}
quota   n.   Quote {f}
quotation   n.   Zitat {n}
quote   v.   Anführungszeichen {n}
quotient   n.   Quotient {m}

R

rabbit   n.   Hase {m}
rabble   n.   Gesindel {n}
rabid   adj. wütend
rabies   n.   Tollwut {f}
race   n.   Rennen {n}
race   v.   rennen
racial   adj. rassisch
racialism   n.   Rassismus {m}
rack   n.   Zahnstange {f}
racket   n.   Schläger {m}
racketeer   n.   Erpresser {m}
racy   adj. schmissig
radar   n.   Radar {m,n}
radial   adj. radial
radiance   n.   Glanz {m}
radiant adj. strahlend
radiate v.   strahlen
radiation   n.   Strahlung {f}
radical adj. radikal
radio   n.   Radio {n}
radioactive adj. radioaktiv
radiography n.   Röntgenaufnahme {f}
radiology   n.   Strahlenforschung {f}
radish   n.   Radieschen {n}
radium n.   Radium {n}
radius   n.   Radius {m}
raffle   n.   Verlosung {f}

raft	n.	Holzfloß {n}	
rag	n.	Unfug {m}	
rage	n.	Wut {f}	
ragged	adj.	zerlumpt	
raid	n.	Razzia {f}	
rail	n.	Reling {f}	
railing	n.	Geländer {n}	
raillery	n.	Spötterei {f}	
railway	n.	Bahn {f}	
rain	n	Regen {m}	
rainbow	n.	Regenbogen {m}	
raincoat	n.	Regenmantel {m}	
rainfall	n.	Niederschlag {m}	
rainforest	n.	Regenwald {m}	
rainy	adj.	regnerisch	
raise	v.	errichten	
raisin	n.	Rosine {f}	
rake	n.	Harke {f}	
rally	n.	Rallye {f}	
ram	n.	Ramme {f}	
ramble	v.	umherstreifen	
ramification	n.	Verästelung {f}	
ramify	v.	verästeln	
ramp	n.	Rampe {f}	
rampage	v.	toben	
rampant	adj.	wild	
rampart	n.	Wall {m}	
ramshackle	adj.	baufällig	
ranch	n.	Farm {f}	
rancid	adj.	ranzig	
rancour	n.	Groll {m}	
random	adj.	zufällig	
range	n.	Bandbreite {f}	
ranger	n.	Förster {m}	

rank	n.	Grad {m}	
rank	v.	gereihen	
rankle	v.	fressen	
ransack	v.	durchstöbern	
ransom	n.	Lösegeld {n}	
rant	v.	lärmen	
rap	v.	plappern	
rapacious	adj.	raubgierig	
rape	v.	vergewaltigen	
rapid	adj.	rasch	
rapidity	n.	Schnelligkeit {f}	
rapier	n.	Rapier {n}	
rapist	n.	Vergewaltiger {m}	
rapport	n.	Übereinstimmung {f}	
rapprochement	n.	Wiederannäherung {f}	
rapt	adj.	versunken	
rapture	n.	Taumel {m}	
rare	adj.	rar	
raring	adj.	bereit	
rascal	n.	Lausebengel {m}	
rash	adj.	voreilig	
rasp	n.	Raspel {f}	
raspberry	n.	Himbeere {f}	
rat	n.	Ratte {f}	
ratchet	n.	Ratsche {f}	
rate	n.	Anteil {m}	
rather	adv.	eher	
ratify	v.	ratifizieren	
rating	n.	Leistungsfähigkeit {f}	
ratio	n.	Verhältnis {n}	
ration	n.	Zuteilung {f}	
rational	adj.	vernünftig	
rationale	n.	Grundprinzip {n}	
rationalism	n.	Rationalismus {m}	

rationalize	v.	rationalisieren
rattle	v.	scheppern
raucous	adj.	rau
ravage	v.t.	verwüsten
rave	v.	auftrennen
raven	n.	Rabe {m}
ravenous	adj.	gefräßig
ravine	n.	Klamm {f}
raw	adj.	roh
ray	n.	Strahl {m}
raze	v.	auslöschen
razor	n.	Rasiermesser {n}
reach	v.	ergreifen
react	v.	reagieren
reaction	n.	Reaktion {f}
reactionary	adj.	reaktionär
reactor	n.	Reaktor {m}
read	v.	lesen
reader	n.	Leser {m}
readily	adv.	bereit
reading	n.	Ablesung {f}
readjust	v.	wiederanpassen
ready	adj.	fertig
reaffirm	v.	beteuern
real	adj.	tatsächlich
realism	n.	Realismus {m}
realistic	adj.	realistisch
reality	n.	Wirklichkeit {f}
realization	n.	Ausführung {f}
realize	v.	durchführen
really	adv.	wirklich
realm	n.	Reich {n}
ream	n.	Aufreiben {n}
reap	v.	ernten

reaper	n.	Mäher {m}
reappear	v.	wiederauftreten
reappraisal	n.	Bewertung {f}
rear	n.	Rückseite {f}
rearrange	v.	umdirigieren
reason	n.	Verstand {m}
reasonable	adj.	vernünftig
reassess	v.	umwerten
reassure	v.	versichern
rebate	n.	Rabatt {m}
rebel	v.	rebellieren
rebellion	n.	Rebellion {f}
rebellious	adj.	aufrührerisch
rebirth	n.	Wiedergeburt {f}
rebound	v.	Rückprall {m}
rebuff	v.	zurückweisen
rebuild	v.	erneuern
rebuke	v.	tadeln
recall	v.	zurückrufen
recap	v.	rekapitulieren
recapitulate	v.	zusammenfassen
recapture	v.	wiedernehmen
recede	v.	zurücktreten
receipt	n.	Empfang {m}
receive	v.	empfangen
receiver	n.	Empfänger {m}
recent	adj.	neue
recently	adv.	neulich
receptacle	n.	Steckerbuchse {f}
reception	n.	Empfang {m}
receptionist	n.	Sprechstundenhilfe {f}
receptive	adj.	aufnahmefähig
recess	n.	Unterbrechung {f}
recession	n.	Rezession {f}

recessive	adj.	nachlassen	
recharge	v.	nachladen	
recipe	n.	Rezept {n}	
recipient	n.	Empfänger {m}	
reciprocal	adj.	wechselseitig	
reciprocate	v.	vergelten	
recital	n.	Vortrag {m}	
recite	v.	vortragen	
reckless	adj.	unbekümmert	
reckon	v.t.	meinen	
reclaim	v.	zurückfordern	
reclamation	n.	Zurückforderung {f}	
recline	v.	lehnen	
recluse	n.	Einsiedler {m}	
recognition	n.	Erkennung {f}	
recognize	v.i.	erkennen	
recoil	v.	Rückstoß {m}	
recollect	v.	erinnern	
recollection	n.	Erinnerung {f}	
recommend	v.	empfehlen	
recommendation	n.	Empfehlung {f}	
recompense	v.	belohnen	
reconcile	v.	versöhnen	
reconciliation	n.	Versöhnung {f}	
recondition	v.	erneuern	
reconsider	v.	überdenken	
reconstitute	v.	wiederherstellen	
reconstruct	v.	wiederaufbauen	
record	n.	Schallplatte {f}	
recorder	n.	Aufnahmegerät {m}	
recount	v.	nachzählen	
recoup	v.	entschädigen	
recourse	n.	Rückgriff {m}	
recover	v.	erholen	

recovery	n.	Genesung {f}	
recreate	v.	wiederschaffen	
recreation	n.	Wiederherstellung {f}	
recrimination		n.Gegenbeschuldigung	
{f} recruit	v.	rekrutieren	
rectangle	n.	Rechteck {n}	
rectangular	adj.	rechtwinklig	
rectification	n.	Verbesserung {f}	
rectify	v.	verbessern	
rectitude	n.	Geradheit {f}	
rectum	n.	Mastdarm {m}	
recumbent	adj.	liegend	
recuperate	v.	erholen	
recur	v.	wiederkehren	
recurrence	n.	Wiederholung {f}	
recurrent	adj.	wiederkehrend	
recycle	v.	verwerten	
red	adj.	rot	
reddish	adj.	rötlich	
redeem	v.	tilgen	
redemption	n.	Tilgung {f}	
redeploy	v.	umgruppieren	
redolent	adj.	duftend	
redouble	v.	verdoppeln	
redoubtable	adj.	furchtbar	
redress	v.	beseitigen	
reduce	v.	vermindern	
reduction	n.	Verkleinerung {f}	
reductive	adj.	verkleinernd	
redundancy	n.	Redundanz {f}	
redundant	adj.	überflüssig	
reef	n.	Riff {n}	
reek	v.	rauchen	
reel	n.	Band {n}	

refer v.	berichten
referee n.	Schiedsrichter {m}
reference n.	Bezugnahme {f}
referendum n.	Volksbegehren {n}
refill v.	auffüllen
refine v.	verfeinern
refinement n.	Verfeinerung {f}
refinery n.	Raffinerie {f}
refit v.	ausbessern
reflect v.	reflektieren
reflection n.	Reflexion {f}
reflective adj.	reflektierend
reflex n.	Reflex {m}
reflexive adj.	reflexiv
reflexology n.	Reflexologie {f}
reform v.	verbessern
reformation n.	Reformation {f}
reformer n.	Reformer {m}
refraction n.	Refraktion {f}
refrain v.t.	zurückhalten
refresh v.	auffrischen
refreshment n.	Erfrischung {f}
refrigerate v.	kühlen
refrigeration n.	Kältetechnik {f}
refrigerator n.	Kühlschrank {m}
refuge n.	Zuflucht {f}
refugee n.	Flüchtling {m}
refulgence adj.	Glanz {m}
refulgent adj.	glänzen
refund v.	rückzahlen
refund n.	Rückzahlung {f}
refurbish v.	aufpolieren
refusal n.	Weigerung {f}
refuse v.	weigern

refuse n.	Ablehnung {f}
refutation n.	Gegenargument {n}
refute v.	widerlegen
regain v.	zurückgewinnen
regal adj.	königlich
regard v.	betrachten
regarding prep.	betreffend
regardless adv.	ungeachtet
regenerate v.	regenerieren
regeneration n.	Regenerierung {f}
regent n.	Regent {m}
reggae n.	Reggae {n}
regicide n.	Königsmord {m}
regime n.	Regime {n}
regiment n.	Regiment {n}
region n.	Gebiet {n}
regional adj.	lokal
register n.	Register {n}
registrar n.	Standesbeamte {m,f}
registration n.	Eintragung {f}
registry n.	Register {n}
regress v.	zurückgehen
regret n.	Bedauern {n}
regrettable adj.	bedauerlich
regular adj.	regelrecht
regularity n.	Vorschriftsmäßigkeit {f}
regularize v.	regeln
regulate v.	regeln
regulation n.	Vorschrift {f}
regulator n.	Regler {m}
rehabilitate v.	rehabilitieren
rehabilitation n.	Rehabilitation {f}
rehearsal n.	Probe {f}
rehearse v.	proben

151

reign	v.	regieren	**relic**	n.	Relikt {n}
reimburse	v.	entschädigen	**relief**	n.	Linderung {f}
rein	n.	Zügel {m}	**relieve**	v.	erleichtern
reincarnate	v.	reinkarnieren	**religion**	n.	Religion {f}
reinforce	v.	verstärken	**religious**	adj.	religiös
reinforcement	n.	Verstärkung {f}	**relinquish**	v.	loslassen
reinstate	v.	wiedereinsetzen	**relish**	v.	genießen
reinstatement	n.	Wiedereinsetzung {f}	**relocate**	v.	zurücksetzen
reiterate	v.	wiederholen	**reluctance**	n.	Abneigung {f}
reiteration	n.	Wiederholung {f}	**reluctant**	adj.	zurückhaltend
reject	v.	zurückweisen	**rely**	v.	vertrauen
rejection	n.	Rückweisung {f}	**remain**	v.	bleiben
rejoice	v.	frohlocken	**remainder**	n.	Restbestand {m}
rejoin	v.	vereinigen	**remains**	n.	Rest {m}
rejoinder	n.	Erwiderung {f}	**remand**	v.	zurückschicken
rejuvenate	v.	verjüngen	**remark**	v.	merken
rejuvenation	n.	Verjüngung {f}	**remarkable**	adj.	beachtenswert
relapse	v.	zurückfallen	**remedial**	adj.	abhelfend
relate	v.	berichten	**remedy**	n.	Heilmittel {n}
relation	n.	Beziehung {f}	**remember**	v.	erinnern
relationship	n.	Relation {f}	**remembrance**	n.	Erinnerung {f}
relative	adj.	relativ	**remind**	v.	mahnen
relativity	n.	Relativität {f}	**reminder**	n.	Mahnschreiben {n}
relax	v.	entspannen	**reminiscence**	n.	Reminiszenz {f}
relaxation	n.	Entspannung {f}	**reminiscent**	adj.	erinnernd
relay	n.	Relais {n}	**remiss**	adj.	lässig
release	v.	auslösen	**remission**	n.	Vergebung {f}
relegate	v.	verweisen	**remit**	v.	erlassen
relent	v.	nachgeben	**remittance**	n.	Geldüberweisung {f}
relentless	adj.	unbarmherzig	**remnant**	n.	Überrest {m}
relevance	n.	Sachlichkeit {f}	**remonstrate**	v.	protestieren
relevant	adj.	einschlägig	**remorse**	n.	Gewissensbiss {m}
reliable	adj.	verlässlich	**remote**	adj.	fern
reliance	n.	Vertrauen {n}	**removable**	adj.	abnehmbar

152

removal	*n.*	Abnahme {f}
remove *v.*		abtragen
remunerate *v.*		belohnen
remuneration	*n.*	Belohnung {f}
remunerative	*adj.*	lohnend
renaissance *n.*		Wiedergeburt {f}
render *v.*		huldigen
rendezvous *n.*		Verabredung {f}
renegade	*n.*	Überläufer {m}
renew *v.*		erneuern
renewal	*adj.*	erneuernd
renounce	*v.t.*	verzichten
renovate	*v.t.*	renovieren
renovation	*n.*	Renovierung {f}
renown *n.*		Glorie {f}
renowned	*adj.*	berühmt
rent	*n.*	Hausmiete {f}
rental	*n.*	Mietbetrag {m}
renunciation	*n.*	Verzicht {m}
reoccur *v.*		wiedergeschehen
reorganize *v.*		reorganisieren
repair *v.*		reparieren
repartee	*n.*	Schlagfertigkeit {f}
repatriate	*v.*	zurückführen
repatriation *n.*		Rückführung {f}
repay *v.*		zurückzahlen
repayment	*n.*	Rückzahlung {f}
repeal *v.*		aufheben
repeat *v.*		wiederholen
repel *v.*		abweisen
repellent	*adj.*	Abwehrmittel {n}
repent *v.*		bereuen
repentance	*n.*	Reue {f}
repentant	*adj.*	wiederholbar

repercussion	*n.*	Rückschlag {m}
repetition	*n.*	Wiederholung {f}
replace *v.*		auswechseln
replacement	*n.*	Ersatz {m}
replay *v.*		wiederholen
replenish	*v.*	auffüllen
replete *adj.*		reichlich
replica *n.*		Nachbildung {f}
replicate	*v.*	kopieren
reply *v.*		antworten
report *v.*		berichten
reportage	*n.*	Reportage {f}
reporter	*n.*	Reporter {m}
repose *v.*		ruhen
repository	*n.*	Aufbewahrungsort {m}
repossess	*v.*	wiedernehmen
reprehensible	*adj.*	tadelnswert
represent	*v.*	repräsentieren
representation	*n.*	Repräsentation {f}
representative	*adj.*	Stellvertretend
repress *v.*		unterdrücken
repression	*n.*	Unterdrückung {f}
reprieve	*v.*	befristen
reprimand	*v.*	rügen
reprint *v.*		umdrucken
reprisal *n.*		Repressalie {f}
reproach	*v.*	vorwerfen
reprobate	*n.*	verurteilen
reproduce	*v.*	reproduzieren
reproduction	*n.*	Wiedergabe {f}
reproductive	*adj.*	fruchtbar
reproof *n.*		Vorwurf {m}
reprove *v.*		tadeln
reptile	*n.*	Reptil {n}

153

republic	n.	Republik {f}
republican	adj.	republikanisch
repudiate	v.	ablehnen
repudiation	n.	Verstoßung {f}
repugnance	n.	Widerwille {m}
repugnant	adj.	widerlich
repulse	v.	abwehren
repulsion	n.	Abstoßung {f}
repulsive	adj.	abstoßend
reputation	n.	Ansehen {n}
repute	n.	Leumund {m}
request	n.	Anfrage {f}
requiem	n.	Seelenmesse {f}
require	v.	verlangen
requirement	n.	Bedingung {f}
requisite	n.	Requisit {n}
requisition	n.	Erfordernis {f}
requite	v.t.	vergelten
rescind	v.	aufheben
rescue	v.	retten
research	n.	Forschung {f}
resemblance	n.	Ähnlichkeit {f}
resemble	v.	gleichen
resent	v.	verübeln
resentment	n.	Ärger {m},
reservation	n.	Reservat {n}
reserve	v.	bewahren
reservoir	n.	Sammelbecken {n}
reshuffle	v.	umschütteln
reside	v.	wohnen
residence	n.	Residenz {f}
resident	n.	Ortsansässiger
residential	adj.	resident
residual	adj.	restlich

residue	n.	Abfallprodukt {n}
resign	v.	aufgeben
resignation	n.	Rücktritt {m}
resilient	adj.	robust
resist	v.	widerstehen
resistance	n.	Widerstand {m}
resistant	adj.	widerstandsfähig
resolute	adj.	entschlossen
resolution	n.	Entschluss {m}
resolve	v.	auflösen
resonance	n.	Resonanz {f}
resonant	adj.	resonant
resonate	v.	nachhallen
resort	n.	Resort {n}
resound	v.	widerhallen
resource	n.	Hilfsquelle {f}
resourceful	adj.	findig
respect	n.	Hinsicht {f}
respectable	adj.	ehrbar
respectful	adj.	respektvoll
respective	adj.	besonders
respiration	n.	Atmung {f}
respirator	n.	Atemgerät {n}
respire	v.	aufatmen
respite	n.	Pause {f}
resplendent	adj.	glänzend
respond	v.	antworten
respondent	n.	Beklagte {m,f}
response	n.	Antwort {f}
responsibility	n.	Verantwortung {f}
responsible	adj.	verantwortungsbewusst
responsive	adj.	ansprechbar
rest	v.	ausruhen
restaurant	n.	Restaurant {n}

154

restaurateur *n.*	Restaurateur {m}	**retire** *v.*	zurücktreten
restful *adj.*	ruhig	**retirement** *n.*	Ruhestand {m}
restitution *n.*	Rückerstattung {f}	**retiring** *adj.*	zurücktretend
restive *adj.*	unruhig	**retort** *v.*	erwidern
restoration *adj.*	Wiedereinsetzung {f}	**retouch** *v.*	retuschieren
restore *v.*	zurückerstatten	**retrace** *v.t.*	zurückverfolgen
restrain *v.*	zurückhalten	**retract** *v.*	zurückziehen
restraint *n.*	Hemmnis {n}	**retread** *v.*	runderneuern
restrict *n.*	einschränken	**retreat** *v.t.*	zurücktreten
restriction *n.*	Restriktion {f}	**retrench** *v.*	abbauen
restrictive *adj.*	einschränkend	**retrenchment** *n.* Ausgabenkürzung {f}
result *n.*	Ergebnis {n}	**retrial** *n.* Wiederaufnahmeverfahren {n}
resultant *adj.*	resultierend	**retribution** *n.*	Vergeltung {f}
resume *v.*	wiederaufnehmen	**retrieve** *v.*	wiederherstellen
resumption *n.*	Wideraufnahme {f}	**retriever** *n.*	Retter {m}
resurgence *n.*	Wiederauferstehung {f}	**retro** *adj.*	retro
resurgent *adj.*	wiederauflebend	**retroactive** *adj.*	rückwirkend
resurrect *v.*	erstehen	**retrograde** *adj.*	rückläufig
retail *n.*	Einzelhandelsabsatz {m}	**retrospect** *n.*	Rückblick {m}
retailer *n.*	Einzelhändler {m}	**retrospective** *adj.*	zurückblickend
retain *v.i.*	beibehalten	**return** *v.*	umstimmen
retainer *n.*	Halter {m}	**return** *n.*	Rücksendung {f}
retaliate *v.*	vergelten	**reunion** *n.*	Wiedervereinigung {f}
retaliation *n.* Vergeltungsmaßnahme {f}	**reunite** *v.*	wiedervereinigen
retard *v.*	verzögern	**reuse** *v.*	wiederverwerten
retardation *n.*	Verzögerung {f}	**revamp** *v.*	umgearbeiten
retarded *adj.*	behindert	**reveal** *v.*	enthüllen
retch *v.*	würgen	**revel** *v.*	feiern
retention *n.*	Spanne {n}	**revelation** *n.*	Preisgebung {f}
retentive *adj.*	zurückhaltend	**revenge** *n.*	Rache {f}
rethink *v.*	umdenken	**revenue** *n.*	Einkommen {n}
reticent *adj.*	verschwiegen	**reverberate** *v.*	zurückstrahlen
retina *n.*	Netzhaut {f}	**revere** *v.*	verehren
retinue *n.*	Gefolge {n}	**revered** *adj.*	verehrt

reverence	n.	Ehrfurcht {f}	rhodium	n.	Rhodium {n}

reverence *n.* Ehrfurcht {f}
reverend *adj.* ehrwürdig
reverent *adj.* ehrerbietig
reverential *adj.* ehrerbietigen
reverie *n.* Träumerei {f}
reversal *n.* Umkehrung {f}
reverse *v.* umsteuern
reversible *adj.* umkehrbar
revert *v.* zurückkehren
review *n.* Kritik {f}
revile *v.* verunglimpfen
revise *v.* überarbeiten
revision *n.* Überarbeitung {f}
revival *n.* Erweckung {f}
revivalism *n.* Wiederbelebung {f}
revive *v.* wiederbeleben
revocable *adj.* widerruflich
revocation *n.* Widerruf {m}
revoke *v.* widerrufen
revolt *v.* auflehnen
revolution *n.* Revolution {f}
revolutionary *adj.* revolutionär
revolutionize *v.* umwälzen
revolve *v.* drehen
revolver *n.* Revolver {m}
revulsion *n.* Ableitung {f}
reward *n.* Belohnung {f}
rewind *v.* umspulen
rhapsody *n.* Rhapsodie {f}
rhetoric *n.* Rhetorik {f}
rhetorical *adj.* phrasenhaft
rheumatic *adj.* rheumatisch
rheumatism *n.* Gelenkrheumatismus {m}
rhinoceros *n.* Nashorn {n}

rhodium *n.* Rhodium {n}
rhombus *n.* Rhombus {m}
rhyme *n.* Reim {m}
rhythm *n.* Rhythmus {m}
rhythmic *adj.* rhythmisch
rib *n.* Rippe {f}
ribbon *n.* Farbband {n}
rice *n.* Reis {m}
rich *adj.* reichhaltig
richly *adv.* wohlhabend
richness *n.* Reichtum {m}
rick *n.* Schober {m}
rickets *n.* Rachitis {f}
rickety *adj.* gebrechlich
rickshaw *n.* Rikscha {f}
rid *v.* loswerden
riddance *n.* Befreitsein {n}
riddle *n.* Rätsel {n}
riddled *adj.* enträtselt
ride *v.* reiten
rider *n.* Reiter {m}
ridge *n.* Rücken {m}
ridicule *n.* Spott {m}
ridiculous *adj.* lächerlich
rife *adj.* verbreitet
rifle *n.* Gewehr {n}
rifle *v.* riffeln
rift *n.* Riss {m}
rig *v.* takeln
rigging *n.* Takelage {f}
right *adj.* rechts
right *n* Recht {n}
righteous *adj.* rechtschaffen
rightful *adj.* rechtmäßig

rigid	adj.	starr	
rigmarole	n.	Geschwätz {n}	
rigorous	adj.	streng	
rigour	n.	Strenge {f}	
rim	n.	Rand {m}	
ring	n.	Klang {m}	
ring	v.	läuten	
ringlet	n.	Haarlocke {f}	
ringworm	n.	Ringelflechte {f}	
rink	n.	Spielfläche {f}	
rinse	v.	spülen	
riot	n.	Aufruhr {m}	
rip	v.	zerreißen	
ripe	adj.	reif	
ripen	v.	reifen	
riposte	n.	Gegenschlag {m}	
ripple	n.	Welligkeit {f}	
rise	v.	aufgehen	
risible	adj.	lachlustig	
rising	n.	Erhebung {f}	
risk	n.	Risiko {n}	
risky	adj.	geheuer	
rite	n.	Ritus {m}	
ritual	n.	Ritual {n}	
rival	n.	Konkurrent {m}	
rivalry	n.	Wettstreit {m}	
riven	n.	gespalten	
river	n.	Fluss {m}	
rivet	n.	Niete {f}	
rivulet	n.	Bach {m}	
road	n.	Weg {m}	
road works	n.	Straßenbau {m}	
roadworthy	adj.	verkehrssicher	
roadster	n.	Röster {m}	

roam	v.	wandern	
roar	n.	Gebrüll {n}	
roar	v.	anbrüllen	
roast	v.	braten	
rob	v.	berauben	
robber	n.	Räuber {m}	
robbery	n.	Raub {m}	
robe	n.	Robe {f}	
robot	n.	Roboter {m}	
robust	adj.	kräftig	
rock	n.	Felsen {m}	
rocket	n.	Rakete {f}	
rocky	adj.	felsig	
rod	n.	Stange {f}	
rodent	n.	Nagetier {n}	
rodeo	n.	Rodeo {n}	
roe	n.	Reh	
rogue	n.	Galgenstrick {m}	
roguery	n.	Gaunerei {f}	
roguish	adj.	schurkisch	
roister	v.	krakellen	
role	n.	Rolle {f}	
roll	v.i.	rollen	
roll	n.	Roulade {f}	
roll-call	n.	Appell {m}	
roller	n.	Walze {f}	
rollercoaster	n.	Achterbahn {f}	
romance	n.	Romanze {f}	
romantic	adj.	romantisch	
romp	v.	tollen	
roof	n.	Dach {n}	
roofing	n.	Bedachung {f}	
rook	n.	Gauner {m}	
rookery	n.	Krähenkolonie {f}	

157

room	*n.*	Raum {m}	**roving** *adj.*	umherstreichend
roomy	*adj.*	geräumig	**row** *n.*	Zeile {f}
roost	*n.*	Schlafplatz {m}	**rowdy** *adj.*	rüpelhaft
rooster	*n.*	Hahn {m}	**royal** *n.*	königlich
root	*n.*	Wurzel {f}	**royalist** *n.*	Royalist {m}

room *n.* Raum {m}
roomy *adj.* geräumig
roost *n.* Schlafplatz {m}
rooster *n.* Hahn {m}
root *n.* Wurzel {f}
rooted *adj.* verwurzelt
rope *n.* Seil {n}
rosary *n.* Rosenkranz {m}
rose *n.* Rose {f}
rosette *n.* Rosette {f}
roster *n.* Liste {f}
rostrum *n.* Rednerbühne {f}
rosy *adj.* rosig
rot *v.* verfaulen
rota *n.* Dienstliste {f}
rotary *adj.* umlaufend
rotate *v.* rotieren
rotation *n.* Drehung {f}
rote *n.* Routine {f}
rotor *n.* Läufer {m}
rotten *adj.* morsch
rouge *n.* Rouge {n}
rough *adj.* grob
roulette *n.* Roulette {n}
round *adj.* rund
roundabout *n.* Karussell {n}
rounded *adj.* abgerundet
roundly *adv.* rund
rouse *v.* wecken
rout *n.* Rotte {f}
route *n.* Strecke {f}
routine *n.* Routine {f}
rove *v.* ausfasern
rover *n.* Wandernde {m,f}

roving *adj.* umherstreichend
row *n.* Zeile {f}
rowdy *adj.* rüpelhaft
royal *n.* königlich
royalist *n.* Royalist {m}
royalty *n.* Lizenzgebühr {f}
rub *v.* abreiben
rubber *n.* Kautschuk {m}
rubbish *n.* Müll {m}
rubble *n.* Bruchstein {m}
rubric *n.* Rubrik {m}
ruby *n.* Rubin {m}
rucksack *n.* Rucksack {m}
ruckus *n.* Unruhe {f}
rudder *n.* Ruder {n}
rude *adj.* unanständig
rudiment *n.* Rudiment {n}
rudimentary *adj.* rudimentär
rue *v.* bereuen
rueful *adj.* reuig
ruffian *n.* Grobian {m}
ruffle *v.* sträuben
rug *n.* Vorleger {m}
rugby *n.* Rugby {n}
rugged *adj.* robust
ruin *n.* Ruine {f}
ruinous *adj.* verderblich
rule *n.* Regel {f}
rule *v.* herrschen
ruler *n.* Lineal {n}
ruling *n.* Entscheidung {f}
rum *n.* Rum {m}
rumble *v.* rumpeln
rumbustious *adj.* derb

ruminant	adj.	meditativ
ruminate	v.	wiederkäuen
rumination	n.	Wiederkäuen {n}
rummage	v.	stöbern
rummy	n.	Romme {n}
rumour	n.	Gerücht {n}
rumple	v.	zerknüllen
rumpus	n.	Krawall {m}
run	n.	Lauf {m}
run	v.	laufen
runaway	adj.	ausgerissen
rundown	adj.	Heruntergewirtschaftet
runway	n.	Rollbahn {f}
rung	n.	Stufe {f}
runnel	n.	Rinnsal {n}
runner	n.	Läufer {m}
runny	adj.	fließend
rupture	v.t.	zerreißen
rural	adj.	ländlich
ruse	n.	Kniff {m}
rush	v.	eilen
rusk	n.	Zwieback {m}
rust	n.	Rost {m}
rustic	adj.	bäuerlich
rusticate	v.	relegieren
rustication	n.	Landzurückgezogenheit {f}
rusticity	n.	Ländlichkeit {f}
rustle	v.	rascheln
rusty	adj.	rostig
rut	n.	Brunst {f}
ruthless	adj.	skrupellos
rye	n.	Roggen {m}

S

Sabbath	n.	Sabbat {m}
sabotage	v.	sabotieren
sabre	n.	Säbel {m}
saccharin	n.	Süßstoff {m}
saccharine	adj.	zuckersüß
sachet	n.	Kissen {n}
sack	n.	Sack {m}
sack	v.	entlassen
sacrament	n.	Sakrament {n}
sacred	adj.	heilig
sacrifice	n.	Opfer {n}
sacrifice	v.	opfern
sacrificial	adj.	opfernd
sacrilege	n.	Frevel {m}
sacrilegious		adj.	entweihend
sacrosanct	adj.	geheiligt
sad	adj.	betrübt
sadden	v.	betrüben
saddle	n.	Sattel {m}
saddler	n.	Sattler {m}
sadism	n.	Sattler {m}
sadist	n.	Sadist {m}
safari	n.	Safari {f}
safe	adj.	sicher
safe	n.	Safe {m}
safeguard	n.	Schutzvorrichtung {f}
safety	n.	Sicherheit {f}
saffron	n.	Safran {m}
sag	v.	senken
saga	n.	Saga {f}
sagacious	adj.	scharfsinnig
sagacity	n.	Scharfsinn {m}
sage	n.	Salbei {m}

sage	adj.	klug
sail	n.	Segel {n}
sail	v.	segeln
sailor	n.	Matrose {m}
saint	n.	Heilige {m,f}
saintly	adj.	heilig
sake	n.	Sake {m}
salable	adj.	verkaufsfähig
salad	n.	Salat {m}
salary	n.	Gehalt {n}
sale	n.	Verkauf {m}
salesman	n.	Händler {m}
salient	adj.	hervorragend
saline	adj.	salzig
salinity	n.	Salzigkeit {f}
saliva	n.	Speichel {m}
sallow	adj.	farblos
sally	n.	Aufbrechung {f}
salmon	n.	Lachs {m}
salon	n.	Salon {m}
saloon	n.	Kneipe {f}
salsa	n.	Salsa {n}
salt	n.	Salz {n}
salty	adj.	salzig
salutary	adj.	gesund
salutation	n.	Gruß {m}
salute	n.	Salut {m}
salvage	v.	retten
salvation	n.	Rettung {f}
salver	n.	Tablett {n}
salvo	n.	Salve {f}
Samaritan	n.	Samariter {m}
same	adj.	derselbe
sample	n.	Kostprobe {f}

sampler	n.	Probierer {m}
sanatorium	n.	Sanatorium {n}
sanctification	n.	Heiligung {f}
sanctify	v.	heiligen
sanctimonious	adj.	scheinheilig
sanction	v.	sanktionieren
sanctity	n.	Heiligkeit {f}
sanctuary	n.	Heiligtum {n}
sanctum	n.	Allerheiligstes {n}
sand	n.	Sand {m}
sandal	n.	Sandale {f}
sandalwood	n.	Sandelholz {n}
sander	n.	Zander {m}
sandpaper	n.	Schleifpapier {n}
sandwich	n.	Sandwich {n}
sandy	adj.	sandig
sane	adj.	zurechnungsfähig
sangfroid	n.	Kaltblütigkeit {f}
sanguinary	adj.	grausam
sanguine	adj.	heiter
sanitarium	n.	Kurort {m}
sanitary	adj.	gesundheitlich
sanitation	n.	Sanierung {f}
sanitize	v.	hygienisieren
sanity	n.	Vernunft {f}
sap	n.	Saft {m}
sapling	n.	Grünschnabel {m}
sapphire	n.	Saphir {m}
sarcasm	n.	Sarkasmus {m}
sarcastic	adj.	sarkastisch
sarcophagus	n.	Sarkophag {m}
sardonic	adj.	sardonisch
sari	n.	Sari
sartorial	adj.	elegant

sash	n.	Schärpe {f}	savoury	adj. schmackhaft
Satan	n.	Satan {m}	saw	n. Säge {f}
satanic	adj.	satanisch	saw	v. sehen
Satanism	n.	Satanismus {m}	sawdust	n. Sägemehl {n}
satchel	n.	Schulmappe {f}	saxophone	n. Saxophon {n}
sated	adj.	gesättigt	say	v. sagen
satellite	n.	Satellit {m}	saying	n. Sprichwort {m}
satiable	adj.	sättigend	scab	n. Krätze {f}
satiate	v.	sättigen	scabbard	n. Scheide {f}
satiety	n.	Sattheit {f}	scabies	n. Krätze {f}
satin	n.	Satin {m}	scabrous	adj. heikel
satire	n.	Satire {f}	scaffold	n. Schafott {n}
satirical	adj.	satirisch	scaffolding	n. Grundlage {f}
satirist	n.	Satiriker {m}	scald	v. verbrühen
satirize	v.	verspotten	scale	n. Skalierung {f}
satisfaction	n.	Befriedigung {f}	scallop	n. Kammmuschel {f}
satisfactory	adj.	befriedigend	scalp	n. Skalp {m}
satisfy	v.	befriedigen	scam	n. Betrug {m}
saturate	v.	sättigen	scamp	n. Schuft {m}
saturation	n.	Sättigung {f}	scamper	v.t. hetzen
Saturday	n.	Samstag {m}	scan	v. untersuchen
saturnine	adj.	düster	scanner	n. Scanner {m}
sauce	n.	Soße {f}	scandal	n. Skandal {m}
saucer	n.	Untersatz {m}	scandalize	v. anecken
saucy	adj.	schlüpfrig	scant	adj. knapp
sauna	n.	Sauna {f}	scanty	adj. dürftig
saunter	v.	schlendern	scapegoat	n. Sündenbock {m}
sausage	n.	Wurst {f}	scar	n. Narbe {f}
savage	adj.	wild	scarce	adj. selten
savagery	n.	Wildheit {f}	scarcely	adv. kaum
save	v.	retten	scare	v. verscheuchen
savings	n.	Ersparnisse {pl}	scarecrow	n. Vogelscheuche {f}
saviour	n.	Retter {m}	scarf	n. Kopftuch {n}
savour	v.t.	geniessen	scarlet	n. Scharlach {m}

scarp *n.*	Eskarpe {f}	
scary *adj.*	erschreckend	
scathing *adj.*	vernichtend	
scatter *v.*	zerstreuen	
scavenge *v.*	reinigen	
scenario *n.*	Szenario {n}	
scene *n.*	Szene {f}	
scenery *n.*	Szenerie {f}	
scenic *adj.*	landschaftlich	
scent *n.*	Duftstoff {m}	
sceptic *n.*	Skeptiker {m}	
sceptical *adj.*	skeptisch	
sceptre *n.*	Zepter {n}	
schedule *n.*	Zeitplan {m}	
schematic *adj.*	schematisch	
scheme *n.*	Schema {n}	
schism *n.*	Spaltung {f}	
schizophrenia *n.*	Schizophrenie {f}	
scholar *n.*	Gelehrte {m,f}	
scholarly *adj.*	wissenschaftlich	
scholarship *n.*	Stipendium {n}	
scholastic *adj.*	akademisch	
school *n.*	Schule {f}	
sciatica *n.*	Ischias {m}	
science *n.*	Wissenschaft {f}	
scientific *adj.*	wissenschaftlich	
scientist *n.*	Wissenschaftler {m}	
scintillating *adj.*	funkelnd	
scissors *n.*	Schere {f}	
scoff *v.i.*	verspotten	
scold *v.*	schelten	
scoop *n.*	Baggereimer {m}	
scooter *n.*	Roller {m}	
scope *n.*	Umfang {m}	

scorch *v.*	stechen	
score *n.*	Filmmusik {f}	
score *v.*	schaffen	
scorer *n.*	Schützer {m}	
scorn *n.*	Verachtung {f}	
scornful *adj.*	verächtlich	
scorpion *n.*	Skorpion {m}	
Scot *n.*	Schotte {m}	
scot-free *adv.*	ungeschoren	
scoundrel *n.*	Schurke {m}	
scour *v.*	umherstreifen	
scourge *n.*	Geißel {f}	
scout *n.*	Pfadfinder {m}	
scowl *n.*	Gesichtsausdruck {m}	
scrabble *v.*	krabbeln	
scraggy *adj.*	rau	
scramble *v.*	klettern	
scrap *n.*	Schrott {m}	
scrape *v.*	kratzen	
scrappy *adj.*	rauflustige	
scratch *v.t.*	kratzen	
scrawl *v.*	kritzeln	
scrawny *adj.*	dürr	
screech *n.*	Schreierei {f}	
scream *v.*	schreien	
screed *n.*	Estrich {m}	
screen *n.*	Bildschirm {m}	
screw *n.*	Bulle {m}	
screwdriver *n.*	Schraubenzieher {m}	
scribble *v.*	kritzeln	
scribe *n.*	Anreißer {m}	
scrimmage *n.*	Handgemenge {n}	
scrimp *v.*	bemessen	
script *n.*	Drehbuch {n}	

scripture	n.	Manuskript {n}	seat	n.	Amtssitz {m}
scroll	n.	Bildschirmrollen {n}	seating	n.	Fundament {n}
scrooge	n.	Geizhals {m}	secede	v.	getrennen
scrub	v.	scheuern	secession	n.	Sezession {f}
scruffy	adj.	unsauber	seclude	v.	abschließen
scrunch	v.	knirschen	secluded	adj.	abschließen
scruple	n.	Skrupel {pl}	seclusion	n.	Abgeschlossenheit {f}
scrupulous	adj.	ängstlich	second	adj.	zweiter
scrutinize	v.	prüfen	secondary	adj.	sekundär
scrutiny	n.	Prüfung {f}	secrecy	n.	Heimlichkeit {f}
scud	v.	jagen	secret	adj.	geheim
scuff	v.	schlurfen	secretariat	n.	Sekretariat {n}
scuffle	n.	Gewühl {n}	secretary	n.	Sekretär
sculpt	v.	formen	secrete	v.	absondern
sculptor	n.	Skulpteur {m}	secretion	n.	Absonderung {f}
sculptural	adj.	bildhauerisch	secretive	adj.	verschwiegen
sculpture	n.	Bildhauerei {f}	sect	n.	Sekte {f}
scum	n.	Abschaum {m}	sectarian	adj.	Sektierer {m}
scurrilous	adj.	gemein	section	n.	Abschnitt
scythe	n.	Sense {f}	sector	n.	Sektor {m}
sea	n.	Meer {n}	secular	adj.	weltlich
seagull	n.	Seemöwe {f}	secure	adj.	sicher
seal	n.	Robbe {f}	security	n.	Sicherheit {f}
sealant	n.	Dichtungsmittel {n}	sedan	n.	Sänfte {f}
seam	n.	Naht {f}	sedate	adj.	gesetzt
seamless	adj.	nahtlos	sedation	n.	Beruhigung {f}
seamy	adj.	gesäumt	sedative	n.	Beruhigungsmittel {n}
sear	v.	versegen	sedentary	adj.	sesshaft
search	v.	suchen	sediment	n.	Ablagerung {f}
seaside	n.	Strand {m}	sedition	n.	Aufwiegelung {f}
season	n.	Jahreszeit {f}	seditious	adj.	aufwiegelnd
seasonable	adj.	zeitgemäß	seduce	v.	verführen
seasonal	adj.	jahreszeitlich	seduction	n.	Verführung {f}
seasoning	n.	Würze {f}	seductive	adj.	verführerisch

163

sedulous	*adj.*	eifrig
see	*v.*	sehen
seed	*n.*	Saat {f}
seedy	*adj.*	schäbig
seek	*v.i.*	suchen
seem	*v.*	scheinen
seemly	*adj.*	geziemend
seep	*v.*	tropfen
seer	*n.*	Seher {m}
see-saw	*n.*	Schaukelbrett {n}
segment	*n.*	Segment {n}
segregate	*v.*	trennen
segregation	*n.*	Trennung {f}
seismic	*adj.*	seismisch
seize	*v.*	ergreifen
seizure	*n.*	Ergreifung {f}
seldom	*adv.*	selten
select	*v.*	auswählen
selection	*n.*	Auswahl {f}
selective	*adj.*	trennscharf
self	*n.*	selbst
selfish	*adj.*	egoistisch
selfless	*adj.*	selbstlos
self-made	*adj.*	selbstgemacht
sell	*v.*	verkaufen
seller	*n.*	Verkäufer {m}
selvedge	*n.*	Webkante {f}
semantic	*adj.*	semantisch
semblance	*n.*	Anschein {m}
semen	*n.*	Samenflüssigkeit {f}
semester	*n.*	Semester {m}
semicircle	*n.*	Halbkreis {m}
semicolon	*n.*	Semikolon {n}
seminal	*adj.*	fruchtbar

seminar	*n.*	Seminar {n}
semitic	*adj.*	semitisch
senate	*n.*	Senat {m}
senator	*n.*	Senator {m}
senatorial	*adj.*	senatorial
send	*v.*	senden
senile	*adj.*	greisenhaft
senility	*n.*	Senilität {f}
senior	*adj.*	älter, Senior {m}
seniority	*n.*	Alter {n}
sensation	*n.*	Wahrnehmung {f}
sensational	*adj.*	spektakulär
sensationalize	*v.*	aufsehenerregen
sense	*n.*	Sinn {m}
senseless	*adj.*	sinnlos
sensibility	*n.*	Sensibilität {f}
sensible	*adj.*	spürbar
sensitive	*adj.*	sensibel
sensitize	*v.*	empfindlichen
sensor	*n.*	Sensor {m}
sensory	*adj.*	sensorisch
sensual	*adj.*	sinnlich
sensualist	*n.*	Sensualist {m}
sensuality	*n.*	Sinnlichkeit {f}
sensuous	*adj.*	sinnenfreudig
sentence	*n.*	Urteilsspruch {m}
sententious	*adj.*	geschwollen
sentient	*adj.*	empfindend
sentiment	*n.*	Empfindung {f}
sentimental	*adj.*	gefühlsduselig
sentinel	*n.*	Hinweiszeichen {n}
sentry	*n.*	Wachposten {m}
separable	*adj.*	trennbar
separate	*v.*	gesondern

separation	n.	Abscheidung {f}
separatist	n.	Separatist {m}
sepsis	n.	Blutvergiftung {f}
September	n.	September {m}
septic	adj.	septisch
sepulchral	adj.	düster
sepulchre	n.	Grab {n}
sepulture	n.	Begräbnis {n}
sequel	n.	Folge {f}
sequence	n.	Serie {f}
sequential	adj.	folgerichtig
sequester	v.	absondern
serene	adj.	heiter
serenity	n.	Heiterkeit {f}
serf	n.	Leibeigene {m,f}
serge	n.	Serge {f}
sergeant	n.	Feldwebel {m}
serial	adj.	hintereinander
serialize	v.	anordnen
series	n.	Serie {f}
serious	adj.	ernstzunehmend
sermon	n.	Predigt {f}
sermonize	v.	predigen
serpent	n.	Schlange {f}
serpentine	adj.	gewunden
serrated	adj.	gezahnt
servant	n.	Dienstmädchen {f}
serve	v.	servieren
server	n.	Diener {m}
service	n.	Bedienung {f}
serviceable	adj.	gebrauchsfähig
serviette	n.	Serviette {f}
servile	adj.	unterwürfig
servility	n.	Unterwürfigkeit {f}

serving	n.	Portion {f}
sesame	n.	Sesam {m}
session	n.	Sitzung {f}
set	v.	einsetzen
set	n.	Zusammenstellung {f}
settee	n.	Sofa {n}
setter	n.	Vorstehhund {m}
setting	n.	Umgebung {f}
settle	v.	einziehen
settlement	n.	Vereinbarung {f}
settler	n.	Siedler {m}
seven	adj. & n.	sieben
seventeen	adj. & n.	siebzehn
seventeenth	adj. & n.	siebzehnte
seventh	adj. & n.	siebente
seventieth	adj. & n.	siebzigste
seventy	adj. & n.	siebzig
sever	v.	ernst
several	adj. & pron.	verschieden
severance	n.	Abbruch {m}
severe	adj.	streng
severity	n.	Strenge {f}
sew	v.	nähen
sewage	n.	Abwasser {n}
sewer	n.	Kanalisationsrohr {n}
sewerage	n.	Kanalisation {f}
sex	n.	Geschlecht {n}
sexism	n.	Sexismus {m}
sexton	n.	Kirchendiener {m}
sextuplet	n.	Sechsling {m}
sexual	adj.	sexuell
sexuality	n.	Sexualität {f}
sexy	adj.	sexy
shabby	adj.	schäbig

165

shack n.	Schuppen {m}	**shaven** adj.	rasiert
shackle n.	Schäkel {m}	**shaving** n.	Rasur {f}
shade n.	Schatten {m}	**shawl** n.	Umhang {m}
shade v.	schattieren	**she** pron.	sie
shadow n.	Schatten {m}	**sheaf** n.	Bündel {n}
shadowy a.	schattenhaft	**shear** v.	scheren
shady adj.	schattig	**sheath** n.	Futteral {n}
shaft n.	Schacht {m}	**shed** n.	Baracke {f}
shag n.	Krähenscharbe {f}	**sheen** n.	Glanz {m}
shake v.	schütteln	**sheep** n.	Schaf {n}
shaky adj.	wacklig	**sheepish** adj.	schüchtern
shall v.	sollen	**sheer** adj.	hauchdünn
shallow adj.	seicht	**sheet** n.	Platte {f}
sham n.	Fälschung {f}	**shelf** n.	Einlegeboden {m}
shamble v.	watscheln	**shell** n.	Muschel {f}
shambles n.	Schlachtbank {f}	**shelter** n.	Schutzdach {n}
shame n.	Schande {f}	**shelve** v.	lagern
shameful adj.	schändlich	**shepherd** n.	Schafhirt {m}
shameless adj.	schamlos	**shield** n.	Schild {n}
shampoo n.	Haarwaschmittel {n}	**shift** v.	abwälzen
shank n.	Wasserläufer {m}	**shiftless** adj.	hilflos
shanty n.	Schuppen {m}	**shifty** adj.	gerissen
shape n.	Form {f}	**shimmer** v.	schimmern
shapeless adj.	formlos	**shin** n.	Schienbein {n}
shapely adj.	wohlgeformt	**shine** v.	glänzen
shard n.	Scherbe {f}	**shingle** n.	Schindel {f}
share n.	Anteil {m}	**shiny** adj.	glänzend
shark n.	Haifisch {m}	**ship** n.	Schiff {n}
sharp adj.	schaftem	**shipment** n.	Versand {m}
sharpen v.	schärfen	**shipping** n.	Versendung {f}
sharpener n.	Schärfer {m}	**shipwreck** n.	Schiffbruch {m}
shatter v.t.	zerrütten	**shipyard** n.	Schiffswerft {f}
shattering adj.	zerrüttend	**shire** n.	Grafschaft {f}
shave v.	rasieren	**shirk** v.	drücken

166

shirker	n.	Drückeberger {m}	shrapnel	n.	Schrapnell {n}

shirker *n.* Drückeberger {m}
shirt *n.* Hemd {n}
shiver *v.* schlottern
shoal *n.* Schar {f}
shock *n.* Stoß {m}
shock *v.* schockieren
shocking *adj.* schockierend
shoddy *adj.* kitschig
shoe *n.* Schuh {m}
shoestring *n.* Schuhsenkel {pl}
shoot *v.* schießen
shooting *n.* Jagd {f}
shop *n.* Laden {m}
shopkeeper *n.* Geschäftsinhaber {m}
shoplifting *n.* Ladendiebstahl {m}
shopping *n.* Einkaufen {n}
shore *n.* Küste {f}
short *adj.* kurz
shortage *n.* Kürzung {f}
shortcoming *n.* Mangel {m}
shortcut *n.* Kurzbezeichnung {f}
shorten *v.* verkürzen
shortfall *n.* Fehlbetrag {m}
shortly *adv.* bald
should *v.* sollten
shoulder *n.* Schulter {f}
shout *v.i.* schreiend
shove *v.* schaufeln
shovel *n.* Schaufel {f}
show *v.* Vorstellung {f}
showcase *n.* Vitrine {f}
showdown *n.* Showdown {m}
shower *n.* Krise {f}
showy *adj.* prächtig

shrapnel *n.* Schrapnell {n}
shred *n.* Stückchen {n}
shrew *n.* Spitzmaus {f}
shrewd *adj.* scharfsinnig
shriek *v.* kreischen
shrill *adj.* schrill
shrine *n.* Heiligengrab {n}
shrink *v.* einschränken
shrinkage *n.* Zusammenschrumpfen
{n} shrivel *v.* schrumpeln
shroud *n.* Leichentuch {n}
shrub *n.* Busch {m}
shrug *v.* achselzucken
shudder *v.* schaudern
shuffle *v.t.* schieben
shun *v.t.* meiden
shunt *v.* Nebenschluss {m}
shut *v.* geschlossen
shutter *n.* Verschluss {m}
shuttle *n.* Pendelverkehr {m}
shuttlecock *n.* Federball {m}
shy *adj.* schüchtern
sibilant *adj.* zischend
sibling *n.* Geschwister {pl}
sick *adj.* krank
sickle *n.* Sichel {f}
sickly *adj.* kränklich
sickness *n.* Krankheit {f}
side *n.* Seite {f}
sideline *n.* Seitenlinie {f}
siege *n.* Belagerung {f}
siesta *n.* Siesta {f}
sieve *n.* Sieb {n}
sift *v.* siebend

sigh	*v.i.*	seufen
sight	*n.*	Sehenswürdigkeit {f}
sighting	*n.*	Ziel {n}
sightseeing	*n.*	Besichtigung {f}
sign	*n.*	Zeichen {n}
signal	*n.*	Signal {n}
signatory	*n.*	Signatur {f}
signature	*n.*	Unterschrift {f}
significance	*n.*	Bedeutung {f}
significant	*adj.*	bedeutsamen
signification	*n.*	Sinn {m}
signify	*v.*	bedeuten
silence	*n.*	Stille {f}
silencer	*n.*	Schalldämpfer {m}
silent	*adj.*	still
silhouette	*n.*	Schattenbild {n}
silicon	*n.*	Silizium {n}
silk	*n.*	Seide {f}
silken	*adj.*	seidenweich
silkworm	*n.*	Seidenraupe {f}
silky	*adj.*	seidenartig
sill	*n.*	Türschwelle {f}
silly	*adj.*	albern
silt	*n.*	Schlamm {m}
silver	*n.*	Silber {n}
similar	*adj.*	gleich
similarity	*n.*	Ähnlichkeit {f}
simile	*n.*	Gleichnis {n}
simmer	*v.*	sieden
simper	*v.*	albern
simple	*adj.*	einfältig
simpleton	*n.*	Naivling {m}
simplicity	*n.*	Einfachheit {f}
simplification	*n.*	Vereinfachung {f}

simplify	*v.*	vereinfachen
simulate	*v.*	simulieren
simultaneous	*adj.*	gleichzeitig
sin	*n.*	Sünde {f}
since	*prep.*	seitdem
sincere	*adj.*	aufrichtig
sincerity	*n.*	Aufrichtigkeit {f}
sinecure	*n.*	Ruheposten {m}
sinful	*adj.*	sündhaft
sing	*v.*	singen
singer	*a.*	Sänger {m}
single	*adj.*	einzeln
singlet	*n.*	Unterhemd {n}
singleton	*n.*	Singleton
singular	*adj.*	singulär
singularity	*n.*	Einzigartigkeit {f}
singularly	*adv.*	singularisch
sinister	*adj.*	unheimlich
sink	*v.*	sinken
sink	*n.*	Spültisch {m}
sinner	*n.*	Sünder {m}
sinuous	*adj.*	gewunden
sinus	*n.*	Stirnhöhle {f}
sip	*v.*	schlürfen
siphon	*n.*	Siphon {m}
sir	*n.*	Herr {m}
siren	*n.*	Sirene {f}
sissy	*n.*	Weichling {m}
sister	*n.*	Schwester {f}
sisterhood	*n.*	Schwesternschaft {f}
sisterly	*adj.*	schwesterlich
sit	*v.*	sitzen
site	*n.*	Standort {m}
sitting	*n.*	Sitzung {f}

situate	v.	aufstellen
situation	n., a	Lebenslage {f}
six	adj.& n.	sechs
sixteen	adj. & n.	sechzehn
sixteenth	adj. & n.	sechzehnte
sixth	adj. & n.	sechste
sixtieth	adj. & n.	sechzigste
sixty	adj. & n.	sechzig
size	n.	Größe {f}
sizeable	adj.	groß
sizzle	v.	zischen
skate	n.	Schlittschuh {m}
skateboard	n.	Skateboard {n}
skein	n.	Strang {m}
skeleton	n.	Skelett {n}
sketch	n.	Skizze {f}
sketchy	adj.	unzureichend
skew	v.	verdrehen
skewer	n.	Spieß {m}
ski	n.	Ski {m}
skid	v.	rutschen
skilful	adj.	geschickt
skill	n.	Geschick {n}
skilled	adj.	fachgerecht
skim	v.	blättern
skimp	adj.	kurz halten
skin	n.	Haut {f}
skinny	adj.	mager
skip	v.	überspringen
skipper	n.	Schiffer {m}
skirmish	n.	Plänkelei {f}
skirt	n.	Rock {m},
skirting	adj.	herumgehend
skit	n.	herumgehend

skittish	adj.	ungebärdig
skittle	n.	Kegel {m}
skull	n.	Schädel {m}
sky	n.	Himmel {m}
skylight	n.	Oberlicht {n}
skyscraper	n.	Wolkenkratzer {m}
slab	n.	Bramme {f}
slack	adj.	flau
slacken	v.	entspannen
slag	n.	Schlacke {f}
slake	v.t.	stillen
slam	v.	zuknallen
slander	n.	Ehrenkränkung {f}
slanderous	adj.	verleumderisch
slang	n.	Jargon {m}
slant	v.	neigen
slap	v.t.	schlagen
slash	v.	schlitzen
slat	n.	Lamelle {f}
slate	n.	Schieferplatte {f}
slattern	n.	Schlampe {f}
slatternly	adj.	schlampige
slaughter	n.	Massaker {n}
slave	n.	Sklave {f}
slavery	n.	Sklaverei {f}
slavish	adj.	sklavisch
slay	v.	erschlagen
sleaze	n.	Widerling {m}
sleazy	adj.	widerlich
sledge	n.	Schlitten {m}
sledgehammer	n.	Vorschlaghammer {m}
sleek	adj.	geschmeidig
sleep	n.	Schlaf {m}
sleeper	n.	Schwelle {f}

sleepy	*adj.*	schläfrig	**slowly**	*adv.*	langsam

sleepy *adj.* schläfrig
sleet *n.* Schneeregen {m}
sleeve *n.* Hülse {f}
sleigh *n.* Schlitten {m}
sleight *n.* Geschicklichkeit {f}
slender *adj.* schlank
sleuth *n.* Spürhund {m}
slice *n.* Brotscheibe {f}
slick *adj.* poliert
slide *v.* abgleiten
slight *adj.* schwach
slightly *adv.* geringfügig
slim *adj.* schlank
slime *n.* Schlamm {m}
slimy *adj.* schleimig
sling *n.* Armschlinge {f}
slink *v.* schleichen
slip *v.* ausgleiten
slipper *n.* Hausschuh {m}
slippery *adj.* glitschig
slit *v.t.* schlitzen
slither *v.* schlitteren
slob *n.* Schlumper {m}
slobber *v.* geifern
slogan *n.* Werbespruch {m}
slope *v.* neigen
sloppy *adj.* schlampig
slot *n.* Einwurf {m}
sloth *n.* Faulheit {f}
slothful *adj.* faul
slouch *v.* krumm dasitzen
slough *n.* Abrieb {m}
slovenly *adj.* schlampig
slow *adj.* langsam

slowly *adv.* langsam
slowness *n.* Langsamkeit {f}
sludge *n.* Abwasserschlamm {m}
slug *n.* Kugel {f}
sluggard *n.* Faulenzer {m}
sluggish *adj.* faul
sluice *n.* Schleuse {f}
slum *n.* Elendsviertel {n}
slumber *v.* schlummern
slump *v.* plumpsen
slur *v.* verschleifen
slurp *v.* schlürfen
slush *n.* Schneematsch {m}
slushy *adj.* matschig
slut *n.* Flittchen {n}
sly *adj.* schlau
smack *n.* Geschmack {m}
small *adj.* klein
smallpox *n.* Pocken {pl}
smart *adj.* pfiffig
smarten *v.* aufwachen
smash *v.* zertrümmern
smashing *adj.* kaputt schlagend
smattering *n.* Oberflächlichkeiten {pl}
smear *v.* anschmieren
smell *n.* Geruch {m}
smelly *adj.* muffig
smidgen *n.* kleine Menge
smile *v.* lächeln
smirk *v.* grinsen
smith *n.* Schmied {m}
smock *n.* Kittel {m}
smog *n.* Smog {m}
smoke *n.* Rauch {m}

smoky *adj.*	rauchig	**snobbish**	*adj.*	protzig
smooch *v.*	schmusen	**snooker**	*n.*	Snooker {n}
smooth *adj.*	straff	**snooze** *v.*		dösen
smoothie *n.*	Smoothie {m}	**snore** *n.*		Schnarcher {m}
smother *v.*	ersticken	**snorte** *v.*		schnarchen
smoulder *v.*	schwelen	**snout** *n.*		Schnauze {f}
smudge *v.*	beschmutzen	**snow** *n.*		Schnee {m}
smug *adj.*	süffisant	**snowball**	*n.*	Schneeball {m}
smuggle *v.*	schmuggeln	**snowy** *adj.*		schneeig
smuggler *n.*	Schmuggler {m}	**snub** *v.*		anfahren
snack *n.*	Imbiss {m}	**snuff** *v.*		schnupfen
snag *n.*	Baumstumpf {m}	**snuffle** *v.*		schnuppern
snail *n.*	Schnecke {f}	**snug** *adj.*		mollig
snake *n.*	Schlange {f}	**snuggle**	*v.*	kuscheln
snap *v.*	schnappen	**so** *adv.* so		
snapper *n.*	Schnapper {m}	**soak** *v.*		durchnässen
snappy *adj.*	bissig	**soap** *n.*		Seife {f}
snare *n.*	fangen	**soapy** *adj.*		seifig
snarl *v.*	knurren	**soar** *v.i.*		aufsteigen
snatch *v.*	greifen	**sob** *v.*		schluchzen
snazzy *adj.*	pfiffig	**sober** *adj.*		nüchtern
sneak *v.*	heranschleichen	**sobriety**	*n.*	Ernsthaftigkeit {f}
sneaker *n.*	Tennisschuhe {pl}	**soccer** *n.*		Fußball {m}
sneer *n.*	Spott {m}	**sociability**	*n.*	Gemütlichkeit {f}
sneeze *v.i.*	niesen	**sociable**	*adj.*	gesellig
snide *adj.*	abfällig	**social** *adj.* sozial		
sniff *v.*	schnüffeln	**socialism**	*n.*	Sozialismus {m}
sniffle *v.*	schnüffeln	**socialist**	*n. & adj.* Sozialist {m}	
snigger *v.*	kichern	**socialize**	*v.*	sozialisieren
snip *v.*	schnippeln	**society** *n.*		Gesellschaft {f}
snipe *n.*	Schnepfe {f}	**sociology**	*n.*	Soziologie {f}
snippet *n.*	Schnipsel {n}	**sock** *n.*		Socke {f}
snob *n.*	Snob {m}	**socket** *n.*		Steckschlüssel {m}
snobbery *n.*	Snobismus {m}	**sod** *n.*		Rasenstück {n}

soda	n.	Mineralwasser {n}
sodden	adj.	durchweicht
sodomy	n.	Sodomie {f}
sofa	n.	Sofa {n}
soft	adj.	sanft
soften	v.	aufweichen
soggy	adj.	feucht
soil	n.	Boden {m}
sojourn	n.	Aufenthalt {m}
solace	n.	Trost {m}
solar	adj.	solar
solder	n.	Lötmaschine {f}
soldier	n.	Soldat {m}
sole	n.	Sohle {f}
solely	adv.	einzig
solemn	adj.	feierlich
solemnity	n.	Festlichkeit {f}
solemnize	v.	feiern
solicit	v.	bewerben
solicitation	n.	Bewerbung {f}
solicitor	n.	Rechtsanwalt
solicitous	adj.	bekümmert
solicitude	n.	Besorgtheit {f}
solid	adj.	fest
solidarity	n.	Verbundenheit {f}
soliloquy	n.	Selbstgespräch {n}
solitaire	n.	Solitär {n}
solitary	adj.	einsam
solitude	n.	Einsamkeit {f}
solo	n.	Solo {n}
soloist	n.	Solist {m}
solubility	n.	Löslichkeit {f}
soluble	adj.	löslich
solution	n.	Lösung {f}

solve	v.	lösen
solvency	n.	Zahlungsfähigkeit {f}
solvent	n.	Lösungsmittel {n}
sombre	adj.	düster
some	adj.	manche
somebody	pron.	jemand
somehow	adv.	irgendwie
someone	pron.	irgendjemand
somersault	n.	Salto {m}
something	pron.	etwas
somewhat	adv.	irgendwas
somewhere	adv.	irgendwo
somnambulism	n.	Nachtwandeln {n}
somnambulist	n.	Schlafwandler {m}
somnolence	n.	Schlafsucht {f}
somnolent	adj.	schläfrig
son	n.	Sohn {m}
song	n.	Lied {n}
songster	n.	Sänger {m}
sonic	adj.	akustisch
sonnet	n.	Sonett {n}
sonority	n.	Klangfülle {f}
soon	adv.	bald
soot	n.	Ruß {m}
soothe	v.	lindern
sophism	n.	Sophismus {m}
sophist	n.	Sophist {m}
sophisticate	v.	komplizieren
sophisticated	adj.	kompliziert
sophistication	n.	Ausgereiftheit {f}
soporific	adj.	ermüdend
sopping	adj.	triefend
soppy	adj.	durchweicht
sorbet	n.	Sorbet {n}

172

sorcerer	n. Zauberer {m}	spaniel n.	Wachtelhund {m}
sorcery n.	Zauberei {f}	Spanish	n. spanisch
sordid adj.	schmutzig	spank v.	verhauen
sore adj.	wund	spanking adj.	mächtig
sorely adv.	schlimm	spanner n.	Schraubenschlüssel {m}
sorrow n.	Leid {n}	spare adj.	überflüssig
sorry adj.	betrübt	sparing adj.	schonend
sort n.	Art {f}	spark n.	Funke {m}
sortie n.	Ausfall {m}	sparkle v.	prickeln
sough v.	rauschen	sparkling adj.	funkelnd
soul n.	Seele {f}	sparrow n.	Sperling {m}
soulful adj.	seelenvoll	sparse adj.	wenig
soulless adj.	seelenlos	spasm n.	Krampf {m}
soul mate	n. Seelenfreund {m}	spasmodic adj.	krampfhaft
sound n.	Ton {m}	spastic adj.	spastisch
soundproof adj.	schalldicht	spat n.	Gamasche {f}
soup n.	Suppe {f}	spate n.	Flut {f}
sour adj.	sauer	spatial adj.	räumlich
source n.	Ursprung {m}	spatter v.	bespritzen
souse v.	eintauchen	spawn v.	hervorbringen
south n.	Süden {m}	spay v.	entfernen
southerly adj.	südlich	speak v.	sprechen
southern adj.	südländisch	speaker n.	Sprecher {m}
souvenir n.	Andenken {n}	spear n.	Speer {m}
sovereign n.	Souverän {m}	spearhead n.	Speerspitze {f}
sovereignty n.	Souveränität {f}	spearmint n.	Grüne Minze {f}
sow n.	Sau {f}	special adj.	besonderes
spa n.	Kurort {m}	specialist n.	Fachmann {m}
space n.	Raum {m}	speciality n.	Spezialfach {n}
spacious adj.	geräumig	specialization n.	Spezialisierung {f}
spade n.	Spaten {m}	specialize v.	spezialisieren
spam n.	Frühstücksfleisch {n}	species n.	Spezies {f}
span n.	Spanne {f}	specific adj.	spezifisch
Spaniard n.	Spanier {m}	specification n.	Beschreibung {f}

specify v.	angeben	spinach n.	Spinat {m}
specimen n.	Muster {n}	spinal adj.	spinal
specious adj.	trügerisch	spindle n.	Spindel {f}
speck n.	Fleckchen {n}	spindly adj.	spindel
speckle n.	Speckle {m}	spine n.	Buchrücken {m}
spectacle n.	Schauspiel {n}	spineless adj.	wirbellos
spectacular adj.	eindrucksvoll	spinner n.	Spinner {m}
spectator n.	Zuschauer {m}	spinster n.	Junggesellin {f}
spectral adj.	gespenstisch	spiral adj.	spirale
spectre n.	Gespenst {n}	spire n.	Turmspitze {f}
spectrum n.	Spektrum {n}	spirit n.	Geist {m}
speculate v.	spekulieren	spirited adj.	lebendig
speculation n.	Spekulation {f}	spiritual adj.	geistlich
speech n.	Sprache {f}	spiritualism n.	Spiritismus {m}
speechless adj.	sprachlos	spiritualist n.	Spiritualist {m}
speed n.	Geschwindigkeit {f}	spirituality n.	Geistlichkeit {f}
speedway n.	Motorradrennbahn {f}	spit n.	Spucke {f}
speedy adj.	schnell	spite n.	Gehässigkeit {f}
spell v.t.	buchstabieren	spiteful adj.	gehässig
spellbound adj.	verzaubert	spittle n.	Speichel {m}
spelling n.	Schreibweise {f}	spittoon n.	Spucknapf {m}
spend v.	aufwenden	splash v.	anspritzen
spendthrift n.	Verschwender {m}	splatter v.	bespritzten
sperm n.	Sperma {n}	splay v.	ausbreiten
sphere n.	Sphäre {f}	spleen n.	Ärger {m}
spherical adj.	sphärisch	splendid adj.	großartig
spice n.	Gewürz {n}	splendour n.	Glorie {f}
spicy adj.	würzig	splenetic adj.	verdrießlich
spider n.	Spinne {f}	splice v.	verbinden
spike n.	Stift {m}	splint n.	Splint {m}
spiky adj.	stachelig	splinter n.	Span {m}
spill v.	umschütten	split v.	zersplitten
spillage n.	Verschüttung {f}	splutter v.	stottern
spin v.	drehen	spoil v.	verderben

174

spoiler	n.	Verderber	{m}
spoke	n.	Radspeiche	{f}
spokesman	n.	Sprecher	{m}
sponge	n.	Schwamm	{m}
sponsor	n.	Kostenträger	{m}
sponsorship	n.	Patenstelle	{f}
spontaneity	n.	Spontaneität	{f}
spontaneous	adj.	spontan	
spool	n.	Bandspule	{f}
spoon	n.	Löffel	{m}
spoonful	n.	Löffel	{m}
spoor	n.	Spur	{f}
sporadic	adj.	unregelmäßig	
spore	n.	Sporen	{pl}
sport	n.	Sport	{m}
sporting	adj.	sport...	
sportive	adj.	mutwillig	
sportsman	n.	Sportler	{m}
spot	n.	Stelle	{f}
spotless	adj.	fleckenlos	
spousal	adj.	häuslich	
spouse	n.	Ehegatte	{m}
spout	n.	Tülle	{f}
sprain	v.t.	verstauchen	
sprat	n.	Sprotte	{f}
sprawl	v.	ausbreiten	
spray	n.	Sprühwasser	{n}
spread	v.	spreizen	
spreadsheet	n.	Tabellenkalkulation	{f}
spree	n.	Spaß	{m}
sprig	n.	Zweigchen	{n}
sprightly	adj.	lebhaft	
spring	v.	springen	
sprinkle	v.i.	berieseln	

sprinkler	n.	Sprengapparate	{pl}
sprinkling	n.	Berieselungsanlage	{f}
sprint	v.	sprinten	
sprinter	n.	Sprinter	{m}
sprout	v.	entsprießen	
spry	adj.	hurtig	
spume	n.	Schaum	{m}
spur	n.	Vorschneider	{m}
spurious	adj.	störend	
spurn	v.	ablehnen	
spurt	v.	plappern	
sputum	n.	Sputum	{n}
spy	n.	Spion	{m}
squabble	n.	Streithammel	{m}
squad	n.	Gruppe	{f}
squadron	n.	Staffel	{f}
squalid	adj.	schmutzig	
squall	n.	Schreihals	{m}
squander	v.	verschleudern	
square	n.	Platz	
squash	v.	zerquetschen	
squat	v.i.	hocken	
squawk	v.	quäken	
squeak	n.	quietschen	
squeal	n.	verraten	
squeeze	v.	quetschen	
squib	n.	Frosch	{m}
squid	n.	Tintenfisch	{m}
squint	v.	schielen	
squire	n.	Knappe	{m}
squirm	v.	herauswinden	
squirrel	n.	Eichhörnchen	{n}
squirt	v.	verspritzen	
squish	v.	quetschen	

175

stab	v.	erstechen
stability	n.	Dauerhaftigkeit {f}
stabilization	n.	Stabilisierung {f}
stabilize	v.	stabilisieren
stable	adj.	beständig
stable	n.	Pferdestall {m}
stack	n.	Stapel {m}
stadium	n.	Stadion {n}
staff	n.	Personal {n}
stag	n.	Hirsch {m}
stage	n.	Bühne {f}
stagecoach	n.	Postkutsche {f}
stagger	v.	wanken
staggering	adj.	wankend
stagnant	adj.	stillstehend
stagnate	v.	stagnieren
stagnation	n.	Stillstand {m}
staid	adj.	ruhig
stain	v.t.	beflecken
stair	n.	Treppe {f}
staircase	n.	Treppenhaus {n}
stake	n.	Anteil {m}
stale	adj.	fad
stalemate	n.	Patt {n}
staleness	n.	Schalheit {f}
stalk	n.	Stengel {m}
stalker	n.	Pirschjäger {m}
stall	n.	Verkaufsstand {m}
stallion	n.	Zuchthengst {m}
stalwart	adj.	robust
stamen	n.	Staubbeutel {m}
stamina	n.	Stehvermögen {n}
stammer	v.	stammeln
stamp	n.	Kennzeichen {n}

stamp	v.	abstempeln
stampede	n.	Exodus {m}
stance	n.	Haltung {f}
stanchion	n.	Wagenrunge {f}
stand	v.	stehen
standard	n.	Maßstab {m}
standardization	n.	Standardisierung {f}
standardize	v.	normieren
standing	n.	Stellung {f}
standpoint	n.	Standpunkt {m}
standstill	n.	Stillstand {m}
stanza	n.	Stanze {f}
staple	n.	Heftklammer {f}
staple	v.	klammern
stapler	n.	Heftklammer {f}
star	n.	Stern {m}
starch	n.	Stärke {f}
starchy	adj.	steif
stare	v.	starren
stark	adj.	krass
starlet	n.	Sternchen {n}
startling	n.	Star {m}
starry	adj.	sternhell
start	v.	starten
starter	n.	Anlasser {m}
startle	v.	aufschrecken
starvation	n.	Hungertod {m}
starve	v.	hungern
stash	v.	verstecken
state	n.	Staat {m}
stateless	adj.	zustandlos
stately	adj.	stattlich
statement	n.	Stellungnahme {f}
statesman	n.	Staatsman {m}

static	adj.	elektrostatisch	steeple n.		Kirchturm {m}
statically	adv.	elektrostatisch	steeplechase n.		Hindernisrennen {n}
station n.		Station {f}	steer	v.	Rind {n}
stationary	adj.	feststehend	stellar	adj.	sternenförmig
stationer	n.	Schreibwarenhändler	stem	n.	Vorbau {m}
{m} stationery	n.	Schreibwaren {pl}	stench n.		Gestank {m}
statistical	adj.	statistisch	stencil n.		Matrize {f}
statistician n.		Statistiker {m}	stenographer	n.	Stenograph {m}
statistics	n.	Statistik {f}	stenography	n.	Stenografie {f}
statuary	n.	Bildhauerkunst {f}	stentorian	adj.	stentorisch
statue n.		Standbild {n}	step	n.	Schritt {m}
statuesque	adj.	statuesk	steppe n.		Steppe {f}
statuette	n.	Statue {f}	stereo n.		Stereoanlage {f}
stature n.		Gestalt {f}	stereophonic	adj.	stereophonisch
status n.		Zustand {m}	stereoscopic	adj.	stereoskopisch
statute n.		Satzung {f}	stereotype	n.	stereoskopisch
statutory	adj.	satzungsgemäß	sterile	adj.	keimfrei
staunch	adj.	zuverlässig	sterility n.		Keimfreiheit {f}
stave n.		Strophe {f}	sterilization n.		Sterilisation {f}
stay	v.	bleiben	sterilize	v.	sterilisieren
stead n.		Stelle {f}	sterling	n.	Sterling
steadfast	adj.	fest	stern	adj.	ernst
steadiness n.		Zuverlässigkeit {f}	sternum	n.	Brustbein {m}
steady	adj.	ordentlich	steroid n.		Steroid {n}
steak n.		Beefsteak {n}	stertorous	adj.	röchelnd
steal	v.	bestehlen	stethoscope	n.	Stethoskop {n}
stealth n.		Heimlichkeit {f}	stew	n.	Eintopfgericht {n}
stealthily	adv.	heimlich	steward	n.	Flugbegleiter {m}
stealthy	adj.	heimlich	stick	n.	Schläger {m}
steam n.		Wasserdampf {m}	sticker n.		Aufkleber {m}
steamer	n.	Dampfer {m}	stickleback n.		Stichling {m}
steed n.		Ross {n}	stickler n.		Verfechter {m}
steel	n.	Stahl {m}	sticky	adj.	klebrig
steep	adj.	abschüssig	stiff	adj.	eingerostet

stiffen	*v.*	steifen	**stoke**	*v.*	schüren
stifle	*v.*	ersticken	**stoker**	*n.*	Heizer {m}
stigma	*n.*	Brandmal {n}	**stole**	*n.*	Stola {f}
stigmata	*n.*	Stigmata {n}	**stolid**	*adj.*	stur
stigmatize	*v.*	stigmatisieren	**stomach**	*n.*	Magen {m}
stile	*n.*	Steigen {pl}	**stomp**	*n.*	Bolzen {m}
stiletto	*n.*	Stöckelschuh {m}	**stone**	*n.*	Stein {m}
still	*adj.*	noch	**stony**	*adj.*	steinig
stillborn	*n.*	totgeboren	**stooge**	*n.*	Strohmann {m}
stillness	*n.*	Stille {f}	**stool**	*n.*	Stuhl {m}
stilt	*n.*	Pfeiler {m}	**stoop**	*v.*	beugen
stilted	*adj.*	gestelzt	**stop**	*v.*	anhalten
stimulant	*n.*	Anregungsmittel {n}	**stoppage**	*n.*	Sperrung {f}
stimulate	*v.*	erregen	**stopper**	*n.*	Stöpsel {m}
stimulus	*n.*	Reizmittel {n}	**storage**	*n.*	Speicherung {f}
sting	*n.*	Stich {m}	**store**	*n.*	Lager {n}
stingy	*adj.*	geizen	**storey**	*n.*	Stock {m}
stink	*v.*	stinken	**stork**	*n.*	Storch {m}
stint	*n.*	Pensum {n}	**storm**	*n.*	Sturm {m}
stipend	*n.*	Gehalt {n}	**stormy**	*adj.*	heftig
stipple	*v.*	tüpfeln	**story**	*n.*	Erzählung {f}
stipulate	*v.*	vereinbaren	**stout**	*adj.*	beleibt
stipulation	*n.*	Vereinbarung {f}	**stove**	*n.*	Küchenherd {m}
stir	*v.*	rühren	**stow**	*v.*	verdrücken
stirrup	*n.*	Steigbügel {m}	**straddle**	*v.*	spreizen
stitch	*n.*	Nadelstich {m}	**straggle**	*v.*	umherstreifen
stitch	*v.*	absteppen	**straggler**	*n.*	Nachzügler {m}
stock	*n.*	Aktien {pl}	**straight**	*adj.*	gerade
stockbroker	*n.*	Börsenmakler {m}	**straighten**	*v.*	gerade werden
stockade	*n.*	Lattenzaun {m}	**straightforward**	*adj.*	ehrlich
stocking	*n.*	Strumpf {m}	**straightway**	*adv.*	schnurstracks
stocklist	*n.*	Lagerliste {f}	**strain**	*v.*	anspannen
stocky	*adj.*	untersetzt	**strain**	*n.*	Bakterienstamm {m}
stoic	*n.*	Stoiker {m}	**strained**	*adj.*	angespannt

strait	*adj.*	schmal
straiten *v.i.*		beschränken
strand	*v.*	stranden
strange *adj.*		fremd
stranger	*n.*	Fremde {m,f}
strangle	*v.*	strangulieren
strangulation	*n.*	Strangulierung {f}
strap	*n.*	Zugband {n}
strapping	*adj.*	schnallend
stratagem	*n.*	List {f}
strategic	*adj.*	strategisch
strategist	*n.*	Stratege {m}
strategy	*n.*	Strategie {f}
stratify *v.*		schichten
stratum *n.*		Schicht {f}
straw	*n.*	Stroh {n}
strawberry	*n.*	Erdbeere {f}
stray	*v.*	verirren
streak	*n.*	Strähne {f}
streaky *adj.*		streifig
stream	*n.*	Strom {m}
streamer	*n.*	Luftschlange {f}
streamlet	*n.*	Bächlein {n}
street	*n.*	Straße
strength	*n.*	Stärke {f}
strengthen *v.*		bestärken
strenuous	*adj.*	tüchtig
stress	*n.*	Spannung {f}
stress *v.t.*		betonen
stretch *v.*		spannen
stretch *n.*		Strecke {f}
stretcher	*n.*	Trage {f}
strew *v.*		streuen
striation	*n.*	Streifenbildung {f}

stricken	*adj.*	streiken
strict	*adj.*	streng
strictly	*adv.*	strenges
stricture	*n.*	Verengung {f}
stride	*v.*	schreiten
strident *adj.*		scharf
strife	*n.*	Unfriede {m}
strike	*v.*	streiken
striker	*n.*	Streikende {m,f}
striking *adj.*		auffallend
string	*n.*	Zeichenkette {f}
stringency	*n.*	Strenge {f}
stringent	*adj.*	zwingend
stringy *adj.*		zäh
strip	*v.t.*	streifen
stripe	*n.*	Streifen {pl}
stripling	*n.*	Bürschchen {n}
stripper	*n.*	Schälmaschine {f}
strive	*v.*	eifern
strobe	*n.*	Abtastimpuls {m}
stroke	*n.*	Schlaganfall {m}
stroll	*v.*	bummeln
strong	*adj.*	stark
stronghold	*n.*	Feste {f}
strop	*v.*	abziehen
stroppy *adj.*		patzig
structural	*adj.*	strukturell
structure	*n.*	Bauweise {f}
strudel *n.*		Strudel {m}
struggle	*v.*	kämpfen
strum	*v.*	klimpern
strumpet	*n.*	Dirne {f}
strut	*n.*	Stütze {f}
stuart	*n.*	Einzelaktion {m}

stub	n.	Abriss {m}	stylized	adj. stilisiert
stubble	n.	Stoppel {m}	stylus	n. Griffel {m}
stubborn	adj.	starrköpfig	stymie	v. hindern
stucco	n.	Stuck {m}	styptic	adj. blutstillend
stud	n.	Knauf {m}	suave	adj. sanft
stud	v.	besetzen	subaltern	n. Untergeordnete {m}
student	n.	Schulkind {n}	subconscious	adj. unterbewusst
studio	n.	Studio {n}	subcontract	v. subunternehmung
studious	adj.	fleißig	subdue	v. bändigen
study	n.	Fleiß {m}	subedit	v. redigieren
study	v.	studieren	subject	n. unterwerfen
stuff	n.	Zeug {n}	subjection	n. Unterwerfung {f}
stuffing	n.	Füllung {f}	subjective	adj. subjektiv
stuffy	adj.	stickig	subjudice	adj. unterurteilen
stultify	v.	blamieren	subjugate	v. bezwingen
stumble	v.	stolpern	subjugation	n. Unterwerfung {f}
stump	n.	Stumpf {m}	subjunctive	adj. konjunktiv
stun	v.	blenden	sublet	v.t. untervermieten
stunner	n.	Mordsding {n}	sublimate	v. sublimieren
stunning	adj.	betäubend	sublime	adj. erhaben
stunt	v.	verkrüppeln	subliminal	adj. unterbewusst
stupefy	v.	verblüffen	submarine	n. Unterseeboot {n}
stupendous	adj.	erstaunlich	submerge	v. untertauchen
stupid	adj.	blöd	submerse	v. untertauchen
stupidity	n.	Dummheit {f}	submersible	adj. untertauchbar
stupor	n.	Stumpfheit {f}	submission	n. Unterbreitung {f}
sturdy	adj.	stämmig	submissive	adj. unterwürfig
stutter	v.	stottern	submit	v. fügen
sty	n.	Gerstenkorn {n}	subordinate	adj. unterordnet
stygian	adj.	stygisch	subordination	n. Abhängigkeit {f}
style	n.	Stil {m}	suborn	v. anstiften
stylish	adj.	stilvoll	subscribe	v. abonnieren
stylist	n.	Stilist {m}	subscript	adj. tiefgestellt
stylistic	adj.	stilistisch	subscription	n. Indizierung {f}

180

subsequent *adj.* nachfolgend
subservience *n.* Unterwürfigkeit {f}
subservient *adj.* dienstbar
subside *v.* sinken
subsidiary *adj.* ergänzend
subsidize *v.* sinken
subsidy *n.* Subvention {f}
subsist *v.* unterhalten
subsistence *n.* Lebensunterhalt {m}
subsonic *adj.* unterschall
substance *n.* Substanz {f}
substantial *adj.* stofflich
substantially *adv.* wesentlich
substantiate *v.* begründen
substantiation *n.* Begründung {f}
substantive *adj.* substantiell
substitute *n.* Ersatz {m}
substitution *n.* Platzhalter {m}
subsume *v.* fassen
subterfuge *n.* Ausflucht {f}
subterranean *adj.* unterirdisch
subtitle *n.* Untertitel {m}
subtle *adj.* feinsinnig
subtlety *n.* Feinheit {f}
subtotal *n.* Zwischensumme {f}
subtract *v.* abziehen
subtraction *n.* Subtraktion {f}
subtropical *adj.* subtropisch
suburb *n.* Vorstadt {f}
suburban *adj.* vorstädtisch
suburbia *n.* Vorort {m}
subversion *n.* Umsturz {m}
subversive *adj.* zersetzend
subvert *v.i.* zerrütten

subway *n.* Unterführung {f}
succeed *v.* gelingen
success *n.* Erfolg {m}
successful *adj.* erfolgreich
succession *n.* Folge {f}
successive *adj.* folgend
successor *n.* Nachfolger {m}
succinct *adj.* prägnant
succour *n.* Hilfe {f}
succulent *adj.* saftig
succumb *v.* unterliegen
such *adj.* derartig
suck *v.* saugen
sucker *n.* Säugling {m}
suckle *v.* säugen
suckling *n.* Säugling {m}
suction *n.* Absaugung {f}
sudden *adj.* plötzlich
suddenly *adv.* plötzlich
Sudoku *n.* Sudoku {m}
sue *v.t.* verklagen
suede *n.* Wildleder {n}
suffer *v.i.* erdulden
sufferance *n.* Duldung {f}
suffice *v.* ausreichen
sufficiency *n.* Zulänglichkeit {f}
sufficient *adj.* hinlänglich
suffix *n.* Nachsilbe {f}
suffocate *v.* ersticken
suffocation *n.* Erstickung {f}
suffrage *n.* Stimmrecht {n}
suffuse *v.* bedecken
sugar *n.* Zucker {m}
suggest *v.* vorschlagen

181

suggestible *adj.* vorschlagend
suggestion *n.* Vorschlag {m}
suggestive *adj.* sinnvoll
suicidal *adj.* selbstmörderisch
suicide *n.* Selbstmord {m}
suit *n.* Gesuch {n}
suitability *n.* Angemessenheit {f}
suitable *adj.* zweckmäßig
suite *n.* Gefolge {n}
suitor *n.* Freier {m}
sulk *v.* schmollen
sullen *adj.* mürrisch
sully *v.* beflecken
sulphur*n.* Schwefel {m}
sultana *n.* Sultanin {f}
sultry *adj.* schwül
sum *n.* Betrag {m}
summarily *adv.* formalitätenlos
summarize *v.* zusammenfassen
summary *n.* Inhaltsangabe {f}
summer *n.* Sommer {m}
summit*n.* Gipfel {m}
summon *v.* vorladen
summons *n.* Vorladung {f}
sumptuous *adj.* üppig
sun *n.* Sonne {f}
sundae*n.* Früchte-Eisbecher {m}
Sunday*n.* Sonntag {m}
sunder *v.* trennen
sundry *adj.* allerlei
sunken *adj.* versunken
sunny *adj.* sonnig
super *adj.* super
superabundance*n.* Überfluss {m}

superabundant *adj.* überreichlich
superannuation *n.* Pensionierung {f}
superb *adj.* herrlich
supercharger *n.* Gebläse {n}
supercilious *adj.* hochmütig
superficial *adj.* oberflächlich
superficiality *n.* Oberflächlichkeit {f}
superfine *adj.* extrafein
superfluity *n.* Überfluss {m}
superfluous*adj.* überflüssig
superhuman *adj.* übermenschlich
superimpose *v.* überlagern
superintend*v.* beaufsichtigen
superintendence*n.* Oberaufsicht {f}
superintendent *n.* Inspektor {m}
superior *adj.* oberer
superiority *n.* Übermacht {f}
superlative *adj.* äußerst
supermarket *n.* Supermarkt {m}
supernatural *adj.* übersinnlich
superpower*n.* Supermacht {f}
superscript *adj.* hochgestellt
supersede *v.* ersetzen
supersonic *adj.* Überschall
superstition*n.* Aberglaube {m}
superstitious *adj.* abergläubisch
superstore *n.* Laden {m}
supervene *v.* hinzukommen
supervise *v.* beaufsichtigen
supervision *n.* Aufsicht {f}
supervisor *n.* Dienstvorgesetzte {m,f}
supper *n.* Abendessen {n}
supplant *v.* verdrängen
supple *adj.* gefügig

supplement	n.	Zusatz {m}
supplementary	adj.	ergänzend
suppliant	n.	Bittsteller {m}
supplicate	v.	anflehen
supplier	n.	Kreditor {m}
supply	v.	liefern
support	v.	unterstützen
support	n.	Auflage {f}
suppose	v.	vermuten
supposition	n.	Voraussetzung {f}
suppository	n.	Zäpfchen {n}
suppress	v.	unterdrücken
suppression	n.	Zerschlagung {f}
suppurate	v.	eitern
supremacy	n.	Überlegenheit {f}
supreme	adj.	höchst
surcharge	n.	Preisaufschlag {m}
sure	adj.	sicher
surely	adv.	sicherlich
surety	n.	Bürgschaft {f}
surf	n.	Brandung {f}
surface	n.	Fläche {f}
surfeit	n.	Übersättigung {f}
surge	n.	Stromstoß {m}
surgeon	n.	Chirurg {m}
surgery	n.	Operation {f}
surly	adj.	verdrießlich
surmise	v.t.	vermuten
surmount	v.	übersteigen
surname	n.	Nachname {m}
surpass	v.	übertreffen
surplus	n.	Überschuss {m}
surprise	n.	Überraschung {f}
surreal	adj.	surrealistisch

surrealism	n.	Surrealismus {m}
surrender	v.	aufgeben
surrender	n.	Kapitulation {f}
surreptitious	adj.	betrügerisch
surrogate	n.	Ersatz {m}
surround	v.	umfangen
surroundings	n.	Umgebungen {pl}
surtax	n.	Steuerzuschlag {m}
surveillance	n.	Überwachung {f}
survey	v.t.	überblicken
surveyor	n.	Vermesser {m}
survival	n.	Überleben {n}
survive	v.	überleben
susceptible	adj.	empfänglich
suspect	v.	vermuten
suspect	n	Verdächtige {m}
suspend	v.	aufgeschoben
suspense	n.	Spannung {f}
suspension	n.	Aufschub {m}
suspicion	n.	Verdacht {m}
suspicious	adj.	misstrauisch
sustain	v.	aushalten
sustainable	adj.	tragbar
sustenance	n.	Unterhalt {m}
suture	n.	Zunähung {f}
svelte	adj.	schlank
swab	n.	Schwabe {m}
swaddle	v.	wickeln
swag	n.	Beute {f}
swagger	v.	schwadronieren
swallow	v.	schlucken
swamp	n.	Sumpf {m}
swan	n.	Schwan {m}
swank	v.	angeben

183

swanky	v.	angeberisch	
swap	v.	tauschen	
swarm	n.	Schwarm {m}	
swarthy	adj.	dunkeln	
swashbuckling	adj.	Säbelrasslerisch	
swat	v.	totschlagen	
swathe	n.	Schwaden {m}	
sway	v.	schaukeln	
swear	v.	schwören	
sweat	n.	Schweiß {m}	
sweater	n.	Pullover {m}	
sweep	v.	fegen	
sweeper	n.	Kehrer {m}	
sweet	adj.	süß	
sweet	n.	Nachtisch {m}	
sweeten	v.	versüßen	
sweetheart	n.	Liebling {m}	
sweetmeat	n.	Bonbon {n}	
sweetener	n.	Süßstoff {m}	
sweetness	n.	Lieblichkeit {f}	
swell	v.	schwellen	
swell	n.	Schwellen {n}	
swelling	n.	Schwellung {f}	
swelter	v.	verschmachten	
swerve	v.	ausweichend	
swift	adj.	schnell	
swill	v.	spülen	
swim	v.	schwimmen	
swimmer	n.	Schwimmer {m}	
swindle	v.	schwindeln	
swindler	n.	Schwindler {m}	
swine	n.	Schwein {n}	
swing	n.	Schaukel {f}	
swing	v.	schaukeln	

swinging	adj.	schaukelnd	
swipe	v.	klauen	
swirl	v.	wirbeln	
swish	adj.	sausend	
switch	n.	schalten	
swivel	v.	drehen	
swoon	v.	schwinden	
swoop	v.	schnappen	
sword	n.	Schwert {n}	
sybarite	n.	Schlemmer {m}	
sycamore	n.	Zuckerahorn {m}	
sycophancy	n.	Kriecherei {f}	
sycophant	n.	Kriecher {m}	
syllabic	adj.	silbenbildend	
syllable	n.	Silbe {f}	
syllabus	n.	Lehrplan {m}	
syllogism	n.	Vernunftschlüsse {f}	
sylph	n.	Luftgeist {m}	
sylvan	adj.	waldig	
symbiosis	n.	Symbiose {f}	
symbol	n.	Symbol {n}	
symbolic	adj.	symbolisch	
symbolism	n.	Symbolik {f}	
symbolize	v.	symbolisieren	
symmetrical	adj.	symmetrisch	
symmetry	n.	Symmetrie {f}	
sympathetic	adj.	sympathisch	
sympathize	v.	sympathisieren	
sympathy	n.	Beileid {n}	
symphony	n.	Sinfonie {f}	
symposium	n.	Symposium {n}	
symptom	n.	Symptom {n}	
symptomatic	adj.	symptomatisch	
synchronize	v.	synchronisieren	

synchronous	*adj.*	gleichzeitig
syndicate	*n.*	Arbeitsgemeinschaft {f}
syndrome	*n.*	Syndrom {n}
synergy	*n.*	Synergie {f}
synonym	*n.*	Synonym {n}
synonymous	*adj.*	synonym
synopsis	*n.*	Übersicht {f}
syntax	*n.*	Satzbau {m}
synthesis	*n.*	Synthese {f}
synthesize	*v.*	aufbauen
synthetic	*adj.*	künstlich
syringe	*n.*	Spritze {f}
syrup	*n.*	Sirup {m}
system	*n.*	System {n}
systematic	*adj.*	planmäßig
systematize	*v.*	systematisieren
systemic	*adj.*	systemisch

T

tab	*n.*	Streifen {m}
table	*n.*	Tisch {n}
tableau	*n.*	Bild {n}
tablet	*n.*	Tablette {f}
tabloid	*n.*	Boulevardzeitung {f}
taboo	*n.*	Tabu {m}
tabular	*adj.*	flach
tabulate	*v.*	tabellarisieren
tabulation	*n.*	Aufgliederung {f}
tabulator	*n.*	Tabulator {m}
tachometer	*n.*	Geschwindigkeitsmesser{m}
tacit	*adj.*	still
taciturn	*adj.*	schweigsam
tack	*n.*	Stift {m}
tackle	*v.t.*	anpacken

tacky	*adj.*	billig
tact	*n.*	Takt {m}
tactful	*adj.*	taktvoll
tactic	*n.*	Taktik {f}
tactician	*n.*	Taktiker {m}
tactical	*adj.*	taktisch
tactile	*adj.*	fühlbar
tag	*n.*	Kennzeichen {n}
tail	*n.*	Ende {n}
tailor	*n.*	Schneider {m}
taint	*v.*	verderben
take	*v.*	nehmen
takeaway	*n.*	Imbissstube {f}
takings	*n.*	Aufregungen {pl}
talc	*n.*	Talk {m}
tale	*n.*	Fabel {f}
talent	*n.*	Begabung {f}
talented	*adj.*	begabt
talisman	*n.*	Talisman {m}
talk	*v.*	sprechen
talkative	*adj.*	geschwätzig
tall	*adj.*	groß
tallow	*n.*	Talg {m}
tally	*n.*	Zähler {m}
talon	*n.*	Abriss {m}
tamarind	*n.*	Tamarinde {f}
tambourine	*n.*	Tamburin {n}
tame	*adj.*	zahm
tamely	*adv.*	zahm
tamp	*v.*	zustopfen
tamper	*v.*	einmischen
tampon	*n.*	Tampon {n}
tan	*v.*	gerben
tandem	*n.*	Reihe {f}

tang	n.	Angel {f}	
tangent	n.	Tangens {m}	
tangerine	n.	Mandarine {f}	
tangible	adj.	greifbar	
tangle	v.t.	verwirren	
tank	n.	Behälter {m}	
tanker	n.	Tankwagen {m}	
tanner	n.	Gerber {m}	
tannery	n.	Gerberei {f}	
tantalize	v.	peinigen	
tantamount	adj.	gleichbedeutend	
tantrum	n.	Wutanfall {m}	
tap	n.	Zapfstelle {f}	
tapas	n.	Tapas {n}	
tape	n.	Tonband {n}	
tape	v.i.	kleben	
taper	v.	zuspitzen	
tapestry	n.	Wandteppich {m}	
tappet	n.	Nockenstößel {m}	
tar	n.	Teer {m}	
tardy	adj.	langsam	
target	n.	Ziel {n}	
tariff	n.	Tarif {m}	
tarn	n.	Bergsee {m}	
tarnish	v.	trüben	
tarot	n.	Tarock {n}	
tarpaulin	n.	Zeltbahn {f}	
tart	n.	Törtchen {m}	
tartar	n.	Weinstein {m}	
task	n.	Aufgabe {f}	
tassel	n.	Quast {m}	
taste	n.	Geschmack {m}	
taste	v.	schmecken	
tasteful	adj.	geschmackvoll	

tasteless	adj.	geschmacklos	
tasty	adj.	schmackhaft	
tatter	n.	Lumpen {m}	
tattle	n.	Tratsch {m}	
tattoo	n.	Tattoo {n}	
tatty	adj.	schmuddelig	
taunt	n.	Spott {m}	
taut	adj.	gespannt	
tavern	n.	Gasthaus {n}	
tawdry	adj.	billig	
tax	n.	Gebühr {f}	
taxable	adj.	umsatzsteuerlich	
taxation	n.	Besteuerung {f}	
taxi	n.	Taxi {n}	
taxi	v.	einschätzen	
taxonomy	n.	Taxonomie {f}	
tea	n.	Tee {m}	
teach	v.	unterrichten	
teacher	n.	Lehrer {m}	
teak	n.	Teak {n}	
team	n.	Mannschaft {f}	
tear	v.	reißen	
tear	n.	Träne {f}	
tearful	adj.	tränenvoll	
tease	v.	reizen	
teat	n.	Brustwarze {f}	
technical	adj.	technisch	
technicality	n.	Formsache {f}	
technician	n.	Techniker {m}	
technique	n.	Verfahren {n}	
technological	adj.	technologisch	
technologist	n.	Technologe {m}	
technology	n.	Technik {f}	
tedious	adj.	nervtötend	

tedium	*n.*	Langeweile {f}	
teem	*v.*	wimmeln	
teenager	*n.*	Jugendliche {m,f}	
teens	*adj.*	Flegeljahre {pl}	
teeter	*v.*	wippen	
teethe	*v.*	wippen	
teetotal	*adj.*	enthaltsam	
teetotaller	*n.*	Abstinenzler {m}	
telecast	*v.t.*	übertragen	

telecommunications *n.*
Nachrichtentechnik {f}

telegram	*n.*	Telegramm {n}	
telegraph	*n.*	Telegraf {m}	
telegraphic	*adj.*	telegraphisch	
telegraphy	*n.*	Telegrafie {f}	
telepathic	*adj.*	telepathisch	
telepathist	*n.*	Telepathist {m}	
telepathy	*n.*	Gedankenübertragung {f}	
telephone	*n.*	Telefon {m}	
teleprinter	*n.*	Fernschreiber {m}	
telescope	*n.*	Teleskop {n}	
teletext	*n.*	Teletext {n}	
televise	*v.*	übertragen	
television	*n.*	Fernsehen {n}	
tell	*v.*	sagen	
teller	*n.*	Erzähler {m}	
telling	*adj.*	erzählend	
telltale	*adj.*	verräterisch	
temerity	*n.*	Unbesonnenheit {f}	
temper	*n.*	Gemütsart {f}	
temperament	*n.*	Temperament {n}	
temperamental	*adj.*	veranlagungsgemäß	
temperance	*n.*	Mäßigung {f}	
temperate	*adj.*	gemäßigt	

temperature	*n.*	Temperatur {f}	
tempest	*n.*	Gewitter {n}	
tempestuous	*adj.*	stürmisch	
template	*n.*	Zeichenschablone {f}	
temple	*n.*	Bethaus {n}	
tempo	*n.*	Tempo {n}	
temporal	*adj.*	zeitlich	
temporary	*adj.*	kurzzeitig	
temporize	*v.*	abwarten	
tempt	*v.*	verlocken	
temptation	*n.*	Versuchung {f}	
tempter	*n.*	Versucher {m}	
ten	*adj. & adv.*	zehn	
tenable	*adj.*	haltbar	
tenacious	*adj.*	klebrig	
tenacity	*n.*	Zähigkeit {f}	
tenancy	*n.*	Mietverhältnis {n}	
tenant	*n.*	Mieter {m}	
tend	*v.*	abzielen	
tendency	*n.*	Absicht {f}	
tendentious	*adj.*	tendenziös	
tender	*adj.*	zart	
tender	*n.*	Ausschreibung {f}	
tendon	*n.*	Sehne {f}	
tenement	*n.*	Wohnung {f}	
tenet	*n.*	Lehre {f}	
tennis	*n.*	Tennis {n}	
tenor	*n.*	Tenor {m}	
tense	*adj.*	verkrampft	
tensile	*adj.*	dehnbar	
tension	*n.*	Spannung {f}	
tent	*n.*	Zelt {n}	
tentacle	*n.*	Tentakel {m}	
tentative	*adj.*	provisorisch	

187

tenterhook *n.* Spannhaken {m}	**testicle** *n.* Hoden {pl}
tenth *adj. & n.* zehnter	**testify** *v.* bezeugen
tenuous *adj.* dünn	**testimonial** *n.* Zeugnis {n}
tenure *n.* Besitztitel {m}	**testimony** *n.* Bezeugung {f}
tepid *adj.* lau	**testis** *n.* Hoden {pl}
term *n.* Semester {n}	**testosterone** *n.* Testosteron {n}
termagant *n.* Zankteufel {m}	**testy** *adj.* reizbar
terminal *adj.* terminal	**tetchy** *adj.* gereizt
terminate *v.* beenden	**tether** *v.t.* anbinden
termination *n.* Ende {n}	**text** *n.* Text {m}
terminological *adj.* terminologisch	**textbook** *n.* Lehrbuch {n}
terminology *n.* Terminologie {f}	**textual** *adj.* inhaltlich
terminus *n.* Endstelle {f}	**textile** *n* Gewebe {n}
termite *n.* Termite {f}	**texture** *n.* Beschaffenheit
terrace *n.* Terrasse {f}	**thank** *v.* danken
terracotta *n.* Terrakotta {f}	**thankful** *adj.* dankbar
terrain *n.* Terrain {n}	**thankless** *adj.* undankbar
terrestrial *adj.* terrestrisch	**that** *pron. & adj.* dasjenige
terrible *adj.* furchtbar	**thatch** *n.* Dachstroh {n}
terrier *n.* Terrier {m}	**thaw** *v.* tauen
terrific *adj.* schrecklich	**the** *adj.* das
terrify *v.* erschrecken	**theatre** *n.* Theater {n}
territorial *adj.* territorial	**theatrical** *adj.* theatralisch
territory *n.* Gebiet {n}	**theft** *n.* Diebstahl {m}
terror *n.* Terror {m}	**their** *adj.* ihr
terrorism *n.* Terrorismus {m}	**theism** *n.* Theismus {n}
terrorist *n.* Terrorist {m}	**them** *pron.* ihnen
terrorize *v.* terrorisieren	**thematic** *adj.* thematisch
terry *n.* Frotteehandtuch {n}	**theme** *n.* Thema {n}
terse *adj.* gedrängt	**themselves** *pron.* sich selbst
tertiary *adj.* Tertiär	**then** *adv.* dann
test *n.* Probe {f}	**thence** *adv.* daher
testament *n.* Testament {n}	**theocracy** *n.* Theokratie {f}
testate *adj.* testiert	**theodolite** *n.* Theodolit

188

theologian *n.* Theologe {m}	thirteenth *adj. & n.* dreizehnte
theology *n.* Theologie {f}	thirtieth *adj. & n.* dreißigste
theorem *n.* Lehrsatz {m}	thirty *adj. & n.* dreißig
theoretical *adj.* theoretisch	this *pron. & adj.* diese
theorist *n.* Theoretiker {m}	thistle *n.* Distel {f}
theorize *v.* theorisieren	thither *adv.* dorthin
theory *n.* Theorie {f}	thong *n.* Stringtanga {m}
theosophy *n.* Theosophie {f}	thorn *n.* Dorn {m}
therapeutic *adj.* therapeutisch	thorny *adj.* dornig
therapist *n.* Therapeut {m}	thorough *adj.* vollständig
therapy *n.* Therapie {f}	thoroughfare *n.* Verkehrsstraße {f}
there *adv.* dort	though *conj.* obschon
thermal *adj.* thermisch	thoughtful *adj.* fürsorglich
thermodynamics *n.* Thermodynamik {f}	thoughtless *adj.* gedankenlos
thermometer *n.* Thermometer {n}	thousand *adj. & n.* tausend
thermos *n.* Thermosflasche {f}	thrall *n.* Leibeigene {m,f}
thermosetting *n.* Duroplastpresse {f}	thrash *v.* verprügeln
thermostat *n.* Temperaturregler {m}	thread *n.* Faden {m}
thesis *n.* These {f}	threat *n.* Bedrohung {f}
they *pron.* sie {pl}	threaten *v.* bedrohen
thick *adj.* dicht	three *adj. & n.* drei
thicken *v.* verdicken	thresh *v.* dreschen
thicket *n.* Dickicht {n}	threshold *n.* Schwelle {f}
thief *n.* Dieb {m}	thrice *adv.* dreimal
thigh *n.* Schenkel {m}	thrift *n.* Sparsamkeit {f}
thimble *n.* Fingerhüte {pl}	thrifty *adj.* geizig
thin *adj.* dünn	thrill *n.* Nervenkitzel {m}
thing *n.* Ding {n}	thriller *n.* Krimi {m}
think *v.* denken	thrive *v.* gedeihen
thinker *n.* Denker {m}	throat *n.* Hals {m}
third *adj.* dritte	throaty *adj.* rau
thirst *n.* Durst {m}	throb *v.* klopfen
thirsty *adj.* durstig	throes *n.* Geburtswehen {pl}
thirteen *adj. & n.* dreizehn	throne *n.* Thron {m}

189

throng	n.	Gedränge {n}	
throttle	n.	Gashebel {m}	
through	prep. &adv.	hindurch	
throughout	prep.	durchweg	
throw	v.	schmeißen	
thrush	n.	Drossel {f}	
thrust	v.	schieben	
thud	v.	aufschlagen	
thug	n.	Gangster {m}	
thumb	n.	Daumen {m}	
thunder	n.	Donner {m}	
thunderous	adj.	gewitterschwül	
Thursday	n.	Donnerstag {m}	
thus	adv.	folglich	
thwart	v.	hintertreiben	
thyroid	n.	Schilddrüse {f}	
tiara	n.	Tiara {f}	
tick	n.	Ticken {n}	
ticket	n.	Fahrkarte {f}	
ticking	n.	Drell {m}	
tickle	v.	kitzeln	
ticklish	adj.	kitzlig	
tidal	adj.	flutwelle	
tiddly	n.	Knirps {m}	
tide	n.	Flutwelle {f}	
tidings	n.	Nachricht {f}	
tidiness	n.	Ordnungsliebe {f}	
tidy	adj.	aufgeräumt	
tie	v.	binden	
tie	n.	Schnürer {m}	
tied	adj.	verschnürt	
tier	n.	Etage {f}	
tiger	n.	Tiger {m}	
tight	adj.	traff	

tighten	v.	festmachen	
tile	n.	Fliesen {m}	
till	prep.	bis	
tiller	n.	Ackerfräse {f}	
tilt	v.	kippen	
timber	n.	Nutzholz {n}	
time	n.	Zeit {f}	
timely	adj.	zeitgemäß	
timid	adj.	furchtsam	
timidity	n.	Furchtsamkeit {f}	
timorous	adj.	ängstlich	
tin	n.	Dose {f}	
tincture	n.	Tinktur {f}	
tinder	n.	Zunder {m}	
tinge	n.	Tönung {f}	
tingle	v.	klingen	
tinker	v.	basteln	
tinsel	n.	Lametta {n}	
tint	n.	Farbe {f}	
tiny	adj.	winzig	
tip	n.	Tipp {m}	
tipple	v.	zechen	
tipster	n.	Schwips {m}	
tipsy	adj.	angeheitert	
tiptoe	v.	schleichen	
tirade	n.	Tirade {f}	
tire	v.	ermüden	
tired	adj.	müde	
tireless	adj.	unermüdlich	
tiresome	adj.	ermüdend	
tissue	n.	Gewebe {n}	
titanic	adj.	titanisch	
titbit	n.	Leckerbissen {m}	
tithe	n.	Zehnte {m}	

titillate v.	kitzeln
titivate v.	schniegeln
title n.	Titel {m}
titled adj.	tituliert
titular adj.	titular
to prep.	zum
toad n.	Kröte {f}
toast n.	Toastbrot {n}
toaster n.	Toaster {m}
tobacco n.	Tabak {m}
today adv.	heute
toddle v.	schwanken
toddler n.	Kleinkind {n}
toe n.	Zehe {f}
toffee n.	Sahnebonbon {n}
tog n.	zusammen
toga n.	Toga {f}
together adv.	gemeinsam
toggle n.	Klöppel {m}
toil v.i.	quälen
toilet n.	Toilette {f}
toiletries n.	Toilettensache {f}
toils n.	schuften
token n.	Zeichen {n}
tolerable adj.	erträglich
tolerance n.	Toleranz {f}
tolerant adj.	tolerante
tolerate v.	zulassen
toleration n.	Duldung {f}
toll n.	Zoll {m}
tomato n.	Tomate {f},
tomb n.	Grab {n}
tomboy n.	Wildfang {m}
tome n.	Wälzer {m}

tomfoolery n.	Albernheit {f}
tomorrow adv.	morgen
ton n.	Tonne {f}
tone n.	Klang {m}
toner n.	Toner {n}
tongs n.	Zange {f}
tongue n.	Zunge {f}
tonic n.	Stärkungsmittel {n}
tonight adv.	heute Nacht
tonnage n.	Tonnage {f}
tonsil n.	Mandel {f}
tonsure n.	Tonsur {f}
too adv.	auch
tool n.	Werkzeug {n}
tooth n.	Zahn {m}
toothache n.	Zahnschmerz {m}
toothless adj.	zahnlos
toothpaste n.	Zahnpaste {f}
toothpick n.	Zahnstocher {m}
top n.	Gipfel {m}
topaz n.	Topas {m}
topiary n.	Formschnitt {m}
topic n.	Thema {n}
topical adj.	thematisch
topless adj.	busenfrei
topographer n.	Topograph {m}
topographical adj.	topographisch
topography n.	Topographie {f}
topping n.	Garnierung {f}
topple v.	stürzen
tor n.	Tor {n}
torch n.	Fackel {f}
toreador n.	Stierfechter {m}
torment n.	Qual {f}

tormentor	*n.*	Quäler {m}		**towards**	*prep.*	zu
tornado	*n.*	Tornado {m}		**towel**	*n.*	Handtuch {n}
torpedo	*n.*	Torpedo {n}		**towelling**	*n.*	abreibend
torpid	*adj.*	betäubt		**tower**	*n.*	Turm {m}
torrent	*n.*	Sturzflut {f}		**town**	*n.*	Stadt {f}
torrential	*adj.*	sturzflutartig		**township**	*n.*	Bürgerschaft {f}
torrid	*adj.*	glühend		**toxic**	*adj.*	giftig
torsion	*n.*	Verwindung {f}		**toxicology**	*n.*	Toxikologie {f}
torso	*n.*	Oberkörper {m}		**toxin**	*n.*	Giftstoff {m}
tort	*n.*	Schadensersatzrecht {n}		**toy**	*n.*	Spielzeug {n}
tortoise	*n.*	Schildkröte {f}		**trace**	*v.t.*	nachweisen
tortuous	*adj.*	gewunden		**traceable**	*adj.*	nachweislich
torture	*n.*	Qual {f}		**tracing**	*n.*	Verfolgung {f}
toss	*v.*	schleudern		**track**	*n.*	Fußspur {f}
tot	*n.*	Knirps {m}		**tracksuit**	*n.*	Trainingsanzug {m}
total	*adj.*	ganz		**tract**	*n.*	Gebiet {n}
total	*n.*	Gesamtbetrag {m}		**tractable**	*adj.*	lenkbar
totalitarian	*adj.*	totalitär		**traction**	*n.*	Ziehen {n}
totality	*n.*	Gesamtheit {f}		**tractor**	*n.*	Traktor {m}
tote	*v.*	schleppen		**trade**	*n.*	Geschäft {n}
totter	*v.*	wackeln		**trademark**	*n.*	Handelszeichen {n}
touch	*v.*	berühren		**trader**	*n.*	Händler {m}
touching	*adj.*	berührend		**tradesman**	*n.*	Gewerbetreibende {m}
touchy	*adj.*	zickig		**tradition**	*n.*	Tradition {f}
tough	*adj.*	schwierig		**traditional**	*adj.*	traditionell
toughen	*v.*	rühren		**traditionalist**	*n.*	Traditionalist {m}
toughness	*n.*	Zähigkeit {f}		**traduce**	*v.*	verleumden
tour	*n.*	Tour {f}		**traffic**	*n.*	Verkehr {m}
tourism	*n.*	Fremdenverkehr {m}		**trafficker**	*n.*	Traffiker {m}
tourist	*n.*	Tourist {m}		**trafficking**	*n.*	Handel {m}
tournament	*n.*	Turnier {n}		**tragedian**	*n.*	Tragiker {m}
tousle	*v.*	zausen		**tragedy**	*n.*	Tragödie {f}
tout	*v.*	werben		**tragic**	*adj.*	tragisch
tow	*v.*	getreideln		**trail**	*n.*	Trampelpfad {m}

trailer	n.	Anhänger {m}	
train	n.	Eisenbahn {f}	
train	v.	trainieren	
trainee	n.	Praktikant {m}	
trainer	n.	Trainer {m}	
training	n.	Ausbildung {f}	
traipse	v.	latschen	
trait	n.	Zug {m}	
traitor	n.	Verräter {m}	
trajectory	n.	Flugbahn {f}	
tram	n.	Straßenbahn {f}	
trammel	v.	fesseln	
tramp	v.	strolchen	
trample	v.	trampeln	
trampoline	n.	Trampolin {n}	
trance	n.	Trance {f}	
tranquil	adj.	ruhig	
tranquillity	n.	Ruhe {f}	
tranquillize	v.	beruhigen	
transact	v.	abwickeln	
transaction	n.	Transaktion {f}	
transatlantic	adj.	transatlantisch	
transceiver	n.	Empfänger {m}	
transcend	v.	überschreiten	
transcendent	adj.	überweltlich	
transcendental	adj.	transzendent	
transcontinental	adj.	Transkontinental	
transcribe	v.	abschreiben	
transcript	n.	Kopie {f}	
transcription	n.	Transkription {f}	
transfer	v.	übertragen	
transferable	adj.	überführbar	
transfiguration	n.	Umgestaltung {f}	
transfigure	v.	umgestalten	

transform	v.	umwandeln	
transformation	n.	Umformung {f}	
transformer	n.	Transformator {m}	
transfuse	v.	übertragen	
transfusion	n.	Transfusion {f}	
transgress	v.	übertreten	
transgression	n.	Übertretung {f}	
transient	adj.	vorübergehend	
transistor	n.	Transistor {m}	
transit	n.	Übergang {m}	
transition	n.	Überleitung {f}	
transitive	adj.	transitiv	
transitory	adj.	vorbeigehend	
translate	v.	übersetzen	
translation	n.	Übersetzung {f}	
transliterate	v.	transkribieren	
translucent	adj.	durchsichtig	
transmigration	n.	Auswanderung {f}	
transmission	n.	Übersetzung {f}	
transmit	v.	übermitteln	
transmitter	n.	Sender {m}	
transmute	v.	verwandeln	
transparency	n.	Transparenz {f}	
transparent	adj.	erkennbar	
transpire	v.	schwitzen	
transplant	v.	verpflanzen	
transport	v.	Transport {m}	
transportation	n.	Beförderungsmittel {n}	
transporter	n.	Transporter {m}	
transpose	v.	versetzen	
transsexual	n.	Transsexuelle {m,f}	
transverse	adj.	quer	
transvestite	n.	Transvestit {m}	
trap	n.	Falle {f}	

193

trapeze *n.*	Trapez {n}		**trendy** *adj.*	schick
trash *n.*	Quatsch {m}		**trepidation** *n.*	Angst {f}
trauma *n.*	Trauma {n}		**trespass** *v.*	übertreten
travel *v.*	reisen		**tress** *n.*	Flechte {f}
traveller *n.*	Reisende {m}		**trestle** *n.*	Stütze {f}
travelogue *n.*	Reisebericht {m}		**trial** *n.*	Erprobung {f}
traverse *v.*	durchqueren		**triangle***n.*	Dreieck {n}
travesty *n.*	Travestie {f}		**triangular** *adj.*	Dreieck {n}
trawler *n.*	Fischdampfer {m}		**triathlon** *n.*	Triathlon {m}
tray *n.*	Ablagekasten {m}		**tribal** *adj.*	stammes
treacherous *adj.*	trügerisch		**tribe** *n.*	Stamm {m}
treachery *n.*	Verrat {m}		**tribulation** *n.*	Drangsal {f}
treacle *n.*	Sirup {m}		**tribunal***n.*	Strafgericht {n}
tread *v.*	zertreten		**tributary** *n.*	Nebenfluss {m}
treadmill *n.*	Tretmühle {f}		**tribute** *n.*	Abgabe {f}
treason*n.*	Landesverrat {m}		**trice** *n.*	Null {f}
treasure *n.*	Schatz {m}		**triceps** *n.*	Trizeps {m}
treasurer *n.*	Schatzmeister {m}		**trick** *n.*	Streich {m}
treasury *n.*	Staatskasse {f}		**trickery***n.*	Betrügerei {f}
treat *v.*	behandeln		**trickle** *v.*	verrennen
treatise*n.*	Abhandlung {f}		**trickster** *n.*	Gauner {m}
treatment *n.*	Behandlung {f}		**tricky** *adj.*	verzwickt
treaty *n.*	Vertrag {m}		**tricolour** *n.*	Trikoloren
treble *adj.*	dreifach		**tricycle***n.*	Dreirad {n}
tree *n.*	Baum {m}		**trident** *n.*	Dreizack {m}
trek *n.*	Treck {m}		**trier** *n.*	Prüfer {m}
trellis *n.*	Gitter {n}		**trifle** *n.*	Kleinigkeit {f}
tremble*v.*	zittern		**trigger** *n.*	Auslöseimpuls {m}
tremendous*adj.*	fürchterlich		**trigonometry** *n.*	Trigonometrie {f}
tremor *n.*	Zittern {n}		**trill** *n.*	Trill {m}
tremulous *adj.*	zitternd		**trillion** *adj & n.*	Trillion {f}
trench *n.*	Schützengraben {m}		**trilogy** *n.*	Trilogie {f}
trenchant *adj.*	scharf		**trim** *v.*	pflegen
trend *n.*	Trend {m}		**trimmer** *n.*	Beschneider {m}

trimming	n.	Beschneiden {n}
trinity n.		Dreifaltigkeit {f}
trinket n.		Zeug {n}
trio n.		Terzett {n}
trip v.		verdreifachen
trIpartite	adj.	dreiseitig
triple n.		dreimalig
triplet n.		Drilling {m}
triplicate	adj.	verdreifachten
tripod n.		Stativ {n}
triptychn.		Triptychon {n}
trite	adj.	abgedroschen
triumph	n.	Sieg {m}
triumphal	adj.	triumphierend
triumphant	adj.	erfolgreich
trivet	n.	Dreifuß {m}
trivia	n.	Plattheit {f}
trivial	adj.	unbedeutend
troll	n.	Troll {m}
trolley	n.	Wagen {m}
troop	n.	Trupp {m}
troopern.		Reiter {m}
trophy	n.	Siegeszeichen {n}
tropic	n.	Wendekreis {m}
tropicaladj.		tropisch
trot	v.	trotten
trotter	n.	Traber {m}
trouble n.		Störung {f}
troubleshooting	n.Problembehandlung {f}	
troublesome	adj.	mühevoll
trough	n.	Mulde {f}
trouncev.		verprügeln
troupe	n.	Komödiant {m}
trousers	n.	Hosen {pl}

trousseau	n.	Brautaussteuer {f}
trout	n.	Forelle {f}
trowel	n.	Spachtel {m}
Troy	n.	Troia
truant	n.	Bummler {m}
truce	n.	Waffenruhe {f}
truck	n.	Lastkraftwagen {m}
trucker n.		Fernlastfahrer {m}
truculent	adj.	wild
trudge v.		schleppen
true	adj.	wahr
truffle	n.	Trüffel {m}
trug	n.	Zustand {m}
truism	n.	Binsenwahrheit {f}
trump	n.	Trumpf {m}
trumpet	n.	Trompete {f}
truncate	v.	stutzen
truncheon	n.	Knüppel {m}
trundle v.		trudeln
trunk	n.	Schrankkoffer {m}
truss	n.	Dachstuhl {m}
trust	n.	Vertrauen {n}
trustee	n.	Sachwalter {m}
trustful adj.		vertrauensvoll
trustworthy	adj.	kreditfähig
trusty	adj.	treu
truth	n.	Wahrheit {f}
truthful adj.		wahrhaft
try	v.	versuchen
trying	adj.	anstrengend
tryst	n.	Stelldichein {n}
tsunami	n.	Tsunami {m}
tub	n.	Wanne {f}
tube	n.	Untergrundbahn {f}

tubercle	*n.*	Tuberkelbazilus {m}
tuberculosis	*n.*	Tuberkulose {f}
tubular *adj.*	röhrenförmig
tuck	*v.*	zurückstreifen
Tuesday	*n.*	Dienstag {m}
tug	*v.*	zerren
tuition	*n.*	Unterricht {m}
tulip	*n.*	Tulpe {f}
tumble	*v.*	hinfallen
tumbler *n.*	Wäschetrockner {m}
tumescent *adj.*	schwellend
tumour *n.*	Tumor {m}
tumult	*n.*	Unruhe {f}
tumultuous *adj.*	tosend
tun	*n.*	Fass {n}
tune	*n.*	Lied {n},
tuner	*n.*	Tuner {m}
tunic	*n.*	Waffenrock {m}
tunnel	*n.*	Stollen {m}
turban	*n.*	Turban {m}
turbid *adj.*	trüb
turbine *n.*	Turbine {f}
turbocharger	*n.*	Turbolader {m}
turbulence	*n.*	Turbulenz {f}
turbulent	*adj.*	stürmisch
turf	*n.*	Torf {m}
turgid *adj.*	geschwollen
turkey	*n.*	Truthahn {f}
turmeric	*n.*	Gelbwurz {f}
turmoil *n.*	Getümmel {n}
turn	*v.*	schalten
turner	*n.*	Dreher {m}
turning *n.*	Abdrehen {n}
turnip	*n.*	Rübe {f}

turnout *n.*	Vertreibung {f}
turnover	*n.*	Umsatz {m}
turpentine	*n.*	Terpentin {n}
turquoise	*n.*	türkis
turtle	*n.*	Schildkröte {f}
tusk	*n.*	Fangzahn {m}
tussle	*n.*	Kampf {m}
tutelage	*n.*	Vormundschaft {f}
tutor	*n.*	Begleiter {m}
tutorial *n.*	Anleitung {f}
tuxedo *n.*	Smoking {m}
tweak	*v.*	zwicken
twee	*adj.*	zuckersüß
tweed	*n.*	Tweed
tweet	*v.*	sprechen
tweeter *n.*	Hochtonlautsprecher {m}
tweezers	*n.*	Pinzette {f}
twelfth *adj.&n.*	zwölfte
twelve *adj.&n.*	zwölf
twentieth	*adj.&n.*	zwanzigste
twenty *adj.&n.*	zwanzig
twice	*adv.*	zweimal
twiddle *v.*	drehen
twig	*n.*	Zweig {m}
twilight *n.*	Dämmerung {f}
twin	*n.*	Zwilling {m}
twine	*n.*	Faden {m}
twinge	*n.*	Stechen {n}
twinkle *v.*	funkel
twirl	*v.*	wirbeln
twist	*v.*	winden
twitch	*v.*	zupfen
twitter	*v.*	zwitschern
two	*adj.&n.*	zwei

twofold *adj.*	zweifach
tycoon *n.*	Manager {m}
type *n.*	Typ {m}
typesetter *n.*	Setzer {m}
typhoid *n.*	Typhus {m}
typhoon *n.*	Taifun {m}
typhus *n.*	Typhus {m}
typical *adj.*	typisch
typify *v.*	verkörpern
typist *n.*	Schreiber {m}
tyrannize *v.*	tyrannisieren
tyranny *n.*	Gewaltherrschaft {f}
tyrant *n.*	Tyrann {m}
tyre *n.*	Reifen {m}

U

ubiquitous *adj.*	allgegenwärtig
udder *n.*	Euter {n}
ugliness *n.*	Hässlichkeit {f}
ugly *adj.*	hässlich
ulcer *n.*	Geschwür {n}
ulterior *adj.*	jenseitig
ultimate *adj.*	äußerster
ultimately *adv.*	schließlich
ultimatum *n.*	Ultimatum {n}
ultra *pref.*	radikal
ultramarine *n.*	ultramarin
ultrasonic *adj.*	Überschall...
ultrasound *n.*	Ultraschall {m}
umber *n.*	Umber {n}
umbilical *adj.*	nabel
umbrella *n.*	Regenschirm {m}
umpire *n.*	Obmann {m}
unable *adj.*	unfähig

unanimity *a.*	Einstimmigkeit {f}
unaccountable *adj.*	unzahlbar
unadulterated *adj.*	naturbelassen
unalloyed *adj.*	unvermischt
unanimous *adj.*	einmütig
unarmed *adj.*	waffenlos
unassailable *adj.*	unangreifbar
unassuming *adj.*	bescheiden
unattended *adj.*	unerwartete
unavoidable *adj.*	unausweichlich
unaware *adj.*	unversehens
unbalanced *adj.*	unsymmetrisch
unbelievable *adj.*	unglaublich
unbend *v.*	entspannen
unborn *adj.*	ungeboren
unbridled *adj.*	ungezügelt
unburden *v.*	entlassen
uncalled *adj.*	unaufgefordert
uncanny *adj.*	unheimlich
unceremonious *adj.*	Ungezwungen
uncertain *adj.*	unsicher
uncharitable *adj.*	lieblos
uncle *n.*	Onkel {m}
unclean *adj.*	unrein
uncomfortable *adj.*	ungemütlich
uncommon *adj.*	ungewöhnlich
uncompromising *adj.*	Kompromisslos
unconditional *adj.*	unbedingt
unconscious *adj.*	unbewusst
uncouth *adj.*	grob
uncover *v.*	freigeben
unctuous *adj.*	salbungsvoll
undeceive *v.*	aufklären
undecided *adj.*	unentschieden

197

undeniable	adj.	unbestreitbar
under	prep.	unter
underarm	adj.	Unterarm {m}
undercover	adj.	geheim
undercurrent	n.	Unterströmung {f}
undercut	v.	unterbieten
underdog	n.	Unterlegene {m,f}
underestimate	v.	unterschätzen
undergo	v.	unterziehen
undergraduate	n.	Student {m}
underground	adj.	Untergrund {m}
underhand	adj.	heimlich
underlay	v.	zugrundelagen
underline	v.t.	unterstreichen
underling	n.	Untergeordnete {m,f}
undermine	v.	untergraben
underneath	prep.	unterhalb
underpants	n.	Unterhosen {pl}
underpass	n.	Unterführung {f}
underprivileged	adj.	Unterprivilegiert
underrate	v.	unterschätzen
underscore	v.	unterstreichen
undersigned	adj.	unterschreiben
understand	v.t.	verstehen
understanding	n.	Verstehen {n}
understate	v.	untertreiben
undertake	v.	übernehmen
undertaker	n.	Leichenbestatter {m}
underwear	n.	Unterwäsche {f}
underworld	n.	Unterwelt {f}
underwrite	v.	unterschreiben
undesirable	adj.	unerwünscht
undo	v.	abbinden
undoing	n.	Annullieren {n}

undone	adj.	abgebunden
undress	v.	auskleiden
undue	adj.	unzulässig
undulate	v.	wellen
undying	adj.	unsterblich
unearth	v.	ausgraben
uneasy	adj.	unbehaglich
unemployable	adj.	unbrauchbar
unemployed	adj.	arbeitslos
unending	adj.	endlos
unequalled	adj.	beispielslos
uneven	adj.	ungleichmäßig
unexceptionable	adj.	untadelig
unexceptional	adj.	ausnahmslos
unexpected	adj.	unerwartet
unfailing	adj.	zuverlässig
unfair	adj.	unlauter
unfaithful	adj.	untreu
unfit	adj.	ungeeignet
unfold	v.	entfalten
unforeseen	adj.	ungeahnt
unforgettable	adj.	unvergesslich
unfortunate	adj.	unglücklich
unfounded	adj.	haltlos
unfurl	v.	entfalten
ungainly	adj.	unbeholfen
ungovernable	adj.	zügellos
ungrateful	adj.	undankbar
unguarded	adj.	ungeschützt
unhappy	adj.	unglücklich
unhealthy	adj.	ungesund
unheard	adj.	ungehört
unholy	adj.	unheilig
unification	n.	Vereinheitlichung {f}

uniform	*adj.* gleichförmig	unnecessary	*adj.* unnötig
unify	*v.* vereinheitlichen	unnerve	*v.* entnerven
unilateral	*adj.* einseitig	unorthodox	*adj.* unorthodox
unimpeachable	*adj.* unantastbar	unpack	*v.* ausgepacken
uninhabited	*adj.* unbewohnt	unpleasant	*adj.* unangenehm
union	*n.* Verein {m}	unpopular	*adj.* unbeliebt
unionist	*n.* Gewerkschaftler {m}	unprecedented	*adj.* beispiellos
unique	*adj.* einzigartig	unprepared	*adj.* unvorbereitet
unisex	*adj.* eingeschlechtig	unprincipled	*adj.* gewissenlos
unison	*n.* Einklang {m}	unprofessional	*adj.* laienhaft
unit	*n.* Gebühreneinheit {f}	unqualified	*adj.* unqualifiziert
unite	*v.* vereinigen	unreasonable	*adj.* unvernünftig
unity	*n.* Einheit {f}	unreliable	*n* unglaubwürdig
universal	*adj.* universal	unreserved	*adj.* uneingeschränkt
universality	*adv.* Allgemeingültigkeit {f}	unrest	*n.* Unruhen {f}
universe	*n.* Universum {n}	unrivalled	*adj.* unerreicht
university	*n.* Universität {f}	unruly	*adj.* unbändig
unjust	*adj.* ungerecht	unscathed	*adj.* unbeschädigt
unkempt	*adj.* verwahrlos	unscrupulous	*adj.* gewissenlos
unkind	*adj.* unfreundlich	unseat	*v.* absetzen
unknown	*adj.* unwissend	unselfish	*adj.* selbstlos
unleash	*v.* entfesseln	unsettle	*v.* beunruhigen
unless	*conj.* wenn nicht	unshakeable	*adj.* unerschütterlich
unlike	*prep.* ungleichartig	unskilled	*adj.* ungelernt
unlikely	*adj.* unwahrscheinlich	unsocial	*adj.* unsozial
unlimited	*adj.* unbeschränkt	unsolicited	*adj.* unaufgefordert
unload	*v.* ausladen	unstable	*adj.* instabil
unmanned	*adj.* bedienungsfrei	unsung	*adj.* unbesungen
unmask	*v.* entlarven	unthinkable	*adj.* undenkbar
unmentionable	*adj.* unaussprechlich	untidy	*adj.* unordentlich
unmistakable	*adj.* unverwechselbar	until	*prep.* bis
unmitigated	*adj.* vollständig	untimely	*adj.* vorzeitig
unmoved	*adj.* ungerührt	untold	*adj.* unsagbar
unnatural	*adj.* unnatürlich	untouchable	*adj.* unangreifbar

untoward	adj. ungefügig	upturn n.	Wendung {f}
unusual	adj. unüblich	upward adv.	aufwärts
unutterable adj. unaussprechlich		urban adj.	kommunal
unveil v.	enthüllen	urbane adj.	höflich
unwarranted	adj. unberechtigt	urbanity n.	Urbanität {f}
unwell adj.	unwohl	urchin n.	Bengel {m}
unwilling	adj. widerwillig	urge v.	drängen
unwind v.	abwickeln	urgent adj.	vordringlich
unwise adj.	unklug	urinal n.	Pissoir {n}
unwittingly adv. unabsichtlich		urinary adj.	urinierend
unworldly	adj. unweltlich	urinate v.	urinieren
unworthy	adj. unwürdig	urine n.	Urin {m}
up adv. aufwärts		urn n.	Urne {f}
upbeat adj. Auftakt {m}		usable adj.	verwertbar
upbraid adj. schimpfend		usage n.	Anwendung {f}
upcoming	adj. demnächst	use v.t.	anwenden
update v.	aktualisieren	useful adj.	brauchbar
upgrade	v. verbessern	useless adj.	zwecklos
upheaval	n. Umbruch {m}	user n.	Benutzer {m}
uphold v.	aufrechterhalten	usher n.	Gerichtsdiener {m}
upholster	v. polstern	usual adj.	üblich
upholstery	n. Polstermöbel {n}	usually adv.	üblicherweise
uplift v.	hochheben	usurp v.	aneignen
upload v.	hochladen	usurpation n.	Usurpation {f}
upper adj.	oberer	usury n.	Wucher {m}
upright adj. stramm		utensil n.	Gerät {n}
uprising	n. Erhebung {f}	uterus n.	Gebärmutter {f}
uproar n.	Erregung {f}	utilitarian	adj. utilitaristisch
uproarious	adj. tobend	utility n.	Nützlichkeit {f}
uproot v.	entwurzeln	utilization n.	Verwertung {f}
upset v.	bestürzen	utilize v.	ausnutzen
upshot n.	Ergebnis {n}	utmost adj.	äußerst
upstart n.	Neureiche {m}	utopia n.	Utopie {f}
upsurge	n. Aufwallung {f}	utopian adj.	utopisch

200

utter *adj.* äußern

utterance *n.* Äußerung {f}

uttermost *adj. & n.* äußerst

V

vacancy *n.* Leere {f}

vacant *adj.* leerstehend

vacate *v.* räumen

vacation *n.* Urlaub {m}

vaccinate *v.* impfen

vaccination *n.* Impfung {f}

vaccine *n.* Impfstoff {m}

vacillate *v.* schwanken

vacillation *n.* Unschlüssigkeit {f}

vacuous *adj.* leer

vacuum *n.* Leerraum {m}

vagabond *n.* Strolch {m}

vagary *n.* Einfall {m}

vagina *n.* Scheide {f}

vagrant *n.* Landstreicher {m}

vague *adj.* vage

vagueness *n.* Verschwommenheit {f}

vain *adj.* eingebildet

vainglorious *adj.* prahlerisch

vainly *adv.* vergeblich

valance *n.* Volant {m}

vale *n.* Abschied {m}

valediction *n.* Abschied {m}

valency *n.* Wertigkeit {f}

valentine *n.* Valentinsgruß {m}

valet *n.* Kammerdiener {m}

valetudinarian *n.* kränklich

valiant *adj.* tapfer

valid *adj.* zulässig

validate *v.* bestätigen

validity *n.* Gültigkeit {f}

valise *n.* Reisetasche {f}

valley *n.* Tal {n}

valour *n.* Heldenmut {m}

valuable *adj.* wertvoll

valuation *n.* Bewertung {f}

value *n.* Wert {m}

valve *n.* Ventil {n}

vamp *n.* Flickwerk {n}

vampire *n.* Vampir {m}

van *n.* Lastwagen {pl}

vandal *n.* Vandal {m}

vandalize *v.* zerstören

vane *n.* Schaufel {f}

vanguard *n.* Vortrupp {m}

vanish *v.* entschwinden

vanity *n.* Einbildung {f}

vanquish *v.* besiegen

vantage *n.* Vorteil {m}

vapid *adj.* fad

vaporize *v.* verdampfen

vapour *n.* Dampf {m}

variable *adj.* variabel

variance *n.* Abweichung {f}

variant *n.* Variante {f}

variation *n.* Veränderung {f}

varicose *adj.* varikös

varied *adj.* verschieden

variegated *adj.* belebt

variety *n.* Auswahl {f}

various *adj.* verschiedenartig

varlet *n.* Knappe {m}

varnish *n.* Lack {m}

201

vary	*v.*	variierend	**venerate**	*v.*	ehren
vascular	*adj.*	vasculär	**veneration**	*n.*	Verehrung {f}
vase	*n.*	Vase {f}	**venetian**	*adj.*	venetianer
vasectomy	*n.*	Vasectomie {f}	**vengeance**	*n.*	Rache {f}
vassal	*n.*	Vasall {m}	**vengeful**	*adj.*	racheschnauben
vast	*adj.*	ausgedehnt	**venial**	*adj.*	verzeihlich
vaudeville	*n.*	Variete {n}	**venom**	*n.*	Gift {n}
vault	*n.*	Gewölbe {n}	**venomous**	*adj.*	giftig
vaunted	*adj.*	gerühmt	**venous**	*adj.*	giftiges
veal	*n.*	Kalbfleisch {n}	**vent**	*n.*	Entlüftung {f}
vector	*n.*	Vektor {m}	**ventilate**	*v.*	ventilieren
veer	*n.*	Drehen {n}	**ventilation**	*n.*	Belüftung {f}
vegan	*n.*	Vegetarier {m}	**ventilator**	*n.*	Lüftungsanlage {f}
vegetable	*n.*	Gemüse {n}	**venture**	*n.*	Risiko {n}
vegetarian	*n.*	vegetarisch	**venturesome**	*adj.*	kühn
vegetate	*v.*	vegetieren	**venue**	*n.*	Schauplatz {m}
vegetation	*n.*	Bewuchs {m}	**veracious**	*adj.*	wahrhaft
vegetative	*adj.*	vegetativ	**veracity**	*n.*	Wahrhaftigkeit {f}
vehement	*adj.*	stürmisch	**veranda**	*n.*	Veranda {f}
vehicle	*n.*	Fahrzeug {n}	**verb**	*n.*	Verb {n}
vehicular	*adj.*	fahrzeug	**verbal**	*adj.*	mündlich
veil	*n.*	Schleier {m}	**verbally**	*adv.*	verbal
vein	*n.*	Vene {f}	**verbalize**	*v.*	formulieren
velocity	*n.*	Geschwindigkeit {f}	**verbatim**	*adv.*	wörtlich
velour	*n.*	Velours {n}	**verbiage**	*n.*	Wortschwall {m}
velvet	*n.*	Samt {m}	**verbose**	*adj.*	wortreich
velvety	*adj.*	samtig	**verbosity**	*n.*	Wortfülle {f}
venal	*adj.*	käuflich	**verdant**	*adj.*	unreif
venality	*n.*	Käuflichkeit {f}	**verdict**	*n.*	Urteilsspruch {m}
vend	*v.*	verkaufen	**verge**	*n.*	Rand {m}
vendetta	*n.*	Vendetta {f}	**verification**	*n.*	Überprüfung {f}
vendor	*n.*	Lieferant {m}	**verify**	*v.*	prüfen
veneer	*n.*	Lieferant {m}	**verily**	*adv.*	wahrlich
venerable	*adj.*	ehrwürdig			

verisimilitude	*n.* Wahrscheinlichkeit {f}		vex	*v.* ärgern
veritable	*adj.* wahrhaft		vexation	*n.* Ärger {m}
verity	*n.* Wahrheit {f}		via	*prep.* über
vermillion	*n.* Zinnober {m}		viable	*adj.* lebensfähig
vermin	*n.* Ungeziefer {n}		viaduct	*n.* Viadukt {n}
vernacular	*n.* Mundart {f}		vial	*n.* Fläschchen {n}
vernal	*adj.* frühlingshaft		viands	*n.* Lebensmittel {pl}
versatile	*adj.* vielseitig		vibe	*n.* Ausstrahlung {f}
versatility	*n.* Vielseitigkeit {f}		vibrant	*adj.* schwingend
verse	*n.* Vers {m}		vibraphone	*n.* Vibraphon {n}
versed	*adj.* bewandert		vibrate	*v.* vibrieren
versification	*n.* Versbau {m}		vibration	*n.* Erschütterung {f}
versify	*v.* dichten		vibrator	*n.* Vibrator {m}
version	*n.* Version {f}		vicar	*n.* Kaplan {m}
verso	*n.* Rückseite {f}		vicarious	*adj.* stellvertretend
versus	*prep.* gegen		vice	*n.* Laster {n}
vertebra	*n.* Wirbel {m}		viceroy	*n.* Vizekönig {m}
vertebrate	*n.* Wirbeltier {n}		vice-versa	*adv.* umgekehrt
vertex	*n.* Scheitel {m}		vicinity	*n.* Nachbarschaft {f}
vertical	*adj.* vertikal		vicious	*adj.* lasterhaft
vertiginous	*adj.* schwindelnd		vicissitude	*n.* Wandel {m}
vertigo	*n.* Schwindel {m}		victim	*n.* Schlachtopfer {n}
verve	*n.* Schwung {m}		victimize	*v.* opfern
very	*adv.* sehr		victor	*n.* Sieger {m}
vesicle	*n.* Bläschen {n}		victorious	*adj.* siegreich
vessel	*n.* Gefäß {n}		victory	*n.* Sieg {m}
vest	*n.* Weste {f}		victualler	*n.* Lieferant {m}
vestibule	*n.* Vorraum {m}		victuals	*n.* Esswaren {pl}
vestige	*n.* Spur {f}		video	*n.* Video {n}
vestment	*n.* Gewand {n}		vie	*v.* wetteifernd
vestry	*n.* Gemeindesaal {m}		view	*n.* Ansicht {f}
veteran	*n.* Veteran {m}		vigil	*n.* Wachsein {n}
veterinary	*adj.* veterinär		vigilance	*n.* Wachsamkeit {f}
veto	*n.* Einspruch {m}		vigilant	*adj.* wachsam

vignette	*n.*	Vignette {f}
vigorous	*adj.*	energisch
vigour *n.*		Kraft {f}
Viking *n.*		Wikinger {m}
vile	*adj.*	wertlos
vilify	*v.*	schmähen
villa	*n.*	Villa {f}
village *n.*		Dorf {n}
villager *n.*		Dorfbewohner {m}
villain *n.*		Bösewicht {m}
vindicate	*v.*	verteidigend
vindication	*n.*	Rechtfertigung {f}
vine	*n.*	Rebe {f}
vinegar *n.*		Essig {m}
vintage *n.*		Lese {f}
vintner *n.*		Weinhändler {m}
vinyl	*n.*	Vinyl {n}
violate *v.*		verletzend
violation	*n.*	Verletzung {f}
violence	*n.*	Heftigkeit {f}
violent *adj.*		gewaltsam
violet	*n.*	Veilchen {n}
violin	*n.*	Violine {f}
violinist	*n.*	Geiger {m}
virago *n.*		Mannweib {n}
viral	*adj.*	viral
virgin	*n.*	Jungfrau {f}
virginity	*n.*	Jungfräulichkeit {f}
virile	*adj.*	männlich
virility	*n.*	Potenz {f}
virtual *adj.*		virtuell
virtue	*n.*	Wirksamkeit {f}
virtuous	*adj.*	tugendhaft
virulence	*n.*	Giftigkeit {f}

virulent *adj.*		virulent
virus	*n.*	Virus {m}
visa	*n.*	Visum {n}
visage *n.*		Antlitz {m}
viscid	*adj.*	sämig
viscose *n.*		Viskose {f}
viscount	*n.*	Vicomte {f}
viscountess *n.*		Vicomtesse {f}
viscous	*adj.*	schwerflüssig
visibility	*n.*	Sicht {f}
visible *adj.*		sichtbar
vision *n.*		Sehkraft {f}
visionary	*adj.*	phantastisch
visit	*v.*	besuchen
visitation	*n.*	Heimsuchung {f}
visitor *n.*		Besucher {m}
visor	*n.*	Gesichtsschutzschirm {m}
vista	*n.*	Durchblick {m}
visual *adj.*		visuell
visualize	*v.*	vorstellen
vital	*adj.*	unerlässlich
vitality *n.*		Lebenskraft {f}
vitalize *v.*		beleben
vitamin *n.*		Vitamin {n}
vitiate *v.*		beeinträchtigen
viticulture	*n.*	Weinbau {m}
vitreous	*adj.*	glasartig
vitrify	*v.*	verglasen
vitriol	*n.*	Vitriol {n}
vituperation *n.*		Beschimpfung {f}
vivacious	*adj.*	lebhaft
vivacity *n.*		Lebhaftigkeit {f}
vivarium	*n.*	Tiergehege {n}
vivid	*adj.*	klar

vivify	v.	klar
vixen	n.	Füchsin {f}
vocabulary	n.	Vokabel {f}
vocal	adj.	klingend
vocalist	n.	Sänger {m}
vocalize	v.	aussprechen
vocation	n.	Berufung {f}
vociferous	adj.	lärmen
vogue	n.	Popularität {f}
voice	n.	Stimme {f}
voicemail	n.	Voicemail {n}
void	adj.	Gefühl {n}
voile	n.	Voile
volatile	adj.	flüchtig
volcanic	adj.	vulkanisch
volcano	n.	Vulkan {m}
volition	n.	Willenskraft {f}
volley	n.	Hagel {m}
volt	n.	Volt {n}
voltage	n.	Voltzahl {f}
voluble	adj.	geläufig
volume	n.	Inhalt {m}
voluminous	adj.	umfangreich
voluntarily	adv.	freiwillig
voluntary	adj.	freiwillig
volunteer	n.	Freiwillige {m,f}
voluptuary	n.	Lüstling {m}
voluptuous	adj.	üppig
vomit	v.	erbrechen
voodoo	n.	Voodoo {n}
voracious	adj.	gefräßig
vortex	n.	Wirbel {m}
votary	n.	Verehrer {m}
vote	n.	Abstimmung {f}

voter	n.	Wähler {m}
votive	adj.	weih
vouch	v.	verbürgen
voucher	n.	Coupon {m}
vouchsafe	v.	gewähren
vow	n.	Schwur {m}
vowel	n.	Vokal {m}
voyage	n.	Seereise {f}
voyager	n.	Reisende {m}
vulcanize	v.	vulkanisieren
vulgar	adj.	abgeschmackt
vulgarian	n.	Unfeinheit {f}
vulgarity	n.	Gemeinheit {f}
vulnerable	adj.	ungeschützt
vulpine	adj.	fuchsartig
vulture	n.	Aasgeier {m}

W

wacky	adj.	exzentrisch
wad	n.	Bausch {m}
waddle	v.	watscheln
wade	v.	waten
wader	n.	Watvogel {m}
wafer	n.	Waffel {f}
waffle	n.	Waffel {f}
waft	v.	wehen
wag	v.	unterhalten
wage	n.	Lohn {m}
wager	n. & v.	Wette {f}
waggle	v.	wackeln
wagon	n.	Waggon {m}
wagtail	n.	Bachstelze {f}
waif	n.	Strandgut {n}
wail	n.	Wehgeschrei {n}

wain *n.*	Wagen {m}	
wainscot *n.*	Täfelung {f}	
waist *n.*	Taille {f}	
waistband *n.*	Hosenbund {m}	
waistcoat *n.*	Weste {f}	
wait *v.*	warten	
waiter *n.*	Kellner {m}	
waive *v.*	aufgeben	
wakeful *adj.*	schlaflos	
walk *v.*	gehen	
wallaby *n.*	Australier {m}	
wallop *v.*	verprügeln	
wally *n.*	Trottel {m}	
walnut *n.*	Walnuss {f}	
walrus *n.*	Walross {n}	
waltz *n.*	Walzer {m}	
wan *adj.*	blass	
wand *n.*	Stab {m}	
wander *v.*	wandern	
wane *v.*	abflauen	
wangle *v.*	drehen	
want *v.*	fehlen	
wanting *adj.*	fehlend	
wanton *adj.*	übermütig	
war *n.*	Krieg {m}	
warble *v.*	trillern	
warbler *n.*	Grasmücke {f}	
ward *n.*	Schutzbefohlene {m,f}	
warden *n.*	Wächter {m}	
warder *n.*	Wärter {m}	
wardrobe *n.*	Garderobe {f}	
ware *n.*	Ware {f}	
warehouse *n.*	Warendepot {n}	
warfare *n.*	Kriegsführung {f}	

warlike *adj.*	streitbar	
warm *adj.*	warm	
warmth *n.*	Wärme {f}	
warn *v.*	warnen	
warning *n.*	Warnung {f}	
warp *v.*	Entstellung {f}	
warrant *n.*	Vollziehungsbefehl {m}	
warrantor *n.*	Gewährsmann {m}	
warranty *n.*	Gewährleistung {f}	
warren *n.*	Kaninchengehege {n}	
warrior *n.*	Krieger {m}	
wart *n.*	Warze {f}	
wary *adj.*	vorsichtig	
wash *v.*	waschen	
washable *adj.*	waschbar	
washer *n.*	Wäscher {m}	
washing *n.*	Wässerigkeit {f}	
wasp *n.*	Wespe {f}	
waspish *adj.*	reizbar	
wassail *n.*	Gelage {n}	
wastage *n.*	Abnutzung {f}	
waste *v.*	verschwenden	
wasteful *adj.*	verschwenderisch	
watch *v.*	beobachten	
watchful *adj.*	wachsam	
watchword *n.*	Kennwort {n}	
water *n.*	Wasser {n}	
waterfall *n.*	Wasserfall {m}	
watermark *n.*	Wasserzeichen {n}	
watermelon *n.*	Wassermelone {f}	
waterproof *adj.*	wasserfest	
watertight *adj.*	wasserdicht	
watery *adj.*	wässrig	
watt *n.*	Watt {n}	

wattage	n.	Wattleistung {f}
wattle	n.	Gitterwerk {n}
wave	v.	wellen
waver	v.	wanken
wavy	adj.	wellig
wax	n.	Wachs {n}
way	n.	Weg {m}
waylay	v.	auflauern
wayward	adj.	launisch
we pron.		wir
weak	adj.	schwach
weaken v.		schwächen
weakling	n.	Schwächling {m}
weakness	n.	Schwachheit {f}
weal	n.	Wohl {n}
wealth	n.	Reichtum {m}
wealthy adj.		reich
wean	v.	entwöhnen
weapon	n.	Waffe {f}
wear	v.	tragen
wearisome	adj.	ermüdend
weary	adj.	müde
weasel	n.	Wiesel {m}
weather	n.	Wetter {n}
weave	v.	weben
weaver	n.	Weber {m}
web	n.	Netz {n}
webby	adj.	schwimmhäutig
webpage	n.	Webpage {f}
website n.		Website {f}
wed	v.	heiraten
wedding	n.	Hochzeit {f}
wedge	n.	Stück {n}
wedlock	n.	Ehe {f}

Wednesday	n.	Mittwoch {m}
weed	n.	Unkraut {n}
week	n.	Woche {f}
weekday	n.	Wochentag {m}
weekly	adj.	wochentlich
weep	v.	weinen
weepy	adj.	weinend
weevil	n.	Rüsselkäfer {m}
weigh	v.	wiegen
weight	n.	Gewicht {n}
weighting	n.	Abwägung {f}
weightlifting		n.Gewichtheben {n}
weighty	adj.	schwerwiegend
weir	n.	Wehr {n}
weird	adj.	bizarr
welcome	n.	Willkommen {n}
weld	v.	schweißen
welfare n.		Fürsorge {f}
well	adv.	gesund
well	n.	Brunnen {m}
wellington	n.	Gummistiefel {pl}
welt	n.	Rahmen {m}
welter	n.	Allerlei {n}
wen	n.	Zyste {f}
wench	n.	Frauenzimmer {n}
wend	v.	wenden
west	n.	Westen {m}
westerly		adv. westlich
western	adj.	westlich
westerner	n.	Westländer {m}
westernize	v.	verwestlichen
wet	adj.	feucht
wetness	n.	Nässe {f}
whack	v.	verhauen

whale	n.	Wal {m}	whinge v.	wimmern
whaler	n.	Walfänger {m}	whinny adj.	wiehernd
whaling	n.	Walfang {m}	whip n.	Geißel {f}
wharf	n.	Kai {m}	whir v.	schwirren
wharf age	n.	Kaianlage {f}	whirl n.	Taumel {m}
what	pron. & adj.	was	whirligig n.	Taumelkäfer {m}
whatever	pron.	was auch immer	whirlpool n.	Whirlwanne {f}
wheat	n.	Weizen {m}	whirlwind n.	Wirbelwind {m}
wheaten	adj.	weizen	whirr v.	schwirren
wheedle	v.	abbetteln	whisk v.	wischen
wheel	n.	Rad {n}	whisker n.	Backenbart {m}
wheeze v.		keuchen	whisky n.	Whisky {m}
whelk	n.	Wellhornschnecke {f}	whisper v.	flüstern
whelm	v.	überschütten	whist n.	Whist {m}
whelp	n.	Welpe {m}	whistle n.	Pfiff {m}
when	adv.	wenn	whit n.	Teilchen {n}
whence adv.		woher	white adj.	weiß
whenever	conj.	wann immer	whitewash v.	tünchen
where	adv.	wo	whither adv.	wohin
whereabouts	adv.	wo herum	whiting n.	Wittling {m}
whereas	adv.	hingegen	whittle v.	schnibbel
whet	v.	wetzen	whiz v.	zischen
whether	conj.	ob	who pron.	wer
whey	n.	Käsewasser {n}	whoever	pron. wer immer
which	pron. & adj.	welch	whole adj.	ganz
whichever	pron.	welche	whole-hearted	adj. ernsthaft
whiff	n.	Luftzug {m}	wholesale n.	Großhandel {m}
while	n.	Weile {f}	wholesaler n.	Großhändler {m}
whilst	conj.	indes	wholesome adj.	gesund
whim	n.	Laune {f}	wholly adv.	gänzlich
whimper	v.	winseln	whom pron.	wen
whimsical	adj.	launisch	whoop n.	Ruf {m}
whimsy n.		Laune {f}	whopper	n. Rummel {m}
whine	n.	Heulen {n}	whore n.	Nutte {f}

whose *adj. & pron.*	wessen
why *adv.*	warum
wick *n.*	Docht {m}
wicked *adj.*	schlimm
wicker *n.*	Korbwaren {pl}
wicket *n.*	Törchen {n}
wide *adj.*	weit
widen *v.*	erweitern
widespread *adj.*	weitverbreitet
widow *n.*	Witwe {f}
widower *n.*	Witwer {m}
width *n.*	Breite {f}
wield *v.*	ausüben
wife *n.*	Ehefrau {f}
wig *n.*	Perücke {f}
wiggle *v.*	wackeln
Wight *n.*	Wicht {m}
wigwam *n.*	Wigwam {n}
wild *adj.*	wild
wilderness *n.*	Wildnis {f}
wile *n.*	List {f}
wilful *adj.*	beabsichtigt
will *v.*	wollen
willing *adj.*	bereitwillig
willingness *adj.*	Willigkeit {f}
willow *n.*	Weide {f}
wily *adj.*	schlau
wimble *n.*	Bohrer {m}
wimple *n.*	Wimpel {m}
win *v.*	gewinnen
wince *v.*	zucken
winch *n.*	Winde {f}
wind *n.*	Wind {m}
windbag *n.*	Windbeutel

winder *n.*	Winde {f}
windlass *n.*	Ladewinde {f}
windmill *n.*	Windrad {n}
window *n.*	Fenster {n}
windy *adj.*	windig
wine *n.*	Wein {m}
winery *n.*	Weinkellerei {f}
wing *n.*	Flügel {m}
wink *v.*	zwinkern
winkle *n.*	Uferschnecke {f}
winner *n.*	Gewinner {m}
winning *adj.*	gewinnend
winnow *v.*	aussortieren
winsome *adj.*	gefällig
winter *n.*	Winter {m}
wintry *adj.*	winterlich
wipe *v.*	wischen
wire *n.*	Leitung {f}
wireless *adj.*	drahtlos
wiring *n.*	Verdrahtung {f}
wisdom *n.*	Weisheit {f}
wise *adj.*	verständig
wish *v.*	wunschen
wishful *adj.*	sehnsüchtig
wisp *n.*	Strohbündel {n}
wisteria *n.*	Blauregen {m}
wistful *adj.*	sehnsüchtig
wit *n.*	Verstand {m}
witch *n.*	Hexe {f}
witchcraft *n.*	Zauberei {f}
witchery *n.*	Hexerei {f}
with *prep.*	mit
withal *adv.*	obendrein
withdraw *v.*	zurückziehen

209

withdrawal	*n.*	Rückzug {m}	**wooden**	*adj.* hölzern
withe	*n.*	Zweig {m}	**woodland**	*n.* Waldgelände {n}
wither	*v.*	verblühen	**woof**	*n.* Einschlag {m}
withhold	*v.*	zuruckhalten	**woofer**	*n.* Tieftonlautsprecher {m}
within	*prep.*	im innern	**wool**	*n.* Wolle {f}
without	*prep.*	ohne	**woollen**	*adj.* wollig
withstand	*v.*	widerstehen	**woolly**	*adj.* wollig
witless	*adj.*	witzlos	**woozy**	*adj.* benebelt
witness	*n.*	Zeuge {f}	**word**	*n.* Wort {n}
witter	*v.*	schwafeln	**wording**	*n.* Wortlaut {m}
witticism	*n.*	Witz {m}	**wordy**	*adj.* wortreich
witty	*adj.*	witzig	**work**	*n.* Arbeit {f}
wizard	*n.*	Zauberer {m}	**workable**	*adj.* betriebsfähig
wizened	*adj.*	schrumplig	**workaday**	*adj.* alltäglich
woad	*n.*	Blaufarbstoff {m}	**worker**	*n.* Arbeiter {m}
wobble	*v.*	schwanken	**working**	*n.* Arbeitsgang {m}
woe	*n.*	Leid {n}	**workman**	*n.* Arbeitsmann {m}
woeful	*adj.*	elend	**workmanship**	*n.* Mannschaft {f}
wok	*n.*	Wok {m}	**workshop**	*n.* Werkstatt {f}
wold	*n.*	Heideland {n}	**world**	*n.* Welt {f}
wolf	*n.*	Wolf {m}	**worldly**	*adj.* weltlich
woman	*n.*	Frau {f}	**worm**	*n.* Wurm {m}
womanhood	*n.*	Weiblichkeit {f}	**wormwood**	*n.* Wermut {m}
womanize	*v.*	weibisch machend	**worried**	*adj.* besorgt
womb	*n.*	Schoß {m}	**worrisome**	*adj.* lästig
wonder	*v.*	wundern	**worry**	*v.* beunruhigen
wonderful	*adj.*	wundervoll	**worse**	*adj.* schlechter
wondrous	*adj.*	wundersam	**worsen**	*v.* verschlechtern
wonky	*adj.*	wacklig	**worship**	*n.* verehren
wont	*n.*	Gewohnheit {f}	**worshipper**	*n.* Anbeter {m}
wonted	*adj.*	gewohnt	**worst**	*adj.* schlechteste
woo	*v.*	werben	**worsted**	*n.* Kammgarn {n}
wood	*n.*	Holz {n}	**worth**	*adj.* wert
wooded	*adj.*	bewaldet	**worthless**	*adj.* wertlos

worthwhile	adj.	wertvoll	
worthy	adj.	würdig	
would	v.	würde	
would-be	adj.	wäre	
wound	n.	Wunde {f}	
wrack	n.	Wrack {n}	
wraith	n.	Gespenst {n}	
wrangle	n.	Streit {m}	
wrap	v.	einwickeln	
wrapper	n.	Buchumschlag {m}	
wrath	n.	Zorn {m}	
wreak	v.	treiben	
wreath	n.	Gebinde {n}	
wreathe	v.	winden	
wreck	n.	Schiffbruch {m}	
wreckage	n.	Wrackgut {n}	
wrecker	n.	Strandräuber {m}	
wren	n.	Zaunkönig {m}	
wrench	v.	reißen	
wrest	v.	entreißen	
wrestle	v.	ringen	
wrestler	n.	Ringkämpfer {m}	
wretch	n.	Kerl {m}	
wretched	adj.	jämmerlich	
wrick	n.	Hals {m}	
wriggle	v.	schlängeln	
wring	v.	abbringen	
wrinkle	n.	Furche {f}	
wrist	n.	Handgelenk {n}	
writ	n.	Erlass {m}	
write	v.	schreiben	
writer	n.	Schriftsteller {m}	
writhe	v.	krümmen	
writing	n.	Schriftzug {m}	

wrong	adj.	falsch	
wrongful	adj.	unrechtmäßig	
wry	adj.	schief	

X

xenon	n.	Xenon {n}	
xenophobia	n.	Fremdenfeindlichkeit {f}	
Xerox	n.	Xerox {n}	
Xmas	n.	Weihnachten {pl}	
x-ray	n.	Röntgenanalyse {f}	
xylophagous	adj.	xylophag	
xylophilous	adj.	xylophil	
xylophone	n.	Xylophon {n}	

Y

yacht	n.	Jacht {f}	
yachting	n.	Segelklub {m}	
yachtsman	n.	Segler {m}	
yak	n.	Grunzochse {m}	
yam	n.	Süßkartoffel {f}	
yap	v.	quasseln	
yard	n.	Hof {m}	
yarn	n.	Garn {n}	
yashmak	n.	Yasmak {m}	
yaw	v.	gieren	
yawn	v.	gähnen	
year	n.	Jahr {n}	
yearly	adv.	jährlich	
yearn	v.	sehnen	
yearning	n.	Sehnsucht {f}	
yeast	n.	Backhefe {f}	
yell	n.	Schrei {m}	
yellow	adj.	gelb	
yelp	n.	Gekläff {n}	

211

Yen	*n.*	Yen {m}
yeoman	*n.*	Freibauer {m}
yes	*excl.*	Ja
yesterday	*adv.*	Gestern
yet	*adv.*	noch
yeti	*n.*	Yeti {m}
yew	*n.*	Eibe {f}
yield	*v.*	gewinnen
yob	*n.*	Halbstarker {m}
yodel	*v.*	jodeln
yoga	*n.*	Joga {n}
yogi	*n.*	Jogi
yogurt	*n.*	Joghurt {m}
yoke	*n.*	Gabel {f}
yokel	*n.*	Tölpel {m}
yolk	*n.*	Eidotter {n}
yonder	*adj.*	jener
yonks	*n.*	Ewigkeit {f}
yore	*n.*	Gewohnheit {f}
you	*pron.*	Du
young	*adj.*	jung
youngster	*n.*	Junge {m}
your	*adj.*	dein
yourself	*pron.*	selbst
youth	*n.*	Jugend {f}
youthful	*adj.*	jugendlich
yowl	*n.*	jaulen
yummy	*adj.*	lecker

zealous	*adj.*	eifrig
zebra	*n.*	Zebra {n}
zebra crossing	*n.*	Zebrastreifen {pl}
zenith	*n.*	Zenit {m}
zephyr	*n.*	Zephir
zero	*adj.*	Null {f}
zest	*n.*	Lust {f}
zigzag	*n.*	Zickzack {n}
zilch	*n.*	Nichts {n}
zinc	*n.*	Zink {n}
zing	*v.*	kritisieren
zip	*n.*	Reißverschluss {m}
zircon	*n.*	Zirkon {m}
zither	*n.*	Zither {f}
zodiac	*n.*	Tierkreis {m}
zombie	*n.*	Zombie {m}
zonal	*adj.*	zonen
zone	*n.*	Zone {f}
zoo	*n.*	Tierpark {m}
zoological	*adj.*	zoologisch
zoologist	*n.*	Zoologe {m}
zoology	*n.*	Tierkunde {f}
zoom	*v.*	zoomen

Z

zany	*adj.*	verrückt
zap	*v.*	abknallen
zeal	*n.*	Eifer {m}
zealot	*n.*	Zelot

GERMAN - ENGLISH

A

Aasgeier {m} *n.* vulture
ab *prep.* from
Abarbeitung {f} *n.* execution
abbaubar *adj.* biodegradable
abbauen *v.* retrench
abbestellen *v.* countermand
abbetteln *v.* wheedle
abbinden *v.* undo
abbitten *v.* beg
abbrechen *v.i* abort
abbringen *v.* wring
abbröckeln *v.* crumble
Abbruch {m} *n.* severance
Abdankung {f} *n.* abdication
abdestillieren *v.* distil
abdominal *a.* abdominal
Abdrehen {n} *n.* turning
abeaufen *v.* expire
Abend {m} *n.* evening
Abenddämmerung {f}*n.* dusk
Abendessen {n} *n.* supper
Abendkleid {n} *n.* gown
Abendland {n} *n.* occident
Abenteuer {n} *n.* adventure
abenteuerlich *adj.* adventurous
aber *conj.* but
Aberglaube {m} *n.* superstition
abergläubisch *adj.* superstitious
Aberkennung {f} *n.* denial
abfahren *v.* depart
abfahrend *adj.* outgoing
Abfall {m} *n.* litter
abfällig *adj.* snide

Abfallprodukt {n} *n.* residue
abfangen *v.* intercept
abfertigen *v.* dispatch
Abfindung {f} *n.* indemnity
abflauen *v.* wane
abforsten *v.* deforest
abführen *v.* purge
abführend *adj.* purgative
Abführmittel {n} *n.* laxative
Abgabe {f} *n.* duty
Abgabe {f} *n.* tribute
abgebunden *adj.* undone
abgedroschen *adj.* hackneyed
abgedroschen *adj.* trite
Abgeltung {f} *n.* lieu
abgemagert *adj.* emaciated
abgeneigt *adj.* averse
abgeneigt *adj.* indisposed
abgeneigt *adj.* loath
abgerundet *adj.* rounded
Abgesandte {m} *n.* delegate
Abgeschlossenheit {f} *n.* seclusion
abgeschmackt *adj.* vulgar
abgesondert *adv.* apart
abgießen *v.* decant
Abgleich {m} *n.* adjustment
Abgleich {m} *n.* balance
abgleiten *v.* slide
abgrasen *v.* graze
Abgrenzung {f} *n.* demarcation
Abgrund {m} *n.* abyss
abhalten *v. t* detain
Abhaltung {f} *n.* disincentive
Abhandlung {f} *n.* treatise
Abhang {m} *n.* declivity

215

abhängen	v.	depend		abonnieren	v.	subscribe
abhängig	adj.	dependent		abordnen	v.	deregulate
Abhängige {m,f}	n.	dependant		Abordnung {f}	n.	deputation
Abhängigkeit {f}	n.	subordination		abrasiv	adj.	abrasive
abheben v.t.		lift		abraten	v.	dissuade
abhelfend	adj.	remedial		abrechnen	v.	deduct
abklären v.		clarify		abreiben v.		rub
abknallen	v.	zap		abreibend	n.	towelling
Abkomme {m}	n.	descendant		Abreise {f}	n.	departure
Abkommen {n}	n.	agreement		Abrieb {m}	n.	abrasion
Abkürzung {f}	n.	abbreviation		Abrieb {m}	n.	slough
Ablagefach {n}	n.	pigeonhole		Abriss {m}	n.	stub
Ablagekasten {m} n.		tray		Abriss {m}	n.	talon
Ablagerung {f}	n.	sediment		abrüstend	v.	disarm
ablassen v.		desist		Abrüstung {f} n.		disarmament
Ablauf {m}	n.	expiry		Absage {f}	n.	cancellation
ablaufen v.		proceed		Absatz {m}	n.	paragraph
ablehnen	v. t.	decline		Absaugung {f}	n.	suction
ablehnen	v.	dislike		abschaffen	v.t	abolish
ablehnen	v.	repudiate		Abschaffung {f}	n.	abolition
ablehnen	v.	spurn		Abschaum {m}	n.	scum
Ablehnung {f}	n.	refuse		Abscheidung {f}	n.	separation
ableiten	v.	deduce		Abscheu {f}	n.	abhorrence
ableiten	v.	derive		Abscheu {m,f}	n.	odium
Ableitung {f}	n.	revulsion		abscheulich	adj.	abominable
Ableitung {f}	adj.	derivative		abscheulich	adj.	heinous
ablenken v.		deflect		abscheulich	adj.	hideous
ablenken	v. t	divert		abscheulich	adj.	outrageous
Ablesung {f}	n.	reading		abschieben	v. t	deport
ablösen v.		detach		Abschied {m} n.		vale
Abmessung {f}	n.	dimension		Abschied {m} n.		valediction
Abnahme {f}	n.	removal		abschließen	v.	seclude
abnehmbar	adj.	removable		abschließen	adj.	secluded
Abneigung {f}	n.	reluctance		Abschnitt	n.	section
Abnutzung {f}	n.	wastage		Abschnitt {m} n.		article

Abschnitt {m}*n.*	chapter	abstandsgleich	*adj.*	equidistant

Abschnitt {m}*n.* chapter
Abschnitt {m}*n.* episode
abschrecken *v.* deter
Abschreckungsmittel {n}*n.* deterrent
abschreiben *v.* transcribe
Abschrift {f} *n.* copy
abschürfend *v.* excoriate
abschüssig *adj.* steep
abschweifen *v.* digress
abschweifend *adj.* discursive
abschwellendesMittel *n.*decongestant
abschwenken*v.* deviate
abschwören *v.* abjure
abschwören *v.* forswear
absehbar *adj.* conceivable
abseits *adj.* offside
absetzen *v.* discharge
absetzen *v.* unseat
absichern *v.* fuse
Absicht {f} *n.* intent
Absicht {f} *n.* intention
Absicht {f} *n.* purpose
Absicht {f} *n.* tendency
absichtlich *adj.* intentional
absolut *adj.* absolute
Absolution {f} *n.* absolution
Absolvent {m} *n.* alumnus
absondern *v.* secrete
absondern *v.* sequester
absondern *v.* excrete
Absonderung {f} *n.* secretion
Absperrung {f} *n.* barrier
Abstammung {f} *n.* ancestry
Abstammung {f} *n.* lineage
Abstammung {f} *n.* parentage

abstandsgleich *adj.* equidistant
abstempeln *v.* stamp
absteppen *v.* stitch
Abstimmung {f} *n.* vote
Abstinenzler {m} *n.* teetotaller
Abstoß {m} *n.* disgust
abstoßen *v.* forbid
abstoßend *adj.* repulsive
Abstoßung {f} *n.* repulsion
abstrakt *adj.* abstract
Abstrich {m} *n.* deduction
Abstufung {f} *n.* gradation
Abstufung {f} *n.* nuance
absurd *adj.* absurd
Abszess {m} *n.* abscess
Abt {m} *n.* abbot
Abtastimpuls {m} *n.* strobe
Abtei {f} *n.* abbey
Abteilung {f} *n.* compartment
abtragen *v.* remove
Abtreibung {f} *n.* abortion
Abtretung {f} *n.* cession
Abtrünnige {m,f} *n.* apostate
abtupfen *v.* dab
Abwägung {f}*n.* weighting
abwälzen *v.* shift
abwarten *v.* temporize
Abwasser {n}*n.* sewage
Abwasserschlamm {m}*n.* sludge
abwechseln *v.t.* alternate
abwedeln *v. t* dodge
abwegig *adj.* devious
abwehren *v.* fend
abwehren *v.* repulse
Abweichung {f} *n.* discrepancy

217

Abweichung {f}	adj.	deviant
Abweichung {f}	n.	variance
abweisen	v.	repel
abwenden	v.	avert
abwerfen	v.	drop
abwerten	v.	devalue
abwesend	adj.	absent
abwesend	adv.	away
Abwesende {m,f}	n.	absentee
Abwesenheit {f}	n.	absence
abwickeln	v.	transact
abwickeln	v.	unwind
Abzahlung {f}n.		instalment
Abzeichen {n}	n.	badge
Abzeichen {n}	n.	emblem
Abzeichen {n}	n.	logo
abziehen v.		strop
abziehen v.		subtract
abzielen v.		tend
Abzug {m}	n.	outlet
abzüglich	prep.	minus
Abzweigung {f}	n.	diversion
Acajoubaum {m}	n.	cashew
Achat {m}	n.	agate
Achse {f}n.		axis
Achse {f}n.		axle
achselzucken v.		shrug
acht adj. & n.		eight
Achteck {n}	n.	octagon
Achtelmeile {f}	n.	furlong
Achtelnote {f}v.		quaver
Achterbahn {f}	n.	rollercoaster
achtsam adj.		attentive
achtsam adj.		observant
Achtung {f}	n.	attention

achtzehn adj. & n.		eighteen
achtzig adj. & n.		eighty
Achtzigjähriger {m}n.		octogenarian
Acker {m}	n.	acre
Ackerbau {m}n.		agriculture
ackerbautreibend adj.		agricultural
Ackerfräse {f}n.		tiller
acrylsauer	adj.	acrylic
Actinium {n}	n.	actinium
Adaptierung {f}	n.	adaptation
adelig	adj.	noble
Adelsgeschlecht {n}n.		nobility
Adjektiv {n}	n.	adjective
Adler {m}	n.	eagle
Adlige {m}	n.	nobleman
Admiral {m}	n.	admiral
adoptieren	v.	adopt
Adoption {f}	n.	adoption
Adressbuch {n}	n.	directory
adrett	adj.	dapper
adsorbieren	v.	adsorb
Advent {m}	n.	advent
Adverb {n}	n.	adverb
Affe {m} n.		ape
Affe {m} n.		monkey
affektiert adj.		finicky
Affinität {f}	n.	affinity
afrikanisch	adj.	African
After {m}n.		anus
Aggregat {n} n.		aggregate
aggressiv	adj.	aggressive
Ägide {f} n.		aegis
agieren	v.	act
Agnostiker {m}	n.	agnostic
Agnostizismus {m}n.		nescience

Ahnentafel {f}n.	pedigree
ähnlich prep.	like
Ähnlichkeit {f}	n.	likeness
Ähnlichkeit {f}	n.	resemblance
Ähnlichkeit {f}	n.	similarity
Ahnung {f}	n.	intuition
ahnungsvoll adj.	ominous
Ahorn {m}	n.	maple
Akademie {f} n.	academy
akademisch adj.	academic
akademisch adj.	scholastic
Akne {f} n.	acne
Akrobat {m} n.	acrobat
akrobatisch adj.	acrobatic
Aktenordner {m}	n.	file
Aktentasche {f}	n.	portfolio
Aktien {pl}	n.	stock
aktiv adj.	active
aktivieren v.	activate
Aktivist {m} n.	activist
Aktivkohle {f}n.	charcoal
aktualisieren v.	update
Akupunktur {f}	n.	acupuncture
Akustik {f} adj.	acoustic
akustisch adj.	audible
akustisch adj.	sonic
akustisches Zeichenn.	beep
Akzent {m} n.	accent
akzentuieren v.	accentuate
Akzession {f} n.	accession
Alarm {m} n	alarm
alarmieren v	alarm
albern adj.	ludicrous
albern adj.	silly
albern v.	simper

alberne adj.	footling
Albernheit {f} n.	absurdity
Albernheit {f} n.	tomfoolery
Album {n} n	album
Alchemie {f} n.	alchemy
Algebra {f} n.	algebra
alias adv.	alias
Alibi {n} n.	alibi
alkali n.	alkali
Alkohol {m} n.	alcohol
alkoholisch adj.	alcoholic
Alkoholsucht {f} n.	dipsomania
Allbekanntheit {f} n.	notoriety
alle adj. all
Allee {f} n.	alley
Allegorie {f} n.	allegory
allein adv.	alone
allein adj.	lonely
Alleinsein {n} n.	loneliness
allerdings adv.	indeed
Allergie {f} n.	allergy
Allergiestoffe {pl} n.	allergen
allergisch adj.	allergic
Allerheiligstes {n} n.	sanctum
allerlei adj.	sundry
Allerlei {n} n.	welter
Allgegenwart {f} n.	omnipresence
allgegenwärtig adj.	omnipresent
allgegenwärtig adj.	ubiquitous
allgemein adj.	common
Allgemeingültigkeit{f} adv.	universality
allgewaltig adj.	omnipotent
Allheilmittel {n} n.	panacea
Allianz {f} n.	alliance
Alligator {m} n.	alligator

Alliteration {f}	*n.*	alliteration
Allmacht {f}	*n.*	omnipotence
allmächtige	*adj.*	almighty
alltäglich *adj.*	ordinary	
alltäglich *adj.*	workaday	
allumfassend *adj.*	overall	
allwissend	*adj.*	omniscient
Allwissenheit {f}	*n.*	omniscience
Almanach {n} *n.*	almanac	
Almosen {pl} *n.*	alms	
Anteil {m}	*n.*	proportion
Alpha {m}	*n.*	alpha
Alphabet {n}	*n.*	alphabet
alphabetisch *adj.*	alphabetical	
Alpin	*adj.*	alpine
Alptraum {m} *n.*	nightmare	
alt *adj.*	old	
Altar {m} *n.*	altar	
älter *adj.*	elder	
Alter {n} *n.*	age	
Alter {n} *n.*	seniority	
älter, Senior {m}	*adj.*	senior
alternativ	*adj.*	alternative
Altersdiskriminierung {f} *n.*	ageism	
altersschwach	*adj.*	decrepit
ältlich *adj.*	elderly	
altmodisch *adj.*	obsolete	
Altruismus {m}	*n.*	altruism
Aluminium {n}	*n.*	aluminium
am besten *adj.*	best	
am Vorabend *adv.*	overnight	
Amalgam {n} *n.*	amalgam	
Amazone {f} *n.*	amazon	
ambitioniert *adj.*	ambitious	
ambivalent *adj.*	ambivalent	

Amboss {m}	*n.*	anvil
Ambulanz {f}	*n.*	ambulance
Ameise {f}	*n.*	ant
Amnesie {f}	*n.*	amnesia
Amnestie {f}	*n.*	amnesty
Amok {m}	*adv.*	amok
amoralisch	*adj.*	amoral
Amperezahl {f}	*n.*	ampere
Amphibie {f}	*n.*	amphibian
Amphitheater {n}	*n.*	amphitheatre
Amt {n}	*n.*	function
amtieren *v.*	officiate	
amtlich *adj.*	functional	
amtlich *adj.*	ministerial	
Amtsenthebungsverfahren {n} *n.*		
impeachment		
Amtssitz {m} *n.*	seat	
Amulett {n}	*n.*	amulet
an *prep.*	at	
an *prep.*	on	
an Land *adv.*	ashore	
Anachronismus {m} *n.*	anachronism	
anal	*adj.*	anal
analog *adj.*	analogous	
analog *adj.*	analogue	
Analogie {f}	*n.*	analogy
Analphabet {m}	*n.*	alliterate
Analphabet {m}	*n.*	illiterate
Analphabetentum {n} *n.*	illiteracy	
Analyse {f}	*n.*	analysis
analysieren *v.*	analyse	
Analytiker {m}	*n.*	analyst
analytisch *adj.*	analytical	
Anämie {f}	*n.*	anaemia
Ananas {f}	*n.*	pineapple

Anarchie {f}	n.	anarchy
Anarchismus{f}	n.	anarchism
Anarchist {m}n.		anarchist
Anästhesie {f}	n.	anaesthesia
Anästhetikum {n}	n.	anaesthetic
Anatomie {f}	n.	anatomy
anbeten	v.	hallow
Anbeter {m}	n.	worshipper
anbetungswürdig	adj.	adorable
anbietend	adj.	biddable
Anbieter {m}	n.	bidder
anbinden	v.t.	tether
Anbindung {f}	n.	binding
anblinzeln	v.	blink
anblitzen v.i		glare
anbrennen	v.	burn
anbrennend	adj.	burning
anbrüllen	v.	roar
andächtig	adj.	devout
Andenken {n}n.		keepsake
Andenken {n}n.		memento
Andenken {n}n.		souvenir
ander	adj.	another
anderes	adj. & pron.	other
ändern	v.t.	modify
Änderung {f}	n.	modification
Änderung {f}	n.	mutation
andeuten	v.	insinuate
Andeutung {f}	n.	inkling
Andeutung {f}	n.	insinuation
Androide {m} n.		android
Androide {m} n.		anecdote
anecken	v.	scandalize
aneignen	v.	usurp
anerkennen	v.	acknowledge

anerkennenswert	adj.	creditable
anfahren v.		snub
anfällig	adj.	prone
Anfang {m}	n.	beginning
Anfang {m}	n.	commencement
Anfang {m}	n.	outset
anfangen	v.	commence
Anfänger {m} n.		amateur
Anfänger {m} n.		novice
anfänglich	adj.	initial
anfechten	v.	arrange
anfertigen	v.	make
anflehen v.t.		implore
anflehen v.		supplicate
Anforderungszeichen {n}v.		prompt
Anfrage {f}	n.	request
anfügen v.		annex
anfügen v.		attach
Anführer {m} n.		chief
Anführungszeichen {n}v.		quote
Angabe {f}	n.	information
angaffen v.		gape
angeben v.		specify
angeben v.		swank
angeberisch v.		swanky
angeboren	adj.	congenital
angeboren	adj.	inborn
angeboren	adj.	innate
angeborene	adj.	inbred
Angebot {n}	n.	bargain
Angebot {n}	n.	offering
angegeben	adj.	given
angeheitert	adj.	tipsy
Angeklagte {f}		n.defendant
Angel {f} n.		tang

angelehnt	adv.	ajar
angemessen	adj.	adequate
Angemessenheit {f}n.		adequacy
Angemessenheit {f}n.		suitability
angenehm	adj.	agreeable
angenehm	adj.	pleasant
angenommen	adj.	adoptive
angespannt	adj.	strained
angestammt	adj.	ancestral
Angina {f}	n.	angina
angleichen	v.	adapt
angleichend	adj.	approximate
Angleichung {f}	n.	assimilation
Angliederung {f}	n.	incorporation
angreifen	v.	grab
angreifend	adj.	offensive
Angreifer {m} n.		aggressor
Angreifer {m} n.		offender
angrenzen	v.	abut
angrenzen	v.	adjoin
Angriff {m}	n.	aggression
Angriff {m}	n.	onset
Angriff {m}	n.	onslaught
Angst {f} n.		agitation
Angst {f} n.		excitement
Angst {f} n.		fright
Angst {f} n.		trepidation
ängstlich	adj.	anxious
ängstlich	adj.	scrupulous
ängstlich	adj.	timorous
anhaften v.		adhere
anhalten v.		stop
Anhang {m}	n.	appendage
Anhang {m}	n.	appendix
anhangen	v.	append

Anhänger {m}	n.	devotee
Anhänger {m}	n.	trailer
Anhänglichkeit {f}n.		adherence
anhäufen	v.	accumulate
Anhäufung {f}	n.	conglomeration
anheften v.		clinch
anheimelnd	adv.	quaintly
anhören v.		listen
Animation {f} n.		animation
animieren	v.	animate
animiert adj.		animated
Anissamen {m}	n.	aniseed
Anker {m}	n.	anchor
Ankergrund {m}	n.	anchorage
Anklage {f}	n.	accusation
Anklage {f}	n.	indictment
Anklagebank {f}	n.	dock
anklagenv.		denounce
anklagenv.		impeach
anklagenv.		indict
Anklageschrift {f} n.		bill
ankommen	v.	arrive
ankündigen	v.	announce
Anlage {f}	n.	attachment
Anlasser {m} n.		starter
Anleihe {f}	n.	bond
Anleihe {f}	n.	debenture
anleiten v.		instruct
Anleitung {f}	n.	guide
Anleitung {f}	n.	tutorial
anmarschieren	v.	approach
anmaßen	v.	arrogate
anmaßen	adj.	overbearing
anmaßend	adj.	overweening
Anmaßung {f}	n.	pretension

German		English
anmeldepflichtig	*adj.*	notifiable
anmerken	*v.*	annotate
Anmerkung {f}	*n.*	comment
Anmut {f}	*n.*	grace
annähern	*adj.*	appropriate
Annahme {f}	*n.*	acceptance
Annalen {pl}	*n.*	annals
annehmbar	*adj.*	acceptable
annehmbar	*adj.*	passable
annehmen	*v.*	accept
annehmen	*v.*	assume
annullieren	*v.*	annul
Annullieren {n}	*n.*	undoing
Annullierung {f}	*n.*	nullification
Anode {f}	*n.*	anode
anomal	*adj.*	aberrant
Anomalie {f}	*n.*	anomaly
Anonymität {f}	*n.*	anonymity
anordnen	*v. t*	dispose
anordnen	*v.*	serialize
Anordnung {f}	*n.*	order
anormal	*adj.*	anomalous
anpacken	*v.t.*	grapple
anpacken	*v.t.*	tackle
anpassen	*v.*	accommodate
anpassen	*v.*	adjust
anpassen	*v.*	assimilate
anpassen	*v.*	conform
anpassen	*v.*	customize
anprangen	*v.*	decry
anraten	*v.*	advise
anregen	*v.*	inspire
Anregungsmittel {n}	*n.*	stimulant
anreichern	*v.*	enrich
Anreise {f}	*n.*	arrival
Anreißer {m}	*n.*	scribe
anreizend	*adj.*	incentive
anrempeln	*v.t.*	jostle
Anruf {m}	*n.*	buzz
ansammeln	*v.*	amass
Ansaugung {f}	*n.*	intake
Anschaffung {f}	*n.*	acquisition
Anschein {m}	*n.*	appearance
Anschein {m}	*n.*	semblance
Anschlagbrett {n}	*n.*	noticeboard
Anschlussbox {f}	*n.*	modem
anschmiegen	*v.*	cling
anschmieren	*v.*	smear
Anschrift {m}	*n.*	address
Ansehen {n}	*n.*	kudos
Ansehen {n}	*n.*	reputation
Ansetzungsform {f}	*n.*	heading
Ansicht {f}	*n.*	view
anspannen	*v.*	strain
Anspielung {f}	*n.*	allusion
ansprechbar	*adj.*	responsive
ansprechen	*v.*	accost
ansprechen	*v.t.*	appeal
anspritzen	*v.*	splash
anspruchsvoll	*adj.*	pretentious
Anstalt {f}	*n.*	establishment
Anstalt {f}	*n.*	institution
Anstand {m}	*n.*	decency
Anstand {m}	*n.*	decorum
anständig	*adj.*	decent
anständig	*adj.*	decorous
anstarren	*v.*	gaze
anstechend	*adj.*	broach
anstecken	*v.*	infect
ansteckend	*adj.*	contagious

ansteckend	adj.	infectious
Ansteckung {f}	n.	contagion
Ansteckung {f}	n.	infection
anstellen v.t		hire
anstiften v.		instigate
anstiften v.		suborn
anstimmen	v.	intone
Anstoß {m}	n.	impetus
anstößen	v.	nudge
anstößig adj.		obnoxious
anstrengend	adj.	arduous
anstrengend	adj.	trying
anstürmen	v.	assail
Antarktis {f}	adj.	Antarctic
Anteil {m}	n.	allotment
Anteil {m}	n.	portion
Anteil {m}	n.	rate
Anteil {m}	n.	share
Anteil {m}	n.	stake
anteilmäßig	adj.	proportionate
Antenne {f}	n.	aerial
Antenne {f}	n.	antenna
anti n.		anti
Antibiotikum {n}	n.	antibiotic
antik	adj.	antique
Antiklimax {f} n.		anticlimax
Antilope {f}	n.	antelope
Antioxidant {n}	n.	antioxidant
Antipathie {f} n.		antipathy
antiquarisch	adj.	antiquarian
Antiquität {f}	n.	antiquity
antiseptisch	adj.	antiseptic
Antithese {f}	n.	antithesis
Antlitz {m}	n.	visage
Antonym {n}	n.	antonym

Antragsteller {m}	n.	claimant
antreiben	v.	actuate
antreiben	v.	goad
antreiben	v.	impel
Antwort {f}	n.	answer
Antwort {f}	n.	response
antworten	v.	reply
antworten	v.	respond
anvertrauen	v.	entrust
anwachsen	v.	increase
Anwalt {m}	n.	advocate
anwenden	v.t.	use
anwendet	v.t.	apply
Anwendung {f}	n.	usage
anwesend	adv.	aboard
Anwesenheit {f}	n.	presence
anwidernd	adj.	cloying
Anzeichen {n}	n.	indication
Anzeichen {n}	n.	portent
anzeigen v.		indicate
anziehen v.		attract
Anziehungskraft {f}		n. gravity
Anziehungspunkt {m} n.		cynosure
Anzug {m}	n.	costume
Anzug {m}	n.	garment
anzünden	v.	kindle
anzweifeln	v.	discredit
Äon {m} n.		aeon
Apathie {f}	n.	apathy
Aperitif {m}	n.	appetizer
Apfel {m}	n.	apple
Apfelsaft {m} n.		cider
Apokalypse {f}	n.	apocalypse
apoplektisch	adj.	apoplectic
Apostel {m}	n.	apostle

Apotheke {f}	n.	pharmacy
Appell {m}	n.	plea
Appell {m}	n.	roll-call
Appetit {m}	n.	appetite
appetitlich	adj.	delicious
Appetitlosigkeit {f}	n.	anorexia
applaudieren v.		applaud
Applaus {m}	n.	applause
Aprikose {f}	n.	apricot
Aquarium {n} n.		aquarium
aquatisch	adj.	aquatic
Äquator {m}	n.	equator
Ära {f}	n.	era
Araber {m}	n.	Arab
arabisch n.		Arabian
arabisch n.		Arabic
Arbeit {f} n.		labour
Arbeit {f} n.		work
Arbeiter {m}	n.	labourer
Arbeiter {m}	n.	worker
arbeitsam	adj.	industrious
arbeitsam	adj.	laborious
Arbeitsergebnis {n}	n.	output
Arbeitsgang {m}	n.	action
Arbeitsgang {m}	n.	operation
Arbeitsgang {m}	n.	working
Arbeitsgemeinschaft {f}n.		syndicate
Arbeitskräfte {pl}	n.	manpower
arbeitslos	adj.	unemployed
Arbeitsmann {m}	n.	workman
Archäologie {f}	n.	archaeology
Arche {f} n.		ark
Architekt {m} n.		architect
Architektur {f}	n.	architecture
Archiv {n}	n.	archives

Archivierung {f}	n.	filings
Arena {f} n.		arena
Ärger {m}	v.t.	fret
Ärger {m}	n.	spleen
Ärger {m}	n.	vexation
Ärger {m},	n.	resentment
ärgerlich adj.		fretful
ärgern	v.	exasperate
ärgern	v.	infuriate
ärgern	v.	vex
Argument {n} n.		argument
argumentieren	v.	argue
Aristokrat {m}	n.	aristocrat
Aristokratie {f}	n.	aristocracy
Arithmetik {f} n.		arithmetic
arithmetisch	adj.	arithmetical
Arktis {f} n.		Arctic
arm adj.		poor
Armada {m}	n.	armada
Armaturenbretter {pl} n.		dashboard
Armband {n}	n.	bracelet
Armlehne {f}	n.	arm
Armreif {m}	n.	bangle
Armschlinge {f}	n.	sling
Armut {f}n.		poverty
Ärobic {f}	n.	aerobics
Aroma {f}	n.	aroma
Aromatherapie {f} n.		aromatherapy
Ärosol {n}	n.	aerosol
Arsen {n}	n.	arsenic
Arsenal {n}	n.	arsenal
Art {f}	n.	sort
Artefakt {n}	n.	artefact
Arterie {f}	n.	artery
Arthritis {f}	n.	arthritis

German		English
Artikel {m}	n.	item
Artillerie {f}	n.	artillery
Artillerie {f}	n.	ordnance
Artischocke {f}	n.	artichoke
Arzneiausgabe {f}	n.	dispensary
Arzt {m}	n.	medic
Arzt {m}	n.	physician
As {n}	n.	ace
Asbest {m}	n.	asbestos
Asche {f}n.		ash
aseptisch	adj.	aseptic
asiatisch adj.		Asian
Aspekt {m}	n.	aspect
assemblieren v.		assemble
Assistant	n.	assistant
assistieren	v.	assist
Assonanz {f}	n.	assonance
Ast {m}	n.	bough
Ast {m}	n.	branch
Asteroid {m}	n.	asteroid
Ästhetik {f}	n.	aesthetics
ästhetisch	adj.	aesthetic
Asthma {n}	n.	asthma
Astigmatismus {m}		n. astigmatism
Astrologe {m}		n. astrologer
Astrologie {f} n.		astrology
Astronaut {m}		n. astronaut
Astronom {m}		n. astronomer
Atem {m}	n.	breath
Atemgerät {n}		n. respirator
Atheismus {m}		n. atheism
Atheist {m}	n.	atheist
Athlet {m}	n.	athlete
Atlas {m}n.		atlas
atmen	v.	breathe

German		English
Atmosphäre {f}	n.	atmosphere
Atmung {f}	n.	respiration
Atoll {n}	n.	atoll
Atom {n}n.		atom
atomar	adj.	atomic
Attache {m}	n.	attaché
Attitüde {f}	n.	attitude
Attraktion {f}	n.	attraction
ätzend	adj.	caustic
Au {f}	n.	meadow
Aubergine {f}	n.	aubergine
auch	adv.	also
auch	adv.	too
Audio {n}	n.	audio
Aue {f}	n.	mead
aufatmen	v.	respire
aufbauen	v.	synthesize
Aufbesserung {f}	n.	amelioration
aufbewahren v.		preserve
Aufbewahrungsort {m} n.		repository
aufblasen	v.	bloat
aufblasen	v.	inflate
aufbrechen	v.	decamp
Aufbrechung {f}	n.	sally
aufdrängen	v.	obtrude
aufdringlich	adj.	brash
aufdringlich	adj.	pushy
aufdrucken	v.	imprint
aufeinander wirken	v.	interact
Aufenthalt {m}	n.	sojourn
Aufenthaltsraum {m}n.		lounge
auferlegend	adj.	imposing
Auferlegung {f}	n.	imposition
auffallend	adj.	conspicuous
auffallend	adj.	garish

auffallend	adj.	striking	
auffangend	adj.	catching	
Auffassung {f}	n.	conception	
Auffassungskraft {f}n.		perception	
auffinden	v.	found	
Aufforstung {f}	n.	afforestation	
auffrischen	v.	refresh	
Aufführung {f}	n.	conduct	
auffüllen v.		refill	
auffüllen v.		replenish	
Aufgabe {f}	n.	exercise	
Aufgabe {f}	n.	task	
aufgeben	v.	capitulate	
aufgeben	v.	resign	
aufgeben	v.	surrender	
aufgeben	v.	waive	
aufgebracht	adj.	angry	
aufgehen	v.	rise	
aufgeräumt	adj.	tidy	
aufgeschoben	v.	suspend	
aufgießen	v.	infuse	
Aufgliederung {f}	n.	classification	
Aufgliederung {f}	n.	tabulation	
aufhängen	v.i.	hang	
Aufhänger {m}	n.	hanger	
aufhäufen	v.	agglomerate	
aufheben	v.	abrogate	
aufheben	v.	repeal	
aufheben	v.	rescind	
aufhellen	v.	brighten	
aufhetzen	v.	incite	
aufklären	v.	undeceive	
Aufklärung {f}	n.	clarification	
Aufkleber {m}n.		sticker	
Auflage n.		edition	

Auflage {f}	n.	layer	
Auflage {f}	n.	support	
auflauern	v.	waylay	
auflehnen	v.	revolt	
auflösen v.		resolve	
aufnahmefähig	adj.	receptive	
Aufnahmegerät {m}	n.	recorder	
Aufpasser {m}	n.	overseer	
aufpolieren	v.	refurbish	
aufrechterhalten	v.	maintain	
aufrechterhalten	v.	uphold	
Aufregungen {pl}	n.	takings	
Aufreiben {n} n.		ream	
aufreizend	adj.	provocative	
aufrichtig	adj.	candid	
aufrichtig	adj.	sincere	
Aufrichtigkeit {f}	n.	candour	
Aufrichtigkeit {f}	n.	sincerity	
Aufruf {m}	n.	calling	
Aufruf {m}	n.	invocation	
aufrufen v.		invoke	
Aufruhr {m}	n.	insurrection	
Aufruhr {m}	n.	riot	
aufrührerisch adj.		inflammatory	
aufrührerisch adj.		rebellious	
Aufrüstung {f}	n.	armament	
aufsässig	adj.	insubordinate	
Aufsatz {m}	n.	composition	
aufsaugen	v.	imbibe	
Aufsaugung {f}	n.	aspiration	
aufschieben v.		adjourn	
aufschlagen v.		thud	
aufschrecken v.		startle	
Aufschrei {m}n.		outcry	
Aufschrift {f}	n.	inscription	

227

Aufschub {m}n.	postponement
Aufschub {m}n.	suspension
Aufsehen {n} n.	furore
aufsehenerregen	v.	sensationalize
Aufseher {m} n.	custodian
Aufseher {m} n.	inspector
Aufsicht {f} n.	supervision
aufsteigen v.i.	soar
aufstellen v.	situate
aufstellend adj.	embattled
Aufstieg {m} n.	ascent
aufstoßen v.	belch
aufstreben v.	aspire
Auftakt {m} adj.	upbeat
auftauchen v.	bob
auftauchen v.	emerge
Auftauchen {n}	n.	loom
auftrennen v.	rave
auftreten v.	occur
aufwachen v.	smarten
Aufwallung {f}	n.	upsurge
Aufwand {m} n.	expense
Aufwand {m} n.	outlay
aufwändig adj.	complex
aufwändig adj.	costly
aufwärts adv. up
aufwärts adv. upward
aufwecken v.	arouse
aufweichen v.	soften
aufwenden v.	spend
Aufwendung {f}	n.	expenditure
aufwiegelnd adj.	seditious
Aufwiegelung {f}	n.	sedition
aufzählen v. t	enumerate
Aufzeichnung {f} n.	chronicle

aufziehen v.	foster
Augapfel {m} n.	eyeball
Auge {n}, n.	eye
Augenblick {m} n.	moment
augenblicklich adj.	instant
augenblicklich ádj.	instantaneous
Augenhöhle {f} n.	orbit
Augenlicht {n} n.	eyesight
Augenwasser {n} n.	eyewash
Augenzeuge {m} n.	eyewitness
August {m} n	August
Auktion {f} n.	auction
Aula {f} n.	auditorium
aus adv. off
ausatmen v.	exhale
ausbessern v.	refit
ausbeuten v. t	exploit
Ausbildung {f} n.	education
Ausbildung {f} n.	training
ausbleichend adj. bleach
Ausblick {m} n.	outlook
ausbrechen v.	erupt
ausbreiten v.	splay
ausbreiten v.	sprawl
Ausbruch {m} n.	outbreak
Ausbruch {m} n.	outburst
ausbrüten v.	incubate
ausbürgern n.	expatriate
ausdauern v.i.	persevere
Ausdehnung {f} n.	expanse
Ausdehnung {f} n.	extension
ausdenken v.	devise
Ausdruck {m}n.	expression
ausdrücken v.	enunciate
ausdrücken v.	express

ausdrücklich *adj.* explicit
Ausdrucksweise {f}*n.* parlance
Ausdrucksweise {f}*n.* phraseology
auseinander *adv.* asunder
Auseinandersetzung {f}*n.* quarrel
auseinandertreiben *v.* disperse
auserwählen *v.* elect
Ausfall {m} *n.* blackout
Ausfall {m} *n.* sortie
ausfällen*v.* precipitate
ausfasern *v.* rove
Ausflucht {f} *n.* elusion
Ausflucht {f} *n.* subterfuge
Ausflug {m} *n.* excursion
Ausflug {m} *n.* jaunt
Ausflug {m} *n.* outing
ausfransen *v.* fray
ausführen *v.* execute
ausführen *v.* perform
Ausführung {f} *n.*accomplishment
Ausführung {f} *n.* implement
Ausführung {f} *n.* realization
Ausgabenkürzung{f}*n.* retrenchment
Ausgangssperre {f} *n.* curfew
ausgearbeitet*adj.* elaborate
ausgeben *v.* emit
ausgebeult *adj.* baggy
ausgedehnt *adj.* vast
ausgeführt *adj.* accomplished
ausgenommen *prep.* barring
ausgepacken *v.* unpack
ausgeprägt *adj.* distinct
ausgereift *adj.* mellow
Ausgereiftheit {f} *n.* sophistication
ausgerissen *adj.* runaway

Ausgesetztsein {n} *n.* exposure
Ausgestoßen {m} *n.* outcast
Ausgestoßene {m,f} *n.* pariah
ausgewichen *n.* quibble
ausgezeichnet *adj.* excellent
ausgleichen *v. t* equalize
ausgleichen *v.* offset
Ausgleichsprozess {m}*n.* netting
ausgleiten *v.* slip
ausgliedern *v.* outsource
ausgraben *v.* excavate
ausgraben *v.* unearth
aushalten *v.* endure
aushalten *v.* sustain
aushöhlend *adj.* hollow
Aushöhlung {f} *n.* cavity
auskleiden *v.* undress
ausladen*v.* unload
Ausländer {m} *n.* foreigner
Auslassung {f} *n.* omission
ausleihen *v.* borrow
ausleihen *v.* lend
Auslieferung {f} *n.* delivery
Auslistung {f}*n.* dump
auslöschen *v.* efface
auslöschen *v.* eliminate
auslöschen *v.* extinguish
auslöschen *v.* raze
Auslöseimpuls {m} *n.* trigger
auslösen*v.* initiate
auslösen*v.* release
Auslösereiz {m} *n.* cue
Auslosung {f}*n.* assignment
Ausmaß {n} *n.* extent
Ausmauerung {f} *n.* cladding

229

ausmeißeln	v.	gouge
ausnahmslos	adj.	unexceptional
ausnutzen	v.	utilize
ausplaudern	v.	blab
Ausprägung {f}	n.	characteristic
ausrangieren	v.	discard
ausreichen	v.	suffice
ausreichend	adj.	enough
ausrenken	v.	dislocate
ausrichten	v.	align
ausrotten	v.	eradicate
ausrotten	v.	extirpate
Ausruf {m}	n.	exclamation
ausrufen	v.	exclaim
ausruhen	v.	rest
ausrüsten	v.	equip
Ausrüstung {f}	n.	apparatus
Ausrüstung {f}	n.	outfit
Ausrutscher {m}	n.	gaffe
aussagekräftig	adj.	expressive
Aussätzige {m,f}	n.	leper
ausschlaggeben	v. t	determine
ausschließen	v. t.	debar
ausschließen	v.	exclude
ausschließend	adj.	prohibitive
ausschließlich	adj.	exclusive
Ausschmückung{f}	n.	ornamentation
Ausschnitt {m}	n.	notch
Ausschreibung {f}	n.	tender
Ausschuss {m}	n.	committee
Ausschuss {m}	n.	junk
Ausschweifung {f}	n.	debauchery
ausschwitzen	v.	exude
außen	n.	outside
Außenposten {m}	n.	outpost

Außenseiter {m}	n.	outsider
Außenseiter {m};	n.	misfit
außer	prep.	except
außer sich	adj.	frantic
außerdem	adv.	furthermore
außerdem	adv.	moreover
äußere	adj.	outer
außergewöhnlich	adj.	extraordinary
außerhalb	adj.	outboard
Außerirdischer {m}	adj.	alien
äußerlich	adj.	exterior
äußerlich	adj.	outward
äußern	adj.	utter
äußerst	adj.	superlative
äußerst	adj.	utmost
äußerst	adj. & n.	uttermost
äußerster	adj.	ultimate
Äußerung {f}	n.	utterance
Aussichtspunkt {m}	n.	gazebo
aussichtsvoll	adj.	promising
aussortieren	v.	winnow
Aussprache {f}	n.	pronunciation
aussprechen	v.	vocalize
aussprechend	v.	pronounce
ausstatten	v.	endow
Ausstattung {f}	n.	accoutrement
Ausstattung {f}	n.	equipment
Ausstattung {f}	n.	environment
ausstellen	v.	exhibit
Ausstellung {f}	n.	exhibition
ausstoßen	v.	ejaculate
ausstoßen	v.	ovulate
Ausstrahlung {f}	n.	charisma
Ausstrahlung {f}	n.	vibe
Austausch {m}	v.	interchange

austauschen *v. t* exchange
Auster {f}   *n.*   oyster
Australier {m}   *n.*   wallaby
australisch   *n.*   Australian
Austritt {m}   *n.*   exit
ausüben *v.*   wield
auswachsen *v.*   outgrow
Auswahl {f}   *n.*   selection
Auswahl {f}   *n.*   variety
auswählen *v.*   select
auswandern *v.*   emigrate
Auswanderung {f} *n.* transmigration
auswärts *adv.* outwardly
auswechseln *v.*   replace
ausweichen *v. t* evade
ausweichend *v.*   swerve
ausweichende   *adj.* evasive
ausweisen   *v. t* expel
auswerten   *v. i* evaluate
Auswirkung {f}   *n.*   effect
Auswirkung {f}   *n.*   impact
Auswirkung {f}   *n.*   outcome
auszanken   *v.*   berate
Auszeichnung {f} *n.*   accolade
Auszeichnung {f} *n.*   distinction
Auszug {m}   *n.*   excerpt
authentisch   *adj.* authentic
Autismus {m} *n.*   autism
Auto {n} *n.*   car
Autobahn {f}   *n.*   motorway
Autobiografie {f}   *n.*   autobiography
Autobus {m} *n.*   bus
Autofahrer {m}   *n.*   motorist
Autograph {m}   *n.*   autograph
Autokrat {m}   *n.*   autocrat

Autokratie {f} *n.*   autocracy
autokratisch *adj.* autocratic
automatisch *adj.* automatic
autonom *adj.* autonomous
Autopsie {f}   *n.*   autopsy
Aversion {f}   *n.*   aversion
Avokado {f}   *n.*   avocado
Axt {f}   *n.*   axe
Azetat {n}   *n.*   acetate
Azeton {n}   *n.*   acetone
Azidität {f}   *n.*   acidity

B

Baby {n} *n.*   baby
Bach {m}*n.*   brook
Bach {m}*n.*   rivulet
Bächlein {n}   *n.*   streamlet
Bachstelze {f}   *n.*   wagtail
Backe {f}*n.*   cheek
backen {v}   *v.*   bake
Backenbart {m}   *n.*   whisker
Backenzahn {m}   *n.*   molar
Bäcker {m}   *n.*   baker
Bäckerei {f}   *n.*   bakery
Backhefe {f}   *n.*   yeast
Backpflaume {f}   *n.*   prune
Backstein {m}   *n.*   brick
Bad {n}   *n.*   bath
baden *v.*   bathe
Badestrand {m}   *n.*   beach
Baggereimer {m}   *n.*   scoop
Baguette {n} *n.*   baguette
Bahn {f} *n.*   railway
Bahre {f}*n.*   bier
Bäkerei {f}   *n.*   patisserie

231

Bakterien {pl}	*n.*	bacteria	**Barbar** {m}	*n.*	barbarian
Bakterienstamm {m}	*n.*	strain	**barbarisch**	*adj.*	barbaric
bald *adv.*		shortly	**Barde** {f}	*n.*	bard
bald *adv.*		soon	**Bargeld** {m}	*n.*	cash
Balken {m}	*n.*	joist	**Barometer** {n}	*n.*	barometer
Balkon {m}	*n.*	balcony	**Baron** {m}	*n.*	baron
Ball {m}	*n.*	ball	**Barrakuda** {f}	*n.*	barracuda
Ballade {f}	*n.*	ballad	**Barriere** {f}	*n.*	barrage
Ballaststoff {m}	*n.*	fibre	**Barsch** {m}	*n.*	perch
Ballen {m}	*n.*	bale	**Bart** {m}	*n.*	beard
Ballett {n}	*n.*	ballet	**Basar** {m}	*n.*	bazaar
Ballungsgebiet {n}	*n.*	conurbation	**Basilika** {f}	*n.*	basilica
Balsam	*n.*	conditioner	**Basilikum** {n}	*n.*	basil
Balsam {n}	*n.*	balm	**Basis** {f}	*n.*	base
Balsam {n}	*n.*	balsam	**Basis** {f}	*n.*	basis
Bambus {n}	*n.*	bamboo	**Bass** {m}	*n.*	bass
banal *adj.*		banal	**Bastard** {m}	*n.*	bastard
banal *adj.*		commonplace	**basteln** *v.*		tinker
Banane {f}	*n.*	banana	**Bastion** {f}	*n.*	bastion
Band {n}	*n.*	reel	**Bataillon** {n}	*n.*	battalion
Bandbreite {f}	*n.*	range	**Batist** {m}	*n.*	batik
Bändchen {n}	*n.*	booklet	**Batist** {m}	*n.*	cambric
Bande {f}	*n.*	gang	**Batterie** {f}	*n.*	battery
bändigen *v.*		subdue	**Bau** {m}	*n.*	fabric
Bandspule {f}	*n.*	spool	**Bauch** {m}	*n.*	abdomen
bange *adj.*		funky	**Bauch** {m}	*n.*	belly
Banjo {n}	*n.*	banjo	**bauen** *v.*		build
Bank {f}	*n.*	bank	**bauen** *v.*		construct
Bankett {n}	*n.*	banquet	**Bauer** {m}	*n.*	pawn
Bankier {m}	*n.*	banker	**Bauer** {m}	*n.*	peasant
bankrott *adj.*		bankrupt	**bäuerlich**	*adj.*	rustic
Bankrott {m}	*n.*	bankruptcy	**Bauernhof** {m}	*n.*	farm
Bär {m}	*n.*	bear	**Bauernlümmel** {m}	*n.*	bumpkin
Baracke {f}	*n.*	barrack	**baufällig** *adj.*		dilapidated
Baracke {f}	*n.*	shed	**baufällig** *adj.*		ramshackle

Baugruppe {f}	n.	assembly
Baum {m}	n.	tree
baumeln v. i.	dangle
Baumstamm {m}	n.	bole
Baumstumpf {m}	n.	snag
Baumwolle {f}	n.	cotton
Bausatz {m}	n.	kit
Bausch {m}	n.	wad
Bautischler {m}	n.	carpenter
Bauunternehmer {m}n.	contractor
Bauweise {f}	n.	structure
beabsichtigen	v.	intend
beabsichtigt adj.	deliberate
beabsichtigt adj.	wilful
beachtenswert	adj.	remarkable
Beachtung {f}v.	heed
Beachtung {f}n.	observance
Beamter {m}	n.	officer
beängstigen v.	frighten
beansprechen	v.	engross
beantwortbar adj.	answerable
bearbeiten	v.	edit
beaufsichtigen	v.	oversee
beaufsichtigen	v.	superintend
beaufsichtigen	v.	supervise
Beaufsichtigende {m,f}n.	peer
beben v.	quake
Becher {m}	n.	mug
Becken {n}	n.	basin
Becken {n}	n.	bowl
Becken {n}	n.	pelvis
bedachtsam adj.	considerate
Bedachung {f}	n.	roofing
Bedarfsartikel {m} n.	commodity
bedauerlich adj.	deplorable

bedauerlich	adj.	regrettable
Bedauern {n} n.	regret
bedecken	v.	suffuse
bedenken	v.	consider
Bedenken {n} n.	qualm
bedenklich	adj.	apprehensive
bedenklich	adj.	questionable
bedeuten	v.	signify
bedeutsamen adj.	significant
Bedeutung {f}	n.	meaning
Bedeutung {f}	n.	prominence
Bedeutung {f}	n.	significance
bedeutungslos	adj.	insignificant
Bedienstete {m,f}	n.	attendant
Bedienung {f}n.	service
bedienungsfrei	adj.	unmanned
bedingt adj.	conditional
Bedingung {f}	n.	condition
Bedingung {f}	n.	requirement
bedrohen	v.	threaten
Bedrohung {f}	n.	threat
bedrücken	v.	depress
Bedürfnis {n} n.	necessity
bedürfnislos adj.	frugal
Beefsteak {n} n.	steak
beeilen v.	hasten
beeindrucken v.	impress
beeinträchtigen	v.	impair
beeinträchtigen	v.	vitiate
beeinträchtigt	adj.	affected
beenden v.	conclude
beenden v.	terminate
beenden	v.	finish
Beerdigung {f}	n.	funeral
Beere {f} n.	berry

233

befähigen	v.	empower
befähigen	v.	quantify
Befähigung {f}	n.	qualification
Befehl {m}	n.	instruction
befehlen	v.	command
befestigen	v.t.	affix
befestigen	v.	fasten
befestigen	v.	fix
Befestigungsorgan {n}n.		fixture
befeuchten	v.	moisturize
beflecken	v.t.	stain
beflecken	v.	sully
befördern	v.	promote
Beförderung {f}	n.	advancement
Beförderung {f}	n.	preferment
Beförderung {f}	n.	promotion
Beförderungsmittel{n}n.transportation
Befrachtung {f}	n.	charter
Befragen {n}	v.	consult
befreien	v.	enfranchise
befreien	v.	extricate
befreien	v.	liberate
Befreier {m}	n.	liberator
Befreitsein {n}	n.	riddance
Befreiung {f}	n.	liberation
befreunden	v.	befriend
befriedigen	v.	satisfy
befriedigend	adj.	satisfactory
Befriedigung {f}	n.	satisfaction
befristen	v.	reprieve
befruchten	v.	fertilize
Befugnisübergabe {f}n.		devolution
befürchten	v.	misgive
befürchtend	adj.	afraid
Befürchtung {f}	n.	fear

Befürchtung {f}	n.	misgiving
begabt	adj.	gifted
begabt	adj.	talented
Begabung {f} n.		ability
Begabung {f} n.		aptitude
Begabung {f} n.		talent
begatten v.		copulate
begeben v.		betake
begegnen	v.	encounter
begehbarer Schrankn.		closet
begehren	v.	covet
begeistern	v.	enthral
Begeisterung {f}	n.	enthusiasm
Begierde {f}	n.	lust
begierig	adj.	avid
begierig	adj.	desirous
Beginn {m}	n.	inception
beginnen	v.	begin
beglaubigen	v.	accredit
beglaubigen	v.	attest
beglaubigt	adj.	accredited
begleiten	v.	accompany
begleiten	v.	attend
Begleiter {m} n.		tutor
Begleitung {f}n.		accompaniment
Begleitung {f}n.		backing
Begleitung {f}n.		escort
beglückwünschen v.		congratulate
beglückwünschen v.		felicitate
Beglückwünschung{f}n.congratulation
Begräbnis {n}n.		sepulture
begreifen	v.	comprehend
begrenzen	v.	confine
begrenzen	v.	delineate
Begrenzung {f}	n.	border

Begrenzung {f}	n.	limitation
Begriff {m}	n.	notion
begrifflich	adj.	notional
begriffsstutzig	adj.	obtuse
begründen	v.	substantiate
Begründung {f}	n.	substantiation
Begrüßung {f}	n.	greeting
begünstigen	v.	abet
begünstigen	v.t.	advantage
behalten	v.	keep
Behälter {m}	n.	crib
Behälter {m}	n.	tank
behandeln	v.t	handle
behandeln	v.	treat
Behandlung {f}	n.	treatment
Behang {m}	n.	hanging
beharren	v.	persist
beharrlich	adj.	persistent
Beharrlichkeit {f}	n.	perseverance
behaupten	v.	allege
behaupten	v.	assert
behaupten	v.	purport
Behauptung {f}	n.	allegation
Behausung {f}	n.	dwelling
beherrschend	adj.	dominant
behilflich	adj.	helpful
behindert	n.	handicapped
behindert	adj.	retarded
Behinderung {f}	n.	handicap
behördlich	adj.	magisterial
behutsam	adv.	gingerly
bei	prep.	for
beibehalten	v.i.	retain
Beichte {f}	n.	confession
beichten	v.	confess

beide	adj. & pron.	both
Beifall {m}	n.	plaudits
Beifügung {f}	n.	addendum
beige	n.	beige
Beihilfen {pl}	n.	aids
Beilage {f}	n.	enclosure
Beileid {n}	n.	condolence
Beileid {n}	n.	sympathy
Bein {n}	n.	leg
beinahe	adv.	nearly
beipflichten	v.	agree
beirren	v.	mislead
beispiellos	adj.	unprecedented
beispielslos	adj.	unequalled
beißen	v.	bite
beißend	adj.	biting
Beißende {f}	n.	pungency
Beitrag {m}	n.	contribution
beitragen	v.	contribute
beitreten	v.	accede
Beize {f}	n.	marinade
beizen	v.	corrode
Bekämpfung {f}	n.	combat
bekannt geben	v.	notify
bekanntmachen	v.	acquaint
Bekanntmachung{f}n.		announcement
Bekanntschaft {f}	n.	acquaintance
bekennen	v.	avow
beklagen	v.	bemoan
beklagenswert	adj.	lamentable
Beklagte {m,f}	n.	respondent
Beklemmung {f}	n.	anxiety
bekommen	v.	get
bekräftigen	v.	affirm
bekräftigen	v.	corroborate

235

bekräftigen	v.	fortify
Bekräftigung {f}	n.	affirmation
bekümmern	v.	grieve
bekümmert	adj.	solicitous
bekunden	v.	evince
Belag {m}	n.	lining
belagert	adj.	beleaguered
Belagerung {f}	n.	siege
belasten	v.	encumber
belästigen	v.	bother
belästigen	v.	harass
belästigen	v.	molest
belästigen	v.	pester
Belästigung {f}	n.	molestation
Belästigung {f}	n.	nuisance
belauschen	v.	overhear
beleben	v.	enliven
beleben	v.	liven
beleben	v.	vitalize
belebt	adj.	variegated
belegen	v.	allocate
beleibt	adj.	corpulent
beleibt	adj.	stout
beleidigen	v.	offend
beleidigend	adj.	abusive
Beleidigung {f}	n.	affront
Beleidigung {f}	n.	indignity
Beleuchtung {f}	n.	illumination
Beleuchtung {f}	n.	lighting
belichten	v.	expose
Beliebtheit {f}	n.	popularity
Bellen {n}	n.	bark
Belobigung {f}	n.	commendation
belohnen	v.	recompense
belohnen	v.	remunerate

Belohnung {f}	n.	remuneration
Belohnung {f}	n.	reward
Belüftung {f}	n.	ventilation
bemerkbar	adj.	noticeable
bemerken	v.	perceive
bemerkenswert	adj.	notable
bemerkenswert	adj.	noteworthy
bemessen	v.	scrimp
bemitleiden	v.	commiserate
bemühen	v.	endeavour
bemühen	v.	exert
benachrichtigen	v.	apprise
benachrichtigen	v.	inform
benachteiligen	v.	discriminate
Benachteiligung {f}		n.disadvantage
benebelt	adj.	woozy
Benefizium {n}	n.	benefice
benehmen	v.	behave
beneidenswert	adj.	enviable
Benennung {f}	n.	denomination
Bengel {m}	n.	urchin
benötigen	v.	need
Benutzer {m}	n.	user
Benzin {n}	n.	gas
Benzin {n}	n.	petrol
Benzinkanister {m}	n.	jerry can
beobachten	v.	observe
beobachten	v.	watch
Beobachtung {f}	n.	observation
bequem	adj.	convenient
bequem	adj.	modest
Beratung {f}	n.	briefing
Beratung {f}	n.	consultation
berauben	v.	bereaved
berauben	v.	deprive

berauben	v.	rob
beraubend	adj.	bereft
berauschen	v.	intoxicate
berauscht	adj.	befuddled
Berechnung {f}	n.	calculation
berechtigen	v.	entitle
Berechtigungsnachweis {m} n.		
credentials		
Bereich {m}	n.	purview
bereit	adj.	raring
bereit	adv.	readily
bereiten v.		prepare
bereits	adv.	already
bereitwillig	adj.	willing
Bereitwilligkeit {f}	n.	alacrity
bereuen v.		repent
bereuen v.		rue
Bergamotte {f}	n.	bergamot
Bergmann {m}	n.	miner
Bergsee {m}	n.	tarn
Bergsteiger {m}	n.	mountaineer
Bergsteigerei {f}	n.	mountaineering
Bericht {m}	n.	bulletin
berichten	v.	refer
berichten	v.	relate
berichten	v.	report
berieseln	v.i.	sprinkle
Berieselungsanlage {f}n.		sprinkling
Bernstein {m}n.		amber
berüchtigt	prep.	notorious
Beruf {m}	n.	occupation
Beruf {m}	n.	profession
berufen v.		convene
beruflich adj.		occupational
Berufung {f}	n.	vocation

beruhigen	v.	appease
beruhigen	v.i	hush
beruhigen	v.	pacify
beruhigen	v.	quieten
beruhigen	v.	tranquillize
beruhigt adj.		becalmed
Beruhigung {f}	n.	sedation
Beruhigungsmittel {n}n.		sedative
berühmt adj.		famous
berühmt adj.		renowned
Berühmtheit {f}	n.	celebrity
berühren v.		touch
berührend	adj.	touching
besänftigen	v.	mollify
beschädigen v.		maul
Beschädigung {f}	n.	damage
Beschädigung {f}	n.	injury
Beschaffenheit	n.	texture
Beschaffenheit {f} n.		character
Beschaffenheit {f} n.		consistency
Beschaffung {f}	n.	procurement
beschäftigen v.		employ
beschäftigen v.		engage
Beschäftigte {m,f} n.		employee
beschämt	adj.	abashed
beschämt	adj.	ashamed
beschämt	v.	embarrass
beschauen	v.	inspect
bescheiden	adj.	unassuming
bescheinigen v.		certify
Bescheinigung {f} n.		certificate
Beschichtung {f}	n.	coating
Beschickung {f}	n.	load
beschimpfen v.t.		insult
Beschimpfung {f}	n.	vituperation

Beschlagenheit {f}n.	proficiency		Besetzung {f} v.	cast
beschlagnahmen v.	impound		Besichtigung {f} n.	sightseeing
beschlagnehmen v.	confiscate		besiegen v. t.	defeat
beschleunigen v.	accelerate		besiegen v.	discomfit
beschleunigen v.	quicken		besiegen v.	vanquish
Beschleuniger {m}	n. accelerator		Besitz {m} n.	domain
beschlossen adj.	decided		besitzanzeigend adj.	possessive
beschmutzen v.	pollute		besitzen v.	possess
beschmutzen v.	smudge		Besitzer n.	owner
beschmutzt adj.	bedraggled		Besitzer {m} n.	proprietor
beschneiden v.	circumcise		Besitzergreifung {f} n.	occupancy
Beschneiden {n} n.	trimming		Besitznahme {f} n.	appropriation
Beschneider {m} n.	trimmer		Besitztitel {m} n.	tenure
beschränken v.i.	straiten		Besitztum {n}n.	estate
beschränkt adj.	parochial		Besitzübertragung {f}n.	demise
beschreiben v.	describe		besonderes adj.	special
Beschreibung {f} n.	description		Besonderheit {f} n.	exception
Beschreibung {f} n.	specification		besonders adj.	particular
beschriften v.	inscribe		besonders adj.	respective
beschuldigen v.	accuse		besorgen v.	provide
beschuldigen v.i.	incriminate		Besorgnis {f} n.	apprehension
beschützen v.	patronize		besorgt adj.	worried
Beschwerde {f} n.	complaint		Besorgtheit {f} n.	solicitude
beschwichtigen v.	allay		Besprechung {f} n.	discussion
beschwichtigen v.	placate		bespritzen v.	dabble
beseitigen v.	nullify		bespritzen v.	spatter
beseitigen v.	redress		bespritzten v.	splatter
Besen {m} n.	besom		besser adj.	better
Besen {m} n.	broom		beständig adj.	perennial
Besessenheit {f} n.	obsession		beständig adj.	stable
Besessenheit {f} n.	possession		Bestandteil {m} n.	component
besetzen v.	occupy		Bestandteil {m} n.	ingredient
besetzen v.	stud		bestärken v.	strengthen
Besetzer {m} n.	occupant		bestärkt adj.	assured
Besetzung {f}n.	allocation		bestätigen v.	confirm

bestätigen	v.	probate
bestätigen	v.	validate
Bestätigung {f}	n.	confirmation
bestechen	v. t.	bribe
bestehen aus	v.	consist
bestehlen	v.	steal
bestellt	adj.	bespoke
Bestellung {f}	n.	mail order
Besteuerung {f}	n.	taxation
bestimmen	v.	appoint
bestimmen	v.	parse
bestimmend	adj.	determinant
bestimmt	adj.	certain
bestimmt	adj.	definite
Bestimmung {f}	n.	appointment
bestrafen	v.	chastise
bestrafen	v.	penalize
bestrafen	v.	punish
bestrahlen	v.	irradiate
bestürmen	v.	bombard
bestürzen	v.	upset
bestürzt	adj.	aghast
Bestürzung {f}	n.	consternation
Bestürzung {f}	n.	dismay
Besuch {m}	n.	attendance
besuchen	v.	visit
Besucher {m}	n.	visitor
besudeln	v.	besmirch
betätigen	v.	operate
betäuben	v.	daze
betäubend	adj.	deafening
betäubend	adj.	stunning
betäubt	adj.	torpid
Betäubungsmittel {n}	n.	narcotic
beteiligen	v.	enlist

beteiligen	v.	participate
Beteiligung {f}	n.	participation
beten	v.	pray
beteuern	v.	assure
beteuern	v.	reaffirm
Beteuerung {f}	n.	protestation
Bethaus {n}	n.	temple
Beton {m}	n.	concrete
betonen	v.	emphasize
betonen	v.t.	stress
Betonung {f}	n.	emphasis
betören	v.	infatuate
Betörung {f}	n.	infatuation
betrachten	v.	contemplate
betrachten	v.	regard
Betrachter {m}	n.	browser
beträchtlich	adj.	considerable
Betrachtung {f}	n.	contemplation
Betrag {m}	n.	quantum
Betrag {m}	n.	sum
betreffen	v.	concern
betreffend	prep.	concerning
betreffend	prep.	regarding
betreiben	v.	prosecute
Betrieb {m}	n.	business
betriebsfähig	adj.	workable
Betriebswerk {n}	n.	depot
betrüben	v.	aggrieve
betrüben	v.	sadden
betrübt	adj.	sad
betrübt	adj.	sorry
Betrug {m}	n.	deceit
Betrug {m}	n.	fraud
Betrug {m}	n.	scam
betrügen	v.	cheat

239

betrügen v.　deceive
betrügen v.　defraud
Betrügerei {f} n.　trickery
betrügerisch adj.　deceitful
betrügerisch adj.　fraudulent
betrügerisch adj.　surreptitious
betrunken adj.　groggy
Bett {n} n.　bed
Bettdecke {f} n.　duvet
betteln adj.　mendicant
Bettenstation {f} n.　inpatient
Bettler {m} n.　beggar
Bettung {f} n.　bedding
beugen v.　stoop
beunruhigen v.　perturb
beunruhigen v.　unsettle
beunruhigen v.　worry
beurteilend v.　criticize
Beurteilung {f} n.　judgement
Beute {f} n.　booty
Beute {f} n.　loot
Beute {f} n.　prey
Beute {f} n.　swag
Beutel {m} n.　pouch
Beuteltier {m}n.　marsupial
bevölkern v.　populate
Bevölkerung {f} n.　population
Bevölkerungsüberschuss {m} n.
　overspill
Bevollmächtigte {m,f}n.　commissioner
bevorstehend adj.　forthcoming
bevorzugt adj.　preferential
bewacht adj.　guarded
bewahren v.　reserve
Bewahrung {f} n.　conservation

Bewahrung {f}　n.　preservation
Bewährung {f}　n.　probation
bewaldet adj.　wooded
bewandert adj.　versed
bewässern v.　irrigate
Bewässerung {f}　n.　irrigation
bewegen v.　affect
bewegen v.　budge
bewegen v.　move
Beweggrund {m}　n.　motivation
beweglich adj.　agile
beweglich adj.　movable
beweglich adj.　moving
Bewegung {f} n.　motion
Bewegung {f} n.　movement
bewegungslos adj.　motionless
beweisen v.　prove
beweiskräftig adj.　argumentative
bewerben v.　solicit
Bewerber {m}n.　applicant
Bewerber {m}n.　candidate
Bewerbung {f}　n.　solicitation
bewerten v.　appraise
bewerten v. t　estimate
Bewertung {f}n.　reappraisal
Bewertung {f}n.　valuation
bewilligen v.　allow
bewirten v.　feed
Bewirtung {f} n.　hospitality
bewohnbar adj.　habitable
bewohnbar adj.　inhabitable
bewohnen v.　inhabit
Bewohner {m}　n.　inhabitant
bewölkt adj.　overcast
Bewuchs {m} n.　vegetation

240

German		English
bewundern	v.	admire
bewundernswert	adj.	admirable
Bewunderung {f}	n.	admiration
bewusst	adj.	aware
bewusst	adj.	conscious
bezahlen	v.	disburse
Bezahlung {f}	n.	payment
bezaubern	v.	enchant
bezaubern	v.	fascinate
bezaubernd	adj.	charming
bezeichnen	v. t	denote
bezeichnen	v.	designate
Bezeichnung {f}	n.	notation
bezeugen	v.	testify
Bezeugung {f}	n.	testimony
beziehen	v.	correlate
Beziehung {f}	n.	relation
Bezirk {m}	n.	canton
Bezirk {m}	n.	precinct
Bezugnahme {f}	n.	reference
Bezugspunkt {m}	n.	date
Bezugspunkt {m}	n.	datum
bezwingen	v.	quell
bezwingen	v.	subjugate
BH {m}	n.	bra
bi	comb.	bi
Bibel {f}	n.	Bible
Biber {m}	n.	beaver
Bibliothek {f}	n.	library
Bibliothekar {m}	n.	librarian
biegen	v.	flex
biegen	v.	inflect
Biene {f}	n.	bee
Bienenhaus {n}	n.	apiary
Bienenstock {m}	n.	hive

German		English
Bier {n}	n.	beer
Biest {n}	n.	beast
bieten	v.	bid
bifokal	adj.	bifocal
Bigamie {f}	n.	bigamy
Bikini {m}	n.	bikini
Bild {n}	n.	image
Bild {n}	n.	tableau
bilden	v.	educate
Bilder {pl}	n.	imagery
bildhaften	adj.	pictorial
Bildhauerei {f}	n.	sculpture
bildhauerisch	adj.	sculptural
Bildhauerkunst {f}	n.	statuary
Bildlegende {f}	n.	caption
bildlich	adj	figurative
Bildmaterial {n}	n.	footage
Bildschirm {m}	n.	monitor
Bildschirm {m}	n.	screen
Bildschirmrollen {n}	n.	scroll
Bildung {f}	n.	development
Billard {n}	n.	billiards
billig	adj.	cheap
billig	adj.	inexpensive
billig	adj.	tacky
billig	adj.	tawdry
bimsen	v.	pounce
binär	adj.	binary
Binde {f}	n.	fascia
Bindehautentzündung {f}	n.	conjunctivitis
binden	v.	bind
binden	v.	tie
Bindestrich {m}	n.	hyphen
Binnenland {n}	adj.	inland

binokular	*adj.*	binocular	
Binsenwahrheit {f}		*n.*	truism
Biochemie {f} *n.*		biochemistry	
Biodiversität {f}		*n.*	biodiversity
Biographie {f}		*n.*	biography
Biologe {m}	*n.*	biologist	
Biologie {f}	*n.*	biology	
Biopsie {f}	*n.*	biopsy	
Birke {f} *n.*	birch		
Birne {f} *n.*	pear		
Birnenmost {m}		*n.*	perry
bis *prep.*	till		
bis *prep.*	until		
Bischof {m} *n.*	bishop		
bisexuell *adj.*	bisexual		
bisher *adv.*	hitherto		
Bissen {m}	*n.*	morsel	
bissig *adj.*	snappy		
Bit {n}	*n.*	bit	
Bitte {f} *n.*	petition		
bitten *v.*	please		
bitter *adj.*	bitter		
Bitterkeit {f}	*n.*	acrimony	
Bittsteller {m}*n.*	suppliant		
bizarr *adj.*	bizarre		
bizarr *adj.*	weird		
Bizeps {pl}	*n.*	biceps	
blähend *adj.*	flatulent		
blamieren *v.*	stultify		
Bläschen {n} *n.*	vesicle		
Blase {f} *n.*	bladder		
blasen *v.*	blow		
Blasen {pl}	*adj.*	cystic	
blass *adj.*	pale		
blass *adj.*	wan		

Blatt {n} *n.*	leaf		
blättern *v.*	skim		
blau *adj.* blue			
Blaufarbstoff {m} *n.*		woad	
Blauregen {m}	*n.*	wisteria	
bleiben *n.*	abode		
bleiben *v.*	remain		
bleiben *v.*	stay		
bleichen *v.*	blanch		
Bleistift {m}	*n.*	pencil	
Blende {f}	*n.*	aperture	
blenden *v. t.*	dazzle		
blenden *v.*	stun		
Blick {m}*n*	look		
blind *adj.*	blind		
Blinddarmentzündung {f} *n.*			
appendicitis			
Blindenschrift {f}	*n.*	Braille	
Blindheit {f} *n.*	blindness		
Blitz {m} *n.*	lightening		
blitzen *v.*	flash		
Blitzkrieg {m}*n.*	blitz		
Block {m}	*n.*	block	
Blockade {f} *n.*	blockade		
Blockierung {f}	*n.*	blockage	
blöd *adj.*	dumb		
blöd *adj.*	stupid		
Blödmann {m}	*n.*	idiot	
Blog {n} *n.*	blog		
blond *adj.*	blonde		
blühen *v.*	bloom		
blühen *v.*	flourish		
blumen *adj.*	floral		
Blumenblatt {n}	*n.*	petal	
Blumenkohl {m}	*n.*	cauliflower	

Blumenstrauß {m} n. bouquet
Blumenzwiebel {f} n. bulb
Bluse {f} n. blouse
Blut {n} n. blood
Blut {n} n. gore
Blutandrang {m} n. plethora
Blutbad {n} n. carnage
Blüte {f} n. blossom
Blüte {f} n. flower
Blutegel {m} n. leech
bluten v. bleed
blüten adj. flowery
Blütenstaub {m} n. pollen
blutig adj. bloody
Blutkreislauf {m} n. circulation
Blutschande {f} n. incest
blutstillend adj. styptic
Blutsverwandtschaft {f}n. kinship
Blutung {f} n. haemorrhage
Blutvergießen {n} n. bloodshed
Blutvergiftung {f} n. sepsis
Bock {m} n. buck
Boden {m} n. soil
Bogen {m} n. arc
Bogen {m} n. bow
Bogengang {m} n. arcade
Bogenschütze {m}n. archer
Bohne {f} n. bean
Bohrer {m} n. wimble
Boje {f} n. buoy
Bollwerk {n} n. bulwark
Bolzen {m} n. bolt
Bolzen {m} n. stomp
Bombage {f} n. camber
bombastisch adj. grandiose

bombastisch adj. overblown
Bombe {f} n. bomb
Bombenangriff {m} n. bombardment
Bomber {m} n. bomber
Bommel {f,m}n. bobble
Bonbon {n} n. candy
Bonbon {n} n. sweetmeat
Bonus {m} n. premium
Boot {n} n. boat
Bordstein {m} n. kerb
Börsenmakler {m} n. stockbroker
Borste {f} n. bristle
böse adj. naughty
Bösewicht {m} n. villain
Bosheit {f} n. malice
böswillig adj. malicious
Botengang {m} n. errand
Botschaft {f} n. embassy
Botschafter {m} n. ambassador
Boulevard {n}n. boulevard
Boulevardzeitung {f}n. tabloid
Box {f} n. pit
Boxen {n} n boxing
Boxer {m} n. boxer
boykottieren v. boycott
Bramme {f} n. slab
Brand {m} n. blaze
Brandblase {f} n. blister
Brandmal {n} n. brand
Brandmal {n} n. stigma
Brandstiftung {f} n. arson
Brandung {f} n. surf
braten v. fry
braten v. roast

243

Bratensoße {f}	*n.*	gravy
brauchbar	*adj.*	useful
Braue {f} *n.*	brow	
brauen *v.*	brew	
Brauerei {f}	*n.*	brewery
braun	*n.*	brown
Braunkohle {f}	*n.*	lignite
Braut {f} *n.*	bride	
Brautaussteuer {f} *n.*	trousseau	
Bräutigam {m}	*n.*	bridegroom
brautlich *adj.*	bridal	
brechen *v.*	breach	
brechen *v.t*	fracture	
Brei {m} *n.*	porridge	
Brei {m} *n.*	pulp	
breit *adj.*	broad	
Breite {f} *n.*	breadth	
Breite {f} *n.*	latitude	
Breite {f} *n.*	width	
Bremse {f}	*n.*	brake
Brenner {m}	*n.*	burner
Brennmaterial {n} *n.*	fuel	
Brennofen {m}	*n.*	kiln
Bresche {f}	*n.*	crack
Bretzel {m}	*n.*	pretzel
Brief {m} *n.*	letter	
Briefträger {m}	*n.*	postman
Briefwechsel {m}	*n*	correspondence
Brigade {f}	*n.*	brigade
Brigadier {m} *n.*	brigadier	
Brillenschlange {f}	*n.*	cobra
bringen *v.*	bring	
brisant *adj.*	controversial	
britisch *adj.*	British	
Brocken {m} *n.*	hunk	

bröcklig *adj.*	friable	
Brokat {n}	*n.*	brocade
Brokkoli {m}	*n.*	broccoli
Brombeere {f}	*n.*	blackberry
bronchial	*adj.*	bronchial
Bronze {f}	*n.*	bronze
Broschüre {f} *n.*	brochure	
Brot {n} *n.*	bread	
Brotkrume {f},	*n.*	crumb
Brotscheibe {f}	*n.*	slice
Bruch {m}	*n.*	fraction
brüchig *adj.*	fragile	
Bruchstein {m}	*n.*	rubble
Bruchstelle {f}	*n.*	breakage
Brücke {f}	*n.*	bridge
Bruder {m}	*n.*	brother
brüderlich	*adj.*	fraternal
Brüderschaft {f}	*n.*	brotherhood
Brüderschaft {f}	*n.*	fraternity
brüllen *v.*	bellow	
brummen	*v.*	hum
Brünette {f}	*n.*	brunette
Brunnen {m} *n.*	fountain	
Brunnen {m} *n.*	well	
Brunst {f}	*n.*	rut
Brust-	*adj.*	mammary
Brust {f} *n.*	breast	
Brustbein {m}	*n.*	sternum
Brustwarze {f}	*n.*	teat
Brut {f}	*n.*	brood
brutal *adj.*	harsh	
brutal *adj.*	brutal	
Buch {n} *n.*	book	
Buche {f}	*n.*	beech
Bücherfreund {m} *n.*	bibliophile	

buchgelehrt	adj.	bookish
Buchhalter {m}	n.	accountant
Buchhaltung {f}	n.	accountancy
Buchhändler {m}	n.	bookseller
Buchrücken {m}	n.	spine
buchstabieren	v.t.	spell
Buchumschlag {m}	n.	wrapper
Buckel {m}	n.	hump
Bückling {m}	n.	bloater
Büffel {m}	n.	buffalo
Buffet {n}	n.	buffet
Bühne {f}	n.	stage
Bühnenausstattung {f}	n.decor	
Bulldogge {f}	n.	bulldog
Bulle {m}n.	screw	
bummeln	v.	stroll
Bummler {m}	n.	truant
Bündel {n}	n.	bundle
Bündel {n}	n.	sheaf
Bungalow {n}n.	bungalow	
Bunker {m}	n.	bunker
Buntstift {m}	n.	crayon
Bürger {m}	n.	commoner
Bürgermeister {m}n.	mayor	
Bürgerpflicht {f}	n.	civics
Bürgerschaft {f}	n.	township
Burggraben {m}	n.	moat
Bürgschaft {f}	n.	bail
Bürgschaft {f}	n.	surety
Büro {n} n.	bureau	
Büro {n} n.	office	
Bürokrat {m} n.	bureaucrat	
Bürokratie {f}n.	bureaucracy	
Bürschchen {n}	n.	stripling
Bursche {m}	n.	bloke

Bürste {f}	n.	brush
Busch {m}	n.	bush
Busch {m}	n.	shrub
buschig adj.	bushy	
Busen {m}	n.	bosom
Busen {m}	n.	bust
busenfrei	adj.	topless
Bussard {m}	n.	buzzard
Butter {f}n.	butter	
Butterfass {n}	v.	churn
Byte {n}	n.	byte

C

Cadmium {n}n.	cadmium	
Café {n}	n.	cafe
Cafeteria {f}	n.	cafeteria
Calcium (Kalzium) {n}n.	calcium	
Camcorder {m}	n.	camcorder
Campus {m}	n.	campus
Candela n.	candela	
Cannabis {m}n.	cannabis	
Casanova {m}	n.	Casanova
Cellulite {f}	n.	cellulite
Celsius n.	Celsius	
Cent n.	cent	
Champagner {m}	n.	champagne
Chaos {n}	n.	chaos
chaotisch	adj.	chaotic
charismatisch	adj.	charismatic
Chauvinismus {m}n.	chauvinism	
chauvinist	n. &adj.	chauvinist
Chefkoch {m}n.	chef	
Chefsteward {m}	n.	purser
Chemie {f}	n.	chemistry

German		English
Chemiker {m}*n.*		chemist
chemisch	*adj.*	chemical
Chemotherapie {f}*n.*		chemotherapy
Chili {m} *n.*		chilli
Chinin {n}	*n.*	quinine
Chip {m} *n.*		chip
Chirurg {m}	*n.*	surgeon
Chlor {n}*n.*		chlorine
Chloroform {n}	*n.*	chloroform
Cholera {f}	*n.*	cholera
Chor {m}*n.*		choir
Chor {m}*n.*		chorus
choral	*adj.*	choral
Christentum {n}	*n.*	Christianity
christlich {adj}	*adj.*	Christian
Christus {m} *n.*		Christ
Chrom {n}	*n.*	chrome
chronisch	*adj.*	chronic
Chronograph {m} *n.*		chronograph
Chronologie {f}	*n.*	chronology
Chutney {n}	*n.*	chutney
Clone {n}	*n.*	clone
Clown {m}	*n.*	clown
Club {m} *n.*		club
Cocktail {n}	*n.*	cocktail
Collage {f}	*n.*	collage
Computer {m}	*n.*	computer
computerisieren	*v.*	computerize
Container {m}	*n.*	container
Coupé {n}	*n.*	coupe
Coupon {m}	*n.*	coupon
Coupon {m}	*n.*	voucher
Creme {f}	*n.*	cream
Cursor {m}	*n.*	cursor
Cyberspace {m}	*n.*	cyberspace

D

German		English
dabei	*adv.*	nearby
Dach {n} *n.*		roof
Dachboden {m}	*n.*	loft
Dachkammer {f}	*n.*	garret
Dachstroh {n}	*n.*	thatch
Dachstube {f}*n.*		attic
Dachstuhl {m}	*n.*	truss
daher	*adv.*	thence
dahinter *prep.*		behind
Dame {f} *n.*		dame
Dame {f} *n.*		lady
Dame {f} *n.*		madam
Damenunterwäsche {f}*n.*		lingerie
Damm {m}	*n.*	causeway
Dämmerung {f}	*n.*	twilight
Dampf {m}	*n.*	vapour
Dampfer {m}	*n.*	damper
Dampfer {m}	*n.*	steamer
Dämpfer {m}	*n.*	muffler
daneben *adv.*		aside
danebenliegend	*adj.*	adjacent
dankbar	*n.*	grateful
dankbar	*adj.*	thankful
Dankbarkeit {f}	*n.*	appreciation
danken	*v.*	thank
Danksagung {f}	*n.*	acknowledgement
dann	*adv.*	then
Darlehen {n}	*n.*	credit
Darm {m}	*n.*	bowel
Darm {m}	*n.*	gut
Darm {m}	*n.*	intestine
Darmverstopfung {f}*n.*		constipation
Darsteller {m}*n.*		performer

German		English
Darstellung {f}	n.	embodiment
Darstellung {f}	n.	portrayal
das adj.		the
dasjenige	pron. & adj.	that
Dateienverküpfung {f}n.		concatenation
Daten {pl}	n.	data
Datenbank {f}n.		database
Datenbasis {f}	n.	pool
Dauer {f} n.		duration
dauerhaft	adj.	lasting
Dauerhaftigkeit {f}n.		stability
dauernd adj.		continual
Daumen {m}	n.	thumb
dazwischenkommenv.		intervene
Debatte {f}	n.	debate
debattieren	v. t.	debate
Debüt {n}	n.	debut
Debütant {m} n.		debutante
Decke {f}n.		mantle
Deckel {m}	n.	cover
decken	v.	cover
deckungsgleich	adj.	congruent
defensiv adj.		defensive
defilieren	v. t	defile
definieren	v.	define
Definition {f}	n.	definition
degradieren	v.	degrade
degradieren	v.	demote
dehnbar adj.		malleable
dehnbar adj.		tensile
dein adj.		your
Déjà-Vu {n}	n.	déjà vu
Dekade {f}	n.	decade
dekadent	adj.	decadent

German		English
Dekan {m}	n.	dean
deklassieren v.		declassify
dekomprimieren	v.	decompress
dekonstruieren	v.	deconstruct
dekorativ	adj.	decorative
Dekret {n}	n.	decree
Delegation {f}n.		delegation
Delikatesse {f}	n.	delicacy
Delta {n} n.		delta
dementieren v.		disclaim
demnächst	adj.	upcoming
demobilisieren	v.	demobilize
Demografie {f}	n.	demography
Demokratie {f}	n.	democracy
demokratischadj.		democratic
demolieren	v.	demolish
demonstrieren	v.	demonstrate
demontieren v.		dismantle
demoralisieren	v.	demoralize
Demoskop {m}	n.	pollster
Demut {f}	n.	humility
demütig adj.		humble
denken	v.	think
Denker {m}	n.	thinker
Denkmal {n}	n.	memorial
Denkmal {n}	n.	monument
Denkschrift {f}	n.	memoir
denkwürdig adj.		memorable
dennoch adv.		however
dennoch adv.		nevertheless
Denunziant {m}	n.	informer
Denunziation {f}	n.	denunciation
Deo {n}	n.	antiperspirant
Deodorant {n}	n.	deodorant
Depot {n}	n.	deposit

deprimiert *adj.* glum
deputierend *v.* depute
derartig *adj.* such
derb*adj.* rumbustious
derselbe *adj.* same
desgleichen *adv.* likewise
desillusionieren *v.* disenchant
desillusionieren *v.* disillusion
desinfizieren *v.* disinfect
desinfizieren *v.* fumigate
desorganisieren *v.* disorientate
Despot {m} *n.* despot
Dessert {n} *n.* dessert
destabilisieren *v.* destabilize
Detail {n}*n.* detail
Detektiv {m} *n.* detective
deuten *v.* portend
deutlich *adj.* clear
deutlich *adj.* lucid
deutlich *adj.* obvious
deutlich *adj.* perspicuous
Deutsche {f} *n.* German
Dezember {m} *n.* December
dezentralisieren *v.* decentralize
Dezibel {n} *n.* decibel
dezimal *adj.* decimal
dezimieren *v.* decimate
dezimieren *v.* deplete
Diadem {n} *n.* coronet
Diagnose {f} *n.* diagnosis
diagnostizieren *v.* diagnose
Diagramm {n}*n.* diagram
Dialyse {f} *n.* dialysis
Diamant {m} *n.* diamond
Diameter {m} *n.* diameter

Diaspora {f} *n.* Diaspora
Diät {f} *n.* diet
Diätspezialist {m} *n.* dietitian
dicht *adj.* dense
dicht *adj.* thick
dichten *v.* versify
Dichtung {f} *n.* gasket
Dichtung {f} *n.* poetry
Dichtungsmittel {n} *n.* sealant
dick *adj.* gross
Dickdarm {m}*n.* colon
Dickicht {n} *n.* thicket
dickköpfig *adj.* bullish
didaktisch *adj.* didactic
Dieb {m} *n.* thief
Diebstahl {m}*n.* theft
Diener {m} *n.* butler
Diener {m} *n.* server
Dienstag {m} *n.* Tuesday
dienstbar *adj.* subservient
Dienstliste {f}*n.* rota
Dienstmädchen {f} *n.* servant
Dienstmädchen {n} *n.* maid
Dienstvorgesetzte {m,f}*n.* supervisor
diese *pron.& adj.* this
Diesel {m} *n.* diesel
diffizil *adj.* difficult
digital *adj.* digital
Diktat {n} *n.* dictate
Diktat {n} *n.* dictation
Diktator {m} *n.* dictator
diktatorisch *adj.* bossy
Dilemma {n} *n.* dilemma
dilettantisch *adj.* amateurish
Ding {n} *n.* gimmick

Ding {n} n. thing
dinieren v. dine
Dinosaurier {m} n. dinosaur
Diplom {n} n. diploma
Diplomat {m} n. diplomat
Diplomatle {f}n. diplomacy
diplomatisch adj. diplomatic
diplomatisch adj. politic
Direktor {m} n. director
Direktor {m} n. headmaster
Direktor {m} n. manager
Dirigent {m} n. conductor
Dirne {f} n. strumpet
dirnenhaft adj. meretricious
Disko {f} n. disco
diskret adj. discreet
diskret adj. discrete
Diskurs {m} n. discourse
Diskussionsleiter {m}n. moderator
diskutieren v. discuss
Disparität {f} n. disparity
dispensieren v. dispense
disputieren v. contend
Disqualifikation {f} n.disqualification
disqualifizieren v. disqualify
Dissertation {f} n. dissertation
Dissident {m}n. dissident
Distel {f} n. thistle
Disziplin {f} n. disciple
disziplinieren n. discipline
dito n. ditto
divergierender v. diverge
Diversität {f} n. diversity
Docht {m} n. wick
Dogma {n} n. dogma

dogmatische adj. dogmatic
Doktor {m} n. doctor
Doktorat {n} n. doctorate
Doktrin {f} n. doctrine
Dokument {n}n. document
dokumentarische n. documentary
Dolch {m} n. dagger
Dollar {m} n. dollar
dolmetschen v. interpret
Dom {m} n. dome
dominieren v. dominate
dominiert adj. henpecked
Donner {m} n. boom
Donner {m} n. thunder
Donnerstag {m} n. Thursday
doofadj. daft
Doppeletagenwohnung {f}n.
maisonette
Doppelfüßer {m} n. millipede
Doppelgänger {m}n. lookalike
Doppelsinnigkeit {f} n. ambiguity
doppelt adj. double
Doppelzüngigkeit {f}n. duplicity
Dorf {n} n. village
Dorfbewohner {m}n. villager
Dorn {m}n. thorn
dornig adj. thorny
dörren v. dehydrate
dort adv. there
dorthin adv. thither
Dose {f} n. tin
dösen v. i doze
dösen v. snooze
Dosis {f} n. dose
Dossier {n} n. dossier

Dozent {m}	n.	lecturer		dreißig	adj. & n.	thirty
Drache {m},	n.	dragon		dreißigste	adj. & n.	thirtieth
Drachen {m}	n.	kite		Dreistigkeit {f}	n	impertinence
Drahtesel {m}n.		bike		Dreizack {m}	n.	trident
drahtlos	adj.	wireless		dreizehn	adj. & n.	thirteen
Drama {n}	n.	drama		dreizehnte	adj. & n.	thirteenth
Dramatiker {m}	n.	dramatist		Drell {m} n.		ticking
Dramatiker {m}	n.	playwright		dreschen	v.	thresh
dramatisch	adj.	dramatic		Dressing {n}	n.	dressing
drängen	v.	urge		Drill {m}	n.	drill
Drangsal {f}	n.	tribulation		Drilling {m}	n.	triplet
drastisch	adj.	drastic		dritte	adj.	third
draußen	adv.	afield		Droge {f}n.		drug
draußen	adj.	outdoor		drohend	adj.	imminent
dreckig	adj.	dirty		drohend	adj.	impending
Drehbank {f}	n.	lathe		Drohung {f}	n.	menace
Drehbuch {n} n.		script		drollig	adj.	droll
drehen	v.	revolve		drollig	adj.	jocose
drehen	v.	spin		Drossel {f}	n.	thrush
drehen	v.	swivel		Druck {m}	n.	pressure
drehen	v.	twiddle		Druckausgabe {f}	n.	printout
drehen	v.	wangle		Drückeberger {m} n.		shirker
Drehen {n}	n.	veer		drucken	v.	print
Dreher {m}	n.	turner		drücken	v.	shirk
Drehung {f}	n.	rotation		Druckerei {f}	n.	printer
drei	adj. & n.	three		druckfest machen v.		pressurize
Dreieck {n}	n.	triangle		druckluftbetätigt	adj.	pneumatic
Dreieck {n}	adj.	triangular		Drüse {f}n.		gland
dreifach	adj.	treble		Dschungel {m}	n.	jungle
Dreifaltigkeit {f}	n.	trinity		Du	pron.	you
Dreifuß {m}	n.	trivet		Duett {n}n.		duet
dreimal	adv.	thrice		duftend	adj.	fragrant
dreimalig	n.	triple		duftend	adj.	redolent
Dreirad {n}	n.	tricycle		Duftstoff {m}	n.	fragrance
dreiseitig	adj.	tripartite		Duftstoff {m}	n.	scent

dulden	v.	acquiesce
dulden	v.	connive
Dulden {n}	n.	bearing
duldsam adj.		indulgent
Duldung {f}	n.	sufferance
Duldung {f}	n.	toleration
dumm	adj.	asinine
dummdreist adj.		impertinent
Dumme {m}	n.	oaf
Dummheit {f} n.		stupidity
Dummi {m}	n.	dummy
Dummkopf {m}	n.	ass
Dummkopf {m}	n.	dullard
dümmlich	adj.	foolish
Dung {m}	n.	dung
Düngemittel {n}	n.	fertilizer
Dünger {m}	n.	manure
dunkel	adj.	dark
dunkel	adj.	dim
dunkel	adj.	obscure
Dunkelheit {f} n.		darkness
Dunkelheit {f} n.		murk
Dunkelheit {f} n.		obscurity
dunkeln adj.		swarthy
dünn	adj.	tenuous
dünn	adj.	thin
Duo {n}	n.	duo
durch	adv.	across
durch	prep.	by
Durchblick {m}	n.	perspective
Durchblick {m}	n.	vista
durchdrang	v.	pierce
durchdringen v.		penetrate
durchdringen v.		pervade
Durchfall {m} n.		diarrhoea

Durchfallen {n}	n.	failing
durchführbar adj.		practicable
Durchführbarkeit {f}n.		practicability
durchführen	v.	realize
Durchgang {m}	n.	passage
durchgehen	v.	peruse
durchgehend adj.		passing
durchkreuzen v.t.		counter
durchlässig	adj.	permeable
durchnässen	v.	drench
durchnässen	v.	soak
durchprügeln v.		belabour
durchqueren	v.	traverse
durchreisen	v.t.	perambulate
durchschneiden	v.	intersect
Durchschnittsbetrag {m}n.		average
Durchsicht {f}	n.	perusal
durchsichtig	adj.	translucent
durchstöbern v.		ransack
durchweg	prep.	throughout
durchweicht	adj.	sodden
durchweicht	adj.	soppy
durfen	v.	may
dürftig	adj.	paltry
dürftig	adv.	poorly
dürftig	adj.	scanty
Duroplastpresse {f}		n.thermosetting
dürr adj.		arid
dürr adj.		scrawny
Durst {m}	n.	thirst
durstig	adj.	thirsty
Düse {f}	n.	nozzle
Dussel {m}	n.	berk
düster	adj.	dismal
düster	adj.	gloomy

251

düster	adj.	saturnine
düster	adj.	sepulchral
düster	adj.	sombre
Dutzend {n}	n.	dozen
Dynamik {f}	n.	dynamics
dynamisch	adj.	dynamic
Dynamit {n}	n.	dynamite
Dynastie {f}	n.	dynasty

E

Ebbe {f}	n.	ebb
Ebenbild {n}	n.	match
Ebenholz {n}	n.	ebony
Eber {m}	n.	boar
echt adj.		genuine
Echtheit {f}	n.	originality
Edelmut {m}	n.	gallantry
Edelstein {m}	n.	gem
Editor {m}	n.	editor
Efeu {m}	n.	ivy
Egge {f}	n.	harrow
eggend	adj.	harrowing
Ego {n}	n.	ego
Egoismus {m}		n. egotism
egoistisch	adj.	selfish
Ehe {f}	n.	wedlock
Ehebruch {m}n.		adultery
Ehefrau {f}	n.	wife
Ehegatte {m}	n.	spouse
ehelich	adj.	conjugal
ehelich	adj.	marital
ehelich	adj.	matrimonial
ehemalig adj.		ancient
ehemalig adj.		former
ehemalig adj.		quondam

ehemals	adj.	erstwhile
ehemals	adv.	formerly
Ehemann {m} n.		husband
ehemündig	adj.	marriageable
eher adv.		rather
Ehescheidung {f}	n.	divorce
Ehestand {m} n.		matrimony
Ehestifter {m}n.		matchmaker
ehrbar	adj.	respectable
Ehre {f}	n.	honour
ehren	v.	dignify
ehren	v.	venerate
ehrenamtlich	adj.	honorary
Ehrenkränkung {f}n.		libel
Ehrenkränkung {f}n.		slander
Ehrenmann {m}	n.	gentleman
ehrenwert	adj.	honourable
ehrerbietig	adj.	reverent
ehrerbietigen adj.		reverential
Ehrerbietung {f}	n.	deference
Ehrerbietung {f}	n.	obeisance
Ehrfurcht {f}	n.	awe
Ehrfurcht {f}	n.	reverence
Ehrgeiz {m}	n.	ambition
ehrlich	adj.	honest
ehrlich	adj.	straightforward
Ehrlichkeit {f}n.		honesty
Ehrlosigkeit {f}	n.	dishonour
ehrwürdig	adj.	reverend
ehrwürdig	adj.	venerable
Ei {n}	n.	egg
Eibe {f}	n.	yew
Eiche {f} n.		oak
Eichel {f}n.		acorn
Eichhörnchen {n}	n.	squirrel

Eid {m}	n.	oath		ein	adj.	an

Eid {m} *n.* oath
Eidbruch {m} *n.* perjury
Eidechse {f} *n.* lizard
Eidotter {n} *n.* yolk
Eierkrem {f} *n.* custard
Elerkuchen {m} *n.* pancake
Eifer {m} *n.* fervour
Eifer {m} *n.* mettle
Eifer {m} *n.* zeal
eifern *v.* strive
Eifersucht {f} *n.* jealousy
eifersüchtig *adj.* jealous
eiförmig *adj.* ovate
eifrig *adj.* eager
eifrig *adj.* keen
eifrig *adj.* sedulous
eifrig *adj.* zealous
eigen *adj. & pron.* own
Eigenart {f} *n.* quirk
eigenartig *adj.* peculiar
Eigenheit {f} *n.* entity
eigensinnig *adj.* headstrong
Eigenständigkeit {f}
*n.*independence
eigentlich *adv.* actually
Eigentum {n} *n.* belongings
Eigentumsrecht {n} *n.* ownership
Eigentumswohnung {f}*n.*condominium
Eiland {n} *n.* isle
Eilbote {m} *n.* courier
eilen *v.* hurry
eilen *v.* rush
Eimer {m} *n.* bin
Eimer {m} *n.* pail
ein *a.* a

ein *adj.* an
Einarbeitung {f} *n.* induction
einäschern *v.* cremate
einäugig *adj.* monocular
einbalsamieren *v.* embalm
Einbau {m} *n.* fitting
Einberufung {f} *n.* convocation
einbetten *adj.* ingrained
Einbeziehung {f} *n.* inclusion
einbilden *v.t.* imagine
Einbildung {f}*n.* imagination
Einbildung {f}*n.* vanity
Einblick {m} *n.* insight
Einbrecher {m} *n.* burglar
Einbruch {m} *n.* burglary
Einbruch {m} *n.* irruption
Eindämmung {f} *n.* containment
Eindämmung {f} *n.* embankment
eindringen *v.* infiltrate
eindringen *v.* intrude
eindringen *v.* invade
Eindringen {n} *n.* intrusion
Eindringen {n} *n.* penetration
Eindringling {m} *n.* interloper
Eindruck*n.* glimpse
Eindruck {m} *n.* impression
eindrucksvoll *adj.* impressive
eindrucksvoll *adj.* spectacular
eine Weile *adv.* awhile
eines *pron.* oneself
einfach *adj.* facile
einfach *adj.* plain
Einfachheit {f} *n.* simplicity
Einfall {m} *n.* incursion
Einfall {m} *n.* vagary

Einfall {m}	n.	incidence
einfältig	adj.	gawky
einfältig	adj.	simple
einfangen	v. t.	entrap
einflussreich	adj.	influential
einfrieren	v.	freeze
einfügen v.		interlink
Einfühlungsvermögen {n}n.		empathy
Einfuhr {f}	n.	influx
einführen	v.	import
einführen	v.	inaugurate
Eingabe {f}	n.	input
eingebaut	adj.	integral
eingebildet	adj.	cocky
eingebildet	adj.	vain
Eingebildetheit {f} n.		conceit
eingeboren	adj.	aboriginal
eingeboren	adj.	indigenous
Eingebung {f}n.		inspiration
eingedenk	adj.	mindful
eingeführt	adj.	inaugural
eingehakt	adj.	hooked
eingerostet	adj.	stiff
eingesammelt	adj.	collective
eingeschlechtig	adj.	unisex
eingeschlossen	v.	embed
eingeschlossen	v.	encase
eingeschränkt	adj.	limited
eingesetzt	v.	deploy
eingeweiht	adj.	privy
eingewurzelt	adj.	inherent
eingreifen	v.	encroach
Eingriff {m}	n.	interference
Eingriff {m}	n.	intervention
eingriffen	v.	interfere

Einheimischer {m}	n.	native
Einheit {f}	n.	oneness
Einheit {f}	n.	unity
einheitlich	a.	homogeneous
Einkaufen {n}n.		shopping
Einkäufer {m}n.		buyer
Einkaufswagen {m}	n.	cart
Einkaufszentrum {n}n.		mall
einkerben	v.	indent
einkerkern	v.	incarcerate
Einklang {m} n.		unison
einklemmen	v.t.	jam
Einkommen {n}	n.	revenue
einkreisen	v. t	encircle
einladen v.		invite
einladend	adj.	inviting
Einladung {f} n.		invitation
Einlegeboden {m} n.		shelf
einlegen v.		potter
einleitend	adj.	introductory
Einleitung {f} n.		introduction
einlenkend	adj.	peaceable
einleuchtend	adj.	evident
einlullen v.		lull
einmal	adv.	once
einmischen	v.	meddle
einmischen	v.	tamper
einmütig adj.		unanimous
einpflanzen	v.	implant
einräumen	v.	concede
Einrichter {m}	n.	fitter
Einrichtung {f}	n.	facility
eins n.		mono
eins n. & adj.		one
einsam	adj.	lone

einsam	*adj.*	lonesome
einsam	*adj.*	solitary
Einsamkeit {f}	*n.*	solitude
Einsatz {m}	*v.*	insert
einsaugen	*v.*	absorb
einschärfen	*v.*	inculcate
einschätzen	*v.*	taxi
Einschienenbahn {f}	*n.*	monorail
einschiffen	*v. t*	embark
Einschlag {m}	*n.*	woof
einschlägig	*adj.*	pertinent
einschlägig	*adj.*	relevant
einschließen	*v.*	enclose
einschließen	*v.*	immure
einschließen	*v.*	imprison
einschmeicheln	*v.*	endear
einschränken	*n.*	restrict
einschränken	*v.*	shrink
einschränkend	*adj.*	restrictive
Einschränkung {f}	*n.*	constraint
Einschub {m}	*n.*	insertion
einschüchtern	*v.*	hector
einschüchtern	*v.*	overawe
Einschüchterung {f}	*n.*	
intimidation		
einseitig	*adj.*	lopsided
einseitig	*adj.*	unilateral
einsetzbar	*adj.*	applicable
einsetzen	*v.*	set
Einsiedler {m}	*n.*	hermit
Einsiedler {m}	*n.*	recluse
einsilbige	*n.*	monosyllable
Einspeisung {f}	*n.*	feeder
einspritzen	*v.*	inject
Einspruch {f}	*n.*	caveat

Einspruch {m}	*n.*	veto
einstellen	*v.*	enrol
Einstellung {f}	*n.*	cessation
Einstellung {f}	*n.*	engagement
Einstimmigkeit {f}	*a.*	unanimity
einstufen	*v.*	classify
eintauchen	*v.*	immerse
eintauchen	*v.*	souse
eintönig	*adj.*	drab
Eintönigkeit {f}	*n.*	monotony
Eintopf {m}	*n.*	minestrone
Eintopfgericht {n}	*n.*	stew
Eintrag {m}	*v.*	enter
einträglich	*adj.*	gainful
Eintragung {f}	*n.*	entry
Eintragung {f}	*n.*	registration
einträufeln	*v.*	instil
Eintritt {m}	*n.*	entrance
einverstanden	*adj.*	okay
Einwanderer {m}	*n.*	immigrant
einwandern	*v.*	immigrate
einwärts *adj.* inward		
einweihen	*v.*	induct
einweisen	*v.*	introduce
einwenden	*v.*	demur
einwerfen	*v.*	interject
einwickeln	*v.*	wrap
Einwirkung {f}	*n.*	influence
Einwurf {m}	*n.*	objection
Einwurf {m}	*n.*	slot
Einzelaktion {m}	*n.*	stuart
Einzelgänger {m}	*n.*	loner
Einzelgänger {m}	*n.*	maverick
Einzelhandelsabsatz {m}	*n.*	retail
Einzelhändler {m}	*n.*	retailer

255

einzeln *adj.* single
Einzelteil {n} *n.* part
Einzelwerk {n} *n.* monograph
einziehen *v.* settle
einzig *adv.* solely
einzigartig *adj.* inimitable
einzigartig *adj.* unique
Einzigartigkeit {f} *n.* singularity
Eis {n} *n.* ice
Eisberg {m} *n.* iceberg
Eisen {n}*n.* iron
Eisenbahn {f}*n.* train
Eishügel {m} *n.* hummock
eisig *adj.* glacial
eisig *adj.* icy
eisig *adj.* parky
Eisscholle {f} *n.* floe
Eiszapfen {m} *n.* icicle
Eiter {m} *n.* pus
eitern *v.* suppurate
Eiweiß {n} *n.* albumen
Eiweiß {n} *n.* protein
ekelhaft *adj.* fulsome
ekelhaft *adj.* nauseous
eklatant *adj.* flagrant
Ekstase {f} *n.* ecstasy
elastisch*adj.* elastic
Elefant {m} *n.* elephant
elegant *adj.* elegant
elegant *adj.* sartorial
Eleganz {f} *n.* elegance
Elektriker {m}*n.* electrician
elektrisch *adj.* electric
elektrisieren *v.* electrify
Elektrizität {f}*n.* electricity

elektronisch *adj.* electronic
elektrostatisch *adj.* static
elektrostatisch *adv.* statically
Element {n} *n.* element
elementar *adj.* elementary
elend *adj.* abject
elend *adj.* woeful
Elend {n}*n.* distress
Elendsviertel {n} *n.* slum
elf *adj. & n.* eleven
Elfenbein {n} *n.* ivory
Elite {f} *n.* elite
Ellenbogen {m} *n.* elbow
Ellipse {f} *n.* ellipse
Eloquenz {f} *n.* eloquence
Elster {f}*n.* magpie
elterlich *adj.* parental
Elternteil {n} *n.* parent
Email {m} *n.* email
emanzipieren *v. t* emancipate
Embryen {pl} *n.* embryo
Eminenz {f} *n.* eminence
Empfang {m} *n.* receipt
Empfang {m} *n.* reception
empfangen *v.* receive
Empfänger {m} *n.* addressee
Empfänger {m} *n.* listener
Empfänger {m} *n.* receiver
Empfänger {m} *n.* recipient
Empfänger {m} *n.* transceiver
empfänglich *adj.* susceptible
Empfangshalle {f} *n.* foyer
empfehlen *v.* commend
empfehlen *v.* recommend
Empfehlung {f} *n.*recommendation

empfindend	adj.	sentient
empfindlich	adj.	pettish
empfindlichen	v.	sensitize
Empfindung {f}	n.	sentiment
empfindungslos	adj.	numb
Empörung {f} n.		indignation
emsig	adj.	assiduous
Ende {n} n.		tail
Ende {n} n.		termination
endemisch	adj.	endemic
enden	v.	cease
endgültig	adj.	conclusive
endgültig	adj.	final
endlich	adj.	finite
endlos	adj.	infinite
endlos	adj.	interminable
endlos	adj.	unending
Endstelle {f}	n.	terminus
energetisch	adj.	energetic
Energie {f}	n.	energy
energisch	adj.	vigorous
eng adj. narrow		
Engel {m}	n.	angel
Englisch {n}	n.	English
Engstirnigkeit {f}	n.	bigotry
Enklave {f}	n.	enclave
entarten	v.	degenerate
entbehrlich	adj.	dispensable
entblößen	v.	denude
entblößen	v.	divest
entdecken	v.	detect
entdecken	v.	discover
Entdeckung {f}	n.	discovery
Entdeckungsreise {f}	n.	expedition
Ente {f}	n.	duck

enteignen	v.	dispossess
enteignen	v.	expropriate
enteignen	v.	oust
enterben v.		disinherit
entfalten v.		unfold
entfalten v.		unfurl
entfernen	v.	spay
entfernt	adj.	distant
Entfernung {f}	n.	distance
entfesseln	v.	unleash
entflammbar	adj.	combustible
entflammbar	adj.	flammable
entflammbar	adj.	inflammable
entflammen	v.	inflame
entfremden	v.i.	alienate
entfremdet	adj.	estranged
entfrosten	v.	defrost
entführen	v.t.	abduct
entführen	v.	hijack
entführen	v.	kidnap
Entführung {f}	n.	abduction
entgegen	prep.	against
entgegengesetzt	adj.	contrary
entgegenwirken	v.	antagonize
entgegenwirken	v.	counteract
entgeistert	adj.	flabbergasted
entgiften v.		decontaminate
entgiften v.		detoxify
entgleisend	v. t.	derail
Enthaarungsmittel {n}adj.		depilatory
enthalten	v.	abstain
enthalten	v.t.	contain
enthaltsam	adj.	ascetic
enthaltsam	adj.	teetotal
Enthaltung {f}	n.	abstinence

257

enthaupten	v.	behead
entheben	v.	depose
enthüllen	v.	divulge
enthüllen	v.	reveal
enthüllen	v.	unveil
entkeimen	v.	germinate
entkleiden	v.	disrobe
entkoffeiniert	adj.	decaffeinated
entkommen	v.i	escape
entkörperlicht	adj.	disembodied
entkräften	v.	enfeeble
entkräften	v.	invalidate
entkräftet	adj.	effete
entkriminalisieren	v.	decriminalize
entlang	prep.	alongside
entlarven	v.	debunk
entlarven	v.	unmask
entlassen	v.	disband
entlassen	v.	dismiss
entlassen	v.	sack
entlassen	v.	unburden
Entlassener	n.	parole
entlasten	v.	exonerate
entlaufen	v.	elope
entleeren	v.	deflate
entleeren	v.	evacuate
Entleerung {f}	n.	deflation
entlegen	adj.	outlying
Entlüftung {f}	n.	vent
entmachten	v.	disempower
entmannen	v.	emasculate
entmenschlichen	v.	dehumanize
entmutigen	v.	dampen
entmutigen	v.	daunt
entmutigen	v.	deject

entmutigen	v.	discourage
entmutigen	v.	dishearten
entmystifizieren	v.	demystify
entnerven	v.	unnerve
enträtselt	adj.	riddled
entreißen	v.	wrest
entsagen	v.t.	abdicate
entschädigen	v.	recoup
entschädigen	v.	reimburse
Entschädigung {f}	n.	compensation
entschärfen	v.	defuse
entscheiden	v.	decide
entscheidend	adj.	crucial
Entscheidung {f}	n.	decision
Entscheidung {f}	n.	ruling
entscheidungsfreudig	adj.	decisive
entschlossen	adj.	resolute
Entschluss {m}	n.	determination
Entschluss {m}	n.	resolution
entschuldbar	adj.	justifiable
entschuldigen	v.	apologize
Entschuldigung {f}	n.	apology
Entschuldigung {f}	v.	excuse
entschwinden	v.	vanish
entsetzlich	adj.	horrific
entspannen	v.	relax
entspannen	v.	slacken
entspannen	v.	unbend
Entspannung {f}	n.	catharsis
Entspannung {f}	n.	relaxation
entsprechend	adv.	accordingly
entsprechend	n.	obverse
Entsprechung {f}	n.	counterpart
entsprießen	v.	sprout
entspringen	v.	arise

258

entstaatlichen	v.	denationalize
entstehen	v.t.	accrue
entstehen	v.	originate
entstellen	v.	deform
Entstellung {f}	v.	warp
enttäuschend v.		disappoint
entthronen	v.	dethrone
entwässern	v. t	drain
entweder	adv.	either
entweihend	adj.	sacrilegious
entwickeln	v.	develop
entwickeln	v.	envelop
entwickeln	v.	evolve
Entwicklung {f}	n.	evolution
entwirren	v.	disentangle
entwöhnen	v.	wean
Entwurf {m}	n.	concept
Entwurf {m}	n.	draft
Entwurf {m}	n.	outline
entwurzeln	v.	uproot
Entziehung {f}	n.	extraction
entziffern	v.	decipher
entzückend	adj.	delightful
entzünden	v.	ignite
Entzündung {f}	n.	ignition
Entzündung {f}	n.	inflammation
Enzyklopädie {f}	n.	encyclopaedia
Epidemie {f}	n.	epidemic
Epidermis {f}	n.	epidermis
Epilepsie {f}	n.	epilepsy
Epilog {m}	n.	epilogue
Epistel {f}	n.	epistle
Epitome {f}	n.	epitome
Epoche {f}	n.	epoch
Epos {n}	n.	epic

er	pron.	he
erachten v.		deem
erachtend	prep.	considering
erbärmlich	adj.	miserable
erbärmlich	adj.	pathetic
erbärmlich	adj.	piteous
erbarmungslos	adj.	pitiless
Erbe {m} n.		heir
Erbe {n}	n.	bequest
erben	v.	inherit
Erbgut	n.	patrimony
erbieten v.		offer
erblich	adj.	hereditary
erblicken	v.	behold
erbrechen	v.	vomit
erbringen	v.	adduce
Erbschaft {f}	n.	heritage
Erbschaft {f}	n.	inheritance
Erbse {f} n.		pea
Erdball {m}	n.	globe
Erdbeben {n} n.		earthquake
Erdbeere {f}	n.	strawberry
Erdboden {m}	n.	ground
erdig	adj.	earthen
Erdkunde {f}	n.	geography
Erdnuss {f}	n.	peanut
Erdöl {n} n.		petroleum
erdulden v.i.		suffer
Erdwall {m}	n.	mound
Ereignis {n}	n.	happening
erfahren adj.		adept
Erfahrung {f}	n.	experience
erfassen v.		apprehend
erfassen v.		include
erfassen v.		mount

259

erfinden	v.	contrive	ergreifen v.	seize
erfinden	v.	invent	Ergreifung {f} n.	seizure
Erfinder {m}	n.	inventor	Ergründer {m}	n. fathom
Erfindung {f}	n.	figment	erhaben adj. sublime	
Erfindung {f}	n.	invention	Erhabenheit {f}	n. dignity
Erfolg {m}	n.	success	erhälten v. obtain	
erfolgreich	adj.	prosperous	erhältlich	adj. obtainable
erfolgreich	adj.	successful	erheben v. elevate	
erfolgreich	adj.	triumphant	erheben v. levy	
erfordern	v.	necessitate	Erhebung {f}	n. rising
Erfordernis {f}	n.	requisition	Erhebung {f}	n. uprising
erforschen	v.	delve	erheitern v. exhilarate	
erforschen	v.	plumb	erhellen v. lighten	
erforschen	v.	explore	erhöhen v. heighten	
erfreuen v. t.		delight	erholen v. recover	
erfreuen v.		gladden	erholen v. recuperate	
erfreuen v.		gratify	erinnern v. recollect	
erfreulich	adj.	joyous	erinnern v. remember	
Erfrischung {f}	n.	refreshment	erinnernd adj. reminiscent	
erfüllen v.		comply	Erinnerung {f}	n. recollection
erfüllen v.		imbue	Erinnerung {f}	n. remembrance
erfüllen v.		preoccupy	Erinnerungsvermögen {n}n.memory	
erfüllend adj.		prepossessing	erkennbar	adj. perceptible
Erfüllung {f}	n.	fulfilment	erkennbar	adj. transparent
ergänzend	adj.	complementary	erkennen	v. discern
ergänzend	adj.	subsidiary	erkennen	v.i. recognize
ergänzend	adj.	supplementary	Erkenntlichkeit {f} n. gratitude	
Ergänzung {f}n.		addition	Erkenntnis {f}n. cognizance	
Ergebnis {n}	n.	result	Erkennung {f}	n. identification
Ergebnis {n}	n.	upshot	Erkennung {f}	n. recognition
ergebnislos	adj.	inconclusive	Erker {m}	n. bay
Ergebung {f}	n.	acquiescence	erklären v. declare	
Ergötzen {n}	n.	delectation	erklären v. explain	
ergreifen v.		grip	erklären v. meld	
ergreifen v.		reach	erklären v. profess	

260

Erklärung {f}	n.	declaration
Erkrankung {f}	n.	disease
erkundigen	v.	enquire
erkundigen	v.	inquire
Erkundigung {f}	n.	enquiry
Erkundigung {f}	n.	inquiry
Erlass {m}	n.	edict
Erlass {m}	n.	writ
erlassen	v.	remit
Erlaubnis {f}	n.	allowance
Erlaubnis {f}	n.	permission
Erlaubnisschein {m}	v.	permit
erläutern	v. t	elucidate
erleichtern	v.	assuage
erleichtern	v.	facilitate
erleichtern	v.	relieve
erleuchten	v.	enlighten
erleuchten	v.	illuminate
erloschen	adj.	extinct
ermächtigen	v.	authorize
ermahnen	v.	admonish
ermahnen	v.	exhort
ermahnend	adj.	monitory
ermitteln	v.	ascertain
ermöglichen	v.	enable
ermorden	v.	assassinate
Ermordung {f}	n.	assassination
ermüden	v.	tire
ermüdend	adj.	soporific
ermüdend	adj.	tiresome
ermüdend	adj.	wearisome
ermüdend,	v.	irksome
Ermüdung {f}	n.	fatigue
ermuntern	v.	encourage
ermutigen	v.	embolden
ermutigen	v.	hearten
ermutigend	adj.	heartening
Ermutigung {f}	n.	countenance
Ernährung {f}	n.	nourishment
Ernährung {f}	n.	nutrition
Ernennung {f}	n.	nomination
erneuern	v.	rebuild
erneuern	v.	recondition
erneuern	v.	renew
erneuernd	adj.	renewal
erniedrigen	v.	demean
erniedrigen	v.	humiliate
ernst	adj.	earnest
ernst	v.	sever
ernst	adj.	stern
ernsthaft	adj.	whole-hearted
Ernsthaftigkeit {f}	n.	sobriety
ernstzunehmend	adj.	serious
Ernte {f}	n.	crop
Erntearbeiter {m}	n.	harvester
ernten	v.	reap
erobern	v.	conquer
Eroberung {f}	n.	conquest
erodieren	v.	erode
erogen	adj.	erogenous
Erosion {f}	n.	erosion
erotisch	adj.	erotic
erpressen	v.	extort
Erpresser {m}	n.	racketeer
Erpressung {f}	n.	blackmail
Erprobung {f}	n.	trial
Errechnung {f}	n.	computation
erregen	v.	agitate
erregen	v.	stimulate
Erregung {f}	n.	uproar

261

erreichen	v.	achieve
erreichen	v.	attain
Erreichung {f}	n.	attainment
errichten v.		constitute
errichten v.		establish
errichten v.		raise
errichtet adj.		erect
erröten v.		blush
Ersatz {m}	n.	replacement
Ersatz {m}	n.	substitute
Ersatz {m}	n.	surrogate
Erschaffer {m}	n.	creator
erscheinen v.		appear
Erscheinung {f}	n.	guise
erschlagen v.		slay
erschöpfen v.		exhaust
erschöpfend adj.		exhaustive
erschöpft adj.		jaded
erschrecken v.		appal
erschrecken v.		horrify
erschrecken v.		terrify
erschreckend adj.		scary
erschüttern n.		convulse
Erschütterung {f}	n.	vibration
ersetzen v.		supersede
ersinnen v. t		conceive
Ersparnisse {pl}	n.	savings
erst adj.		prim
erst, vorderst adj.		foremost
erstaufgeführt	adj.	premier
erstaunen v.		amaze
Erstaunen {n} n.		astonishment
erstaunlich adj.		prodigious
erstaunlich adj.		stupendous
erstechen v.		stab

erstehen v.		resurrect
ersticken	v.	asphyxiate
ersticken	v.	smother
ersticken	v.	stifle
ersticken	v.	suffocate
Erstickung {f} n.		suffocation
erstrangig	adv.	primarily
ersuchen	v.	beseech
ersuchen	v.	entreat
erträglich	adj.	tolerable
ertrinken v.		drown
eruptiv adj.		igneous
erwachsen	adj.	mature
Erwachsener {m}	n.	adult
Erwählung {f} n.		election
erwähnen	v.	mention
Erwärmung {f}	n.	heating
erwarten v.		await
erwarten v.		bide
erwarten v.		bode
erwarten	v.	expect
erwartungsvoll	adj.	expectant
Erweckung {f}	n.	revival
erweitern	v.	amplify
erweitern	v.	dilate
erweitern	v.	enlarge
erweitern	v.	expand
erweitern	v.	extend
erweitern	v.	widen
erwerben	v.	acquire
erwerben	v.	pre-empt
erwidern v.		retort
Erwiderung {f}	n.	rejoinder
Erz {n}	n.	ore
erzählen v.		narrate

erzählend	adj.	telling
Erzähler {m}	n.	narrator
Erzähler {m}	n.	teller
Erzählung {f}	n.	narration
Erzählung {f}	n.	story
Erzbischof {m}	n.	archbishop
Erzengel {m}	n.	archangel
erzeugen	v.	create
erzeugen	v.	generate
erzeugen	v.	procreate
Erzeuger {m}	n.	originator
Erzeugung {f}	n.	creation
Erzeugung {f}	n.	production
Erzieherin {f}	n.	governess
erzürnen	v.	enrage
erzwingen	v.	enforce
es	pron.	it
Esel {m}	n.	donkey
Esel {m}	n.	jackass
eskalieren	v.	escalate
Eskarpe {f}	n.	scarp
esoterisch	adj.	esoteric
Espresso {m}	n.	espresso
essbar	adj.	eatable
essbar	adj.	edible
essen	v.	eat
Essenz {f}	n.	essence
Essig {m}	n.	vinegar
Essiggurke {f}	n.	pickle
Esslokal {n}	n.	eatery
Essstäbchen {n}	n.	chopstick
Esswaren {pl}	n.	victuals
Estrich {m}	n.	screed
Etage {f}	n.	tier
Ethik {f}	n	ethic

ethisch	adj.	ethical
ethnisch	adj.	ethnic
Ethos {n}	n.	ethos
Etikett {n}	n.	etiquette
etwa	prep.	about
etwas	pron.	anything
etwas	pron.	something
Etymologie {f}	n.	etymology
Eule {f}	n.	owl
Eunuch {m}	n.	eunuch
Euphorie {f}	n.	euphoria
Euro {m}	n.	euro
Europäer {m}	n.	European
Euter {n}	n.	udder
Euthanasie {f}	n.	euthanasia
Evangelium {n}	n.	gospel
eventuell	adv.	perhaps
ewig	adj.	eternal
Ewigkeit {f}	n.	eternity
Ewigkeit {f}	n.	yonks
exakt	adv.	minutely
exaltiert	adj.	eccentric
Examen {n}	n.	examination
Exil {n}	n.	exile
Existenz {f}	n.	existence
existieren	v.	exist
Exmission {f}	n.	eviction
exmittieren	v.	evict
Exodus {m}	n.	stampede
exotisch	adj.	exotic
Experiment {n}	n.	experiment
Experte {m}	n.	expert
explodieren	v.	burst
explodieren	v.	detonate
explodieren	v.	explode

263

Explosion {f} *n.* blast
Explosion {f} *n.* explosion
explosiv *adj.* explosive
Exponent {m}*n.* exponent
exportieren *v. t.* export
extern *adj.* external
extra *adj.* extra
extrafein *adj.* superfine
Extravaganza {f} *n.* extravaganza
Extravertiert {m} *n.* extrovert
extrem *adj.* extreme
Extremist {m}*n.* extremist
extrudieren *v.* extrude
Exzellenz {f} *n.* excellency
exzentrisch *adj.* wacky
Exzess {m} *n.* excess

F

Fabel {f} *n.* fable
Fabel {f} *n.* tale
fabrizieren *v.* fabricate
facettenreich *adj.* multifarious
Fachberater {m} *n.* consultant
fachgerecht *adj.* skilled
Fachhochschule *n.* college
Fachmann {m} *n.* specialist
Fachwerk {n} *n.* framework
Fackel {f} *n.* torch
fad *adj.* stale
fad *adj.* vapid
fade *adj.* insipid
Faden {m} *n.* thread
Faden {m} *n.* twine
fähig *adj.* able
fähig *adj.* capable

Fähigkeit {f} *n.* faculty
Fähigkeit {f} *n.* feature
Fahne {f}*n.* banner
Fahne {f}*n.* flag
Fähre {f} *n.* ferry
fahren *v.* drive
Fahrenheit *n.* Fahrenheit
Fahrer {m} *n.* chauffeur
Fahrer {m} *n.* driver
Fahrgestell {n} *n.* chassis
fahrig *adj.* erratic
Fahrkarte {f} *n.* ticket
Fahrrad {n} *n.* bicycle
Fahrrolle {f} *n.* castor
Fahrstuhl {m}*n.* elevator
fahrzeug *adj.* vehicular
Fahrzeug {n} *n.* craft
Fahrzeug {n} *n.* vehicle
Faktor {m} *n.* factor
falb *adj.* fallow
Falke {f} *n.* falcon
Falke {f} *n.* hawk
Fall {m} *n.* event
Fall {m} *n.* halyard
Fall {m} *n.* instance
Fall {m} *n.* occurrence
Falle {f} *n.* trap
fallen *v.* fall
fallen *v.* fell
Fallgrube {f} *n.* pitfall
Fallschirm {m} *n.* parachute
Fallschirmspringer {pl}*n.* parachutist
falsch *adj.* fake
falsch *adj.* wrong
falsch schwören *v.* perjure

264

falschanwenden	v.	misapply
falschbuchstabieren	v.	misspell
Falschheit {f}	n.	falsehood
falschlesen	v.	misread
Falschspieler {m}	n.	cheat
Fälschung {f}	n.	forgery
Fälschung {f}	n.	fudge
Fälschung {f}	n.	sham
falschunterrichten	v.	misinform
falschzitieren	v.	misquote
Falte {f}	n.	crease
Falte {f}	n.	pleat
falten	v.t	fold
Falter {m}	n.	moth
familiär	adj.	familiar
Familie {f}	n.	family
Fan {m}	n.	bigot
Fan {m}	n.	fan
Fanatiker {m}	n.	fanatic
Fanfare {f}	n.	fanfare
Fang {m}	n.	claw
fangen	v.	catch
fangen	n.	snare
Fänger {m}	n.	captor
Fangzahn {m}	n.	fang
Fangzahn {m}	n.	tusk
fantasievoll	adj.	imaginative
fantastisch	adj.	fantastic
Farbband {n}	n.	ribbon
Farbe {f}	n.	colour
Farbe {f}	n.	paint
Farbe {f}	n.	tint
farbenprächtig	adj.	gaudy
Farbfleck {m}	n.	blob
farblos	n.	colourless

farblos	adj.	sallow
Farbskala {f}	n.	gamut
färbte	n.	dye
Färbung {f}	n.	colouring
Farm {f}	n.	grange
Farm {f}	n.	ranch
Farn {n}	n.	fern
Faschismus {m}	n.	fascism
Fase {f}	n.	bevel
faseln	v.	maunder
Fass {n}	n.	barrel
Fass {n}	n.	cask
Fass {n}	n.	tun
Fassade {f}	n.	facade
fassen	v.	subsume
Fassette {f}	n.	facet
fast	adv.	almost
faul	adj.	idle
faul	adj.	lazy
faul	adj.	slothful
faul	adj.	sluggish
faulenzen	v.	laze
faulenzen	v.	lounge
Faulenzer {m}	n.	idler
Faulenzer {m}	n.	sluggard
Faulheit {f}	n.	sloth
Fauna	n.	fauna
Faust {f}	n.	fist
Fausthandschuh {m}	n.	mitten
favorit	adj.	favourite
Fax {n}	n.	fax
Februar {m}	n.	February
Fechten {n}	n.	fencing
Feder {f}	n.	feather
Federbalg {m}	n.	bellows

265

Federball {m} *n.*	shuttlecock	**feilschen** *v.*	haggle
Federball {n} *n.*	badminton	**Feind {m}** *n.*	enemy
Fegefeuer {n} *n.*	purgatory	**Feind {m}** *n.*	fiend
fegen *v.*	sweep	**Feind {m}** *n.*	foe
Fehde {f} *n.*	feud	**feindlich** *adj.*	adverse
Fehdehandschuh *n.*	gauntlet	**feindlich** *adj.*	inimical
fehlbar *adj.*	fallible	**Feindlichkeit {f}** *n.*	animosity
Fehlbetrag {m} *n.*	deficit	**Feindschaft {f}** *n.*	enmity
Fehlbetrag {m} *n.*	shortfall	**feindselig** *adj.*	hostile
Fehlbogen {m} *n.*	misprint	**Feindseligkeit {f}** *n.*	hostility
fehlen *v.*	want	**feinfühlig** *adj.*	delicate
fehlend *adj.*	amiss	**Feinheit {f}** *n.*	finesse
fehlend *adj.*	wanting	**Feinheit {f}** *n.*	nicety
Fehler {m} *n.*	error	**Feinheit {f}** *n.*	subtlety
Fehler {m} *n.*	mistake	**Feinschmecker {m}** *n.*	gourmet
Fehler {m} *n.*	defect	**feinsinnig** *adj.*	subtle
Fehler {n} *n.*	blunder	**Feld {n}** *n.*	field
fehlerbehebend *adj.*	corrective	**Feldstein {m}** *n.*	boulder
fehlerhaft *adj.*	defective	**Feldwebel {m}** *n.*	sergeant
fehlerhaft *adj.*	faulty	**Felsen {m}** *n.*	rock
Fehlerstelle {f} *n.*	flaw	**felsig** *adj.*	rocky
Fehlgeburt {f} *n.*	miscarriage	**Felsvorsprung {m}** *n.*	cliff
fehlleiten *v.*	misdirect	**feminin** *adj.*	feminine
Fehlschuss {m} *n.*	miss	**Feminismus {m}** *n.*	feminism
fehlzünden *v.*	misfire	**Fenchel {m}** *n.*	fennel
feierlich *adj.*	ceremonial	**feng shui {n}** *n.*	feng shui
feierlich *adj.*	solemn	**Fenster {n}** *n.*	window
feiern *v.*	celebrate	**Fensterflügel {m}** *n.*	casement
feiern *v.*	revel	**Fensterscheibe {f}** *n.*	pane
feiern *v.*	solemnize	**fern** *adv.*	afar
Feiertag {m} *n.*	holiday	**fern** *adj.*	aloof
feige *adj.*	craven	**fern** *adv.*	far
Feige {f} *n.*	fig	**fern** *adj.*	remote
Feigheit {f} *n.*	cowardice	**ferner** *adv.*	further
Feigling {m} *n.*	coward	**Fernlastfahrer {m}** *n.*	trucker

266

Fernschreiber {m} *n.* teleprinter
Fernsehen {n} *n.* television
Ferse {f} *n.* heel
fertig *adj.* ready
Fertigkeit {f} *n.* dexterity
Fertigungsanlage {f}*n.* factory
fesseln *v.* captivate
fesseln *v.* gripe
fesseln *v.* trammel
fest *adj.* firm
fest *adj.* solid
fest *adj.* steadfast
Fest {m} *n.* feast
Fest {n} *n.* celebration
Fest {n} *n.* festival
Feste {f} *n.* stronghold
Festigung {f} *n.* consolidation
Festland {n} *n.* land
festlegen *v.* locate
festlegen *v.* pinpoint
festlich *adj.* convivial
festlich *adj.* festive
Festlichkeit {f} *n.* festivity
Festlichkeit {f} *n.* solemnity
festmachen *v.* belay
festmachen *v.* tighten
Festplattenlaufwerk {n}*n.* hard drive
feststehend *adj.* stationary
feststellbar *adj.* certifiable
Feststellung {f} *n.* assessment
Festung {f} *n.* fortress
Fetisch {m} *n.* fetish
Fett {n} *n.* fat
Fettabsaugung {f} *n.* liposuction
Fettsucht {f} *n.* obesity

feucht *adj.* damp
feucht *adj.* dank
feucht *adj.* humid
feucht *adj.* moist
feucht *adj.* soggy
feucht *adj.* wet
feuchten *v.* moisten
Feuchtigkeit {f} *n.* dampness
Feuchtigkeit {f} *n.* humidity
Feuchtigkeit {f} *n.* moisture
feuchtkalt *adj.* clammy
Feudalismus {m} *n.* feudalism
Feuer {n}*n.* fire
Feuerbestattung {f} *n.* cremation
Feuerpause {f} *n.* ceasefire
Feuerstein {m} *n.* flint
Feuerstelle {f} *n.* hearth
Feuerzeug {n} *n.* lighter
feurig *adj.* fiery
feurig *adj.* mettlesome
Fiasko {n} *n.* fiasco
Fichte {f}*n.* fir
Fieber {n} *n.* fever
fiebernd *adj.* febrile
Fiedel {f}*n.* fiddle
Figurine {f} *n.* figurine
Fiktion {f} *n.* fiction
fiktiv *adj.* fictitious
Film {m} *n.* film
Filmmusik {f} *n.* score
Filter {m}*n.* filter
filtern *v.* filtrate
filtern *v.* percolate
Finalist {m} *n.* finalist
Finanz *n.* finance

Finanzbeamte {m} n.   financier
finanziell adj.   financial
finden   v.   find
findig   adj.   resourceful
Finger {m}   n.   finger
Fingerhüte {pl}   n.   thimble
finster   adj.   murky
Finsternis   n.   eclipse
Firma {m}   n.   employer
Fisch {m}   n.   fish
Fischdampfer {m} n.   trawler
Fischer {m}   n.   fisherman
Fischerei {f}   n.   fishery
Fiskus {m}   n.   exchequer
Fixierung {f}   n.   fixation
Fjord {m}   n.   fjord
flach   adj.   tabular
Fläche {f}   n.   face
Fläche {f}   n.   surface
flackern v.t   flicker
Flamme {f}   n.   flame
Flanke {f}   n.   flank
Flannel {n}   n.   flannel
Fläschchen {n}   n.   flask
Fläschchen {n}   n.   phial
Fläschchen {n}   n.   vial
Flasche {f}   n.   bottle
Flaschenkürbis {m}   n.   gourd
flattern   v.   flutter
flau adj. slack
Flaute {f} n.   doldrums
Flechte {f}   n.   tress
Fleckchen {n} n.   speck
fleckenlos   adj.   spotless
fleckig   adj.   patchy

Fleckigkeit {f} n.   blotch
Fledermaus {f}   n.   bat
Flegel {m}   n.   cub
Flegeljahre {pl}   adj.   teens
flehen   v. t   crave
Flehen {n}   n.   entreaty
Fleisch {n}   n.   flesh
Fleisch {n}   n.   meat
Fleischbrühe {f}   n.   broth
fleischig adj. beefy
fleischlich   adj.   carnal
Fleiß {m} n.   study
fleißig   adj.   diligent
fleißig   adj.   studious
flexibel   adj.   flexible
Flickwerk {n} n.   vamp
Flieder {m}   n.   lilac
fliegen   v.i   fly
Fliegen {n}   n.   aviation
Flieger {m}   n.   aviator
Fliesen {m}   n.   tile
Fließen v.i   flow
fließend adj. fluent
fließend adj. runny
flink adj. nimble
Flinte {f} n.   musket
Flittchen {n}   n.   slut
Flitterwochen {pl} n.   honeymoon
Floh {m} n.   flea
Flora {f}   n.   flora
florieren   v.   prosper
Florist {m}   n.   florist
Flosse {f}   n.   flipper
Flöte {f} n.   flute
Flotte {f} n.   fleet

fluch [m] *n.* curse
Fluch {m} *n.* malediction
flüchten *v.* abscond
flüchten *v.* flee
flüchtig *adj.* volatile
Flüchtling {m} *n.* fugitive
Flüchtling {m} *n.* refugee
Fluchtlinie {f} *n.* non-alignment
Flug {m} *n.* flight
Flugbahn {f} *n.* trajectory
Flugbegleiter {m} *n.* steward
Flügel {m} *n.* wing
Flugplatz {m} *n.* aerodrome
Flugzeug {n} *n.* aeroplane
Flugzeug {n} *n.* plane
Flugzeughalle {f} *n.* hangar
Flunkerei {f} *n.* blarney
fluoreszierend *adj.* fluorescent
Fluorid {n} *n.* fluoride
Fluse {f} *n.* fluff
Fluss {m} *n.* river
flussartig *adj.* fluvial
Flüsschen {n} *n.* creek
Flüssigkeit {f} *n.* liquid
Flüssigkeit {f} *n.* fluid
flüstern *v.* whisper
Flut {f} *n.* spate
flutwelle *adj.* tidal
Flutwelle {f} *n.* tide
Föderal *adj.* federal
Föderation {f}*n.* federation
fokal *adj.* focal
Fokus {m} *n.* focus
Folge {f} *n.* consequence
Folge {f} *n.* sequel

Folge {f} *n.* succession
folgen *v.* ensue
folgen *v.* follow
folgend *adj.* consequent
folgend *adj.* successive
folgerichtig *adj.* sequential
folgern *v.* infer
Folgerung {f} *n.* implication
Folgerung {f} *n.* inference
folgewidrig *adj.* inconsistent
folglich *adv.* thus
folgsam *adj.* obedient
Folgsamkeit {f} *n.* obedience
Förderer {m} *n.* patron
Forderung {f} *n.* demand
Forelle {f} *n.* trout
Form {f} *n.* shape
formal *adj.* formal
formalitätenlos *adv.* summarily
Format {m} *n.* format
Formblatt {n} *n.* form
Formel {f} *n.* formula
formen *v.* sculpt
Formenlehre {f} *n.* morphology
Förmlichkeit {f} *n.* formality
formlos *adj.* amorphous
formlos *adj.* informal
formlos *adj.* shapeless
Formsache {f} *n.* technicality
Formschnitt {m} *n.* topiary
formulieren *v.* formulate
formulieren *v.* verbalize
Forschung {f}*n.* research
Förster {m} *n.* ranger
Forstwissenschaft {f}*n.* forestry

269

fortan *adv.* henceforth
Fortbestand {m} *n.* continuity
Fortbewegung {f} *n.* locomotion
Fortdauer {f} *n.* persistence
Fortführung {f} *n.* continuation
Fortgang {m} *n.* progress
fortlaufend *adj.* consecutive
fortschreiten *v.* advance
fortschreitend *adv.* onward
Fortschritt {m} *n.* advance
Fortschritte {pl} *n.* proceedings
fortschrittlich *adj.* progressive
fortsetzen *v.* continue
fortsetzen *v.* proceeds
fortwährend *adj.* perpetual
Forum {n} *n.* forum
Foto {n} *n.* photo
Fotograf {m} *n.* photographer
Fotografie {f} *n.* photograph
Fotografie {f} *n.* photography
fotografisch *adj.* photographic
Fotokopie {f} *n.* photocopy
fotokopieren *n.* photostat
Fötus {m} *n.* fetus
Fracht {f} *n.* freight
Frage {f} *n.* query
Fragebogen {m} *n.* questionnaire
fragen *v.* ask
fragend *adj.* interrogative
Fragestellung {f} *n.* question
Fragment {n} *n.* fragment
Franchise *n.* franchise
Frankfurter *n.* frankfurter
französisch *adj.* French
fratzenhaft *adj.* grotesque

Frau {f} *n.* woman
Frauenzimmer {n} *n.* wench
Fräulein *n.* miss
Freak {m} *n.* freak
frech *adj.* cheeky
frech *adj.* impudent
Frechheit {f} *n.* insolence
frei *adj.* exempt
frei *adj.* free
Freibauer {m}*n.* yeoman
Freier {m} *n.* suitor
freigeben *v.* uncover
freigebig *adj.* bountiful
freigebig *adj.* lavish
freigebig *adj.* munificent
Freigebigkeit {f} *n.* bounty
Freigebigkeit {f} *n.* largesse
freigestellt *adj.* optional
freigiebig *adj.* generous
Freiheit {f} *n.* freedom
Freiheit {f} *n.* liberty
freiheitlich *adj.* liberal
Freilassung {f} *n.* manumission
freimachen *v.* disengage
freimütig *adj.* outspoken
freisprechen *v.* absolve
freisprechen *v.* acquit
Freispruch {m} *n.* acquittal
Freitag {m} *n.* Friday
freiwillig *adv.* voluntarily
freiwillig *adj.* voluntary
Freiwillige {m,f} *n.* volunteer
Freizeit {f} *n.* leisure
fremd *adj.* strange
fremd, *adj.* foreign

fremdartig   adj.   outlandish
Fremde {m,f}   n.   stranger
Fremdenfeindlichkeit {f}n.
   xenophobia
Fremdenverkehr {m}n.   tourism
frenetisch   adj.   frenetic
fressen   v.   rankle
Fresssucht {f}   n.   bulimia
Freudenfeuer {n}   n.   bonfire
freudig   adj.   glad
freudig   adj.   joyful
Freund {m}   n.   friend
Freundin {f}   n.   lass
freundlich   adj.   affable
freundschaftlich   adj.   amicable
Freundschaftlichkeit {f}n.   amity
Frevel {m}   n.   sacrilege
Friede {m}   n.   peace
Friedensrichter {m}   n.   magistrate
Friedhof {m}   n.   cemetery
Friedhof {m}   n.   graveyard
friedlich   adj.   peaceful
frisch   adj.   fresh
Friseur {m}   n.   barber
Frist {f}   n.   period
frivol   adj.   frivolous
froh adj.   cheery
froh adj.   lucky
fröhlich   adj.   mirthful
Fröhlichkeit {f}   n.   glee
Fröhlichkeit {f}   n.   happiness
Fröhlichkeit {f}   n.   mirth
frohlocken   v.   rejoice
fromm   adj.   godly
fromm   adj.   pious

Front {f}   n.   front
Frosch {m}   n.   frog
Frosch {m}   n.   squib
Frost {m}   n.   frost
frostig   adj.   chilly
frostig   adj.   frosty
Frotteehandtuch {n}n.   terry
Frucht {f}   n.   progeny
fruchtbaradj.   fertile
fruchtbaradj.   fruitful
fruchtbaradj.   reproductive
fruchtbaradj.   seminal
Fruchtbarkeit {f}   n.   fertility
Früchte-Eisbecher {m}n.   sundae
Fruchtknoten {m}   n.   ovary
früh adj.   early
früher   adj.   prior
frühest   adj. & n.   first
frühlingshaft   adj.   vernal
frühreif   adj.   premature
Frühstück {n}n.   breakfast
Frühstücksfleisch {n}n.   spam
frustrieren   v.   frustrate
Fuchs {m}   n.   fox
fuchsartig   adj.   vulpine
Füchsin {f}   n.   vixen
fügen   v.   submit
fühlbar   adj.   palpable
fühlbar   adj.   tactile
fühlen   v.   feel
führen   v.   lead
Führer {m}   n.   leader
Führung {f}   n.   lead
Führung {f}   n.   leadership
Führungskraft {f}   n.   executive

271

füllen	v.	fill
Füllung {f}	n.	filling
Füllung {f}	n.	padding
Füllung {f}	n.	stuffing
Fundament {n}	n.	footing
Fundament {n}	n.	foundation
Fundament {n}	n.	seating
fünf *adj. & n.*		five
fünfzehn *adj. & n.*		fifteen
fünfzig *adj. & n.*		fifty
Funke {m}	n.	spark
funkel	v.	twinkle
funkeln	v.	glitter
funkelnd *adj.*		scintillating
funkelnd *adj.*		sparkling
Funktionär {m}	n.	functionary
funktionsfähig	*adj.*	operative
funktionsunfähig	*adj.*	inoperative
für *prep.*		per
Furche {f}	n.	furrow
Furche {f}	n.	wrinkle
furchtbar*adj.*		formidable
furchtbar*adj.*		redoubtable
furchtbar*adj.*		terrible
furchteinflößend	*adj.*	awesome
fürchten *v.t*		dread
fürchterlich	*adj.*	tremendous
furchtlos*adj.*		fearless
furchtsam	*adj.*	fearful
furchtsam	*adj.*	timid
Furchtsamkeit {f}	n.	timidity
Fürsorge {f}	n.	welfare
fürsorglich	*adj.*	thoughtful
Fuß {m} *n.*		foot
Fußball {m}	n.	football

Fußball {m}	n.	soccer
Fußgänger {m}	n.	pedestrian
Fußgrund {m}	n.	bottom
Fußhebel {m} *n.*		pedal
Fußknöchel {m}	n.	ankle
Fußpunkt {m}*n.*		nadir
Fußring {m}	n.	anklet
Fußrücken {m}	n.	arch
Fußspur {f}	n.	track
Futteral {n}	n.	sheath
futuristisch	*adj.*	futuristic

G

Gabel {f} *n.*		fork
Gabel {f} *n.*		yoke
Gabelfrühstück {n}		n. brunch
gackeln	v.	cackle
Gag {m} *n.*		gag
gähnen	v.	yawn
Gala {f} *n.*		gala
galant	*adj.*	chivalrous
Galaxie {f}	n.	galaxy
Galerie {f}	n.	gallery
Galgen {m}	n.	gallows
Galgenstrick {m}		n. rogue
Galle {f} *n.*		bile
Galle {f} *n.*		gall
gallig	*adj.*	acrid
Gallone {f}	n.	gallon
Galopp {n}	n.	gallop
Gamasche {f}*n.*		leggings
Gamasche {f}*n.*		spat
Gambit {n}	n.	gambit
Gammler {m} *n.*		bum
Gang {m}	n.	gait

Gangster {m} *n.* gangster
Gangster {m} *n.* thug
Ganove {m} *n.* crook
Gans {f} *n.* goose
Gänseblümchen {n} *n.* daisy
ganz *adj.* total
ganz *adj.* whole
Ganze {n} *n.* entirety
gänzlich *adv.* wholly
Garage {f} *n.* garage
Garant {m} *n.* guarantor
garantieren *v.t* guarantee
Garderobe {f} *n.* wardrobe
Garderobenräume {pl}*adv.* backstage
Gardine {f} *n.* curtain
Garn {n} *n.* yarn
garnieren *v.* garnish
Garnierung {f} *n.* topping
Garten {m} *n.* garden
Gartenbau {m} *n.* horticulture
Gärtner {m} *n.* gardener
Gashebel {m}*n.* throttle
Gasse {f} *n.* lane
Gast {m} *n.* guest
gastfreundlich *adj.* hospitable
Gasthaus {n} *n.* inn
Gasthaus {n} *n.* tavern
Gastronomie {f} *n.* gastronomy
Gaudi {m} *n.* jamboree
Gaukler {m} *n.* imposter
Gaukler {m} *n.* juggler
Gaumen {m} *n.* palate
gaumen... *adj.* palatal
Gauner {m} *n.* rook
Gauner {m} *n.* trickster

Gaunerei {f} *n.* roguery
Gaze {f} *n.* gauze
Geächtet {m} *n.* outlaw
gealtert *adj.* aged
Gebäck {n} *n.* pastry
Gebärdensprache {f}*n.* mimicry
Gebärmutter {f} *n.* uterus
Gebäude {n} *n.* building
Gebäude {n} *n.* edifice
geben *v.* give
Gebet {n} *n.* prayer
Gebiet {n} *n.* region
Gebiet {n} *n.* territory
Gebiet {n} *n.* tract
Gebieter {m} *n.* lord
Gebieterin {f} *n.* mistress
gebildet *adj.* literate
Gebinde {n} *n.* wreath
Gebirge {n} *n.* mountain
gebirgig *adj.* mountainous
Gebiss {n} *n.* denture
Gebläse {n} *n.* supercharger
gebogen *adj.* bent
geboren *adj.* born
geboren *adj.* natant
Gebräu {n} *n.* concoction
gebrauchsfähig *adj.* serviceable
gebrechlich *adj.* rickety
Gebrechlichkeit {f} *n.* infirmity
Gebrüll {n} *n.* roar
Gebühr {f} *n.* tax
Gebühreneinheit {f} *n.* unit
gebunden (Buch) *n.* hardback
Geburt {f} *n.* birth
Geburt {f} *n.* nativity

geburts *adj.*	natal	
Geburtshelferin {f}	*n.*	midwife
Geburtswehen {pl}	*n.*	throes
gedankenlos *adj.*	thoughtless	
Gedankensplitter {m} *n.*	aphorism	
Gedankenübertragung {f} *n.*	telepathy	
gedankenvoll *adj.*	pensive	
gedeihen	*n.*	batten
gedeihen	*v.*	thrive
gedemütigen *v.*	abase	
gedenken	*v.*	commemorate
Gedenkfeier {f}	*n.* commemoration	
Gedicht {n}	*n.*	ode
Gedicht {n}	*n.*	poem
Gedränge {n} *n.*	throng	
gedrängt *adj.*	terse	
Gedrängtheit {f}	*n.*	density
Geduld {f}	*n.*	patience
geduldig *adj.*	patient	
Geduldsprobe {f}	*n.*	ordeal
geeignet *adj.*	apt	
Gefahr {f}	*n.*	danger
Gefahr {f}	*n.*	hazard
Gefahr {f}	*n.*	jeopardy
Gefahr {f}	*n.*	peril
gefährden	*v.*	endanger
gefährden	*v.*	imperil
gefährden	*v.*	jeopardize
gefährlich	*adj.*	dangerous
Gefährte {m} *n.*	companion	
gefahrvoll	*adj.*	perilous
gefällig *adj.*	complaisant	
gefällig *adj.*	compliant	
gefällig *adj.*	favourable	
gefällig *adj.*	winsome	

gefälscht	*adj.*	bogus
Gefangene {m,f}	*n.*	prisoner
Gefangener *n.*	captive	
gefangennehmen *v.*	capture	
Gefangenschaft {f}	*n.*	captivity
Gefangenschaft {f}	*n.* confinement	
Gefängnis {n} *n.*	jail	
Gefängnis {n} *n.*	prison	
Gefängniswärter {m} *n.*	jailer	
Gefäß {n}	*n.*	vessel
gefeit *adj.*	immune	
gefertigen	*v.*	manufacture
Gefieder {n}	*n.*	plumage
Geflügel {n}	*n.*	fowl
Geflügel {n}	*n.*	poultry
Gefolge {n}	*n.*	retinue
Gefolge {n}	*n.*	suite
gefräßig *adj.*	gutsy	
gefräßig *adj.*	ravenous	
gefräßig *adj.*	voracious	
gefügig *adj.*	amenable	
gefügig *adj.*	pliable	
gefügig *adj.*	supple	
gefügigen	*v.*	amend
Gefühl {n}	*n.*	emotion
Gefühl {n}	*n.*	feeling
Gefühl {n}	*adj.*	void
gefühlsduselig	*adj.*	sentimental
gefühlserregend	*adj.*	emotive
gefühlsmäßig *adj.*	emotional	
gegen	*prep.*	contra
gegen	*prep.*	versus
Gegenargument {n}	*n.*	refutation
Gegenbeschuldigung {f} *n.* recrimination		

Gegenfeuer {n}	v.	backfire
Gegenkörper {m}	n.	antibody
Gegenmittel {n}	n.	antidote
Gegenmittel {n}	n.	antagonist
Gegensatz {m}	n.	antagonism
Gegensatz {m}	n.	complement
Gegensatz {m}	n.	contrast
Gegenschlag {m}	n.	riposte
gegenseitig	adj.	mutual
Gegensprechanlage {f}n.		intercom
gegenüberliegend adj.		opposite
gegenüberstellen	v.	confront
gegenüberstellen	v.	oppose
Gegenüberstellung {f}n.		
confrontation		
Gegner {m}	n.	adversary
Gegner {m}	n.	opponent
Gehalt {n}	n.	salary
Gehalt {n}	n.	stipend
gehaltlos	adj.	inane
gehärten v.		harden
gehässig adj.		spiteful
Gehässigkeit {f}	n.	spite
geheiligt adj.		sacrosanct
geheim	adj.	secret
geheim	adj.	undercover
Geheimmittel {n}	n.	nostrum
Geheimnis {n}	n.	mystery
Geheimnis {n}	n.	mystique
Geheiß {n}	n.	behest
gehen	v.t	go
gehen	v.	walk
Gehen {n}	n.	going
geheuer adj.		risky
Gehirnerschütterung {f}n.concussion		

Gehör {n}	n.	hearing
gehorchen	v.	obey
gehören v.		pertain
Gehorsamsverweigerung {f}n.		
insubordination		
Gehrungssäge {f}	n.	mitre
Gehweg {m}	n.	promenade
geifern	v.	slobber
Geiger {m}	n.	violinist
Geisel {f}	n.	hostage
Geiser {m}	n.	geyser
Geißel {f}	n.	scourge
Geißel {f}	n.	whip
geißeln	v.	flagellate
Geist {m}	n.	spirit
geistig	adj.	mental
geistlich adj.		spiritual
Geistliche {m,f}	n.	chaplain
Geistliche {m,f}	n.	clergy
Geistlichkeit {f}	n.	spirituality
geizen	adj.	stingy
Geizhals {m}	n.	miser
Geizhals {m}	n.	niggard
Geizhals {m}	n.	scrooge
geizig	adj.	miserly
geizig	adj.	niggardly
geizig	adj.	thrifty
Gejohle {n}	n.	hoot
Gejohle {n}	n.	jubilation
Gekläff {n}	n.	yelp
gekniffen	v.	pinch
Gel n.		gel
Gelächter {n}	n.	guffaw
Gelage {n}	n.	binge
Gelage {n}	n.	wassail

275

Geländer {n} *n.* banisters
Geländer {n} *n.* railing
Gelassenheit {f} *n.* composure
geläufig *adj.* voluble
Geläut {n} *n.* peal
gelb *adj.* yellow
Gelbsucht {f} *n.* jaundice
Gelbwurz {f} *n.* turmeric
Geld {n} *n.* money
Geldbeutel {m} *n.* purse
Geldgier {f} *n.* avarice
Geldüberweisung {f}*n.* remittance
Geldwirtschaft {f} *n.* monetarism
Gelee {n} *n.* jelly
Gelegenheit {f} *n.* occasion
Gelegenheit {f} *n.* opportunity
gelegentlich *adj.* casual
gelegentlich *adj.* occasional
gelehrig *adj.* docile
gelehrt *adj.* erudite
Gelehrte {m,f} *n.* scholar
Geleit {n} *n.* convoy
geleiten *v.* conduct
Gelenkrheumatismus {m}*n.*
rheumatism
gelernt *adj.* learned
geliebt *adj.* beloved
Geliebte {m,f}*n.* lover
Geliebte {m,f}*n.* paramour
gelindert *adj.* emollient
gelingen *v.* succeed
Gelöbnis {n} *n.* plight
Geltungsbereich {m} *n.* ambit
gemächlich *adj.* leisurely
Gemälde {n} *n.* painting

Gemälde {n} *n.* picture
gemäß *adv.* according
gemäß *conj.* after
gemäßigt *adj.* temperate
gemein *adj.* ignoble
gemein *adj.* scurrilous
Gemeinde {n}*n.* commune
Gemeindesaal {m}*n.* vestry
Gemeinheit {f} *n.* vulgarity
Gemeinplatz {m} *n.* bathos
gemeinsam *adv.* together
Gemeinschaft {f} *n.* community
Gemeinschaftsküche {f}*n.* canteen
Gemeinwesen {n} *n.* polity
gemessen *adj.* measured
Gemisch {n} *n.* medley
gemischt *adj.* composite
Gemüse {n} *n.* vegetable
Gemüsehändler {m}*n.* greengrocer
gemütlich *adj.* cosy
gemütlich *adj.* jovial
Gemütlichkeit {f} *n.* sociability
Gemütsart {f} *n.* temper
genau *adj.* precise
genehmigen *v.t.* consent
Genehmigung {f} *n.* approval
Genehmigung {f} *n.* consent
Generation {f} *n.* generation
Generator {m} *n.* generator
generell *adj.* general
Genesung {f} *n.* recovery
genetisch *adj.* genetic
Genie {n} *n.* genius
genießen *v.* enjoy
genießen *v.* relish

geniessen	v.t.	savour	
Genießer {m}	n.	epicure	
Genügsamkeit {f}	n.	modesty	
Genugtuung {f}	n.	gratification	
Genussucht {f}	n.	hedonism	
Geograph {m}	n.	geographer	
geographisch	adj.	geographical	
Geologe {m}	n.	geologist	
Geologie {f}	n.	geology	
Geometrie {f}	n.	geometry	
geometrisch	adj.	geometric	
Gepard {m}	n.	cheetah	
Geplänkel {n}	n.	banter	
Gepränge {n}	n.	pomp	
gerade	adj.	direct	
gerade	adj.	even	
gerade	adj.	just	
gerade	adj.	straight	
gerade werden	v.	straighten	
geradezu	adv.	directly	
Geradheit {f}	n.	rectitude	
Gerät {n}	n.	appliance	
Gerät {n}	n.	utensil	
geräumig	adj.	capacious	
geräumig	adj.	roomy	
geräumig	adj.	spacious	
Geräusch {n}	n.	noise	
geräuschvoll	adj.	noisy	
gerben	v.	tan	
Gerber {m}	n.	tanner	
Gerberei {f}	n.	tannery	
gerecht	adj.	equitable	
Gerechtigkeit {f}	n.	equity	
Gerechtigkeit {f}	n.	justice	
gereihen	v.	rank	

gereizt	adj.	petulant	
gereizt	adj.	tetchy	
Gereiztheit {f}	n.	petulance	
Gericht {n}	n.	dish	
gerichtlich	adj.	forensic	
gerichtlich	adj.	judicial	
gerichtliche Verfügung	n.	injunction	
Gerichtsbarkeit {f}	n.	jurisdiction	
Gerichtsdiener {m}	n.	usher	
Gerichtsvollzieher {m}	n.	bailiff	
gerillt	adj.	corrugated	
geringer	adj.	minor	
geringere	conj.	lest	
geringfügig	adv.	slightly	
Geringfügigkeit {f}	n.	insignificance	
geringschätzig	adj.	contemptuous	
gerissen	adj.	shifty	
Geröll {n}	n.	detritus	
geröstet	adj.	parched	
Gerste {f}	n.	barley	
Gerstenkorn {n}	n.	sty	
Geruch {m}	n.	odour	
Geruch {m}	n.	smell	
Gerücht {n}	n.	rumour	
geruhen	v.	condescend	
geruhen	v.	deign	
gerühmt	adj.	vaunted	
Gerundium {n}	n.	gerund	
gerupfen	v.	pluck	
gesamt	adj.	cumulative	
Gesamtbetrag {m}	n.	total	
Gesamtgewicht {n}	n.	laden	
Gesamtheit {f}	n.	totality	
Gesandte {m,f}	n.	envoy	
gesättigt	adj.	sated	

gesäumt *adj.* seamy
Geschäft {n} *n.* affair
Geschäft {n} *n.* trade
geschäftig *adj.* busy
geschäftsführend *adj.* managerial
Geschäftsführung {f}*n.* management
Geschäftsinhaber {m}*n.* shopkeeper
Geschäftsmann {m} *n.*businessman
geschäftsunfähig *adj.* disabled
geschätzt *adj.* precious
geschehen *v.* happen
Geschenk {n}*n.* gift
Geschenk {n}*n.* present
Geschenkkorb {m} *n.* hamper
Geschichte {f} *n.* history
Geschichte {f} *n.* narrative
geschichtlich *adj.* historical
Geschick {n} *n.* skill
Geschicklichkeit {f} *n.* sleight
geschickt *adj.* adroit
geschickt *adj.* skilful
Geschiedene {m,f} *n.* divorcee
Geschirr {n} *n.* crockery
Geschlecht {n} *n.* gender
Geschlecht {n} *n.* sex
geschlossen *v.* shut
Geschmack {m} *n.* flavour
Geschmack {m} *n.* smack
Geschmack {m} *n.* taste
geschmacklos *adj.* tasteless
geschmackvoll *adj.* tasteful
geschmeidig *adj.* lissom
geschmeidig *adj.* lithe
geschmeidig *adj.* sleek
geschmolzen *adj.* molten

geschnittener Stein *n.* cameo
Geschrei {n} *n.* clamour
Geschrei {n} *n.* hue
geschützt *adj.* proprietary
geschützte *adj.* protective
Geschwätz {n} *n.* gossip
Geschwätz {n} *n.* rigmarole
geschwätzig *adj.* garrulous
geschwätzig *adj.* talkative
Geschwindigkeit {f} *n.* speed
Geschwindigkeit {f} *n.* velocity
Geschwindigkeitsmesser{m} *n.*
tachometer
Geschwister {pl} *n.* sibling
geschwollen *adj.* puffy
geschwollen *adj.* sententious
geschwollen *adj.* turgid
Geschwür {n}*n.* ulcer
gesegnet *adj.* blessed
gesellig *adj.* sociable
Gesellschaft {f} *n.* corporation
Gesellschaft {f} *n.* society
Gesellschaft *n.* association
gesetzeswidrig *adj.* illegal
gesetzgeben *v.* legislate
gesetzgebend *adj.* legislative
Gesetzgeber {m} *n.* legislator
Gesetzgebung {f} *n.* legislation
gesetzlos *adj.* lawless
gesetzmäßig *adj.* constitutional
Gesetzmäßigkeit {f} *n.* legality
gesetzt *adj.* sedate
Gesicht- *adj.* facial
Gesichtsausdruck {m}*n.* scowl
Gesichtsfarbe {f} *n.* complexion

278

Gesichtsschutzschirm {m}n. visor
Gesindel {n} n. rabble
gesondern v. separate
gespalten n. riven
gespannt adj. agog
gespannt adj. taut
Gespenst {n} n. ghost
Gespenst {n} n. spectre
Gespenst {n} n. wraith
gespenstisch adj. spectral
Gespräch {n} n. conversation
Gespräch {n} n. dialogue
Gesprächspartner {m} n.
  interlocutor
Gestalt {f} n. figure
Gestalt {f} n. stature
Gestänge {n} n. linkage
Gestank {m} n. stench
Geste {f} n. gesture
gestelzt adj. stilted
Gestern adv. yesterday
gestorben adj. deceased
gestrandet adj. aground
Gesuch {n} n. suit
gesund adj. hale
gesund adj. healthy
gesund adj. salutary
gesund adv. well
gesund adj. wholesome
Gesundheit {f} n. health
gesundheitlich adj. sanitary
Gesundheitspflege {f}n. hygiene
Getöse {n} n. din
Getränk {n} n. beverage
Getreide {n} n. cereal

Getreide {n} n. corn
getreideln v. tow
Getreidespeicher {m}v. garner
getrennen v. secede
Getriebe {f} n. gear
Getue {n} n. ado
Getümmel {n}n. turmoil
Gewachs {n} n. growth
Gewächs {n} n. plant
gewähren v. grant
gewähren v. vouchsafe
Gewährleistung {f} n. warranty
Gewährsmann {m} n. warrantor
Gewaltherrschaft {f}n. tyranny
gewaltig adj. enormous
gewaltsam adj. forcible
gewaltsam adj. oppressive
gewaltsam adj. violent
Gewalttätigkeit {f} n. outrage
Gewand {n} n. vestment
gewandt adj. deft
Gewebe {n} n textile
Gewebe {n} n. tissue
Gewehr {n} n. gun
Gewehr {n} n. rifle
Geweih {n} n. antler
Gewerbetreibende {m}n. tradesman
Gewerkschaftler {m}n. unionist
Gewicht {n} n. weight
Gewichtheben {n} n. weightlifting
gewinnen v. award
gewinnen v. win
gewinnen v. yield
gewinnend adj. winning
Gewinner {m}n. winner

279

Gewinnsucht {f}　*n.*　lucre
gewiss　*adv.*　certainly
Gewissen {n}　*n.*　conscience
gewissenlos　*adj.*　unprincipled
gewissenlos　*adj.*　unscrupulous
Gewissensbiss {m}　*n.*　remorse
Gewissensbisse {pl}*n.*　compunction
Gewitter {n}　*n.*　tempest
gewitterschwül　*adj.*　thunderous
gewöhnen　*v.t*　acclimatise
gewöhnen　*v.*　accustom
gewöhnen　*v.t.*　habituate
Gewohnheit {f}　*n.*　habit
Gewohnheit {f}　*n.*　wont
Gewohnheit {f}　*n.*　yore
gewöhnlich　*adj.*　customary
gewöhnlich　*adv.*　ordinarily
gewohnt *adj.*　wonted
gewöhnt *adj.*　accustomed
Gewölbe {n}　*n.*　cove
Gewölbe {n}　*n.*　vault
gewölbt *adj.*　concave
Gewühl {n}　*n.*　melee
Gewühl {n}　*n.*　scuffle
gewunden　*adj.*　serpentine
gewunden　*adj.*　sinuous
gewunden　*adj.*　tortuous
Gewürz {n}　*n.*　spice
gezahnt *adj.*　serrated
gezaubern　*v.*　conjure
geziemend　*adj.*　seemly
Gicht {f} *n.*　gout
Gier {f} *n.*　greed
gieren　*v.*　yaw
gierig　*adv.* avidly

gierig　*adj.* greedy
gießen　*v.*　pour
Gießer {m}　*n.*　moulder
Gießerei {m}　*n.*　foundry
Gift {n}　*n.*　poison
Gift {n}　*n.*　venom
giftig　*adj.* poisonous
giftig　*adj.* toxic
giftig　*adj.* venomous
giftiges *adj.* venous
Giftigkeit {f}　*n.*　virulence
Giftstoff {m}　*n.*　toxin
Gigabyte {m} *n.*　gigabyte
Gigant {m}　*n.*　giant
gigantisch　*adj.* gigantic
Gilde {f} *n.*　guild
Gipfel {m}　*n.*　summit
Gipfel {m}　*n.*　top
Gips {m} *n.*　plaster
Giraffe {f}　*n.*　giraffe
Girlande {f}　*n.*　garland
Giro {n} *n.*　giro
Gitarre {f}　*n.*　guitar
Gitter {n}*n.*　grid
Gitter {n}*n.*　lattice
Gitter {n}*n.*　trellis
Gitterwerk {n}　*n.*　wattle
Glanz {m}　*n.*　brilliance
Glanz {m}　*n.*　glamour
Glanz {m}　*n.*　radiance
Glanz {m}　*adj.* refulgence
Glanz {m}　*n.*　sheen
glänzen *adj.* refulgent
glänzen *v.*　shine
glänzend*adj.* lustrous

glänzend *adj.* resplendent	Gleitzeit {f} *n.* flexitime
glänzend *adj.* shiny	Gletscher {m}*n.* glacier
glanzlos *adj.* lacklustre	Glied {n} *n.* limb
Glas {n} *n.* jar	Gliederung {f} *n.* formation
glasartig *adj.* vitreous	Glimmer {m} *n.* mica
Glaser {m} *n.* glazier	glitschig *adj.* slippery
glasieren *v.* glaze	glitzern *v.* glisten
Glasur {f} *n.* icing	Globalisierung {f} *n.* globalization
glatt *adj.* glossy	Glorie {f}*n.* glory
glauben *v.* believe	Glorie {f}*n.* renown
Glauben {m} *n.* belief	Glorie {f}*n.* splendour
Glaubensbekenntnis {n}*n.* creed	Glosse {f} *n.* gloss
glaubhaft *adj.* plausible	glotzen *n.* goggle
Gläubigerin {f} *n.* creditor	Glück {n} *n.* bliss
gleich *adj.* alike	Glück {n} *n.* felicity
gleich *adj.* equal	Glück {n} *n.* fortune
gleich *adj.* similar	Glück {n} *n.* luck
gleichbedeutend *adj.* tantamount	glucken *v.* chuckle
gleichen *v.* resemble	glücklich *adj.* fortunate
gleichförmig *adj.* uniform	glücklich *adj.* happy
Gleichgewicht {n} *n.* equilibrium	glücklich *adj.* providential
gleichgültig *adj.* indifferent	glücklos *adj.* hapless
Gleichgültigkeit {f} *n.*indifference	glücklos *adj.* luckless
Gleichnis {n} *n.* simile	Glücksbringer *n.* fluke
gleichseitig *adj.* equilateral	Glücksfall {m} *n.* bonanza
gleichstellen *v.* equate	glücksverheißend *adj.* auspicious
Gleichstromerzeuger {m}*n.* dynamo	Glückwunsch {m} *n.* felicitation
gleicht *adj.* likely	glühen *v.* glow
Gleichung {f} *n.* equation	glühend *adj.* fervent
gleichwertig *adj.* equivalent	glühend *adj.* torrid
gleichzeitig *adj.* coeval	Glukose {f} *n.* glucose
gleichzeitig *adj.* concomitant	Glyzerin {n} *n.* glycerine
gleichzeitig *adj.* simultaneous	gnädig *adj.* gracious
gleichzeitig *adj.* synchronous	Gold *n.* gold
gleiten *v.* glide	Goldbarren {m} *n.* bullion

golden	*adj.*	golden			
Goldschmied {m}	*n.*		goldsmith		
Golf {m}	*n.*	gulf			
Golf {n}	*n.*	golf			
Gondel {f}	*n.*	gondola			

golden *adj.* golden
Goldschmied {m} *n.* goldsmith
Golf {m} *n.* gulf
Golf {n} *n.* golf
Gondel {f} *n.* gondola
Gong *n.* gong
Gönnerschaft {f} *n.* patronage
Gorilla {m} *n.* gorilla
Gosse {f} *n.* gutter
Gosse {f} *n.* kennel
Gott {m} *n.* god
Götterspeise {f} *n.* ambrosia
gotteslästerlich *adj.* profane
Gottheit {f} *n.* deity
Gottheit {f} *n.* divinity
Göttin {f}n. goddess
göttlich *adj.* divine
Gouverneur {m} *n.* governor
Grab {n} *n.* grave
Grab {n} *n.* sepulchre
Grab {n} *n.* tomb
graben *v.* dig
Grabschrift {f} *n.* epitaph
Grad {m}n. degree
Grad {m}n. rank
Graduierte {m,f} *n.* postgraduate
Graf {m} *n.* earl
grafisch *adj.* graphic
Grafschaft {f} n. county
Grafschaft {f} n. shire
grämlich *adj.* morose
Gramm {n} *n.* gram
Grammatik {f} *n.* grammar
Grammophon {n} *n.* gramophone
Granat {m} *n.* garnet

Granatapfel {m} *n.* pomegranate
Granit {m} *n.* granite
Graph {m} *n.* graph
Graphit {m} *n.* graphite
Gras {n} *n.* grass
Grasbüschel {n} *n.* hassock
grasen *v.* browse
Grashüpfer {m} *n.* grasshopper
Grasmücke {f} *n.* warbler
grässlich *adj.* dire
grässlich *adj.* dreadful
Gratifikation {f} *n.* gratuity
gratis *adv. &adj.* gratis
graun. grey
Gräuel {m} *n.* horror
grauenvoll *adj.* horrid
grausam *adj.* ferocious
grausam *adj.* ghastly
grausam *adj.* horrible
grausam *adj.* sanguinary
Grausamkeit {f} *adv.* cruelty
grausig *adj.* gruesome
grausig *adj.* macabre
gravieren *v.* aggravate
gravieren *v.* engrave
Gravität {f} *n.* gravitas
Gravitation {f} *n.* gravitation
gravitieren *v.* gravitate
greifbar *adj.* tangible
greifen *v.* snatch
greisenhaft *adj.* senile
grelladj. lurid
grenzenlos *adj.* boundless
Grenzenlosigkeit {f} *n.* immensity
Grenzenlosigkeit {f} *n.* infinity

Grenzfläche {f}	n.	interface
Grenzwert {m}	n.	limit
Griff {m} n.	haft
Griff {m} n.	hilt
Griffel {m}	n.	stylus
Grill {m} n.	barbecue
Grill {m} v.	grill
Grille {f} n.	cricket
grimmig adj.	fierce
grinsen v.	grin
grinsen v.	smirk
Grippe {f}	n.	flu
Grippe {f}	n.	influenza
grob	adj.	rough
grob	adj.	uncouth
grob,	adj.	crude
Grobian {m}	n.	ruffian
grölen v.	bawl
Groll {m} n.	dudgeon
Groll {m} n	grudge
Groll {m} n.	rancour
groß	adj.	ample
groß	adj.	big
groß	adj.	large
groß	adj.	megalithic
groß	adj.	sizeable
groß	adj.	tall
großartig adj.	genial
großartig adj.	grand
großartig adv.	greatly
großartig adj.	splendid
Größe {f} n.	quantity
Größe {f} n.	size
Größenordnung {f}	n.	magnitude
Großhandel {m}	n.	wholesale

Großhändler {m}	n.	wholesaler
Großmutter {f}	n.	grandmother
großzügig	adj.	lordly
großzügig	adj.	magnanimous
Großzügigkeit {f}	n.	generosity
Grotte {f} n.	grotto
grübeln v.	ponder
grummeln v.	grumble
grün	adj. & n.	green
Gründer {m}	n.	founder
Grundlage {f} n.	scaffolding
grundlegend n.	basic
grundlos adj.	baseless
grundlos adj.	groundless
Grundprinzip {n}	n.	rationale
grundsätzlich adj.	fundamental
Grundstück {n}	n.	property
Gründung {f} n.	flotation
Grundzustand {m} n.	default
Grüne Minze {f}	n.	spearmint
Grünschnabel {m} n.	sapling
grunzen v.i.	grunt
Grunzochse {m}	n.	yak
Gruppe {f}	n.	group
Gruppe {f}	n.	squad
Gruppierung {f}	n.	alignment
Gruppierung {f}	n.	grouping
Gruß {m} n.	salutation
grüßen n.	greet
Grütze {f}	n.	grout
Guave n.	guava
gucken v.	peek
Guerilla {m}	n.	guerrilla
Gültigkeit {f}	n.	validity
Gummi {m}	n.	gum

283

Gummistiefel {pl}	n.	wellington	Haferflocken {pl}	n.	oatmeal
Gunst {f}n.		favour	Haferflockenplätzchen {n}n.flapjack		
Günstling {m}	n.	minion	Haferschleim {m}	n.	gruel
Gurdwara {f}	n.	gurdwara	Haft {f}	n.	custody
gurgeln	v.	gargle	Häftling {m}	n.	detainee
gurgeln	v.	gurgle	Hagel {m}	n.	hail
Gurt {m}	n.	girth	Hagel {m}	n.	volley
Gürtel {m}	n.	belt	hager	adj.	gaunt
Gürtel {m}	n.	girdle	Hahn {m}	n.	cock
Gurtsatz {m}	n.	harness	Hahn {m}	n.	rooster
gut	adj.	good	Hahnerei {f}	n.	cuckold
Gut {n}	n.	manor	Haifisch {m}	n.	shark
gutgläubig	adj.	bonafide	häkeln	n.	crochet
gütig	adv.	kindly	Haken {m}	n.	crux
Gymnastik {f}n.		gymnastic	Haken {m}	n.	hook
Gynäkologie {f}	n.	gynaecology	halal	adj.	halal

H

			Halbgeschoss {n}	n.	mezzanine
Haar {n}	n.	hair	halbieren	v.	bisect
haarig	adj.	hairy	halbieren	v.	halve
haarig	adj.	hirsute	Halbinsel {f}	n.	peninsula
Haarlocke {f}	n.	ringlet	Halbkreis {m}n.		semicircle
Haarriss {m}	n.	craze	Halbkugel {f}	n.	hemisphere
Haarschnitt {m}	n.	haircut	Halbstarker {m}	n.	yob
Haartracht {f}n.		hairstyle	halluzinieren	v.	hallucinate
Haarwaschmittel {n}n. shampoo			Halogen {n}	n.	halogen
Habe {n}n.		chattel	Hals {m}	adj.	cervical
haben	v.	have	Hals {m}	n.	throat
Habgier {f}	n.	cupidity	Hals {m}	n.	wrick
hacken	v.	hack	Halsband {n}	n.	collar
Haddsch {m}	n.	hajj	Halskette {f}	n.	necklace
Hafen {m}	n.	harbour	Halskette {f}	n.	necklet
Hafen {m}	n.	haven	Halstuch {n}	n.	kerchief
Hafen {m}	n.	port	Halt {m}	v.	halt
Hafer {m}	n.	oat	haltbar	adj.	tenable
			halten	v.t	hold

284

German		English
Halter {m}	*n.*	retainer
haltlos	*adj.*	adrift
haltlos	*adj.*	unfounded
Haltung {f}	*n.*	poise
Haltung {f}	*n.*	stance
Hamburger {m}	*n.*	burger
Hamburger {m}	*n.*	hamburger
Hammel {m}	*n.*	mutton
Hämoglobin {n}	*n.*	haemoglobin
Hamster {m}	*n.*	hamster
Hand {f}	*n.*	hand
Handarbeit {f}	*n.*	handiwork
Handbuch {n}*n.*		compendium
Handbuch {n}*n.*		handbook
Handel {m}	*n.*	commerce
Handel {m}	*n.*	deal
Handel {m}	*n.*	trafficking
handeln	*v. i*	deal
handeln	*v.*	manage
Handelssperre {f}	*n.*	embargo
Handelszeichen {n}	*n.*	trademark
Handelszentrum {n}	*n.*	mart
Händeschütteln {n}	*n.*	handshake
Handfesseln {pl}	*n.*	handcuff
Handgelenk {n}	*n.*	wrist
Handgemenge {n} *n.*		scrimmage
Handgranate {f}	*a.*	grenade
Handlanger {m}	*n.*	henchman
Händler {m}	*n.*	dealer
Händler {m}	*n.*	salesman
Händler {m}	*n.*	trader
Handlesekunst {f} *n.*		palmistry
handlich *adj.*		manageable
Handlung {f}	*n.*	plot
Handschuh {m}	*n.*	glove
Handtasche {f}	*n.*	handbag
Handtuch {n} *n.*		towel
handvoll *n.*		handful
Handwerk {n}*n.*		handicraft
Handwerker {m}	*n.*	artisan
Handwerker {m}	*n.*	craftsman
Handwerker {m}	*n.*	manufacturer
Handzettel {m}	*n.*	handbill
Hang {m}	*n.*	penchant
Hängematte {f}	*n.*	hammock
Hänselei {f}	*n.*	pleasantry
Harem {n}	*n.*	harem
Harfe {f} *n.*		harp
Harke {f} *n.*		rake
Harlekin {m}	*n.*	harlequin
harmlos *adj.*		benign
harmlos *adj.*		harmless
Harmonie {f}	*n.*	harmony
harmonisch *adj.*		harmonious
harmonisieren	*v.*	harmonize
Harmonium {n}	*n.*	harmonium
Harpyie {f	*n.*	harpy
hart *adj.*		hard
hartnäckig *adj.*		insistent
Hase {m}*n.*		hare
Hase {m}*n.*		rabbit
Hasenscharte {f}	*n.*	harelip
hässlich *adj.*		ugly
Hässlichkeit {f}	*n.*	ugliness
hasten	*v.*	bustle
hastig *adj.*		abrupt
hätscheln	*v.*	nuzzle
Hauch {m}	*n.*	puff
hauchdünn *adj.*		sheer
hauen	*v.*	hew

German		English
Haufen {m}	*n.*	cluster
Haufen {m}	*n.*	heap
Haufen {m}	*n.*	lot
häufig	*adj.*	frequent
häufig	*adv.*	often
Häufung {f}	*n.*	accumulation
Hauptbuch {n}	*n.*	ledger
Hauptinhalt {m}	*n.*	gist
Häuptling {m}*n.*		chieftain
Hauptplatine {f}	*n.*	motherboard
Hauptquartier {n}	*n.*	headquarters
hauptsächlich	*adv.*	chiefly
hauptsächlich	*adj.*	major
hauptsächlich	*adj.*	primal
hauptstädtisch	*adj.*	metropolitan
Hauptstoß {m}	*n.*	brunt
Hauptstütze {f}	*n.*	mainstay
Haus {n} *n.*		house
Hausbesitzer {m}	*n.*	landlord
Hausbesitzerin {f} *n.*		landlady
Häuschen {n}*n.*		cottage
Häuschen {n}*n.*		lodge
Hausfrau {f}	*n.*	housewife
haushälterisch	*adj.*	economical
hausieren	*v.*	peddle
Hausierer {m}*n.*		hawker
Hausierer {m}*n.*		pedlar
häuslich *adj.*		domestic
häuslich *adj.*		homely
häuslich *adj.*		spousal
Hausmiete {f}*n.*		rent
Hausschuh {m}	*n.*	slipper
Haustier {n}	*n.*	pet
Haut {f}	*n.*	skin
Hebel {m}	*n.*	lever

German		English
Hebelkraft {f} *n.*		leverage
heben	*v.*	heave
Hecht {m}	*n.*	pike
Hecke {f}*n.*		hedge
heftig	*adj.*	bold
heftig	*adj.*	impetuous
heftig	*adj.*	stormy
Heftigkeit {f}	*n.*	violence
Heftklammer {f}	*n.*	staple
Heftklammer {f}	*n.*	stapler
Hegemonie {f}	*n.*	hegemony
Heide {m}	*n.*	heathen
Heide {m}	*n.*	pagan
Heidekraut {n}	*n.*	heather
Heideland {n}*n.*		heath
Heideland {n}*n.*		wold
heikel	*adj.*	fussy
heikel	*adj.*	queasy
heikel	*adj.*	scabrous
heilbar	*adj.*	curable
heilen	*v. t.*	cure
heilen	*v.*	heal
heilend	*adj.*	curative
heilig	*adj.*	holy
heilig	*adj.*	sacred
heilig	*adj.*	saintly
Heilige {m,f}	*n.*	saint
heiligen	*v.*	sanctify
Heiligengrab {n}		shrine
Heiligenschein {m}	*n.*	aura
Heiligenschein {m}	*n.*	nimbus
Heiligkeit {f}	*n.*	sanctity
Heiligtum {n} *n.*		sanctuary
Heiligung {f}	*n.*	sanctification
Heilmittel {n} *n.*		remedy

Heim {n} *n.*	asylum	
Heimat {f}	*n.*	home
heimlich *adj.*	clandestine	
heimlich *adv.*	stealthily	
heimlich *adj.*	stealthy	
heimlich *adj.*	underhand	
Heimlichkeit {f}	*n.*	secrecy
Heimlichkeit {f}	*n.*	stealth
heimsuchen *v.*	infest	
Heimsuchung {f}	*n.*	visitation
heimtückisch *adj.*	dastardly	
heimtückisch *adj.*	perfidious	
heiraten *v.*	marry	
heiraten *v.*	wed	
heiser *adj.*	hoarse	
heiß *adj.*	hot	
heiter *adj.*	alacritous	
heiter *adj.*	blithe	
heiter *adj.*	cheerful	
heiter *adj.*	gay	
heiter *adj.*	merry	
heiter *adj.*	sanguine	
heiter *adj.*	serene	
Heiterkeit {f}	*n.*	hilarity
Heiterkeit {f}	*n.*	joviality
Heiterkeit {f}	*n.*	serenity
Heizer {m}	*n.*	stoker
Heizfaden {m}	*n.*	filament
Heizform {f}	*n.*	mould
Heizung {f}	*n.*	heater
Hektar {m}	*n.*	hectare
hektisch *adj.*	hectic	
Held {m} *n.*	hero	
heldenhaft *adj.*	heroic	
Heldenmut {m}	*n.*	valour

Heldin {f}	*n.*	heroine
helfen *v.*	help	
helfend *n.*	helping	
Helfer {m}	*n.*	aide
hell *adj.*	bright	
Helm {m}*n.*	helmet	
Hemd {n}	*n.*	shirt
hemmen *v.*	obstruct	
Hemmnis {n} *n.*	restraint	
Hemmung {f} *n.*	inhibition	
Henna {f,n}	*n.*	henna
Henne {f}	*n.*	hen
Hepatitis {f}	*n.*	hepatitis
herabsetzen *v.*	depreciate	
Herabsetzung {f}	*v.*	detract
heranschaffen	*v.*	cater
heranschleichen	*v.*	sneak
heraus *adv.*	forth	
heraus *adv.*	out	
herausfordern	*v.*	defy
Herausforderung {f}*n.*	defiance	
Herausforderung {f}*n.*	provocation	
herausplatzen	*v.*	blurt
herauswinden	*v.*	squirm
herausziehen *v. t*	extract	
herb*adj.*	dry	
Herberge {f}	*n.*	hostel
Herbst {m}	*n.*	autumn
Herde {f}*n.*	herd	
Hering {m}	*n.*	herring
Herkunft {f}	*n.*	provenance
hermetisch *adj.*	hermetic	
Herpes {f}	*n.*	herpes
Herr {m} *n.*	sir	
herrisch *adj.*	authoritative	

287

herrlich *adj.* magnificent
herrlich *adj.* superb
Herrlichkeit {f} *n.* grandeur
Herrschaft {f} *n.* dominion
Herrschaft {f} *n.* mastery
herrschen *v.* rule
herrschend *adj.* prevalent
Hersteller {m}*n.* producer
Herstellung {f} *n.* making
herum *adv.* around
herumgehend *adj.* skirting
herumgehend *n.* skit
herumtanzen *v.* gambol
herumwursteln *v.* bumble
heruntergewirtschaftet*adj.* rundown
herunterkommen *v.* descend
hervorbringen *v.* spawn
hervorheben *v. t* distinguish
hervorheben *v.* highlight
hervorlocken *v.* elicit
hervorragend *adj.* eminent
hervorragend *adj.* outstanding
hervorragend *adj.* pre-eminent
hervorragend *adj.* salient
hervorrufen *v.* evoke
Herz {n} *n.* heart
Herzeleid {n} *n.* heartbreak
herzhaft *adj.* hearty
Herzklopfen {n} *n.* palpitation
herzkrank *adj.* cardiac
herzlich *adj.* cordial
herzlos *adj.* heartless
Herzschmerz {m} *n.* heartache
Herzschrittmacher {m}*n.*
    pacemaker

heterosexuell *adj.* heterosexual
hetzen *v.t.* scamper
Heu {n} *n.* hay
Heuchelei {f} *n.* hypocrisy
heucheln *v.* feign
Heuchler {m} *n.* hypocrite
heulen *v.* blub
heulen *n.* howl
Heulen {n} *n.* whine
Heuschrecke {f} *n.* locust
heute *adv.* today
heute Nacht *adv.* tonight
Hexe {f} *n.* hag
Hexe {f} *n.* witch
Hexerei {f} *n.* witchery
Hexogen {n} *n.* hexogen
hier *adv.* here
hier herum *adv.* hereabouts
hierdurch *adv.* hereby
hierher *adv.* hither
Hilfe {f} *n.* succour
Hilfe {f} -erste*n.* first aid
hilfend *adj.* auxiliary
Hilfestellung {f} *n.* assistance
hilflos *adj.* helpless
hilflos *adj.* shiftless
hilfsbedürftig *adj.* needy
Hilfsmittel {n}*n.* jig
Hilfsquelle {f}*n.* resource
Himbeere {f} *n.* raspberry
Himmel {m} *n.* heaven
Himmel {m} *n.* sky
Himmelszelt {n} *n.* firmament
himmlisch *adj.* celestial
himmlisch *adj.* heavenly

hinausschießen	v.	overshoot
hindern	v.	stymie
Hindernis {n}	v.	baulk
Hindernis {n}	n.	impediment
Hindernis {n}	n.	obstacle
Hindernisrennen {n}	n.	steeplechase
hindurch prep. &adv.		through
hinein	prep.	in
hinfallen	v.	tumble
hingeben	v.	devote
Hingebung {f}	n.	devotion
hingegen	adv.	whereas
hingezogen	adj.	protracted
hinlänglich	adj.	sufficient
hinreißen	v.	enrapture
hinrichten	v.	electrocute
Hinsicht {f}	n.	respect
Hinstellen {n}	n.	placement
hinten	adv.	aft
Hinterbacke {f}	n.	buttock
hintereinander	adj.	serial
Hintergrund {m}	n.	background
Hinterhalt {m}	n.	ambush
hinterher	adv.	after
Hinterlassenschaft {f}	n.	legacy
Hinterteil {n}	adj.	posterior
hintertreiben	v.	thwart
hinunterschlingen	v.	gulp
Hinweis {m}	n.	clue
Hinweis {m}	n.	pointing
hinweisen	v.t.	allude
hinweisend	adj.	indicative
Hinweiszeichen {n}	n.	sentinel
hinwerfen	v.t.	jot
Hinzufügung {f}	n.	annexation

hinzukommen	v.	supervene
Hirn {n}	n.	brain
Hirnhautentzündung {f}	n.	meningitis
Hirsch {m}	n.	deer
Hirsch {m}	n.	stag
Hirse {f}	n.	millet
Histogram {f}	n.	histogram
Historiker {m}	n.	historian
historisch	adj.	historic
Hobby {n}	n.	fad
Hobby {n}	n.	hobby
hoch	adj.	high
hoch	adv.	highly
hochgestellt	adj.	superscript
hochheben	v.	uplift
Hochkomma {n}	n.	apostrophe
hochladen	v.	upload
Hochmut {m}	n.	arrogance
hochmütig	adj.	cavalier
hochmütig	adj.	supercilious
Hochofen {m}	n.	furnace
höchst	n.	most
höchst	adj.	supreme
höchste	adj.	paramount
Hochtonlautsprecher {m}	n.	tweeter
hochtrabend	adj.	lofty
Hochzeit {f}	n.	wedding
hochzeitlich	adj.	nuptial
hochziehen	v.	hoist
hocken	v.	cower
hocken	v.i.	squat
Höcker {m}	n.	knob
Hockey {n}	n.	hockey
Hockstellung {f}	v.	crouch
Hoden {pl}	n.	testicle

289

Hoden {pl}   *n.*   testis
Hof {m}   *n.*   court
Hof {m}   *n.*   yard
Hoffnung {f}   *n.*   hope
hoffnungslos *adj.* hopeless
hoffnungsvoll   *adv.* hopefully
höflich   *adj.* courteous
höflich   *adj.* debonair
höflich   *adj.* polite
höflich   *adj.* urbane
Höflichkeit {f}*n.*   politeness
Höfling {m}   *n.*   courtier
Hofraum {m}   *n.*   courtyard
Höhe {f}   *n.*   altitude
Höhe {f}   *n.*   height
Höhe {f}   *n.*   Highness
Hohepriester {m}   *n.*   pontiff
Höhepunkt {m}   *n.*   acme
Höhepunkt {m}   *n.*   climax
Höhepunkt {m}   *n.*   heyday
Höhle {f} *n.*   cave
Höhle {f} *n.*   cavern
Höhle {f} *n.*   den
hold *adj.* meek
holen   *v.*   fetch
holistisch   *adj.* holistic
Hölle {f}   *n.*   hell
Hölle {f}   *n.*   pandemonium
höllisch *adj.* infernal
Holmium {n}   *n.*   holmium
Holocaust {n}*n.*   holocaust
Hologram {n}*n.*   hologram
holperig *adj.* bumpy
Holz {n}   *n.*   wood
hölzern *adj.* wooden

Holzfloß {n}   *n.*   raft
Homöopath {m}   *n.*   homoeopath
Homöopathie {f}   *n.*   homeopathy
Homophobie {f}   *n.*   homophobia
homosexuell *n.*   homosexual
Honig {m}   *n.*   honey
Honigwabe {f}   *n.*   honeycomb
horchen *v.*   hark
Horde {f}*n.*   horde
hören   *v.*   hear
Horizont {m}   *n.*   horizon
horizontal   *adj.* horizontal
Hormon {n}   *n.*   hormone
Horn {n} *n.*   cornet
Horn {n} *n.*   horn
Hörnchen {n}*n.*   croissant
Hornhaut {f}   *n.*   cornea
Hornisse {f}   *n.*   hornet
Horoskop {n}*n.*   horoscope
horrend *adj.* horrendous
Höschen {pl}   *n.*   panties
Hose {f}   *n.*   pantaloon
Hosen {pl}   *n.*   trousers
Hosenbund {m}   *n.*   waistband
Hospiz {n}   *n.*   hospice
Hostess {f}   *n.*   hostess
Hotel {n}*n.*   hotel
Hub {m}   *n.*   hub
hübsch   *adj.* handsome
hübsch   *adj.* nice
hübsch   *adj.* pretty
Hübschheit {f}   *n.*   prettiness
Hubschrauber {m}*n.*   helicopter
Hubschrauberlandeplatz {m}*n.*
   heliport

Hüfte {f} *n.*	haunch
Hüfte {f} *n.*	hip
Hügel {m} *n.*	hill
Hügelchen {n} *n.*	hillock
Huhn {n} *n.*	chicken
huldigen *v.*	render
Huldigung {f} *n.*	homage
Hülle {f} *n.*	hull
Hülse {f} *n.*	husk
Hülse {f} *n.*	sleeve
Humanismus {m} *n.*	humanism
humanitär *adj.*	humanitarian
Hummer {m} *n.*	lobster
Humor {m} *n.*	humour
Humorist {m} *n.*	humorist
humoristisch *adj.*	humorous
humpeln *v.*	hobble
Hund {m} *n.*	dog
hundeartig *adj.*	canine
hundert *adj.& n.*	hundred
hundertgradig *adj.*	centigrade
Hundertjahrfeier {f} *n.*	centennial
Hundeschnauze {f} *n.*	muzzle
Hündin {f} *n.*	bitch
Hunger {m} *n.*	hunger
hungern *v.*	starve
Hungersnot {f} *n.*	famine
Hungertod {m} *n.*	starvation
hungrig *adj.*	hungry
Hupensignal {n} *n.*	honk
hüpfen *v.*	frisk
hüpfen *v.*	hop
Hürde {f} *n.*	hurdle
hurtig *adj.*	spry
husten *v.*	cough

Hut {m} *n.*	hat
Hüter {m} *n.*	guardian
Hütte {f} *n.*	cot
Hütte {f} *n.*	hovel
Hütte {f} *n.*	hut
Hyäne {f} *n.*	hyena
Hydrant {n} *n.*	hydrant
hydratisieren *v.*	hydrate
hydraulisch *adj.*	hydraulic
hygienisieren *v.*	sanitize
Hymne {f} *n.*	anthem
Hymne {f} *n.*	hymn
hyperaktiv *adj.*	hyperactive
Hyperbel {f} *n.*	hyperbole
Hypertonie {f} *n.*	hypertension
Hypnose {f} *n.*	hypnosis
Hypnose {f} *n.*	hypnotism
hypnotisch *adj.*	mesmeric
hypnotisieren *v.*	hypnotize
hypnotisieren *v.*	mesmerize
Hypotenuse {f} *n.*	hypotension
Hypothek {f} *n.*	mortgage
Hypothekar {m} *n.*	mortgagee
Hypothekenschuldner {m} *n.* mortgagor
Hypothese {f} *n.*	hypothesis
hypothetisch *adj.*	hypothetical
Hysterie {f} *n.*	hysteria
hysterisch *adj.*	hysterical

I

ich *pron.*	I
ich *pron.*	me
ideal *n.*	ideal
idealerweise *adv.*	ideally

idealisieren v. idealize
Idealismus {m} n. idealism
Idealist {m} n. idealist
idealistisch adj. idealistic
Idee {f} n. idea
identifizieren v. identify
identisch adj. identical
Identität {f} n. identity
Ideologie {f} n. ideology
idiomatisch adj. idiomatic
idiotisch adj. idiotic
Idol {n} n. idol
Idylle {f} n. idyll
Iglu {n} n. igloo
Ignorant {m} n. ignoramus
ignorieren v. ignore
ihm pron. him
Ihn pron. himself
ihnen pron. them
ihr pron. her
ihr adj. their
ihre pron. hers
ihrer pron. herself
Ikone {f} n. icon
Illusion {f} v.t. illusion
illusorisch adj. fatuous
illusorisch adj. illusory
illuster adj. illustrious
Illustration {f}n. illustration
illustrieren n. illustrate
im Gange adv. afoot
im innern prep. within
imaginär adj. imaginary
Imbiss {m} n. snack
Imbissstube {f} n. takeaway

Imitator {m} n. imitator
imitieren v. imitate
immanent adj. immanent
immanent adj. intrinsic
Immatrikulation {f} n. matriculation
immatrikulieren v. matriculate
immens adj. immense
immer adv. always
immer adv. forever
Immigration {f} n. immigration
immunisieren v. immunize
Immunologie {f} n. immunology
Imperialismus {m}n. imperialism
impfen v. inoculate
impfen v. vaccinate
Impfstoff {m} n. vaccine
Impfung {f} n. inoculation
Impfung {f} n. vaccination
implizieren v. imply
implizit adj. implicit
implodieren v. implode
imponieren v. impose
Importeur {m} n. importer
impotent adj. impotent
Impotenz {f} n. impotence
improvisieren v. improvise
Impuls {m} n. impulse
impulsiv adj. impulsive
in prep. into
in Flammen adj. aflame
in Mengeadj. galore
inaktiv adj. inactive
inaktiv adj. inert
inbrünstig adj. fervid

indes *adv.* meanwhile
indes *conj.* whilst
Index {m} *n.* index
Indigo {n} *n.* indigo
Indikator {m} *n.* indicator
indirekt *adj.* indirect
indisch *n.* Indian
indiskret *adj.* indiscreet
Indiskretion {f} *n.* indiscretion
Indisziplin {f} *n.* indiscipline
Individualismus {m}*n.* individualism
Individualität {f} *n.* individuality
individuell *adj.* individual
Indizierung {f} *n.* subscription
indossieren *v.* endorse
Industrie {f} *n.* industry
industriell *adj.* industrial
Infanterie {f} *n.* infantry
Inflation {f} *n.* inflation
infolgedessen *adv.* hence
informativ *adj.* informative
Infrastruktur {f} *n.* infrastructure
Infusion {f} *n.* infusion
Ingenieur {m}*n.* engineer
Ingwer {m} *n.* ginger
Inhalation {f} *n.* inhaler
inhalieren *v.* inhale
Inhalt {m} *n.* content
Inhalt {m} *n.* volume
inhaltlich *adj.* textual
Inhaltsangabe {f} *n.* précis
Inhaltsangabe {f} *n.* summary
Initiative {f} *n.* initiative
Injektion {f} *n.* injection
inklusive*adj.* inclusive

inkompetent *adj.* incompetent
inkorrekt*adj.* incorrect
inmitten *adj.* midst
innen *adj.* indoor
Innenhof {m} *n.* patio
innerbetrieblich *adj.* internal
inner *adj.* interior
Innereien {pl}*n.* entrails
innerlich*adj.* inner
Innern *n.* inside
innerst *adj.* inmost
innerst *adj.* innermost
innovieren *v.* innovate
Insasse {m} *n.* inmate
insbesonders*adv.* especially
Insekt {n} *n.* bug
Insekt {n} *n.* insect
Insektengift {n} *n.* insecticide
Insektenkunde {f} *n.* entomology
Insel {f} *n.* island
Inselchen {n} *n.* islet
Insistenz {f} *n.* insistence
insistieren *v.* insist
Inspektion {f}*n.* inspection
Inspektor {m}*n.* superintendent
instabil *adj.* unstable
installieren *v.* install
Installierung {f} *n.* installation
instandsetzen *v.* mend
Instinkt {n} *n.* instinct
instinktiv *adj.* instinctive
Institut {n} *n.* institute
Instrument {n} *n.* instrument
Instrumentalist {m}
        *n.*instrumentalist

293

instrumentell *adj.* instrumental
insular *adj.* insular
Insulin {n} *n.* insulin
Intellekt {m} *n.* intellect
intellektuell *adj.* intellectual
intelligent *adj.* intelligent
Intelligenz {f} *n.* intelligence
Intensität {f} *n.* intensity
intensiv *adj.* acute
intensiv *adj.* intense
intensiv *adj.* intensive
interessant *adj.* interesting
Interessengruppe {f}*n.* lobby
international *adj.* international
Internet {n} *n.* internet
internieren *v.* intern
Interpret {m} *n.* interpreter
interrassisch *adj.* interracial
Intervall {n} *n.* interval
inthronisieren *v.* enthrone
intim *adj.* intimate
Intimität {f} *n.* intimacy
intolerant *adj.* intolerant
Intranet {n} *n.* intranet
intransitiv *adj.* intransitive
intrigieren *v.* intrigue
introvertiert *n.* introvert
Invasion {f} *n.* invasion
Inventar {n} *n.* inventory
invertiert*adj.* inverse
investieren *v.t.* invest
Investition {f} *n.* investment
inzwischen *adv.* meantime
irdisch *adj.* mundane
irgendeiner *adj.* any

irgendjemand*pron.* anyone
irgendjemand*pron.* someone
irgendwas *adv.* somewhat
irgendwie *adv.* anyhow
irgendwie *adv.* somehow
irgendwo *adv.* anywhere
irgendwo *adv.* somewhere
Ironie {f} *n.* irony
ironisch *adj.* ironical
irre *adj.* mad
irrelevant *adj.* irrelevant
irren *v.* err
irrend *adj.* errant
irreredend *adj.* delirious
Irrfahrt {f} *n.* odyssey
Irrglaube {m} *n.* misbelief
irritativ *n.* irritant
irritieren *v.* irritate
Irrsinn {m} *n.* insanity
Irrsinn {m} *n.* lunacy
irrtümlich *adj.* erroneous
Ischias {m} *n.* sciatica
Islam {m} *n.* Islam
Isobar {n} *n.* isobar
Isolator {m} *n.* insulator
isolieren *v.* insulate
isolieren *v.* isolate
Isolierung {f} *n.* isolation

J

Ja *excl.* yes
Jacht {f} *n.* yacht
Jachthafen {m} *n.* marina
Jacke {f} *n.* jerkin
Jackett {n} *n.* coat

Jackett {n}	n.	jacket
Jackpot {m}	n.	jackpot
Jade {m,f}	n.	jade
Jagd {f}	n.	shooting
Jagdbeute {f}	n.	quarry
Jagdhund {m}	n.	hound
jagen	v.	hunt
jagen	v.	scud
Jäger {m}	n.	hunter
Jahr {n}	n.	year
Jahresrente {f}	n.	annuity
Jahrestag {m}	n.	anniversary
Jahreszeit {f}	n.	season
jahreszeitlich	adj.	seasonal
Jahrhundert {n}	n.	centenary
Jahrhundert {n}	n.	century
jährlich	adj.	annual
jährlich	adv.	yearly
Jahrtausend {n}	n.	millennium
jämmerlich	adj.	wretched
Januar {m}	n.	January
Jargon {m}	n.	jargon
Jargon {m}	n.	slang
Jasmin {m}	n.	jasmine
Jauche {f}	n.	muck
jaulen	n.	yowl
Jazz {m}	n.	jazz
Jeans {f}	n.	jeans
jede	adj.	each
jeder	adj.	every
Jeep {m}	n.	jeep
jemals	adv.	ever
jemand	pron.	somebody
jener	adj.	yonder
jenseitig	adj.	ulterior

jenseits	adv.	beyond
jetzig	adj.	current
jetzt	adv.	now
Jockey {m}	n.	jockey
jodeln	v.	yodel
Joga {n}	n.	yoga
Joggen	v.	jog
Joghurt {m}	n.	yogurt
Jogi	n.	yogi
jonglieren	v.	juggle
Journalismus {m}	n.	journalism
Journalist {m}	n.	journalist
jubeln	v. t.	cheer
jubelnd	adj.	jubilant
Jubiläum {n}	n.	jubilee
Jubiläum {n}	n.	bicentenary
jucken	v.i.	itch
juckend	adj.	itchy
Judo {n}	n.	judo
Jugend {f}	n.	adolescence
Jugend {f}	n	boyhood
Jugend {f}	n.	youth
jugendlich	adj.	juvenile
jugendlich	adj.	youthful
Jugendliche {m,f}	n.	teenager
Juli {m}	n.	July
Jumbo {m}	adj.	jumbo
jung	adj.	young
Junge {m}	n.	boy
Junge {m}	n.	youngster
junger Hund		pup
Jungfrau {f}	n.	virgin
Jungfräulichkeit {f}	n.	virginity
Junggeselle {m}	n.	bachelor
Junggesellin {f}	n.	spinster

295

Jüngling {m} n.   lad
Juni {m} n.   June
junior adj.   junior
Jupiter n.   Jupiter
Jurist {m}   n.   jurist
Jury {m} n.   jury
Justierung {f}n.   justification
Justizgewalt {f}   n.   judiciary
Jute {f} n.   jute
Juwel {n}   n.   jewel
Juwelier {m} n.   jeweller
Juwelierwaren {pl}   n.   jewellery

K

Kabarett {n}   n.   cabaret
Kabel {n}n.   cable
Kabine {f}   n.   cabin
Kabinett {n}   n.   cabinet
Kadaver n.   cadaver
Kadaver {m}   n.   cadaver
Kader {m}   n.   cadre
Kadett {m}   n.   cadet
Käfer {m}   n.   beetle
Kaffee {m}   n.   coffee
Kaffeemaschine {f}   n.   percolator
Kaftan {m}   n.   kaftans
Kai {m} n.   quay
Kai {m} n.   wharf
Kaianlage {f} n.   wharf age
Kaiser {m}   n.   emperor
Kaiserin {f}   n.   empress
kaiserlich adj.   imperial
Kaiserreich {n}   n.   empire
Kaiserschnitt {m} n.   caesarean
Kakao {m}   n.   cacao

Kakao {m}   n.   cocoa
Kakerlake {f} n.   cockroach
Kaktus {m}   n.   cactus
Kalb {n} n.   calf
Kalbfleisch {n}   n.   veal
Kaleidoskop {n}   n.   kaleidoscope
Kalender {m} n.   calendar
Kaliber {n}   n.   calibre
kalibrieren v.   calibrate
Kalkulationsfehler {m}n. miscalculation
Kalligraphie {f}   n.   calligraphy
Kalorie {f}   n.   calorie
kalt adj. cold
kalt adj. frigid
Kaltblütigkeit {f}   n.   sangfroid
Kältegefühl {n}   n.   chill
Kältetechnik {f}   n.   refrigeration
Kamel {n}   n.   camel
Kamera {f}   n.   câmera
Kamerad {m} n.   comrade
Kameradschaft {f}n.   fellowship
Kameradschaftsgeist {m}n.
   camaraderie
Kamm {m}   n.   comb
Kammer {f}   n.   chamber
Kammerdiener {m}   n.   valet
Kammerherr {m}   n.   chamberlain
Kammgarn {n}   n.   worsted
Kammmuschel {f} n.   scallop
Kampagne {f}n.   campaign
Kampf {m}   n.   battle
Kampf {m}   n.   tussle
Kampfansage {f}   n.   challenge
kämpfen v.t   fight
kämpfen v.   struggle

Kampfer {m}	*n.*	camphor	**Kaplan** {m}	*n.*	vicar
Kämpfer {m}	*n*	combatant	**Kaprize** {f}	*n.*	caprice
kämpferisch	*adj.*	militant	**Kaprize** {f}	*n.*	fancy
Kanal {m}	*n.*	canal	**Kapsel** {f}	*n.*	capsule
Kanal {m}	*n.*	channel	**kaputt**	*adj.*	broken
Kanalisation {f}	*n.*	sewerage	**kaputtschlagend**	*adj.*	smashing
Kanalisationsrohr {n}*n.*		sewer	**kaputtmachen**	*v.*	knacker
Kanalisationsschacht {m}*n.*			**Kapuze** {f}	*n.*	hood
manhole			**Karaffe** {f}	*n.*	decanter
Kandidat {m} *n.*		aspirant	**Karambolage** {f}	*n.*	collision
Kandidat {m} *n.*		nominee	**Karamell** {n}	*n.*	caramel
Känguru {n} *n.*		kangaroo	**Karaoke** {n}	*n.*	karaoke
Kaninchenbau {m}		burrow	**Karat** {n}*n.*		carat
Kaninchengehege {n}*n.*		warren	**Karate** {n}	*n.*	karate
Kanister {m}	*n.*	can	**karbonisiert**	*adj.*	carbonate
Kanister {m}	*n.*	canister	**Kardamom** {n}	*n.*	cardamom
Kannibale {m}	*n.*	cannibal	**Kardinal** {m}	*n.*	cardinal
Kanone {f}	*n.*	cannon	**Kardiographie** {f}	*n.*	cardiograph
Kante {f} *n.*		edge	**Kardiologie** {f}	*n.*	cardiology
Kanter {m}	*n.*	canter	**Karikatur** {f}	*n*	caricature
Kanzel {f}	*n.*	cockpit	**karmesinrot**	*n.*	crimson
Kanzel {f}	*n.*	pulpit	**karminrot**	*n.*	carmine
Kanzleigericht {n} *n.*		Chancery	**Karneval** {m}	*n.*	carnival
Kanzler {m}	*n.*	chancellor	**Karotte** {f}	*n.*	carrot
Kapazität {f}	*n.*	capacity	**karpal**	*adj.*	carpal
Kapelle {f}	*n.*	chapel	**Karriere** {f}	*n.*	career
Kapital {n}	*n.*	capital	**Karte** {f} *n.*		card
Kapital {n}	*n.*	fund	**Karte** {f} *n.*		map
Kapitalertragsteuer {f}*n.*		dividend	**Kartell** {n}	*n.*	cartel
kapitalisieren *v.*		capitalize	**Kartoffel** {f}	*n.*	potato
Kapitalismus {m} *n.*		capitalism	**Karton** {m}	*n.*	cardboard
Kapitalist {m}*n. &adj.*		capitalist	**Karussell** {n} *n.*		roundabout
Kapitän {m}	*n.*	commander	**kaschieren**	*v.*	conceal
Kapitänsamt {n}	*n.*	captaincy	**kaschiert**	*adj.*	clad
Kapitulation {f}	*n.*	surrender	**Kaschmir** {m}*n.*		cashmere

297

Käse {m}n.   cheese
Käsewasser {n}   n.   whey
Kasino {n}   n.   casino
Kassenbeamte {m}   n.   cashier
Kasserolle {f}n.   casserole
Kastanie {f}   n.   chestnut
Kastanie {f}   n.   conker
Kastanienbraun   n.   maroon
Kaste {f} n.   caste
kasteien v.   chasten
Kastell {n}   n.   fort
Kasten {m}   n.   coffer
Kasten {m}   n.   hutch
kastrieren   v.   castrate
kastrieren   v.   geld
Katalog {m}   n.   catalogue
Katalysator {m}   n.   catalyst
katalysieren v.   catalyse
Katarakt {m}   n.   cataract
Katastrophe {f}   n.   calamity
Katastrophe {f}   n.   cataclysm
Katastrophe {f}   n.   catastrophe
Katastrophe {f}   n.   debacle
Katechismus {m}   n.   catechism
Kategorie {f}   n.   category
Kategorie {f}   n.   predicament
kategorisch adj. categorical
kategorisieren   v.   categorize
Kathedrale {f}n.   cathedral
katholisch   adj. catholic
Kätzchen {n} n.   kitten
Kätzchen {n} n.   kitty
Katze {f} n.   cat
Katzenjammer {m}n.   hangover
katzig   n.   catty

Kauderwelsch {n} n.   lingo
Kauderwelsch redenv.   gibber
kauen   v.   chew
kaufen   v.   buy
kaufen   v.   purchase
käuflich adj. mercenary
käuflich adj. venal
Käuflichkeit {f}   n.   venality
Kaufmann {m}   n.   merchant
kaufmännisch   adj. commercial
kaufmännisch   adj. mercantile
Kaufmanns-Und {n}   n.
  ampersand
kaukasisch   adj. Caucasian
kaum   adv. barely
kaum   adv. scarcely
Kausalität {f} n.   causality
Kautschuk {m}   n.   rubber
kauzig   adj. grumpy
Kavalier {m}   adj. gallant
Kavalkade {f} n.   cavalcade
Kebab {m}   n.   kebab
Kegel {m}   n.   skittle
kegelförmig   adj. conical
Kehlkopf {m} n.   larynx
Kehrer {m}   n.   sweeper
keifen   v.t.   nag
Keim {m}n.   germ
keimfrei adj. sterile
Keimfreiheit {f}   n.   sterility
kein pron.   none
Keks {m}n.   biscuit
Keks {m}n.   cookie
Keks {m}n.   cracker
Kelch {m}   n.   chalice

Kelch {m}	*n.*	goblet
Keller {m}	*n.*	cellar
Kellergeschoss {n}	*n.*	basement
Kellner {m}	*n.*	waiter
keltisch *adj.*		Celtic
Kennsatz {m} *n.*		label
Kenntnis {f}	*n.*	knowledge
Kennwort {n} *n.*		watchword
Kennzeichen {n}	*n.*	stamp
Kennzeichen {n}	*n.*	tag
Kennzeichnung {f}	*n.*	marking
kentern *v.*		capsize
Keramik {f}	*n.*	ceramic
Kerbe {f} *n.*		dent
Kerbe {f} *n.*		nick
Kerker {m}	*n.*	dungeon
Kerl {m} *n.*		guy
Kerl {m} *n.*		wretch
Kernstück {n}*n.*		core
Kerosin {n}	*n.*	kerosene
Kerze {f} *n.*		candle
Kessel {m}	*n.*	cauldron
Kessel {m}	*n.*	kettle
Kette {f} *n.*		chain
keuchen *v.i*		gasp
keuchen *v.*		pant
keuchen *v.*		wheeze
Keuschheit {f}	*n.*	chastity
Keyboard {n} *n.*		keyboard
Kichererbse {f}	*n.*	chickpea
kichern *v.t.*		giggle
kichern *v.*		snigger
Kiefer {f} *v.*		pine
Kiel {m} *n.*		keel
Kiesel {m}	*n.*	gravel

Kieselstein {m}	*n.*	pebble
Kilobyte {n} *n.*		kilobyte
Kilogramm {n}	*n.*	kilo
Kilometer {m}*n.*		kilometre
Kilometerleistung {f}*n.*		mileage
Kimono {m}	*n.*	kimono
Kind {n} *n.*		child
Kind {n} *n.*		kid
Kindchen {n} *n.*		chit
Kinderarzt {m}	*n.*	paediatrician
Kindergarten {m} *n.*		kindergarten
Kinderhort {m}	*n.*	crèche
kinderleicht *adj.*		foolproof
Kindermädchen {n}	*n.*	nanny
Kinderwagen {m} *n.*		buggy
Kinderwagen {m} *n.*		pram
Kinderzimmer {n} *n.*		nursery
Kindesmord {m}	*n.*	infanticide
Kindheit {f}	*n.*	childhood
Kindheit {f}	*n.*	infancy
kindisch *adj.*		childish
kindisch *adj.*		infantile
Kindlein {n}	*n.*	babe
kindlich *adj.*		puerile
kinetisch*adj.*		kinetic
Kinn {n} *n.*		chin
Kino {n} *n*		cinema
Kino {n} *n.*		movies
kippen *v.*		tilt
Kirche {f}	*n.*	church
Kirchendiener {m}*n.*		sexton
Kirchenlied {n}	*n.*	chant
Kirchenschiff {n}	*n.*	nave
Kirchgemeinde {f}*n.*		parish
Kirchhof {m} *n.*		churchyard

kirchlich adj.	clerical	**klassisch** adj.	classic
Kirchturm {m} n.	steeple	**klassischer** adj.	classical
Kissen {n} n.	cushion	**klatschen** v.	clap
Kissen {n} n.	pillow	**Klaue {f}** n.	hoof
Kissen {n} n.	sachet	**klauen** v.	swipe
Kiste {f} n.	case	**Klause {f}** n.	hermitage
Kiste {f} n.	crate	**Klausel {f}** n.	clause
kitschig adj.	shoddy	**Klaustrophobie {f}**n.	claustrophobia
Kittel {m} n.	smock	**Klavier {n}** n.	piano
kitzeln v.	tickle	**kleben** v.	cleave
kitzeln v.	titillate	**kleben** v.i.	tape
kitzlig adj.	ticklish	**klebrig** adj.	sticky
Klage {f} n.	lament	**klebrig** adj.	tenacious
klagen v.	bewail	**Klebstoff {m}** n.	adhesive
klagen v.	claim	**Kleid {n}** v.	dress
klagen v.	complain	**Kleid {n}** n.	frock
Kläger {m} n.	petitioner	**kleiden** v.	attire
Kläger {m} n.	plaintiff	**kleiden** v.	clothe
Klamm {f} n.	ravine	**Kleidung {f}** n.	apparel
Klammer {f} n.	bracket	**Kleidung {f}** n.	clothes
Klammer {f} n.	parenthesis	**Kleidung {f}** n.	clothing
klammern v.	staple	**klein** adj.	minuscule
Klang {m} n.	ring	**klein** adj.	small
Klang {m} n.	tone	**klein** adj.	little
Klangfülle {f} n.	sonority	**kleine Menge** n.	smidgen
klangvolladj.	melodious	**kleiner** adj.	lesser
Klappentext {m} n.	blurb	**Kleinigkeit {f}**n.	trifle
klapsen v.	flip	**Kleinkind {n}** n.	infant
klar adv.	clearly	**Kleinkind {n}** n.	toddler
klar adj.	vivid	**kleinstädtisch** adj.	provincial
klar v.	vivify	**Kleister {m}** n.	paste
Klarheit {f} n.	lucidity	**Klementine** n.	Clementine
Klärung {f} n.	clearance	**Klemmbacke {f}** n.	jaw
Klärung {f} n.	purification	**Klemme {f}** n.	clip
Klasse {f} n.	class	**Klempner {m}**n.	plumber

Kleriker {m}	n.	cleric
klettern v.i		climb
klettern v.		scramble
Klick {m}n.		click
Klima {n}n.		climate
klimpern v.		strum
Klinge {f}	n.	blade
Klingel {f}	n.	bell
klingeln v.		jingle
klingen v.		tingle
klingend adj.		vocal
Klinik {f} n.		clinic
Klo {n}	n.	loo
Kloben {m}	n.	log
klopfen v.		knock
klopfen v.		palpitate
klopfen v.		throb
Klöppel {m}	n.	toggle
Klosett {n}	n.	lavatory
Kloster {n}	n.	convent
Kloster {n}	n.	monastery
klösterlich	adj.	monastic
Klotz {m}n.		chunk
klotzig adj.		bulky
Klubjacke {f} n.		blazer
klug adj.		clever
klug adj.		sage
Klugheit {f}	n.	prudence
klüglich adj.		prudential
Klumpen {m} n.		clot
Klumpen {m} n.		gob
Klumpen {m},n.		nugget
Klüpfel {m}	n.	mallet
knabbern	v.	nibble
knacken v.		crack

Knallkörper {m}	n.	banger
knapp	adj.	bare
knapp	adj.	concise
knapp	adj.	curt
knapp	adj.	scant
Knappe {m}	n.	squire
Knappe {m}	n.	varlet
Knappheit {f} n.		paucity
knarr	n.	creak
knarren v.		creak
Knauf {m}	n.	stud
knechtisch	adj.	menial
Kneifzange {f}	n.	pincer
Kneipe {f}	n.	pub
Kneipe {f}	n.	saloon
kneten	v.	knead
Knick {m}	n.	kink
Knie {n} n.		knee
Kniehosen {pl}	n.	breeches
knien	v.	kneel
Kniesehne {f}n.		hamstring
Kniff {m}n.		knack
Kniff {m}n.		ruse
kniffen v.		nip
Knirps {m}	n.	tot
Knirps {m}	n.	tiddly
knirschen	v.	scrunch
knistern v.		crackle
knittern v.		crinkle
Knoblauch {m}	n.	garlic
Knöchel {m}	n.	knuckle
Knochen {m} n.		bone
knöcherne	adj.	bony
Knopf {m}	n.	button
Knorpel {m}	n.	cartilage

German		English
Knospe {f}	*n.*	bud
knospen *v.*		burgeon
Knoten {m}	*n.*	knot
Knoten {m}	*n.*	node
knotig *adj.*		knotty
Know-how {n}	*n.*	expertise
Knüppel {m}	*n.*	billet
Knüppel {m}	*n.*	bludgeon
Knüppel {m}	*n.*	cudgel
Knüppel {m}	*n.*	truncheon
knurren *v.*		growl
knurren *v.*		snarl
knusprig *adj.*		crisp
Koalition {f}	*n.*	coalition
Koaxialkabel {n}	*v.*	coax
Kobalt {n}	*n.*	cobalt
Kobold {m}	*n.*	bogey
Kobold {m}	*n.*	elf
Kobold {m}	*n.*	hobgoblin
Koch {m}	*n.*	cook
kochen *v.*		cook
kochen *v.i.*		boil
Kocher {m}	*n.*	boiler
Kocher {m}	*n.*	cooker
Kode {m}	*n.*	code
Köder {m}	*n.*	bait
ködern *n.*		decoy
ködern *v.*		lure
Koedukation {f}	*n.*	co-education
Koeffizient {m}	*n.*	coefficient
Koexistenz {f}	*n.*	coexistence
koexistieren *v.*		coexist
Koffer {m}	*n.*	bag
Koffer {m}	*n.*	chest
kohabitieren *v.*		cohabit

German		English
Kohäsion {f}	*n.*	cohesion
Kohlehydrat {n}	*n.*	carbohydrate
Kohlenbergwerk {n}	*n.*	colliery
kohlensäurehaltig *adj.*		fizzy
Kohlenstoff {m}	*n.*	carbon
Kokain {n}	*n.*	cocaine
Kokarde {f}	*n.*	cockade
kokettieren *v.i*		flirt
Kokon {m}	*n.*	cocoon
Kokosnuss {f}	*n.*	coconut
Kokosraspel {f}	*n.*	flake
Kokoswandplatte {f}	*n.*	coir
Koks {m}	*n.*	coke
Kolben {m}	*n.*	piston
Kolik {f}	*n.*	colic
Kollateral	*n.*	collateral
kollationieren *v.*		collate
Kollege {m}	*n.*	colleague
Kollektor {m}	*n.*	collector
kollidieren *v.*		collide
Kollusion {f}	*n.*	collusion
Kölnisch Wasser {n}	*n.*	cologne
kolonial *adj.*		colonial
Koloss {m}	*n.*	hulk
Koma {n}	*n.*	coma
Kombination {f}	*n.*	combination
Komet {m}	*n.*	comet
Komfort {m}	*n.*	convenience
komisch *adj.*		comic
komisch *adj.*		funny
komisch *adj.*		quizzical
Komma {n}	*n.*	comma
Kommandant {m}	*n.*	commandant
Kommandotruppe {f}	*n.*	commando
kommen *v.*		come

Kommentar {m}	n.	commentary
Kommentator {m}	n.	commentator
Kommode {f}	n.	commode
kommunal	adj.	communal
kommunal	adj.	urban
Kommunlkant {m}	n.	communicant
Kommunion {f}	n.	communion
Kommunismus {m}		n.communism
Komödiant {m}	n.	troupe
Komödie {f}	n	comedy
kompakt adj.	compact	
Kompass {m} n.	compass	
kompensieren	v.	compensate
Komplikation {f}	n.	complication
Kompliment {n}	n.	compliment
Komplize {m} n.	accomplice	
komplizieren v.	complicate	
komplizieren v.	sophisticate	
kompliziert	adj.	intricate
kompliziert	adj.	sophisticated
Komponist {m}	n.	composer
Kompost {m} n.	compost	
komprimieren	v.	compress
Kompromiss {m}	n.	compromise
kompromisslos		adj.uncompromising
Kondensator {m}	n.	capacitor
kondensieren v.	condense	
Konditorwaren {pl}		n.confectionery
kondolieren	v.	condole
Kondom {n}	n.	condom
Konfekt {n}	n.	confection
Konferenz {f} n.	conference	
Konfiguration {f}	n.	configuration
Konfiszierung {f}	n.	confiscation
Konflikt {m} n.	conflict	

Konglomerat n.	conglomerate	
Kongress {m}n.	congress	
König {m}	n.	king
Königin {f}	n.	queen
königlich	adj.	regal
königlich	n.	royal
Königreich {n}	n.	kingdom
Königsmord {m}	n.	regicide
konjugieren	v.	conjugate
konjunktiv	adj.	subjunctive
Konkubine {f}n.	concubine	
Konkurrent {m}	n.	competitor
Konkurrent {m}	n.	rival
konkurrenzfähig	adj.	competitive
konkurrieren v.	compete	
konnen v.	can	
könnte v.	might	
Konsens {m} n.	consensus	
konservativ	adj.	conservative
Konservatorium {n}		n.conservatory
konservieren v. t	conserve	
Konservierungsmittel {f}n.preservative		
konsistent	adj.	consistent
konsolidierung	v.	consolidate
Konsonant {m}	n.	consonant
konstant adj.	constant	
Konstanz {f}	n.	permanence
Konstellation {f}	n.	constellation
Konstitution {f}	n.	constitution
konstruieren v.	construe	
Konstruktion {f}	n.	construction
konstruktiv	adj.	constructive
Konsul {m}	n.	consul
konsularisch	n.	consular
Konsulat {n}	n.	consulate

Kontakt {m} *n.* contact
Konterbande {f} *n.* contraband
Kontinent {m} *n.* continent
kontinental *adj.* continental
kontinuierlich*adj.* continuous
Konto {m} *n.* account
Kontoinhaber {m} *n.* depository
Kontrollabschnitt {m}*n.* counterfoil
Kontrolle {f} *n.* control
Kontroverse {f} *n.* controversy
Kontusion {f} *n.* contusion
Konus {m} *n.* cone
Konvention {f} *n.* convention
konvergieren *v.* converge
Konzentration {f} *n.* concentration
konzentrieren*v.* concentrate
Konzert {n} *n.* concert
Kooperation {f} *n.* cooperation
koordinieren *v. t* coordinate
Koordinierung {f} *n.* coordination
Kopf {n} *n.* head
köpfen *v.* decapitate
Kopfhörer {m} *n.* headphone
Kopfschmerz {m} *n.* headache
Kopftuch {n} *n.* scarf
Kopie {f} *n.* transcript
kopieren*v.* copy
kopieren*v.* replicate
Kopierer {m} *n.* copier
Koralle {f} *n.* coral
Korb {m}*n.* basket
Korbwaren {pl} *n.* wicker
Kordon {m} *n.* cordon
Koriander {m} *n.* coriander
Korinthe {f} *n.* currant

Korken {m} *n.* cork
Körnchen {n} *n.* granule
Kornspeicher {m} *n.* granary
Körper {m} *n.* body
Körper {m} *n.* carcass
Körperbau {m} *n.* physique
körperlich *adv.* bodily
körperlich *adj.* physical
Körperverletzung {f}*n.* assault
Korporal {m} *n.* corporal
Korps *n.* corps
korpulent *adj.* obese
korregieren *v.* correct
korrekt *adj.* proper
Korrektur {f} *n.* correction
Korrektur {f} *n.* patch
Korrelation {f} *n.* correlation
Korrespondent {f} *n.* correspondent
korrespondieren *v.* correspond
Korridor {m} *n.* corridor
Korrosion {f} *n.* corrosion
korrosiv *adj.* corrosive
korrupt *adj.* corrupt
Korruption {f}*n.* corruption
Kortison {n} *n.* cortisone
koscher *adj.* kosher
Kosmetikerin {f} *n.* beautician
kosmetisch *adj.* cosmetic
kosmisch *adj.* cosmic
Kosmologie {f} *n.* cosmology
kosmopolit *adj.* cosmopolitan
Kosmos {m} *n.* cosmos
Kost {f} *n.* fare
kosten *v.* cost
Kostenrahmen {m} *n.* budget

Kostenträger {m}	n.	sponsor
köstlich	adj.	delectable
Kostprobe {f}	n.	sample
Kotentleerung {f}	n.	dejection
Krabbe {f}		n. crab
krabbeln	v.	scrabble
Kraft {f}	n.	power
Kraft {f}	n.	vigour
Kraftfahrzeug {n}	n.	automobile
Kraftfutter {n}n.		pellet
kräftig	adj.	forceful
kräftig	adj.	hefty
kräftig	adj.	husky
kräftig	adj.	lusty
kräftig	adj.	robust
kraftlos	adj.	feeble
kraftlos	adj.	infirm
kraftlos	adj.	nerveless
kraftvoll	adj.	powerful
Krähe {f} n.		crow
Krähenkolonie {f}	n.	rookery
Krähenscharbe {f}n.		shag
krakellen v.		roister
Krämer {m}	n.	monger
Krampf {m}	n.	cramp
Krampf {m}	n.	spasm
krampfhaft	adj.	spasmodic
Kran {m}n.		crane
krank	adj.	ill
krank	adj.	sick
Kranke	n.	invalid
kränkeln	v.	ail
kränkelnd	adj.	ailing
kränken	v.	mortify
Krankenhaus {n}	n.	hospital

Krankenschwester {f}n.		nurse
Krankhaftigkeit {f}n.		morbidity
Krankheit {f}	n.	illness
Krankheit {f}	n.	malady
Krankheit {f}	n.	sickness
kränklich	adj.	peaky
kränklich	adj.	sickly
kränklich	n.	valetudinarian
krass	adj.	stark
Krätze {f}	n.	scab
Krätze {f}	n.	scabies
kratzen	v.	scrape
kratzen	v.t.	scratch
Kraut {n}n.		cabbage
Kraut {n}n.		herb
Krawall {m}	n.	rumpus
Krawatte {f}	n.	cravat
Krebs {m}	n.	cancer
kreditfähig	adj.	trustworthy
Kreditor {m}	n.	supplier
Kreide {f}	n.	chalk
Kreidetafel {f}n.		blackboard
Kreis {m}	n.	circle
kreischen	v.	shriek
kreisen	v.	gyrate
kreisförmig	adj.	circular
kreisförmig	adj.	orbital
Kreisumfang {m}	n.	circumference
Krematorium {n}	n.	crematorium
Kreuz {n}	n.	cross
Kreuzblume {f}	n.	finial
Kreuzblume {f}	n.	flab
Kreuzfahrt {f} v.		cruise
Kreuzfahrtschiff {n}	n.	cruiser
Kreuzgang {m}	n.	cloister

Kreuzkümmel {m} *n.*	cumin
Kreuzzug {f} *n.*	crusade
kriechen *v.*	crawl
Kriechen *v.*	creep
kriechen *v.*	cringe
kriechen *v.*	grovel
Kriecher {m} *n.*	creeper
Kriecher {m} *n.*	sycophant
Kriecherei {f} *n.*	sycophancy
Krieg {m} *n.*	war
Krieger {m} *n.*	warrior
kriegerisch *adj.*	bellicose
kriegerisch *adj.*	martial
Kriegsbeil {n}*n.*	hatchet
Kriegsfanfare {f} *adj.*	clarion
Kriegsführung {f} *n.*	warfare
Krimi {m} *n.*	thriller
Kriminologie {f} *n.*	criminology
Krippe {f} *n.*	manger
Krise {f} *n.*	shower
Kristall {m} *n.*	crystal
Kriterium {n} *n.*	criterion
Kritik {f} *n.*	criticism
Kritik {f} *n.*	review
Kritiker {m} *n.*	censor
Kritiker {m} *n.*	critic
kritisch *adj.*	critical
kritische Abhandlung*n.*	critique
kritisieren *v.*	zing
kritzeln *v.*	scrawl
kritzeln *v.*	scribble
Krokodil {n} *n.*	crocodile
krönen *v.*	crown
Krönung {f} *n.*	coronation
Kröte {f} *n.*	toad

Krücke {f} *n.*	crutch
Krug {m}*n.*	jug
krumm *adv.*	awry
krumm *adj.*	crooked
krumm dasitzen *v.*	slouch
krümmen *v.*	writhe
Krümmung {f} *v.*	bend
Krümmung {f} *n.*	curve
Krüppel {m} *n.*	cripple
Kruste {f} *n.*	crust
Krypta {f} *n.*	crypt
kubisch *adj.*	cubical
Küche {f} *n.*	cuisine
Küche {f} *n.*	kitchen
Kuchen {m} *n.*	cake
Kuchenblech {n} *n.*	griddle
Küchenherd {m} *n.*	stove
Kuckuck {m} *n.*	cuckoo
Küfer {m} *n.*	cooper
Kugel {f} *n.*	bullet
Kugel {f} *n.*	orb
Kugel {f} *n.*	slug
Kuh {f} *n.*	cow
kühl *adj.*	cool
kühlen *v.*	refrigerate
Kühler {m} *n.*	cooler
Kühlmittel {n}*n.*	coolant
Kühlschrank {m} *n.*	fridge
Kühlschrank {m} *n.*	refrigerator
kühn *adj.*	hardy
kühn *adj.*	venturesome
Kuhstall {m} *n.*	byre
kulinarisch *adj.*	culinary
Kulisse {f} *n.*	backdrop
Kulissenwagen {m} *n.*	chariot

kulminierend	v.	culminate	
Kult {m}	n.	cult	
kultivieren	v.	cultivate	
Kultur {f}	n.	culture	
kulturell	adj.	cultural	
kulturfähig	adj.	arable	
Kummer {m}	n.	grief	
kümmerlich	adj.	puny	
Kümmernis {n}	n.	grievance	
Kumpel {m}	n.	chum	
Kumpel {m}	n.	fellow	
Kumpel {m}	n.	pal	
Kunde {m}	n.	client	
Kunde {m}	n.	customer	
Kundgebung {f}	n.	manifestation	
kündigen	v.	cancel	
Kündigung {f}	n.	notice	
Kung fu {m}	n.	kung fu	
Kunst {f}	n.	art	
Kunstflug {m}	n.	aerobatics	
Kunstgriff {m}	n.	artifice	
Künstler {m}	n.	artist	
künstlerisch	adj.	artistic	
künstlich	adj.	artificial	
künstlich	adj.	factitious	
künstlich	adj.	synthetic	
künstlich...	comb.	cyber	
Kunststück {m}	n.	feat	
kunstvoll	adj.	artful	
Kupfer {n}	n.	copper	
Kürbis {m}	n.	pumpkin	
Kurier {m}	n.	messenger	
Kurort {m}	n.	sanitarium	
Kurort {m}	n.	spa	
kursiv	adj.	cursive	

Kursiv	adj.	italic
Kurtisane {f}	n.	courtesan
kurz adj.	brief	
kurz adj.	short	
kurz halten	adj.	skimp
Kurzbezeichnung {f}n.	shortcut	
Kürze {f} n.	brevity	
kürzen	v.t.	abbreviate
kürzen	v.	curtail
kurzsichtig	adj.	myopic
kurzsichtig	adj.	purblind
Kurzsichtigkeit {f} n.	myopia	
Kürzung {f}	n.	shortage
kurzzeitig	adj.	temporary
kuschelig	adj.	cuddly
kuscheln v.	nestle	
kuscheln v.	snuggle	
küssen	v.t.	kiss
Küste {f} n.	coast	
Küste {f} n.	shore	
Küstenfahrer {m}	n.	coaster

L

labial	adj.	labial
Labor {n}	n.	laboratory
Labyrinth {n} n.	labyrinth	
Labyrinth {n} n.	maze	
lächeln	v.	smile
lachen	v.	laugh
Lachen {n}	n.	laughter
lächerlich	adj.	laughable
lächerlich	adj.	preposterous
lächerlich	adj.	ridiculous
lachlustig	adj.	risible
Lachs {m}	n.	salmon

307

Lack {m} *n.*	enamel	
Lack {m} *n.*	lacquer	
Lack {m} *n.*	varnish	
Lacrosse {n} *n.*	lacrosse	
Ladegerät {n} *n.*	charger	
laden *n.*	charge	
laden *v.*	download	
Laden {m} *n.*	boutique	
Laden {m} *n.*	shop	
Laden {m} *n.*	superstore	
Ladendiebstahl {m}	*n.*shoplifting	
Ladewinde {f}*n.*	windlass	
Ladung {f} *n.*	cargo	
Ladung {f} *v.*	charge	
Lage {f} *n.*	position	
Lager {n}*n.*	camp	
Lager {n}*n.*	store	
Lagerbier {n} *n.*	lager	
Lagerfass {n} *n.*	keg	
Lagerliste {f} *n.*	stocklist	
lagern *v.*	shelve	
Lagune {f} *n.*	lagoon	
lahm *adj.*	gammy	
lahm *adj.*	lame	
lahmen *v.*	limp	
lähmen *v.*	paralyse	
Lähmung {f} *n.*	palsy	
Laib {n} *n.*	loaf	
Laie {f} *n.*	layman	
laienhaft *adj.*	unprofessional	
Lakai {m} *n.*	lackey	
lakonisch *adj.*	laconic	
Lamelle {f} *n.*	slat	
Lametta {n} *n.*	tinsel	
Lamm {n} *n.*	lamb	

Lampe {f} *n.*	lamp	
lancieren *v.*	launch	
Land {n} *n.*	country	
landen *v.t.*	alight	
landen *v.*	disembark	
Landesgrenze {f} *n.*	frontier	
Landesregierung {f}*n.*	government	
Landesverrat {m} *n.*	treason	
Landhaus {n} *n.*	chateau	
ländlich *adj.*	rural	
Ländlichkeit {f} *n.*	rusticity	
Landplage {f} *n.*	pest	
Landplage {f} *n.*	plague	
Landschaft {f} *n.*	landscape	
landschaftlich *adj.*	scenic	
Landsmann {m} *n.*	compatriot	
Landstreicher {m} *n.*	vagrant	
Landstreitkräfte {f} *n.*	army	
Landung {f} *n.*	descent	
Landung {f} *n.*	landing	
Landvolk {n} *n.*	peasantry	
Landwirt {m} *n.*	farmer	
Landwirtschaft {f} *n*	husbandry	
landwirtschaftlich *adj.*	agrarian	
Landzurückgezogenheit {f} *n.* rustication		
Länge {f}*n.*	length	
Länge {f}*n.*	longitude	
Langeweile {f} *n.*	tedium	
langlebig *adj.*	durable	
Langlebigkeit {f} *n.*	longevity	
längs *prep.*	along	
langsam *adj.* slow		
langsam *adv.* slowly		
langsam *adj.* tardy		

Langsamkeit {f}	*n.*	slowness	
langweilen	*v.*	bore	
langwierig	*adj.*	lengthy	
langwierig	*adj.*	long	
Lanze {f} *n.*	lance		
Lanzenreiter {m}	*n.*	lancer	
Lanzette {f}	*n.*	lancet	
Lappen {m}	*n.*	lobe	
Lärm {m}n.	breeze		
Lärm {m}n.	fuss		
Lärm {m}n.	hubbub		
lärmen	*v.*	rant	
lärmen	*adj.*	vociferous	
lärmend *adj.*	blatant		
Larve {f} *n.*	larva		
Lasagne {f}	*n.*	lasagne	
Laschung {f}	*n.*	lashings	
Laser {m}	*n.*	laser	
lassen	*v.*	let	
lässig	*adj.*	nonchalant	
lässig	*adj.*	remiss	
Lässigkeit {f}	*n.*	nonchalance	
Last {f}	*n.*	burden	
Laster {n}	*n.*	vice	
lasterhaft	*adj.*	vicious	
Lasterhaftigkeit {f}		*n.* profligacy	
lästig	*adj.*	onerous	
lästig	*adj.*	worrisome	
Lastkahn {m} *n.*	barge		
Lastkraftwagen {m}		*n.*	lorry
Lastkraftwagen {m}		*n.*	truck
Lastposten {m}	*n.*	debit	
Lastwagen {pl}	*n.*	van	
Laterne {f}	*n.*	lantern	
Latrine {f}	*n.*	latrine	

latschen *v.*	traipse		
Latte {f} *n.*	lath		
Lattenzaun {m}	*n.*	stockade	
Latz {m} *n.*	bib		
lau *adj.*	tepid		
Laube {f}n.	arbour		
Laube {f}n.	bower		
Laubsägemaschine {f}n.		jigsaw	
Laubwerk {n} *n.*	foliage		
Lauch {m}	*n.*	leek	
lauern	*v.*	lurk	
Lauf {m} *n.*	run		
laufen	*v.*	run	
Läufer {m}	*n.*	rotor	
Läufer {m}	*n.*	runner	
Laufsteg {m} *n.*	gangway		
Laufwerk {n} *n.*	device		
laugen	*v.*	leach	
Laune {f}n.	whim		
Laune {f}n.	whimsy		
launisch *adj.*	capricious		
launisch *adj.*	moody		
launisch *adj.*	wayward		
launisch *adj.*	whimsical		
Laus {f} *n.*	louse		
Lausebengel {m}	*n.*	rascal	
laut *adv.* aloud			
laut *adj.* loud			
Laute {f} *n.*	lute		
läuten	*v.*	ring	
lauwarm *adj.*	lukewarm		
Lava {f} *n.*	lava		
Lavendel {m} *n.*	lavender		
Lawine {f}	*n.*	avalanche	
Laxheit {f}	*n.*	laxity	

Leasingnehmer {m} *n.* lessee
leben *v.* live
Leben {n} *n.* life
lebendig *adj.* alive
lebendig *adj.* lively
lebendig *adj.* spirited
Lebendigkeit {f} *n.* agility
lebensfähig *adj.* viable
Lebenskraft {f} *n.* buoyancy
Lebenskraft {f} *n.* vitality
Lebenslage {f} *n.*, *a* situation
lebenslänglich *adj.* lifelong
Lebensmittel {n} *n.* food
Lebensmittel {pl} *n.* viands
Lebensmittelgeschäft {n}*n.* grocery
Lebensmittelhändler {m}*n.* grocer
Lebensraum {m} *n.* habitat
Lebensunterhalt {m}*n.* livelihood
Lebensunterhalt {m}*n.* subsistence
Lebensweise {f} *n.* living
Leber {f} *n.* liver
Lebewesen {n} *n.* creature
Lebewohl *n.* adieu
lebewohl *excl.* goodbye
Lebewohl {n} *interj.* farewell
lebhaft *adj.* brisk
lebhaft *adj.* mercurial
lebhaft *adj.* perky
lebhaft *adj.* sprightly
lebhaft *adj.* vivacious
Lebhaftigkeit {f} *n.* vivacity
leblos *adj.* inanimate
leblos *adj.* lifeless
lecken *v.* lick
lecker *adj.* yummy

Leckerbissen {m} *n.* titbit
Leder {n}*n.* leather
leer *adj.* devoid
leer *adj.* empty
leer *adj.* vacuous
Leere {f} *n.* vacancy
Leerraum {m}*n.* vacuum
leerstehend *adj.* vacant
legalisieren *v.* legalize
Legasthenie {f} *n.* dyslexia
legen *v.* lay
legen *v.* put
Legende {f} *n.* legend
Legierung {f} *n.* alloy
Legion {f} *n.* legion
Legislative {f}*n.* legislature
Legitimierung {f} *n.* legitimacy
Lehmstein {m} *n.* adobe
lehnen *v.* lean
lehnen *v.* recline
Lehrbuch {n} *n.* textbook
Lehre {f} *n.* tenet
Lehrer {m} *n.* instructor
Lehrer {m} *n.* teacher
Lehrling {m} *n.* apprentice
Lehrplan {m} *n.* syllabus
Lehrsatz {m} *n.* theorem
Leibeigene {m,f} *n.* serf
Leibeigene {m,f} *n.* thrall
Leibwache {f}*n* bodyguard
Leiche {f} *n.* corpse
Leichenbegräbnis {n}*n.* burial
Leichenbestatter {m}*n.* undertaker
Leichenhalle {f} *n.* mortuary
Leichenschauhaus {n}*n.* morgue

Leichentuch {n}	*n.*	shroud
Leichenwagen {m}	*n.*	hearse
leicht	*adv.*	lightly
leichtgläubig	*adj.*	gullible
Leichtgläubigkeit {f}	*adv.*	credulity
Leichtigkeit {f}	*n.*	ease
Leichtsinn {m}	*n.*	levity
leichtsinnig	*adj.*	careless
leichtsinnig	*adj.*	flippant
Leid {n}	*n.*	affliction
Leid {n}	*n.*	sorrow
Leid {n}	*n.*	woe
Leidenschaft {f}	*n.*	passion
leidenschaftlich	*adj.*	impassioned
leidenschaftlich	*adj.*	passionate
leidenschaftslos	*adj.*	dispassionate
leider	*conj.*	alas
Leier {f}	*n.*	lyre
Leihe {f}	*n.*	loan
Leim {m}	*n.*	glue
Leine {f}	*n.*	leash
Leinen {n}	*n.*	linen
Leinwand {f}	*n.*	canvas
leise	*adj.*	quiet
Leiste {f}	*n.*	groin
leisten	*v.t.*	afford
Leistenbruch {m}	*n.*	hernia
Leistung {f}	*n.*	performance
Leistungsfähigkeit {f}	*n.*	capability
Leistungsfähigkeit {f}	*n.*	efficiency
Leistungsfähigkeit {f}	*n.*	rating
Leiter {f}	*n.*	ladder
Leitstrahl {m}	*n.*	beam
Leitung {f}	*n.*	wire
Lektion {f}	*n.*	lesson

Lektüre {f}	*n.*	lecture
Lende {f}	*n.*	loin
lenkbar	*adj.*	tractable
Lenkung {f}	*n.*	guidance
Leopard {m}	*n.*	leopard
Lepra {f}	*n.*	leprosy
Lerche {f}	*n.*	lark
lernen	*v.*	learn
Lernende {m,f}	*n.*	learner
Lernprozeß {m}	*n.*	learning
lesbar	*adj.*	legible
Lesbierin {f}	*n.*	lesbian
Lese {f}	*n.*	vintage
Lesemarke {f}	*n.*	bookmark
lesen	*v.*	read
Leser {m}	*n.*	reader
Lethargie {f}	*n.*	lethargy
lethargisch	*adj.*	lethargic
letzte	*adj.*	last
leuchtend	*adj.*	luminous
Leuchtfeuer {n}	*n.*	beacon
Leuchtgeschoss {n}	*n.*	flare
Leuchtkörper {m}	*n.*	luminary
leugnen	*v. i.*	deny
Leumund {m}	*n.*	repute
Leute {pl}	*n.*	gentry
Leute {pl}	*n.*	people
Leuteschinder {m}	*n.*	martinet
Leutnant {m}	*n.*	lieutenant
lexikalisch	*adj.*	lexical
Lexikon {n}	*n.*	lexicon
Libido {f}	*n.*	libido
Licht {n}	*n.*	light
liebäugeln	*v.*	ogle
Liebe {f}	*n.*	love

German		English
Liebelei {f}	*n.*	dalliance
liebenswert	*adj.*	lovable
liebenswürdig	*adj.*	amiable
lieber	*adj.*	dear
liebestrunken	*adj.*	besotted
Liebesverhältnis {n}	*n.*	liaison
Liebeswerben {n}	*n.*	courtship
liebevoll	*adj.*	affectionate
liebhaft	*adj.*	lovely
liebkosen	*v.*	caress
liebkosen	*v.*	fondle
lieblich	*adj.*	cozy
Lieblichkeit {f}	*n.*	charm
Lieblichkeit {f}	*n.*	sweetness
Liebling {m}	*n.*	darling
Liebling {m}	*n.*	sweetheart
lieblos	*adj.*	uncharitable
Lied {n}	*n.*	song
Lied {n},	*n.*	tune
liederlich	*adj.*	lewd
liederlich	*adj.*	profligate
Lieferant {m}	*n.*	vendor
Lieferant {m}	*n.*	veneer
Lieferant {m}	*n.*	victualler
liefern	*v.*	deliver
liefern	*v.*	purvey
liefern	*v.*	supply
Liege {f}	*n.*	chaise
Liege {f}	*n.*	couch
Liege {f}	*n.*	liege
liegend	*adj.*	recumbent
Liegeplatz {m}	*n.*	berth
Liegewagen {m}	*n.*	couchette
Liegewiese {f}	*n.*	lawn
Liga {f}	*n.*	league

German		English
Ligament {n}	*n.*	ligament
Lilie {f}	*n.*	lily
Limerick {m}	*n.*	limerick
Limette {f}	*n.*	lime
Limonade {f}	*n.*	lemonade
Limousine {f}	*n.*	limousine
lindern	*v.*	alleviate
lindern	*v.*	soothe
Linderung {f}	*n.*	alleviation
Linderung {f}	*n.*	relief
Lineal {n}	*n.*	ruler
links	*n.*	left
Linkshänder {m}	*n.*	leftist
Linse {f}	*n.*	lens
Linse {f}	*n.*	lentil
Lippe {f}	*n.*	lip
Liquidation {f}	*n.*	liquidation
lispeln	*v.*	lisp
List {f}	*n.*	guile
List {f}	*n.*	ploy
List {f}	*n.*	stratagem
List {f}	*n.*	wile
Liste {f}	*n.*	roster
Liste(schwarze) {f}	*n.*	blacklist
listig	*adj.*	crafty
Liter {m}	*n.*	litre
literarisch	*adj.*	literary
Literatur {f}	*n.*	literature
Literaturangabe {f}	*n.*	bibliography
Litschi {f}	*n.*	lychee
Lizenz {f}	*n.*	licence
Lizenzgebühr {f}	*n.*	royalty
Lizenznehmer {m}	*n.*	licensee
loben	*v. i*	compliment

loben	v.	laud
loben	v.t.	praise
lobenswert	adj.	commendable
löblich	adj.	laudable
Lobschrift {f}	n.	panegyric
Loch {n}	n.	hole
Locke {f}	n.	curl
locken	v.	entice
locker	adj.	lax
locker	adj.	loose
lockern	v.	limber
lockern	v.	loosen
Lockung {f}	n.	allure
lodernd	adv.	ablaze
Löffel {m}	n.	spoon
Löffel {m}	n.	spoonful
Logarithmus {m}	n.	logarithm
Logik {f}	n.	logic
logisch	adj.	logical
Logistik {f}	n.	logistics
Lohn {m}	n.	fee
Lohn {m}	n.	wage
lohnend	adj.	remunerative
lokal	adj.	regional
Lokal {n}	n.	premises
lokalisieren	v.	localize
Lokomotive {f}	n.	locomotive
Lorbeerbaum {m}	n.	laurel
löschen	v.	erase
löschen	v.	quench
Lösegeld {n}	n.	ransom
lösen	v.	solve
loslassen	v.	relinquish
löslich	adj.	soluble
Löslichkeit {f}	n.	solubility

Lösung {f}	n.	solution
Lösungsmittel {n}	n.	solvent
loswerden	v.	rid
Lotion {f}	n.	lotion
Lötmaschine {f}	n.	solder
Lotterie {f}	n.	lottery
Lotus {m}	n.	lotus
Louvre {n}	n.	Louvre
Löwe {m}	n.	Leo
Löwe {m}	n.	lion
Löwenzahn {m}	v.	dandelion
loyal	adj.	loyal
Loyalist {m}	n.	loyalist
Lücke {f}	n.	gap
Lücke {f}	n.	lacuna
Luft {f}	n.	air
Luftballon {m}	n.	balloon
Luftblase {f}	n.	bubble
Luftfahrttechnik {f}	n.	aeronautics
Luftfahrzeug {n}	n.	aircraft
Luftgeist {m}	n.	sylph
luftig	adj.	airy
Luftschlange {f}	n.	streamer
luftsiegelig	adj.	morganatic
Luftspiegelung {f}	n.	mirage
Lüftungsanlage {f}	n.	ventilator
Luftzug {m}	n.	whiff
Luftzug {m}	n.	draught
lügen	v.	belie
lügen	v.	lie
Lügner {m}	n.	liar
lukrativ	adj.	lucrative
Lümmel {m}	n.	boor
Lümmel {m}	n.	lout
Lumpen {m}	n.	tatter

Lunge {f}n. lung
Lunge {f} n. lunge
Lungenentzündung {f}n.
     pneumonia
Lust {f} n. zest
Lüster {m} n. chandelier
Lüster {m} n. lustre
lüstern adj. lascivious
Lustigkeit {f} n. gaiety
Lüstling {m} n. voluptuary
lustlos adj. listless
Lutscher {m} n. lollipop
luxuriös adj. luxurious
luxus adj. deluxe
Luxus {m} n. luxury
Lymphe {f} n. lymph
lynchen v. lynch
Lyrik {f} n. lyric
Lyriker {m} n. lyricist
lyrisch adj. lyrical

M

Macho {m} adj. macho
Macht {f}n. force
mächtig adj. mighty
mächtig adj. spanking
Machtspruch {m} n. dictum
Machtvollkommenheit {f}n. authority
Mädchen {n} n. girl
mädchenhaft adj. girlish
Mafia {f} n. Mafia
Magd {f} n. maiden
magen- adj. gastric
Magen {m} n. stomach
Magensäuremittel {n}adj. antacid

magenta n. magenta
mager adj. meagre
mager adj. skinny
Magie {f}n. magic
Magnat {n} n. magnate
Magnet {m} n. magnet
magnetisch adj. magnetic
Magnetismus {m} n. magnetism
Mahagonibaum {m} n. mahogany
mähen v. mow
Mäher {m} n. reaper
Mahl {n} n. dinner
Mahl {n} n. meal
Mähne {f} n. crest
Mähne {f} n. mane
mahnen v. remind
Mahnschreiben {n} n. reminder
Mai {m} n. May
Maid {f} n. damsel
Majestät {f} n. majesty
majestätisch adj. majestic
makaber adj. grim
mäkelig adj. censorious
mäkelig adj. dainty
makellos adj. immaculate
makellos adj. impeccable
Makler {m} n. broker
Malaria {f} n. malaria
Maler {m} n. painter
Malheur {n} n. mishap
maligne adj. malignant
Malz {n} n. malt
Mama {f}n. mum
Mammon {m} n. mammon
Mammut {m} n. mammoth

314

mampfen	v.	munch
Manager {m}	n.	tycoon
manche	adj.	some
Mandarine {f}	n.	tangerine
Mandat {n}	n.	mandate
Mandel {f}	n.	almond
Mandel {f}	n.	tonsil
Mangan {n}	n.	manganese
Mangel {m}	n.	dearth
Mangel {m}	n.	deficiency
Mangel {m}	n.	fault
Mangel {m}	n.	lack
Mangel {m}	n.	privation
Mangel {m}	n.	shortcoming
mangelhaft	adj.	deficient
mangelhaft	adj.	inadequate
Mangelhaftigkeit {f}	n.	
imperfection		
Mango	n.	mango
Manieriertheit {f}	n.	mannerism
Manifest {n}	n.	manifesto
Maniküre {f}	n.	manicure
manipulieren	v.	manipulate
mannbar	a.	nubile
Männchen {n}	n.	male
mannhaft	adj.	manful
männlich	adj.	manly
männlich	adj.	masculine
männlich	adj.	virile
Männlichkeit {f}	n.	manhood
Mannschaft {f}	n.	crew
Mannschaft {f}	n.	team
Mannschaft {f}	n.	workmanship
Mannschaftskapitän {m}	n.	captain
Mannweib {n}	n.	virago

Manöver {n}	n.	manoeuvre
Manschette {f}	n.	cuff
Mantel {m}	n.	cloak
Mantel {m}	n.	mantel
Mantra {n}	n.	mantra
manuell	adj.	manual
Manuskript {n}	n.	manuscript
Manuskript {n}	n.	scripture
Marathonlauf {m}	n.	marathon
märchenhaft	adj.	fabulous
Margarine {f}	n.	margarine
marginal	adj.	marginal
Marienkäfer {m}	n.	ladybird
marin	adj.	marine
marinieren	v.	marinate
Marionette {f}	n.	marionette
Marionette {f}	n.	puppet
maritim	adj.	maritime
Marke {f}	n.	marker
Markierung {f}	n.	blip
Markierung {f}	n.	mark
Markise {f}	n.	marquee
Markt {m}	n.	market
Marktlücke {f}	n.	opening
Marktplatz {m}	n.	piazza
Marmelade {f}	n.	jam
Marmelade {f}	n.	marmalade
marmorieren	v.	mottle
Mars {m}	n.	Mars
Marsch {f}	n	marsh
marschieren	v.	march
Marshmellow	n.	marshmallow
Märtyrer {m}	n.	martyr
Martyrium {n}	n.	martyrdom
Marxismus {m}	n.	Marxism

März {m} *n.*	march	**Matriarchat {n}** *n.*	matriarch
Marzipan {n} *n.*	marzipan	**Matrix {f}** *n.*	matrix
Mascara {f} *n.*	mascara	**Matrize {f}** *n.*	stencil
Maschenweite {f} *n.*	mesh	**Matrone {m}** *n.*	matron
Maschine {f} *n.*	machine	**Matrose {m}** *n.*	sailor
Maschinerie {f} *n.*	machinery	**matschig** *adj.*	slushy
Masern {pl} *n.*	measles	**Matte {f}** *n.*	mat
Maske {f} *n.*	mask	**Mauer {f}** *n.*	mural
Maskerade {f} *n.*	masquerade	**Mauerwerk {n}** *n.*	masonry
Maskottchen {n} *n.*	mascot	**Maulbeerbaum {m}** *n.*	mulberry
Masochismus {m} *n.*	masochism	**Maultier {n}** *n.*	mule
Maß {n} *n.*	gauge	**Maulwurf {m}** *n.*	mole
Maß {n} *n.*	measure	**Maurer {m}** *n.*	mason
Massage {f} *n.*	massage	**Maus {f}** *n.*	mouse
Massaker {n} *n.*	massacre	**Mäuse {pl}** *n.*	lolly
Massaker {n} *n.*	slaughter	**mausen** *v.*	pilfer
Masse {f} *n.*	bulk	**mausern** *v.*	moult
Masseur {m} *n.*	masseur	**Mausoleum {n}** *n.*	mausoleum
Mäßigung {f} *n.*	moderation	**maximal** *n.*	maximum
Mäßigung {f} *n.*	temperance	**maximieren** *v.*	maximize
massiv *adj.*	massive	**Mayonnaise {f}** *n.*	mayonnaise
maßlos *adj.*	immoderate	**Mechanik {f}** *n.*	mechanics
Maßstab {m} *n.*	standard	**Mechaniker {m}** *n.*	mechanic
Mast {m} *n.*	mast	**mechanisch** *adj.*	mechanical
Mastdarm {m} *n.*	rectum	**Mechanismus {m}** *n.*	mechanism
mästen *v.*	cram	**meckern** *v. i*	bleat
mastizieren *v.*	masticate	**Medaille {f}** *n.*	medal
masturbieren *v.*	masturbate	**Medaillon {n}** *n.*	locket
Matador {m} *n.*	matador	**Media {f}** *n.*	media
Materialismus {m} *n.*	materialism	**Medikament {n}** *n.*	medication
Mathematik {f} *n.*	mathematics	**meditativ** *adj.*	ruminant
Mathematiker {m} *n.*	mathematician	**mediterran** *adj.*	Mediterranean
mathematisch *adj.*	mathematical	**meditieren** *v.*	meditate
Matinee {pl} *n.*	matinee	**Medium {n}** *n.*	medium
Matratze {f} *n.*	mattress	**Medizin {f}** *n.*	medicine

medizinisch	*adj.*	medical
medizinisch	*adj.*	medicinal
Meduse {f}	*n.*	jellyfish
Meer {n} *n.*		sea
Meeresschnecke {f}	*n.*	conch
mega	*adj.*	mega
Megabyte {n} *n.*		megabyte
Megafon {n} *n.*		megaphone
Megahertz {n}	*n.*	megahertz
Megalith {n} *n.*		megalith
Megapixel {n}*n.*		megapixel
Mehl {n} *n.*		flour
mehlig	*adj.*	mealy
mehr	*adj.*	more
Mehraufwand {m}	*adv.*	overhead
mehrdeutig	*adj.*	equivocal
mehrfach	*adj.*	manifold
mehrfach	*adj.*	plural
Mehrfachbetrieb {m}	*n.*	multiplex
mehrgebärend	*adj.*	multiparous
Mehrheit {f}	*n.*	majority
Mehrheit {f}	*n.*	plurality
meiden	*v.t.*	shun
Meile {f}	*n.*	mile
Meilenstein {m}	*n.*	milestone
mein	*pron.*	mine
mein	*adj.*	my
meinen	*v.*	mean
meinen	*v.*	opine
meinen	*v.t.*	reckon
Meinung {f}	*n.*	opinion
Meißel {m}	*n.*	chisel
Meister {m}	*n.*	champion
Meister {m}	*n.*	master
meistern *v.*		cope

meistern *v.*		manhandle
Meisterwerk {n}	*n.*	masterpiece
Melamin {n}	*n.*	melamine
Melassesirup {m}	*n.*	molasses
Melodie {f}	*n.*	melody
melodisch	*adj.*	melodic
Melodrama {n}	*n.*	melodrama
melodramatisch	*adj.*	melodramatic
Melone {f}	*n.*	melon
Membrane {f} *n.*		membrane
Memorandum {n}	*n.*	memorandum
Menge {f}	*n.*	crowd
Menge {f}	*n.*	multitude
Menge {f}	*pron.*	plenty
Menopause {f}	*n.*	menopause
Mensch {m}	*n.*	man
menschenfreundlich	*adj.*	
philanthropic		
Menschenkunde {f}	*n.*	
anthropology		
Menschheit {f}	*n.*	mankind
menschlich	*adj.*	human
Menschlichkeit {f} *n.*		humanity
Menstruation {f}	*n.*	menstruation
menstruell	*adj.*	menstrual
Mentalität {f} *n.*		mentality
Mentor {m}	*n.*	mentor
Menü {n}*n.*		menu
Mergel {m}	*n.*	marl
Meridian {m} *n.*		meridian
merkbar *adj.*	appreciable	
Merkblatt {n} *n.*		leaflet
Merkblatt {n} *n.*		pamphlet
Merkblatter {m}	*n.*	pamphleteer
merken *v.*		remark

317

Merkmal {m}	n.	cachet
Merkwürdigkeit {f}	n.	curiosity
Messbecher {m}	n.	beaker
Messe {f}	n.	mass
messen	v.	measure
messen	v.	mete
Messer {n}	n.	knife
Messgehilfe {f}	n.	acolyte
Messgerät {n}	n.	meter
Messias {m}	n.	messiah
Messing {n}	n.	brass
Messlatte {f}	n.	latte
Messung {f}	n.	measurement
Metall {n}	n.	metal
metallisch	adj.	metallic
Metallurgie {f}	n.	metallurgy
Metapher {n}	n.	metaphor
Metaphysik {f}	n.	metaphysics
metaphysisch	adj.	metaphysical
Meteor {m}	n.	meteor
meteorisch	adj.	meteoric
Meter {m,n}	n.	metre
Methode {f}	n.	method
Methodologie {f}	n.	methodology
metrisch	adj.	metric
metrisch	adj.	metrical
Metropole {f}	n.	metropolis
Metzger {m}	n.	butcher
Meute {f}	n.	mob
Meuterei {f}	n.	mutiny
Miasma {n}	n.	miasma
miauend	v.	mew
miefig	adj.	musty
mies	adj.	lousy
Miesmacher {m}	n.	defeatist

Mietbetrag {m}	n.	rental
Miete {f}	n.	lease
Mieter {m}	n.	tenant
Mietverhältnis {n}	n.	tenancy
Miezchen {n}	n.	puss
Migräne {f}	n.	migraine
Mikrobiologie {f}	n.	microbiology
Mikrochip {m}	n.	microchip
Mikrochirurgie {f}	n.	microsurgery
Mikrofilm {m}	n.	microfilm
Mikrometer {n}	n.	micrometer
Mikrophon {n}	n.	microphone
Mikroprozessor {m}	n.	microprocessor
Mikroskop {n}	n.	microscope
mikroskopisch	adj.	microscopic
Mikrowelle {f}	n.	microwave
Milbe {f}	n.	mite
Milch {f}	n.	milk
Milchgeschäft {n}	n.	dairy
milchig	adj.	milky
Milchshake {m}	n.	milkshake
Milchzucker {m}	n.	lactose
mild	adj.	gentle
Milieu {n}	n.	milieu
Militant {m}	n.	militant
militärisch	adj.	military
Miliz {f}	n.	militia
Milliardär {m}	n.	billionaire
Milliarde {f}	n.	billion
Milligramm {n}	n.	milligram
Millimeter {m,n}	n.	millimetre
Million {f}	n.	million
Millionär {m}	n.	millionaire
Milzbrand {m}	n.	anthrax
Mimik {f}	n.	mimic

Minarett {n} *n.*	minaret
Minderheit {f} *n.*	minority
Minderung {f} *n.*	depreciation
Minderwertigkeit {f} *n.*	inferiority
Mindestbetrag {m} *n.*	minim
Mineral {n} *n.*	mineral
Mineralogie {f} *n.*	mineralogy
Mineralwasser {n} *n.*	soda
mini *adj.* mini
Miniatur {f} *n.*	miniature
Minibus {m} *n.*	minibus
Minicab {n} *n.*	minicab
minimal *adj.* minimal
Minimum {n} *n.*	minimum
Minirock {m} *n.*	miniskirt
Ministerium {n} *n.* ministry
Minuspunkt {m} *n* demerit
Minute {f} *n.* minute
minuziös *adj.* meticulous
Minze {f} *n.* mint
mischen *v.t* mash
mischen *v.* mingle
Mischling {m} *n.* hybrid
Mischling {m} *n.* mongrel
Mischmasch {m} *n.* hotchpotch
Mischmasch {m} *n.* jumble
Mischpult {n} *n.* mixer
Mischung {f} *n.* melange
miserabel *adj.* abysmal
missachten *v. t* disregard
missachten *v.* disobey
Missallianz {f} *n.* misalliance
Missbildung {f} *n.* deformity
Missbildung {f} *n.* malformation
missbilligen *v.* deprecate

missbilligen *v.i* frown
missbilligend *v.* disapprove
missbrauchen *v.* abuse
missbrauchen *v.* misuse
missdeuten *v.* misconstrue
missdeuten *v.* misinterpret
Missetat {f} *n.* misdeed
Missetäter {m} *n.* malefactor
missfallen *v.* displease
Missfallen {n} *n.* disapproval
Missfallen {n} *n.* disfavour
Missfallen {n} *n.* displeasure
Missgeschick {n} *n.* adversity
Missgeschick {n} *n.* misadventure
Missgeschick {n} *n.* misfortune
misshandeln *v.* maltreat
misshandeln *v.* mishandle
Missionar {m} *n.* missionary
misslingen *v.* fail
misslingen *v.* miscarry
misstrauen *v.* mistrust
Misstrauen {n} *n.* distrust
misstrauisch *adj.* suspicious
Missverständnis {n} *n.* misapprehension
Missverständnis {n} *n.* misconception
Missverständnis {n} *n.* misunderstanding
missverstehen *v.* misapprehend
missverstehen *v.* misconceive
missverstehen *v.* misunderstand
Misswirtschaft {f} *n.* maladministration
Misswirtschaft {f} *n.* mismanagement
Mistelzweig {m} *n.* mistletoe
mit *prep.* with

mit Widerhaken *adj.* barbed
Mitarbeit {f} *n.* collaboration
Mitgift {f}*n.* dowry
Mitglied {n} *n.* member
Mitgliedschaft {f} *n.* membership
Mithilfe {f} *n.* aid
Mitleid {m} *n.* mercy
Mitleid {m} *n.* pity
Mitleid {n} *n.* charity
Mitleid {n} *n.* compassion
mitleidig *adj.* merciful
mitleidig *adj.* pitiful
Mitschuld {f} *n.* complicity
mitschuldig *adj.* complicit
Mittag {m} *n.* midday
Mittag {m} *n.* noon
Mittagessen {n} *n.* lunch
Mittagessen {n} *n.* luncheon
Mitte {f} *n.* centre
mitteilbar *adj.* communicable
mitteilen *v.* communicate
Mitteilung {f} *n.* communication
Mittel *adj.* middle
Mittel *adv.* midway
Mittel {n}*n.* means
mittelalterlich *adj.* medieval
Mittellinie {f} *adj.* median
mittellos *adj.* destitute
mittellos *adj.* penniless
mittelmäßig *adj.* mediocre
mittelmäßig *adj.* middling
mittelmäßig *adj.* moderate
Mittelmäßigkeit {f}*n.* mediocrity
Mittelpfosten {m} *n.* mullion
Mittelsmann {m} *n.* middleman

mittenunter *prep.* amid
Mitternacht {f} *n.* midnight
mittler *adj.* mid
Mittwoch {m} *n.* Wednesday
mitwirken *v.* concur
mixen *v.* mix
Mixer {m} *n.* blender
Möbel {n} *n.* furniture
Möbelspediteur {m} *n.* mover
mobil *adj.* mobile
mobilisieren *v.* mobilize
Mobilität {f} *n.* mobility
Mobiltelefon {n} *n.* cellphone
möblieren *v.* furnish
Möblierung {f} *n.* furnishing
Modalität {f} *n.* modality
Mode {f} *n.* fashion
Model {n} *n.* model
moderieren *v.* compere
moderig *adj.* frowsty
modern *adj.* latter
modern *adj.* modern
Moderne {f} *n.* modernity
modernisieren *v.* modernize
Modernismus {m} *n.* modernism
modisch *adj.* fashionable
modisch *adj.* modish
Modistin {f} *n.* milliner
Modul {n} *n.* module
modulieren *v.* modulate
Modus {m} *n.* mode
möglich *adj.* possible
Möglichkeit {f} *n.* chance
Möglichkeit {f} *n.* contingency
Möglichkeit {f} *n.* possibility

Möglichkeit {f}	*n.*	potentiality
Mokka {m}	*n.*	mocha
Molekül {n}	*n.*	molecule
molekular	*adj.*	molecular
mollig	*adj.*	plump
mollig	*adj.*	snug
Moment {m}	*n.*	momentum
momentan	*adj.*	momentary
Monarch {m}	*n.*	monarch
Monarchie {f}	*n.*	monarchy
Monat {m}	*n.*	month
monatlich	*adj.*	monthly
Mönch {m}	*n.*	monk
Mönchtum {n}	*n.*	monasticism
mond	*adj.*	lunar
Mond {m}	*n.*	moon
Mondlicht {n}	*n.*	moonlight
Mondsichel {f}	*n.*	crescent
monetär	*adj.*	monetary
monochrom	*n.*	monochrome
Monogamie {f}	*n.*	monogamy
Monogramm {n}	*n.*	monogram
Monokel {n}	*n.*	monocle
Monolith {m}	*n.*	monolith
Monolog {m}	*n.*	monologue
monophon	*adj.*	monophonic
Monopol {n}	*n.*	monopoly
monopolisieren	*v.*	monopolize
Monopolist {m}	*n.*	monopolist
Monotheismus {m}	*n.*	monotheism
Monotheist {m}	*n.*	monotheist
monoton	*adj.*	monotonous
Monster {m}	*n.*	monster
Monsun {m}	*n.*	monsoon
Montag {m}	*n.*	Monday

Montage {f}	*n.*	montage
monumental	*adj.*	monumental
Moor {n}	*n.*	bog
Moor {n}	*n.*	moor
Moos {n}	*n.*	moss
Moped {n}	*n.*	moped
Mopp {m}	*n.*	mop
Moral {f}	*n.*	morale
moralisch	*adj.*	moral
moralisieren	*v.*	moralize
Moralist {m}	*n.*	moralist
Moräne {f}	*n.*	moraine
Morast {m}	*n.*	morass
morbid	*adj.*	morbid
Mord {m}	*n.*	homicide
Mord {m}	*n.*	murder
Mörder {m}	*n.*	assassin
Mörder {m}	*n.*	murderer
mörderisch	*adj.*	gory
Mordsding {n}	*n.*	stunner
morgen	*adv.*	tomorrow
Morgen {m}	*n.*	morning
Morgenrot {n}	*n.*	dawn
Morphium {n}	*n.*	morphine
morsch	*adj.*	rotten
Mörser {m}	*n.*	mortar
Mosaik {n}	*n.*	mosaic
Moschee {f}	*n.*	mosque
Moschus {m}	*n.*	musk
Moskowiter {pl}	*n.*	muscovite
Moslem {m}	*n.*	Muslim
Motel {n}	*n.*	motel
Motiv {n}	*n.*	motif
Motiv {n}	*n.*	motive
motivieren	*v.*	motivate

321

Motor {m}	n.	engine	
Motor {m}	n.	motor	
Motorrad {n}	n.	motorcycle	
Motorradrennbahn {f}n.		speedway	
Motto {n}n.		motto	
Mousse {f}	n.	mousse	
Möwe {f} n.		gull	
Mozzarella {f}n.		mozzarella	
müde	adj.	tired	
müde	adj.	weary	
muffig	adj.	fusty	
muffig	adj.	smelly	
Mühe {f} n.		effort	
muhen	v.	moo	
mühevoll	adj.	troublesome	
Mühle {f}n.		mill	
Mulatte {m}	n.	mulatto	
Mulde {f}n.		trough	
Müll {m}	n.	garbage	
Müll {m}	n.	rubbish	
Mullah {m}	n.	mullah	
multikulturell adj.		multicultural	
Multimedia	n.	multimedia	
Multiplikation {f}	n.	multiplication	
multiplizieren v.		multiply	
Mumie {f}	n.	mummy	
mumifizieren v.		mummify	
Mumps {m}	n.	mumps	
Mund {m}	n.	mouth	
Mundart {f}	n.	dialect	
Mundart {f}	n.	idiom	
Mundart {f}	n.	vernacular	
Mundgeruch {m}	n.	halitosis	
mündlich	adj.	oral	
mündlich	adj.	verbal	

mündliche	adv.	orally	
Mundtuch {n}n.		napkin	
mundvoll	n.	mouthful	
Mungo {m}	n.	mongoose	
Munition {f}	n.	ammunition	
Munition {f}	n.	munitions	
Münster {m}	n.	minster	
munter	adj.	jaunty	
munter werden	v.	perk	
Münze {f}	n.	coin	
Münzwesen {n}	n.	coinage	
Murmel {f}	n.	marble	
murmeln v.		mumble	
murmeln v.		mutter	
mürrisch adj.		fractious	
mürrisch adj.		sullen	
Mus {n}	n.	mush	
Muschel {f}	n.	mussel	
Muschel {f}	n.	shell	
Muse {f} n.		muse	
Museum {n}	n.	museum	
Museumsdirektor {m}n.		curator	
Musik {f}n.		music	
musikalisch	adj.	musical	
Musiker {m}	n.	musician	
Muskel {m}	n.	muscle	
Muskelentzündung {f}n.		myosis	
Muskelschmerzen {pl}n.		myalgia	
Musketier {m}	n.	musketeer	
muskulös	adj.	muscular	
Müsli {n}n.		muesli	
Musselin {m}n.		muslin	
müssen v.		must	
müßig	adj.	otiose	
Mustang {m}	n.	mustang	

Muster {n}   *n.*   specimen
Musterknabe {m}   *n.*   paragon
mustern   *v.*   muster
Mut {m}   *n.*   boldness
Mut {m}   *n.*   courage
mutig   *adj.*   courageous
mutig   *adj.*   gamely
mutlos   *adj.*   despondent
mutlos   *adj.*   dispirited
Mutter {f}   *n.*   mother
mütterlich   *adj.*   maternal
mütterlich   *adj.*   motherly
Muttermord {m}   *n.*   matricide
Mutterschaft {f}   *n.*   maternity
Mutterschaft {f}   *n.*   motherhood
mutwillig *adj.*   sportive
Mütze {f} *n.*   bonnet
Mütze {f} *n.*   cap
Myriade {f}   *n.*   myriad
Myrre {f} *n.*   myrrh
Myrte {f} *n.*   myrtle
mysteriös   *adj.*   mysterious
Mystik {f}   *n.*   mysticism
mystisch *adj.*   mystical
mythisch   *adj.*   mythical
Mythologie {f}   *n.*   mythology
mythologische   *adj.*   mythological
Mythos {n}   *n.*   myth

N

nabel   *adj.*   umbilical
Nabob {m}   *n.*   nabob
Nachahmung {f}   *n.*   imitation
Nachbar {m}   *n.*   neighbour
nachbarlich   *adj.*   neighbourly

Nachbarschaft {f}   *n.*   vicinity
Nachbesprechung {f}   *v.*   debrief
Nachbildung {f}   *n.*   effigy
Nachbildung {f}   *n.*   replica
nachdem   *prep.*   after
nachdenklich *adj.*   meditative
nachdrücklich   *adj.*   emphatic
nacheifern   *v. t*   emulate
nachfolgen   *adv.*   consecutively
nachfolgend *adj.*   subsequent
Nachfolger {m}   *n.*   follower
Nachfolger {m}   *n.*   successor
Nachforschung {f} *n.*   investigation
nachgeben   *v.*   indulge
nachgeben   *v.*   relent
nachgemacht *adj.*   counterfeit
nachhallen   *v.*   resonate
Nachhängen {n}   *n.*   lagging
nachher   *adv.*   hereafter
Nachhinein   *n.*   hindsight
nachladen   *v.*   recharge
nachlassen   *adj.*   recessive
nachlässig   *adj.*   inattentive
nachlässig   *adj.*   negligent
Nachlässigkeit {f}   *n.*   negligence
Nachname {m}   *n.*   surname
Nacho {m}   *n.*   nacho
Nachricht {f}   *n.*   message
Nachricht {f}   *n.*   tidings
Nachrichtentechnik{f}   *n.*
    telecommunications
Nachschrift {f}   *n.*   postscript
Nachsicht {f}   *n.*   clemency
Nachsicht {f}   *n.*   indulgence
Nachsicht {f}   *n.*   leniency

323

nachsichtig	*adj.*	clement
nachsichtig	*adj.*	lenient
Nachsilbe {f}	*n.*	suffix
nächste	*adj.*	nearest
nächster	*adj.*	proximate
nächstes	*adj.*	next
Nacht {f}	*n.*	night
Nachteil {m}	*n.*	drawback
nachteilig	*adj.*	derogatory
nachteilig	*adj.*	prejudicial
Nachthemd {n}	*n.*	nightie
Nachtigall {f}	*n.*	nightingale
Nachtisch {m}	*n.*	sweet
nächtlich	*adj.*	nocturnal
Nachtwandeln {n}	*n.*	somnambulism
nachvollziehbar	*adj.*	comprehensible
nachweisen	*v.t.*	trace
nachweislich	*adj.*	traceable
Nachwelt {f}	*n.*	posterity
Nachwuchs {m}	*n.*	junior
Nachwuchs {m}	*n.*	offspring
nachzählen	*v.*	recount
nachziehen	*v.*	draw
Nachzügler {m}	*n.*	straggler
Nacken {m}	*n.*	nape
Nacken {m}	*n.*	neck
nackt	*adj.*	callow
nackt	*adj.*	naked
nackt	*adj.*	nude
Nacktheit {f}	*n.*	nudity
Nadel {f}	*n.*	needle
Nadel {f}	*n.*	pin
Nadelstich {m}	*n.*	stitch
Nagel {m}	*n.*	nail
Nagetier {n}	*n.*	rodent

nah	*adj.*	close
nahe	*adv.*	near
nahe	*adv.*	nigh
nähen	*v.*	sew
nähern	*v.i.*	near
Näherung {f}	*n.*	proximity
Nahkampf {m}	*n.*	infighting
nähren	*v.*	nourish
nahrhaft	*adj.*	nutritious
nahrhaft,	*adj.*	nutritive
Nährstoff {m}	*n.*	nutrient
Naht {f}	*n.*	fin
Naht {f}	*n.*	seam
nahtlos	*adj.*	seamless
Naivität {f}	*n.*	naivety
Naivling {m}	*n.*	simpleton
Name {m}	*n.*	name
namenlos	*adj.*	anonymous
namens	*n.*	behalf
Namensirrtum {m}	*n.*	misnomer
Namensvetter {m}	*n.*	namesake
namentlich	*adj.*	nominal
nämlich	*n.*	namely
Naphthalin {n}	*n.*	naphthalene
Narbe {f}	*n.*	scar
Narr {m}	*n.*	fool
Narzisse {f}	*n.*	daffodil
Narzisse {f}	*n.*	narcissus
Narzissmus {m}	*n.*	narcissism
nasal	*adj.*	nasal
Nase {f}	*n.*	nose
Nasenloch {n}	*n.*	nostril
Nasenstüber {m}	*n.*	fillip
Nashorn {n}	*n.*	rhinoceros
Nässe {f}	*n.*	wetness

Nation {f}	*n.*	nation
national *adj.*	national
Nationalismus {m}*n.*	nationalism
Nationalist {m}	*n.*	nationalist
Natur {f} *n.*	nature
naturalisieren*v.*	naturalize
Naturalisierung {f}*n.*	naturalization
Naturalist {m}*n.*	naturalist
naturbelassen	*adj.*	unadulterated
Naturismus {m}	*n.*	naturism
natürlich *adj.*	natural
nautisch *adj.*	nautical
naval	*adj.*	naval
Navigation {f}*n.*	navigation
Nebel {m}	*n.*	fog
Nebel {m}	*n.*	mist
Nebelfleck {m}	*n.*	nebula
nebelhaft	*adj.*	hazy
nebelhaft	*adj.*	misty
nebelig *adj.*	nebulous
neben *prep.*	beside
nebeneinander	*adv.*	abreast
Nebenfluss {m}	*n.*	tributary
Nebengebäude {n}	*n.*	outhouse
Nebenlinie {f} *n.*	byline
Nebenschluss {m}*v.*	shunt
Neffe {m}	*n.*	nephew
Negation {f}	*n.*	negation
negativ *adj.*	negative
Negativität {f}*n.*	negativity
Neger {m}	*n.*	negro
Negerin {f}	*n.*	negress
nehmen *v.*	take
Neid {m} *n.*	envy
neidisch *adj.*	envious

neidisch *adj.*	grudging
neigen	*v.*	incline
neigen	*v.*	slant
neigen	*v.*	slope
Neigung {f}	*n.*	inclination
Neigung {f}	*n.*	liking
Neigung {f}	*n.*	proclivity
nein *adv.* nay
Nektar {m}	*n.*	nectar
Nektarine {f}	*n.*	nectarine
Nelke {f} *n.*	clove
Nemesis {f}	*n.*	nemesis
Nenner {m}	*n.*	denominator
neoklassisch *adj.*	neoclassical
Neon {n} *n.*	neon
Neptunium {n}	*n.*	Neptune
Nerv {m} *n.*	Nerve
nerven *v.*	annoy
Nervenfaserbündel {pl}*n.*
	commissure
Nervenkitzel {m}	*n.*	thrill
nervös	*adj.*	edgy
nervös	*adj.*	nervous
nervösen	*adj.*	nervy
nervtötend	*adj.*	tedious
Nerz {m} *n.*	mink
Nessel {f}	*n.*	nettle
Nest {n} *n.*	nest
Nesthäkchen {n}	*n.*	nestling
nett *adj.* natty
Netz {n} *n.*	net
Netz {n} *n.*	web
Netzhaut {f}	*n.*	retina
Netzwerk {n} *n.*	network
neu *adj.* new

neue	adv.	anew
neue	adj.	recent
Neuerung {f}	n.	innovation
neugierig	adj.	curious
neugierig	adj.	inquisitive
neugierig	adj.	nosy
neugierig sein	v.	pry
Neuigkeit {f}	n.	novelty
Neuigkeiten {pl}	n.	news
neulich	adv.	lately
neulich	adv.	newly
neulich	adv.	recently
Neuling {m}	n.	neophyte
neun	adj. & n.	nine
neunte	adj. & n.	ninth
neunzehn	adj. & n.	nineteen
neunzehnte	adj. & n.	nineteenth
neunzig	adj. & n.	ninety
neunzigste	adj. & n.	ninetieth
neural	adj.	neural
Neureiche {m}	n.	upstart
Neurologe {m}	n.	neurologist
Neurologie {f}	n.	neurology
Neurose {f}	n.	neurosis
neurotisch	adj.	neurotic
neutral	adj.	neutral
neutralisieren	v.	neutralize
Neutron {n}	n.	neutron
nicht	adj.	no
nicht	adv.	not
nicht zustimmend	v.	disagree
Nichtbeachtung {f}	n.	oblivion
Nichte {f}	n.	niece
nichts	pron.	nothing
Nichts {n}	n.	zilch

Nichtsein {n}	n.	nonentity
Nichtübereinstimmung {f}	n.	mismatch
Nichtübereinstimmung {f}	n. nonconformist	
Nickel {n}	n.	nickel
Nicken {n}	v.	nod
Niederschlag {m}	n.	rainfall
niederwerfend	adj.	prostrate
Niederwerfung {f}	n.	prostration
niedlich	adj.	neat
niedrig	adj.	low
niedriger	adj.	lower
niemals	adv.	never
niemand	pron.	nobody
Niere {f}	n.	kidney
niesen	v.i.	sneeze
Niete {f}	n.	rivet
Nigger {m}	n.	nigger
Nihilismus {n}	n.	nihilism
Nikotin {n}	n.	nicotine
nirgendwohin	adv.	nowhere
Nirvana {n}	n.	nirvana
Nische {f}	n.	alcove
Nische {f}	n.	niche
Niveau {n}	n.	level
Nixe {f}	n.	mermaid
noch	adj.	still
noch	adv.	yet
nochmals	adv.	again
Nockenstößel {m}	n.	tappet
nölitisch	adj.	Neolithic
Nomade {n}	n.	nomad
nomadisch	adj.	nomadic
Nomenklatur {f}	n.	nomenclature
nominieren	v.	nominate

Nonne {f}	*n.*	nun
Nonnenkloster {n} *n.*		nunnery
nonstop *adj.*	nonstop	
Noppe {f}	*n.*	nap
Norden {m}	*n.*	north
nördlich *adj.*	Nordic	
nördlich *adj.*	northerly	
nördlich *adj.*	northern	
Norm {f} *n.*	norm	
normal *adj.*	normal	
normalerweise	*adv.* naturally	
normalisieren *v.*	normalize	
Normalität {f} *n.*	normalcy	
normativ *adj.*	normative	
normieren	*v.*	standardize
Nostalgie {f}	*n.*	nostalgia
Not {f}	*n.*	misery
Not {f}	*n.*	hardship
Notar {m}	*n.*	notary
Note {f}	*n.*	note
notiert *adj.*	noted	
nötig *adj.*	needful	
Notiz {f}	*n.*	memo
Notiz {f}	*n.*	notification
Notizbuch {n} *n.*	diary	
Notizbuch {n} *n.*	notebook	
Notsituation {f}	*n.*	emergency
Notstand {m} *n.*	crisis	
notwendigerweise *adv.* necessarily		
Nougat {m,n} *n.*	nougat	
Novelle {f}	*n.*	novelette
November {m}	*n.*	november
nüchtern *adj.*	demure	
nüchtern *adj.*	sober	
Nudeln {pl}	*n.*	noodles

Nudeln {pl}	*n.*	pasta
Nudist {m}	*n.*	nudist
nuklear *adj.*	nuclear	
Null {f}	*n.*	nil
Null {f}	*n.*	nought
Null {f}	*adj.*	null
Null {f}	*n.*	trice
Null {f}	*adj.*	zero
numerisch	*adj.*	numerical
Nummer {f}	*n.*	number
nur *adj.* mere		
nur *adv.* only		
Nutte {f} *n.*	whore	
nützen	*v.*	avail
Nutzholz {n}	*n.*	timber
nützlich *adj.*	beneficial	
nützlich *adj.*	handy	
Nützlichkeit {f}	*n.*	utility
nutzlos *adj.*	abortive	
nutzlos *adj.*	needless	
Nylon {n}	*n.*	nylon
Nymphe	nymph	

O

Oase {f} *n.*	oasis	
ob *conj.* whether		
oben	*adv.* above	
oben	*adv.* aloft	
obendrein	*adv.* withal	
Oberaufsicht {f}	*n.*	superintendence
oberer *adj.*	superior	
oberer *adj.*	upper	
oberflächlich *adj.*	superficial	
oberflächliche	*adj.*	cursory
oberflächliche	*adj.*	perfunctory

Oberflächlichkeit {f}   n.superficiality
Oberflächlichkeiten {pl}   n.
   smattering
oberhalb *prep.*   above
Oberhaupt {n}   *n.*   boss
Oberkörper {m}   *n.*   torso
Oberlicht {n}   *n.*   skylight
Oberschwelle {f}   *n.*   lintel
Oberschwingung {f}   *n.*   overtone
Oberst {m}   *n.*   colonel
obgleich *conj.* albeit
Objekt {n}   *n.*   object
objektiv *adj.* objective
obliegend   *adj.*   incumbent
obligatorisch *adj.* compulsory
obligatorisch *adj.* mandatory
Obmann {m}   *n.*   umpire
obschon *conj.* though
Obst {n}   *n.*   fruit
Obstgarten {m}   *n.*   orchard
obszön *adj.* obscene
obwohl *conj.* although
Ochse {m}   *n.*   bullock
Ochse {m}   *n.*   ox
Octree {m}   *n.*   octree
öde *adj.* bleak
oder*conj.*   or
Ofen {m}*n.*   oven
offen   *adj.*   frank
offen   *adj.*   open
offen   *adv.* openly
offenbar *adj.* apparent
offenbar *adj.* manifest
offenkundig *adj.* overt
öffentlich   *adj.* public

offiziell   *adj.* official
offiziell   *adv.* officially
offshore *adj.* offshore
oftmal   *adv.* oft
ohne   *prep.*   without
Ohr {n}   *n.*   ear
Ökologie {f}   *n.*   ecology
Oktavband {m}   *n.*   octavo
Oktave {f}   *n.*   octave
Oktober {m}   *n.*   October
Öl {n}   *n.*   oil
ölig *adj.* oily
Oligarchie {f} *n.*   oligarchy
Olive {f}   *n.*   olive
Olympiasieger {m}   *n.*   medallist
olympisch   *adj.* Olympic
Omelette {n}   *n.*   omelette
Omnibus {n}   *n.*   omnibus
Onkel {m}   *n.*   uncle
onkelhaft   *adj.* avuncular
Onomatopöie {f}   *n.*   onomatopoeia
Ontologie {f} *n.*   ontology
Onyx {m}   *n.*   onyx
Opal {m} *n.*   opal
Oper {f} *n.*   opera
Operation {f} *n.*   surgery
operativ *adj.* operational
Operator {m} *n.*   operator
Opfer {n}*n.*   sacrifice
Opfergabe {f} *n.*   oblation
opfern   *v.*   immolate
opfern   *v.*   sacrifice
opfern   *v.*   victimize
opfernd *adj.* sacrificial
Opium {n}   *n.*   opium

328

Opportunismus {m}   n. opportunism
Optiker {m}   n.   optician
optimal   adj. optimum
optimieren   v.   optimize
Optimismus {m}   n.   optimism
Optimist {m}   n.   optimist
optimistisch   adj. optimistic
optisch   adj. optic
Orakel {n}   n.   oracle
orakelhaft   adj. oracular
Orange {n}   n.   orange
Orchester {n} n.   orchestra
orchestral   adj. orchestral
Orchidee {f}   n.   orchid
ordentlich   adv. fairly
ordentlich   adj. steady
Ordnungsliebe {f} n.   tidiness
ordnungsmäßig   adv. duly
Organisation {f}   n.   organization
organisch   adj. organic
organisch   n.   organism
organisieren v.   organize
Orgasmus {m}   n.   orgasm
Orgel {f} n.   organ
Orgie {f} n.   orgy
Orient {m}   n.   east
Orient {m}   n.   orient
orientieren   v.   orientate
Origami {f}   n.   origami
original   adj. original
Ornament {n} n.   ornament
Ort {m}   n.   place
orthodoxe   adj. orthodox
Orthodoxie {f}   n.   orthodoxy

Orthopädie {f}   n.   orthopaedics
örtlich   adj. local
Örtlichkeit {f} n.   locality
Ortsansässiger   n.   resident
Ortskurve {f} n.   locus
Osman {m}   n.   ottoman
Ostblock {m} n.   bloc
Osteopathie   n.   osteopathy
österlich adj. eastern
Ostern {n}   n.   Easter
östlich   adj. oriental
Otter {m}n.   otter
Ouvertüre {f}   n.   overture
oval adj. oval
Ovation {f}   n.   ovation
Oxid {n}   n.   oxide
Ozean {m}   n.   ocean
ozeanisch   adj. oceanic
Ozon {n} n   ozone

P

Paar {n}   n.   couple
Paar {n}   n.   pair
Pack {n} n.   pack
Päckchen {n} n.   parcel
packen   v. t. clutch
Pädagoge {m}   n.   pedagogue
Pädagogik {pl}   n.   pedagogy
Paddelboot {n}   n.   canoe
Pädiatrie {f}   n.   paediatrics
Pädophile {m,f}   n.   paedophile
Pagode {f}   n.   pagoda
Paisleymuster {n} n.   paisley
Paket {n}n.   package
Paket {n}n.   packet

Pakt {m}	n.	covenant
Palast {m}	n.	palace
palastartig	adj.	palatial
Palette {f}	n.	palette
Palette {f}	n.	pallet
Palme {f}n.		palm
Panda {m}	n.	panda
Paneel {n}	n.	panel
Panik {f} n.		panic
Pankreas {n} n.		pancreas
Panorama {n}n.		panorama
Pantheismus {m}	n.	pantheism
pantheist	adj.	pantheist
Panther {m}	n.	panther
Pantomime {f}	n.	mime
Pantomime {f}	n.	pantomime
Panzer {m}	n.	armour
Panzerfaust {f}	n.	bazooka
Papa {m}n		dad
Papagei {m}	n.	parrot
Pappel {f}	n.	poplar
Paprika {m}	n.	capsicum
Papst {m}	n.	pope
päpstlich	adj.	papal
Papsttum {n} n.		papacy
Parabel {m}	n.	parable
Parade {f}	n.	parade
paradierend	v.	flaunt
Paradies {n}	n.	paradise
paradox adj. paradoxical		
Paradox {m}	n.	paradox
Paraffin {n}	n.	paraffin
Parallele {f}	n.	parallel
Parallelogramm {n}		n.
parallelogram		

Paralyse {f}	n.	paralysis
paralytisch	adj.	paralytic
Parameter {m}	n.	parameter
Parasit {m}	n.	parasite
Parfüm {n}	n.	perfume
parfümiert	adv.	perfume
Pari n.		par
parieren v.		parry
Parität {f}	n.	parity
Park {m} n.		park
Parlament {n}n.		parliament
Parlamentarier {m} n.parliamentarian		
parlamentarisch	adj.	parliamentary
Parodie {f}	n.	parody
Parodontose {f}	n.	pyorrhoea
Parteienvertretend (zwei)		adj.
bipartisan		
Parteilichkeit {f}	n.	partiality
partiell adj. partial		
Partikel {n}	n.	particle
Partner {m}	n.	mate
Partnerschaft {f}	n.	partnership
Party {f} n.		fete
Party {f} n.		party
Passagier {m}	n.	passenger
passiv adj. passive		
passt,	adj.	fit
Pastell {n}	n.	pastel
Pastetchen {n}	n.	patty
Pastete {f}	n.	pasty
pasteurisiert adj. pasteurized		
Pastor {m}	n.	parson
pastoral adj. pastoral		
Patenkind {n}n.		godchild
Patenstelle {f}	n.	sponsorship

Patent {n}   *n.*   patent
Pathologie {f} *n.*   pathology
Pathos {m}   *n.*   pathos
Patient   *n.*   outpatient
Patient {m}   *n.*   patient
Patin {f}   *n.*   godmother
Patriarch {m} *n.*   patriarch
Patriot {m}   *n.*   patriot
patriotisch   *adj.*   patriotic
Patriotismus {m}   *n.*   patriotism
Patt {n}   *n.*   stalemate
patzig   *adj.*   stroppy
Pause {f} *n.*   intermission
Pause {f} *n.*   pause
Pause {f} *n.*   respite
Pavian {m}   *n.*   baboon
Pavillon {m}   *n.*   pavilion
Pazifik {m}   *n.*   pacific
Pazifist {m}   *n.*   pacifist
Pecan {m}   *n.*   pecan
Pechvogel {m}   *n.*   jinx
Pedant {m}   *n.*   pedant
pedantisch   *adj.*   pedantic
Pediküre {f}   *n.*   pedicure
Pein {f}   *n.*   anguish
peinigen *v.*   tantalize
peinlich *adj.*   awkward
peitschen   *v.*   flog
peitschen   *v.*   lash
Pelikan {m}   *n.*   pelican
Pelz {m} *n.*   fur
Pendel {n}   *n.*   pendulum
pendeln *v.*   commute
Pendelverkehr {m}   *n.*   shuttle
Penis {m}   *n.*   penis

Penny {m}   *n.*   penny
Pension {f}   *n.*   pension
Pensionierung {f} *n.*   superannuation
Pensum {n}   *n.*   stint
Pentagon {n} *n.*   pentagon
Penthouse {n}   *n.*   penthouse
peptisch *adj.*   peptic
perfekt *adj.*   perfect
perforieren   *v.*   perforate
periodisch   *adj.*   cyclic
periodisch   *adj.*   periodic
periodische *adj.*   periodical
Peripherie {f} *n.*   periphery
Perle {f}   *n.*   pearl
perlen   *v.*   fizz
perlend *adj.*   beady
Permutation {f}   *n.*   permutation
Person {f}   *n.*   person
Personal {n}   *n.*   personnel
Personal {n}   *n.*   staff
Personifikation {f} *n.*   impersonation
personifizieren   *v.*   personify
persönlich   *adj.*   personal
Persönlichkeit {f} *n.*   personage
Persönlichkeit {f} *n.*   personality
Perücke {f}   *n.*   wig
pervers *adj.*   perverse
Perversion {f} *n.*   perversion
pervertieren   *v.*   pervert
Pervertiertheit {f} *n.*   perversity
Pessimist {m}   *n.*   pessimist
pessimistisch   *adj.*   pessimistic
Pessismismus {m}   *n.*   pessimism
Pesthauch {m}   *n.*   blight
Pestizid {n}   *n.*   pesticide

331

Pfadfinder {m}	*n.*	scout
Pfahl {m}*n.*		picket
Pfahl {m}*n.*		pole
Pfandleiher {m}	*n.*	pawnbroker
Pfandrecht {n}	*n.*	lien
Pfanne {f}	*n.*	pan
Pfarrer {m}	*n.*	minister
Pfarrer {m}	*n.*	pastor
Pfau {m} *n.*		peacock
Pfauenhenne {f}	*n.*	peahen
Pfeffer {m}	*n.*	pepper
Pfefferminz {n}	*n.*	peppermint
Pfeife {f} *n.*		pipe
Pfeil {m} *n.*		dart
Pfeiler {m}	*n.*	pier
Pfeiler {m}	*n.*	pillar
Pfeiler {m}	*n.*	stilt
Pferd {n}*n.*		horse
Pferdestall {m}	*n.*	stable
Pferdestärke *n.*		horsepower
Pfiff {m} *n.*		whistle
pfiffig	*adj.*	smart
pfiffig	*adj.*	snazzy
Pfirsich {m}	*n.*	peach
Pflanzenkunde {f} *n.*		botany
Pflanzung {f} *n.*		plantation
pflastern *v.*		pave
Pflaume {f}	*n.*	plum
Pflegekraft {f}*n.*		carer
pflegen	*v.*	groom
pflegen	*v.*	nurture
pflegen	*v.*	trim
Pflicht {f}	*n.*	obligation
pflichtgemäß *adj.*		dutiful
pflücken *v.*		pick

Pflug {m}	*n.*	plough
Pflüger {m}	*n.*	ploughman
Pforte {f}*n.*		portal
Pförtner {m}	*n.*	porter
Pfote {f} *n.*		paw
Pfund *n.*		pound
Pfund {n}	*n.*	quid
Pfütze {f}*n.*		puddle
Phänomen {n}	*n.*	phenomenon
phänomenal *adj.*		phenomenal
Phantasie {f} *n.*		fantasy
phantasiereich	*adj.*	fanciful
phantasieren *v.*		fantasize
phantastisch *adj.*		visionary
Phantom {n} *n.*		phantom
Pharmazeut {m}	*n.*	pharmacist
Pharmazeutisch *adj.*		pharmaceutical
Phase {f}*n.*		phase
Philanthrop {m}	*n.*	philanthropist
Philanthropie {f}	*n.*	philanthropy
Philatelie {f}	*n.*	philately
Philologe {m}*n.*		philologist
Philologie {f}	*n.*	philology
philologisch *adj.*		philological
Philosoph {m}	*n.*	philosopher
Philosophie {f}	*n.*	philosophy
philosophischen *adj.*		philosophical
phlegmatisch *adj.*		phlegmatic
Phobie {f}	*n.*	phobia
phonetisch	*adj.*	phonetic
Phönix {m}	*n.*	phoenix
Phosphat {n} *n.*		phosphate
Phosphor {n} *n.*		phosphorus
phrasenhaft	*adj.*	rhetorical
Physik {f}	*n.*	physics

German		English
Physiognomie {f}	*n.*	physiognomy
Physiotherapie {f}	*n.*	physiotherapy
Pianist {m}	*n.*	pianist
Pickel {m}	*n.*	pimple
picken	*v.i.*	peck
Picknick {n}	*n.*	picnic
piekfein	*adj.*	posh
piepsen	*v.*	cheep
piepsen	*v.*	peep
Piepsen {n}	*n.*	bleep
Pietät {f}	*n.*	piety
pietätlos	*adj.*	impious
Pigment {n}	*n.*	pigment
pikant	*adj.*	piquant
Piktogramm {n}	*n.*	pictograph
Pilger {m}	*n.*	pilgrim
Pilgerschaft {f}	*n.*	pilgrimage
Pille {f}	*n.*	pill
Pilot {m}	*n.*	pilot
Pilz {m}	*n.*	mushroom
Pilz {m}	*n.*	fungus
Pinguin {m}	*n.*	penguin
Pinne {f}	*n.*	helm
Pinzette {f}	*n.*	tweezers
Pionier {m}	*n.*	pioneer
Pipette {f}	*n.*	pipette
Pirat {m}	*n.*	pirate
Pirschjäger {m}	*n.*	stalker
Pissoir {n}	*n.*	urinal
Pistole {f}	*n.*	pistol
Pistolentasche {f}	*n.*	holster
pittoresk	*adj.*	picturesque
Pivot {n}	*n.*	pivot
Pixel {n}	*n.*	pixel
Pizza {f}	*n.*	pizza

German		English
Plackerei {f}	*v.*	grind
plädieren	*v.*	plead
Plakat {n}	*n.*	placard
Plan {m}	*n.*	plan
Planet {m}	*n.*	planet
planetar	*adj.*	planetary
planieren	*v.t.*	flatten
Planke {f}	*n.*	plank
Plänkelei {f}	*n.*	skirmish
planmäßig	*adj.*	systematic
Planung {f}	*n.*	design
plappern	*v.*	burble
plappern	*v.*	gab
plappern	*v.*	jabber
plappern	*v.*	rap
plappern	*v.*	spurt
Plastik {f}	*n.*	plastic
Plateau {n}	*n.*	plateau
Platin {n}*n.*		platinum
platonisch	*adj.*	platonic
Platte {f}	*n.*	ledge
Platte {f}	*n.*	sheet
Plattheit {f}	*n.*	trivia
Platz	*n.*	square
Platzhalter {m}	*n.*	substitution
Plauderei {f}	*v. i.*	chat
plaudern	*v.*	prattle
Plaza {f}	*n.*	plaza
plebejisch	*adj.*	plebeian
Plebiszit {n}	*n.*	plebiscite
Plinthe {f}	*n.*	plinth
plötzlich	*adj.*	sudden
plötzlich	*adv.*	suddenly
Pluderhosen {pl}	*n.*	bloomers
plump	*adj.*	clumsy

Plumps {m}	n.	bump
plumpsen	v.	slump
plumpsen	v.	flop
Plünderer {m}	n.	marauder
plündern v.		maraud
plündern v.		plunder
Plüsch {m}	n.	plush
Pöbel {m}	n.	populace
pochieren	v.	poach
Pocken {pl}	n.	smallpox
Podcast {n}	n.	podcast
Podium {n}	n.	dais
Podium {n}	n.	platform
Podium {n}	n.	podium
Poet {m} n.		poet
Pokal {f} n.		cup
Poker {m}	n.	poker
polar	adj.	polar
Polemik {f}	n.	polemic
poliert	adj.	slick
Politik {f}n.		politics
Politiker n.		politician
politisch adj.		political
Politur {f}	n.	polish
Polizei {f}	n.	police
Polizeiaufgebot {n}	n.	platoon
Polizeidirektor {m}	n.	marshal
Polizeitruppe {f}	n.	constabulary
Polizist {m}	n.	constable
Polizist {m}	n.	policeman
Poller {m}	n.	bollard
Polohemd {n}n.		polo
Polstermöbel {n}	n.	upholstery
polstern v.		upholster
Polyandrie {f}n.		polyandry

polygam adj.		polygamous
Polygamie {f} n.		polygamy
Polygraph {m}	n.	polygraph
Polytechnik n.		polytechnic
Polytheismus {m} n.		polytheism
polytheistisch	adj.	polytheistic
Pomp {m}	n.	pageant
Pony {n} n.		pony
Pop {m} v.		pop
Popelin {m}	n.	poplin
populär adj.		popular
popularisieren	v.	popularize
Popularität {f}	n.	vogue
Pore {f} n.		pore
Pornographie {f}	n.	pornography
porös	adj.	cavernous
Portier {m}	n.	janitor
Portion {f}	n.	serving
Porto {n}n.		postage
Portrait {n}	n.	portrait
porträtieren	v.	portray
Porträtphotographie {f}		
	n.	portraiture
Porzellan {n} n.		china
Porzellan {n} n.		porcelain
posieren v.		pose
positiv adj.		positive
Posse {f}n.		burlesque
Posse {f}n.		farce
Possen {pl}	n.	antic
Possen {pl}	n.	prank
Post {f} n.		mail
postalisch	adj.	postal
Postamt {f}	n.	postoffice
Poster {n}	n.	poster

posthum *adj.* posthumous
Postkarte {f} *n.* postcard
Postkutsche {f} *n.* stagecoach
Postleitzahl {f} *n.* postcode
Postmeister {m} *n.* postmaster
postmortal *n.* postmortem
postulieren *v.* posit
potent *adj.* potent
potentiell *adj.* potential
Potenz {f} *n.* potency
Potenz {f} *n.* virility
Präambel {f} *n.* preamble
prächtig *adj.* glorious
prächtig *adj.* showy
prachtvoll *adj.* gorgeous
Prädestination {f} *n.* predestination
Prädikat {n} *n.* predicate
Prafekt *n.* prefect
Präfix {n} *n.* prefix
pragmatisch *adj.* pragmatic
Pragmatismus {m} *n.* pragmatism
prägnant *adj.* succinct
prähistorisch *adj.* prehistoric
prahlen *v.* boast
prahlen *v.* brag
prahlerisch *adj.* vainglorious
praktikabel *adj.* feasible
Praktikant {m} *n.* trainee
Praktiker {m} *n.* practitioner
praktisch *adj.* practical
praktizieren *v.* practise
Prälat {n} *n.* prelate
Praline {f} *n.* praline
Prämie {f} *n.* bonus
Prämie {f} *n.* prize

Prämisse {f} *n.* premise
Präposition {f} *n.* preposition
präsent *adj.* present
Präsentation {f} *n.* presentation
präsentieren *v.* present
Präsident {m} *n.* president
präsidential *adj.* presidential
präsidieren *v.* preside
Präzedenzfall {m} *n.* precedent
Präzision {f} *n.* precision
Präzisionsschütze {m} *n.* marksman
predigen *v.* preach
predigen *v.* sermonize
Prediger {m} *n.* preacher
Predigt {f} *n.* sermon
Preis {m} *n.* price
Preisaufschlag {m} *n.* surcharge
Preisgebung {f} *n.* revelation
Preisträger {m} *n.* laureate
Prellung {f} *n.* bruise
Premiere {f} *n.* premiere
pressen *v.* press
Prestige {n} *n.* prestige
prestigevoll *adj.* prestigious
prickeln *v.* sparkle
Priester {m} *n.* priest
Priesterschaft {f} *n.* priesthood
primär *adj.* main
Primat {m} *n.* primate
primitiv *adj.* primitive
Prinz {m} *n.* prince
Prinzessin {f} *n.* princess
Prinzgemahl {m} *n.* consort
Prinzip {n} *n.* principle
Prinzipal {m} *n.* principal

prinzlich *adj.* princely
Priorität {f} *n.* precedence
Priorität {f} *n.* priority
Prisma {n} *n.* prism
privat *adj.* private
privatisieren *v.* privatize
Privatsphäre {f} *n.* privacy
proaktiv *adj.* proactive
Probe {f} *n.* probe
Probe {f} *n.* proof
Probe {f} *n.* rehearsal
Probe {f} *n.* test
Probekandidat {m} *n.* probationer
proben *v.* rehearse
Probierer {m} *n.* sampler
Problem {n} *n.* problem
problematisch *adj.* problematic
Problembehandlung {f} *n.* troubleshooting
Produkt {n} *n.* product
produktiv *adj.* productive
Produktivität {f} *n.* productivity
professionell *adj.* professional
Professor {m} *n.* professor
Profi {m} *n.* pro
Profil {n} *n.* moulding
Profil {n} *n.* profile
Profilsehne {f} *n.* chord
Profit {m} *n.* profit
Prognose {f} *n.* prognosis
Programm {n} *n.* programme
Projekt {n} *n.* project
Projektil {n} *n.* projectile
Projektion {f} *n.* projection
Projektor {m} *n.* projector

Proklamation {f} *n.* proclamation
proklamieren *v.* proclaim
prolabieren *v.* prolapse
Prolet {m} *n.* cad
Prolog {m} *n.* prologue
Prominente {m} *adj.* prominent
promovieren *n.* graduate
Pronomen {n} *n.* pronoun
Propaganda {f} *n.* advertisement
Propaganda {f} *n.* propaganda
propagieren *v.* publicize
Propeller {m} *n.* propeller
prophetisch *adj.* prophetic
prophezeien *v.* prophesy
Prophezeier {m} *n.* prophet
Prophezeiung {f} *n.* prediction
Prophezeiung {f} *v.* presage
Prophezeiung {f} *n.* prophecy
proportional *adj.* proportional
Prosa {f} *n.* prose
prosaisch *adj.* prosaic
Prosperität {f} *n.* prosperity
Prostituierte {m,f} *n.* prostitute
Prostitution {f} *n.* prostitution
Protest {m} *n.* protest
protestieren *v.* remonstrate
Protokoll {n} *n.* protocol
Prototyp {m} *n.* prototype
protzig *adj.* snobbish
Provinz {f} *n.* province
provisorisch *adj.* provisional
provisorisch *adj.* tentative
provozieren *v.* provoke
Prozedur {f} *n.* procedure
Prozentsatz {m} *n.* percentage

Prozessführer {m} n.	litigant
prozessieren v.	litigate
Prozession {f}	n.	procession
Prozessliste {f}	n.	docket
prüde	adj.	crass
Prüde {f} n.	prude
prüfen v.	canvass
prüfen v.	check
prüfen v.	examine
prüfen v.	scrutinize
prüfen v.	verify
prüfen sich	v.	introspect
Prüfer {m}	n.	trier
Prüfling {m}	n.	examinee
Prüfung {f}	n.	exam
Prüfung {f}	n.	scrutiny
Prunk {m}	n.	pageantry
prunkvoll	adj.	pompous
Psalm {m}	n.	psalm
Pseudonym {n}	n.	alias
Pseudonym {n}	n.	pseudonym
Psyche {f}	n.	psyche
Psychiater {m}	n.	psychiatrist
Psychiatrie {f}	n.	psychiatry
psychisch	adj.	psychic
Psychologe {m}	n.	psychologist
Psychologie {f}	n.	psychology
psychologisch	adj.	psychological
Psychopathe {m}	n.	psychopath
Psychose {f} n.	psychosis
Psychotherapie {f}	n.psychotherapy
pubertär adj.	adolescent
Pubertät {f}	n.	puberty
Pudding {m} n.	pudding
Puder {n}	n.	powder

Puff {m} n.	brothel
Pufferspeicher {m}	n.	cache
Pullover {m} n.	sweater
Puls {m} n.	pulse
pulsieren v.	pulsate
Pulsschlag {m}	n.	pulsar
Pulsschlag {m}	n.	pulsation
Pumpe {f}	n.	pump
Punkt {m}	n.	dot
Punkt {m}	n.	point
pünktlich	adj.	punctual
Pünktlichkeit {f}	n.	punctuality
Puppe {f}	n.	doll
Purist {m}	n.	purist
Puritaner {m} n.	puritan
puritanisch	adj.	puritanical
Purpurr n.	purple
Pustel {f}n.	blain
Putsch {m}	n.	coup
Pygmäe {m}	n.	pygmy
Pyjama {f}	n.	pyjamas
Pyramide {f}	n.	pyramid
Pyromanie {f}n.	pyromania
Pythonschlange {f} python

Q

Quacksalber {m}	n.	charlatan
Quacksalberei {f}	n.	quackery
Quadrant {m} n.	quadrant
quaken n.	croak
quaken v.i.	quack
quäken v.	squawk
Quäker {m}	n.	quaker
Qual {f}	n.	agony
Qual {f}	n.	pain

Qual {f}	n.	torment	
Qual {f}	n.	torture	
quälen	v.	afflict	
quälen	v.	agonize	
quälen	v.	obsess	
quälen	v.i.	toil	
Quäler {m}	n.	tormentor	
qualifizieren	v.	qualify	
Qualität {f}	n.	quality	
qualitativ	adj.	qualitative	
quantitativ	adj.	quantitative	
Quarantäne {f}	n.	quarantine	
Quark {n}	n.	quark	
Quart {f} n.		quart	
Quartett {n}	n.	quartet	
Quartier {f}	n.	cantonment	
Quarz {m}	n.	quartz	
quasseln v.		yap	
Quast {m}	n.	tassel	
Quatsch {m}	n.	bunk	
Quatsch {m}	n.	trash	
Quecksilber {n}		n.	mercury
queradj.		oblique	
queradj.		transverse	
Querbehang {m}		n.	pelmet
quetschen	v.	squeeze	
quetschen	v.	squish	
quietschen	n.	squeak	
Quinärzahl {f}n.		quin	
Quintessenz {f}		n.	quintessence
quittadj.	quits		
Quitte {f}n.		quince	
Quiz {n} n.		quiz	
Quorum {n}	n.	quorum	
Quote {f}n.		quota	

Quotient {m}	n.	quotient	

R

Rabatt {m}	n.	discount	
Rabatt {m}	n.	rebate	
Rabe {m}n.		raven	
Rache {f}n.		revenge	
Rache {f}n.		vengeance	
rächen	v.	avenge	
racheschnauben	adj.	vengeful	
Rachitis {f}	n.	rickets	
rackern	v.	moil	
Rad {n}	n.	wheel	
Radar {m,n}	n.	radar	
Radfahrer {m}		n.	cyclist
radial	adj.	radial	
Radieschen {n}		n.	radish
radikal	adj.	radical	
radikal	pref.	ultra	
Radio {n}		n.	radio
radioaktiv	adj.	radioactive	
Radium {n}	n.	radium	
Radius {m}	n.	radius	
Radschüssel {f}		n.	disc
Radspeiche {f}		n.	spoke
Radzahn {m} n.		cog	
Raffinerie {f} n.		refinery	
Rahmen {m}	n.	frame	
Rahmen {m}	n.	welt	
Rakete {f}	n.	rocket	
Raketengeschoss {n}		n.	missile
Rallye {f}n.		rally	
Ramme {f}	n.	ram	
Rampe {f}	n.	ramp	
Rampenlicht {n}		n.	limelight

338

Rand {m}	n.	boundary
Rand {m}	n.	brim
Rand {m}	n.	brink
Rand {m}	n.	fringe
Rand {m}	n.	rim
Rand {m}	n.	verge
Randgebiet {n}	n.	outskirts
Range {f}	n.	minx
Rangordnung {f}	n.	hierarchy
ranzig	adj.	rancid
Rapier {n}	n.	rapier
rar	adj.	rare
rasch	adj.	rapid
rascheln v.		rustle
Rasenstück {n}	n.	sod
rasieren v.		shave
Rasiermesser {n}	n.	razor
rasiert	adj.	shaven
Raspel {f}	n.	rasp
Rassentrennung {f}	n.	apartheid
rassisch	adj.	racial
Rassismus {m}	n.	racialism
Rasterung {f} n.		grating
Rasur {f} n.		shaving
Rat {m}	n.	council
raten	v.	counsel
Ratgeber {m} n.		counsellor
ratifizieren	v.	ratify
rationalisieren	v.	rationalize
Rationalismus {m}n.		rationalism
ratlos	v.	perplex
Ratlosigkeit {f}	n.	perplexity
ratsam	adj.	advisable
Ratsche {f}	n.	ratchet
Ratschlag {m}	n.	advice

Ratschlag {m}	n.	counsel
Rätsel {n}	n.	enigma
Rätsel {n}	n.	riddle
Ratsmitglied {n}	n.	councillor
Ratte {f} n.		rat
rau adj.		gnarled
rau adj.		raucous
rau adj.		scraggy
rau adj.		throaty
Raub {m}	n.	robbery
Räuber {m}	n.	bandit
Räuber {m}	n.	predator
Räuber {m}	n.	robber
raubgierig	adj.	rapacious
Raubpressung {f} adj.		bootleg
Raubtier {n}	n.	carnivore
Rauch {m}	n.	fume
Rauch {m}	n.	smoke
rauchen v.		reek
Rauchfass {n}	n.	censer
rauchig	adj.	smoky
Raufbold {m} n.		bully
rauflustige	adj.	scrappy
Raum {m}	n.	room
Raum {m}	n.	space
räumen v.		vacate
Raumfahrt {f} n.		aerospace
räumlich adj.		spatial
raunen v.		murmur
Raupe {f}	n.	caterpillar
Rausch {m}	n.	intoxication
rauschen	v.	sough
Razzia {f}	n.	raid
reagieren	v.	react
Reaktion {f}	n.	reaction

reaktionär	adj.	reactionary
Reaktor {m}	n.	reactor
Realismus {m}	n.	realism
realistisch	adj.	realistic
Rebe {f}	n.	vine
Rebell {m}	n.	insurgent
rebellieren	v.	rebel
Rebellion {f}	n.	rebellion
rebellisch	adj.	mutinous
rechnen	v.	calculate
rechnen	v.	compute
Rechner {m}	n.	calculator
Rechnung {f}	n.	invoice
Rechnungsprüfung {f}	n.	audit
Recht {n}	n	right
Rechteck {n}	n.	rectangle
rechteckig	adj.	oblong
rechtfertigen	v.	justify
Rechtfertigung {f}	n.	vindication
rechtlich	adj.	legal
rechtmäßig	adj.	lawful
rechtmäßig	adj.	legitimate
rechtmäßig	adj.	rightful
rechts	adj.	right
Rechtsanwalt	n.	attorney
Rechtsanwalt	n.	lawyer
Rechtsanwalt	n.	solicitor
Rechtsanwalt {m}	n.	barrister
rechtschaffen	adj.	righteous
Rechtschaffenheit {f}	n.	probity
Rechtsgültigkeit {f}	n.	authenticity
Rechtsverletzung {f}	n.	infringement
Rechtswissenschaft {f}	n.	jurisprudence
Rechtswissenschaft {f}	n.	law

rechtwinklig	adj.	rectangular
rechtzeitig	adj.	opportune
redaktionell	adj.	editorial
Rede {f}	n.	oration
Redekunst {f}	n.	oratory
Redewendung {f}	n.	locution
Redewendung {f}	n.	phrase
redigieren	v.	subedit
Redner {m}	n.	orator
Rednerbühne {f}	n.	rostrum
Redundanz {f}	n.	redundancy
reduzieren	v.	cut
reduzieren	v.	diminish
reflektieren	v.	reflect
reflektierend	adj.	reflective
Reflex {m}	n.	reflex
Reflexion {f}	n.	reflection
reflexiv	adj.	reflexive
Reflexologie {f}	n.	reflexology
Reformation {f}	n.	reformation
Reformer {m}	n.	reformer
Refraktion {f}	n.	refraction
Regel {f}	n.	rule
regeln	v.	regularize
regeln	v.	regulate
regelrecht	adj.	regular
Regen {m}	n	rain
Regenbogen {m}	n.	rainbow
regenerieren	v.	regenerate
Regenerierung {f}	n.	regeneration
Regenguss {m}	n.	downpour
Regenmantel {m}	n.	mackintosh
Regenmantel {m}	n.	raincoat
Regenschirm {m}	n.	umbrella
Regent {m}	n.	regent

Regenwald {m}	*n.*	rainforest	Reihe {f} *n.*	tandem
Reggae {n}	*n.*	reggae	Reihen {pl}	*n.*	queue
regieren *v.*	govern	Reim {m}*n.*	rhyme
regieren *v.*	reign	rein *adj.* chaste
Regierungsgewalt {f}	*n.* governance	rein *adj.* pure
Reglme {n}	*n.*	regime	Reinheit {f}	*n.*	purity
Regiment {n} *n.*	regiment	reinigen *v.*	cleanse
Register {n}	*n.*	register	reinigen *v.*	defecate
Register {n}	*n.*	registry	reinigen *v.*	purify
Regler {m}	*n.*	regulator	reinigen *v.*	scavenge
regnerisch	*adj.*	rainy	Reinigung {f} *n.*	purgation
Reh *n.* roe	reinkarnieren *v.*	reincarnate
Rehabilitation {f} *n.*	rehabilitation	Reinlichkeit {f}	*n.*	cleanliness
rehabilitieren *v.*	rehabilitate	Reis {m} *n.* rice
Reibeisen {n} *n.*	grater	Reise {f} *n.*	journey
reiben *v.t* grate	Reisebericht {m} *n.*	travelogue
Reibung {f}	*n.*	friction	Reiseführer {m}	*n.*	guidebook
reich *adj.* wealthy	Reisegepäck {n}	*n.*	baggage
Reich {n}*n.*	realm	Reisegepäck {n}	*n.*	luggage
reichhaltig	*adj.*	comprehensive	reisen *v.* travel
reichhaltig	*adj.*	rich	Reisende {m} *n.*	traveller
reichlich *adj.*	abundant	Reisende {m} *n.*	voyager
reichlich *adj.*	copious	Reisepass {m}	*n.*	passport
reichlich *adj.*	opulent	Reisetagebuch {n}*n*	itinerary
reichlich *adj.*	replete	Reisetasche {f}	*n.*	valise
Reichtum {m}*n.*	opulence	Reisetasche {f};	*n.*	holdall
Reichtum {m}*n.*	richness	Reiseziel {n} *n.*	destination
Reichtum {m}*n.*	wealth	reißen *v.* tear
reif *adj.* ripe	reißen *v.* wrench
Reife {f} *n.*	maturity	Reißverschluss {m}	*n.*	zip
reifen *v.* ripen	reiten *v.*	bestride
Reifen {m}	*n.*	hoop	reiten *v.*	ride
Reifen {m}	*n.*	tyre	Reiter {m}	*adj.* equestrian
Reifenpanne {f}	*n.*	puncture	Reiter {m}	*n.*	rider
Reihe {f} *n.*	array	Reiter {m}	*n.*	trooper

341

Reiterei {f}	*n.*	cavalry	
reizbar	*adj.*	irritable	
reizbar	*adj.*	testy	
reizbar	*adj.*	waspish	
reizen	*v.i*	excite	
reizen	*n.*	pique	
reizen	*v.*	tease	
Reizmittel {n}	*n.*	stimulus	
reizvoll	*adj.*	attractive	
rekapitulieren	*v.*	recap	
rekeln	*v.*	loll	
rekrutieren	*v.*	recruit	
Relais {n}	*n.*	relay	
Relation {f}	*n.*	relationship	
relativ	*adj.*	relative	
Relativität {f}	*n.*	relativity	
relegieren	*v.*	rusticate	
Religion {f}	*n.*	religion	
religiös	*adj.*	religious	
Relikt {n}	*n.*	relic	
Reling {f}	*n.*	rail	
Reminiszenz {f}	*n.*	reminiscence	
Rennbahn {f}	*n.*	course	
rennen	*v.*	race	
Rennen {n}	*n.*	race	
renovieren	*v.t.*	renovate	
Renovierung {f}	*n.*	renovation	
Rentner {m}	*n.*	pensioner	
reorganisieren	*v.*	reorganize	
reparieren	*v.*	repair	
Reportage {f}	*n.*	reportage	
Reporter {m}	*n.*	reporter	
Repräsentation {f}	*n.*	representation	
repräsentieren	*v.*	represent	
Repressalie {f}	*n.*	reprisal	

Reproduktion {f}	*n.*	facsimile	
reproduzieren	*v.*	reproduce	
Reptil {n}	*n.*	reptile	
Republik {f}	*n.*	republic	
republikanisch	*adj.*	republican	
Requisit {n}	*n.*	requisite	
Reservat {n}	*n.*	reservation	
resident	*adj.*	residential	
Residenz {f}	*n.*	residence	
resonant	*adj.*	resonant	
Resonanz {f}	*n.*	resonance	
Resort {n}	*n.*	resort	
respektlos	*adj.*	dismissive	
Respektlosigkeit {f}	*n.*	disrespect	
respektvoll	*adj.*	respectful	
Ressort {n}	*n.*	department	
Rest {m}	*n.*	remains	
Restaurant {n}	*n.*	restaurant	
Restaurantgast {m}	*n.*	diner	
Restaurateur {m}	*n.*	restaurateur	
Restbestand {m}	*n.*	remainder	
Reste {pl}	*n.*	pickings	
restlich	*adj.*	residual	
Restriktion {f}	*n.*	restriction	
resultierend	*adj.*	resultant	
retro	*adj.*	retro	
retten	*v.*	rescue	
retten	*v.*	salvage	
retten	*v.*	save	
Retter {m}	*n.*	retriever	
Retter {m}	*n.*	saviour	
Rettung {f}	*n.*	salvation	
Rettungssanitäter {m}	*n.*	paramedic	
Reue {f}	*n.*	penance	

Reue {f} *n.* repentance
reuig *adj.* penitent
reuig *adj.* rueful
Revier {n} *n.* district
Revolution {f}*n.* revolution
revolutionär *adj.* revolutionary
Revolver {m} *n.* revolver
Rezept {n} *n.* recipe
Rezession {f} *n.* recession
Rhapsodie {f}*n.* rhapsody
Rhetorik {f} *n.* elocution
Rhetorik {f} *n.* rhetoric
rheumatisch *adj.* rheumatic
Rhodium {n} *n.* rhodium
Rhombus {m}*n.* lozenge
Rhombus {m}*n.* rhombus
rhythmisch *adj.* rhythmic
Rhythmus {m} *n.* rhythm
Richter {m} *n.* judge
richtig *adj.* accurate
richtig *adj.* correct
richtig *adj.* exact
Richtlinie {f} *n.* directive
Richtung {f} *n.* direction
Richtung {f} *n.* line
Richtungspfeil {m} *n.* arrow
Ricke {f} *n.* doe
riechend *adj.* odorous
Riefe {f} *n.* groove
Riegel {m} *n.* bar
Riese {m} *n.* colossus
Riesentier {n}*n.* behemoth
riesig *adj.* colossal
riesig *adj.* huge
Riff {n} *n.* reef

riffeln *v.* rifle
Rikscha {f} *n.* rickshaw
Rind {n} *v.* steer
Rindfleisch {n} *n.* beef
Rindvieh {n} *n.* cattle
Ringelblume {f} *n.* marigold
Ringelflechte {f} *n.* ringworm
ringen *v.* wrestle
Ringkämpfer {m} *n.* wrestler
Ringwerfen {n} *n.* hoopla
Rinnsal {n} *n.* runnel
Rippe {f} *n.* rib
Risiko {n} *n.* risk
Risiko {n} *n.* venture
riskant *adj.* hazardous
Riss {m} *n.* cleft
Riss {m} *n.* rift
Ritter {m} *n.* knight
Ritterschaft {f} *n.* knighthood
Rittertum {n} *n.* chivalry
rittlings *prep.* astride
Ritual {n} *n.* ritual
Ritus {m} *n.* rite
Rizinusöl {n} *a.* castor oil
Robbe {f} *n.* seal
Robe {f} *n.* robe
Roboter {m} *n.* robot
robust *adj.* resilient
robust *adj.* rugged
robust *adj.* stalwart
röchelnd *adj.* stertorous
Rock {m}, *n.* skirt
Rodeo {n} *n.* rodeo
Roggen {m} *n.* rye
roh *adj.* raw

343

Röhre {f} n. duct
röhrenförmig adj. tubular
Rohrstutzen {m} n. nipple
Rollbahn {f} n. runway
Rolle {f} n. persona
Rolle {f} n. role
rollen v.i. roll
Rollenantrieb {m} n. capstan
Rollenbesetzung {f} n. casting
Roller {m} n. scooter
Rolltreppe {f} n. escalator
Roman {m} n. novel
Romanschriftsteller {m} n. novelist
romantisch adj. romantic
Romanze {f} n. romance
Romme {n} n. rummy
Röntgenanalyse {f} n. x-ray
Röntgenaufnahme {f} n.radiography
rosa adj. pink
Rose {f} n. rose
Rosenkranz {m} n. rosary
Rosette {f} n. rosette
rosig adj. rosy
Rosine {f} n. raisin
Ross {n} n. steed
Rost {m} n. rust
Röster {m} n. roadster
rostig adj. rusty
rot adj. red
Rote Beete {f} n. beetroot
rotieren v. rotate
rötlich adj. reddish
Rotte {f} n. rout
Rouge {n} n. rouge
Roulade {f} n. roll

Roulette {n} n. roulette
Routine {f} n. routine
Routine {f} n. rote
Rowdy {m} n. hooligan
Royalist {m} n. royalist
Rübe {f} n. beet
Rübe {f} n. turnip
Rubin {m} n. ruby
Rubrik {m} n. rubric
ruchlos adj. nefarious
ruckartig adj. fitful
Rückblick {m} n. retrospect
rücken v. hitch
Rücken {m} n. ridge
Rückerstattung {f}n. restitution
Rückführung {f} n. repatriation
Rückgrat {n} n. backbone
Rückgriff {m} n. recourse
Rückhand {f} n. backhand
rückläufig adj. retrograde
Rückprall {m}v. rebound
Rucksack {m} n. backpack
Rucksack {m} n. rucksack
Rückschlag {m} n. repercussion
rückschlagig adj. atavistic
Rückseite {f} n. backside
Rückseite {f} n. rear
Rückseite {f} n. verso
Rücksendung {f} n. return
Rücksichtnahme {f} n.consideration
rücksichtslos adj. inconsiderate
rücksichtslos adj. irrespective
Rückstand {m} n. backlog
Rückstoß {m}v. recoil
Rücktritt {m} n. resignation

rückwärts	adv.	aback
rückwärts	adj.	backward
Rückweisung {f}	n.	rejection
rückwirkend	adj.	retroactive
Rückwirkung {f},	n.	backlash
rückzahlen	v.	refund
Rückzahlung {f}	n.	refund
Rückzahlung {f}	n.	repayment
Rückzug {m}	n.	withdrawal
Ruder {n}	n.	oar
Ruder {n}	n.	rudder
Rudiment {n}	n.	rudiment
rudimentär	adj.	rudimentary
Ruf {m}	n.	whoop
rufen	v.	call
Rugby {n}	n.	rugby
rügen	v.	reprimand
Ruhe {f}	n.	quietetude
Ruhe {f}	n.	tranquillity
ruhen	v.	repose
Ruheposten {m}	n.	sinecure
Ruhestand {m}	n.	retirement
ruhig	adj.	restful
ruhig	adj.	staid
ruhig	adj.	tranquil
Ruhm {m}	n.	fame
Ruhr {f}	n.	dysentery
rühren	v.	stir
rühren	v.	toughen
rührselig	adj.	maudlin
Rührstange {f}	n.	paddle
Ruine {f}	n.	ruin
Rum {m}	n.	rum
Rummel {m}	n.	whopper
Rummel {m}	n.	hype

Rumpelkammer {f}	n.	limbo
rumpeln	v.	rumble
rund	adj.	round
rund	adv.	roundly
Runde {f}	n.	bout
runderneuern	v.	retread
runter	adv.	down
rüpelhaft	adj.	rowdy
Rüschen	n.	frill
Ruß {m}	n.	soot
Rüsselkäfer {m}	n.	weevil
rutschen	v.	skid
rütteln	v.	jiggle
rütteln	v.t.	jolt

S

Saal {m}	n.	hall
Saat {f}	n.	seed
Saat-Lein {m}	n.	linseed
Sabbat {m}	n.	Sabbath
sabbeln	v.	dote
Säbel {m}	n.	sabre
säbelrasslerisch	adj.	swashbuckling
sabotieren	v.	sabotage
sachkundig	adj.	competent
sachlich	adv.	objectively
sächlich	adj.	neuter
Sachlichkeit {f}	n.	relevance
Sachwalter {m}	n.	trustee
Sack {m}	n.	kith
Sack {m}	n.	sack
Sackgasse {f}	n.	impasse
Sadist {m}	n.	sadist
Safari {f}	n.	safari
Safe {m}	n.	safe

345

Safran {m}	*n.*	saffron	**Samenkern** {m}	*n.*	kernel
Saft {m}	*n.*	juice	**Samenkorn** {n}	*n.*	grain
Saft {m}	*n.*	liquor	**sämig**	*adj.*	viscid
Saft {m}	*n.*	sap	**Sammelbecken** {n}		*n.* reservoir
saftig	*adj.*	juicy	**sammeln** *v.*		collect
saftig	*adj.*	lush	**sammeln** *v.*		glean
saftig	*adj.*	succulent	**Sammlung** {f} *n.*		collection
Saga {f}	*n.*	saga	**Samstag** {m}	*n.*	Saturday
Säge {f}	*n.*	saw	**Samt** {m}*n.*		velvet
Sägemehl {n} *n.*		sawdust	**samtig**	*adj.*	velvety
sagen	*v.*	say	**Sanatorium** {n}	*n.*	sanatorium
sagen	*v.*	tell	**Sand** {m}*n.*		sand
sagenhaft	*adj.*	legendary	**Sandale** {f}	*n.*	sandal
Sahnebonbon {n}	*n.* toffee		**Sandelholz** {n}	*n.*	sandalwood
Sahnetorte {f}	*n.*	gateau	**sandig**	*adj.* sandy	
Sake {m}*n.*		sake	**Sandwich** {n} *n.*		sandwich
Sakrament {n}	*n.*	sacrament	**sanft**	*adj.*	bland
Salat {m}*n.*		salad	**sanft**	*adj.*	mild
Salatgurke {f}*n.*		cucumber	**sanft**	*adj.*	placid
Salbe {f} *n.*		ointment	**sanft**	*adj.*	soft
Salbei {m}	*n.*	sage	**sanft**	*adj.*	suave
salben	*v.*	anoint	**Sänfte** {f}	*n.*	sedan
salbungsvoll	*adj.* unctuous		**Sänger** {m}	*a.*	singer
Salon {m}	*n.*	salon	**Sänger** {m}	*n.*	songster
Salsa {n}*n.*		salsa	**Sänger** {m}	*n.*	vocalist
Salto {m}*n.*		somersault	**Sanierung** {f} *n.*		sanitation
Salut {m}*n.*		salute	**sanktionieren** *v.*		sanction
Salve {f} *n.*		salvo	**Saphir** {m}	*n.*	sapphire
Salz {n} *n.*		salt	**sardonisch**	*adj.* sardonic	
salzig	*adj.*	saline	**Sargtuch** {n} *n.*		pall
salzig	*adj.*	salty	**Sari** *n.*	sari	
Salzigkeit {f}	*n.*	salinity	**Sarkasmus** {m}	*n.*	sarcasm
Salzlauge {f}	*n.*	brine	**sarkastisch**	*adj.* sarcastic	
Samariter {m}*n.*		Samaritan	**Sarkophag** {m}	*n.*	sarcophagus
Samenflüssigkeit {f}*n.* semen			**Satan** {m}	*n.*	Satan

satanisch *adj.* satanic	**sausend** *adj.* swish
Satanismus {m} *n.* Satanism	**Saxophon {n}** *n.* saxophone
Satellit {m} *n.* satellite	**Scanner {m}** *n.* scanner
Satin {m} *n.* satin	**schäbig** *adj.* dingy
Satire {f} *n.* satire	**schäbig** *adj.* measly
Satiriker {m} *n.* satirist	**schäbig** *adj.* poky
satirisch *adj.* satirical	**schäbig** *adj.* seedy
Sattel {m} *n.* saddle	**schäbig** *adj.* shabby
Sattelplatz {m} *n.* paddock	**Schabracke {f}** *n.* caparison
Sattheit {f} *n.* satiety	**Schach {n}** *n.* chess
sättigen *v.* satiate	**Schachmatt {n}** *n* checkmate
sättigen *v.* saturate	**Schacht {m}** *n.* shaft
sättigend *adj.* satiable	**Schachtel {f}** *n.* box
Sättigung {f} *n.* saturation	**Schachtel {f}** *n.* carton
Sattler {m} *n.* saddler	**Schädel {m}** *n.* skull
Sattler {m} *n.* sadism	**Schaden {m}** *n.* detriment
Satz {m} *n.* proposition	**Schaden {m}** *n.* harm
Satzbau {m} *n.* syntax	**Schaden {m}** *n.* mischief
Satzung {f} *n.* statute	**Schaden {m}** *n.* prejudice
satzungsgemäß *adj.* statutory	**schadenfroh** *adj.* mischievous
Sau {f} *n.* sow	**Schadensersatzrecht {n}** *n.* tort
sauber *adj.* clean	**Schadensminderung {f}**
sauer *adj.* sour	*n.*mitigation
Sauerstoff {m} *n.* oxygen	**schädigen** *v.* injure
Säuferwahnsinn {m} *n.* delirium	**schädlich** *adj.* deleterious
saugen *v.* suck	**schädlich** *adj.* injurious
säugen *v.* lactate	**schädlich** *adj.* malign
säugen *v.* suckle	**Schadstofffahne {f}** *n.* plume
Säugetier {n} *n.* mammal	**Schaf {n}** *n.* sheep
Säugling {m} *n.* sucker	**schaffen** *v.* score
Säugling {m} *n.* suckling	**Schafhirt {m}** *n.* shepherd
Säulengang {m} *n.* portico	**Schafott {n}** *n.* scaffold
Saum {m} *n.* hem	**schaftem** *adj.* sharp
Sauna {f} *n.* sauna	**Schakal {m}** *n.* jackal
Säure {f} *n.* acid	**Schäkel {m}** *n.* shackle

347

Schale {f}   n.   peel
Schale {f}   n.   pod
schälen v.   pare
Schalheit {f}   n.   staleness
Schalldämpfer {m}   n.   silencer
schalldicht   adj.   soundproof
Schallplatte {f}   n.   record
Schallwand {f}   v.   baffle
Schälmaschine {f}n.   stripper
schalten n.   switch
schalten v.   turn
Schaltkäfig {m}   n.   cage
Schaltung {f} n.   circuit
Schalung {f}   n.   casing
schamlos   adj.   shameless
schamm adj.   pubic
Schamröte {f}n.   blusher
Schande {f}   n.   disgrace
Schande {f}   n.   disrepute
Schande {f}   n.   shame
Schandfleck {m}   n.   blot
schändlich   adj.   harmful
schändlich   adj.   ignominious
schändlich   adj.   infamous
schändlich   adj.   shameful
Schar {f} n.   flock
Schar {f} n.   shoal
Scharbockskraut {n}   n. celandine
scharf   adj.   poignant
scharf   adj.   strident
scharf   adj.   trenchant
Schärfe {f}   n.   keenness
Schärfe {f}   n.   poignancy
schärfen v.   sharpen
Schärfer {m}   n.   sharpener

Scharfsinn {m}   n.   acumen
Scharfsinn {m}   n.   sagacity
scharfsinnig adj. astute
scharfsinnig adj. sagacious
scharfsinnig adj. shrewd
scharfzüngig adj. acerbic
Scharlach {m}   n.   scarlet
Scharnier {n} n.   hinge
Schärpe {f}   n.   sash
Schatten {m} n.   shade
Schatten {m} n.   shadow
Schattenbild {n}   n.   silhouette
schattenhaft a.   shadowy
schattieren v.   shade
schattig adj. shady
Schatz {m}   n.   hoard
Schatz {m}   n.   treasure
Schatzamt {n}   n.   bursary
schätzen v.   appreciate
schätzen v.   cherish
Schatzmeister {m}n.   bursar
Schatzmeister {m}n.   treasurer
Schätzung {f}n.   esteem
Schaubild {n}n.   chart
schaudern   v.   shudder
Schaufel {f}   n.   shovel
Schaufel {f}   n.   bucket
Schaufel {f}   n.   vane
schaufeln   v.   shove
Schaufensterpuppe {f}n.
    mannequin
Schaukel {f}   n.   swing
Schaukelbrett {n}   n.   see-saw
schaukeln   v.   sway
schaukeln   v.   swing

348

schaukelnd	*adj.*	swinging	
Schaum {m}	*n.*	froth	
Schaum {m}	*n.*	lather	
Schaum {m}	*n.*	spume	
Schaumstoff {m}	*n.*	foam	
Schaumünze {f}	*n.*	medallion	
Schauplatz {m}	*n.*	locale	
Schauplatz {m}	*n.*	venue	
Schauspiel {n}	*n.*	spectacle	
Schauspieler {m}	*n.*	actor	
Schauspieler {m}	*n.*	comedian	
Schauspielerei {f}	*n.*	acting	
Schauspielerin {f}	*a.*	actress	
Scheck {m}	*n.*	cheque	
scheckig	*adj.*	brindle	
scheckig	*adj.*	motley	
Scheibe {f}	*n.*	pulley	
Scheide {f}	*n.*	scabbard	
Scheide {f}	*n.*	vagina	
scheiden	*v. t*	dissolve	
schein...	*adj.*	pseudo	
scheinen	*v.*	seem	
Scheingrund {m}	*n.*	pretext	
scheinheilig	*adj.*	sanctimonious	
Scheinwerfer {m}	*n.*	floodlight	
Scheinwerfer {m}	*n.*	headlight	
Scheitel {m}	*n.*	vertex	
Scheitelpunkt {m}	*n*	apex	
Scheiterhaufen {m}		*n.*	pyre
schelten	*v.*	chide	
schelten	*v.*	scold	
Schema {n}	*n.*	scheme	
schematisch	*adj.*	schematic	
Schenkel {m}	*n.*	thigh	
schenken	*v.*	bestow	

schenken	*v.*	donate	
scheppern	*v.*	rattle	
Scherbe {f}	*n.*	shard	
Schere {f}	*n.*	scissors	
scheren	*v.*	shear	
Scherz {m}	*n.*	hoax	
Scherz {m}	*n.*	joke	
scherzen	*v.i.*	frolic	
scherzen	*n.*	jest	
Scherzfrage {f}		*v. t*	conundrum
scherzhaft	*adj.*	jocular	
scheuchen	*v.*	flush	
scheuern	*v.*	scrub	
Scheuklappen {pl}	*n.*	blinkers	
Scheune {f}	*n.*	barn	
scheußlich	*adj.*	atrocious	
scheußlich	*adj.*	nasty	
Schicht {f}	*n.*	ply	
Schicht {f}	*n.*	stratum	
schichten	*v.*	laminate	
schichten	*v.*	stratify	
schick	*adj.*	chic	
schick	*adj.*	trendy	
Schicklichkeit {f}	*n.*	propriety	
Schicksal {n}	*n.*	destiny	
Schicksal {n}	*n.*	fate	
Schicksal {n}	*n.*	karma	
schicksalhaft	*adj.*	fateful	
schieben	*v.*	push	
schieben	*v.t.*	shuffle	
schieben	*v.*	thrust	
Schiebergeschäfte {pl}	*n.*		
profiteering			
Schiebung {f}	*n.*	graft	

349

Schiedsgerichtsbarkeit {f}
n. arbitration

Schiedsmann {m} *n.* arbiter

Schiedsrichter {m} *n.* arbitrator

Schiedsrichter {m} *n.* referee

schief *adv.* askance

schief *adj.* wry

Schieferplatte {f} *n.* slate

schielen *v.* squint

Schienbein {n} *n.* shin

schießen *v.* shoot

Schiff {n} *n.* ship

schiffbar *adj.* navigable

Schiffbruch {m} *n.* shipwreck

Schiffbruch {m} *n.* wreck

schiffen *v.* navigate

Schiffer {m} *n.* mariner

Schiffer {m} *n.* skipper

Schifffahrt {f} *n.* navy

Schiffswerft {f} *n.* shipyard

Schikane {f} *n.* chicanery

Schikane {f} *n.* harassment

Schild {n} *n.* shield

Schilddrüse {f} *n.* thyroid

schildern *v.* depict

Schildkröte {f} *n.* tortoise

Schildkröte {f} *n.* turtle

schillernd *adj.* lucent

Schimmer {m} *v.* gleam

Schimmer {m} *v.* glimmer

schimmern *v.* shimmer

Schimpanse {m} *n.* chimpanzee

schimpfend *adj.* upbraid

Schimpfwort {n} *n.* invective

Schindel {f} *n.* shingle

Schinder {m} *n.* oppressor

Schinken {m} *n.* ham

Schinkenspeck {m} *n.* bacon

Schirmherrschaft {f} *n.* protectorate

Schizophrenie {f} *n.* schizophrenia

Schlachtbank {f} *n.* shambles

Schlachtopfer {n} *n.* victim

Schlacke {f} *n.* dross

Schlacke {f} *n.* slag

Schlaf {m} *n.* sleep

schlafend *adj.* asleep

schlaff *v.* droop

schlaff *adj.* flaccid

Schlaflied {n} *n.* lullaby

schlaflos *adj.* wakeful

Schlafplatz {m} *n.* roost

schläfrig *adj.* sleepy

schläfrig *adj.* somnolent

Schlafsaal {m} *n.* dormitory

Schlafsucht {f} *n.* somnolence

Schlafwandler {m} *n.* somnambulist

Schlag {m} *n.* bang

Schlag {m} *v.* beat

Schlaganfall {m} *n.* stroke

Schlägel {m} *n.* hammer

schlagen *v.* flap

schlagen *v.* flick

schlagen *v.* pummel

schlagen *v.* punch

schlagen *v.t.* slap

Schläger {m} *n.* racket

Schläger {m} *n.* stick

Schlägerei {f} *n.* affray

Schlägerei {f} *n.* brawl

German		English
Schlagfertigkeit {f}	*n.*	repartee
schlaksig	*adj.*	gangling
schlaksig	*adj.*	lanky
Schlamassel {m}	*n.*	mess
Schlamm {m}	*n.*	silt
Schlamm {m}	*n.*	slime
Schlammfang {m}	*n.*	gully
Schlampe {f}	*n.*	frump
Schlampe {f}	*n.*	slattern
schlampig	*adj.*	blowsy
schlampig	*adj.*	sloppy
schlampig	*adj.*	slovenly
schlampige	*adj.*	slatternly
Schlange {f}	*n.*	serpent
Schlange {f}	*n.*	snake
schlängeln	*v.*	meander
schlängeln	*v.*	wriggle
schlank	*adj.*	slender
schlank	*adj.*	slim
schlank	*adj.*	svelte
schlapp	*adj.*	flabby
schlappig	*adj.*	floppy
schlau	*adj.*	cunning
schlau	*adj.*	sly
schlau	*adj.*	wily
Schlauch {m}	*n.*	hose
Schlaufe {f}	*n.*	loop
schlecht	*adv.*	badly
schlechtbehandeln	*v.*	mistreat
schlechtbenehmen	*v.*	misbehave
schlechter	*adj.*	worse
schlechteste	*adj.*	worst
schlechtregieren	*v.*	misrule
schleichen	*v.*	slink
schleichen	*v.*	tiptoe
Schleier {m}	*n.*	haze
Schleier {m}	*n.*	veil
Schleifmaschine {f}	*n.*	grinder
Schleifpapier {n}	*n.*	sandpaper
Schleim {m}	*n.*	mucilage
Schleim {m}	*n.*	mucus
schleimig	*adj.*	mucous
schleimig	*adj.*	slimy
Schlemmer {m}	*n.*	sybarite
schlendern	*v.*	amble
schlendern	*v.*	saunter
schleppen	*v.*	tote
schleppen	*v.*	trudge
Schleppen {n}	*n.*	haulage
schleudern	*v.*	hurl
schleudern	*v.*	toss
Schleuse {f}	*n.*	sluice
schlicht	*adj.*	artless
schlichten	*v.*	arbitrate
schließlich	*adv.*	eventually
schließlich	*adv.*	ultimately
schlimm	*adj.*	bad
schlimm	*adv.*	sorely
schlimm	*adj.*	wicked
Schlinge {f}	*n.*	noose
Schlitten {m}	*n.*	sledge
Schlitten {m}	*n.*	sleigh
schlitteren	*v.*	slither
Schlittschuh {m}	*n.*	skate
schlitzen	*v.*	slash
schlitzen	*v.t.*	slit
Schloss {n}	*n.*	castle
schlottern	*v.*	shiver
Schlucht {f}	*n.*	canyon
schluchzen	*v.*	sob

351

Schluckauf {m}	n.	hiccup
schlucken	v.	swallow
schlummern	v.	drowse
schlummern	v.	slumber
Schlumper {m}	n.	slob
Schlupfanorak {m}	n.	pullover
Schlüpfer {pl}n.		knickers
schlüpfrig	adj.	saucy
Schlupfwinkel {m}n.		nook
schlurfen	v.	scuff
schlürfen	v.	sip
schlürfen	v.	slurp
Schluss {m}	n.	end
Schlüssel {m}	n.	key
Schlüsselloch {n}	n.	keyhole
Schlussfolgerung {f}	n.	conclusion
schmachten	v.	languish
schmackhaft	adj.	nutty
schmackhaft	adj.	palatable
schmackhaft	adj.	savoury
schmackhaft	adj.	tasty
schmähen	v.	vilify
schmal	adj.	strait
schmecken	v.	taste
Schmeichelei {f}	n.	adulation
schmeicheln	v.	cajole
schmeicheln	v.	flatter
schmeißen	v.	throw
schmeltzen	v.	melt
schmelzen	v.	liquefy
Schmerzen {pl}	n.	ache
schmerzhaft	adj.	painful
schmerzlich	adj.	grievous
Schmerzstiller {m}	n.	painkiller
Schmerztablette {f}	n.	analgesic

Schmetterling {m}n.		butterfly
schmettern	v.	blare
Schmied {m}	n.	blacksmith
Schmied {m}	n.	smith
schmieden	v.t	forge
schmiegsam,	adj.	pliant
schmieren	v.	daub
schmieren	v.	lubricate
Schmierfett {n}	n.	grease
Schmierstoff {m}	n.	lubricant
Schmierung {f}	n.	lubrication
Schminke {f}	n.	make-up
schmissig	adj.	racy
schmollen	v.	sulk
Schmuckanhänger {m}n.		pendant
schmücken	v.	decorate
schmückend	adj.	ornamental
schmucklos	adj.	bald
schmuddelig	adj.	tatty
schmuggeln	v.	smuggle
Schmuggler {m}	n.	smuggler
schmusen	v.	smooch
Schmutz {m}	n.	filth
Schmutz {m}	n.	grime
Schmutz {m}	n.	mud
schmutzig	adj.	foul
schmutzig	adj.	sordid
schmutzig	adj.	squalid
Schnabel {m}n.		beak
Schnalle {f}	n.	buckle
schnallend	adj.	strapping
schnappen	v.	nab
schnappen	v.	snap
schnappen	v.	swoop
Schnapper {m}	n.	snapper

Schnapsbrennerei {f}	*n.*	distillery
schnarchen	*v.*	snorte
Schnarcher {m}	*n.*	snore
schnattern	*v.*	chatter
Schnauze {f}	*n.*	snout
Schnecke {f}	*n.*	snail
Schnee {m}	*n.*	snow
Schneeball {m}	*n.*	snowball
schneeig	*adj.*	snowy
Schneematsch {m}	*n.*	slush
Schneeregen {m}	*n.*	sleet
Schneesturm {m}	*n.*	blizzard
Schneidemaschine {f}	*n.*	guillotine
Schneiden {n}	*n.*	cutting
schneidend	*adj.*	incisive
Schneider {m}	*n.*	tailor
schnell	*adv.*	apace
schnell	*adj.*	fast
schnell	*adj.*	quick
schnell	*adv.*	quickly
schnell	*adj.*	speedy
schnell	*adj.*	swift
Schnellgang {m}	*n.*	overdrive
Schnelligkeit {f}	*n.*	fastness
Schnelligkeit {f}	*n.*	rapidity
Schnellstraße {f}	*n.*	highway
Schnepfe {f}	*n.*	snipe
schnibbel	*v.*	whittle
schniegeln	*v.*	titivate
schnippeln	*v.*	snip
Schnipsel {n}	*n.*	snippet
Schnitzel {m}	*n.*	cutlet
schnitzen	*v.*	carve
Schnitzlerei {f}	*n.*	carvery
schnüffeln	*v.*	sniff

schnüffeln	*v.*	sniffle
schnupfen	*v.*	snuff
schnuppern	*v.*	snuffle
Schnürer {m} *n.*		tie
Schnurrbart {m}	*n.*	moustache
Schnurren	*v.*	purr
schnurstracks	*adv.*	straightway
Schober {m} *n.*		rick
schockieren	*v.*	shock
schockierend	*adj.*	shocking
Schokolade {f}	*n.*	chocolate
schön	*adj.*	beautiful
schön	*adj.*	fair
schön	*adj.*	fine
schonend	*adj.*	sparing
Schönheit	*n.*	beauty
Schönheit {f} *n.*		belle
Schönheitsfehler {m} *n.*		blemish
Schönheitspflege {f} *n.*		cosmetic
schöpferisch	*adj.*	creative
Schöpflöffel {m}	*n.*	ladle
Schornstein {m}	*n.*	chimney
Schoß {m}	*n.*	lap
Schoß {m}	*n.*	womb
Schotte {m}	*n.*	Scot
Schottenrock {m} *n.*		kilt
schräg	*adv.*	askew
Schräge {f}	*n.*	cant
Schrank {m}	*n.*	cupboard
Schrank {m}	*n.*	locker
Schrankkoffer {m} *n.*		trunk
Schrapnell {n}	*n.*	shrapnel
Schraubenmutter {f}	*n.*	nut
Schraubenschlüssel {m}	*n.*	spanner

353

Schraubenzieher {m}   n.
  screwdriver
Schrecken {m}   n.   amazement
Schreckenstat {f}   n.   atrocity
schrecklich   adj.   awful
schrecklich   adj.   cruel
schrecklich   adj.   terrific
Schrei {m}   n.   cry
Schrei {m}   n.   yell
schreiben   v.   write
Schreiber {m}n.   clerk
Schreiber {m}n.   typist
Schreibfeder {f}   n.   nib
Schreibwagen {m}n.   carriage
Schreibwaren {pl} n.   stationery
Schreibwarenhändler {m}n.
  stationer
Schreibweise {f}   n.   spelling
schreien v.   scream
schreiend   v.i.   shout
Schreierei {f} n.   screech
Schreihals {m}   n.   squall
Schreiner {m}n.   joiner
schreiten   v.   stride
Schriftart {f}   n.   font
Schriftsteller {m}   n.   writer
Schriftzug {m}   n.   writing
schrill   adj.   shrill
Schritt {m}   n.   step
Schrittmesser {m}n.   pedometer
schroff   adj.   brusque
Schroffheit {f}   n.   asperity
Schrott {m}   n.   scrap
schrumpeln   v.   shrivel
schrumplig   adj.   wizened

Schub {m}   n.   batch
schüchtern   adj.   coy
schüchtern   adj.   sheepish
schüchtern   adj.   shy
Schuft {m}   n.   scamp
schuften v.   plod
schuften n.   toils
Schuh {m}   n.   shoe
Schuhsenkel {pl}   n.   shoestring
Schuld {f}   n.   debt
Schuld {f}   n.   guilt
schuldbewusst   adj.   guilty
schulden   v.   owe
Schulden {pl}n.   arrears
schuldend   adj.   owing
schuldenfrei   adj.   afloat
schuldig adj.   due
Schuldige {m,f}   n.   culprit
schuldigen   v.   blame
Schuldner {m}   n.   debtor
Schule {f}   n.   school
Schüler {m}   n.   pupil
Schulkind {n}n.   student
Schulmappe {f}   n.   satchel
Schulnote {f} n.   grade
Schulter {f}   n.   shoulder
Schuppen {m}   n.   shack
Schuppen {m}   n.   shanty
Schuppen {pl}   n.   dandruff
schüren v.   stoke
Schurke {m}   n.   knave
Schurke {m}   n.   miscreant
Schurke {m}   n.   scoundrel
schurkisch   adj.   roguish
schürren v.   poke

Schurz {m}	*n.*	apron	**schwanger**	*adj.*	pregnant
Schuster {m}	*n.*	cobbler	**Schwangerschaft** {f}	*n.*	gestation
Schutt {m}	*n.*	debris	**Schwangerschaft** {f}	*n.*	pregnancy
schütteln	*v.*	joggle	**Schwangerschaftsverhütung** {f}*n.*		
schütteln	*v.*	shake	contraception		
Schutz {m}	*n.*	protection	**schwanken**	*v.*	falter
Schutzbefohlene {m,f}*n.*		ward	**schwanken**	*v.*	fluctuate
Schutzdach {n}	*n.*	shelter	**schwanken**	*v.*	toddle
schützen*v.*		protect	**schwanken**	*v.*	vacillate
Schützengraben {m}*n.*		trench	**schwanken**	*v.*	wobble
Schützer {m}	*n.*	scorer	**Schwanken** {n}	*v.*	dither
Schutzgebiet {n}	*n.*	dependency	**schwankend**	*adj.*	fickle
Schutzvorrichtung {f}*n.*		safeguard	**Schwankungsbreite** {f}*n.*		jitters
Schutzwall {m}	*n.*	barricade	**Schwarm** {m}*n.*		bevy
Schutzwall {m}	*n.*	firewall	**Schwarm** {m}*n.*		swarm
Schwabe {m}	*n.*	swab	**Schwärmer** {m}	*n.*	enthusiastic
schwach	*adj.*	faint	**schwärmerisch**	*adj.*	quixotic
schwach	*adj.*	feckless	**schwarz**	*adj.*	black
schwach	*adj.*	languid	**schwärzen**	*v.*	blacken
schwach	*adj.*	slight	**schwatzen**	*n.*	pattern
schwach	*adj.*	weak	**schwätzen**	*v.t.*	gabble
schwache	*adj.*	flimsy	**schweben**	*v.*	hover
schwächen	*v.*	debilitate	**schwebend**	*adj.*	pending
schwächen	*v.*	weaken	**Schwefel** {m}	*n.*	sulphur
Schwächezustand {m}	*n.*	debility	**schweigsam**	*adj.*	taciturn
Schwachheit {f}	*n.*	weakness	**Schwein** {n}	*n.*	pig
Schwachkopf {m}	*n.*	moron	**Schwein** {n}	*n.*	swine
Schwächling {m}	*n.*	weakling	**Schweinefett** {n}	*n.*	lard
Schwachsinn {m}	*n.*	dementia	**Schweinefleisch** {n}	*n.*	pork
Schwachsinn {m}	*n.*	idiocy	**Schweiß** {m}	*n.*	sweat
Schwaden {m}	*n.*	swathe	**schweißen**	*v.*	weld
schwadronieren	*v.*	swagger	**schwelen**	*v.*	smoulder
schwafeln	*v.*	witter	**Schwelle** {f}	*n.*	sleeper
Schwamm {m}	*n.*	sponge	**Schwelle** {f}	*n.*	threshold
Schwan {m}	*n.*	swan	**schwellen**	*v.*	swell

Schwellen {n}*n.*	swell	
schwellend *adj.*	tumescent	
Schwellung {f}	*n.*	lump
Schwellung {f}	*n.*	swelling
schwer *adj.*	heavy	
schwer *adj.*	leaden	
schwerfällig *adj.*	cumbersome	
schwerflüssig *adj.*	viscous	
schwerlich *adv.*	hardly	
Schwermut {m}	*n.*	melancholia
Schwert {n}	*n.*	sword
Schwertlilie {f}	*n.*	iris
Schwerverbrecher {m} *n.*	felon	
schwerverständlich *adj.*	abstruse	
schwerwiegend *adj.*	weighty	
Schwester {f} *n.*	sister	
schwesterlich *adj.*	sisterly	
Schwesternschaft {f}*n.*	sisterhood	
Schwiegermutter {f}*n.*	mother-in-law	
Schwiegertochter {f}*n.*	daughter-in-law	
schwielig, *adj.*	callous	
schwierig *adj.*	catchy	
schwierig *adj.*	tough	
Schwierigkeit {f}	*n.*	difficulty
schwimmen *v.*	float	
schwimmen *v.*	swim	
schwimmend *adj.*	buoyant	
Schwimmer {m}	*n.*	swimmer
schwimmhäutig *adj.*	webby	
Schwindel {m}	*n.*	vertigo
schwindeln *v.*	swindle	
schwindelnd *adj.*	vertiginous	
schwinden *v. t*	dwindle	
schwinden *v.*	swoon	
Schwindler {m}	*n.*	swindler

schwindlig *adj.*	giddy	
schwingen *v.*	brandish	
schwingen *v.*	oscillate	
schwingend *adj.*	vibrant	
Schwingung {f}	*n.*	oscillation
Schwingungszahl {f}*n.*	frequency	
Schwips {m} *n.*	tipster	
schwirren *v.*	whir	
schwirren *v.*	whirr	
schwitzen *v.t.*	perspire	
schwitzen *v.*	transpire	
schwören *v.*	swear	
schwül *adj.*	muggy	
schwül *adj.*	sultry	
Schwung {m}*n.*	panache	
Schwung {m}*n.*	verve	
Schwur {m}	*n.*	vow
sechs *adj.&n.*	six	
Sechsling {m}	*n.*	sextuplet
sechste *adj. & n.*	sixth	
sechzehn *adj. & n.*	sixteen	
sechzehnte *adj. & n.*	sixteenth	
sechzig *adj. & n.*	sixty	
sechzigste *adj. & n.*	sixtieth	
See {m} *n.*	lake	
Seele {f} *n.*	soul	
Seelenfreund {m} *n.*	soul mate	
seelenlos *adj.*	soulless	
Seelenmesse {f} *n.*	requiem	
seelenvoll *adj.*	soulful	
Seemann {m}*n.*	navigator	
Seemöwe {f} *n.*	seagull	
Seepolyp {m}*n.*	octopus	
Seeräuberei {f} *n.*	piracy	
Seereise {f} *n.*	voyage	

Segel {n}*n.* sail
Segelflieger {m} *n.* glider
Segelklub {m} *n.* yachting
segeln *v.* sail
Segen {m} *n.* blessing
Segler {m} *n.* yachtsman
Segment {n} *n.* segment
segnen *v.* bless
segnen *v.* consecrate
Segnung {f} *n.* benediction
sehen *v.* look
sehen *v.* saw
sehen *v.* see
Sehenswürdigkeit {f} *n.* sight
Seher {m} *n.* seer
Sehkraft {f} *n.* vision
Sehne {f}*n.* tendon
sehnen *v.* yearn
sehnlich *adj.* ardent
Sehnsucht {f}*n.* longing
Sehnsucht {f}*n.* yearning
sehnsüchtig *adj.* wishful
sehnsüchtig *adj.* wistful
sehr*adv.* very
seicht *adj.* shallow
Seide {f} *n.* floss
Seide {f} *n.* silk
Seidel {m} *n.* pint
seidenartig *adj.* silky
Seidenraupe {f} *n.* silkworm
seidenweich *adj.* silken
Seife {f} *n.* soap
seifig *adj.* soapy
Seil {n} *n.* rope
sein *v.* be

seine *adj.* his
seismisch *adj.* seismic
seitdem *prep.* since
Seite {f} *n.* page
Seite {f} *n.* side
Seitengewehr {n} *n.* bayonet
Seitenlinie {f} *n.* sideline
Seitenrand {m} *n.* margin
Seitenschiff {n} *n.* aisle
Seitenzahl {f} *n.* folio
Sekretär *n.* secretary
Sekretariat {n} *n.* secretariat
Sekte {f} *n.* sect
Sektierer {m} *adj.* sectarian
Sektor {m} *n.* sector
sekundär *adj.* secondary
selbst *pron.* itself
selbst *pron.* myself
selbst *n.* self
selbst *pron.* yourself
Selbstbewusstsein {n} *n.* aplomb
selbstgefällig *adj.* complacent
selbstgemacht *adj.* self-made
Selbstgespräch {n} *n.* soliloquy
selbstlos*adj.* selfless
selbstlos*adj.* unselfish
Selbstmord {m} *n.* suicide
selbstmörderisch *adj.* suicidal
Selbstprüfung {f} *n.* introspection
selbstständig*adj.* independent
Seligkeit {f} *n.* beatitude
selten *adj.* infrequent
selten *adj.* scarce
selten *adv.* seldom
Seltsamkeit {f} *n.* oddity

357

German		English
semantisch	*adj.*	semantic
Semester {m} *n.*		semester
Semester {n} *n.*		term
Semikolon {n}	*n.*	semicolon
Seminar {n} *n.*		seminar
semitisch	*adj.*	semitic
Senat {m}	*n.*	senate
Senator {m}	*n.*	senator
senatorial	*adj.*	senatorial
Sendbote {m}*n.*		emissary
senden *v.*		send
Sender {m}	*n.*	transmitter
Sendschreiben {n}	*n.*	missive
Sendung {f}	*n.*	mission
Senf {m} *n.*		mustard
Senilität {f}	*n.*	senility
senken *v.*		sag
senkrecht	*adj.*	perpendicular
Sennhütte {f} *n.*		chalet
Sense {f}*n.*		scythe
sensibel *adj.*		sensitive
Sensibilität {f}	*n.*	sensibility
Sensor {m}	*n.*	sensor
sensorisch	*adj.*	sensory
Sensualist {m}	*n.*	sensualist
Separatist {m}	*n.*	separatist
September {m}	*n.*	September
septisch *adj.*		septic
Serge {f} *n.*		serge
Serie {f} *n.*		sequence
Serie {f} *n.*		series
servieren *v.*		serve
Servierplatte {f}	*n.*	platter
Serviette {f}	*n.*	serviette
Sesam {m}	*n.*	sesame

German		English
sesshaft *adj.*		sedentary
Setzer {m}	*n.*	compositor
Setzer {m}	*n.*	typesetter
Seuche {f}	*n.*	pestilence
seufen *v.i.*		sigh
Sexismus {m}	*n.*	sexism
Sexualität {f} *n.*		sexuality
sexuell *adj.*		sexual
sexy *adj.*		sexy
Sezession {f} *n.*		secession
Showdown {m}	*n.*	showdown
sich betragen *v.*		comport
sich freuen *v.*		gloat
sich selbst *pron.*		themselves
sich sonnen *v.*		bask
Sichel {f}*n.*		sickle
sicher *adj.*		safe
sicher *adj.*		secure
sicher *adj.*		sure
Sicherheit {f} *n.*		certitude
Sicherheit {f} *n.*		immunity
Sicherheit {f} *n.*		safety
Sicherheit {f} *n.*		security
sicherlich *adv.*		surely
sichern *v.*		ensure
Sicht {f} *n.*		prospect
Sicht {f} *n.*		visibility
sichtbar *adj.*		visible
sickern *v.i.*		ooze
sie *pron.*		she
sie {pl} *pron.*		they
Sieb {n} *n.*		sieve
sieben *adj. & n.*		seven
siebend *v.*		sift
Siebeneck {n}	*n.*	heptagon

siebente *adj. & n.* seventh
siebzehn *adj. & n.* seventeen
siebzehnte *adj. & n.* seventeenth
siebzig *adj. & n.* seventy
siebzigste *adj. & n.* seventieth
sieden *v.* simmer
Siedler {m} *n.* settler
Siedlung {f} *n.* colony
Sieg {m} *n.* triumph
Sieg {m} *n.* victory
Sieger {m} *n.* victor
Siegeszeichen {n}*n.* trophy
siegreich *adj.* victorious
Siesta {f}*n.* siesta
Signal {n} *n.* signal
Signatur {f} *n.* signatory
Silbe {f} *n.* syllable
silbenbildend *adj.* syllabic
Silber {n} *n.* silver
Silizium {n} *n.* silicon
simulieren *v.* simulate
simultan *adj.* concurrent
Sinfonie {f} *n.* symphony
singen *v.* sing
Singleton *n.* singleton
singulär *adj.* singular
singularisch *adv.* singularly
sinken *v.* sink
sinken *v.* subside
sinken *v.* subsidize
Sinn {m} *n.* sense
Sinn {m} *n.* signification
sinnenfreudig *adj.* sensuous
sinnentstellen *v.* distort
Sinngedicht {n} *n.* epigram

sinnlich *adj.* sensual
Sinnlichkeit {f} *n.* sensuality
sinnlos *adj.* pointless
sinnlos *adj.* senseless
sinnvoll *adj.* suggestive
Siphon {m} *n.* siphon
Sippe {f} *n.* clan
Sippe {f} *n.* kin
Sirene {f} *n.* siren
Sirup {m} *n.* syrup
Sirup {m} *n.* treacle
Sittenlosigkeit {f} *n.* immorality
Sittlichkeit {f}*n.* morality
Sitzbank {f} *n.* bench
sitzen *v.* sit
Sitzung {f} *n.* session
Sitzung {f} *n.* sitting
Sitzwaschbecken {n} *n.* bidet
Skalierung {f}*n.* scale
Skalp {m} *n.* scalp
Skandal {m} *n.* scandal
Skateboard {n} *n.* skateboard
Skelett {n} *n.* skeleton
Skeptiker {m}*n.* sceptic
skeptisch *adj.* sceptical
Ski {m} *n.* ski
Skizze {f} *n.* sketch
Sklave {f} *n.* slave
Sklaverei {f} *n.* slavery
sklavisch *adj.* slavish
Skorpion {m} *n.* scorpion
Skrupel {pl} *n.* scruple
skrupellos *adj.* ruthless
Skulpteur {m}*n.* sculptor
Smaragd {m} *n.* emerald

359

Smog {m}   *n.*   smog
Smoking {m} *n.*   tuxedo
Smoothie {m}*n.*   smoothie
Snob {m}   *n.*   snob
Snobismus {m}   *n.*   snobbery
Snooker {n} *n.*   snooker
so   *adv.* as
so   *adv.* so
Socke {f}*n.*   sock
Sockel {m}   *n.*   pedestal
Sodbrennen {n}   *n.*   heartburn
Sodomie {f} *n.*   sodomy
Sofa {n} *n.*   settee
Sofa {n} *n.*   sofa
Sohle {f} *n.*   sole
Sohn {m}   *n.*   son
solar   *adj.* solar
Soldat {m}   *n.*   soldier
Solist {m}   *n.*   soloist
Solitär {n}   *n.*   solitaire
sollen   *v.*   shall
sollten   *v.*   should
Solo {n} *n.*   solo
Sommer {m} *n.*   summer
Sommersprosse {f}   *n.*   freckle
Sommerwende {f} *adj.* midsummer
Sonett {n}   *n.*   sonnet
Sonne {f}   *n.*   sun
Sonnenschirm {m}   *n.*   parasol
sonnig *adj.* sunny
Sonntag {m} *n.*   Sunday
sonst   *adv.* else
sonstig *adv.* otherwise
Sophismus {m}   *n.*   sophism
Sophist {m}   *n.*   sophist

Sorbet {n}   *n.*   sorbet
Sorge {f} *n.*   care
sorgenlos   *adj.* carefree
sorgfältig   *adj.* careful
sorgfältig   *adj.* painstaking
Sorte {f} *n.*   kind
sortiert   *adj.* assorted
Sortiment {n} *n.*   assortment
Soße {f} *n.*   sauce
Souffleur {m} *n.*   prompter
Soutane {f} *n.*   cassock
Souverän {m}*n.*   sovereign
Souveränität {f}   *n.*   sovereignty
sozial   *adj.* social
Sozialhilfeempfänger {m}*n.* pauper
sozialisieren *v.*   socialize
Sozialismus {m}   *n.*   socialism
Sozialist {m} *n.* & *adj.* socialist
Soziologie {f}*n.*   sociology
Spachtel {f} *n.*   filler
Spachtel {m} *n.*   trowel
Spaltung {f} *n.*   schism
Span {m}*n.*   splinter
Spanier {m} *n.*   Spaniard
spanisch*n.*   Spanish
Spanne {f}   *n.*   span
Spanne {n}   *n.*   retention
spannen *v.*   stretch
Spannhaken {m} *n.*   tenterhook
Spannung {f} *n.*   stress
Spannung {f} *n.*   suspense
Spannung {f} *n.*   tension
Spannungsspitze {f}   *n.*   glitch
Spannungsverstärker {m}   *n.*
   booster

Spargel {m}	*n.*	asparagus	
Sparren {m}	*n.*	chevron	
Sparsamkeit {f}	*n.*	parsimony	
Sparsamkeit {f}	*n.*	thrift	
Spaß {m}*n.*	fun		
Spaß {m}*n.*	spree		
Spaßmacher {m}	*n.*	jester	
spastisch	*adj.*	spastic	
spät *adj.* late			
Spaten {m}	*n.*	spade	
Speckbauch {m}	*n.*	paunch	
Speckle {m}	*n.*	speckle	
Spediteur {m}*n.*	carrier		
Spedition {f}	*n.*	conveyance	
Speer {m}	*n.*	spear	
Speerspitze {f}	*n.*	spearhead	
Speichel {m}	*n.*	saliva	
Speichel {m}	*n.*	spittle	
Speicherung {f}	*n.*	storage	
Speiseeis {n} *n.*	ice-cream		
Speisekammer {f} *n.*	larder		
Speisekammer {f} *n.*	pantry		
spektakulär *adj.*	sensational		
Spektrum {n} *n.*	spectrum		
Spekulation {f}	*n.*	speculation	
spekulieren *v.*	speculate		
Spender {m}	*n.*	donor	
Sperling {m}	*n.*	sparrow	
Sperma {n}	*n.*	sperm	
Sperre {f}	*n.*	gate	
Sperre {f}	*n.*	latch	
Sperrung {f}	*n.*	stoppage	
Spezialfach {n}	*n.*	speciality	
spezialisieren	*v.*	specialize	
Spezialisierung {f}*n.*	specialization		

Spezies {f}	*n.*	species	
spezifisch	*adj.*	specific	
Sphäre {f}	*n.*	sphere	
sphärisch	*adj.*	spherical	
Spiegel {m}	*n.*	mirror	
Spiel {n} *n.*	game		
Spiel {n} *v.i.*	play		
Spieler {m}	*n.*	gambler	
Spieler {m}	*n.*	player	
Spielerei {f}	*n.*	bauble	
Spielfläche {f}	*n.*	rink	
Spielplatz {m}	*n.*	playground	
Spielzeug {n} *n.*	toy		
Spieß {m}	*n.*	skewer	
spinal *adj.* spinal			
Spinat {m}	*n.*	spinach	
spindel *adj.* spindly			
Spindel {f}	*n.*	spindle	
Spinne {f}	*n.*	spider	
Spinnennetz {n}	*n.*	cobweb	
Spinner {m}	*n.*	spinner	
Spion {m}	*n.*	spy	
Spionage {f}	*n.*	espionage	
spirale *adj.* spiral			
Spiritismus {m}	*n.*	spiritualism	
Spiritualist {m}	*n.*	spiritualist	
Spitze {f}*n.*	peak		
Spitze {f}*n.*	lace		
spitzenartig *adj.* lacy			
Spitzmaus {f} *n.*	shrew		
Spitzname {m}	*n.*	nickname	
Splint {m}	*n.*	splint	
Split {m} *n.*	grit		
Splitterpartei {f}	*n.*	faction	
spontan *adj.* spontaneous			

Spontaneität {f}	*n.*	spontaneity	**Springer {m}**	*n.*	jack
Sporen {pl}	*n.*	spore	**Springer {m}**	*n.*	jumper
Sport {m}	*n.*	sport	**sprinten** *v.*	sprint	
sport...	*adj.*	sporting	**Sprinter {m}**	*n.*	sprinter
Sportler {m}	*n.*	sportsman	**Spritze {f}**	*n.*	syringe
sportlich *adj.*	athletic		**spritzig** *adj.*	nippy	
Spott {m}	*n.*	ridicule	**spröde** *adj.*	brittle	
Spott {m}	*n.*	sneer	**Sprossen {n}** *n.*	germination	
Spott {m}	*n.*	taunt	**Sprössling {m}**	*n.*	offshoot
spotten *v.*	jeer		**Sprotte {f}**	*n.*	sprat
Spötterei {f}	*n.*	mockery	**Sprühregen {m}**	*n.*	drizzle
Spötterei {f}	*n.*	raillery	**Sprühwasser {n}**	*n.*	spray
Sprache {f}	*n.*	language	**Sprung {m}**	*n.*	fissure
Sprache {f}	*n.*	speech	**Spucke {f}**	*n.*	spit
sprachlich	*adj.*	linguistic	**Spucknapf {m}**	*n.*	spittoon
sprachlos	*adj.*	mute	**spülen** *v.*	rinse	
sprachlos	*adj.*	speechless	**spülen** *v.*	swill	
Sprachwissenschaftler {m}*n.*linguist			**Spültisch {m}** *n.*	sink	
sprechen *v.*	speak		**Spund {m}**	*n.*	bung
sprechen *v.*	talk		**Spur {f}** *n.*	spoor	
sprechen *v.*	tweet		**Spur {f}** *n.*	vestige	
Sprecher {m} *n.*	speaker		**spürbar** *adj.*	sensible	
Sprecher {m} *n.*	spokesman		**Spürhund {m}**	*n.*	beagle
Sprechstundenhilfe {f} *n.*receptionist			**Spürhund {m}**	*n.*	sleuth
spreizen *v.*	spread		**Sputum {n}**	*n.*	sputum
spreizen *v.*	straddle		**Staat {m}***n.*	state	
Sprengapparate {pl}	*n.*	sprinkler	**Staatenbund {m}**	*n.*	commonwealth
sprenkeln *v.*	dapple		**Staatenbund {m}**	*n.*	confederation
Sprichwort {m}	*n.*	maxim	**Staatsangehörigkeit {f}***n.*	citizenship	
Sprichwort {m}	*n.*	proverb	**Staatsanwalt {m}**	*n.*	prosecutor
Sprichwort {m}	*n.*	saying	**Staatsanwaltschaft {f}***n.*		
sprichwörtlich	*adj.*	proverbial	prosecution		
springen *v.*	bounce		**Staatsbürger {m}** *n.*	citizen	
springen *v.i*	jump		**staatsbürgerlich** *adj.*	civic	
springen *v.*	spring		**Staatsbürgerschaft {f}***n.*	nationality	

Staatskasse {f}   *n.*   treasury
Staatsman {m}   *n.*   statesman
Stab {m} *n.*   baton
Stab {m} *n.*   wand
stabilisieren   *v.*   stabilize
Stabilisierung {f}   *n.*   stabilization
Stachel {m}   *n.*   prickle
Stachelbeere {f}   *n.*   gooseberry
stachelig*adj.*   spiky
Stachelschwein {n}   *n.*   porcupine
Stadion {n}   *n.*   stadium
Stadt {f} *n.*   city
Stadt {f} *n.*   town
Stadtbezirk {m}   *n.*   municipality
Stadtgemeinde {f} *n.*   borough
städtisch   *adj.*   municipal
Stadtteil {m}   *n.*   neighbourhood
Staffel {f}   *n.*   squadron
stagnieren   *v.*   stagnate
Stahl {m}*n.*   steel
Staket {n}   *n.*   paling
Stallung {f}   *n.*   mews
Stamm {m}   *n.*   tribe
stammeln   *v.*   stammer
stammes*adj.*   tribal
Stammgast {m}   *n.*   habitué
stämmig *adj.*   sturdy
Stand {m}   *n.*   booth
Standardisierung {f}*n.*   standardization
Standbild {n} *n.*   statue
Standesbeamte {m,f}*n.*   registrar
ständig   *adj.*   permanent
Standort {m}   *n.*   location
Standort {m}   *n.*   site
Standpunkt {m}   *n.*   post

Standpunkt {m}   *n.*   standpoint
Stange {f}   *n.*   rod
Stanze {f}   *n.*   stanza
stanzen   *v.*   emboss
Stapel {m}   *n.*   stack
Star {m}   *n.*   startling
stark   *adj.*   strong
Stärke {f}   *n.*   forte
Stärke {f}   *n.*   starch
Stärke {f}   *n.*   strength
Stärkungsmittel {n}   *n.*   tonic
starr   *adj.*   rigid
starren   *v.*   stare
starrköpfig   *adj.*   obstinate
starrköpfig   *adj.*   stubborn
starten   *v.*   start
Station {f}   *n.*   station
Statistik {f}   *n.*   statistics
Statistiker {m}   *n.*   statistician
statistisch   *adj.*   statistical
Stativ {n}*n.*   tripod
stattdessen   *adv.*   instead
stattlich *adj.*   stately
Statue {f}   *n.*   statuette
statuesk *adj.*   statuesque
Staub {m}   *n.*   dust
Staubbeutel {m}   *n.*   stamen
Stäubchen {pl}   *n.*   mote
Staubsauger {m}   *n.*   hoover
Staubtuch {n}*n.*   duster
Stauchung {f}*n.*   compression
Staudamm {m}   *n.*   dam
Stauwasser {n}   *n.*   backwater
stechen   *v.*   jab
stechen   *v.*   prick

363

stechen	v.	scorch	stellvertretend	adj. representative
Stechen {n}	n.	pang	stellvertretend	adj. vicarious
Stechen {n}	n.	twinge	Stempel {m} n.	hallmark
stechend	adj.	pungent	Stengel {m} n.	stalk

stechen v. scorch
Stechen {n} n. pang
Stechen {n} n. twinge
stechend adj. pungent
Stechkahnfahrer {m} n. punter
Stechmücke {f} n. gnat
Stechmücke {f} n. mosquito
Stechpalme {f} n. holly
Stecker {m} n. plug
Steckerbuchse {f} n. receptacle
Steckmodul {n} n. cartridge
Steckschlüssel {m} n. socket
stehen v. stand
Stehvermögen {n} n. stamina
steif adj. starchy
steifen v. stiffen
Steigbügel {m} n. clamp
Steigbügel {m} n. stirrup
steigen v. ascend
Steigen {pl} n. stile
steigend adj. ascendant
Steigung {f} n. gradient
Stein {m}n. stone
Steinbruch {m} n. mine
steinig adj. stony
Steinkiste {f} n. cist
Steinkohle {f}n. coal
Stelldichein {n} n. tryst
Stelle {f} n. spot
Stelle {f} n. stead
Stellung {f} n. job
Stellung {f} n. posture
Stellung {f} n. standing
Stellungnahme {f} n. statement
stellvertretend adj. acting

stellvertretend adj. representative
stellvertretend adj. vicarious
Stempel {m} n. hallmark
Stengel {m} n. stalk
Stenografie {f} n. stenography
Stenograph {m} n. stenographer
stentorisch adj. stentorian
Steppdecke {f} n. quilt
Steppe {f} n. steppe
Sterbeanzeige {f} n. obituary
Sterbefall {m}n. decease
sterben v. die
sterbend adj. moribund
Sterblichkeit {f} n. mortality
Stereoanlage {f} n. stereo
stereophonisch adj. stereophonic
stereoskopisch adj. stereoscopic
stereoskopisch n. stereotype
Sterilisation {f} n. sterilization
sterilisieren v. sterilize
Sterling n. sterling
Stern {m} n. asterisk
Stern {m} n. star
Sternchen {n}n. starlet
sternenförmig adj. stellar
sternförmig adj. astral
sternhell adj. starry
Sternkunde {f} n. astronomy
Sternwarte {f}n. observatory
Steroid {n} n. steroid
Stethoskop {n} n. stethoscope
Steuereinheit {f} n. controller
steuerrechtlich adj. fiscal
Steuerzuschlag {m} n. surtax
Stich {m}n. sting

Stichelei {m} *n.* quip
Stichling {m} *n.* stickleback
Stichtage {pl} *n.* deadline
Stickerei {f} *n.* embroidery
stickig *adj.* stuffy
Stickstoff {m}*n.* nitrogen
Stiefel {m} *n.* boot
Stier {m} *n.* bull
Stierfechter {m} *n.* toreador
Stift {m} *n.* pen
Stift {m} *n.* spike
Stift {m} *n.* tack
Stiftsherr {m} *n.* canon
Stigmata {n} *n.* stigmata
stigmatisieren *v.* stigmatize
Stil {m} *n.* style
Stilblüte {f} *n.* howler
stilisiert *adj.* stylized
Stilist {m} *n.* stylist
stilistisch *adj.* stylistic
still *adj.* calm
still *adj.* silent
still *adj.* tacit
Stille {f} *n.* silence
Stille {f} *n.* stillness
stillen *v.t.* slake
Stillstand {m}*n.* stagnation
Stillstand {m}*n.* standstill
stillstehend *adj.* stagnant
stilvoll *adj.* stylish
Stimme {f} *n.* voice
Stimmengewirr {n} *n.* Babel
Stimmrecht {n} *n.* suffrage
Stimmung {f} *n.* mood
Stimmungsmensch {m}*n.* monody

stinken *v.* stink
Stipendium {n} *n.* scholarship
Stirn {f} *n.* forehead
Stirnhöhle {f} *n.* sinus
stöbern *v.* rummage
Stock {m} *n.* cane
Stock {m} *n.* storey
Stöckelschuh {m} *n.* stiletto
Stockwerk {n} *n.* floor
Stoff {m}*n.* matter
stofflich *adj.* substantial
Stoffwechsel {m} *n.* metabolism
stöhnen *v.* groan
stöhnen *v.* moan
Stoiker {m} *n.* stoic
Stola {f} *n.* stole
Stollen {m} *n.* tunnel
stolpern *v.* stumble
stolz *adj.* proud
Stolz {m}*n.* pride
Stoppel {m} *n.* stubble
Stöpsel {m} *n.* peg
Stöpsel {m} *n.* stopper
Storch {m} *n.* stork
störend *adj.* spurious
störend {f} *adj.* dysfunctional
Störgeräusch {n} *v.* babble
störrisch*adj.* mulish
Störung {f} *n.* trouble
Stoß {m}*n.* pile
Stoß {m}*n.* shock
Stoßdämpfer {m} *n.* buffer
stoßen *v.* hustle
Stoßstange {f} *n.* bumper
stottern *v.* splutter

365

stottern *v.*	stutter
strafbar *adj.*	culpable
Strafe {f} *n.*	penalty
Strafe {f} *n.*	punishment
strafend *adj.*	punitive
straff *adj.*	smooth
straffällig *adj.*	delinquent
Strafgericht {n} *n.*	tribunal
Straflosigkeit {f} *n.*	impunity
strafmildern *v.*	mitigate
strafrechtlich *adj.*	penal
Strahl {m} *n.*	jet
Strahl {m} *n.*	ray
strahlen *v.*	radiate
strahlend *adj.*	brilliant
strahlend *adj.*	radiant
Strahlenforschung {f} *n.*	radiology
Strahlung {f} *n.*	radiation
Strähne {f} *n.*	hank
Strähne {f} *n.*	streak
strähnig *adj.*	lank
stramm *adj.*	upright
Strand {m} *n.*	seaside
stranden *v.*	strand
Strandgut {n} *n.*	waif
Strandräuber {m} *n.*	wrecker
Strang {m} *n.*	skein
strangulieren *v.*	strangle
Strangulierung {f} *n.*	strangulation
Straße *n.*	street
Straße {f} *n.*	avenue
Straßenbahn {f} *n.*	tram
Straßenbau {m} *n.*	road works
Straßenkreuzung {f} *n.*	crossing
Straßenpflaster {n} *n.*	pavement

Stratege {m} *n.*	strategist
Strategie {f} *n.*	policy
Strategie {f} *n.*	strategy
strategisch *adj.*	strategic
sträuben *v.*	ruffle
Strauß {m} *n.*	bunch
Strauß {m} *n.*	ostrich
Streber {m} *n.*	nerd
Strecke {f} *n.*	route
Strecke {f} *n.*	stretch
Streich {m} *n.*	escapade
Streich {m} *n.*	trick
Streifblick {m} *v.i.*	glance
Streifen *v.*	patrol
streifen *v.t.*	strip
Streifen {m} *n.*	tab
Streifen {pl} *n.*	stripe
Streifenbildung {f} *n.*	striation
streifig *adj.*	streaky
Streifzug {m} *n.*	foray
streiken *adj.*	stricken
streiken *v.*	strike
Streikende {m,f} *n.*	striker
Streit {m} *n.*	wrangle
streitbar *adj.*	warlike
streiten *v. i*	dispute
Streiter {m} *n.*	fighter
Streitfall {m} *n.*	issue
Streithammel {m} *n.*	squabble
streitig *adj.*	debatable
streitig *adj.*	moot
streitlustig *adj.*	belligerent
Streitsache {f} *n.*	litigation
streitsüchtig *adj.*	contentious
streitsüchtig *adj.*	quarrelsome

streng	adj.	austere
streng	adj.	rigorous
streng	adj.	severe
streng	adj.	strict
Strenge {f}	n.	rigour
Strenge {f}	n.	severity
Strenge {f}	n.	stringency
strenges adv.	strictly	
streuen v.	strew	
Streugerät {n}	n.	distributor
Strick {m}	n.	cord
Strick {m}	n.	halter
stricken v.	knit	
Strickjacke {f}	n.	cardigan
striegel {m}	n.	curry
Stringtanga {m}	n.	thong
Stroh {n}n.	straw	
Strohbündel {n}	n.	wisp
Strohmann {m}	n.	stooge
Strolch {m}	n.	vagabond
strolchen v.	tramp	
Strom {m}	n.	stream
Stromstärke {f}	n.	current
Stromstoß {m}	n.	surge
Strömung {f} n.	flux	
Strophe {f}	n.	stave
strotzen v.i.	abound	
Strudel {m}	n.	strudel
strukturell	adj.	structural
Strumpf {m}	n.	stocking
Strumpfband {n}	n.	garter
Strumpfware {f}	n.	hosiery
Stuck {m}	n.	stucco
Stück {n}n.	piece	
Stück {n}n.	wedge	

Stückchen {n}	n.	shred
stückweise	adv.	piecemeal
Student {m}	n.	undergraduate
Studienplan {m}	n.	curriculum
studieren	v.	study
Studio {n}	n.	studio
Stufe {f} n.	pace	
Stufe {f} n.	rung	
stufenweise	adj.	gradual
Stuhl {m}	n.	stool
Stümper {m}	n.	cobble
stumpf	adj.	blunt
stumpf	adj.	dull
Stumpf {m}	n.	stump
Stumpfheit {f}	n.	stupor
Stunde {f}	n.	hour
stupsen v.	prod	
stur adj.	stolid	
Sturheit {f}	n	obstinacy
Sturm {m}	n.	gale
Sturm {m}	n.	storm
stürmisch	adj.	tempestuous
stürmisch	adj.	turbulent
stürmisch	adj.	vehement
stürzen v.	plummet	
stürzen v.	topple	
Sturzflut {f}	n.	torrent
sturzflutartig	adj.	torrential
Stute {f} n.	mare	
Stütze {f}n.	column	
Stütze {f}n.	pad	
Stütze {f}n.	prop	
Stütze {f}n.	strut	
Stütze {f}	n.	trestle
stutzen v.	lop	

stutzen	v.	truncate	Sünder {m}	n.	sinner
Stutzer {m}	n.	dandy	sündhaft adj.	sinful	
Stützpunkt {m}	n.	fulcrum	super	adj.	super
stygisch adj.	stygian		Supermacht {f}	n.	superpower
subjektiv adj.	subjective		Supermarkt {m}	n.	supermarket
sublimieren	v.	sublimate	Suppe {f}	n.	soup
substantiell	adj.	substantive	Surrealismus {m}	n.	surrealism
Substantiv {n}	n.	noun	surrealistisch adj.	surreal	
Substanz {f}	n.	substance	süß adj.	cute	
Subtraktion {f}	n.	subtraction	süß adj.	sweet	
subtropisch adj.	subtropical		Süßkartoffel {f}	n.	yam
subunternehmung v.	subcontract		Süßstoff {m}	n.	saccharin
Subvention {f}	n.	subsidy	Süßstoff {m}	n.	sweetener
Suche {f} n.	quest		Symbiose {f}	n.	symbiosis
suchen	v.	search	Symbol {n}	n.	symbol
suchen	v.i.	seek	Symbolik {f}	n.	symbolism
Sucht {f} n.	addiction		symbolisch	adj.	symbolic
süchtig adj.	addicted		symbolisieren	v.	symbolize
Süchtige {m,f}	n.	addict	Symmetrie {f} n.	symmetry	
Süden {m}	n.	south	symmetrisch adj.	symmetrical	
südländisch adj.	southern		sympathisch adj.	congenial	
südlich adj.	southerly		sympathisch adj.	likeable	
Sudoku {m}	n.	Sudoku	sympathisch adj.	sympathetic	
süffisant adj.	smug		sympathisieren	v.	sympathize
Sühne {f}	n.	atonement	Symposium {n}	n.	symposium
sühnen	v.	atone	Symptom {n} n.	symptom	
sühnen	v.	expiate	symptomatisch	adj.	symptomatic
Sultanin {f}	n.	sultana	synchronisieren	v.	synchronize
Summe {f}	n.	amount	Syndrom {n} n.	syndrome	
Summer {m} n.	buzzer		Synergie {f}	n.	synergy
summieren	v.	add	synonym	adj.	synonymous
Sumpf {m}	n.	mire	Synonym {n} n.	synonym	
Sumpf {m}	n.	swamp	Synthese {f}	n.	synthesis
Sünde {f}	n.	sin	System {n}	n.	system
Sündenbock {m}	n.	scapegoat	systematisch adj.	methodical	

systematisch *adj.* orderly
systematisieren *v.* systematize
systemisch *adj.* systemic
Szenario {n} *n.* scenario
Szene {f}*n.* scene
Szenerie {f} *n.* scenery

T

Tabak {m} *n.* tobacco
tabellarisieren *v.* tabulate
Tabellenkalkulation {f}*n.*
spreadsheet
Tablett {n} *n.* salver
Tablette {f} *n.* tablet
Tabu {m}*n.* taboo
Tabulator {m}*n.* tabulator
tadeln *v.* censure
tadeln *v.* rebuke
tadeln *v.* reprove
tadelnswert *adj.* reprehensible
Täfelchen {n} *n.* platelet
Täfelung {f} *n.* wainscot
Tag {m} *n.* day
Tageblatt {n} *n.* journal
Tagesordnung {f} *n.* agenda
täglich *adj.* daily
Tagung {f} *n.* meeting
Taifun {m} *n.* typhoon
Taille {f} *n.* bodice
Taille {f} *n.* waist
Takelage {f} *n.* rigging
takeln *v.* rig
Takt {m} *n.* tact
Taktik {f}*n.* tactic
Taktiker {m} *n.* tactician

taktisch *adj.* tactical
taktvoll *adj.* tactful
Tal {n} *n.* ale
Tal {n} *n.* dale
Tal {n} *n.* dell
Tal {n} *n.* valley
Talent {n} *n.* flair
Talg {m} *n.* tallow
Talisman {m} *n.* talisman
Talk {m} *n.* talc
Tamarinde {f} *n.* tamarind
Tamburin {n} *n.* tambourine
Tampon {n} *n.* tampon
Tangens {m} *n.* tangent
Tankwagen {m} *n.* tanker
Tante {f} *n.* aunt
Tanz {m} *v.* dance
Tänzer {m} *n.* dancer
Tapas {n} *n.* tapas
tapfer *adj.* brave
tapfer *adj.* valiant
Tapferkeit {f} *n.* bravery
Tapferkeit {f} *n.* fortitude
Tapferkeit {f} *n.* prowess
Tarif {m} *n.* tariff
Tarock {n} *n.* tarot
Tasche {f} *n.* pocket
Taschenbuch {n} *n.* paperback
Taschenlampe {f} *n.* flash light
Taschentuch {n} *n.* handkerchief
tasten *v.* grope
Tatenlosigkeit {f} *n.* inaction
Tätigkeit {f} *n.* activity
Tatsache {f} *n.* fact
tatsächlich *adj.* actual

369

tatsächlich	adj.	real
tätscheln	v.	pat
Tattoo {n}	n.	tattoo
Tau {m}	n.	dew
taub	adj.	deaf
Taube {f}	n.	pigeon
tauchen	v. t	dip
tauchen	v.	dive
tauchen	v.	plunge
tauen	v.	thaw
Taufe {f}	n.	baptism
taufen	v.	baptize
Täufer {m}	n.	Baptist
Taufpate {f}	n.	godfather
Taumel {m}	n.	rapture
Taumel {m}	n.	whirl
Taumelkäfer {m}	n.	whirligig
tauschen	v.	swap
täuschen	v.	beguile
täuschen	v.	bluff
täuschen	v.	delude
täuschen	v.	hoodwink
täuschen	v.	mystify
täuschen	v.	pretend
täuschend	adj.	deceptive
Tauschgeschäft {n}	v.	barter
Täuschung {f}	n.	deception
Täuschung {f}	n.	fallacy
tausend	adj. & n.	thousand
Tausendfuß {m}	n.	centipede
Taxi {n}	n.	cab
Taxi {n}	n.	taxi
Taxonomie {f}	n.	taxonomy
Teak {n}	n.	teak
Technik {f}	n.	technology

Techniker {m}	n.	technician
technisch	adj.	technical
technische Spielerei {f}	n.	gadget
Technologe {m}	n.	technologist
technologisch	adj.	technological
Tee {m}	n.	tea
Teedose {f}	n.	caddy
Teer {m}	n.	tar
Teesemmel {f}	n.	muffin
Teich {m}	n.	hamlet
Teich {m}	n.	pond
Teig {m}	n.	dough
Teilchen {n}	n.	bun
Teilchen {n}	n.	modicum
Teilchen {n}	n.	whit
teilen	v.	divide
Teilhaberschaften {pl}	n.	cahoots
teilnahmslos	adj.	impassive
teilnehmen	v.	partake
Teilnehmer {m}	n.	participant
Teilnehmer {m}	n.	partner
teilweise	adv.	partly
Telefon {m}	n.	telephone
Telefon {n}	n.	phone
Telegraf {m}	n.	telegraph
Telegrafie {f}	n.	telegraphy
Telegramm {n}	n.	telegram
telegraphisch	adj.	telegraphic
telepathisch	adj.	telepathic
Telepathist {m}	n.	telepathist
Teleskop {n}	n.	telescope
Teletext {n}	n.	teletext
Teller {m}	n.	plate
Temperament {n}	n.	temperament

Temperatur {f}   *n.*   temperature
Temperaturregler {m}   *n.*   thermostat
Tempo {n}   *n.*   tempo
tendenziös   *adj.*   tendentious
Tennis {n}   *n.*   tennis
Tennisschuhe {pl} *n.*   sneaker
Tenor {m}   *n.*   tenor
Tentakel {m}   *n.*   tentacle
Teppich {m}   *n.*   carpet
Termin {m}   *n.*   date
terminal *adj.* terminal
Terminologie {f}   *n.*   terminology
terminologisch   *adj.* terminological
Termite {f}   *n.*   termite
Terpentin {n} *n.*   turpentine
Terrain {n}   *n.*   terrain
Terrakotta {f} *n.*   terracotta
Terrasse {f}   *n.*   terrace
terrestrisch   *adj.* terrestrial
Terrier {m}   *n.*   terrier
territorial*adj.* territorial
Terror {m}   *n.*   terror
terrorisieren *v.*   terrorize
Terrorismus {m}   *n.*   terrorism
Terrorist {m} *n.*   terrorist
Tertiär   *adj.* tertiary
Terzett {n}   *n.*   trio
Testament {n}   *n.*   testament
Testamentsvollstrecker {m } *n.*
    executor
testiert *adj.* testate
Testosteron {n}   *n.*   testosterone
teuer   *adv.* dearly
teuer   *adj.* expensive
Teufel {m}   *n.*   demon

Teufel {m}   *n.*   devil
Text {m} *n.*   text
Theater {n}   *n.*   theatre
theatralisch   *adj.* theatrical
Theismus {n} *n.*   theism
Thema {n}   *n.*   theme
Thema {n}   *n.*   topic
thematisch   *adj.* thematic
thematisch   *adj.* topical
Theodolit   *n.*   theodolite
Theokratie {f} *n.*   theocracy
Theologe {m} *n.*   theologian
Theologie {f}   *n.*   theology
Theoretiker {m}   *n.*   theorist
theoretisch   *adj.* theoretical
Theorie {f}   *n.*   theory
theorisieren *v.*   theorize
Theosophie {f}   *n.*   theosophy
Therapeut {m}   *n.*   therapist
therapeutisch*adj.* therapeutic
Therapie {f}   *n.*   therapy
thermisch   *adj.* thermal
Thermodynamik {f}*n.*
    thermodynamics
Thermometer {n}   *n.*   thermometer
Thermosflasche {f}   *n.*   thermos
These {f}*n.*   thesis
Thron {m}   *n.*   throne
Thronhimmel {m} *n.*   canopy
Tiara {f} *n.*   tiara
Ticken {n}   *n.*   tick
tief *adj.* deep
Tiefe {f}   *n.*   depth
tiefgefühlt   *adj.* heartfelt
tiefgestellt   *adj.* subscript

371

Tiefgründigkeit {f} n.	profundity		toben v.	rampage

Tiefgründigkeit {f} n. profundity
Tiefkühltruhe {f} n. freezer
tiefsinnig adj. profound
Tieftonlautsprecher {m} n.woofer
Tier {n} n. animal
Tier {n} n. brute
Tierfutter {n} n. fodder
Tiergehege {n} n. vivarium
tierisch adj. beastly
tierisch adj. bestial
Tierkreis {m} n. zodiac
Tierkunde {f} n. zoology
Tierpark {m} n. zoo
Tierpfleger {m} n. keeper
Tiger {m}n. tiger
tilgen v. liquidate
tilgen v. obliterate
tilgen v. redeem
Tilgung {f} n. deletion
Tilgung {f} n. redemption
Tinktur {f} n. tincture
Tinte {f} n. ink
Tintenfisch {m} n. squid
Tipp {m} n. hint
Tipp {m} n. tip
Tirade {f}n. tirade
Tisch {m} n. desk
Tisch {n}n. table
titanisch adj. titanic
Titel {m} n. title
titular adj. titular
tituliert adj. titled
Toastbrot {n} n. toast
Toaster {m} n. toaster
toben v. bluster

toben v. rampage
tobend adj. uproarious
Tochter {f} n. daughter
Tod {m} n. death
todgeweiht adj. fey
tödlich adj. deadly
tödlich adj. fatal
tödlich adj. lethal
tödlich adj. mortal
Toga {f} n. toga
Toilette {f} n. toilet
Toilettensache {f} n. toiletries
tolerant adj. permissive
tolerante adj. tolerant
Toleranz {f} n. tolerance
toll adj. jazzy
toll adj. madcap
toll adj. great
Tolle {f} n. quiff
tollen v. romp
Tollhaus {n} n. bedlam
Tollwut {f} n. rabies
Tölpel {m} n. jay
Tölpel {m} n. yokel
Tomate {f}, n. tomato
Tomatensauce {f} n. ketchup
Ton {m} n. chime
Ton {m} n. clay
Ton {m} n. sound
Tonband {n} n. tape
Toner {n} n. toner
Tonhöhe {f} n. pitch
Tonnage {f} n. tonnage
Tonne {f} n. ton
Tonsur {f} n. tonsure

372

Tönung {f}	*n.*	tinge
Topas {m}	*n.*	topaz
Topf {m} *n.*	pot
Topfdeckel {m}	*n.*	lid
Töpfer {m}	*n.*	pottery
Topograph {m}	*n.*	topographer
Topographie {f}	*n.*	topography
topographisch	*adj.*	topographical
Tor {n}	*n.*	goal
Tor {n}	*n.*	tor
Törchen {n}	*n.*	wicket
Torf {m} *n.*	turf
torkeln *v.*	lurch
Tornado {m}	*n.*	tornado
Torpedo {n}	*n.*	torpedo
Törtchen {m} *n.*	tart
Torte {f}	*n.*	pie
Torwart {m}	*n.*	goalkeeper
tosend	*adj.*	tumultuous
tot	*adj.*	dead
totalitär	*adj.*	totalitarian
töten	*v.*	kill
Totenschrein {m}	*n.*	coffin
Totenstadt {f}*n.*	necropolis
totgeboren	*n.*	stillborn
totschlagen	*v.*	swat
Tötung {f}	*n.*	killing
Tour {f}	*n.*	tour
Tourist {m}	*n.*	tourist
Toxikologie {f}	*n.*	toxicology
traben	*v.*	lope
Traber {m}	*n.*	trotter
Tracht {f}	*n.*	garb
Tracht {f}	*n.*	livery
Tradition {f}	*n.*	tradition

Traditionalist {m}	*n.*	traditionalist
traditionell	*adj.*	traditional
traff	*adj.*	tight
Traffiker {m}	*n.*	trafficker
Tragbalken {m}	*n.*	girder
Tragband {n} *n.*	brace
tragbar	*adj.*	portable
tragbar	*adj.*	sustainable
träge	*adj.*	indolent
Trage {f} *n.*	stretcher
tragen	*v.t*	bear
tragen	*v.*	carry
tragen	*v.*	wear
Tragflügelboot {n}*n.*	hydrofoil
Trägheit {f}	*n.*	idleness
Trägheit {f}	*n.*	inertia
Tragiker {m}	*n.*	tragedian
tragisch *adj.*	tragic
Tragödie {f}	*n.*	tragedy
Trainer {m}	*n.*	coach
Trainer {m}	*n.*	trainer
trainieren	*v.*	train
Trainingsanzug {m}	*n.*	tracksuit
Traktor {m}	*n.*	tractor
trampeln *v.*	trample
Trampelpfad {m}	*n.*	trail
Trampolin {n}*n.*	trampoline
Trance {f}	*n.*	trance
Träne {f} *n.*	tear
tränenreich	*adj.*	lachrymose
tränenvoll	*adj.*	tearful
Transaktion {f}	*n.*	transaction
transatlantisch	*adj.*	transatlantic
Transformator {m}*n.*	transformer
Transfusion {f}	*n.*	transfusion

German			English
Transistor {m}	n.	transistor
transitiv adj.	transitive
transkontinental adj.	transcontinental
transkribieren v.	transliterate
Transkription {f}	n.	transcription
Transparenz {f}	n.	transparency
Transpiration {f}	n.	perspiration
Transport {m}	n.	portage
Transport {m}	v.	transport
Transportbehälter {m}	n.	casket
Transporter {m}	n.	transporter
Transsexuelle {m,f}	n.transsexual
Transvestit {m}	n.	transvestite
transzendent adj.	transcendental
Trapez {n}	n.	trapeze
Trassant {m} n.	drawer
Tratsch {m}	n.	tattle
Trauende {m,f}	n.	mourner
Trauerarbeit {f}	n.	mourning
trauern v.	mourn
Traum {m}	n.	dream
Trauma {n}	n.	trauma
Träumerei {f} n.	reverie
traurig adj.	mournful
traurig adj.	plaintive
Trauung {f}	n.	marriage
Travestie {f}	n.	travesty
Treck {m}	n.	trek
treffen v.	meet
treffend adj.	apposite
Treffer {m}	v.	hit
treiben v.	drift
treiben v.	wreak
Trend {m}	n.	trend
trennbar adj.	separable

German			English
trennen v.	disconnect
trennen v.	segregate
trennen v.	sunder
trennscharf adj.	selective
Trennung {f}	n.	detachment
Trennung {f}	n.	division
Trennung {f}	n.	parting
Trennung {f}	n.	segregation
Trennwand {f}	n.	partition
Treppe {f}	n.	stair
Treppenhaus {n}	n.	staircase
treten v.	kick
Tretmühle {f} n.	treadmill
treu adj.	faithful
treu adj.	trusty
treubrüchig adj.	disloyal
treulos adj.	faithless
Triathlon {m} n.	triathlon
Trichter {m}	n.	funnel
Trieb {m}n.	desire
triefend adj.	sopping
Trigonometrie {f}	n.	trigonometry
Trikoloren n.	tricolour
Trikot {n}	n.	jersey
Trill {m} n.	trill
trillern v.	warble
Trillion {f}	adj & n.	trillion
Trilogie {f}	n.	trilogy
trinken v. t	drink
Triptychon {n}	n.	triptych
trist adj.	forlorn
triumphierend adj.	triumphal
Trizeps {m}	n.	triceps
Trockener {m}	n.	dryer
Trockenheit {f}	n.	drought

374

trödeln	v.	dally
trödeln	v.	loiter
trödeln	v.	niggle
Troia	n.	Troy
Troll {m} n.		troll
Trommel {f}	n.	drum
Trompete {f}	n.	trumpet
tropfen	v.	seep
Tropfen {m}	v. i	drip
tropisch adj.		tropical
Trost {m}	n.	comfort
Trost {m}	n.	solace
trösten	v.	comfort
trösten	v. t.	console
trostlos adj.		cheerless
trostlos adj.		disconsolate
trostlos adj.		dreary
trostlos adj.		inconsolable
trostreich	adj.	comfortable
Trottel {m}	n.	jerk
Trottel {m}	n.	wally
trotten	v.	trot
trotzprep.		despite
trotz alledem a.		nonetheless
trüb adj.	fishy
trüb adj.	turbid
trüben	v.	tarnish
Trübsinn {m} n.		gloom
trudeln	v.	trundle
Trüffel {m}	n.	truffle
trügerisch	adj.	elusive
trügerisch	adj.	specious
trügerisch	adj.	treacherous
Trumpf {m}	n.	trump
Trunkenbold {m}	adj.	drunkard

Trupp {m}	n.	band
Trupp {m}	n.	troop
Truthahn {f}	n.	turkey
Tsunami {m} n.		tsunami
Tuberkelbazilus {m}	n.	tubercle
Tuberkulose {f}	n.	tuberculosis
Tuch {n} n.		blanket
Tuch {n} n.		cloth
tüchtig adj.		proficient
tüchtig adj.		strenuous
Tugend {f}	n.	goodness
tugendhaft	adj.	virtuous
Tülle {f} n.		spout
Tulpe {f} n.		tulip
Tumor {m}	n.	tumour
tun v.	do
tünchen v.	whitewash
Tuner {m}	n.	tuner
tüpfeln	v.	stipple
Tür {f}	n.	door
Turban {m}	n.	turban
Turbine {f}	n.	turbine
Turbolader {m}	n.	turbocharger
Turbulenz {f} n.		turbulence
türkis	n.	turquoise
Turm {m}	n.	tower
Turmspitze {f}	n.	spire
Turner {m}	n.	gymnast
Turnhalle {f} n.		gymnasium
Turnier {n}	n.	tournament
Türschwelle {f}	n.	sill
Türsteher {m}n.		bouncer
Tweed	n.	tweed
Typ {m} n.		type
Typhus {m}	n.	typhoid

375

Typhus {m}	*n.*	typhus
typisch	*adj.*	typical
Tyrann {m}	*n.*	tyrant
tyrannisieren	*v.*	tyrannize

Ü

übel *adj.*		evil
Übelkeit {f}	*n.*	nausea
übellaunig	*adj.*	feisty
über *adv.*		about
über *pref.*		hyper
über *prep.*		of
über *prep.*		via
über Bord	*adv.*	overboard
überallhin	*adv.*	abroad
überaltert	*adj.*	outdated
überarbeiten	*v.*	revise
überarbeitet	*adj.*	overwrought
Überarbeitung {f}	*n.*	revision
Überblick {m} *n.*		overview
überblicken	*v.t.*	survey
überboten	*v.*	outbid
überdauern	*v.*	outlast
überdenken	*v.*	reconsider
Überdosis {f}	*n.*	overdose
übereifrig	*adj.*	officious
übereinstimmen	*v.*	accord
übereinstimmen	*v.*	coincide
Übereinstimmung {f}	*n.*	accordance
Übereinstimmung {f}	*n.*	concord
Übereinstimmung {f}	*n.*	concordance
Übereinstimmung {f}	*n.*	conformity
Übereinstimmung {f}	*n.*	rapport
überfallen	*v.*	attack
überfällig	*adj.*	overdue

Überfluss {m} *n.*		abundance
Überfluss {m} *n.*		profusion
Überfluss {m} *n.*		superabundance
Überfluss {m} *n.*		superfluity
überflüssig	*adj.*	redundant
überflüssig	*adj.*	spare
überflüssig	*adj.*	superfluous
überfordern	*v.*	overcharge
überführbar	*adj.*	transferable
Überführung {f}	*n.*	overpass
Übergang {m}	*n.*	transit
übergeben	*v.*	consign
Übergewicht {n}	*n.*	preponderance
überglücklich *adj.*		overjoyed
übergroß *adj.*		outsize
überhängend *adj.*		pendent
überhäufe	*n.*	glut
überhäufen	*v.*	besiege
überheblich	*adj.*	arrogant
überholen	*v.*	outstrip
überholen	*v.*	overtake
überholend	*v.*	overhaul
überladen	*adj.*	flamboyant
überladen	*v.*	ornate
überlagern	*v.*	superimpose
überlappen	*v.*	overlap
überlassen	*v.*	cede
überlasten	*v.*	overburden
überlasten	*v.*	overload
Überlastung {f}	*n.*	congestion
Überlauf {m} *v.*		overflow
Überläufer {m}	*n.*	renegade
überleben	*v.*	outlive
überleben	*v.*	survive
Überleben {n} *n.*		survival

überlegen	v.	cogitate	Überschrift {f}	n.	headline
Überlegenheit {f}	n.	pre-eminence	überschritten	v.	exceed
Überlegenheit {f}	n.	supremacy	Überschuss {m}	n.	surplus
Überlegung {f}	n.	deliberation	überschüssig	adj.	excessive
Überleitung {f}	n.	transition	überschütten	v.	whelm
Überlieferung {f}	n.	deliverance	Überschwang {m}	n.	ardour
Überlieferung {f}	n.	lore	überschwemmen	v.	inundate
überlisten	v.	outwit	Überschwemmung {f}	n.	flood
Übermacht {f}	n.	superiority	überseeisch	adv.	overseas
Übermantel {m}	n.	overcoat	übersehen	v.	overlook
übermäßig	adv.	overly	übersetzen	v.	compile
übermäßig	adj.	profuse	übersetzen	v.	translate
übermenschlich	adj.	herculean	Übersetzung {f}	n.	translation
übermenschlich	adj.	superhuman	Übersetzung {f}	n.	transmission
übermitteln	v.	transmit	Übersicht {f}	n.	oversight
übermütig	adj.	wanton	Übersicht {f}	n.	synopsis
übernehmen	v.	undertake	Übersichtlichkeit {f}	n.	clarity
Überprüfung {f}	n.	verification	übersinnlich	adj.	supernatural
Überraschung {f}	n.	surprise	Überspanntheit {f}	n.	extravagance
überreden	v.	persuade	überspielen	v.	overact
überreichlich	adj.	superabundant	überspringen	v.	leap
Überrest {m}	n.	remnant	überspringen	v.	skip
überrollen	v.	overrun	übersteigen	v.	surmount
Übersättigung {f}	n.	surfeit	überstrahlen	v.	outshine
Überschall	adj.	supersonic	Überstunde {f}	n	overtime
Überschall...	adj.	ultrasonic	übertölpeln	v.	dupe
überschatten	v.	overshadow	übertragen	v. t	broadcast
überschätzen	v.	overestimate	übertragen	v.	convert
überschätzen	v.	overrate	übertragen	v.	devolve
überschäumend	adj.	ebullient	übertragen	v.t.	telecast
überschäumend	adj.	exuberant	übertragen	v.	televise
überschreiten	v.	outrun	übertragen	v.	transfer
überschreiten	v.	overstep	übertragen	v.	transfuse
überschreiten	v.	transcend	übertreffen	v.	excel
überschrieben	v.	override	übertreffen	v.	outclass

übertreffen	v.	outdo
übertreffen	v.	surpass
übertreiben	v.	overdo
Übertreibung {f}	n.	exaggeration
übertreten	v.	transgress
übertreten	v.	trespass
Übertretung {f}	n.	transgression
übertrieben	v.	exaggerate
übervorteilen	v.	overreach
Überwacht	adj.	invigilate
Überwachung {f}	n.	surveillance
Überwachungseinrichtung {f} n.		
invigilator		
überwältigen	v.	overpower
überwältigen	v.	overwhelm
überweltlich	adj.	transcendent
überwiegen	v.	outweigh
überwiegen	v.	overbalance
überwiegen	v.	preponderate
überwiegen	v.	prevail
überwinden	v.	overcome
überwintern	v.	hibernate
überwuchernd	adj.	overgrown
überzeugen	v.	convince
Überzeugung {f}	n.	persuasion
überziehen	v.	overdraw
Überziehung {f}	n.	overdraft
üblich	adj.	usual
üblicherweise	adv.	usually
übriggeblieben	adj.	extant
Übung {f}	n.	practice

U

Uferschnecke {f}	n.	winkle
Uhr {f}	n.	clock

Ultimatum {n}n.		ultimatum
ultramarin	n.	ultramarine
Ultraschall {m}	n.	ultrasound
um Geld spielen	v.	gamble
umarmen	v.	embrace
Umarmung {f}	v.	hug
Umber {n}	n.	umber
Umbruch {m} n.		upheaval
umdenken	v.	rethink
umdirigieren	v.	rearrange
umdrucken	v.	reprint
Umfang {m}	n.	complexity
Umfang {m}	n.	scope
umfangen	v.	surround
umfangreich	adj.	voluminous
umfassen	v.	comprise
umfassend	adj.	global
umfasst	v.	enfold
Umformung {f}	n.	transformation
Umfrage {f}	n.	poll
umganglich	adj.	colloquial
umgearbeiten	v.	revamp
umgeben	v.	encompass
umgebend	adj.	ambient
Umgebung {f}	n.	entourage
Umgebung {f}	n.	setting
Umgebungen {pl}	n.	surroundings
umgehen	v.	elude
Umgehung {f}	n.	bypass
Umgehung {f}	n.	evasion
umgekehrt	adv.	vice-versa
umgestalten	v.	transfigure
Umgestaltung {f}	n.	transfiguration
umgruppieren	v.	redeploy
Umhang {m}	n.	cape

Umhang {m}	n.	shawl
umherspringen	v.	cavort
umherstreichend	adj.	roving
umherstreifen	v.	ramble
umherstreifen	v.	scour
umherstreifen	v.	straggle
umhertasten	v.	fumble
umhüllen	v.	muffle
umkehrbar	adj.	reversible
umkehren	v.	invert
Umkehrung {f}	v.	converse
Umkehrung {f}	n.	reversal
umklammern	v.	clasp
umkommen	v.	perish
umlaufend	adj.	rotary
Umriss {m}	v.	contort
umrissen	n.	contour
Umsatz {m}	n.	turnover
umsatzsteuerlich	adj.	taxable
Umschläge {m}	n.	envelope
umschreiben	v.	circumscribe
umschreiben	v.	paraphrase
umschütteln	v.	reshuffle
umschütten	v.	spill
umseitig	adv.	overleaf
Umsetzung {f}	n.	conversion
umsichtig	adj.	canny
umspulen	v.	rewind
Umstand {m}	n.	circumstance
Umstand {m}	n.	conjuncture
umsteuern	v.	reverse
umstimmen	v.	return
umstoßen	v.	overturn
Umstürz {m}	n.	subversion
umstürzen	v.	overthrow

umwälzen	v.	revolutionize
umwandeln	v.	transform
Umweg {m}	n.	detour
umwerten	v.	reassess
unabsehbar	adj.	incalculable
unabsichtlich	adv.	unwittingly
unabwendbar	adj.	inevitable
unangebracht	adj.	inappropriate
unangebracht	adj.	inopportune
unangenehm	adj.	unpleasant
unangreifbar	adj.	unassailable
unangreifbar	adj.	untouchable
unanständig	adj.	indecent
unanständig	adj.	rude
Unanständigkeit {f}	n.	indecency
unantastbar	adj.	inviolable
unantastbar	adj.	unimpeachable
unartikuliert	adj.	inarticulate
unaufgefordert	adj.	uncalled
unaufgefordert	adj.	unsolicited
unaufhaltsam	adj.	irresistible
unaufhörlich	adj.	ceaseless
unauflöslich	adj.	insoluble
unaufrichtig	adj.	disingenuous
unaufrichtig	adj.	insincere
Unaufrichtigkeit {f}	adv.	insincerity
unausgefüllt	adj.	blank
unaussprechlich	adj.	unmentionable
unaussprechlich	adj.	unutterable
unausweichlich	adj.	unavoidable
unbändig	adj.	unruly
unbarmherzig	adj.	relentless
unbedeutend	adj.	petty
unbedeutend	adj.	trivial
unbedingt	adj.	imperative

unbedingt	*adj.*	unconditional
unbefahrbar	*adj.*	impassable
Unbehagen {n}	*n.*	discomfort
unbehaglich	*adj.*	uneasy
unbeholfen	*adj.*	ungainly
unbekümmert	*adv.*	gaily
unbekümmert	*adj.*	mindless
unbekümmert	*adj.*	reckless
unbeliebt	*adj.*	unpopular

Unbequemlichkeit {f}*n.*inconvenience

unberechtigt	*adj.*	unwarranted
unbeschädigt*adj.*		intact
unbeschädigt*adj.*		unscathed
unbescheiden	*n.*	immodest
Unbescheidenheit {f}*a.*		immodesty
Unbescholtenheit {f}*n.*		integrity
unbeschränkt*adj.*		unlimited
unbeschreiblich	*adj.*	indescribable
unbesiegbar	*adj.*	invincible
unbesonnen	*adj.*	imprudent
Unbesonnenheit {f}	*n.*	temerity
Unbeständigkeit {f}	*n.*	instability
unbestechlich	*adj.*	incorruptible
unbestreitbar *adj.*		indisputable
unbestreitbar *adj.*		undeniable
unbesungen	*adj.*	unsung
unbeweglich	*adv.*	immovable
unbeweglich	*adj.*	inflexible
unbewohnt	*adj.*	uninhabited
unbewusst	*adj.*	unconscious
unbezahlbar	*adj.*	priceless
unbrauchbar	*adj.*	unemployable
und *conj.* and		
undankbar	*adj.*	thankless
undankbar	*adj.*	ungrateful

Undankbarkeit {f}	*n.*	ingratitude
undenkbar	*adj.*	unthinkable
undeutlich	*adj.*	indistinct
Undichtigkeit {f}	*v.*	leak
undurchdringlich	*adj.*	impervious
undurchführbar	*adj.*	impracticable
undurchsichtig	*adj.*	opaque
Undurchsichtigkeit {f}	*n.*	opacity
unehelich	*adj.*	illegitimate
Unehre {f}	*n.*	ignominy
unehrlich	*adj.*	dishonest
uneingeschränkt	*adj.*	unreserved
uneinig	*adj.*	discordant
Uneinigkeit {f}	*n.*	disagreement
unempfänglich	*adj.*	insensible
unentgeltlich	*adj.*	gratuitous
unentrinnbar	*adj.*	inescapable
unentschieden	*adj.*	undecided
Unentschiedenheit {f}	*n.*	abeyance
unentschlossen	*adj.*	irresolute
unentschuldbar	*adj.*	inexcusable
unentwirrbar	*adj.*	inextricable
unerbittlich	*adj.*	adamant
unerbittlich	*adj.*	implacable
unerbittlich	*adj.*	inexorable
Unerfahrenheit {f}	*n.*	inexperience
unerklärlich	*adj.*	inexplicable
unerlässlich	*adj.*	essential
unerlässlich	*adj.*	vital
unermüdlich	*adj.*	tireless
unerreicht	*adj.*	unrivalled
unersättlich	*adj.*	insatiable
unersätzlich	*adj.*	irreplaceable
unerschöpflich	*adj.*	inexhaustible
unerschrocken	*adj.*	dauntless

unerschrocken	*adj.*	intrepid	ungeeignet	*adj.*	inapplicable
unerschütterlich	*adj.*	unshakeable	ungeeignet	*adj.*	ineligible
unerschwinglich	*adj.*	exorbitant	ungeeignet	*adj.*	unfit
unerträglich	*adj.*	insupportable	ungefügig	*adj.*	untoward
unerträglich	*adj.*	intolerable	ungehalten	*adj.*	indignant
unerwartet	*adj.*	unexpected	ungeheuer	*adj.*	monstrous
unerwartete	*adj.*	unattended	Ungehörigkeit {f}	*n.*	impropriety
unerwünscht	*adj.*	undesirable	ungehorsam	*adj.*	disobedient
unfähig	*adj.*	incapable	ungehört	*adj.*	unheard
unfähig	*adj.*	unable	ungelernt	*adj.*	unskilled
unfähig machend	*v.*	disable	ungemütlich	*adj.*	uncomfortable
Unfähigkeit {f}	*n.*	disability	ungenau	*adj.*	inaccurate
Unfähigkeit {f}	*n.*	inability	ungenau	*adj.*	inexact
Unfähigkeit {f}	*n.*	incapacity	ungenügend	*adj.*	insufficient
Unfall {m}	*n.*	mischance	ungeordnet	*adj.*	disorganized
unfassbar	*adj.*	intangible	ungerade	*adj.*	odd
unfehlbar	*adj.*	infallible	ungerecht	*adj.*	unjust
Unfeinheit {f}	*n.*	vulgarian	Ungerechtigkeit {f}	*n.*	injustice
Unfreiheit {f}	*n.*	bondage	ungerührt	*adj.*	unmoved
unfreiwillig	*adj.*	involuntary	ungeschlechtlich	*adj.*	asexual
unfreundlich	*adj.*	unkind	ungeschliffen	*adj.*	coarse
Unfriede {m}	*n.*	strife	ungeschoren	*adv.*	scot-free
unfruchbar	*adj.*	infertile	ungeschützt	*adj.*	unguarded
unfruchtbar	*adj.*	barren	ungeschützt	*adj.*	vulnerable
Unfug {m}	*n.*	rag	ungestüm	*adj.*	boisterous
unfügsam	*adj.*	intractable	ungesund	*adj.*	unhealthy
unfühlbar	*adj.*	impalpable	ungewöhnlich	*adj.*	uncommon
ungastlich	*adj.*	inhospitable	Ungeziefer {n}	*n.*	vermin
ungeachtet	*prep.*	notwithstanding	Ungezogenheit {f}	*n.*	misbehaviour
ungeachtet	*adv.*	regardless	ungezügelt	*adj.*	unbridled
ungeahnt	*adj.*	unforeseen	ungezwungen	*adj.*	unceremonious
ungebärdig	*adj.*	skittish	Unglaube {m}	*n.*	disbelief
ungeboren	*adj.*	unborn	unglaublich	*adj.*	incredible
ungeduldig	*adj.*	impatient	unglaublich	*adj.*	unbelievable
ungeeignet	*adj.*	improper	unglaubwürdig	*n*	unreliable

ungleichartig *prep.*		unlike
Ungleichgewicht {n}	*n.*	imbalance
Ungleichheit {f}	*n.*	inequality
Ungleichheit {f}	*n.*	odds
ungleichmäßig	*adj.*	uneven
Unglück {n}	*n.*	disaster
unglücklich	*adj.*	unfortunate
unglücklich	*adj.*	unhappy
Unglücksfall {m}	*n.*	accident
ungünstig	*adj.*	inauspicious
unhaltbar	*adj.*	indefensible
unheilbar	*adj.*	incurable
unheilig *adj.*		unholy
unheilvoll	*adj.*	disastrous
unheimlich	*adj.*	sinister
unheimlich	*adj.*	uncanny
unhöflich	*adj.*	discourteous
unhöflich	*adj.*	impolite
unhörbar *adj.*		inaudible
universal	*adj.*	universal
Universität {f} *n.*		university
Universum {n}	*n.*	universe
unklar	*adj.*	ambiguous
unklar	*adj.*	indefinite
unklug	*adj.*	unwise
unkörperlich	*adj.*	immaterial
Unkraut {n}	*n.*	weed
unkündbar	*adj.*	irredeemable
unlauter *adj.*		unfair
unleserlich	*adj.*	illegible
Unleserlichkeit {f} *n.*		illegibility
unlogisch	*adj.*	illogical
unmenschlich		*adj.* inhuman
unmessbar	*adj.*	immeasurable
unmittelbar	*adj.*	immediate

unmittelbar	*adj.*	ocular
unmöglich	*adj.*	impossible
Unmöglichkeit {f}	*n.*	impossibility
unmoralisch	*adj.*	immoral
unnatürlich	*adj.*	unnatural
unnormal	*adj.*	abnormal
unnötig *adj.*		unnecessary
unordentlich	*adj.*	messy
unordentlich	*adj.*	untidy
Unordnung {f}	*n.*	disorder
unorthodox	*adj.*	unorthodox
unparteiisch	*adj.*	impartial
Unpässlichkeit {f} *n.*		ailment
Unpässlichkeit {f} *n.*		malaise
unpersönlich *adj.*		impersonal
unpraktisch	*adj.*	impractical
unqualifiziert *adj.*		unqualified
unrechtmäßig		*adj.* wrongful
unregelmäßig *adj.*		irregular
unregelmäßig *adj.*		sporadic
Unregelmäßigkeit {f}	*n.*	irregularity
unreif	*adj.*	immature
unreif	*adj.*	verdant
Unreife {f}	*n.*	immaturity
unrein	*adj.*	impure
unrein	*adj.*	unclean
unrichtig *adj.*		false
Unruhe {f}	*n.*	commotion
Unruhe {f}	*n.*	disquiet
Unruhe {f}	*n.*	ruckus
Unruhe {f}	*n.*	tumult
Unruhen {f}	*n.*	unrest
unruhig *adj.*		restive
uns selbst	*pron.*	ourselves
unsagbar	*adj.*	untold

unsauber	adj.	scruffy
unschätzbar	adj.	invaluable
unscheinbar	adj.	inconspicuous
Unschlüssigkeit {f}	n.	vacillation
Unschuld {f}	n.	innocence
unschuldig	adj.	innocent
unschwer	adj.	easy
unser	adj.	our
unsicher adj.	insecure
unsicher adj.	precarious
unsicher adj.	uncertain
Unsicherheit {f}	n.	insecurity
unsichtbar	adj.	invisible
Unsinn {m}	n.	nonsense
unsozial adj.	antisocial
unsozial adj.	unsocial
unsterblich	adj.	immortal
unsterblich	adj.	undying
Unsterblichkeit {f} n.	immortality
Unstimmigkeit {f} v.	dissent
unsymmetrisch	adj.	unbalanced
untadelig	adj.	unexceptionable
Untat {f} n.	malpractice
untätig adj.	quiescent
unteilbar adj.	indivisible
unten	prep.	below
unten	adj.	lowly
unter	adj.	nether
unter	prep.	under
Unterarm {m} adj.	underarm
unterbewusst adj.	subconscious
unterbewusst adj.	subliminal
unterbieten v.	undercut
unterbrechen v.	break
unterbrechen v.	discontinue

unterbrechen v.	interrupt
Unterbrechung {f} n.	interception
Unterbrechung {f} n.	interruption
Unterbrechung {f} n.	recess
Unterbreitung {f} n.	submission
unterbrochen adj.	intermittent
Unterdruck {m}	n.	depression
unterdrücken v.	oppress
unterdrücken v.	repress
unterdrücken v.	suppress
Unterdrückung {f} n.	oppression
Unterdrückung {f} n.	repression
Unterernährung {f}	n. malnutrition
Unterführung {f}	n.	subway
Unterführung {f}	n.	underpass
Untergang {m}	n.	downfall
untergeordnet	adj.	ancillary
untergeordnet	adj.	inferior
Untergeordnete {m,f}	n.	underling
Untergeordnete {m}	n.	subaltern
untergraben v.	undermine
Untergrund {m}	adj.	underground
Untergrundbahn {f}	n.	tube
unterhalb	adv.	beneath
unterhalb	prep.	underneath
Unterhalt {m} n.	alimony
Unterhalt {m} n.	sustenance
unterhalten v.	entertain
unterhalten v.	subsist
unterhalten v.	wag
unterhalten v.	amuse
Unterhaltung {f}	n.	entertainment
Unterhändler {m} n.	negotiator
Unterhemd {n}	n.	singlet

Unterhose {f} n.	pants	
Unterhosen {pl}	n.	underpants
unterirdisch adj.	subterranean	
unterjochen v.	enslave	
Unterkleid {n}n.	petticoat	
Unterkunft {f} n.	housing	
Unterkunft {f} n.	lodging	
unterlassen v.	forbear	
unterlassen v.	omit	
Unterlegene {m,f} n.	underdog	
unterliegen v.	succumb	
Untermieter {m}	n.	lodger
Unternehmen {n} n.	company	
Unternehmer {m} n.	entrepreneur	
Unternehmung {f} n.	enterprise	
unterordnet adj.	subordinate	
unterprivilegiert	adj.underprivileged	
Unterredung {f}	n.	parley
Unterricht {m}	n.	tuition
unterrichten v.	teach	
Untersatz {m}n.	saucer	
unterschall adj.	subsonic	
unterschätzen	v.	underestimate
unterschätzen	v.	underrate
unterscheiden	v.	differ
unterschiedlich	adj.	different
unterschlagen	v.	misappropriate
Unterschlagung {f}n.	misappropriation	
unterschreiben	adj.	undersigned
unterschreiben	v.	underwrite
Unterschrift {f}	n.	signature
Unterseeboot {n} n.	submarine	
untersetzt adj.	stocky	
unterstellen v.	impute	
unterstreichen	v.	punctuate

unterstreichen	v.t.	underline
unterstreichen	v.	underscore
Unterströmung {f} n.	undercurrent	
unterstützen v.	espouse	
unterstützen v.	support	
untersuchen v.	investigate	
untersuchen v.	scan	
Untersuchung {f} n.	exploration	
Untersuchung {f} n.	inquest	
Untersuchung {f} n.	inquisition	
Untersuchungsrichter {m} n.coroner		
Untertanentreue {f}	n.	allegiance
untertauchbar	adj.	submersible
untertauchen v.	submerge	
untertauchen v.	submerse	
Untertitel {m} n.	subtitle	
untertreiben v.	understate	
unterurteilen adj.	subjudice	
untervermieten	v.t.	sublet
Unterwäsche {f}	n.	underwear
Unterwelt {f} n.	underworld	
unterwerfen n.	subject	
Unterwerfung {f}	n.	subjection
Unterwerfung {f}	n.	subjugation
unterwürfig adj.	servile	
unterwürfig adj.	submissive	
Unterwürfigkeit {f}n.	servility	
Unterwürfigkeit {f}n.	subservience	
unterziehen v.	undergo	
untrennbar adj.	inseparable	
untreu adj.	unfaithful	
unüberbrückbar adj.insurmountable		
unüberlegt adj.	indiscriminate	
unüberlegt adj.	injudicious	
unüblich adj.	unusual	

unumgänglich   *adj.* indispensable
unumkehrbar *adj.* irreversible
unveränderbar   *adj.* immutable
unveränderlich   *adj.* invariable
unverbesserlich   *adj.* incorrigible
unverdaulich *adj.* indigestible
unvereinbar *adj.* irreconcilable
unvergesslich   *adj.* unforgettable
unvergleichbar   *adj.* incomparable
unvergleichlich   *adj.* peerless
unvergleichlich   *adj.* nonpareil
unverhältnismäßig *adj.* disproportionate
unverheiratet *adj.* celibate
unvermischt *adj.* unalloyed
unvernünftig *adj.* irrational
unvernünftig *adj.* unreasonable
unverschämt *adj.* insolent
Unverschämtheit {f}   *n.* infamy
unversehens *adj.* unaware
unverträglich *adj.* incompatible
unverwechselbar *adj.* unmistakable
unverwundbar   *adj.* invulnerable
unverzüglich *adv.* forthwith
unvollständig *adj.* imperfect
unvollständig *adj.* incomplete
unvorbereitet *adj.* unprepared
Unvoreingenommenheit {f} *n.*
   impartiality
unvorsichtig *adj.* improvident
unwahrscheinlich *adj.* implausible
unwahrscheinlich *adj.* improbable
unwahrscheinlich *adj.* unlikely
unweltlich   *adj.* unworldly
unwiderlegbar   *adj.* irrefutable
unwiderruflich   *adj.* irrevocable

unwirksam   *adj.* ineffective
unwirksam   *adj.* inefficient
unwissend   *adj.* ignorant
unwissend   *adj.* unknown
Unwissenheit {f}   *n.* ignorance
unwohl *adj.* unwell
unwürdig   *adj.* unworthy
unzahlbar   *adj.* unaccountable
unzählig *adj.* innumerable
unzähmbar   *adj.* indomitable
Unze {f}   *n.* ounce
unzüchtig   *adj.* licentious
Unzüchtigkeit {f}   *n.* obscenity
unzufrieden   *adj.* disaffected
unzufrieden   *adj.* malcontent
Unzufriedenheit {f}   *n.* discontent
Unzufriedenheit {f} *n.* dissatisfaction
unzugänglich *adj.* impenetrable
unzulässig   *adj.* inadmissible
unzulässig   *adj.* undue
unzureichend *adj.* sketchy
unzusammenhängend *adj.* incoherent
üppig   *adj.* luscious
üppig   *adj.* luxuriant
üppig   *adj.* sumptuous
üppig   *adj.* voluptuous
uralt *adj.* immemorial
Urbanität {f}   *n.* urbanity
Urin {m}   *n.* urine
urinieren *v.* urinate
urinierend   *adj.* urinary
Urkunde {f}   *n.* deed
Urlaub {m}   *n.* vacation
Urne {f}   *n.* urn
Ursache {f}   *n.* cause

ursächlich	adj.	causal
Ursprung {m} n.	genesis
Ursprung {m} n.	origin
Ursprung {m} n.	source
ursprünglich	adj.	pristine
urteilen	v.	adjudicate
urteilsfähig	adj.	judicious
Urteilsspruch {m} n.	sentence
Urteilsspruch {m} n.	verdict
urzeitlich	adj.	primeval
Usurpation {f}	n.	usurpation
usw. -und so weiter	adv.	et cetera
utilitaristisch	adj.	utilitarian
Utopie {f}	n.	utopia
utopisch	adj.	utopian

V

vage	adj.	vague
Valentinsgruß {m} n.	valentine
Vampir {m}	n.	vampire
Vandal {m}	n.	vandal
variabel	adj.	variable
Variante {f}	n.	variant
Variete {n}	n.	vaudeville
variierend	v.	vary
varikös	adj.	varicose
Vasall {m}	n.	vassal
vasculär	adj.	vascular
Vase {f}	n.	vase
Vasectomie {f}	n.	vasectomy
Vater {m}	n.	father
väterlich	adj.	paternal
Vatermord {m}	n.	parricide
Vatermord {m}	n.	patricide
Vaterschaft {f}	n.	paternity

Vegetarier {m}	n.	vegan
vegetarisch	n.	vegetarian
vegetativ	adj.	vegetative
vegetieren	v.	vegetate
Veilchen {n}	n.	violet
Vektor {m}	n.	vector
Velours {n}	n.	velour
Vendetta {f}	n.	vendetta
Vene {f} n.	vein
venetianer	adj.	venetian
Ventil {n} n.	valve
ventilieren	v.	ventilate
verableugnend	v.	disown
Verabredung {f}	n.	rendezvous
verabscheuen	v.	abhor
verabscheuen	v.	abominate
verabscheuen	v.	detest
verabscheuen	v.	loathe
verabscheun v.	nauseate
verachten	v.	despise
verachten	v.	disdain
verächtlich	adj.	despicable
verächtlich	adj.	scornful
Verachtung {f}	n.	contempt
Verachtung {f}	n.	scorn
verallgemeinern	v.	generalize
veraltend	adj.	obsolescent
veraltet	adj.	antiquated
veraltet	adj.	archaic
veraltet	adj.	outmoded
Veranda {f}	n.	porch
Veranda {f}	n.	veranda
veränderlich	adj.	mutable
veränderlicher	adj.	mutative
verändern	v.	alter

verändern	v.	mutate	Verbesserung {f}	n.	improvement
Veränderung {f}	n.	alteration	Verbesserung {f}	n.	rectification
Veränderung {f}	v.	change	verbeugen	v.	bow
Veränderung {f}	n.	variation	verbilligen	v. t.	cheapen
Verankerung {f}	n.	moorings	verbinden	v.	conflate
veranlagen	v.	assess	verbinden	v.	connect
Veranlagung {f}	n.	idiosyncrasy	verbinden	v.	peer
veranlagungsgemäß adj. temperamental			verbinden	v.	splice
veranlassen	v.	induce	verbinden (Augen)	v.	blindfold
Veranlassung {f}	n.	inducement	Verbinder {m}	n.	merger
verantwortlich	adj.	accountable	verbindlich	adj.	obligatory
Verantwortung {f}	n.	responsibility	verbindlich	adj.	obliging
Verantwortungsbewusst adj.			Verbindlichkeit {f}	n.	commitment
responsible			Verbindlichkeit {f}	n.	courtesy
verantwortungslos adj. irresponsible			Verbindung {f}	n.	compound
Verarbeitung {f}	n.	manipulation	Verbindung {f}	n.	conjunction
verärgert adj.	disgruntled		Verbindung {f}	n.	connection
Verärgerung {f}	n.	huff	Verbindung {f}	n.	junction
verarmen	v.	impoverish	Verbindung {f}	n.	peerage
verästeln	v.	ramify	Verbindungspunkt {m} n.		juncture
Verästelung {f}	n.	ramification	Verbindungsstelle {f}	n.	joint
verausgeben	v.	expend	verbittern	v.	embitter
Verb {n}	n.	verb	verblassen	v.i	fade
verbal	adv.	verbally	verblenden	v. t	blend
verbannen	v.	banish	verblödet	adj.	gaga
verbannen	v.	ostracize	verblüffen	v.	astound
Verbannung {f}	n.	banishment	verblüffen	v.	stupefy
verbessern	v.	ameliorate	verblüft adj.	nonplussed	
verbessern	v.	emend	verblühen	v.	wither
verbessern	v.	improve	verborgen	adj.	latent
verbessern	v.	meliorate	verborgen	n.	occult
verbessern	v.	rectify	Verbot {n}	n.	prohibition
verbessern	v.	reform	verboten v.	ban	
verbessern	v.	upgrade	verboten adj.	illicit	
Verbesserung {f}	n.pl.	amendment	verboten v.	prohibit	

387

German		English
Verbrauch {m}	*n.*	consumption
verbrauchen *v.*		consume
Verbraucher {m}	*n.*	consumer
Verbrauchssteuer {f}	*n.*	excise
Verbrechen {n}	*n.*	crime
Verbrecher {m}	*n.*	criminal
verbreiten *v.*		diffuse
verbreiten *v.*		propagate
verbreitet *adj.*		rife
Verbreitung {f}	*n.*	propagation
Verbrennung {f}	*n.*	combustion
verbrühen *v.*		scald
verbunden *v.*		incorporate
verbünden *v.*		federate
verbunden *v.*		bound
Verbundenheit {f} *n.*		solidarity
verbündet *adj.*		allied
Verbündete {m,f}	*n.*	ally
verbürgen *v.*		vouch
Verdacht {m} *n.*		suspicion
Verdächtigte {m}	*n*	suspect
verdammenswert *adj.*		damnable
Verdammung {f}	*n.*	doom
verdampfen *v.*		evaporate
verdampfen *v.*		vaporize
verdarb *adj.*		addled
verdauen *v.*		digest
Verdauung {f}	*n.*	digestion
Verdauungsstörung {f} *n.*		dyspepsia
Verdauungsstörung {f} *n.*		indigestion
Verdeck {n}	*n.*	deck
verderben *v.*		deprave
verderben *v.*		spoil
verderben *v.*		taint
Verderben {n}	*n.*	bane
Verderben {n}	*n.*	perdition
Verderber {m}	*n.*	spoiler
verderblich *adj.*		noxious
verderblich *adj.*		pernicious
verderblich *adj.*		ruinous
verdicken *v.*		thicken
verdienen *v. t.*		deserve
verdienen *v.*		earn
Verdienst {m}*n.*		income
Verdienst {n} *n.*		merit
verdienstlich *adj.*		meritorious
verdoppeln *v.*		redouble
Verdopplung {f}	*n.*	duplex
verdorben *adj.*		putrid
Verdrahtung {f}	*n.*	wiring
verdrängen *v.*		supplant
verdrehen *v.*		misrepresent
verdrehen *v.*		skew
verdreifachen *v.*		trip
verdreifachten	*adj.*	triplicate
verdrießlich *adj.*		splenetic
verdrießlich *adj.*		surly
verdrossen *adj.*		querulous
verdrücken *v.*		stow
Verdruss {m} *n.*		annoyance
verdunkeln *v.*		darken
verdünnen *v.*		dilute
verdutzend *v.*		disconcert
verehren *v.*		enshrine
verehren *v.*		revere
verehren *n.*		worship
verehren *v.t.*		adore
Verehrer {m} *n.*		votary
verehrt *adj.*	revered
Verehrung {f} *n.*		adoration

Verehrung {f} *n.*	veneration	**verfaulen**	*v.*	fester
Vereidigter {m}	*n.*	juror	**verfaulen**	*v.*	rot
Verein {m}	*n.*	union	**verfechten**	*v.*	advocate

Verehrung {f} *n.* veneration   verfaulen *v.* fester
Vereidigter {m} *n.* juror   verfaulen *v.* rot
Verein {m} *n.* union   verfechten *v.* advocate
vereinbaren *v.* stipulate   Verfechter {m} *n.* stickler
vereinbart *adj.* concerted   Verfehlung {f} *n.* lapse
Verelnbarung {f} *n.* arrangement   Verfehlung {f} *n.* misconduct
Vereinbarung {f} *n.* settlement   verfeinern *v.* refine
Vereinbarung {f} *n.* stipulation   Verfeinerung {f} *n.* refinement
vereinfachen *v.* simplify   verfinstern *v.* obfuscate
Vereinfachung {f} *n.* simplification   verfluchen *v.* darn
vereinheitlichen *v.* unify   verfolgen *v.* beset
Vereinheitlichung {f} *n.* unification   verfolgen *v.* chase
vereinigen *v.* amalgamate   verfolgen *v.* haunt
vereinigen *v.* associate   verfolgen *v.* persecute
vereinigen *v.* combine   verfolgen *v.* pursue
vereinigen *v.* join   verfolgt *adj.* haunted
vereinigen *v.* rejoin   Verfolgung {f} *n.* persecution
vereinigen *v.* unite   Verfolgung {f} *n.* pursuance
vereinigt *adj.* confederate   Verfolgung {f} *n.* pursuit
vereinigt *adj.* corporate   Verfolgung {f} *n.* tracing
Vereinigung {f} *n.* consortium   verfrachtet *adj.* chartered
vereint *adj.* conjunct   verfügbar *adj.* available
vereiteln *v.* foil   verfügbar *adj.* disposable
Verengung {f} *n.* stricture   Verfügung {f} *n.* disposal
Vererbung {f} *n.* heredity   verführen *v.* debauch
verewigen *v.* immortalize   verführen *v.* seduce
verewigen *v.t.* perpetuate   verführerisch *adj.* seductive
Verfahren {n} *n.* technique   Verführung {f} *n.* seduction
Verfall {m} *n.* disrepair   vergangen *adj.* bygone
verfallen *v. i* decay   Vergangenheit {f} *adj.* past
verfälschen *v.* adulterate   vergänglich *adj.* perishable
Verfälschung {f} *n.* adulteration   vergären *v.* ferment
verfärben *v.* discolour   Vergärung {f} *n.* fermentation
Verfasser *n.* author   vergeblich *adv.* vainly
Verfassung {f} *n.* fettle   Vergeblichkeit {f} *n.* futility

389

Vergebung {f}	n.	remission
vergehen	v.	elapse
vergehen	v.	pass
Vergehen {n} n.		misdemeanour
vergelten	v.	reciprocate
vergelten	v.t.	requite
vergelten	v.	retaliate
Vergeltung {f}	n.	retribution
Vergeltungsmaßnahme {f}n.		retaliation
vergessen	v.	forget
vergesslich	adj.	forgetful
vergesslich	adj.	oblivious
Vergewaltiger {m} n.		rapist
vergewaltigen	v.	rape
verglasen	v.t.	glass
verglasen	v.	vitrify
Vergleich {m} n.		comparison
vergleichen	v.	compare
vergleichen	v.	confer
vergleichen	v.	liken
vergleichend	adj.	comparative
vergnügt adj.		hilarious
vergnügt adj.		jolly
Vergnügung {f}	n.	amusement
Vergnügung {f}	n.	pleasure
vergolden	v.	gild
vergoldet	adj.	gilt
vergöttern	v.	deify
vergöttern	v.	idolize
Vergötterung {f}	n.	idolatry
vergraben	v.	bury
vergrößern	v.	magnify
Vergrößerung {f}	v.	augment
Vergütung {f} n.		emolument
Vergütung {f} n.		perquisite

verhaften	v.	arrest
Verhalten {n} n.		behaviour
Verhalten {pl}n.		manner
verhaltensgestört	adj.	maladjusted
Verhältnis {n}n.		ratio
verhandeln	v.	negotiate
Verhandlung {f}	n.	negotiation
Verhängnis {n}	n.	fatality
verhasst adj.		hateful
verhasst adj.		odious
verhätscheln	v.	cuddle
verhauen	v.	spank
verhauen	v.	whack
verheeren	v.	devastate
verheimlichen	v.	dissimulate
verheiraten	v.	mar
verherrlichen	v.	exalt
verherrlichen	v.	glorify
verhexen	v.	bewitch
verhindern	v.	forestall
verhindern	v.	hinder
verhindern	v.	impede
verhindern	v.	inhibit
verhindern	v.	prevent
Verhinderung {f}	n.	hindrance
verhören v.		interrogate
verhungert	adj.	famished
Verhütung {f} n.		prevention
Verhütungsmittel {n}	n.	contraceptive
verirren v.		stray
Verirrung {f}	n.	aberration
verjüngen	v.	rejuvenate
Verjüngung {f}	n.	rejuvenation
verkalkulieren	v.	miscalculate
verkapseln	v.	encapsulate

Verkauf {m}	n.	sale	verkürzen	v.	shorten
verkaufen	v.	sell	Verlagsbuchhändler {m}	n.	publisher
verkaufen	v.	vend	verlangen	v.	require
Verkäufer {m}n.		seller	verlangend	adj.	demanding
verkäuflich	adj.	negotiable	verlängern	v.	elongate
verkaufsfähig adj.		salable	verlängern	v.	prolong
Verkaufsstand {m}	n.	stall	Verlängerung {f}	n.	prolongation
Verkehr {m}	n.	intercourse	verlangsamen	v.	decelerate
Verkehr {m}	n.	traffic	verlassen	v.t.	abandon
verkehrsreich adj.		congested	verlassen	v.	forsake
verkehrssicher	adj.	roadworthy	verlassen	v.t.	leave
Verkehrsstraße {f} n.		thoroughfare	verlassen	v.	quit
verkennen	v.	misjudge	verlässlich	adj.	reliable
verklagbar	adj.	actionable	verlautbaren	v.	disclose
verklagen	v.t.	sue	verlegen v.		confuse
Verkleidung {f}	n.	facing	verlegen v.		mislay
Verkleidung {f}	n.	fairing	verlegen v.		misplace
verkleinern	v.	belittle	Verlegenheit {f}	n.	quandary
verkleinernd	adj.	reductive	verleiten v.		misguide
Verkleinerung {f}	v.	decrease	verletzen v.		hurt
Verkleinerung {f}	n.	reduction	verletzen v.		infringe
Verklemmung {f}	n.	deadlock	verletzend	v.	violate
verknöchern v.		ossify	Verletzung {f}n.		violation
verknüpfen	v.	affiliate	verleumden	v.	defame
Verknüpfung {f}	n.	nexus	verleumden	v.	traduce
verkörperlichen	v.	materialize	verleumderisch	adj.	slanderous
verkörpern	v.	impersonate	Verleumdung {f}	n.	calumny
verkörpern	v.	typify	Verleumdung {f}	n.	defamation
verkörpert	adj.	incarnate	Verleumdung {f}	n.	obloquy
Verkörperung {f}	n.	incarnation	Verleumdungen {pl}	n.	aspersions
Verkörperung {f}	n.	personification	verlieben	v. t	enamour
verkrampft	adj.	tense	verliebt	adj.	amatory
verkrüppeln	v.	stunt	verliebt	adj.	amorous
verkündigen	v.	promulgate	verliebt	adj.	fond
verkürzen	v.t	abridge	verlieren v.		lose

Verlinkung {f}n.	link	Vermummung {f} n.	mummer
Verlobte {m} n.	fiancé	vermuten v.i	guess
verlocken v.	tempt	vermuten v.	hunch
verlockt adj.	alluring	vermuten v.	presume
verlogen adj.	mendacious	vermuten v.	suppose
verloren adv.	astray	vermuten v.t.	surmise
Verlosung {f} n.	raffle	vermuten v.	suspect
Verlust {m} n.	bereavement	Vermutung {f} n.	assumption
Verlust {m} n.	casualty	Vermutung {f} n.	presumption
Verlust {m} n.	leakage	Vermutung {f} n. &v.	conjecture
Verlust {m} n.	loss	vernachlässigbar adj.	negligible
vermachen v.	bequeath	vernachlässigen v.	neglect
vermasseln v.	bungle	vernein v.	negate
vermasseln v.	muddle	vernichten v.	annihilate
vermeiden v.	avoid	vernichtend adj.	scathing
vermeiden v.	beware	Vernichtung {f} n.	annihilation
Vermeidung {f} n.	avoidance	Vernunft {f} n.	sanity
vermeintlich adj.	putative	vernünftig adj.	rational
vermenschlichen v.	humanize	vernünftig adj.	reasonable
Vermesser {m} n.	surveyor	Vernunftschlüsse {f} n.	syllogism
Vermieter {m}n.	lessor	veröffentlichen v.	publish
vermindern v.t.	abate	Veröffentlichung {f} n.	publication
vermindern v. t.	decrement	verordnen v.	enact
vermindern v.	reduce	Verordnung {f} n.	ordinance
Verminderung {f} n.	diminution	Verordnung {f} n.	prescription
Vermischung {f} n.	amalgamation	Verpackung {f} n.	packing
Vermischung {f} n.	mixture	verpatzen v.	mull
vermitteln v.	conciliate	Verpfändung {f} n.	pledge
vermitteln v.	intercede	verpflanzen v.	transplant
vermitteln v.	liaise	verpflichten v.	oblige
vermitteln v.	mediate	verpflichtet adj.	beholden
vermitteln v.	procure	verpflichtet adj.	liable
Vermittlung {f} n.	agency	verpflichtet adj.	obligated
Vermittlung {f} n.	mediation	Verpflichtung {f} n.	liability
Vermögen {n}n.	asset	Verpflichtung {f} n.	onus

verprassen	v.	guzzle
verprügeln	v.	baste
verprügeln	v.	lambast
verprügeln	v.	thrash
verprügeln	v.	trounce
verprügeln	v.	wallop
Verrat {m}	n.	betrayal
Verrat {m}	n.	treachery
verraten v.		betray
verraten n.		squeal
Verräter {m}	n.	traitor
verräterisch	adj.	telltale
verrennen	v.	trickle
verringern	v.	lessen
verringern	v.	minimize
verrückt adj.		crazy
verrückt adj.		zany
Verrücktheit {f}	n.	folly
verrufen adj.		disreputable
Vers {m} n.		verse
versagen	v.	malfunction
Versager {m} n.		failure
versammeln	v.	congregate
versammeln	v.	gather
Versammlung {f}	n.	assemblage
Versand {m}	n.	shipment
Versbau {m}	n.	versification
verschämt	adj.	bashful
verschanzen v.		entrench
verscheuchen		v. scare
verschieben	v.	defer
verschieben	v. t	displace
verschieben	v.	postpone
verschieden	adj.	diverse
verschieden	adj. & pron.	several

verschieden	adj.	varied
verschiedenartig	adj.	heterogeneous
verschiedenartig	adj.	miscellaneous
verschiedenartig	adj.	various
Verschiedenheit {f}	n.	difference
verschiedentlich	adv.	occasionally
verschlechtern	v.	debase
verschlechtern	v.	deteriorate
verschlechtern	v.	worsen
verschleifen v.		slur
Verschleppung {f} n.		procrastination
verschleudern	v.	squander
verschlimmernd	adj.	pejorative
Verschlimmerung {f}	n.	aggravation
verschlingen v.		devour
verschlingen v.		gobble
Verschluss {m}	n.	breech
Verschluss {m}	n.	closure
Verschluss {m}	n.	lock
Verschluss {m}	n.	shutter
verschlüsseln	v.	encode
verschlüsseln	v.	encrypt
verschmachten	v.	swelter
verschmelzen	v.	merge
Verschmelzung {f}	n.	fusion
Verschmutzung {f}	n.	dirt
Verschmutzung {f}	n.	pollution
verschnürt	adj.	tied
verschollen	adj.	missing
verschönern v.		beautify
verschönern v.		embellish
Verschönerung {f}	n.	glorification
verschüchtern	v.	intimidate
verschuldet	adj.	indebted
Verschüttung {f}	n.	spillage

393

verschwenden	v.	waste
Verschwender {m}	n.	spendthrift
verschwenderisch adj.		extravagant
verschwenderisch adj.		prodigal
verschwenderisch adj.		wasteful
verschwiegen	adj.	reticent
verschwiegen	adj.	secretive
verschwindend	v.	disappear
verschwommen	adj.	muzzy
Verschwommenheit {f}	n.	vagueness
verschwören	v.	conspire
Verschwörer {m}	n.	conspirator
Verschwörung {f}	n.	conspiracy
versegen	v.	sear
versehentlich adj.		accidental
versehentlich adj.		inadvertent
versenden	v.	convey
Versendung {f}	n.	shipping
Versessener	n.	geek
versetzen	v.	transpose
verseuchen	v.	contaminate
versichern	v.	insure
versichern	v.	reassure
Versicherung {f}	n.	insurance
Versicherungsstatistiker {m}	n.	actuary
versinken	v.	engulf
Version {f}	n.	version
versöhnen	v.	propitiate
versöhnen	v.	reconcile
Versöhnung {f}	n.	reconciliation
Versorgung {f}	n.	accommodation
Verspaar {n}	n.	couplet
verspätet	adj.	belated
verspotten	v.	deride

verspotten	v.	lampoon
verspotten	v.	mock
verspotten	v.	satirize
verspotten	v.i.	scoff
verspotten	v.	gibe
verspritzen	v.	squirt
verstaatlichen	v.	nationalize
Verstaatlichung {f}	n.	nationalization
Verstand {m}	n.	mind
Verstand {m}	n.	reason
Verstand {m}	n.	wit
verständig	adj.	prudent
verständig	adj.	wise
verständlich	adj.	intelligible
Verständnis {n}	n.	comprehension
verstärken	v.	boost
verstärken	v.	intensify
verstärken	v.	reinforce
Verstärker {m}	n.	amplifier
Verstärkung {f}	n.	amplification
Verstärkung {f}	n.	reinforcement
verstauchen	v.t.	sprain
Versteck {n}	n.	lair
verstecken	v.t	hide
verstecken	v.	stash
versteckt	adj.	covert
verstehen	v.t.	understand
Verstehen {n}	n.	understanding
versteinern	v.	petrify
Versteinerung {f}	n.	fossil
Verstellung {f}	v.	disguise
verstockt	adj.	obdurate
Verstocktheit {f}	n.	obduracy
verstopfen	v.	occlude

Verstopfung {f}	n.	obstruction
verstorben	adj.	defunct
Verstörtheit {f}	n.	distraction
Verstoß {m}	n.	offence
verstoßen	v.	contravene
Verstoßung {f}	n.	repudiation
verstümmeln v.		garble
verstümmeln v.		maim
verstümmeln v.		mutilate
Verstümmelung {f}	n.	mayhem
Verstümmelung {f}	n.	mutilation
Versuch {m}	n.	essay
versuchen	v.	attempt
versuchen	v.	try
Versucher {m}	n.	tempter
Versuchung {f}	n.	temptation
versunken	adj.	rapt
versunken	adj.	sunken
versüßen	v.	sweeten
vertagen v.		prorogue
Vertagung {f} n.		adjournment
vertan	adj.	mistaken
verteidigen	v.	defend
verteidigend v.		vindicate
Verteidigung {f}	n.	defence
verteilen v.		distribute
verteufeln	v.	demonize
Vertieftsein {n}	n.	preoccupation
Vertiefung {f} n.		immersion
vertikal	adj.	vertical
Vertilgung {f} n.		obliteration
Vertrag {m}	n.	contract
Vertrag {m}	n.	indenture
Vertrag {m}	n.	pact
Vertrag {m}	n.	treaty

vertraglich	adj.	contractual
verträglich	adj.	compatible
Vertrauen	v.	confide
vertrauen	v.	rely
Vertrauen {n} n.		confidence
Vertrauen {n} n.		faith
Vertrauen {n} n.		reliance
Vertrauen {n} n.		trust
vertrauensvoll	adj.	confident
vertrauensvoll	adj.	trustful
vertraulich	adj.	confidential
vertraut adj.		conversant
Vertraute {m} n.		confidant
vertreiben	v.	dislodge
vertreiben	v. t	eject
Vertreibung {f}	n.	expulsion
Vertreibung {f}	n.	turnout
vertretbar	adj.	defensible
Vertreter {m} n.		locum
Vertreter {m} n.		deputy
Vertretung {f} n.		proxy
Vertrieb {m}	n.	marketing
vertrödeln	v.	dawdle
verübeln v.		resent
verüben v.		commit
verüben v.		perpetrate
verunglimpfen	v.	denigrate
verunglimpfen	v.	revile
Verunreinigung {f}n.		impurity
verunstalten v.		deface
Veruntreuung {f}	n.	infidelity
verurteilen	v.	condemn
verurteilen	v.	convict
verurteilen	v.	damn
verurteilen	n.	reprobate

Verurteilung {f}	n.	condemnation
Verurteilung {f}	n.	conviction
Verurteilung {f}	n.	damnation
vervielfältig	adj.	duplicate
Vervollständigung {f}	n.	completion
verwahrlos	adj.	unkempt
verwalten	v.	administer
Verwalter {m} n.		administrator
Verwalter {m} n.		caretaker
Verwaltung {f}	n.	administration
Verwaltungseinrichtung {f}n.		
quango		
verwaltungsmäßigadj.		administrative
verwandeln	v.	convert
verwandeln	v.	transmute
verwandt	adj.	akin
verwandt	adj.	cognate
Verwandtschaft {f}	n.	affiliation
Verwechslung {f}	n.	confusion
verweichlicht	adj.	effeminate
verweigernd	v.	disallow
verweilen	v.i	abide
verweilen	v.	linger
verweilend	adj.	abiding
verweisen	v.	relegate
Verwendung {f}	n.	application
verwerfen	v.	overrule
verwerfen	v.	quash
verwertbar	adj.	usable
verwerten	v.	recycle
Verwertung {f}	n.	utilization
verwestlichen	v.	westernize
verwickeln	v. t	entangle
verwickeln	v.	implicate
verwickeln	v.	involve

Verwicklung {f}	n.	imbroglio
Verwindung {f}	n.	torsion
Verwirkung {f}	v.	forfeit
verwirren	v.t	bewilder
verwirren	v.	distract
verwirren	v.	disturb
verwirren	v.	fluster
verwirren	v.t.	puzzle
verwirren	v.t.	tangle
verwirrend	v.	disarrange
verwirrt	adj.	bemused
verwirrte, gestört	adj.	deranged
verwischen	v.	blur
Verworfene {m,f}	n.	castaway
verworren	adj.	promiscuous
verwunderlichen	v.	astonish
verwurzelt	adj.	rooted
verwüsten	v.t.	ravage
Verwüstung {f}	n.	havoc
verzahnen	v.	interlock
verzärteln	v.	pamper
verzaubert	adj.	spellbound
Verzeichnis {n}	n.	list
verzeihen	v.	forgive
verzeihlich	adj.	pardonable
verzeihlich	adj.	venial
Verzeihung {f}	n.	pardon
verzetteln	v.	fritter
Verzicht {m}	n.	renunciation
verzichten	v.t.	renounce
verzichten auf	v.	forgo
verziehen	v.	condone
Verzierung {f}n.		decoration
verzinken	v.i.	galvanize
verzögern	v. t	delay

verzögern	v.	lag
verzögern	v.	retard
Verzögerung {f}	n.	retardation
verzweifelt	adj.	desperate
Verzweiflung {f}	n.	despair
verzwickt	adj.	tricky
Veteran {m}	n.	veteran
veterinär adj.		veterinary
Vetter {m}	n.	cousin
Vetternwirtschaft {f}	n.	nepotism
Vetternwirtschaft {f}	n.	partisan
Viadukt {n}	n.	viaduct
Vibraphon {n}	n.	vibraphone
Vibrator {m}	n.	vibrator
vibrieren v.		vibrate
Vicomte {f}	n.	viscount
Vicomtesse {f}	n.	viscountess
Video {n}n.		video
Viehweide {f} n.		pasture
viel pron.		much
viele	adj.	many
vielfach adj.		multiple
Vielfachheit {f}	n.	multiplicity
vielförmig	adj.	multiform
Vielfraß {m}	n.	glutton
Vielfraß {m}	n.	gourmand
vielleicht adv.		maybe
vielseitig adj.		multilateral
vielseitig adj.		versatile
Vielseitigkeit {f}	n.	versatility
vielsprachig	adj.	polyglot
vier adj.& n.		four
Vierbeiner {m}	n.	quadruped
Viereck {n}	a.	quadrangle
viereckig n.		quadrangular

vierfach n.		quad
vierfach adj.		quadruple
Vierling {m}	n.	quadruplet
vierseitig	n.	quadrilateral
Viertel {n}	n.	quarter
vierteljährlich adj.		quarterly
Viertelnote {f}n.		crotchet
viertes adj.& n.		fourth
vierzehn adj.& n.		fourteen
vierzehn Tage	n.	fortnight
vierzig adj.& n.		forty
Vignette {f}	n.	vignette
Villa {f}	n.	mansion
Villa {f}	n.	villa
Vinyl {n} n.		vinyl
Violine {f}	n.	violin
viral adj.		viral
virtuell	adj.	virtual
virulent	adj.	virulent
Virus {m}	n.	virus
Viskose {f}	n.	viscose
visuell	adj.	visual
Visum {n}	n.	visa
Vitamin {n}	n.	vitamin
Vitrine {f}	n.	showcase
Vitriol {n}	n.	vitriol
Vizekönig {m}	n.	viceroy
Vlies {n} n.		fleece
Vogel {m}	n.	bird
Vogelgrippe {f}	n.	bird flu
Vogelhaus {n}	n.	aviary
Vogelscheuche {f}n.		scarecrow
Voicemail {n} n.		voicemail
Voile	n.	voile
Vokabel {f}	n.	vocabulary

Vokal {m}   *n.*   vowel
Volant {m}   *n.*   valance
Volk*n.*   folk
volkreich   *adj.*   populous
Volksbegehren {n}   *n.*
  referendum
Volkswirtschaftslehre {f} *n.* economics
Volkszählung {f}   *n.*   census
voll *adj.* fraught
voll *adj.* full
vollbringen   *v.*   accomplish
vollenden   *v.*   consummate
Vollendung {f}   *n.*   achievement
Völlerei {f}   *n.*   gluttony
Völlerei {f}   *n.*   piggery
völlig   *adj.*   arrant
vollkommen   *adv.*   altogether
Vollkommenheit {f}   *n.*   perfection
vollständig   *adj.*   complete
vollständig   *adj.*   entire
vollständig   *adv.*   outright
vollständig   *adj.*   thorough
vollständig   *adj.*   unmitigated
vollziehen   *v.*   fulfil
Vollziehungsbefehl {m}   *n.* warrant
Volt {n}   *n.*   volt
Voltzahl {f}   *n.*   voltage
voneinander abhängig *adj.*
  interdependent
Voodoo {n}   *n.*   voodoo
Vorabend {m}*n.*   eve
vorahnen   *v.*   anticipate
vorangehen   *v.*   precede
vorantreiben   *v.*   expedite
vorantreiben   *v.*   propel

Vorarbeiter {m}   *n.*   foreman
Vorausnahme {f}   *n.*   anticipation
voraussagen *v.t* forecast
voraussagen *v.* prognosticate
voraussehen *v.* foresee
voraussetzen *v.* presuppose
Voraussetzung {f} *n.* prerequisite
Voraussetzung {f} *n.* presupposition
Voraussetzung {f} *n.* supposition
Voraussicht {f}   *n.*   foreknowledge
voraussichtlich   *adv.*   probably
voraussichtlich   *adj.*   prospective
Vorbau {m}   *n.*   stem
Vorbedeutung {f} *n.* omen
Vorbedingung {f} *n.* precondition
Vorbehalt {m}*n.*   proviso
vorbeigehend*adj.* transitory
vorbereitend *adj.* preparatory
Vorbereitung {f}   *n.*   preparation
vorbeugen   *v.*   obviate
vorbeugend   *adj.* precautionary
Vorbild {n}   *n.*   example
Vorblick {m}   *n.*   foresight
Vorbote {m}   *n.*   forerunner
Vorbote {m}   *n.*   herald
vordatieren   *v.*   antedate
Vordenker {m}   *n.*   mastermind
Vorderarm {m}   *n.*   forearm
Vorderbänkler {m}*n.* frontbencher
Vorderbein {n}   *n.*   foreleg
vordergründig   *adj.* ostensible
vordringlich *adj.* urgent
vorehelich   *adj.* premarital
voreilig *adj.* heady
voreilig *adj.* rash

398

voreingenommen *adj.* biased
Vorenthaltung {f} *n.* detention
vorfabriziert *adj.* prefabricated
Vorfahr {m} *n.* ancestor
Vorfahr {m} *n.* forebear
Vorfahr {m} *n.* forefather
Vorfall {m} *n.* incident
Vorführung {f} *n.* demonstration
vorfürsorglich *adj.* provident
Vorgang {m} *n.* process
Vorgänger {m} *n.* predecessor
Vorhalle {f} *n.* atrium
Vorhängeschloss {n} *n.* padlock
vorher *adv.* ago
vorher *adv.* before
vorherbestimmen *v.* predetermine
vorhergehend *adj.* foregoing
vorherig *adj.* previous
Vorherrschaft {f} *n.* predominance
vorherrschen *v.* predominate
Vorherrschen {n} *n.* prevalence
vorherrschend *adj.* predominant
vorhersagen *v.* foretell
vorhersagen *v.* predict
Vorherwissen {n} *n.* prescience
Vorkämpfer {m} *n.* protagonist
Vorkehrung {f} *n.* provision
Vorkenntnis {f} *n.* precognition
vorladen *v.* summon
Vorladung {f} *n.* summons
vorläufig *n.* interim
vorläufig *adj.* preliminary
vorlegen *v.* propound
Vorleger {m} *n.* rug
vorletzt *adj.* penultimate

Vorliebe {f} *n.* preference
Vormundschaft {f} *n.* tutelage
vorn *adv.* ahead
vorn *adj.* fore
Vorname {m} *n.* forename
vornehm *adj.* courtly
vornehm *adj.* genteel
vornehme Herkunft *n.* gentility
vornehmlich *adj.* especial
Vorort {m} *n.* suburbia
Vorrang {m} *n.* antecedent
Vorrang {m} *n.* primacy
Vorrang {m} *n.* priory
Vorrat {m} *n.* armoury
Vorrat {m} *n.* hoarding
Vorraum {m} *n.* vestibule
Vorrecht {n} *n.* prerogative
Vorrecht {n} *n.* privilege
Vorreiter {m} *n.* outrider
Vorrichtung {f} *n.* contrivance
Vorsatz {m} *n.* premeditation
vorsätzen *v.* premeditate
vorsätzlich *adv.* purposely
Vorschau {f} *n.* preview
Vorschlag {m} *n.* proposal
Vorschlag {m} *n.* suggestion
vorschlagen *v.* propose
vorschlagen *v.* suggest
vorschlagend *adj.* suggestible
Vorschlaghammer {m} *n.*
    sledgehammer
Vorschneider {m} *n.* spur
vorschreiben *v.* prescribe
Vorschrift {f} *n.* precept
Vorschrift {f} *n.* regulation

399

German		English
Vorschriftsmäßigkeit {f}	*n.*	regularity
Vorsehung {f}	*n.*	providence
Vorsicht {f}	*n.*	caution
vorsichtig	*adj.*	chary
vorsichtig	*adj.*	circumspect
vorsichtig	*adj.*	wary
Vorsitz {m}	*n.*	chair
Vorsitzende {m}	*n.*	chairman
Vorsorgemaßnahme {f}	*n.*	precaution
vorsorglich,	*adj.*	preventive
Vorspannung {f}	*n.*	bias
Vorspiel {n}	*n.*	foreplay
Vorspiel {n}	*n.*	prelude
Vorsprechung {f}	*n.*	audition
Vorstadt {f}	*n.*	suburb
vorstädtisch	*adj.*	suburban
Vorstand {m}	*n.*	board
vorstehen	*v.*	protrude
Vorsteherdrüse {f}	*n.*	prostate
Vorstehhund {m}	*n.*	setter
vorstellen	*v.*	envisage
vorstellen	*v.*	visualize
Vorstellung {f}	*v.*	show
Vorstellungsgespräch {n}	*n.*	interview
Vortäuschung {f}	*n.*	pretence
Vorteil {m}	*n.*	advantage
Vorteil {m}	*n.*	benefit
Vorteil {m}	*n.*	interest
Vorteil {m}	*n.*	vantage
vorteilhaft	*adj.*	advantageous
vorteilhaft	*adj.*	profitable
Vortrag {m}	*n.*	recital
vortragen	*v.*	declaim
vortragen	*v.*	recite
Vortrefflichkeit {f}	*n.*	excellence
Vortrupp {m}	*n.*	vanguard
vorüber	*prep.*	over
vorübergehend	*adj.*	transient
vorurteilen	*v.*	prejudge
vorwerfen	*v.*	reproach
Vorwort {n}	*n.*	foreword
Vorwort {n}	*n.*	preface
Vorwurf {m}	*n.*	reproof
vorzeitig	*adj.*	untimely
vorziehen	*v.*	prefer
Vulkan {m}	*n.*	volcano
vulkanisch	*adj.*	volcanic
vulkanisieren	*v.*	vulcanize

W

German		English
Waage {f}	*n.*	Libra
Wachposten {m}	*n.*	sentry
Wachs {n}	*n.*	wax
wachsam	*adj.*	alert
wachsam	*adj.*	vigilant
wachsam	*adj.*	watchful
Wachsamkeit {f}	*n.*	vigilance
Wachsein {n}	*n.*	vigil
wachsen	*v.i.*	grow
Wachstum {n}	*n.*	accretion
Wachtel {f}	*n.*	quail
Wachtelhund {m}	*n.*	spaniel
Wächter {m}	*v.*	guard
Wächter {m}	*n.*	warden
wackeln	*v.*	totter
wackeln	*v.*	waggle
wackeln	*v.*	wiggle
wacklig	*adj.*	shaky
wacklig	*adj.*	wonky
Waffe {f}	*n.*	weapon

Waffel {f}*n.*	wafer	
Waffel {f}*n.*	waffle	
waffenlos	*adj.*	unarmed
Waffenrock {m}	*n.*	tunic
Waffenruhe {f}	*n.*	truce
Waffenstillstand {m}	*n.*	armistice
wagemutig	*adj.*	daring
wagen *v.*	dare	
Wagen {m}	*n.*	trolley
Wagen {m}	*n.*	wain
Wagenrunge {f}	*n.*	stanchion
Waggon {m} *n.*	wagon	
Wahl {f} *n.*	option	
wahlberechtigt	*adj.*	elective
wählen *v. t*	choose	
wählen *v.*	opt	
Wähler {m}	*n.*	voter
Wählerschaft {f}	*n.*	electorate
wahlfähige	*adj.*	eligible
Wahlgang {m}	*n.*	ballot
Wahlkreis {m}	*n.*	constituency
Wahlmöglichkeit {f}	*n.*	choice
Wählscheibe {f}	*n.*	dial
Wahn {m}	*n.*	delusion
Wahnsinn {m}	*n.*	frenzy
Wahnsinn {m}	*n.*	mania
wahnsinnig	*adj.*	demented
wahnsinnig	*adj.*	insane
Wahnsinnige {m,f}*n.*	lunatic	
Wahnsinnige {m,f}*n.*	maniac	
wahr	*adj.*	true
während *prep.*	during	
wahrhaft *adj.*	truthful	
wahrhaft *adj.*	veracious	
wahrhaft *adj.*	veritable	

Wahrhaftigkeit {f}	*n.*	veracity
Wahrheit {f}	*n.*	truth
Wahrheit {f}	*n.*	verity
wahrlich *adv.*	verily	
wahrnehmbar*adj.*	perceptible	
wahrnehmend	*adj.*	perceptive
wahrnehmend	*adj.*	percipient
Wahrnehmung {f} *n.*	sensation	
Wahrsager {m}	*n.*	palmist
wahrscheinlich	*adj.*	probable
Wahrscheinlichkeit {f}	*n.*	likelihood
Wahrscheinlichkeit {f}	*n.*	probability
Wahrscheinlichkeit {f}	*n.*	
verisimilitude		
Währung {f}	*n.*	currency
Wahrung {f}	*n.*	keeping
Waise {m}	*n.*	orphan
Waisenhaus {n}	*n.*	orphanage
Wal {m} *n.*	whale	
Wald {m}*n.*	forest	
Waldgelände {n} *n.*	woodland	
Waldhorn {n} *n.*	bugle	
waldig	*adj.*	sylvan
Waldwiese {f}*n.*	glade	
Walfang {m} *n.*	whaling	
Walfänger {m}	*n.*	whaler
Wall {m} *n.*	rampart	
Walnuss {f}	*n.*	walnut
Walross {n}	*n.*	walrus
Walze {f}*n.*	roller	
Walzer {m}	*n.*	waltz
Wälzer {m}	*n.*	tome
Wälzfräser {m}	*n.*	hob
Wandel {m}	*n.*	vicissitude
wandern *v.*	flit	

401

wandern *v.*	migrate	
wandern *v.*	roam	
wandern *v.*	wander	
Wandernde {m,f} *n.*	rover	
Wanderung {f}	*n.*	hike
Wanderung {f}	*n.*	migration
Wandlung {f} *n.*	metamorphosis	
Wandschmiererei{f}	*n.*	graffiti
Wandteppich {m} *n.*	tapestry	
wanken *v.*	stagger	
wanken *v.*	waver	
wankend *adj.*	staggering	
wann immer *conj.*	whenever	
Wanne {f}	*n.*	tub
wäre *adj.*	would-be	
Ware {f} *n.*	merchandise	
Ware {f} *n.*	ware	
Warendepot {n}	*n.*	warehouse
Warenmarkt {m}	*v.*	produce
Warensendung {f} *n.*	consignment	
warm *adj.*	warm	
Wärme {f}	*n.*	heat
Wärme {f}	*n.*	warmth
Wärmedämmung {f}	*n.*	insulation
warnen *v.*	warn	
warnend *adj.*	cautionary	
Warnung {f}	*n.*	premonition
Warnung {f}	*n.*	warning
warten *v.*	wait	
Wärter {m}	*n.*	warder
Wartung {f}	*n.*	maintenance
warum *adv.*	why	
Warze {f} *n.*	wart	
was *pron. & adj.*	what	
was auch immer *pron.*	whatever	

waschbar	*adj.*	washable
waschen *v.*	launder	
waschen *v.*	mope	
waschen *v.*	wash	
Wäscher {m} *n.*	washer	
Wäscherei {f} *n.*	laundry	
Wäschetrockner {m}	*n.*	tumbler
Waschmittel {n}	*n.*	detergent
Waschsalon {m}	*n.*	launderette
Waschung {f} *n.*	ablutions	
Wasser {n}	*n.*	water
Wasserdampf {m} *n.*	steam	
wasserdicht *adj.*	watertight	
Wasserfall {m}	*n.*	cascade
Wasserfall {m}	*n.*	waterfall
wasserfest *adj.*	waterproof	
Wassergraben {m}	*n.*	ditch
Wässerigkeit {f}	*n.*	washing
Wasserläufer {m} *n.*	shank	
Wassermelone {f} *n.*	watermelon	
Wasserrinne {f}	*n.*	gullet
Wasserstoff {m}	*n.*	hydrogen
Wasserzeichen {n}	*n.*	watermark
wässrig *adj.*	aqueous	
wässrig *adj.*	watery	
waten *v.*	wade	
watscheln *v.*	shamble	
watscheln *v.*	waddle	
Watt {n} *n.*	watt	
wattierte *adj.*	quilted	
Wattleistung {f}	*n.*	wattage
Watvogel {m} *n.*	wader	
weben *v.*	weave	
Weber {m}	*n.*	weaver
Webkante {f} *n.*	selvedge	

Webpage {f}	*n.*	webpage
Website {f}	*n.*	website
wechseln	*v.*	interrelate
wechselseitig *adj.*	reciprocal
Wechselwirkung {f}	*n.*	interplay
wecken *v.*	awake
wecken *v.*	rouse
weder *adj.*	neither
weder noch *conj.&adv.*	nor
Weg {m} *n.*	path
Weg {m} *n.*	road
Weg {m} *n.*	way
Wegbereiter {m}	*n.*	innovator
Wegbereiter {m}	*n.*	precursor
Wegerich {m} *n.*	plantain
wehen *v.*	waft
Wehgeschrei {n} *n.*	wail
Wehmut {f} *n.*	melancholy
Wehr {n} *n.*	weir
weibisch machend	*v.*	womanize
weiblich *adj.*	female
Weiblichkeit {f}	*n.*	womanhood
Weichling {m}	*n.*	sissy
Weide {f} *n.*	willow
weigern *v.*	refuse
Weigerung {f} *n.*	refusal
weih *adj.*	votive
Weihnachten {n} *n.*	Christmas
Weihnachten {pl} *n.*	Xmas
Weihnachtslied {n}	*n.*	carol
Weihrauch {m}	*n.*	incense
weil *conj.* because
Weile {f} *n.*	while
Wein {m} *n.*	wine
Weinbau {m} *n.*	viticulture

Weinbrand {m}	*n.*	brandy
weinen *v.*	cry
weinen *v.*	weep
weinend *adj.* weepy
Weinhändler {m}	*n.*	vintner
Weinkellerei {f}	*n.*	winery
Weinstein {m}	*n.*	tartar
Weintraube {f}	*n.*	grape
Weisheit {f}	*n.*	wisdom
weiß *adj.* white
Weißdorn {m} *n.*	hawthorn
Weißkäse {m} *n.*	curd
Weisung {f}	*n.*	commission
weit *adj.* wide
Weiten {pl}	*n.*	amplitude
weiter *adv.&adj.*	forward
weitergeben *v.*	impart
weitest *adj.&adv.*	furthest
weitverbreitet *adj.* widespread
weizen *adj.* wheaten
Weizen {m}	*n.*	wheat
welch *pron.&adj.*	which
welche *pron.*	whichever
wellen *v.*	undulate
wellen *v.*	wave
Wellhornschnecke {f} *n.* whelk
wellig *adj.* wavy
Welligkeit {f} *n.*	ripple
Welpe {m}	*n.*	puppy
Welpe {m}	*n.*	whelp
Welt {f} *n.*	earth
Welt {f} *n.*	world
Weltenbummler {m}	*n.* globetrotter
weltlich *adj.* earthly
weltlich *adj.* secular

weltlich *adj.* worldly
Weltuntergang {m}   *n.* Armageddon
wen *pron.*   whom
Wendekreis {m}   *n.*   tropic
wenden *v.*   wend
Wendung {f} *n.*   upturn
wenig   *adj.*   few
wenig   *adj. & pron.*   less
wenig   *adj.* sparse
wenigsten   *adj.& pron.*   least
wenn   *conj.* if
wenn   *adv.* when
wenn nicht   *conj.* unless
wer *pron.*   who
wer immer   *pron.*   whoever
Werbegeschenk {n}   *n.* freebie
werben *v.*   advertise
werben *v.*   tout
werben *v.*   woo
Werbeprospekt {n}   *n.*   prospectus
Werbespruch {m} *n.*   slogan
Werbung {f} *n.*   publicity
werden *v.*   become
werdend *adj.* nascent
werfen *v.*   fling
werfen *v.*   pelt
Werfer {m}   *n.*   pitcher
Werkstatt {f} *n.*   workshop
Werkstoff {m}*n.*   material
Werkzeug {n} *n.*   tool
Wermut {m}   *n.*   wormwood
wert *adj.* worth
Wert {m} *n.*   value
Wertigkeit {f} *n.*   valency
wertlos *adj.* nugatory

wertlos   *adj.* vile
wertlos   *adj.* worthless
wertvoll *adj.* valuable
wertvoll *adj.* worthwhile
Wesen {n}   *n.*   being
wesentlich   *adj.* principal
wesentlich   *adv.* substantially
Wespe {f}   *n.*   wasp
wessen *adj. & pron.*   whose
Weste {f}*n.*   vest
Weste {f}*n.*   waistcoat
Westen {m}   *n.*   west
Westländer {m}   *n.*   westerner
westlich *adj.* occidental
westlich *adv.* westerly
westlich *adj.* western
Wettbewerb {m}   *n.*   competition
Wette {f} *n. & v.*   wager
wetteifernd *v.*   vie
wetten *v.*   bet
Wetter {n}   *n.*   weather
Wetterkunde {f}   *n.*   meteorology
Wettkampf {m}   *n.*   contest
Wettkämpfer {m}   *n.*   contestant
Wettstreit {m}*n.*   contention
Wettstreit {m}*n.*   rivalry
wetzen *v.*   whet
Whirlwanne {f}   *n.*   Jacuzzi
Whirlwanne {f}   *n.*   whirlpool
Whisky {m}   *n.*   whisky
Whist {m}   *n.*   whist
Wicht {m}   *n.*   Wight
wichtig   *adj.* important
wichtig   *adj.* momentous
wichtig   *adj.* necessary

Wichtigkeit {f}   n.   importance
wichtigste   adj.   prime
Wichtigtuerei {f}   n.   pomposity
wickeln   v.   swaddle
Wicklung {f}   n.   coil
Wideraufnahme {f}   n. resumption
Widerhaken {m}   n.   barb
Widerhall {m} n.   echo
widerhallen   v.   resound
widerlegen   v.   confute
widerlegen   v.   disprove
widerlegen   v.   refute
widerlich adj.   loathsome
widerlich adj.   repugnant
widerlich adj.   sleazy
Widerling {m} n.   sleaze
Widerruf {m}   n.   revocation
widerrufen   v.   revoke
widerruflich   adj.   revocable
widersetzlich   adj.   obstructive
widersprechen   v.   contradict
Widerspruch {m}   n.   contradiction
Widerspruch {m}   n.   opposition
Widerstand {m}   n.   resistance
widerstandsfähig   adj.   resistant
widerstehen   v.   resist
widerstehen   v.   withstand
widerstreiten   v.   militate
widerwärti   adj.   objectionable
widerwärtig,   adj.   disagreeable
Widerwille {m}   n.   distaste
Widerwille {m}   n.   repugnance
widerwillig   adj.   unwilling
widmen   v.   dedicate
Widmung {f}   n.   dedication

wie   adv. how
wieder   adv.   afresh
Wiederannäherung {f}
    n. rapprochement
wiederanpassen   v.   readjust
wiederaufbauen   v.   reconstruct
Wiederauferstehung {f}   n.
    resurgence
wiederauflebend   adj.   resurgent
Wiederaufnahmeverfahren {n} n. retrial
wiederaufnehmen v.   resume
wiederauftreten   v.   reappear
wiederbeleben   v.   revive
Wiederbelebung {f}   n.   revivalism
wiedereinsetzen   v.   reinstate
Wiedereinsetzung {f}   n. reinstatement
Wiedereinsetzung {f}   adj.   restoration
Wiedergabe {f}   n.   reproduction
Wiedergabetreue {f}   n.   fidelity
Wiedergeburt {f}   n.   rebirth
Wiedergeburt {f}   n.   renaissance
wiedergeschehen v.   reoccur
wiederherstellen   v.   reconstitute
wiederherstellen   v.   retrieve
Wiederherstellung {f}   n.   recreation
wiederholbar adj. repentant
wiederholen   v.   iterate
wiederholen   v.   reiterate
wiederholen   v.   repeat
wiederholen   v.   replay
Wiederholung {f}   n.   recurrence
Wiederholung {f}   n.   reiteration
Wiederholung {f}   n.   repetition
wiederkäuen v.   ruminate
Wiederkäuen {n}   n.   rumination

wiederkehren *v.*	recur		**Winde** {f}*n.*	winch
wiederkehrend	*adj.* recurrent		**Winde** {f}*n.*	winder
wiedernehmen	*v.* recapture		**Windel** {f}	*n.* diaper
wiedernehmen	*v.* repossess		**Windel** {f}	*n.* nappy
wiederschaffen	*v.* recreate		**winden** *v.*	twist
wiedervereinigen *v.*	reunite		**winden** *v.*	wreathe
Wiedervereinigung {f} *n.*	reunion		**Windhund** {m}	*n.* greyhound
wiederverwerten *v.*	reuse		**windig** *adj.* windy
Wiege {f}*n.*	cradle		**Windrad** {n}	*n.* windmill
wiegen *v.*	dandle		**Windstoß** {m}*n.*	flurry
wiegen *v.*	weigh		**Windstoß** {m}*n.*	gust
wiehern *n.*	neigh		**Wink** {m}*n.*	beck
wiehernd	*adj.* whinny		**Winkel** {m}	*n.* angle
Wiesel {m}	*n.* weasel		**Winkel** {m}	*n.* corner
Wigwam {n}	*n.* wigwam		**Winkelmesser** {m}*n.*	protractor
Wikinger {m} *n.*	Viking		**winken** *v.*	beckon
wild *adj.* feral			**winklig** *adj.* angular
wild *adj.* haggard			**winseln** *v.*	whimper
wild *adj.* rampant			**Winter** {m}	*n.* winter
wild *adj.* savage			**winterlich**	*adj.* wintry
wild *adj.* truculent			**winzig** *adj.* minute
wild *adj.* wild			**winzig** *adj.* tiny
Wildfang {m} *n.*	tomboy		**wippen** *v.*	teeter
Wildheit {f}	*n.* savagery		**wippen** *v.*	teethe
Wildleder {n} *n.*	suede		**wir** *pron.*	we
Wildnis {f}	*n.* wilderness		**Wirbel** {m}	*n.* vertebra
Willenskraft {f}	*n.* volition		**Wirbel** {m}	*n.* vortex
Willigkeit {f} *adj.*	willingness		**wirbellos***adj.* spineless
Willkommen {n}	*n.* welcome		**wirbeln** *v.*	swirl
willkürlich	*adj.* arbitrary		**wirbeln** *v.*	twirl
wimmeln*v.*	teem		**Wirbelsturm** {m}	*n.* hurricane
wimmern	*v.* whinge		**Wirbeltier** {n} *n.*	vertebrate
Wimpel {m}	*n.* wimple		**Wirbelwind** {m}	*n.* whirlwind
Wind {m}*n.*	wind		**wirklich** *adv.* really
Windbeutel	*n.* windbag		**Wirklichkeit** {f}	*n.* reality

wirksam *adj.* effective
Wirksamkeit {f}   *n.*   virtue
Wirkungskraft {f}   *n.*   efficacy
Wirkungsmittel {n}   *n.*   agent
wirkungsvoll *adj.* efficient
Wirrwarr {n}   *v.*   huddle
Wirt {m}   *n.*   host
wirtschaftlich *adj.* economic
Wirtschaftlichkeit {f}   *n.*   economy
wischen *v.* whisk
wischen *v.* wipe
Wisent {m}   *n.*   bison
wissen *v.* know
wissend *n.* intuitive
wissend *adj.* knowing
Wissenschaft {f}   *n.*   science
Wissenschaftler {m}   *n.*   scientist
wissenschaftlich *adj.* scholarly
wissenschaftlich *adj.* scientific
Wittling {m}   *n.*   whiting
Witwe {f} *n.* widow
Witwer {m}   *n.*   widower
Witz {m}   *n.*   witticism
Witzbold {m}   *n.*   buffoon
Witzbold {m}   *n.*   joker
witzig   *adj.* facetious
witzig   *adj.* witty
witzlos   *adj.* witless
wo *adv.* where
wo herum   *adv.* whereabouts
Woche {f}   *n.*   week
Wochentag {m}   *n.*   weekday
wochentlich *adj.* weekly
wogen   *v.*   billow
woher   *adv.* whence

wohin   *adv.* whither
Wohl {n} *n.* weal
wohlgeformt *adj.* shapely
wohlhabend *adj.* affluent
wohlhabend *adv.* richly
Wohlstand {m}   *n.*   affluence
Wohltat {f}   *n.*   boon
Wohltäter {m} *n.* benefactor
wohltätig *adj.* beneficent
wohltätig *adj.* charitable
Wohlwollen {n}   *n.*   benevolence
Wohlwollen {n}   *n.*   goodwill
wohlwollend *adj* benevolent
wohnen *v.* reside
Wohnsitz {m} *n.* domicile
wohnte *v.* dwell
Wohnung {f}   *n.*   apartment
Wohnung {f}   *n.*   habitation
Wohnung {f}   *n.*   tenement
Wohnung{f}   *adj.* flat
Wohnwagen {m}   *n.*   caravan
Wohnzimmer {n}   *n.*   parlour
Wok {m} *n.* wok
Wolf {m} *n.* wolf
Wolke {f} *n.* cloud
Wolkenbruch {m}   *n.*   deluge
Wolkenkratzer {m} *n.* skyscraper
wolkig   *adj.* cloudy
Wolle {f}   *n.* wool
wollen   *v.*   will
wollig   *adj.* woollen
wollig   *adj.* woolly
wollüstig *adj.* lustful
Wonne {f}   *n.*   joy
Wort {n}   *n.*   word

Wörterbuch {n}	n.	dictionary	würdevoll	adj.	dignified

Wörterbuch {n}   n.   dictionary
Wörterverzeichnis {n} n.   glossary
Wortfülle {f}   n.   verbosity
wortgewandt adj.   articulate
Wortlaut {m} n.   wording
wörtlich adj.   literal
wörtlich adv.   verbatim
wortreich   adj.   verbose
wortreich   adj.   wordy
Wortschwall {m}   n.   verbiage
Wortspiel {n} n.   pun
Wortwahl {f} n.   diction
Wrack {n}   n.   wrack
Wrackgut {n} n.   wreckage
Wucher {m} n.   usury
wuchern v.   proliferate
Wucherung {f}   n.   proliferation
Wulst {f} n.   bead
wund   adj. sore
Wunde {f}   n.   wound
Wunder {n}   n.   miracle
Wunderkind {n}   n.   prodigy
wunderlich   adj. quaint
wunderlich   adj. queer
wundern v.i   marvel
wundern v.   wonder
wundersam   adj. wondrous
wundertätig   adj. miraculous
wundervoll   adj. marvellous
wundervoll   adj. wonderful
Wundverband {m} n.   bandage
wunschen   v.   wish
wünschenswert   adj. desirable
würde   v.   would
Würdenträger {m} n.   dignitary

würdevoll   adj. dignified
würdig adj. worthy
Würfel {m}   n.   cube
Würfel {pl}   n.   dice
Wurfspieß {m}   n.   javelin
würgen v.   choke
würgen v.   retch
Wurm {m}   n.   worm
Wurst {f} n.   sausage
Würze {f}n.   condiment
Würze {f}n.   seasoning
Wurzel {f}   n.   root
würzig adj. spicy
wüst   adj. desolate
Wüsten v.   desert
Wut {f}   n.   rage
Wutanfall {m}n.   paddy
Wutanfall {m}n.   tantrum
wütend adj. berserk
wütend adj. furious
wütend adj. rabid

Xenon {n}   n.   xenon
Xerox {n}   n.   Xerox
xylophag   adj. xylophagous
xylophil adj. xylophilous
Xylophon {n} n.   xylophone

Yasmak {m}   n.   yashmak
Yen {m} n.   Yen
Yeti {m} n.   yeti

Z

zackig *adj.* jagged
zäh *adj.* stringy
Zähigkeit {f} *n.* tenacity
Zähigkeit {f} *n.* toughness
Zahl {f} *n.* digit
Zahl {f} *n.* numeral
zahlbar *n.* payable
zahlen *v.* defray
zahlen *v.* pay
zählen *v.* count
zahlenmäßig überlegen *v.* outnumber
Zähler {m} *n.* counter
Zähler {m} *n.* numerator
Zähler {m} *n.* tally
zahllos *adj.* countless
zahllos *adj.* numberless
zahlreich *adj.* numerous
zahlreich *adj.* prolific
Zahlung {f} *n.* capitation
Zahlungsempfänger {m}*n.* payee
Zahlungsfähigkeit {f} *n.* solvency
zahlungsunfähig *adj.* insolvent
Zahlungsunfähigkeit {f} *n.* insolvency
zahm *adj.* tame
zahm *adv.* tamely
Zahn {m}*n.* tooth
Zahnarzt {m} *n.* dentist
zahnärztlich *adj.* dental
Zahnbelag {m} *n.* plaque
Zahnkrone {f}*n.* crown
zahnlos *adj.* toothless
Zahnpaste {f} *n.* toothpaste
Zahnschmerz {m} *n.* toothache
Zahnstange {f} *n.* rack
Zahnstocher {m} *n.* toothpick

Zander {m} *n.* sander
Zange {f}*n.* forceps
Zange {f}*n.* pliers
Zange {f}*n.* tongs
Zank {m}*n.* altercation
zanken *v.* bicker
zänkisch *adj.* cantankerous
Zankteufel {m} *n.* termagant
Zäpfchen {n} *n.* suppository
Zapfen {m} *n.* gudgeon
Zapfstelle {f} *n.* tap
zappeln *v.* flounce
zappeln *v.* flounder
zart *adj.* tender
Zartheit {f} *n.* delicatessen
Zärtlichkeit {f} *n.* endearment
Zauberei {f} *n.* necromancy
Zauberei {f} *n.* sorcery
Zauberei {f} *n.* witchcraft
Zauberer {m} *n.* magician
Zauberer {m} *n.* sorcerer
Zauberer {m} *n.* wizard
Zauberin {f} *n.* fairy
Zauderer {m} *n.* laggard
Zaum {m} *n.* bridle
Zaun {m}*n.* fence
Zaunkönig {m} *n.* wren
zausen *v.* tousle
Zebra {n}*n.* zebra
Zebrastreifen {pl} *n.* zebra crossing
zechen *v.* quaff
zechen *v.* tipple
Zeder {f} *n.* cedar
Zehe {f} *n.* toe
zehn *adj. & adv.* ten

Zehnte {m}	*n.*	tithe		**Zeltbahn {f}**	*n.*	tarpaulin

Zehnte {m} *n.* tithe
zehnter *adj. & n.* tenth
Zeichen {n} *v.* char
Zeichen {n} *n.* sign
Zeichen {n} *n.* token
Zeichenkette {f} *n.* string
Zeichenschablone {f} *n.* template
Zeichensetzung {f} *n.* punctuation
Zeichentrickfilm {m} *n.* cartoon
Zeichnung {f} *n.* drawing
Zeigefinger {m} *n.* forefinger
zeigen *v.* display
Zeile {f} *n.* row
Zeit {f} *n.* time
zeitgemäß *adj.* seasonable
zeitgemäß *adj.* timely
zeitgenössisch *adj.* contemporary
zeitlich *adj.* temporal
zeitlos *adj.* ageless
Zeitplan {m} *n.* schedule
Zeitschrift {f} *n.* magazine
Zeitung {f} *n.* gazette
Zeitung {f} *n.* paper
Zeitungsente {f} *n.* canard
Zeitvertreib {m} *n.* pastime
Zeitzonenkater {m} *n.* jet lag
Zelebrant {m} *n.* celebrant
Zelle {f} *n.* cell
Zelle {f} *n.* cubicle
zellig *adj.* cellular
Zellkern {m} *n.* nucleus
Zellstoff {m} *n.* cellulose
Zelluloid {n} *n.* celluloid
Zelot *n.* zealot
Zelt {n} *n.* tent

Zeltbahn {f} *n.* tarpaulin
Zement {m} *n.* cement
Zenit {m} *n.* zenith
Zensur {f} *n.* censorship
Zentimeter *n.* centimetre
zentral *adj.* central
zentral *adj.* pivotal
zentralisieren *v.* centralize
Zentrum *n.* center
Zephir *n.* zephyr
Zepter {n} *n.* sceptre
zerbrechen *v.* crash
zerbrechlich *adj.* frail
zerbrochen *adj.* broke
zerdrücken *v.* crush
zerebral *adj.* cerebral
Zeremonie {f} *n.* ceremony
zeremoniös *adj.* ceremonious
zerfahren *adj.* disjointed
zerfleischen *v.* lacerate
zerfleischen *v.* mangle
zerhacken *v.* chop
zerhacken *v.* mince
Zerhacker {m} *n.* chopper
zerknitternd *v.* crumple
zerknüllen *v.* rumple
zerlegen *v.* decompose
zerlegen *v.* dissect
zerlumpt *adj.* ragged
zermalmen *v.* crunch
zernagen *v.* gnaw
zerquetschen *v.* squash
zerreiben *v.* bray
zerreißen *v.* disrupt
zerreißen *v.* rip

zerreißen	*v.t.*	rupture
zerren	*v.*	tug
zerrütten *v.t.*		shatter
zerrütten *v.i.*		subvert
zerrüttend	*adj.*	shattering
Zerschlagung {f}	*n.*	suppression
zerschmettern	*v.*	dash
zerschmetternd	*adj.*	dashing
zerschmettert*n.*		batter
zersetzen	*v.*	disintegrate
zersetzend	*adj.*	subversive
Zersetzung {f}	*n.*	decomposition
zersplitten	*v.*	split
zerstören	*v. i*	delete
zerstören	*v.*	destroy
zerstören	*v.*	vandalize
Zerstörer {m} *n.*		destroyer
Zerstörung {f}	*n.*	destruction
zerstreuen	*v.*	dispel
zerstreuen	*v.*	scatter
zerteilend	*v.*	dissipate
zertreten *v.*		tread
zertrümmern *v.*		smash
Zeug {n} *n.*		stuff
Zeug {n} *n.*		trinket
Zeuge {f}*n.*		witness
zeugen	*v.*	beget
Zeugenaussage {f}		*n.* evidence
Zeugnis {n}	*n.*	testimonial
zickig	*adj.*	touchy
Zickzack {n} *n.*		zigzag
Ziege {f} *n.*		goat
Ziegelstein {m}	*n.*	clink
ziehen	*v. t*	drag
ziehen	*v.*	pull

Ziehen {n}	*n.*	traction
Ziel {n}	*n.*	aim
Ziel {n}	*n.*	sighting
Ziel {n}	*n.*	target
zielen	*v.i.*	aim
ziellos	*adj.*	aimless
ziemen	*v.*	befit
ziemlich	*adv.*	quite
zieren	*v.*	adorn
Ziererei {f}	*n.*	affectation
zierlich	*adj.*	graceful
zierlich	*adj.*	petite
Zigarette {f}	*n.*	cigarette
Zigarre {f}	*n.*	cigar
Zigeuner {m} *n.*		gypsy
Zimmerdecke {f}	*n.*	ceiling
Zimmerhandwerk {n}	*n.*	carpentry
Zimt {m} *n.*		cinnamon
Zink {n} *n.*		zinc
Zinne {f} *n.*		pinnacle
Zinnober {m} *n.*		vermillion
Zirkon {m}	*n.*	zircon
zirkulieren	*v.*	circulate
Zirkus {m}	*n.*	circus
zirpen	*v.*	chirp
zischen	*v.i*	hiss
zischen	*v.*	sizzle
zischen	*v.*	whiz
zischend*v.*		fizzle
zischend*adj.*		sibilant
Zisterne {f}	*n.*	cistern
Zitadelle {f}	*n.*	citadel
Zitat {n} *n.*		quotation
Zither {f} *n.*		zither
zitieren	*v.*	cite

411

Zitrone {f}	*n.*	lemon
Zitrus	*n.*	citrus
zitrus	*adj.*	citric
zittern	*v.*	quiver
zittern	*v.*	tremble
Zittern {n}	*n.*	tremor
zitternd	*adj.*	tremulous
zivil *adj.*		civil
Zivilisation {f}	*n.*	civilization
zivilisieren	*v.*	civilize
Zivilist {m}	*n.*	civilian
zögerlich	*adj.*	halting
zögerlich	*adj.*	hesitant
zögern	*v.*	hesitate
zögern	*v.*	procrastinate
Zögern {n}	*n.*	indecision
Zölibat {n}	*n.*	celibacy
Zoll {m}	*n.*	custom
Zoll {m}	*n.*	toll
Zoll {n}	*n.*	inch
Zombie {m}	*n.*	zombie
Zone {f}	*n.*	area
Zone {f}	*n.*	zone
zonen	*adj.*	zonal
Zoologe {m}	*n.*	zoologist
zoologisch	*adj.*	zoological
zoomen	*v.*	zoom
Zopf {m}	*n.*	plait
Zorn {m}	*n.*	anger
Zorn {m}	*n.*	fury
Zorn {m}	*n.*	ire
Zorn {m}	*n.*	wrath
zornig	*adj.*	irate
zu *prep.*		towards
Zubehör {n}	*n.*	adjunct

Zubehör {n}	*n.*	paraphernalia
zubetonieren	*v.t.*	greenery
züchten	*v.*	breed
Zuchthäusler {m}	*n.*	convict
Zuchthengst {m}	*n.*	stallion
züchtigen	*v.*	castigate
zucken	*v.*	wince
Zucker {m}	*n.*	sugar
Zuckerahorn {m}	*n.*	sycamore
Zuckerbäcker {m}	*n.*	confectioner
Zuckerkrankheit {f}	*n.*	diabetes
zuckersüß	*adj.*	saccharine
zuckersüß	*adj.*	twee
Zuckung {f}	*n.*	convulsion
zudringlich	*adj.*	intrusive
zuerst	*adj.*	primary
Zufall {m}	*n.*	coincidence
zufällig	*adj.*	haphazard
zufällig	*adj.*	incidental
zufällig	*adj.*	random
Zuflucht {f}	*n.*	refuge
zufrieden	*adj.*	content
Zufriedenheit {f}	*n.*	contentment
zufügen	*v.*	inflict
Zug {m}	*n.*	trait
Zugabe {f}	*n.*	encore
zugänglich	*adj.*	accessible
Zugband {n}	*n.*	strap
zugehörig	*adj.*	constituent
zugehörig	*adj.*	germane
Zügel {m}	*n.*	rein
zügellos *adj.*		ungovernable
zügeln	*v. t*	curb
Zugeständnis {n}	*n.*	concession
Zugriff {m}	*n.*	access

zugrundelagen	v.	underlay	
Zugvogel {m} n.		migrant	
Zuhörerschaft {f}	n.	audience	
zujubeln	v.	acclaim	
zuknallen	v.	slam	
Zukunft {f}	n.	future	
Zukunft {f}	n.	morrow	
Zulänglichkeit {f}	n.	sufficiency	
zulassen v.		admit	
zulassen v.		tolerate	
zulässig adj.		admissible	
zulässig adj.		permissible	
zulässig adj.		valid	
Zulassung {f} n.		admission	
zum prep.		to	
Zunahme {f}	n.	bulge	
Zunahme {f}	n.	increment	
Zunähung {f}	n.	suture	
Zunder {m}	n.	tinder	
Zündsatz {m} n.		primer	
Zunehmen	v.	gain	
Zuneigung {f} n.		affection	
Zunge {f}n.		lingua	
Zunge {f}n.		tongue	
Zungenlaut {m}	n.	lingual	
zupacken	v.	grasp	
zupfen v.		twitch	
zureagieren	v.	overreact	
zurechnungsfähig adj.		sane	
Zurschaustellung {f}	n.		
ostentation			
zurück n.		back	
zurückblickend	adj.	retrospective	
(zu)rückdatieren	v.	backdate	
zurückerstatten	v.	restore	

zurückfallen v.		relapse	
zurückfordern	v.	reclaim	
Zurückforderung {f}	n.		
reclamation			
zurückführen v.		repatriate	
zurückgehen v.		regress	
zurückgewinnen	v.	regain	
zuruckhalten v.		withhold	
zurückhalten v.t.		refrain	
zurückhalten v.		restrain	
zurückhaltend	adj.	cautious	
zurückhaltend	adj.	reluctant	
zurückhaltend	adj.	retentive	
zurückkehren v.		revert	
zurückrufen v.		recall	
zurückschicken	v.	remand	
zurückschrecken v.		blench	
zurückschrecken v.		boggle	
zurücksetzen v.		relocate	
zurückstrahlen	v.	reverberate	
zurückstreifen	v.	tuck	
zurücktreten v.		recede	
zurücktreten v.		retire	
zurücktreten v.t.		retreat	
zurücktretend	adj.	retiring	
zurückverfolgen	v.t.	retrace	
zurückverfolgen {v}	v.	backtrack	
zurückweichen	v.	flinch	
zurückweisenv.		rebuff	
zurückweisenv.		reject	
zurückzahlen v.		repay	
zurückziehen v.		retract	
zurückziehen v.		withdraw	
zurzeit adv.		presently	
zusammen n.		tog	

zusammen arbeiten	v.	collaborate	Zuschauer {m}	n.	onlooker
zusammen beißen	v.	clench	Zuschauer {m}	n.	spectator
zusammen bindend	v.		Zuschneider {m}	n.	cutter
interconnect			zuschreiben	v.	ascribe
zusammen fließend	adj.	confluent	zuschreiben	v.	attribute
zusammen gefasst	adj.	compendious	Zusicherung {f}	n.	assurance
zusammen hängend	adj.	contiguous	zuspitzen	v.	taper
zusammen ziehen	v.	constrict	zusprechen	v.t.	adjudge
zusammenbrauen	v.	concoct	Zuspruch {m}	n.	consolation
zusammenbrechen	v.	collapse	Zustand {m}	n.	status
zusammenfassen	v.	recapitulate	Zustand {m}	n.	trug
zusammenfassen	v.	summarize	Zuständigkeit {f}	n.	competence
Zusammenfluss {m}	n.	confluence	zustandlos	adj.	stateless
zusammengehören	v.	belong	Zustellungsurkunde {f}	n.	affidavit
zusammengestellen	v.	compose	zustimmen	v.	approve
zusammenhaltend	adj.	cohesive	zustimmen	v.	jibe
Zusammenhang {m}	n.	context	zustimmend	adj.	affirmative
zusammenhängen	v.	cohere	Zustimmung {f}	n.	assent
zusammenhängend	adj.	coherent	Zustimmung {f}	n.	compliance
zusammenklappen	v.	furl	zustopfen	v.	tamp
zusammenprallen	v.	hurtle	zustoßen	v.	befall
Zusammenschrumpfen {n}	n.		zuteilen	v.t.	apportion
shrinkage			Zuteilung {f}	n.	handout
Zusammenstellung {f}	n.	anthology	Zuteilung {f}	n.	ration
Zusammenstellung {f}	n	set	Zutritt {m}	n.	admittance
zusammenstoßen	v.	clash	zuverlässig	adj.	credible
Zusammentreffen {n}	n.	concourse	zuverlässig	adj.	staunch
zusammenwirken	v.	cooperate	zuverlässig	adj.	unfailing
zusammenwirkend	adj.	cooperative	Zuverlässigkeit {f}	n.	steadiness
Zusammenziehung {f}	n.	contraction	zuvor	adv.	beforehand
Zusatz {m}	n.	accessory	zuweisen	v.	assign
Zusatz {m}	n.	supplement	Zuweisung {f}	n.	assignation
zusätzlich	adj.	additional	zuwider	adj.	abhorrent
Zusatzstoff {m}	n.	additive	zuwiesen	v.	allot
Zuschauer {m}	n.	bystander	zuziehen	v.	incur

zuzüglich	*prep.*	plus
Zwang {m}	*n.*	compulsion
Zwangslage {f}	*n.*	exigency
zwangsläufig	*adv.*	perforce
zwanzig	*adj.&n.*	twenty
zwanzigste	*adj.&n.*	twentieth
zwecklos	*adj.*	futile
zwecklos	*adj.*	useless
zweckmäßig	*adj.*	expedient
zweckmäßig	*adj.*	suitable
zwei	*adj.&n.*	two
zweifach	*adj.*	dual
zweifach	*adj.*	twofold
Zweifel {m}	*n.*	doubt
zweifelhaft	*adj.*	dubious
Zweig {m}	*n.*	twig
Zweig {m}	*n.*	withe
Zweigchen {n}	*n.*	sprig
zweijährig	*adj.*	biennial
Zweikampf {m}	*n.*	duel
zweimal	*adv.*	twice
zweimal jährlich	*adj.*	biannual
zweiseitig	*adj.*	bilateral
zweisprachig	*adj.*	bilingual
zweiter	*adj.*	second
Zwerchfell {n}	*n.*	midriff
Zwerg {m}	*n.*	dwarf
Zwerg {m}	*n.*	midget
Zwerg {m}	*n.*	pigmy
zwicken	*v.*	tweak
Zwieback {m}	*n.*	rusk
Zwiebel {f}	*n.*	onion
Zwietracht {f}	*n.*	discord
Zwilling {m}	*n.*	twin
zwingen	*v.*	coerce

zwingen	*v.*	compel
zwingen	*v.*	constrain
zwingend	*adj.*	cogent
zwingend	*adj.*	compulsive
zwingend	*adj.*	stringent
zwinkern	*v.*	wink
zwischen	*prep.*	among
zwischen	*adv.*	between
Zwischenhändler {m}	*n.*	intermediary
zwischenliegen	*adj.*	intermediate
Zwischenprogramm {n}	*n.*	interlude
zwischenrufen	*v.*	heckle
zwischenstaatlich	*n.*	interstate
Zwischensumme {f}	*n.*	subtotal
Zwischenwahl {f}	*n.*	by-election
zwitschern	*v.*	twitter
zwölf	*adj.&n.*	twelve
zwölfte	*adj.&n.*	twelfth
Zyan	*n.*	cyan
Zyanid {n}	*n.*	cyanide
Zyklon {m}	*n.*	cyclone
Zyklus {m}	*n.*	cycle
Zylinder {m}	*n.*	cylinder
Zyniker {m}	*n.*	cynic
Zypresse {f}	*n.*	cypress
Zyste {f}	*n.*	cyst
Zyste {f}	*n.*	wen